Ridgway's Paratroopers
The American Airborne in World War II

Books by Clay Blair

NONFICTION
THE ATOMIC SUBMARINE AND ADMIRAL RICKOVER
THE HYDROGEN BOMB, *with James R. Shepley*
BEYOND COURAGE
VALLEY OF THE SHADOW, *for Ward M. Millar*
NAUTILUS 90 NORTH, *with William R. Anderson*
DIVING FOR PLEASURE AND TREASURE
ALWAYS ANOTHER DAWN, *with A. Scott Crossfield*
THE VOYAGE OF NINA II, *for Robert Marx*
THE STRANGE CASE OF JAMES EARL RAY
SURVIVE!
SILENT VICTORY: THE U.S. SUBMARINE WAR AGAINST JAPAN
THE SEARCH FOR J.F.K., *with Joan Blair*
MacARTHUR
COMBAT PATROL
RETURN FROM THE RIVER KWAI, *with Joan Blair*
A GENERAL'S LIFE, *with Omar N. Bradley*

FICTION
THE BOARD ROOM
THE ARCHBISHOP
PENTAGON COUNTRY
SCUBA!, *with Joan Blair*
MISSION TOKYO BAY, *with Joan Blair*
SWORDRAY'S FIRST THREE PATROLS, *with Joan Blair*

Ridgway's Paratroopers

The American Airborne in World War II

Clay Blair

Naval Institute Press
Annapolis, Maryland

Naval Institute Press
291 Wood Road
Annapolis, MD 21402

First Naval Institute Press edition, 2002

Library of Congress Cataloging-in-Publication Data

Blair, Clay, 1925–
    Ridgway's paratroopers : the American airborne in World
War II / Clay Blair.—Naval Institute Press pbk. ed.
        p.   cm.
    Originally published: Garden City, N.Y. : Dial Press, 1985.
    Includes bibliographical references and index.
    ISBN 1-55750-299-4 (alk. paper)
        1. United States. Army Airborne troops—History.   2. World
War, 1939–1945—Campaigns—Western Front.   3. Ridgway,
Matthew B. (Matthew Bunker) 1895—Military leadership.   I.
Title.
D769.345 .B53 2002
940.54′1273—dc21

                                                    2002070299

Printed in the United States of America on acid-free paper ∞
09 08 07 06 05 04 03 02   8 7 6 5 4 3 2 1

Grateful acknowledgment is made to the following for permission
to reprint their copyrighted material:
Soldier: The Memoirs of Matthew B. Ridgway, by General Matthew
B. Ridgway as told to Harold H. Martin. Copyright ©1956, Harper
& Row Publishers, Inc. Used by permission.
On to Berlin, by James M. Gavin. Copyright ©1978, The Viking
Press. Used by permission.

To Julie Drury, with love—
and gratitude for your support in this and previous endeavors.

Contents

Maps

Designed by Rafael D. Palacios Commelin

Foreword

IN DECEMBER 1950 the United States confronted one of the worst military crises in its history. Following the rout of the North Korean Army in South Korea by the brilliantly conceived Inchon amphibious landing, the U.S. Eighth Army was, in turn, routed by the Red Chinese Army, which poured into North Korea. The Eighth Army, commanded by Walton H. Walker, was driven back pell-mell toward Pusan. A bloody Dunkirk seemed inevitable, with possibly the complete destruction of the Eighth Army. This would have laid open Japan and Formosa to Communist conquest.

In this darkest hour, Eighth Army Commander Walker was killed in a jeep accident. He was immediately replaced by a Pentagon staff officer, Lieutenant General Matthew Bunker Ridgway, who was well known within the professional Army but virtually unknown to the public or to the dispirited GIs in Korea. Wearing a hand grenade on a parachute harness and glistening paratrooper boots, Ridgway arrived on the battlefield with an unflinching determination to turn defeat into victory, disaster into triumph.

In what many considered to be a miracle, he soon did so. Largely by the sheer power and force of his personality, he transformed the "bug-out" Eighth Army from a rabble into a deadly, aggressive fighting force. He stopped the retreat, shifted to the offensive and, over the next four months, inflicted such disastrous punishment on the Red Chinese Army that it was compelled to withdraw from South Korea and negotiate a truce.

The Chairman of the U.S. Joint Chiefs of Staff, Omar N. Bradley, who had led all American armies in the defeat of Hitler's Wehrmacht, wrote: "It is not often in wartime that a single battlefield commander can make a decisive difference. But in Korea, Ridgway would prove to be the exception. His brilliant, driving leadership would turn the tide of battle like no other general's in our military history."[1]

Ridgway, deservedly, became an instant Army hero and a world celebrity. When President Truman fired MacArthur as Supreme Commander, Allied Powers in the Far East, he named Ridgway to succeed him. When Eisenhower resigned from the newly created post of Supreme Commander, Allied Powers in Europe, to run for the presidency, Truman named Ridgway in his place. When Eisenhower was elected President, he appointed Ridgway Chief of Staff of the Army. As such, in 1954, Ridgway was the chief opponent of American military intervention in Indochina within the Eisenhower Administration. His opposition postponed that disastrous course by nearly ten years.[2]

Less well known, but no less fascinating and important, was Ridgway's contribution to the defeat of Germany in World War II. Early in that war, Army Chief of Staff George C. Marshall, who knew Ridgway well, chose him to lead and battle-test a brand-new concept of warfare known as the airborne. Ridgway commanded the first such American unit to enter combat, the famous 82nd Airborne Division, which had spawned the equally famous 101st Airborne Division. Later, as Commanding General, XVIII Airborne Corps, he led all American paratroopers in the war against Germany.

In these earlier commands, Ridgway set the high standards of leadership, courage and resourcefulness for which paratroopers would become famous. He fought in the front lines in Sicily, the Italian mainland, Normandy, the Battle of the Bulge, the Rhine crossing, the Ruhr encirclement and, in the final days, the Elbe crossing and the linkup with the Russians near the Baltic Sea. His battlefield leadership as a division commander in Normandy and as a corps commander in the Bulge and later was no less inspiring and decisive than his leadership in Korea. James M. Gavin, the fighter-intellectual-historian who inherited the 82nd Division from Ridgway, wrote that Ridgway was "undoubtedly the best combat corps commander in the American Army in World War II." Eisenhower was no less full of praise. He wrote: "Ridgway is one of the finest soldiers this war has produced . . . He has never undertaken a job that he has not performed in a soldierly and even brilliant way . . ."[3]

Although I have had full access to Ridgway's private and official papers and he has cooperated by granting interviews and responding to numerous written queries, this book is not an "authorized biography" in the traditional sense. Ridgway did not see the manuscript before publication. Moreover, I have supplemented his substantial contribution by drawing on numerous published histories and memoirs, extensive interviews and/or correspondence with his closest professional associates, and research in official archives—as set forth in detail in "Sources and Acknowledgments."

Clay Blair
Washington Island, Wisconsin
1982–85

Ridgway's Paratroopers
The American Airborne in World War II

PART I

Designation:
Airborne!

ON THE MORNING of December 7, 1941, Lieutenant Colonel Matthew Bunker Ridgway, a professional infantryman on duty in Washington with the War Department General Staff, arrived at Fort Benning, Georgia, for a brief temporary assignment. Benning was a vast, sprawling tract of rolling hills and pine forests in western Georgia, abutting the Chattahoochee River, near Columbus. It was the spiritual home of the Army's infantry branch, a rural military trade school where regulars, reservists, National Guardsmen and a few marines and acceptable foreigners came to learn the finer points of commanding small infantry units such as companies and battalions.[1]

By that time, the war in Europe had been raging for twenty-seven months, and the United States Army, after a slow start, was mobilizing full tilt. Once a sleepy military backwater, Benning had been growing in almost direct proportion to Hitler's conquests. Now it was on a simulated war footing, teeming with tens of thousands of doughboys. A new Officer Candidate School (OCS), designed to transform draftees and volunteers into shavetail lieutenants in three months ("90-day wonders") had been established near the older Infantry School. Out in the boondocks, George S. Patton and his tankers were adapting the blazing tactics of the Nazi *Blitzkrieg* to the U.S. Army. Another group of innovators was shaping doctrine and techniques for the Army's first airborne forces. Elsewhere, in remote areas, weapons specialists were field-testing new infantry small arms.[2]

"Matt" Ridgway, then forty-six years old, had recently been selected for promotion to the rank of full colonel. He had been told unofficially that he would soon receive orders to command one of the Army's new infantry regiments. He had come to Benning for a week's "refresher" course—to dip from Benning's spiritual well; to see all that was new and different and to get his juices flowing.[3]

Ridgway was an impressive figure. In his younger years he was so handsome, physically trim and impeccably attired, he could well have been a soldier conceived in Hollywood. Now, in his middle years, he had the classically mature countenance of a Mediterranean or Latin aristocrat: piercing, deep and wide-set hazel eyes, sharply chiseled and well-proportioned cheekbones and chin, a thin Roman nose and remarkably unblemished swarthy skin. Behatted, he looked a full ten years younger than his true age. Bareheaded, his baldness, reaching to the very top of his skull, added the years back.

He was a fine physical specimen. He stood five feet ten inches and weighed one hundred and seventy-five pounds. He had not been a varsity athlete in his youth, but he had closely associated with athletes at school and thereafter. He had acquired the athlete's pride in keeping physically fit, and he did so by riding horseback, running, swimming, hunting, chopping wood and playing handball and tennis. He ate, drank and smoked (mostly cigars) in moderation. His body was taut, he had great stamina and he was strong. He had immense hands and a proportionately powerful handshake. His posture was ramrod straight. Even while sitting down, he did not slouch or cross his legs.

The most striking feature about Ridgway was the aura of force or determination he radiated. Even his closest associates found this aura difficult to describe. One recalled: "The force that emanated from him was *awesome*. It reminded me of Superman. You had the impression he could knock over a building with a single blow, or stare a hole through a wall, if he wanted to. It was a powerful *presence*. He'd come into a room and you immediately felt it. He couldn't have gotten lost in a crowd if he tried."[4]

In breeding, speech and taste, Ridgway was almost Edwardian, reflecting a polished eastern upper-middle-class background. His forebears, mostly Episcopalians, had been well-to-do New Yorkers, a family of professionals. His paternal grandfather, James Ridgway, had been a surrogate judge in Brooklyn. His father, Thomas Ridgway, born in a pre-Revolutionary British barracks on Staten Island ("Ridgway House," demolished in 1910), was a West Point graduate, an artillery specialist who had retired as a full colonel in 1919. His mother, Julia Starbuck Bunker of Garden City, Long Island, was a concert-class pianist and a collector of *objets d'art*. One uncle, Robert Ridgway, had been the chief design engineer for the New York subway system and a consultant on the urban rail systems built in Chicago and Tokyo. In a social setting, Ridgway was well-mannered, warm, charming and tactful.[5]

Matt Ridgway had never seriously considered any career other than the military. After a comfortable childhood on Army posts and some prep school cramming, he had made a bee line for West Point, determined to be a general. He graduated on April 20, 1917, two weeks after the United States declared war on Germany, eager to test his mettle in the trenches of France, but he was denied that opportunity. By the luck of the draw, he was ordered back to West Point as an instructor in Romance languages, and no amount of string pulling in the War Department could overturn the decision.

It was a bitter, bitter pill. He had missed the Great War and felt humiliated and professionally ruined, his life's goal beyond reach. But that pill may well have been a powerful stimulant. During the ensuing peacetime years, Ridgway attacked the rungs of the Army's ladder with relentless zeal. Within the Army's small peacetime officer corps, he was soon noted and marked a "comer." As the years rolled by, he was selected for all the right graduate schools: two one-year tours at the Infantry School; a two-year stint at the Command and General Staff School, at Fort Leavenworth, Kansas; and finally a year at the prestigious Army War College, at Fort Humphreys, on the Potomac River in Washington, D.C.[6]

Ridgway was uncommonly bright and a quick study. Encouraged by his parents from childhood, he became an obsessive reader. As a cadet, he devoured every military biography and memoir he could lay his hands on. He memorized great martially stirring swaths of Kipling and delighted in quoting him and other patriotic poets. Although he was neither a profound nor an original thinker, he had a facility with words that enabled him to draft complicated war plans and analytical staff papers with comparative ease. Having been assigned to teach Spanish during his World War I tour at West Point, he mastered the language and, during the twenties and thirties, was one of only a half dozen officers in the Regular Army fluent in Spanish. This accomplishment led to several special high-level assignments in Latin America, which broadened his horizons and further enhanced his career.[7]

Along this climb up the ladder, Ridgway formed devout religious convictions and a personal philosophy. The latter he described as "dichotomous." On the one hand he believed that most individuals and societies were motivated by greed, acquisitiveness, a thirst for power and brutality; that until these "inherent human traits" were "drastically altered" wars were inevitable and that the rich and powerful United States would all too often be the "prime target." For that reason, he believed it was imperative that the United States maintain an unassailable military posture. On the other hand, he believed there was some "high, although inscrutable" guiding purpose behind this miserable state of affairs and that every individual had an "inescapable duty" to do whatever lay in his or her power to achieve "a better world order" through nonmilitary endeavors.[8]

Fundamentally, Ridgway was a soldier. He much preferred life in the field to a desk or a classroom. From his earliest years he was a dedicated outdoorsman. He loved to camp out, sleep on the ground, hike endless miles, hunt birds and big game, fly-cast in remote mountain streams, blaze trails through jungles on foot or horseback. But opportunities to savor life in the field had come all too infrequently. Owing to his talent for paperwork, his fluency in Spanish, and the shortage of peacetime field units, he had drawn mostly staff jobs. In his twenty-four years of Army service since graduating from West Point, he had spent only two years in the field directly in command of troops—five companies and a battalion—and never for very long at a stretch.[9]

On those rare occasions when he had commanded troops, Ridgway had excelled. In this, his true element, he demonstrated a pronounced talent for getting men to pull together and for inculcating unit pride. One reason was that he was no tent hog grinding out orders. He was out front all day, exhorting, cajoling, teaching. He drove himself tirelessly from dawn to dusk and often late into the night. His working motto, delivered in a deep commanding voice tinged with a New York accent, was "Haven't got time? Well, get up earlier . . . stay up later at night." He had little patience with human failings and was notoriously outspoken and short-fused. His dedication, zeal and intensity led his sweating GIs to joke: "There's a right way, a wrong way and a Ridgway." The "Ridgway" was the Army way raised to perfection.[10]

He was a professional field soldier with high ideals and principles and unyielding integrity. When it came to military matters, he was not a man who would compromise; he would not hesitate to lay his career on the line rather than do so. A close West Point friend, Russell P. Reeder, Jr., described his soldiering thus: "He was a Twelfth Century knight with a Twentieth Century brain."[11]

He had developed leadership tricks, at least one of which inspired awe: an uncanny memory for names. By graduation from West Point, Ridgway could give, on sight, the first and last names of every cadet in the seven-hundred-man corps. He continued this trick throughout his career in the belief that "calling people by their names had a powerful effect." Many a private, corporal or sergeant who had not seen Ridgway for years had been stunned when he approached them and said, "Hello, Smith! Haven't seen you since . . ." In 1951, the American author James Michener, in a magazine profile of Ridgway, estimated that Ridgway knew the names of "four or five thousand" men, half of them enlisted, and could "recall them without hesitation."[12]

There was yet another aspect about Ridgway that did not go unremarked. The opposite sex found him irresistibly attractive. Whether deserved or not, he had a reputation as something of a Don Juan. That reputation had attached to him during his days at West Point, where he was known to some as "the Black Knight of the Hudson." He had married a New Yorker on graduation, beneath the traditional arch of swords. But that marriage, which produced two daughters, had ended in divorce after thirteen years, a rare and drastic step in the peacetime Army, as elsewhere in American society in the 1930s. He then married another New Yorker (an Army widow) with a young daughter, whom he adopted. Both his divorce and the remarriage evoked gossip. In some Army-wife circles, there were whispers of scorn. To other females, the dark intrigue and scandalous chitchat merely added to Ridgway's fatal charm.[13]

Apart from the critics of his erratic affairs of the heart, a few of Ridgway's fellow officers were put off by his single-mindedness, his zeal, his tendency to evoke the flag and a Divine Being, to needlessly call attention to his accomplishments, or to use big and flowery words and phrases when simple ones would do. To them Ridgway came across as a stuffed shirt and a drudge who took life—and himself—far too seriously. They were resentful that he seemed unable to relax or get drunk or put his feet up or tell a joke. Ridgway willingly conceded the last shortcoming. "Long ago," he told an interviewer, "I eschewed any attempts in trying to be a humorist. I was never able to be funny."[14]

Despite some surface indications to the contrary, Ridgway was at root a modest and at times a self-deprecating man. In private conversation, he was apt to paraphrase an old poem: "When you are beginning to think you're so important, make a fist and stick your arm into a bucket of water up to your wrist. When you take it out, the hole you left is the measure of how much you'll be missed."[15]

That Sunday of December 7 at Fort Benning, Ridgway and a contemporary, C. Ralph Huebner, another "comer" who had also just arrived for a week's refresher course, went to the officers' club for lunch. While they were waiting for a table, someone—Ridgway would never forget the shocked expression on the man's face—came up and told them that the Japanese had just attacked the U.S. Pacific Fleet at Pearl Harbor.

Ridgway and Huebner were stunned. As a senior member of the War Department War Plans Division, Ridgway knew the Japanese had been gearing up for all-out war in the Far East. Before leaving Washington he had helped plot an ominous movement of Japanese convoys southward from staging bases in the Formosa Strait and Indochina toward Malaya, a movement that possibly foreshadowed an attack on the Isthmus of Kra, on the Malay Peninsula. But Pearl Harbor? It seemed inconceivable.

By midafternoon Ridgway was in telephone contact with his Washington office. He confirmed the unbelievable news. It meant, of course, that he had to cancel the temporary duty at Fort Benning and return to Washington without delay. On his way back that night, he thanked his lucky stars that he had already been notified that he was slated for troop duty, that in spite of the catastrophe at Pearl Harbor, the odds were probably good that he would not be trapped in staff duty in Washington, that he would at last have an opportunity to lead troops in battle and remove the "blot" of "no combat service" from his record.[16]

☆2☆

TWENTY-FOUR HOURS after Ridgway arrived at Fort Benning he was back at his desk in the War Plans Division of the War Department. The Department was housed in a row of seedy barracks-like buildings on Constitution Avenue which had been hurriedly thrown up to meet emergency space requirements of World War I. For twenty-two years they had served as "temporary" headquarters for the War and Navy departments. The Army would soon move to the vast, palatial Pentagon, then under construction at a site immediately across the Potomac River in Virginia.[1]

Presiding over the Department was the Secretary of War, Henry L. Stimson, a distinguished and aged Republican hawk who had been Secretary of War for President William Howard Taft, and later Secretary of State for President Herbert Hoover. Roosevelt had enticed Stimson and another Republican hawk, Secretary of the Navy Frank Knox, into his Cabinet in June 1940, in order to build Republican support for his pro-British, anti-Hitler policies and to strengthen his position on Capitol Hill. Despite his advanced years, Secretary Stimson was a strong and energetic administrator, and officers such as Ridgway held him in highest esteem.[2]

Under Stimson, the senior professional Army officer was chief of staff General George Catlett Marshall, whom Roosevelt had appointed to the post in April 1939. Born in Pennsylvania, Marshall was a graduate of the Virginia Military Institute (VMI), in Lexington, Virginia. He had married a Virginian and had adopted the courtly manners and life-style of the Virginia gentleman. He was all Army, all business. In the words of one who knew him well, Marshall was "austere, cold, aloof, succinct, prudish," and he projected a towering sense of authority and quiet force. Like many other officers who knew Marshall well, Ridgway idolized the man. He believed then that Marshall would someday "occupy a place second only to George Washington in the military history of the United States."[3]

To no small degree, Ridgway owed his present position in the prestigious War Plans Division and his recent promotion to colonel to George Marshall. During the peacetime years, they had served together several times. On each of those occasions, Ridgway had made a highly favorable impression on Marshall, although Marshall fretted over Ridgway's tendency to overachieve and to impress superiors, sometimes even at the expense of his health.

They had first met in the field at Tientsin, China, in 1925. Marshall was then executive officer of the 15th Infantry Regiment. Its nominal commander, one Marshall biographer wrote, was an alcoholic who had allowed the regiment to fall into disarray and disrepute. When young Ridgway reported for duty, Marshall, who temporarily commanded the regiment, assigned him to command the headquarters company and asked his help in rescuing the regiment. This was no easy assignment. The regiment was quartered in the middle of Tientsin, a teeming metropolis. The men, as Ridgway later remembered, "had too many luxuries" and indulged in "too much high living." Most of the men were single; the VD rate in the outfit was appalling. It was difficult to find space for training in the nearby countryside, where every square foot was under cultivation. Nonetheless, Ridgway put his hand to the job with his customary intensity. Within a few months Marshall, with the help of Ridgway and others, transformed the regiment from one of the worst into one of the best, and Ridgway earned Marshall's gratitude. In only one respect did Ridgway fail to measure up. In spite of his fluency in Spanish, he had a "very difficult" time with Chinese, a language he was expected to learn on the job. He attributed this failure to a minor hearing disability. His ear "had never been very keen," and he had a particularly hard time "distinguishing the intonations" of the Chinese language.[4]

Three years later, in 1929, Ridgway and Marshall met again at Fort Benning. Marshall was then commandant of the Infantry School, Ridgway a student in the one-year Advanced Course. Marshall's tenure as Benning's commandant would, in time, become the stuff of legends. He set in motion what one of his section chiefs (Omar N. Bradley) would call a "minor revolution," throwing out the outmoded textbooks, field manuals and theories and introducing entirely new teaching techniques. Ridgway and his classmates were among Marshall's first guinea pigs. They judged his new approach superior to any military schooling they had ever received. Ridgway had graduated at the top of his class.[5]

Their paths next crossed during military maneuvers in Michigan in the summer of 1936. Marshall was then the senior instructor of the Illinois National Guard, Ridgway the chief planner on the staff of the Second Army. During this maneuver, Marshall conceived a daunting plan to strike the "enemy" a fatal blow by utilizing a rapid flanking envelopment. To his dismay, he found he did not have nearly enough trucks to carry it out. Ridgway and a cohort, George P. Hayes, saved the day—and helped Marshall win the exercise—by talking General Motors executives in Detroit into lending Marshall two hundred brand-new trucks.

Throughout these maneuvers, Ridgway had worked in Marshall's behalf with feverish intensity. At the end, he was so drained, mentally and physically, that he "fainted" in his bathroom, fell, badly gashed his head and sank into oblivion. The next day friends found him comatose on a blood-soaked bed and rushed him to the hospital. After Ridgway recovered and was packing to leave for the Army War College, he received a letter from Marshall which both commended him and admonished him in a fatherly way to take life easier:

> You personally are to be congratulated for the major success of all the tactical phases of the enterprise and certainly Hayes has commendations coming for handling of a vast number of complications connected with setting up supply and similar arrangements. You two officers did such a perfect job that

there should be some way of rewarding you other than saying it was well done.

I am concerned as to whether you have succeeded in relaxing. I know you have enough brains to perform your military duties in a superior fashion but I doubt very much whether you have enough sense to take care of the human machine—very few men have, and unfortunately when you burn out a fuse you cannot substitute another twenty minutes later. Seriously, you must cultivate the art of playing and loafing; there is no need for you to demonstrate any further you are an energetic, able workman. So I hope you will utilize the remaining days before the War College opens and the first week or two of the War College course to establish the reputation of being something of a dilettante . . .[6]

Ridgway served under Marshall a fourth time in May 1939 in the weeks before Marshall took up his duties as chief of staff; this service led directly to Ridgway's appointment to War Plans.

At that time, President Roosevelt was deeply concerned over the way Hitler was wooing certain Latin American nations, apparently with some degree of success. This had evoked fear in Washington that the courtship might result in firm Third Reich footholds in Latin America. To counter this threat, Roosevelt decided to send Marshall on a "good will" mission to the largest of the Latin nations, Brazil. The news of this assignment reached Marshall simultaneously with the news of his appointment as chief of staff. It came while Marshall was visiting Fourth Army headquarters at the Presidio, in San Francisco, where Ridgway was a staff officer and in whose quarters Marshall was a houseguest.

Marshall knew that Ridgway had served as an adviser to a member of four special diplomatic missions in Latin America and the Philippines and that he was fluent in Spanish, though not in Portuguese, the official language of Brazil. Subsequently he requested the War Department to assign Ridgway to the Brazil mission, which was scheduled to depart New York on U.S. Navy cruiser *Nashville* on May 10, 1939.

Ridgway, flattered to be invited, packed a wardrobe trunk with the many uniforms such a visit demanded and set off by train for New York. On May 5, while in Rock Springs, Wyoming, he received a telegram with shocking news: his seventy-seven-year-old father, who had been living in retirement in San Diego, had died of a heart attack. There was no practical way that Ridgway could attend the funeral and reach New York before the *Nashville* sailed, so he continued on to New York. His older sister, Ruth, and her husband, Norton Meade Beardslee, a retired West Pointer (class of 1909), who lived near San Diego, saw to the funeral arrangements.

The trip to Brazil was thus a tonic. During it, Ridgway's relationship with Marshall grew closer. Ridgway recalled that on the ten-day voyage to Rio de Janeiro he had "many, many hours of quiet talk with Marshall on the forward deck of the ship." In these talks, Marshall exhibited his trust in Ridgway by confiding his most closely held ideas for preparing the then absurdly small and ill-equipped U.S. Army for World War II.

One overriding but secret aim of the mission was to obtain permission from the Brazilian Government for the U.S. Army Air Corps to establish an air route and network of air bases through Brazil as a jumping-off point for a transatlantic air route to Dakar, French West Africa. The network of bases would require that American troops be stationed on Brazilian soil, a radical— and sensitive—proposition. Ultimately Marshall was successful in persuading the Brazilians to approve every aspect of the air system, although the Brazilians insisted that the American troops be solely airmen and that they wear mufti. It was probably well that the Brazilians agreed. Ridgway said later that the War Department had contingency war plans (POT OF GOLD and LILAC) to seize the bases "by force" if necessary.

The mission was deemed an unqualified success. Brazil would remain a staunch "good neighbor" throughout World War II. Ridgway's contribution had been substantial. When Marshall returned to Washington to take over as chief of staff, one of his first moves was to assign Ridgway to the War Plans Division as a Latin American specialist. In that assignment, Ridgway became the chief manager of the Brazilian air routes project, which in time became a vital line of communication for the American armed forces. Later, when the War Plans Division established a formal Latin American section, Ridgway was named to head it.[7]

Another of Ridgway's responsibilities was to dispatch special missions to Latin America, broadening the "good neighbor" policies Marshall had inaugurated in Brazil. It proved to be difficult to find Army officers sufficiently poised, mature and fluent in Spanish to successfully carry out these missions. The search for such men led Ridgway to remember Maxwell Davenport Taylor, a brainy artilleryman who had graduated fourth in the West Point class of 1922 and had been Ridgway's classmate and sometime tennis partner at the Command and General Staff School. A handsome, soft-spoken Missourian, Taylor had a reputation as a diplomat and linguist.

"He had me yanked right out of the War College," Taylor recalled recently with amusement. He had been a member of the class of 1940 at the Army War College—the last class to graduate before the war closed the college down. "I finally graduated *in absentia.* He had these missions running all over South America to find out how we could help the Latins militarily. I'll never forget that experience. The Latins would give us these huge shopping lists, which we couldn't possibly fill. At one point, I wound up in Peru. Darned if the Peruvian admirals didn't present me with a list of things they needed to combat possible German submarines in Lake Titicaca, a land-locked body of water in the Andes foothills."

The assignment to the War Plans Division had drawn Ridgway even closer into the Marshall orbit. "It was a very close relationship," Max Taylor recalled. "Ridgway did not need an appointment. He had unrestricted access to the Old Man. He was one of Marshall's boys."[8]

Marshall continued to worry in his fatherly way about the relentless way Ridgway drove himself and the adverse effect it could have on his health. By the fall of 1940, Ridgway typically had so exhausted himself physically and mentally that he came down with a streptococcal throat—a dangerous infection—and had to go to Walter Reed Army Hospital. After several days in bed, Ridgway grew impatient to return to work and, against doctors' advice, left the hospital. Two days later he had a relapse and returned to Walter Reed for a long stay. Shortly after his readmission, he received a gentle rebuke from Marshall: "I got a note . . . that you were shipped back to the hospital for further treatment . . . I am sorry that you have had this hard luck, but I was afraid you were going to walk into it by forcing your comeback the last time. Please take it more casually this time and do exactly what the doctors say."[9]

THE JAPANESE ATTACK on Pearl Harbor was merely one key move in a well-conceived war plan that unfolded with awesome efficiency. It was immediately followed by devastating air raids and amphibious invasions in the Philippines which drove out the Navy and compelled the ground forces' commander, Douglas MacArthur, to withdraw his troops to Bataan and Corregidor. Other Japanese forces invaded Malaya to attack the British bastion at Singapore from the rear. Still others struck at Hong Kong, Guam and Wake Island, all of which soon fell. For a while, an invasion of Hawaii and even the West Coast of the United States seemed a possibility.

The War Plans Division was swamped in crises. Every man assigned to it worked long, exhausting hours. In addition to his arduous and complex Latin American responsibilities, Ridgway was assigned to prepare a daily summary of the world's battlefronts for Roosevelt, Stimson and Marshall and other top brass. In order to have the summary delivered by 8 A.M., Ridgway had to be in his office by 6 A.M. When that chore was finished, he wrote, "I would go ahead with my regular duties until ten or eleven o'clock at night, a routine that left me a little hollow-eyed."[1]

The men in War Plans had ringside seats to a fascinating period in American history. Their decisions were shaping policy with profound implications. But few prized the assignment; most wanted to get out and command troops. Among the most eager to leave was Ridgway's boss, Leonard T. (Gee) Gerow. Before Pearl Harbor, Marshall had promised Gerow the infantryman's ultimate prize: command of a division. But these plans had been frustrated by a tragedy. On the way to have a quick look at the damage at Pearl Harbor, Gerow's understudy and intended relief, Charles W. Bundy, had been killed in a plane crash. Now, before Gerow could leave, he had to break in a new replacement. Marshall's latest handpicked candidate, a recent Marshall "discovery," was Brigadier General Dwight D. Eisenhower, who had been serving in a staff job in the field and who came to War Plans only reluctantly—determined to get back to the field as quickly as possible.[2]

No man in War Plans was more eager to leave than Matt Ridgway. Before Pearl Harbor, Marshall himself had assured Ridgway he would get command of a regiment. But weeks passed with no word from Marshall. Owing to the heavy new burdens imposed by the war, Ridgway saw Marshall less and less frequently. Had Marshall changed his mind? Would Ridgway be stuck in War Plans for the duration of the war?

Marshall's office was now in the charge of a brilliant, acerbic officer, Walter Bedell Smith, who bore the title Secretary of the General Staff. Smith and his small staff (known collectively as the Secretariat) presided over Marshall's flow of paperwork and appointments and, at Marshall's insistence, made many decisions on his behalf. Ridgway counted Smith among his good friends. They had been classmates at the Command and General Staff School and later the Army War College. At the former, Smith had been a member of a study team Ridgway headed which had presented the decisive World War I Battle of Tannenberg on stage, like a play, complete with dramatic dialogue, sound effects and lighting. More recently, Ridgway had done Smith the favor of giving him his best Latin American envoy, Max Taylor, for a job in the Secretariat, replacing one of Ridgway's classmates, J. Lawton (Joe) Collins.[3]

In his eagerness to get out of War Plans, Ridgway began hounding Smith "every day" to see if Marshall had made a decision. Despite their old acquaintanceship, Smith soon tired of this and became none too sympathetic. One day when Ridgway stuck his head in Smith's door and for the umpteenth time asked, "Any word?" Smith snapped back, "Yes. This morning General Marshall said, and I quote, 'Tell Ridgway I'm tired of seeing him hanging around out there every time my door opens. When I have something for him, I'll send for him.' "[4]

Thus squelched, a "crestfallen" Ridgway returned to the paperwork drudgery in War Plans and waited.

Not until late January 1942 did Marshall send for him. The news he gave Ridgway was positively electrifying. The Army was reactivating the famous 82nd "All-American" Division of World War I. Omar Bradley, a onetime member of Marshall's Secretariat and then the commandant of Fort Benning and the Infantry School, would command the division. Marshall was assigning Ridgway to be Bradley's second-in-command, or assistant division commander (ADC), a job that carried the rank of brigadier general.[5]

It seemed difficult to believe. Ridgway had spent thirteen long years in the rank of captain; eight more long years a major. Now, in a mere eighteen months, he had advanced from lieutenant colonel to brigadier general—spending only about six weeks in the grade of colonel. Moreover, had he been in a position to choose, he could not have come up with a better job or boss than ADC to Omar Bradley, whom Ridgway viewed as one of the ablest officers in the Army. The position of ADC was on-the-job training for command of a division. If Ridgway did well, he might soon move up another notch.[6]

Ridgway returned immediately to his office and emptied his desk and files. There was no farewell ceremony—not even an office lunch—merely a quick good-bye to Gerow, Eisenhower and a few other associates. He jumped into his car and drove to nearby Fort Humphreys, now headquarters for Army Ground Forces (AGF), an organization Marshall had created to oversee the fielding and training of the planned one hundred Army divisions for World War II. The AGF was commanded by a distinguished older general, Lesley J. McNair. His chief of staff, Mark Wayne Clark, also newly promoted to brigadier general, was one of Ridgway's West Point classmates and a close friend. At the Command and General Staff School, Clark had also been a teammate on Ridgway's "Tannenberg" presentation.[7]

At AGF, Ridgway learned that the 82nd Division would assemble and train at Camp Claiborne, a new base outside Alexandria, Louisiana, on the Red River. It was suggested that en route to Claiborne, Ridgway might well profit from a week's "refresher" course at Benning—the very same course he had set out to take on December 7. Omar Bradley was still at Benning, winding up his affairs. A visit to Benning would also provide an opportunity for the two men to huddle and make plans.

Few men have ever left Washington in such great haste. Having no easy means at hand to safeguard the classified papers from his desk and files (some with historic notations such as "OK-FDR"), Ridgway simply burned them while awaiting his orders to be cut, an impetuous act he would regret. Two hours after his meeting with Marshall he was back in his car, crossing the Memorial Bridge, southbound for Benning. His wife, Peggy, would see to the packing and join him at Claiborne.[8]

Brigadier General Omar Bradley, Commandant of the Infantry School and titular boss of all of Fort Benning, was a tall, slim, bespectacled man approaching his forty-ninth birthday—two years older than Ridgway. Bradley was one of the homeliest and most humble men West Point had ever turned out. He had the low-key air of a country schoolteacher and spoke in rural, twangy Midwest vernacular. He was shy, hated to be fussed over, and thus avoided publicity. He was warmhearted, compassionate, had a keen sense of humor and relished the outdoor life, particularly hunting and fishing. His prowess at the poker table was legendary. On the golf course he had few peers within the Regular Army.

Bradley had come to the Army from modest circumstances. His forebears were desperately poor Missouri sodbusters. His self-educated father, a poor country schoolteacher, had died when Bradley, an only surviving child, was fourteen, leaving him and his mother penniless. From that time onward, Bradley had had to earn his own way and help support his mother. He had chosen West Point not because he wanted to be a soldier, but because it offered him a free college education. Like Ridgway—and Eisenhower—he had missed the fighting in France in World War I, but he had matured into one of the smartest and most well-rounded officers of his generation. A year past, Marshall had jump-promoted Bradley from lieutenant colonel to brigadier general and put him in command of Benning. Bradley had thus become the first infantryman of the class of 1915 to make general—ten months ahead of his classmate Eisenhower.[9]

Bradley and Ridgway were longtime professional associates. They had served together, off and on, for ten years. They had overlapped at the Academy for two years, where Bradley had been a star on the varsity baseball and football teams and Ridgway the football-team manager. At West Point both had been members of a secret (and illegal) Greek fraternity, Omicron Pi Phi, composed mostly of cadets involved with athletics. In the ensuing years, they had served together four times—once at West Point, twice at Fort Benning, and more recently in the War Department when Bradley was assigned to Marshall's Secretariat. As fellow instructors at West Point in the early twenties, they had learned to play golf together. At West Point and Benning they had been hunting companions.[10]

Soon after arriving at Benning, Matt Ridgway called on Omar Bradley. Bradley greeted Ridgway with his customary old-shoe geniality. He did not number Ridgway among his most intimate friends—Ridgway was too intense for Bradley's taste—but he had a high regard for him professionally. Decades later, in his autobiography, Bradley wrote that Ridgway was "one of the most charismatic and able officers" in the Army and that he felt "lucky" to have drawn him as ADC.[11]

Bradley was intensely proud that George Marshall, whom he revered, had made him a general and chosen him to be the first in his West Point class to command a division. Outward appearances notwithstanding, Bradley was keenly ambitious, an intense competitor, impatient of fools, braggarts, dilettantes and misfits. Since his West Point days, when athletic activities diverted him from his academic work, Bradley had sought first place in all his postgraduate schools and assignments. He viewed his selection to command the 82nd Division as a singular vote of confidence from Marshall. He intended to fully justify that confidence. The 82nd Infantry Division would be the "best-trained" division in the Army. In this, Bradley's views coincided exactly with those of his newly appointed second in command.[12]

☆4☆

THE 82ND DIVISION had had a brief but proud history. It was activated in World War I and tagged the "All-American" Division, because it was composed of men from all forty-eight states. It had spent more consecutive days in the front lines than any other American division and had suffered 7,422 casualties, including 1,035 killed. Its battle streamers included Lorraine, Saint-Mihiel, Meuse-Argonne. It had many distinguished alumni, including West Pointer Jonathan M. (Skinny) Wainwright, then fighting desperately on Bataan under General Douglas MacArthur. Its most distinguished World War I alumnus was the Tennessee sharpshooter Sergeant Alvin C. York, who had single-handedly broken up an entire German battalion and been awarded the Medal of Honor. He had recently been immortalized by Gary Cooper in the 1941 film *Sergeant York.* After World War I, the division had been deactivated.[1]

The newly activated 82nd Division staff began assembling in Camp Claiborne, Louisiana, in mid to late February 1942. The Ridgways rented a house in Alexandria, from which Ridgway car-pooled to work. They had barely unpacked and settled in when Peggy Ridgway became ill and returned to Washington for a thorough checkup at Walter Reed Army Hospital. After her discharge, on the advice of doctors she remained in Washington as an outpatient for many weeks. Thus began a separation that would last through most of the war.[2]

The 82nd Division, along with two or three others, was to be staffed and trained in an experimental fashion. Theretofore, draftees had been sent to reserve and National Guard units already in existence or to basic training camps to become fillers. The 82nd Division was to be created from scratch, made up of some sixteen thousand draftees who would report to the division directly from civilian life. The draftees would be integrated into the division's paper structure and undergo basic training while the division itself was gradually taking shape. It would be a standard "triangular" unit, with three infantry regiments of three battalions each, and would have its own division artillery.[3]

Owing to its complexity and size, the division artillery was commanded by a brigadier general. He was Joseph May Swing, another handpicked "Marshall man." Swing had been a classmate of Bradley and Eisenhower at West Point and was married to the daughter of onetime Army chief of staff Peyton C. March. At West Point, Swing had been a stunt rider and track star. In the Academy yearbook, *Howitzer,* his classmates described him as "a rough-house kid with a happy-go-lucky disposition" who was "at the bottom of more mischief and practical jokes than any other Kaydet in the place." Although Swing graduated in the top quarter of his class, his classmates believed that had "he boned it," he could have stood even higher, perhaps in the top five or ten.[4]

The tendency to hell-raise stayed with Swing for a long time. One contemporary recalled, "When I was a young captain in Hawaii, I was billeted temporarily in the BOQ, a dreadful place with thin tar-paper walls. Major Swing was also staying there for some reason. Saturday night he and this infantry officer buddy would get skunked. They'd start roughhousing. Well, I'm damned if Swing didn't literally throw this fellow right through the wall of the BOQ."[5]

On duty with troops, Joe Swing was tough as nails, a notorious disciplinarian who inspired awe and fear. "You could almost see flames shooting out of his eyes," a contemporary recalled. Another said, "He was very forceful, very positive. When he said, 'Frog,' something jumped." One day, Swing passed a group of junior officers in the headquarters area and not one man saluted him. "Who *are* those people?" he demanded in a fury. They turned out to be students at the signal school. Swing hauled the signal school instructor—a West Pointer—up before Bradley and, even though the instructor had no responsibility for discipline or military courtesy, "tore him to shreds."[6]

The next-most-senior officer in the 82nd Division was the chief of staff, a full colonel, the executive who presided over the division "Gs" (G-1, personnel; G-2, intelligence; G-3, plans and training; G-4, logistics). It was Bradley's prerogative to choose his own chief of staff. His first choice was not available, so he turned to George van Wyck Pope, who, by all accounts, turned out to be "one of the few personnel mistakes" Bradley ever made. Pope was virtually the only non-West Pointer in the 82nd Division high command. "He was an awfully nice guy," a contemporary recalled, "but he had never really made a strong mark in the Army. He had been in the West Point Tactical Department —teaching cadets calisthenics in the gym—when Brad was a math teacher there and later worked for Brad at Benning. He was one of Brad's hunting and golfing and poker buddies. But it turned out he couldn't make decisions."[7]

Ridgway recruited the next headquarters staffer, the adjutant general, who also doubled in brass as the division G-1.* He was an old acquaintance, Ralph P. Eaton, nicknamed "Doc" because he had been an enlisted stretcher-bearer in the trenches in France in World War I. Doc Eaton would remain close by Ridgway's side for most of World War II and become his most trusted confidant.[9]

On the surface, Doc Eaton seemed an unlikely buddy for Matt Ridgway. He was in many ways his opposite: homely, self-deprecating, a rural Midwesterner with a knack for telling amusing anecdotes, a sort of country slicker. He recalled:

When I got back from service in World War I, I entered the University of Illinois and joined the ROTC and played semi-pro baseball. Word came around that any World War I vet who spent a year overseas could enter West Point *without taking the entrance exam*. I jumped at it—because I could

---

* The other Gs were as follows: G-2, George E. Lynch, West Point 1929 and son of the former chief of infantry; G-3, Willis S. Matthews, West Point 1927; G-4, Truman C. (Tubby) Thorson. Bradley had brought Matthews and Thorson from Benning.[8]

never have passed the exams. I squeaked through the four years and graduated twenty-three from the bottom of my class in 1924. I was a pretty fair pitcher—sidearm and knuckle ball—and very much wanted to play at West Point but the coach turned me down. He wanted only overhand pitchers. That was the biggest disappointment of my young life.

Ridgway and Eaton had served together several times, first with the 9th Infantry at Fort Sam Houston, Texas, then at the Infantry School, then in the Philippines. But they had never become close friends. They had had virtually no contact for ten years. In fact, by 1940, Eaton had left the infantry branch and joined the Army's adjutant general's section. They had not much in common—except a passion for baseball, service in the 9th Infantry and marital difficulties. Eaton, married in 1932, had been divorced after five years and had remarried in 1940.[10]

I'm not certain what I meant to Ridgway [Eaton recalled]. It's a mystery. Maybe it was just common sense. I didn't have many brains but I was blessed with a good ration of plain common sense. And I was something of a Bolshevik—not a by-the-book man. My motto was "Throw the goddamn regulations out of the window and get the job done." We had a lot of jobs to do in a big hurry and there was a tendency on the part of some of the old-timers to get snarled up in red tape—to lose sight of the forest for the trees. Also, he could get wound up pretty tight—tense as hell—and I think he unwound talking to me.

The signal officer of the 82nd Division—he who had been so harshly rebuked by Joe Swing—would become another close associate of Ridgway's. He was Frank Willoughby (Bill) Moorman, a West Pointer in the class of 1934, who was the son of a retired regular Army officer. Moorman was a far different type of man from Eaton—soft-spoken, urbane, intellectually inclined. He was nearly unflappable and was blessed not only with a good ration of common sense, but also a wry sense of humor. Regarding his volcanic encounter with Joe Swing, he recalled with amusement, "The more Swing ranted—tearing me to shreds—the more opaque became Bradley's face. Bradley was like a rock. He could handle Swing. Screwing up my courage, I said to Swing: 'My job is to teach these officers something about communications. It's *your* job to teach them to salute.' Bradley finally said, 'Huumph,' and walked away. And that was that." Moorman may have thus become the only junior officer in the Army to face down Joe Swing.[11]

Eaton and Moorman were deeply impressed by Brigadier General Ridgway. At one point during his career, Eaton, who could be irascible and intolerant, had become so fed up with the "drunkenness and incompetence" of the peacetime Army that he had almost resigned his commission. Ridgway helped restore his faith. "He was an inspiration," Eaton recalled. "Dedicated. Intensely patriotic and moral." Moorman found Ridgway to be "a very striking fellow . . . almost awe-inspiring to a young officer like myself. He would always throw me. Whatever you knew, he knew more. Whatever you did, he could do better."[12]

As brigadier general and the ADC, Ridgway rated an aide-de-camp and a driver. For his aide, he handpicked Don Carlos Faith, Jr., who had just graduated from the Fort Benning OCS, standing in the top ten of his two-hundred-man class. Ridgway later described him as "an awfully likable youngster" with a "winning smile," who had a "superior physique, great athletic ability and an alert mind and positive qualities of leadership." Like Moorman, Faith was an "Army brat"; his father, a brigadier general, had been handpicked by George Marshall to assist Colonel Oveta Culp Hobby in establishing the Women's Army Auxiliary Corps (WAAC). For his driver, Ridgway chose Frank G. Farmer of Moreauville, Louisiana. Both men would remain with Ridgway throughout the war.[13]

Each of the division's three infantry regiments (325th, 326th, 327th) was commanded by a full colonel. With the Army expanding to 100 divisions, qualified regimental commanders with the requisite seniority, professional experience, leadership ability, courage and physical stamina were all too rare. Two of the three regimental commanders, Claudius S. Easley (325th) and Stuart Cutler (326th) were outstanding. The third, George S. Wear (327th), failed to meet the high standards Bradley and Ridgway had set, but owing to the shortage of qualified colonels, he was retained in his command through the division's basic training phase.[14]

Each of the three regiments' three infantry battalions was commanded by a lieutenant colonel. Able battalion commanders were likewise rare. Moreover, inasmuch as it was believed that the casualty rate for battalion commanders would be high, the problem was further complicated by the need to have a "backup" already in place in each battalion (second-in-command, or executive officer), plus several "spares" within each regiment (usually assigned to the regimental headquarters staff). Ideally, each infantry regiment would go into combat with at least ten qualified battalion commanders, or a total of thirty in the three infantry regiments. Owing to the shortage of qualified officers, this ideal was never realized in the 82nd—or any other infantry division—and the continuing search for able battalion commanders would preoccupy Bradley and Ridgway (and all other ground commanders) throughout the war.

The initial cadre for the reactivated 82nd Division—seven hundred junior officers and twelve hundred enlisted men—came from the 9th Infantry Division, commanded by a West Pointer (class of 1909), Jacob L. Devers, at Fort Bragg, North Carolina. These nearly two thousand men reported to Camp Claiborne at about the time the senior staffs were gathering. The bulk of the division—the sixteen thousand draftees—would come directly from reception centers in Alabama, Georgia, Mississippi and Tennessee. The division was officially activated on March 25, 1942, about three weeks after Ridgway's forty-seventh birthday.[15]

Bradley was determined that his draftees would be treated in "an intelligent, humane, understanding way" and made to feel "at home." There would be no stupid, morale-eroding "hurry up and wait" in the 82nd Division. Accordingly, he gave orders to the G-1/adjutant, Doc Eaton, to send teams ahead to the reception centers to meet—and greet—the draftees and, during the train ride to Camp Claiborne, interview and classify them by their civilian specialties (cook, truck driver, carpenter, etc.) and assign them to specific units of the 82nd before arrival. Draftees debarking at Camp Claiborne went directly from the train to preassigned units, hot meals and tents, where they found their equipment and bedding on preassigned cots. Nothing like this had ever been tried before. AGF commander General McNair pronounced it a grand idea and recommended it for the other new divisions, which were coming into being on a schedule slightly behind the 82nd.[16]

The AGF staff had devised a seventeen-week training program for the new divisions. This meant the 82nd should be fully trained and ready for combat by about August 1. As Bradley and Ridgway knew, George Marshall and his chief war planner, Dwight Eisenhower, were then advocating an early invasion of France—perhaps as early as the fall of 1942 but no later than the spring of 1943. This plan was known as ROUNDUP. Although no official orders had come down from Washington, it seemed probable that the 82nd would be assigned to the invasion. Thus Bradley and Ridgway commenced the 82nd Division training schedule with a great sense of urgency and gravity.[17]

Bradley was swamped administratively with organizing, manning, equipping and training the division. One result was that, as Ridgway put it, Bradley "very generously" delegated the responsibility for all aspects of training to Ridgway. Given the shortness of the training schedule, this turned out to be "a full-time job every waking hour of the day." Ridgway, as was his custom, drove himself —and the men—hard.[18]

The first large task was to whip the draftees into prime physical condition. Bradley and Ridgway were shocked to find that at least a third of them were, as Bradley put it, "in appallingly poor physical condition . . . overweight and soft as marshmallows." Only a few were really capable of the hard and sustained physical exertion they would face in combat. Ridgway believed that each man should be "as finely trained as a champion boxer." Soon the entire division, including Bradley, Ridgway and all staff officers, were engaged in an agonizingly tough physical-fitness program: daily calisthenics, long hikes, sporting events, plus workouts on what Ridgway described as an "extremely difficult" obstacle course, consisting of high walls, deep ditches, log barriers, culverts, rope climbs and the like.

Both Bradley and Ridgway, who were in far better shape than most of the draftees, ran the obstacle course from time to time. Once, while doing so, Bradley slipped on a rope swing and fell into a stinking drainage ditch below. Ridgway remarked, "The sight of a two-star general in such a predicament seemed to be a source of vast delight to all ranks, and the incident became one of the memorable highlights of the training period. My first impulse, of course, on seeing my senior in such a fix, was to turn loose and fall in with him, but my decision, made in mid-swing, was that this would be carrying military courtesy too far."[19]

Ridgway resorted to every conceivable means of keeping his body in tone. On his daily rounds in the field he jogged from one unit to the next or rode one of two horses (Greta, a black mare; Brown Gold, a chestnut mare) he had acquired from a converted cavalry unit. During formal unit parades and inspections, he took such long, vigorous strides that shorter-legged officers, such as Stuart Cutler, had to "dog-trot" or "hop-skip" to keep up. In the evenings, at his bachelor bungalow, he chopped logs which were supplied by the division engineers, a vigorous daily routine he continued throughout the war whenever logs could be found.[20]

In the "modern" Army, the sight of Ridgway on horseback evoked considerable barrack-room humor and inspired a lampooning cartoon in a division newspaper. But his horsemanship gave him great mobility in the field and made a strong and lasting impression on many GIs. Thomas J. Catanzaro, then a green recruit, remembered:

We were on the mortar range firing live ammo. We had fired a round when the barrel of our mortar flipped over backwards. General Ridgway was seated astride a large horse, watching the firing. He immediately galloped over, jumped off the horse and demonstrated how to properly anchor the bipod. Having never been in the company of a real-life general before, we were all amazed. Right then and there our pride in our never-before-seen general grew to new heights.[21]

The hard work was soon paying handsome dividends. General McNair and the Army corps command to which the 82nd was assigned administratively, showered compliments on Bradley and Ridgway, and the 82nd became a model for visiting firemen to study. In early April, a mere two weeks after official activation, McNair and Mark Wayne Clark paid the division a visit. Subsequently Clark wrote Ridgway: "General McNair was certainly well pleased with the way the new divisions are coming along and with your fine example the others should certainly whip into shape in rapid fashion."[22]

To build esprit, Bradley and Ridgway emphasized in every possible way the division's distinguished combat record in World War I. Bradley hit upon the idea of inviting Sergeant York to visit the division and talk to the men. York gladly accepted. In preparation for York's visit in early May, Ridgway hastily formed a "division band" composed of draftee-musicians from Cutler's 326th Regiment. One of the three traditional marches the band worked up for the York visit, "The American Soldier," would in time become the division battle song, renamed "All-American Soldier" and later "The Airborne March."

The Sergeant York visit was deemed a huge success. Ridgway assembled the division en masse in an amphitheater. Bradley and an honor guard escorted York to the podium, while the "band" struggled through its limited repertoire. York, an unpretentious man, spellbound the division with his story of how he had wiped out the German battalion (killing twenty German soldiers, capturing another 132, and destroying some thirty-five machine guns). His talk was carried on a nationwide radio hookup. Ridgway recalled: "He created in the minds of farm boys and clerks, youngsters of every station and class, the conviction that an aggressive soldier, well trained and well armed, can fight his way out of any situation."

There was one other useful by-product of the York visit. During his stay, York told Bradley that he had done his most effective shooting at very short range—twenty-five to fifty yards. Not long after York's departure, Bradley had Ridgway build a short-range firing course through the woods, with partially concealed tin cans for targets. This was a radical addition to the standard, static, long-distance firing range. One result was that draftees trained in the 82nd Division became outstanding close-in, quick-firing marksmen.[23]

Following the York visit, Ridgway received wonderful news. It came in a personal letter from Mark Clark, who wrote that "it looked as though" McNair would recommend that Ridgway be given command of his own division the following September. It would mean not only his own division command but also temporary promotion to the two-star rank of major general. Ridgway would be among the first men in his West Point class to receive that honor.[24]

But as it turned out George Marshall had another plan. The 28th National Guard Division, based at nearby Camp Livingston, was in grave difficulties. Mobilized a full year before the 82nd Division, it had made little progress in its training, for various reasons. Marshall decided that the best hope for rescuing the division lay in naming Bradley to command it. He also decreed that when Bradley moved to the 28th Division, Ridgway would be promoted to command the 82nd.[25]

For Ridgway, this was even better news. It meant that he would get command of a division about three to four months earlier than Clark had indicated. Not only that, rather than starting from scratch with a brand-new contingent of draftees and therefore likely to see combat much later, he would take over a division well along in its training schedule. Moreover, by now Ridgway identified strongly with the 82nd Division, just as the men identified him with the division. He had made an emotional as well as a professional commitment to the division. To have left it for another division would have been a personal wrench.

Facing a large headache at the 28th Division, Bradley might well have drawn heavily on the 82nd for help. But apart from his two aides and his driver, he took only three men from the division staff. All three were "Bradley men" whom he had personally brought to the division: chief of staff Van Pope, G-3 Willis Matthews and G-4 Tubby Thorson. The key positions in the 82nd were soon filled: Don F. Pratt replacing Ridgway as the ADC, R. Klemm Boyd (a West Pointer from the class of 1931) replacing Matthews as G-3, and a Reservist, Robert H. Wienecke, replacing Thorson as G-4.[26]

Like Bradley before him, Ridgway had the prerogative of choosing his own chief of staff. His choice was an interesting one: the field artilleryman-intellectual-linguist-diplomat Maxwell Taylor, who was still working in Marshall's Secretariat. Taylor was itching to get into the field. Only recently, Joseph W. (Vinegar Joe) Stilwell, knowing that Taylor had mastered the Japanese language, had asked Taylor to join his military mission to the Far East. Taylor had eagerly accepted, but Marshall refused to let Taylor go with Stilwell. However, Marshall was willing to release Taylor to join the 82nd Division.[27]

The change of command, which took place at noon on June 26, was not accomplished without some emotional heart tugs. McNair had wanted Bradley promoted to corps commander; Bradley did not relish leaving the 82nd to rescue a fumbling National Guard division, but of course he uncomplainingly carried out Marshall's wishes. On Bradley's departure, Ridgway assembled the division in a farewell salute. In a short speech praising Bradley, Ridgway, who reveled in such ceremonies, said that "we attribute our present proud progress to his strength of leadership, his vision, and his patient guidance" and that "in our hearts his name will always be on our rolls."

Bradley, who was made ill at ease by such displays of public sentimentality and who seldom wrote thank-you notes, nonetheless later took the time to write Ridgway: "I hope the division staff realizes how much I appreciate the very fine work they did for me. Every member was a master at his task and I only wish that I could always be so lucky." Ridgway responded: "Of course, you know we all hope still that we will be side by side in action, or that you will be our corps commander, as seems most apt to happen."[28]

Bradley had led the 82nd Division through ninety days of its basic training course. With Ridgway's help he had turned it into a showpiece, one of the best, if not *the* best-trained division in the Army. One reason for this success was that Bradley and Ridgway, as dissimilar in background, temperament and taste as two men could possibly be, had worked well together, Bradley the low-key "inside" administrator, Ridgway the tough, driving "outside" man. Beyond doubt, Bradley had a hand in the decision to name Ridgway as his successor. In return, Bradley earned Ridgway's unflinching loyalty.

☆ 5 ☆

WHEN RIDGWAY took command of the 82nd Division, it was about three quarters of the way through its seventeen-week basic training schedule. By that time summer had come to Camp Claiborne, bringing searing heat and enervating humidity. Neither seemed to faze Ridgway. His new chief of staff, Max Taylor, who reported for duty on July 2, later described Ridgway as "very impressive, very intense. He was highly ambitious, determined to be a great general, go all the way to the top. It was mid-summer and hot as hell and yet he insisted on *running* from place to place on his daily rounds of inspection. What was worse, he expected me to run with him! He'd drop in on a unit on foot, then take off for the next unit on foot. And here was his new chief of staff, trailing behind, puffing away. After one of these visits, I heard that a junior officer said, 'My God! I saw the chief of staff *chasing* the Old Man around the camp!' "[1]

In late July, when the division was in its last days of the training schedule, McNair notified Ridgway that the division would be converted from a normal infantry division to a "motorized" division and would move to Camp Atterbury, Indiana, for further training. Instead of slogging into battle on foot, the division would ride in trucks, presumably in company with fast-moving armored forces. Not long afterward, hundreds of trucks and other vehicles began arriving at Camp Claiborne for the move. They were well received. The designation "motorized" was new and exciting, a fitting distinction for this gung-ho outfit, now virtually ready for combat.[2]

The division had barely adjusted to this abrupt change in mission when Brigadier General Floyd L. Parks, who had replaced Mark Clark as McNair's chief of staff in the AGF, arrived at Claiborne. Parks, an old friend, came into Ridgway's office "wearing an air of mystery" and talking in whispers. The news he brought stood Ridgway on his ear. Marshall had decided to create two airborne divisions immediately—and others later. The 82nd would be one of these and it would provide the bulk of the personnel to build a second, the 101st.

Ridgway was torn. On the one hand he was flattered that the 82nd had been chosen for this special mission. His knowledge of airborne operations at that time was slight. But he did know that this new form of warfare was bold, swift, glamorous and elitist and it held great appeal. On the other hand, he was dismayed that after all his hard work to make it a high-spirited, cohesive fighting unit, his division was now to be ripped apart to provide the bulk of personnel for another division.[3]

Confronted with this new and wholly unexpected challenge, Ridgway first sought to learn all he could about the history, ongoing status and problems of airborne warfare. He soon discovered that there was very little to go on; that, in fact, for all the glamorous publicity attending the parachutists, airborne warfare was still very much in its infancy, its potential still a large unknown.

By 1942, the parachute had been around a long time, but its value as a military weapon had been slow in evolution. Parachutes had first come into limited use in the 1700s, employed by European balloonists as escape devices or for stunting at circuses and carnivals. The first parachute jump from a moving plane was made by an American, Albert Berry, on February 28, 1912. During World War I, when the parachute became commonplace life-saving gear for balloonists and pilots, visionary planners on both sides proposed ideas for utilizing parachute infantry. On the Allied side, the noted Air Force* pilot Brigadier General William (Billy) Mitchell conceived a plan to capture German-held Metz with a horde of parachute infantry which would be dropped into the enemy's rear. But the war ended before his scheme got off the drawing board.

During the twenties and thirties, most of the world's major armies experimented with airborne warfare. Two main theoretical concepts emerged: the use of small commando-like paratrooper units to seize key enemy objectives (bridges, etc.) ahead of advancing armies and the grander scheme of lifting larger regular infantry units by air transport into an "airhead" which had been previously seized by paratrooper shock troops. The Russians were the most innovative and aggressive pioneers in airborne warfare. In 1935, they electrified the world's military establishments when they moved a division of infantry by air across a large segment of the Soviet Union, from Moscow to Vladivostok. In the following year, during war games near Kiev, they created another sensation when two battalions of Red Army airborne forces (equipped with sixteen light field guns and 150 machine guns) airlanded in eight minutes and "seized" their objective within the hour.[4]

Despite these sensational public displays, military experts recognized that this new form of warfare had some severe built-in limitations. Perhaps the greatest was the lack of a suitable aircraft for airborne operations. Military air transports of that era were small, slow, unarmed and vulnerable to enemy air or ground attack. In the United States, for example, the best available aircraft was the twin-engine Douglas DC-3, which had entered commercial service in 1931. The military version, the C-47, enthusiastically misnamed the "Skytrain," had a maximum payload of a mere six thousand pounds. Manned by a pilot, copilot, navigator and crew chief, the C-47 could carry only eighteen paratroopers or regular infantry with equipment. The paratroopers had to leap from a single side door in the left rear fuselage. To transport or drop one regular battalion of infantrymen required about fifty C-47s; a regiment would fill about a hundred fifty. Very large-scale operations would require hundreds or even thousands of aircraft. Even if such numbers of aircraft could be pro-

---

* "Air Force" is used throughout to designate the Army Air Corps, which, in 1947, became the U.S. Air Force.

duced and made available for the purpose, it was clear that airborne operations would never be other than very expensive.

Mass jumps proved to be very difficult. In order to maximize surprise, concentrate force and keep enemy counterfire to a minimum, the drop itself had to be executed with speed and precision theretofore unknown in the military. The landing area, or drop zone (DZ), had to be situated as close as possible to the enemy objective and be free of obstructions such as trees or swamps or open bodies of water. If the ground in the chosen DZ proved to be too hard or rocky, there was a good possibility that a paratrooper, weighted down with heavy gear, would sprain or break an ankle or leg on landing. The weather had to be nearly perfect. Too much cloud cover could defeat the pinpoint navigation necessary to find the enemy objective or completely obscure the DZ. Too much wind—anything above twenty miles per hour—could dash a paratrooper into the ground or brutally drag him across it. The planes had to fly in tight, well-disciplined formations, with no recourse to evasive maneuvers to avoid enemy gunfire, in order to drop the paratroopers en masse at the exact aiming point; otherwise, they might scatter the paratroopers all over the landscape. The planes had to fly very slowly (no more than one hundred twenty miles per hour) and low (about six hundred feet) at the point of drop to minimize both the opening shock of the parachute as it hit the slipstream and the paratrooper's time of descent (when he was most exposed). On the ground, paratroopers had to jettison parachutes, collect gear and form up into cohesive, interlocking combat units—squads, platoons, companies, battalions—before the enemy (however much surprised) could stage a counterattack. Thereafter, the troops had to quickly move to the objective on foot, in strange territory, usually with sketchy maps and communications, and then launch a coordinated assault on the objective.

Such complex and dangerous operations required an elite brand of soldier. He had to be in superb physical condition in order to withstand the shock of the jump and the hard landing. He had to have nerves of steel. For most men, merely jumping from an airplane with a parachute required unusual courage or daredeviltry. To jump from an airplane directly into enemy-held territory with none of the usual military backup such as tanks or artillery covering fire, no organized command headquarters or well-laid communications, no well-defined "front line" with flank protection and possible egress to the rear and no transportation whatsoever, required courage and resourcefulness of an extraordinarily high degree. To be sure, such men could be found in all armies, but if too many were siphoned off to staff elitist paratrooper units, that might dangerously sap the leadership and readiness of the units from which they were drawn.

A more difficult personnel problem proved to be that of recruiting qualified transport pilots. Most pilots had been drawn to military service because they wanted to fly fighter planes. Over the years, many switched, or were switched, to bombers, some with misgivings but many enthusiastically convinced that the bomber alone could win wars. Very few pilots had joined the military service with the aim of flying "troop transports." Troop-transport duty was considered demeaning—the bottom of the pile—and a career dead end. Moreover, flying paratroopers behind enemy lines in slow, unarmed planes was also very dangerous. As a consequence, there was no great rush of volunteers. Air Force leaders, reluctant to send their "best" pilots to troop-transport duty, often turned to the least-motivated pilots.

Slowly some technological improvements were made. To increase the punch and "staying power" of the paratroopers, militarists devised techniques of parachuting (or air dropping) heavier weapons and extra ammunition to the ground. However, in war games, air dropping did not prove to be as effective as promised in the staff papers. The pieces were usually so badly scattered, it was impossible to find all the parts in time to make effective use of the weapon. Follow-up "aerial resupply" required the same high level of precision navigation and pinpoint dropping as the initial paratrooper assault, with the added distraction of flying into the teeth of an "enemy" now fully alerted. It was a rare C-47 crew that could resupply ammo bundles by air drop precisely where needed. All too many bundles wound up in enemy hands.

One promising innovation—at least on paper—was the development of the military glider. These craft, designed to be towed into combat by the transports, were nearly as large as the towing craft. The American version—the Waco CG-4A—was manned by two pilots and fitted with a swinging nose section to facilitate loading and unloading bulky cargo. It had a payload of nearly four thousand pounds and could carry fifteen soldiers or six soldiers and a jeep or a wheeled antitank gun. The theoretical advantages of the glider were several. It could airland ordinary infantrymen, who did not require the long, expensive and complex paratrooper training, directly into enemy-held territory. It eliminated possible landing injuries which paratroopers were prone to sustain. It could put fifteen men—a full squad—down on the ground closely bunched in one place, eliminating the "forming up" delays of the paratroopers, and bring light artillery or antitank weapons or radio-equipped jeeps directly to the battlefield. Four gliders landing close together could disgorge a full platoon instantly ready for combat. Since some paper studies envisioned that one C-47 fully loaded with paratroopers could tow one or two cheap gliders into combat, gliders could double or treble the effectiveness of every C-47, substantially reducing the requirement for C-47s and thus making airborne warfare more cost-effective.

In field tests, gliders proved to be far more difficult—and dangerous—than envisioned. Although the Waco version had a strong frame of small-gauge tubular steel and a sturdy plywood floor (the whole covered with aircraft fabric), gliders were structurally flimsy, unarmed and unarmored, and thus utterly defenseless against enemy ground or air attack. In the early days, some lost wings in flight. They were not difficult to fly, but having no power, once they were cut loose from the tow ship, everything about the descent and landing had to work perfectly. There was no "second chance," no way to "go around" for a new approach. If a preselected landing area proved to be too rough or too small or too muddy, or if the pilot in his anxiety under- or overshot, the result was usually a disastrous crash landing in a heavily loaded vehicle not designed to withstand severe stress. For these and other reasons, gliders would not be received with wildest enthusiasm by the American troops assigned to ride in them.[5]

Despite these considerable limitations, the Russian airborne warfare demonstrations of the 1930s made a strong impact on Hitler and the German General Staff. Hitler ordered Hermann Göring's *Luftwaffe* to organize airborne forces. The task was delegated to a Luftwaffe colonel, Kurt Student, who had been a decorated pilot in World War I and afterward a glider enthusiast. He formed and trained three types of German airborne forces: paratroopers, glider-borne infantry and air-transportable infantry.

When Hitler launched World War II, Student's airborne forces were in the vanguard. German paratroops first jumped into Norway to help seize that country. Employed in the May 1940 attacks on the Netherlands, paratroopers were particularly effective in seizing bridges over the Maas and Waal rivers in front of the advancing *Blitzkrieg*. Similarly, in Belgium, a small force of paratroopers and glider-borne infantry was utilized to capture Fort Eben Emael, a key fortress on the King Albert Canal. Later in the year, when Hitler was poised to invade the British Isles, the British, believing German paratroopers and glider-borne infantry might spearhead the attack, were compelled to divert enormous energy and resources to a defense against this possible threat.

German airborne operations culminated in May 1941, in a massive assault on the British-held Mediterranean island of Crete. For this attack, Student— now a general—assembled a total of twenty-five thousand men, including paratroopers, glider-borne infantry and elements of two mountain divisions which were to be airlanded after the airfields had been captured. Unknown to Student, Crete was strongly defended. A motley collection of about forty-two thousand Allied troops—British, Australian, New Zealand, Palestinian, Greek —had been gathering on the island from various locations. Moreover, thanks to the fact that the British had broken some German military codes, the Allied forces had advance warning of the attack and deployed on full alert. When Student's forces assaulted the island, on May 20, they were very badly mauled. The airborne forces suffered 44 percent casualties—three thousand killed, eight thousand wounded. Aircraft losses were also heavy—about 170 out of 530. Nonetheless, Student's forces overwhelmed the Allied defenses, forcing the British to evacuate the island—another Dunkirk, on a smaller scale. About fifteen thousand British got away, but they had to leave behind some twenty-seven thousand dead, wounded, missing and captured.

The outside world, not privy to Germany's appalling losses on Crete, was stunned by this lightning-like airborne "victory." It appeared that Student's forces had magically materialized out of the sky to pick off an easy, rich plum. The "victory" made a profound impact on George Marshall and the War Department General Staff. It appeared to be a quintessential example of "vertical envelopment." In U.S. Army eyes, Crete, more than any other single factor, "proved" that airborne forces were "here to stay" and led Marshall to initiate plans to field a substantial number of American airborne forces.

Ironically, Crete led to the very opposite course in Berlin. Up to May 1941, Hitler's forces had never suffered such heavy battle casualties. Hitler was shocked. He called Crete a disaster and told the General Staff that "the days of the paratrooper are over." Thereafter, the Germans did not undertake another major airborne operation. Student's existing crack airborne units—and others created later—were held in reserve as potential threats, requiring the Allies to continue extensive defensive precautions. Later these elite units were deployed to battlefronts as regular "light infantry."[6]

The prime mover in U.S. airborne operations was a non-West Pointer, William C. Lee, an old friend of Ridgway's. He was an unlikely zealot. Born in Dunn, North Carolina, on March 12, 1895, he was a homely and lanky "southern gentleman" with a heavy drawl and courtly manners. As a reserve officer, he had commanded a company in France in World War I. After the war he elected to make the Army his career, became a tank expert and in the early thirties spent three years abroad studying and working with French armored outfits. There he had an opportunity to observe German military preparations close at hand. He came away much impressed by Kurt Student's airborne experiments and, on returning to the States, began to gently prod the War Department to conduct similar experiments.[7]

Following German airborne successes in the invasion of the Low Countries in the spring of 1940, Lee was able to convince the War Department to take some concrete steps. On June 25, 1940, the Department established a "test" platoon of fifty volunteer paratroopers at Fort Benning's crude airstrip, Lawson Field, commanded by a West Pointer, William T. Ryder (class of 1936). This little group of brave pioneers, borrowing heavily from what was known of German paratroop operations, blazed the trail. By way of gear, it developed the standard Army backpack parachute (with a twenty-eight-foot nylon canopy), the "reserve" chest-pack chute, sturdy leather "jump boots" and cloth helmets with chin straps. For training purposes, it turned to a modified version of an amusement ride which had first appeared at the New York World's Fair. This was a 250-foot steel tower from which the men were dropped with fully opened parachutes, simulating a landing. By August 16, the platoon was ready for the real thing. That day, Bill Ryder made Army history of a sort by being the first American paratrooper officer to jump from a plane. Private William N. (The Spartan) King followed him, becoming the first American enlisted man to jump.[8]

Meanwhile, Bill Lee was quietly prodding the War Department to dramatically greater efforts. He sold his program, and a month later, on September 16, 1940, the chief of infantry authorized a tenfold increase in paratroopers and established the 501st Parachute Battalion. Command of this unit went to another friend of Ridgway's, a West Pointer renowned for his physical fitness, William M. (Bud) Miley. Descended from generations of West Point graduates on both sides of his family, Miley (class of 1918) had won the Best Gymnast Award at the Academy and had returned there (as Assistant Master of the Sword) to teach the cadets gymnastics, agility and military poise. "He was one of a kind," a contemporary paratrooper recalled. "He could do a standing backflip, things like that. He was the perfect choice to command the 501. We were a wild, hell-for-leather outfit, but we were a bit ragged militarily." Ironically, Miley, overloaded with experimental gear, broke his shoulder on his very first jump.[9]

Under Miley's leadership, the 501st took parachute infantry techniques far beyond the primitive stages developed by Ryder's platoon. The 501st concentrated not so much on merely jumping and surviving, but on military maneuvers on the ground. Units of the battalion made coordinated jumps on specific military objectives and evolved weapons and tactics for capturing them. Despite shortages of nearly everything—weapons, parachutes, aircraft, living quarters, training facilities—Miley made significant progress. Eight months later, when the Germans galvanized the War Department with the airborne seizure of Crete, Miley was ready with field manuals and further expansion plans.

Under Marshall's prodding, expansion came swiftly. The chief of infantry established a Provisional Parachute Group at Benning and named Bill Lee to command it. In the months that followed, Lee established three other parachute battalions—the 502nd, 503rd and 504th—drawing on Miley's 501st for cadres. Benning's commandant, Omar Bradley, an early enthusiast of airborne forces, expanded the base into Alabama to accommodate the influx, and added two more training towers, for a total of four. On November 21, 1941, one of the new battalions, the 502nd, made more history of a sort by becoming the first to jump en masse, a thrilling spectacle conducted at Fort Bragg, North Carolina.[10]

One of Lee's staff recalled:

Lee was known as a tanker, but not as well known as Patton. He was a smart, patient, tolerant, considerate, intelligent and kind man. He struggled with us—we kids wanted to rebuild the world right away. There were all sorts of things we were wild-eyed about and having a great old time doing. Jumping every place under the sun. He let us try anything we wanted to do. And we did. But he applied a governing hand—and good common sense. We thought the world of him. There couldn't have been a better man for that job, in my opinion. In those days we all packed our own parachutes—didn't trust anybody else. We wanted a separate packing shed for each battalion. Gosh, the landscape would have been cluttered with packing sheds. Lee, quite rightly, held us to one shed per regiment and we finally agreed to use packers.[11]

Not long after the Fort Bragg demonstration, Bill Lee nearly killed himself in a parachute jump. He was hospitalized for weeks with a broken back and had to wear a chin-to-waist cast for months. The accident knocked a lot of the wind out of his sails. One of his staffers remarked: "Parachuting was really a young man's game. Bill Lee was a little too old—and not physically rugged enough. After that injury, I don't think Bill was ever the same man." While

Lee was hospitalized, Bud Miley temporarily took command of the Parachute Group.[12]

Profoundly impressed by the German operation at Crete, Marshall foresaw large-scale Allied paratrooper operations. After Pearl Harbor, he authorized a further bold step: the creation of parachute infantry regiments (PIRs), composed of three parachute battalions. Drawing on his four existing parachute battalions for cadres, Bill Lee established six such regiments in the first six months of 1942. Command of one regiment—the 503rd—went to Bud Miley.[13]

The next step was not long in coming: expansion to division-size units. Exactly what size and shape such units should be was the subject of much heated controversy. Lee and Miley wanted hefty divisions, almost as large as the normal infantry divisions, composed mostly of paratroopers and equipped with the usual backup and support troops and "organic" transportation, such as trucks. But AGF commanding general McNair disagreed. From the outset, his mind was set on a small, "greatly stripped-down" division of about eighty-three hundred men, about half the number in a normal infantry division. As McNair saw it, such a division would have one parachute regiment of about two thousand men and two glider regiments of about sixteen hundred men each, plus light artillery and supporting units. The parachutists would jump first and seize an airhead into which the gliders would land. The paratroop regiments would be drawn from the six already authorized; the glider regiments would be ordinary infantry. Since McNair had the final word, his views prevailed.[14]

McNair himself picked the 82nd Division to be the guinea pig division. His reasons for the choice were several. It was a problem-free division nearing the end of its training cycle. Ridgway was intelligent, dynamic and flexible—in many ways the ideal senior officer to help carry out the experiment. The division was conveniently situated: near the paratrooper school at Fort Benning and not too far from Fort Bragg, where the Air Force had established an embryonic Troop Carrier Command.[15]

Bill Lee was the natural choice to command the other airborne division, the 101st, and he was so named. To infuse a man with airborne experience into the top command of the 82nd, Bud Miley, promoted to brigadier general, was named ADC, and the officer who had served in that job barely a month, Don Pratt, was shifted over to be Bill Lee's ADC. Although no one was yet sure what form "airborne artillery" would assume, McNair decided that Joe Swing would stay with the 82nd Division and assigned a newly promoted brigadier general, Anthony C. (Tony) McAuliffe, a West Pointer who stood high in the class of 1919, to be Bill Lee's artillery commander.[16]

☆6☆

FOR MANY DAYS, the future status of the 82nd Division was a closely held secret, known only to a handful of senior staff. The reaction of those in the know was, at first, almost universally negative.

The doubts and questions were numerous. First, there was vast unease—even fear—about airborne operations. To many, jumping out of an airplane into enemy territory seemed the height of madness, perhaps even suicidal. Going in by flimsy glider might be even worse, if that were possible. Second, many believed, as Ridgway had, that it was shortsighted and unwise to break up so fine a division at the peak of its training. Moreover, the breakup posed painful choices: who would go to the 101st; who would stay with the 82nd? Third, it seemed to many completely unfair, or worse, to simply consign the division's infantry units to glider duty at regular pay.* Should not the men be given the right to volunteer? Should they not receive hazardous-duty and flight pay like paratroopers? Fourth, many believed integrating an elitist parachute regiment into the division would cause grave problems. Was it possible, or would it result in an awkward, unbridgeable rift?[1]

If Ridgway had deep inner doubts, he concealed them well. Outwardly he was entirely positive. He professed to be honored that the 82nd Division had been selected for this bold new experimental role. The division had been chosen, he said to one and all, mainly because it was "the best" of the divisions then in training. The 82nd would not disappoint McNair (or Marshall). Every man must put his doubts aside and do his utmost to make the experiment a success.[2]

He soon met, in utmost secrecy, with Bill Lee to divide up the division. By the time they got together, McNair had settled the general-officer assignments —Miley, Pratt, Swing, McAuliffe—but beyond that, everybody else was up for grabs. They decided first that each man would keep his own chief of staff and his principal assistants. That meant that Max Taylor, Doc Eaton, Lynch, Boyd, Wienecke, Moorman and others would stay with the 82nd. Lee kept his newly appointed chief of staff, an early paratrooper volunteer, Charles L. (Bull) Keerans, Jr., and the senior staff he was assembling. They literally tossed a coin for all the rest. Ridgway explained:

Usually in a situation such as this, when you are ordered to furnish a cadre, you pick all your goof-offs and screwballs and send them along to the new command. I wouldn't even consider doing this to my old friend Bill Lee. So I proposed that we take all the ranks and skills in the division and divide them

* Parachute officers received $100 per month extra pay; enlisted men, $50 per month.

into as nearly two equal halves as we could. Then we'd flip a coin, and the man who won could pick the half he wanted. Bill said nothing could be fairer and we did it that way.[3]

McNair had decreed that each of the airborne divisions would be composed of one parachute infantry regiment drawn from the six already in being and two glider regiments (of only two battalions instead of three), created from units of the 82nd Division. He assigned the 504th Parachute Infantry Regiment, commanded by Theodore L. (Ted) Dunn, to Ridgway; the 502nd, commanded by George P. Howell, Jr., to Lee. In the ensuing coin toss, Ridgway was lucky. He "won" the two best glider regiments in the 82nd Division: Easley's 325th and Cutler's 326th. Lee "won" George Wear's 327th Glider Infantry Regiment, together with a battalion each from the 325th and 326th to cadre a new 101st glider regiment, the 401st, commanded by Joseph H. (Bud) Harper.[4]

Soon after the split-up had been settled, Ridgway laid plans to visit Benning. He had two reasons: first, to take a close look at Ted Dunn's 504th Regiment, which was based there and would be coming to the 82nd Division and, secondly, to make a parachute jump. Ridgway told his new ADC, Bud Miley, that if anybody in the division was going to have to jump, "I wanted to be the first to do it."[5]

Many from the staff bravely volunteered to go with Ridgway and make a jump: Joe Swing, Bud Miley, Max Taylor, Doc Eaton, Bill Moorman, among others. Ridgway turned down most of these requests. It had already been decided that the division staff would go into combat by glider. The parachute jump was therefore an "unnecessary risk," he told Eaton with a straight face. But he approved jumps for Swing, Taylor, Miley, Moorman and a few others.[6]

The decision to make this parachute jump must have been a hard one for Ridgway. His marvelous physique had a hidden flaw: a trick back. He attributed it to a severe injury from West Point days. While jumping a horse over hurdles, riding bareback with his eyes closed (as instructed), he had fallen off and landed on the base of a hurdle. Soon, and for a long time thereafter, he had had a blinding pain in his back, "as if somebody had stabbed me there with a bayonet and neglected to remove it." Fearing that if he reported to the hospital he might be washed out of West Point, he gritted his teeth and "locked my back there and stuck it out." But it had never been completely right since, and every now and then—without warning—it would go out, giving Ridgway some "excruciatingly painful moments."[7]

At Benning, Ted Dunn (West Point, 1925) met the distinguished delegation of generals with proper military courtesy. He then turned them over to the commander of his 1st Battalion, Warren R. Williams, a young West Pointer (class of 1938), who would serve as "jumpmaster." Williams gave the group about a half hour of basic instruction and demonstration: a few minutes work in a suspended parachute harness, a few jumps from a raised platform to simulate the shock of hitting the ground, a few practice exits from the door of the C-47 and a rudimentary briefing on how to maneuver the parachute with the risers, collapse it on the ground and shuck the harness.[8]

Ridgway recalled that as he got deeper into the venture he began to get "a little nervous." He later wrote: "It occurred to me that this was an idiotic enterprise that might well get me a broken leg, or worse, and that I was a damned fool to be such an eager beaver, breaking the first rule of an old soldier —which is never to volunteer for anything." He decided there was no need for his aide, Don Faith, to risk a jump, but Faith succeeded, finally, in changing Ridgway's mind.[9]

The party divided for the jump: the generals (and Faith) in the first "stick," the colonels and lower ranks in the second. Under Warren's supervision, the generals boarded the C-47 and took off. The old hand, Bud Miley, back in his element, volunteered to be the "wind dummy": he would jump alone on the first pass over the DZ. If he missed the DZ, the pilot would make corrections for the wind drift for the next pass.[10]

As the plane approached the DZ, a field in Alabama, Miley hooked his static line to the overhead cable and stood in the open door, waiting. When the pilot turned on a green light and rang a shrill bell, Miley leaped out, the static line trailing. His chute canopy popped open and—as Ridgway watched in fascination at the open door—Miley descended gracefully straight into a patch of tall pine trees. To Ridgway, it seemed a disaster.[11]

Ridgway was next up. The pilot swung around and reapproached the DZ, correcting for the wind that had put Miley in the trees. Ridgway stood in the open door, watching the landscape below. When the green light lit and the buzzer sounded, he leaped into the roaring slipstream. When the static line ripped the chute open, he recalled, it "was like the blow of a club across the shoulders." There followed a "wonderful silence"—but not for long. The ground rushed up at alarming speed. In the rush, Ridgway forgot everything he'd been told. He hit the ground, going backward, "with a tooth-rattling crash." The landing impact, he judged, was about "like jumping off the top of a freight car traveling at thirty-five miles an hour onto a hard clay roadbed." Fortunately, Ridgway's trick back did not go out.

Joe Swing jumped next, with no apparent ill effects. Later, when asked how he liked it, he joked, "I'd rather fall off an airplane than a polo pony." As the plane swung around to drop Faith and Williams, Swing and Ridgway gathered up their gear and waited for Miley, who was trekking from the pine forest. When he came up, Ridgway and Swing saw that he was "scratched and bruised" and "grinning a little sheepishly." He congratulated them, and later gave them a parachute patch for their overseas caps. Ridgway mounted his on a field of blue (the infantry color), Swing on a field of red (the field-artillery color). Ridgway concluded: "I was now a parachutist of sorts."[12]

The next stick followed in time, with another jumpmaster, Julian J. Ewell (West Point, 1939), then Assistant Commandant of the Parachute School. Taylor jumped first, Bill Moorman second. Moorman recalled, "They threw us out of the plane like bales of hay. They stood me in the door. I was frozen . . . scared. A sergeant shouted, 'Go!' Then he hit me a terrific whack behind my knees. I shot four feet straight into the air . . ." In Ewell's recollection, "Taylor took a very compressed course and I wanted to be sure that his first jump passed without incident. So I went along and jumped right after him. I was watching him as he landed and a brisk breeze snatched him up in the air and he hit with a terrible crash. (Head first, I think.) I landed nearby and ran over to pick up the pieces but he bounced up apparently unhurt. He was always in good physical condition—which helps."[13]

Later, when he was asked his reaction to parachuting, Taylor said, "When I was sober I never volunteered for paratroopers! But I felt very lucky to have been ordered into it." Moorman had his own interpretation of Taylor's attitude: "He really didn't like to jump out of airplanes, but he liked to be *around* people who jumped out of airplanes."[14]

While the party was at Benning, Ted Dunn was in constant attendance, but he did not jump with either group. Ridgway soon learned that Dunn "had bad knees from old football injuries" and on the rare occasions he jumped, he did so with a special parachute with a thirty-two-foot canopy. Williams, for one, did not believe Dunn was "physically able to lead the 504 in combat," because of those knee injuries. Moorman remembered another problem with Dunn: "After the jump, Dunn took Taylor and me to the Officers' Club for the traditional 'post-jump' celebratory drink. Taylor was carefully sizing up Dunn. After we finished the drink, Dunn appeared eager for another—a little too eager. It was only eleven o'clock in the morning and when Dunn asked Taylor if he wanted another drink, Taylor almost bit his head off."[15]

During the visit, Dunn staged an "airborne demonstration," a fairly large-scale jump. After his men had reached the ground in an impressively executed display of acrobatics, Dunn said, according to Moorman, "Well, that's it." Taylor turned on Dunn angrily. "What do you mean, that's it? They haven't *done* anything." Later, Moorman explained. "Taylor meant they hadn't made any tactical maneuvers on the ground—no military achievement, merely the jump itself. There was this definite feeling that the job ended with the jump. They made the jump; they were all heroes and they went home." Taylor later summed it up: "Everyone was too jump-happy. There was too little emphasis on infantry tactics."[16]

These first impressions were later officially and painfully verified. When McNair's AGF staff subsequently conducted an important inspection of the 504th Regiment, two of the three battalions failed the tests and the third would probably have failed had not Dunn's S-3, Charles W. Kouns, a West Point graduate (1939), taken temporary command for the inspection. The failing battalion commanders had to be relieved of command, and a difficult search for new commanders had to be initiated.[17]

There was one exceptionally impressive young officer in the 504th's upper command. He was the executive officer, a former West Point classmate of Moorman's, Reuben Henry Tucker III. Tucker came from an old Yankee blue-collar family, employed over the generations by the brass mill in Ansonia, Connecticut. Born there on January 29, 1911, Tucker was the third of six children. At age thirteen, he won a local Boy Scout award for bravery and resourcefulness when he pulled his drowning younger brother and a friend from a freezing millpond. In high school, he was an energetic athlete (football, baseball, hockey, swimming), but he made a stronger mark as sports editor of the school newspaper and as president of his social fraternity (whose brothers nicknamed him "Duke" for his very good looks and fastidiousness in dress). But, of course, everyone else in town called him "Tommy," after the Mother Goose rhyme.

Tucker's forebears on both sides of the family had been soldiering since the Revolutionary War. This family "tradition," or perhaps the grim prospect of a life of drudgery in a mill town in the Depression, tilted Tucker toward a military career. After graduation from high school, in 1927, he worked at the brass mill as an apprentice to his father for about a year, then left to attend a West Point prep school, Millard's. He passed the tough West Point examinations in 1929 but did not receive an appointment. After kicking around Wyoming for a year with a survey gang, he tried again in 1930 and, thanks to the political pull of a family friend, he received a congressional appointment to the West Point class of 1934.

Tucker cut a striking military figure at West Point and did well at football, lacrosse and hockey, but he was weak academically. Eleven months after entering the Academy, he was "found" in mathematics and washed out. Tucker was determined to stay in West Point, and after private tutoring, he passed a grueling two-day reexamination and was readmitted as a "turnback" to the class of 1935. He finally graduated, standing 186th in a class of 277. He was married the following day at the West Point chapel beneath the traditional arch of swords.

As a young lieutenant, Tucker served first with the 9th Infantry Regiment in Texas, then with the 33rd Infantry in Panama, where his wife gave birth to the first of five children—all boys. In earlier days, Ridgway had served with both those outfits and felt a special kinship toward the alumni—especially those who had served in the 9th Infantry. But, quite apart from that, the Ridgway staff warmed to Tucker (whom they called "Rube") both because of his airborne professionalism and of his obvious ability as an infantry leader. Moorman remembered: "He was a wonderful athlete and soldier. Fearless. Dedicated. A gung-ho combat officer, exactly the kind of fellow you want when you go to war." Another contemporary described him as "A bluff, jovial little guy, brave as any of them. You liked him right off. Just a grand guy. Very solid. As soon as he came into the room, you'd think: Here's a guy I figure I'd want to have a beer with."[18]

The 82nd Division completed its seventeen-week basic training program in early August. Coincidentally, Ridgway received his promotion to major general at about that same time: August 6. He wore his hard-earned two stars proudly. "He sewed those two stars on the forward left side of his overseas cap," an aide commented. "Ordinarily you had the peak of the cap pointing forward. But Ridgway slightly skewed the cap to the right so that the peak jutted off to one side and the two stars were pointing forward and highly visible." This display of stars forward would become commonplace on steel helmets in the combat zone, but to wear them so on an overseas cap was most unusual. Another officer was struck by the way "the stars came straight at you, right over those piercing eyes, which had the look of a great predatory bird—a golden eagle. On anyone less formidable than Ridgway the forward-facing stars would have looked ridiculous. But on him they looked just right."

One other minor affectation which the men began to notice at this time was Ridgway's somewhat unorthodox salute. An officer in the 325, Wayne Pierce, described it: "The Ridgway salute was done with the hand slightly cupped and bent at the wrist, upper arm and elbow held high, somewhat as though you were shading your right eye. I know of no other general officer who had such a distinctive hand salute—and none so widely imitated by subordinates!"[19]

The division was scheduled for a dramatic full-dress review, a parade for visiting brass, on August 15. Ridgway decided he would utilize that occasion to formally announce the news that the division was to be split up to form two airborne divisions. He spoke from a raised platform, his words broadcast over a P.A. system: "Tomorrow our destinies divide. That which was one division becomes two. That which was one team must be rebuilt into two . . ."[20]

The news was profoundly shocking. First, that the division would be split in two; second, that its various parts would be used to create two airborne divisions. "There were sixteen thousand men standing there," said one witness, "and you could have heard a pin drop. And when Ridgway explained that four *glider* regiments would be formed from the ranks of the regular infantry, I saw a lot of faces go white." One source described the aftershock:

The next morning we had 4,500 men AWOL. Ridgway called me in. He was baffled. He said, "What in the world made them do that?" I said, "You scared the pants off 'em." He couldn't understand why everyone wasn't as fired up as he was—wasn't as patriotic and gung-ho. He couldn't see that they didn't want to go to the 101st. Above all, they didn't want to be gliderists! I knew how they felt. I wasn't happy either—I'm not that brave. I told him not to worry, they'd all be back in three or four days, except the ones who'd have deserted anyway. And they did come back.[21]

$$\star 7 \star$$

THE EARLY HISTORY of the newly created 82nd Airborne Division was somewhat chaotic. In mid-September, Ridgway received orders to move it from
Camp Claiborne to Fort Bragg, where it would be mated with its Air Force
transport, the 52nd Troop Carrier Wing, which was based at nearby Pope
Field. Bill Lee's 101st Airborne Division replaced the 82nd at Claiborne. During this shift, which was completed in mid-October, virtually all training in the
82nd came to a complete halt.

For the first few weeks at Bragg, the division was a revolving door. First it
was ordered to supply a "full quota" of "key personnel" to cadre the newly
forming 98th Infantry Division. Next it had to divest itself of those men who
were, as Ridgway put it, "ill-suited because of lack of airworthiness." That is,
those who had to be classified as "hopeless," either because they had a morbid
fear of flying or because they became airsick. Literally thousands of men left
the division. They were replaced by thousands of raw recruits, who were integrated into Easley's 325th and Cutler's 326th glider infantry regiments.[1]

There were also many changes in the roster of senior officers of the division.
These changes were triggered in part by Marshall's decision to create two more
airborne divisions, the 11th and the 17th. Joe Swing was named to command
the former, Bud Miley the latter. Although it was some time before either man
actually left the division, they were naturally more concerned with their own
embryonic outfits than the 82nd.*

To replace Bud Miley as ADC, Ridgway selected Bill Lee's chief of staff,
Bull Keerans, who was promoted to brigadier general. As it turned out, Keerans was not the best possible choice, often more of a burden than a help. A
contemporary recalled that he was a "smart guy," a graduate of both infantry
and artillery schools. He had begun his airborne career in the early days at
Benning as Bill Lee's plans-and-training officer. But "Bull had a serious drinking problem. He liked to go on a spree every now and then for three or four
days at a stretch. Everybody in the Army knew Bull had a drinking problem
but they all took care of him and protected him. As long as that was kept quiet,
that was all right. But if you happened to be sharing responsibility with him, it
could be wicked."[3]

Beyond that, Ridgway was not entirely happy with his chief of staff, Max
Taylor. One associate described Taylor as "an intellectual, a thinker. He was
fascinated by the intellectual side of things. He liked to see what he could do
with his mind—how far he could push it. And he had an excellent mind. He

* Swing activated the 11th Airborne Division on February 25, 1943; Miley activated the
17th Airborne Division on April 15, 1943.[2]

would walk around things, look at them. He may have gotten emotionally involved, but he didn't show it. He was outwardly very, very cool."[4]

Ridgway respected Taylor's intellectual gifts, but this was not what he needed most at that time. He needed a direct, forceful administrator who could make quick decisions on the thousand and one matters that arose each day. Taylor seemed bored with administration. According to Doc Eaton, Taylor was "just smarter than hell," but he was a field artilleryman and he liked to shoot. Eaton went on: "His idea of being chief of staff was to come in in the morning, spend about fifteen to thirty minutes signing papers, then go down and spend most of the day with the Field Artillery and late in the afternoon, come back to the office and sign some more papers." Meanwhile, the telephone rang all day and Eaton had to take the calls and make the decisions. "I was running the chief of staff's office for him," Eaton said, "as well as doing my own jobs."[5]

When Joe Swing was named to command the 11th Airborne Division, it created a vacancy in the 82nd's artillery. The chief-of-staff problem was solved when the War Department named Max Taylor to replace Swing. Taylor was pleased. The old divisional tables of organization were still in force; the switch meant a promotion to brigadier general.[6]

Ridgway's choice for chief of staff floored everyone, including the man himself, Doc Eaton.

I told him I didn't want the job. He was very shrewd, always planning way ahead. I wasn't that kind of fellow. I simply wasn't that smart and I told him. I said, "I don't want any part of it. I'm too stupid—not smart enough —to be your chief of staff." Of course, I'll never forget his reply. He looked at me with those piercing eyes and said, "I don't want any more *smart* chiefs of staff."†

By the time Taylor became commander of the division artillery, its organization, weapons and tactical concepts had been worked out by airborne personnel and approved by McNair's AGF. The general idea was that each parachute regiment would be supported by one parachute artillery battalion, and each glider regiment would be supported by one glider artillery battalion.[9]

At first, all the airborne artillery battalions were issued the same weapon. It was a curiosity: the Army's 75 mm pack howitzer. Conceived originally for rugged mountain warfare, where it would be packed in by mules, it was designed to be broken down into nine major pieces, each of which was carried by a separate mule. When assembled, the piece weighed only thirteen hundred pounds and fired a thirteen-pound projectile a maximum range of 9,475 yards. It was mounted on a light carriage with hard rubber or wooden wheels and,

---

† Upon Eaton's elevation to chief of staff, Thomas B. Ketterson became G-1, later replaced by Frederick M. Schellhammer. Lynch, Boyd and Wienecke remained as G-2, G-3 and G-4, respectively.[8]

when fully assembled, it could be moved from place to place by the artillery-men.

The parachute and glider artillery battalions were organized around the pack howitzer. Each artillery battalion consisted of three firing batteries (A, B, C) of four howitzers each, for a total of twelve pieces. The parachute artillery battalion weapons were to be parachuted into battle in broken-down state, each of the nine pieces in a separate bundle mounted beneath the planes. Ammo for the howitzers would be parachuted into battle in similar mounted bundles, or in bundles which could be tossed out the fuselage door. On the ground, the howitzer would be moved by hand. The glider artillery battalions, each also organized into three firing batteries, would go into battle with the howitzers fully assembled and stored inside the gliders. Other gliders would bring in jeeps to tow the weapons and/or ammo trailers around the battlefield.

The airborne forces, however, recognizing the limitations of the 75 mm pack howitzer, sought a more powerful artillery piece. They found it in another curiosity, the so-called "infantryman's cannon." This was a standard Army 105 mm howitzer M-1, ("medium," artillery in regular infantry divisions), with a "sawed-off," or "snub-nose," bell (barrel) and a lighter carriage. The snub-nose (called the M-3) 105 howitzer weighed only twenty-four hundred pounds (half as much as the conventional 105), and it fired the standard thirty-three-pound projectile about 8,000 yards. One snub-nose 105 would just barely fit in a glider—with the bell projecting forward into the cockpit between the pilot and copilot. Jeep tows and ammo trailers would come in other gliders.

The snub-nose 105 was indeed a more powerful weapon, but it had certain drawbacks. Owing to its short barrel it did not have much range—not even as much as the 75 mm pack howitzer. This meant it had to be deployed perilously close to the enemy and was thus vulnerable to counterbattery fire from the enemy's longer-range conventional artillery. Nor did it have protective armor. Moreover, the jeep proved to be a marginal tow, just barely able to move the weapon on firm, relatively flat terrain. These shortcomings led to improvisations: twelve standard M-1 105 mm howitzers with stronger tows (3/4- or 2 1/2-ton trucks) would be included in the division's "tail." When the "tail" linked up with the airborne assault forces on the battlefield, the conventional 105 howitzers and tows would be substituted for the snub-nose 105s and the jeep tows.

The airlift required to deliver a battalion of parachute or glider artillery was substantial. Nine C-47s were employed to lift a single firing battery (four how-itzers) of a parachute battalion. Counting the "headquarters battery" (command, communications, etc., but no artillery weapons), each parachute artillery battalion utilized a total of about thirty-six aircraft, almost enough planes to lift a battalion of parachute infantry. Glider artillery battalions, which would come into battle with twelve fully assembled weapons (one per glider) plus twelve jeeps (one per glider) and ammo trailers and artillerymen, utilized an even greater number of C-47s for towing.

The 82nd Airborne Division artillery was initially organized into one parachute (376th) and two glider (319th and 320th) battalions to support its one parachute and two glider regiments. The 376th (twelve pack howitzers) was initially commanded by Paul E. Wright, the 319th (twelve pack howitzers) by William Harry Bertsch, and the 320th (twelve M-3 105 mm snub-nose howitzers, organized into two 6-howitzer battalions, A and B), by Francis A. (Andy) March III, a nephew of former Army chief of staff Peyton C. March (and a first cousin of Joe Swing's wife). However, when Taylor promoted March to be division artillery executive officer, Paul Wright moved from command of the 376th to command of the 320th, and Wilbur M. Griffith replaced Wright as commander of the 376th.‡

In addition to this artillery firepower, the airborne divisions had one so-called glider-borne "antiaircraft" defense battalion, which in time would become more an antitank than an antiaircraft unit. In the 82nd, it was the 80th, commanded by Whitfield Jack. It was composed of three batteries (A, B, C) of the Army's standard 57 mm antitank gun, each with eight guns (a total of twenty-four) and three batteries (D, E, F) of .50 caliber air-cooled machine guns, each with twelve weapons (a total of thirty-six). In theory, each of the three regiments was to be supported by one antitank and one antiaircraft battery. But in practice, the 80th remained under direct control of the division commander to deploy as he saw fit.*

In the meanwhile, Ted Dunn's 504th Parachute Infantry Regiment moved from Benning to Bragg and was officially integrated into the division. After a careful review of Dunn's lack of progress with the regiment, Ridgway relieved Dunn of command, officially and bluntly stating his reason: "Inability to secure results." To replace Dunn, Ridgway chose his exec, Rube Tucker, a decision that won nearly unanimous approval within the 504, but one that raised eyebrows in higher headquarters. Tucker was then only thirty-one years old, perhaps the youngest regimental commander in the Army. Owing to Tucker's youth, Ridgway was unable to secure his promotion to full colonel for another six months.[10]

At about the same time, higher headquarters promoted Claudius Easley, commander of the 325th Glider Infantry Regiment, to brigadier general and ordered him to be ADC of the 96th Infantry Division. Easley's departure left Ridgway with a large and continuing headache: who would command the 325? For about three weeks the regimental exec, Jean D. Scott, a West Point classmate of Doc Eaton's (1924), held the post, but Eaton did not think Scott was the right man for the job: "Every time I called the regimental CP, Scott answered. He should have been out in the field with the men. Ridgway did not like that." They soon began looking for a new man.[11]

Since Ridgway had picked the youthful Rube Tucker to lead the 504, his final choice for commander of the 325 was baffling and controversial—for

‡ The 101st Airborne Division artillery was similarly organized: 377 Parachute Artillery, 321 and 907 Glider Artillery.

* The 101st Airborne Division also had an "antiaircraft" battalion, the 81st, similarly organized and equipped.

different reasons. Colonel Harry Leigh Lewis was a man Ridgway's age who had entered active Army service in 1913, four years before Ridgway. (Lewis had a son, Robert, who joined the 504.) His appointment was not universally well received by the officers in the 325. Behind his back they derisively called him "Lighthorse Harry Leigh." One said, "He was a weak man, looked like a Mr. Milquetoast or a bank teller: short, slim, steel-rimmed glasses, sharp little face, humorless expression." Another, Wayne Pierce, remembered that Lewis "was too old to lead an airborne regiment. He looked old, acted old." Paul L. Turner said, "He was a small man with a fiery temper—a tough old Regular Army officer who was over-age in grade and drank too much whiskey." Teddy H. Sanford described him thus: "He had a runt complex; bounced like a rubber ball and barked a lot." John H. Swenson thought he was "an intelligent man who did some awfully dumb things. He boasted to me that he had been a senior lieutenant in the Army for fourteen years."[12]

Nonetheless, Ridgway had a "warm spot" for Lewis and backed him all the way. One reason was that Ridgway believed that Lewis, despite his weakness as a leader, was good at training men, and at that point Ridgway was hard-pressed for trainers to shape up the revolving-door 325. Another was that Lewis gave Ridgway the impression of being a fearless fighter. Unknown to Ridgway (and almost everyone else) Lewis had a cancer that would soon take his life. Hiding this illness, Lewis was a "ball of fire" in the training fields, a martinet who brooked no nonsense and who was on the job twenty-four hours a day and still had energy enough to lead the regimental square dances on Saturday nights.[13]

All these departures, changes and new arrivals were completed about January 1, 1943. By that time the 82nd Airborne was virtually a brand-new division, with many new men in key command and staff jobs and thousands more newcomers in the ranks. Although much preliminary planning and work had been carried out, Ridgway was not in position to commence "airborne training" for the division as a whole until that date.

Once again he was frustrated. This time the cause was an acute shortage of C-47 troop transports and gliders. This shortage was an old story to Rube Tucker and his paratroopers. They had been cadging rides as best they could for months, but it was a new problem for Ridgway. Despite his zeal and energies, he was not able to overcome it. Throughout the remainder of the war, airborne forces would suffer at every turn from a chronic shortage of all types of airlift.

This shortage of airlift was later traced to three main causes. From the start, McNair simply failed to foresee that large numbers of planes would be necessary for training purposes. As one Air Force historian put it, "Always interested above all in perfecting ground combat training, he believed that a large share of training an airborne division could be accomplished with only one previous trip in a plane or glider." Second, the Air Force simply refused to give transport aircraft a high construction priority. Offensive combat aircraft— fighters and bombers—came first. (In 1942, for example, the Air Force took delivery of 12,634 bombers and 10,780 fighters, but only 1,985 transports of all types.) By the time production of transports was dramatically stepped up (7,013 in 1943), the demand for them was so great worldwide that there were still not enough for the airborne forces, and even these were often diverted to other uses. Third, production of gliders got off to a very slow start and fairly late in the game, too late to keep pace with the formation of airborne divisions.[14]

Full-scale production of the Waco CG-4A glider was not begun until the summer of 1942, a few weeks before the 82nd and 101st airborne divisions were established. The initial Air Force order was for 5,290 gliders, which were to be produced by fifteen factories and delivered by June 1943. However, because of mismanagement, last-minute design changes and tooling-up difficulties, gliders would not come off the production lines in any great quantity until the fall of 1943.

Some gliders from the early production lines were designated for training—ninety for glider-pilot training and 165 for the 82nd and 101st divisions. These figures promised that about eighty gliders would be made available for training the 82nd's two glider regiments. But it never happened. Owing to a misguided decision in the War Department, many early-production gliders were shipped overseas to await the coming of airborne forces. Many others got caught up in air delivery bottlenecks, in part attributable to the chronic shortage of C-47 "tows"; others were grounded by Air Force retrofit orders. A substantial number were lost in test flights, in towing operations or in delivery landings, as well as in airborne training accidents owing to inexperienced pilots. As a result, the 82nd Airborne Division seldom had as many as two dozen gliders fit for training its two regiments, and often the number was far lower.[15]

Ridgway had been the first man from the division to make a parachute jump. Recently he had made a second jump. Now, faced with training two glider regiments, he was determined to be the first of the old hands to ride in a glider. Not to be outdone, Joe Swing went along.

The two generals traveled to Wright Field, near Dayton, Ohio, where some Waco gliders were undergoing modification and testing. The Air Force assigned the generals one of its most experienced glider test pilots, Frederick R. Dent, Jr. (West Point, 1919), who was also an engineer. The glider model Dent was then testing had wheels (like most gliders) and also experimental skids. It was designed to take off on wheels, drop them in flight and then land on the skids, which, it was believed, might be better for rough-terrain landings. Since the wheels were to be discarded in flight, they were not equipped with brakes.[16]

The tow plane, a C-47, warmed up on the runway. The nylon tow rope, three hundred feet long, was attached to a fitting in the tail of the C-47 and to one on the nose of the glider. Each aircraft had a tow-rope release device. These devices, not yet foolproof, sometimes activated in mid-flight, prematurely releasing the glider.

At first all went well. The C-47 pilot gunned engines and began the takeoff roll. The tow rope stretched taut and the glider began to roll on its wheels.

Dent was an excellent pilot and Ridgway had full confidence in him. The C-47 lifted off, and behind it, the glider. It was a somewhat eerie sensation, a noise-less, vibrationless climb behind the mother ship to altitude. At the appointed spot, Dent cut loose the tow rope and the glider soared off on its own, a great ungainly kite.

However, in preparation for the landing, things began to go wrong—badly wrong. When Dent pulled the wheel-release mechanism, it fouled; the wheels would not drop. There was no time to fool with it—the glider was coming down fast. Dent lined up on a runway and the glider touched down, rolling fast —with no brakes. Suddenly a four-engine bomber, propellers turning, loomed ahead on the runway.

Dent cried, "Jump!" Ridgway and Swing needed no further prodding; they dived out the glider door, hitting the concrete runway at an estimated thirty miles an hour. Bruised and skinned, but not otherwise injured, they watched in amazement as some quick-thinking airmen grabbed the wing of the glider and spun it away from a sure collision with the bomber's four whirling propellers.

Ridgway's glider flight had not been all that unusual. Glider accidents seemed to be the rule, rather than the exception. He "limped" back to Bragg, not without some very strong reservations about glider flight. However, he disguised his true feelings and, for morale purposes, went about extolling "the beauties of glider transportation." It was "free flight," that which man had been seeking since the beginning of time. The propaganda fell on deaf ears. The men listened, Ridgway recalled, "but they looked dubious . . . They were being put into gliders willy-nilly, and most of them didn't like it."

What was needed, Ridgway concluded, was a dramatic demonstration that the glider was not a "death trap," as everyone supposed. To that end he ar-ranged to have a legendary aerial stunter, Michael C. (Mike) Murphy, come to Bragg and put on a show for the men. Ridgway bravely climbed into the glider for the demonstration. Cut loose from the tow plane, Murphy, a superb pilot, did indeed dramatically wring out the glider. He did vertical banks and slow rolls and, as a hair-raising finale, three complete loops, coming out of the last one to a perfect landing on the runway, stopping three feet from a prearranged marker.[17]

How many minds this demonstration changed is not recorded. Not many, probably. Most men in the 82nd Airborne Division continued to harbor a dread of gliding. Posters went up on barracks walls in the 325th and 326th regiments with a montage of photographs of crashed gliders captioned: "Join the glider troops! No flight pay. No jump pay. But never a dull moment!" Someone wrote a song, "The Glider Riders," which aptly expressed the feel-ings of the men:

> Once I was infantry, now I'm a dope,
> Riding gliders attached to a rope,
> Safety in landing is only a hope,
> And the pay is exactly the same.[18]

☆ 8 ☆

THE BRITISH AND AMERICAN chiefs of staff were in fundamental disagreement over the best way to defeat Hitler and the German war machine. The British concept was what American planners called an "indirect" or "peripheral" strategy. The British believed that while Hitler was exhausting Germany in his vast and increasingly fruitless land war with Russia, the United States and Britain should: 1) defeat the German U-boat armadas, which were dominating the Atlantic and nearly paralyzing Allied shipping; 2) smash the German war production base to smithereens with massive air bombardments and 3) chip away at the southwestern periphery of the Axis empire in the Balkans, Mediterranean and Middle East. American planners, while generally agreeing with the first two strategic objectives, strongly disagreed with the third, believing instead that the major effort should be put into an early cross-Channel invasion into occupied France, from whence the Allies could drive armies straight at the heart of Germany. This was George Marshall's ROUNDUP plan, with which his chief planner, Dwight Eisenhower, concurred.[1]

Early in the war, the British views on strategy had led them into costly campaigns in the Mediterranean-North African Theater. It began in 1940, when Mussolini's inept army in Libya invaded Egypt. Determined to hold Egypt and the Middle East, the British had committed a large share of their available resources to that area, throwing back the Italians. This, in turn, had led Hitler to send a motorized armored force commanded by one of his most able generals, Erwin Rommel, to North Africa to help the Italians. In a seesaw desert war, Rommel's Afrika Korps had inflicted severe losses on the British, greatly eroding public confidence in Churchill and the British generals.

At the first wartime meeting of Churchill and President Roosevelt—in Washington in December 1941—Churchill and the British staffs urged the "peripheral" land strategy. Churchill proposed a large-scale amphibious landing (GYMNAST) in French Northwest Africa, with the idea of trapping Rommel between these new land forces and British armies in Egypt. Stimson and Marshall vigorously opposed this idea, holding out for ROUNDUP—the "direct" cross-Channel assault on France. In fact, in the early summer of 1942, Marshall sent Eisenhower to London to push preparations for ROUNDUP and to help persuade the British chiefs that it was a better alternative.

In the end, Stimson and Marshall lost the strategy battle. President Roosevelt sided with Churchill and the British staffs and approved the amphibious landing in French Northwest Africa, which was renamed TORCH. The U.S. forces in the British Isles which were earmarked for ROUNDUP were committed to TORCH, along with British forces. Eisenhower was named to command the landings. He, in turn, recruited Mark Clark, Bedell Smith and Alfred M. Gruenther to be his principal planners.

The final plan for TORCH was hastily drawn and less than perfect. British General Bernard L. Montgomery, commanding the British Eighth Army, would jump off from a defensive line at El Alamein and drive Rommel and the Italians westward. Eisenhower's TORCH forces would land in three places in French Northwest Africa: Casablanca, Oran and Algiers, it was hoped against perfunctory or no resistance from the Vichy French, who, it was thought, would quickly come over to the Allied side. Eisenhower's easternmost forces in Algeria would strike some four hundred miles east into Tunisia, setting the trap in Rommel's rear. The success of the enterprise hinged on the Allied forces in Algeria racing to Tunisia before Rommel got there or before the Axis could send reinforcements from Italy.

The execution of the plan was also less than perfect. Montgomery delayed his jump-off at El Alamein week after week, cautiously—too cautiously it seemed to many, including Churchill—building supplies and designing deceptions based on intercepted German military messages. Finally, on October 23, 1942, a mere two weeks before TORCH forces were scheduled to land, he smashed out of El Alamein with the roar of a thousand heavy guns, reeling the Germans and Italians back toward Tunisia. But his follow-up was much too slow and the badly shattered Axis forces had time to regroup and commence a well-executed withdrawal toward Tunisia.

On November 8, at about the time Ridgway was settling the 82nd Airborne Division at Fort Bragg, Eisenhower's TORCH forces landed at Casablanca, Oran and Algiers. The landing at Casablanca, led by George S. Patton, turned out to be a mistake. Contrary to expectations, the French did not swing over to the Allied side but, rather, put up a stiff fight. Moreover, when the brief battle was over, Patton's forces were a thousand miles from the key objective, Tunisia. The landing forces farther east, at Oran, led by American General Lloyd R. Fredendall, met moderate to strong resistance which was soon overcome, but Fredendall's forces were also too far from Tunisia to be of immediate help. The landing forces at Algiers—closest to Tunisia—led by American General Charles W. (Doc) Ryder, met no resistance (the French leader was pro-American), but the "race" to Tunisia, led by British General Kenneth A. N. Anderson, was too slow in getting started and not run hard and fast enough.

Axis leaders were completely surprised by the TORCH landings but soon perceived the intended trap for Rommel in Tunisia. They at once moved reinforcements from Italy—principally Luftwaffe fighters—to Tunisia, stopping Anderson's "race" near the Tunisia-Algeria border, giving Rommel time to withdraw into Tunisia and prepare defensive lines—against both Montgomery and Anderson. In the meantime, Montgomery's pursuit of Rommel had also been too slow and lackluster. The main purpose of TORCH—to trap Rommel before he could establish defensive positions in Tunisia or evacuate to Italy—was not achieved, leaving the Allies to face an entirely new situation.

Hitler and Mussolini now had two choices: to evacuate the Afrika Korps or to reinforce it sufficiently to enable it to inflict a decisive defeat on the Allies.

Neither course appealed to Hitler. Immediate evacuation would be a humiliating defeat for the Axis, with possible grave adverse psychological ramifications in Germany and Italy. To provide the Korps massive supplies would require a major commitment of resources—particularly air and sea power—which Hitler, immersed in the war with Russia, could not spare. The upshot was that Hitler made the cold-blooded decision to sacrifice the Afrika Korps. It would not be evacuated and would get only modest supplies. Its final mission would be to pin down as many Allied air, land and sea forces as possible for as long as possible, denying the use of those forces against Hitler elsewhere, and to inflict the greatest possible casualties.

The battle for Tunisia thus bogged down into a nearly static war of attrition. Montgomery's Eighth Army finally arrived in southern Tunisia, where he lingered at the Mareth Line for another long buildup. In the meantime, Eisenhower reinforced his long (250-mile) north-south Tunisian front with troops and equipment laboriously brought overland by rail and truck from Oran, Casablanca and elsewhere. Cold, rainy winter weather set in, miring tanks, motorized vehicles and aircraft. Eisenhower, having lost the race for Tunisia and facing a grim and costly winter campaign, became ill with "walking pneumonia" and utterly depressed and went about muttering, "Anyone who wants the job of Allied Commander in Chief can have it." That which Marshall and Eisenhower had feared most—a prolonged diversion of Allied resources to a peripheral theater—had occurred. Victory in Tunisia was inevitable; but it was certain to be a long and costly effort.

Amid these grim circumstances, President Roosevelt and Churchill and the combined Allied military staffs met again—at Casablanca in January 1943. By that time the British had become disenchanted with Eisenhower as field commander. They had two principal objectives at Casablanca: to "kick Ike upstairs" and insert British land, air and sea commanders immediately under him to conduct the campaign in Tunisia; and to gain approval for an expansion of the Mediterranean operations to include an invasion of Sicily or Sardinia (preferably Sicily) after Tunisia had been captured and, perhaps later, an invasion of Italy. Despite the most strenuous objections of Marshall, who knew that further operations in the Mediterranean Theater would delay ROUNDUP, the British views prevailed. Eisenhower was indeed kicked upstairs, and a decision to invade Sicily (Operation HUSKY), which would immediately follow victory in Tunisia, was agreed upon. One of Marshall's key war planners who attended the conference wrote: "We came, we listened, and we were conquered."

When Marshall activated the 82nd and 101st airborne divisions, on August 15, 1942, his intent was to incorporate them in the cross-Channel invasion, ROUNDUP, or in operations in France following the invasion. Because Bill Lee and his parachute outfit, the 502nd Regiment, commanded by George Howell, were senior in terms of airborne experience, Marshall decreed that the 101st would be the first airborne outfit committed to combat.[2]

After the Casablanca conference, however, Marshall made two important changes in his plans for airborne operations. First he decided that airborne forces would be employed in HUSKY—the invasion of Sicily. Second he ruled that not the 101st, but the 82nd, would be assigned to HUSKY and thus go into combat first. This news came to the division in early February 1943. Ridgway would say that he did not know why Marshall switched the 82nd for the 101st, but others believed it was because Ridgway pressed Marshall to let him go first and because Ridgway was one of "Marshall's boys."[3]

The news hit the division with the force of a bombshell. HUSKY had initially been set for about June 10. (It was later delayed a month.) Ridgway had about 120 days to finish training the division in airborne operations and get it to North Africa, from whence it would stage for HUSKY. Not only that, Ridgway had to draw up a complex war plan and integrate this plan with those being generated in Washington and Eisenhower's headquarters in North Africa. It seemed impossible that all could be done on such short notice.

The weakest links in the scheme were the glider regiments. Owing to the acute shortage of gliders and glider pilots, there had been no time to properly train the division gliderists. Moreover, although gliders were already being shipped to North Africa, some of them were being earmarked for the British, and it seemed doubtful that there would be enough gliders by D day to lift both Harry Lewis' 325th and Cutler's 326th regiments from North Africa to Sicily. Military prudence dictated the solution to this problem, and it caused another drastic reorganization of the division. They would have to substitute a parachute regiment for one of the glider regiments, changing the division makeup from one parachute regiment and two glider regiments to two parachute regiments and one glider regiment.

Here Ridgway faced another wrenching decision: which glider regiment to let go? Both regiments had been with the division since its inception; Ridgway had helped create them. To now lop off one would be like losing an arm. However, there was no time for sentimentality; not an hour to lose. Ridgway chose to retain Harry Lewis' 325th Regiment. On February 12, 1943, Cutler's 326th Regiment (but not its glider artillery) was transferred out of the division, and eventually sent to yet another new airborne division which was being activated, the 13th.[4]*

To replace the 326th, Ridgway drew the 505th Parachute Infantry Regiment, which was commanded by a young West Pointer, James Maurice Gavin, and which came with the 456th Parachute Artillery Battalion, commanded by Harrison B. Harden, Jr. Activated on June 25, 1942, the 505 had been in existence for about six months and was based nearby at Hoffman, North Carolina. Ridgway could not have been more pleased. He had met Gavin and knew that under Gavin's leadership the 505 was the best of all the parachute regiments. He immediately got off a letter to Gavin "warmly" welcoming the

---

* Although others were planned, the 13th (deliberately activated on Friday, 13 August 1943) was the fifth and last American airborne division to be created in World War II. Its original commander was George W. Griner, soon replaced by Elbridge G. Chapman, a highly decorated World War I veteran and early convert to airborne operations. Cutler, promoted to brigadier general, was named ADC of the 13th Division.[5]

505th to the 82nd Division, making a point to say that the 505th was "highly regarded."[6]

Then thirty-five years old, Gavin was tall and slim ("Slim Jim"), handsome, soft-spoken, a dedicated athlete and a master in the art of leading men. He was also dazzlingly brilliant—considered by some to be a military genius, a *Wunderkind*. In conversation, his mind raced at such breathtaking speed over such a vast canvas that he usually left ordinary soldiers bewildered and fumbling. Ridgway would later write that Gavin was "one of the finest battle leaders, and one of the most brilliant thinkers the Army has ever produced."[7]

Gavin was every inch a soldier and tough as steel. One young West Point lieutenant, reporting to him for the first time at Benning, recalled the encounter as one that made his "hair stand on end." "He snarled, 'You're an officer, huh?' " the officer recalled. "Er, yes sir." Gavin continued, "In this outfit that means you are first out of the door of the airplane and last in the chow line. *You understand that?*" He was one of the "toughest men you ever saw," the officer continued. "God! It was nutty enough to jump out of an airplane with a static line to open your chute. But Gavin was doing free falls—just falling hundreds of feet through the air and opening his chute by hand. He was a phenomenal soldier—you don't see very many of his kind."[8]

Born in Brooklyn, New York, on March 22, 1907, Gavin was the son of Irish immigrant parents, both of whom died before he was two years old, leaving him stranded in a Catholic orphanage. The Catholic Church soon found him foster parents, Martin and Mary Gavin, who were also Irish immigrants, devout Catholics and poor. The Gavins and a great host of Irish relatives settled near Mount Carmel, Pennsylvania, a coal-mining center. Gavin grew up there, working long hours to help support the family. By age eleven, he managed two paper routes and was the local agent for three out-of-town newspapers. By the time he was thirteen, he had added two Sunday routes and had two young employees. When he reached eighth grade, his foster parents thought that was schooling enough and Gavin went to work full time, first as a shoe store clerk, later as a filling station manager, assiduously avoiding work in the coal mines.

Contrary to his foster parents' view, Gavin believed a good education was "fundamental to real advancement." From childhood on he had been an omnivorous reader; had, in fact, read every book in Mount Carmel that he could find. On his seventeenth birthday, he left the Gavin home for New York City to find a means of educating himself. The search soon led to an Army recruiting office, where, after he had signed papers stating he was eighteen, he was sworn in as a private on April 1, 1924. A mere five months later, Gavin was accepted into an Army prep school for West Point examinations. He whizzed through the course, passed the tests and on July 1, 1925, entered the Academy. He graduated in the class of 1929 and entered the peacetime Army, a career that he found vastly appealing and one at which he excelled. He continued to read and study, educating himself. During the thirties, he became an expert in military history and strategy. By the spring of 1940, coincident with the German *Blitzkrieg* through the Low Countries and France, he was an instructor at West Point in the Tactical Department, submitting articles to *Infantry Journal.*

The German parachute operation in 1940 attracted Gavin, as did several articles by Bill Lee in *Infantry Journal.* Bill Ryder, commanding the original fifty-man parachute test platoon, was a good friend; they had served together in the Philippines. In April 1941, Gavin applied for duty with Miley's newly forming 501st Battalion. The West Point superintendent disapproved the request because Gavin had only been at West Point one year and because, the superintendent wrote, Gavin "so far as I know . . . is not peculiarly fitted for this type of duty." However, a very determined Gavin pulled strings in the War Department, and on August 1, 1941, he arrived at Benning for paratroop training. He proved to be more than peculiarly fitted for paratrooper duty— one of the very best. After graduation from the parachute school, he briefly commanded a parachute company. However, when Bill Lee had an opportunity to take his full measure, he pulled Gavin into his headquarters staff, where, among other duties, Gavin was detailed to write the first manual for *The Employment of Airborne Forces.* Soon promoted to chief planning and training officer, Gavin was a natural choice to command one of the parachute regiments when they were created in the spring of 1942. After a brief "crash" course at the Command and General Staff School, Gavin assumed command of the 505 in July, 1942 and was soon promoted to full colonel.

The 505 may well have been one of the best-trained and most highly motivated regiments the Army had ever fielded. "They were awesome," an 82nd Airborne Division staffer recalled. "Every man a clone of the CO, Gavin. Tough? God they were tough! Not just in the field, but twenty-four hours a day. Off-duty they'd move into a bar in little groups and if everyone there didn't get down on their knees in adoration, they'd simply tear the place up. Destroy it. And God help the 'straight legs'† they came across." Doc Eaton thought he had never seen such killers. They reminded him "of a pack of jackals."[9]

Gavin stood by his men with unflinching loyalty. Once, while the regiment was training at Benning, one of his troopers had been arrested for having sexual intercourse with a young lady on the lawn of the courthouse in nearby Phoenix City, Alabama. The Benning post commander had been outraged by this indecency and had demanded to know what Gavin was going to do about it. Gavin's icy reply: "In view of the fact that that young man will be asked to give his life for his country in the next few months, I suggest we give him a medal."[10]

The off-duty horseplay and macho games were not confined to the enlisted men. Gavin remembered his officers as equally rowdy. "When we were in training, the boys were a pretty wild bunch. There was this thing they did to show how tough they were. They'd have a few drinks at the Officers' Club and start jumping off high places, like the balcony onto the dance floor. Then, after a few more drinks, they'd start jumping out of the second floor bathroom

---

† The paratrooper boots caused the trousers to bunch in "baggy" fashion, in contrast to the unbunched, or "straight," trousers, or "legs," of regular GIs.

window, which was about the size of a door on a C-47. They'd get so wild they'd have to send the MPs to the Officers' Club to keep the peace."[11]

Gavin had imbued the 505 with such remarkable esprit and pride that the normal problems of integrating the outfit into the 82nd Airborne Division were magnified manyfold. Some believed that the 505 never was fully integrated, that it stubbornly clung to its own proud identity. A couple of typical incidents were remembered by Bill Moorman: "A young lieutenant came up to Ridgway and saluted and said, 'Sir, Colonel Gavin sends his compliments and told us he wants us to cooperate to the utmost with the 82nd Division.' Ridgway was flabbergasted. 'What do you mean, "cooperate"?' he said. 'You're *part* of the 82nd Division!' " Once, when Bob Hope came to entertain the 82nd Division, by chance his first audience was composed entirely of the 505th Regiment: "Hope walked out on the stage, grabbed the mike and said, 'Well, I'm certainly happy to be here today with the famous 82nd Division!' The men jumped up shouting vehemently, 'No! No! 505 . . . 505 . . . 505.' Hope was dumbfounded. He said, 'Isn't this the 82nd?' The men shouted back, 'No! No! The 505 . . . the 505!' "[12]

According to Moorman, the parachutists of the 505 regarded Harry Lewis' gliderists with utmost scorn. One of Ridgway's morale-building orders therefore became particularly unpopular:

The gliderists wore plain shoes, canvas leggings and a glider patch insignia. That included most of the 82nd's headquarters staff, who would go into combat in gliders. Not too flashy. So Ridgway put out an order that anyone who made one parachute jump could wear jump boots and the parachute insignia. You can believe that just about every staffer, no matter how terrified, made that jump and then swanked around in those high polished jump boots. I'll guarantee you I got mine as soon as the order came down. The paratroopers in the 505 who'd each made at least five jumps in school to qualify—and get jump boots and badges—took great exception to this order. One of them put up a notice on the 505 bulletin board, aping Ridgway's order almost word for word, which said: "Any man in the 505 who makes one glider ride shall be entitled to wear shoes and canvas leggings."[13]

The merger—or attempted merger—of the 505 into the 82nd Division had brought together under one tent three remarkable officers: Ridgway, Taylor and Gavin. They were a rare breed: magnetic, handsome, dynamic, literate, ambitious. In the postwar years, each man would rise to a position of great prominence in the Army. Ridgway and Taylor would be chiefs of staff and Taylor would rise further, to be chairman of the Joint Chiefs. Collectively they would become symbols of the nuclear-age Army of the 1950s, occasionally even referred to as "Ridgway-Taylor-Gavin" to denote a point of view.

They were products of West Point and the peacetime Army, but each was an individualist with a powerful ego and a distinct style of leadership. They frequently clashed, and some of these clashes would open deep wounds. Bill

Moorman, who often saw them together during the war and later, defined their differences with his usual pungent wit:

> Ridgway would cut your throat and then burst into tears. Taylor would cut your throat and think nothing about it. Gavin would cut your throat and then laugh.[14]

PART II
Sicily:
Baptism of Fire

☆9☆

IN EARLY MARCH 1943, George Marshall called Ridgway to Washington for a private talk. He told Ridgway that he wanted him to make a quick air trip to North Africa to talk with Eisenhower and his planners about how best to utilize the 82nd Airborne Division in the invasion of Sicily. The orders suited Ridgway perfectly; he was not satisfied with the scanty information he had about the planning. Leaving the training of the division in the hands of his ADC, Bull Keerans; the chief of staff, Doc Eaton, and his three regimental commanders, Gavin, Tucker and Lewis, Ridgway set off accompanied by his aide, Don Faith, and a small planning staff.

Among the planners was a new Ridgway protégé, Emory S. (Hank) Adams, Jr., the younger of two remarkable sons of the recently retired Adjutant General of the Army, whom Ridgway had known well and admired. Both Adams boys were West Point graduates, the elder, James Y., class of 1935; Hank, class of 1940. Both were 6′ 3″ tall, both had been athletes at the Academy and, owing to the prominence of their father, both were very well connected in the Army. James, a brilliant but eccentric maverick, somewhat in the mold of Lawrence of Arabia, became involved with "special forces," such as the British Commandos and the American Rangers. Hank, a more conventional, team player, briefly joined Jim in Ranger training in the British Isles, then volunteered for the airborne. After he had completed his training, Rube Tucker, a classmate of Jim Adams', chose Hank to be the 504th's regimental S-3, chief of plans and training.

Hank Adams remembered his first encounter with Ridgway:

I made a practice parachute jump at Fort Bragg, landed in a pine tree, then fell to the ground, somewhat groggy. I looked up and here was this two-star general—Ridgway—standing there. I jumped up, saluted, gave my name, then, still groggy, I fell down again. He helped me up and asked if I was General Adams' son. When I said yes, he then proceeded to tell me at some length what a fine man my father was, and how Dad had helped him in the past in certain ways.

In that brief encounter in the woods, I realized what a hell of an impressive leader Ridgway was. You could feel this amazing strength of character. It just emanated. I later learned that it was based on a set of inflexible, uncompromising principles. He had a truly *deep love* for our country, for the Army, for his unit, whatever it might be, and for fighting men. He was physically energetic and ambitious—but he was not motivated by *personal* ambition. No vanity. He would let nothing stand in the way of getting done what was important for the country. Toward that end, too, he had a real understand-

Allied Invasions of North Africa and Sicily

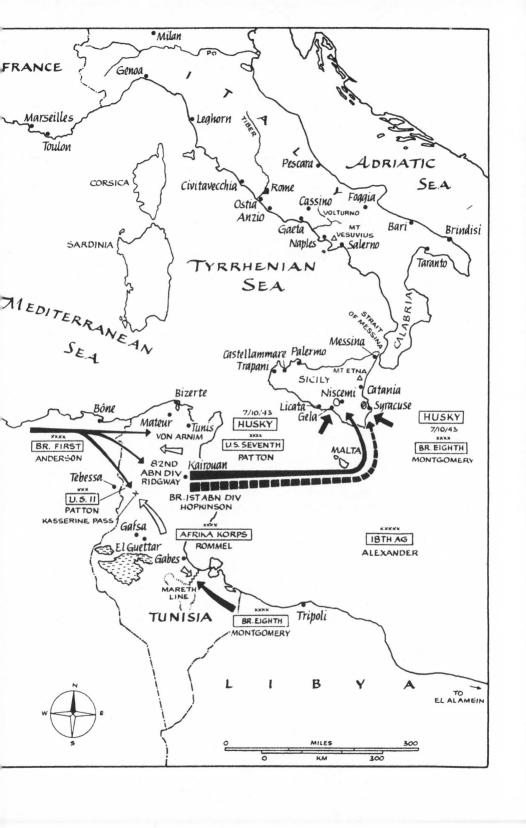

ing of soldiers—what the men needed and how to get it for them, what they could and could not accomplish in a given situation. In that sense, he was also a deeply compassionate man.

I was only a first lieutenant, but after a little while Ridgway became convinced that I was some sort of airborne planner. So he took me along on that first trip to North Africa.

Hank Adams was thus brought into Ridgway's little "family," or inner circle. He was an impressive addition: big, brave, handsome, smart, modest to a fault. Ridgway watchers would note that many of the younger men inducted into the inner circle were, like Ridgway himself, sons of "old Army" generals or colonels. Some would remark that young men like Don Faith, Bill Moorman, and Hank Adams became somewhat like sons to Ridgway.[1]

The flight to North Africa was long and arduous: three days in uncomfortable Air Force transports with frequent changes of planes. Landing at the Maison Blanche Airport, in Algiers, Ridgway went to Eisenhower's headquarters at the St. George's Hotel. There, Bedell Smith, presiding over a large Allied staff composed of American, British and French officers, greeted Ridgway with a long face. It was an unhappy time. The Allies had just suffered a devastating defeat on the Tunisian front. Ridgway had heard some of the grim details in the Pentagon. Now he got the full, unvarnished story.[2]

In accordance with the decisions reached at Casablanca in late January, Eisenhower had been kicked upstairs, and British ground, air and sea commanders had been appointed to run the war in North Africa. The highly regarded British general Harold R. L. G. Alexander, appointed commanding general of the 18th Army Group, took charge of all ground operations. The American forces, loosely and imperfectly organized as II Corps, were commanded by Lloyd Fredendall, who had done a commendable job in leading the TORCH landings at Oran.

The tactical situation favored the Allies in the long term. Rommel's Afrika Korps, withdrawn to the Mareth Line, in southern Tunisia, and caught between Montgomery's Eighth Army and General Kenneth Anderson's First Army, was ultimately doomed. But Hitler wanted to save Rommel for another day. In late January, about the time Alexander took over Allied ground operations, Hitler ordered Rommel home for a good long rest and replaced him with Jürgen von Arnim.

Before leaving North Africa, Rommel conceived a plan to deliver a parting shot at the Allies which, if successful, would significantly delay the destruction of his beloved Afrika Korps. He would first attack the First Army in western Tunisia, then pivot and hit Montgomery's Eighth Army at the Mareth Line. The First Army was green and loosely organized—composed of British, American and some French forces recruited in North Africa. Rommel hurriedly launched the attack on February 14. The Allies were alerted to the upcoming attack by intercepted messages but misinterpreted the data and prepared defenses at the wrong place. Rommel smashed into Fredendall's thin and ineptly held II Corps front in the southern sector and broke through at Kasserine Pass. Rommel had it within his power to crack straight through and rout the First Army, but he did not realize it. Confusion and disorder in the Axis high command discouraged exploitation of the breakthrough. After several days, Rommel withdrew to positions in the Tunisia heartland and left for Germany.

Rommel's brief but effective attack had disgraced the American forces. Some had fought courageously but too many had broken and run, leaving behind vehicles, equipment, ammo and fuel. In the aftermath, Eisenhower relieved Fredendall of command and brought George Patton from Morocco to replace him and put backbone in II Corps. This was merely a temporary assignment for Patton; he had already been named to lead the U.S. forces which would invade Sicily with Montgomery's all-British Eighth Army—after Tunisia was wrapped up. Omar Bradley, who had just arrived in North Africa after straightening out the 28th National Guard Division to serve as Eisenhower's "eyes and ears" on the Tunisian front, would become the permanent II Corps commander after Patton returned to the planning for Sicily.

The American disgrace had put a heavy strain on British-American relationships. The British veterans of North Africa, who had been fighting Rommel for years, were openly contemptuous of American battlefield commanders and the GIs under them. In its first hard battlefield encounter with the German Army, the American corps had fallen on its face. This distrust of the Americans would influence Alexander's planning for future battles, including Sicily. Reacting to the criticism and humiliated by defeat, the Americans were in turn contemptuous of the British and blamed the setback at Kasserine Pass on inept British intelligence and planning.

Ridgway arrived in Algiers on March 8, two days after Eisenhower had relieved Fredendall and put Patton and Bradley in charge of II Corps. Eisenhower was glad to see him. Less than a month earlier, he had suggested Ridgway (along with Bradley and eleven other possibilities) for the "eyes and ears" job. But Eisenhower had no time then to discuss the invasion of Sicily in detail and, in fact, was removed from the day-to-day planning. His mind was naturally focused on the Tunisian front, on restoring the integrity of II Corps. On March 10, when Bradley came to the rear on urgent business, Ridgway joined Eisenhower, Bradley and Smith for afternoon conferences and dinner. During these meetings, Eisenhower suggested that Ridgway return with Bradley to II Corps and spend a week at the front. Ridgway gladly accepted this opportunity to, as he later put it, drink in "the delight of battle."[3]

Eisenhower, as Bradley later wrote, was not an outstanding battlefield manager, but he was a general with rare political and diplomatic gifts. He was determined to make "coalition warfare" work, to prevent a catastrophic breakdown between the American and British high commands. Every American general who visited his GHQ, including Ridgway, got a stern personal warning. Eisenhower would brook not the slightest criticism of the British; anyone who did so would be sent home. Those American generals who displayed willingness to "get along" with the British generals rose high and fast in Eisenhower's command. The Anglophobes—and there were many in the American Army—had to keep their feelings repressed or face certain professional ruin. Many senior Americans, including Patton and Bradley, believed that Eisenhower "went too far" with this policy. They would later write that Eisenhower had been captivated—and captured—by the British.

Ridgway was not an Anglophobe, but he was proud of the professionalism of the American Army. He greatly resented the widespread snobbery in the British officer corps and the slurs and insults British officers leveled at the American GI. It made hackles rise on the back of his neck. However, emulating Bradley, he kept his hostility under tight rein.[4]

Alexander was then reorganizing the Allied forces in Tunisia and putting the final touches on the plan to defeat the Afrika Korps. Basically the plan was what Bradley would describe as a "squeeze" strategy. Montgomery's Eighth Army would push north from the Mareth Line while Alexander's First Army pushed eastward from positions along the western Tunisia border. Owing to a lack of faith in the fighting ability of the GI, Alexander had decided that II Corps would not be given a major role in the forthcoming battle. The corps would be utilized principally in feinting actions and deceptions designed to confuse or mislead Von Arnim.[5]

Ridgway accompanied Bradley back to the Tunisian front—a four-hundred-mile trip. Ridgway recalled: "For the first time I saw the loneliest and most ominous of all landscapes, a battlefield. And I knew for the first time that strange exhilaration that grips a man when he knows that somewhere out there in the distance, hostile eyes are watching him and that at any moment a bullet he may never hear, fired by an enemy he cannot see, may strike him."[6]

Patton had been in command of II Corps only one week, but already this sadly dispirited outfit was smartening up. Patton was a ruthless, earthy, profane leader, seemingly fearless and driven by a kind of bizarre martial spirit. Bradley wrote: "Patton was the most fiercely ambitious man and the strangest duck I have ever known . . . He was unmercifully hard on his men, demanding the utmost in military efficiency and bearing. Most of them respected but despised him." And yet, Bradley wrote, Patton was "one of the most extraordinary fighting generals the Army had ever produced . . ."[7]

Ridgway had first met Patton at Fort Benning a year and a half before. Sharing some of Bradley's reservations about Patton, he would later observe: "Leadership . . . is an art of the first order and it's got to have an infinite variety of adaptation, depending on the person . . . I wouldn't follow any of his [Patton's] techniques of leadership. I couldn't do it. My nature . . . [was] totally different."[8]

The first phase of the "squeeze" strategy was about to begin. Montgomery would jump off from the Mareth Line, driving the Axis forces northward. Patton's II Corps was to "make noise" and "demonstrate," as if launching an attack into the Axis flank, thus relieving pressure on Montgomery's front. In addition, if possible, II Corps was to capture several limited objectives, including Gafsa, El Guettar and Station de Sened. To heighten the effect of the feint, II Corps would jump off three days prior to Montgomery.[9]

On March 17, Alexander and Eisenhower and other VIPs thronged into the II Corps Command Post (CP). The corps was wound tight as a watch spring, determined to redeem itself. Ridgway joined Bradley, who was going with the 1st Armored Division in the drive on Station de Sened. The 1st Armored Division, reinforced by troops from the U.S. 9th Infantry Division, was commanded by Orlando Ward, who had preceded Bedell Smith as head of Marshall's Secretariat and whom both Bradley and Ridgway knew well.[10]

Ridgway and Bradley joined the forward elements of the infantry. In the very first few hours of the day, Bradley was nearly killed when a wheel of his jeep rolled over an Italian mine, which luckily failed to go off. Ridgway also had a close call. As he was riding in a jeep behind a column of closely bunched trucks, a German Messerschmitt fighter, "guns blinking red," strafed the road. The gunner missed Ridgway but blew a truck sky-high before the plane was shot down by a fusillade of GI small-arms fire. The incident burned into Ridgway's mind. After that, he recalled, "I never allowed vehicles to bunch up on the roads."[11]

These initial II Corps feints were successful in that they drew some German forces away from Montgomery's front. The 1st Infantry Division (The Big Red One), commanded by Terry de la Mesa Allen, lured elements of the 10th Panzer Division into El Guettar and, thanks to some decoded German messages, sprung a trap in which thirty-two Tiger tanks were destroyed. This was sweet revenge, but it would take many more weeks of hard fighting to overrun the Afrika Korps and capture Tunisia, delaying the invasion date of Sicily.[12]

Ridgway spent a full week on the Tunisian front with II Corps. It was valuable experience. It gave him a "feel" for battle, a good idea of what was and was not possible. He saw firsthand some of the shortcomings in American training and the inferiority of some American equipment—such as the antitank guns. He met some of the British generals, notably the cool and unflappable Alexander, who would be the overall land commander for Sicily. Like Bradley and others, Ridgway was immensely impressed by Alexander. He would later describe him as "one of the great soldiers of this generation" and "brilliant soldier and a wonderful personality—a talented, versatile gentleman" whose "physical and moral courage" were of "the highest order."[13]

Alexander also was too busy to discuss Sicily except in the most general terms. The detailed planning was going forward at Eisenhower's headquarters in Algiers and at Patton's headquarters in Mostaganem, a seaside city about fifty miles east of Oran. Patton's spearhead for the invasion was to be VI Corps, commanded by Ernest J. (Mike) Dawley, a field artilleryman from the West Point class of 1910, who, like Patton, had fought with distinction in World War I and whom Ridgway had known well at West Point in the early twenties.[14]

Large, mountainous and triangle-shaped, Sicily lies three miles off the toe of Italy's boot. Militarily, the most effective way to seize it would be to invade the toe of the boot, Calabria, isolate the island and block Axis attempts to reinforce it. However, inasmuch as Roosevelt and Churchill had made no decisions about invading the Italian mainland—and George Marshall was still opposed to an invasion—the planners were compelled to treat Sicily as though it were an isolated island sitting in the middle of nowhere. The initial plan was to make simultaneous American and British frontal assaults on the northwest and southeast coasts, then conquer the island in a rapid giant pincers movement. Little or no real consideration had been given to blocking Axis attempts to reinforce the island across the three-mile-wide Strait of Messina.[15]

The role airborne forces would play in the Sicily invasion had been roughed out. Like the general plan itself, airborne operations were to be predominantly British, making full use of Britain's single airborne division, the 1st.

The British 1st Airborne Division, comparable in strength to the 82nd, had come into being in the fall of 1941.* Its first commander had been Frederick Arthur Montague (Boy) Browning, a handsome, elegant and adventurous grenadier who had fought with distinction in World War I and who was married to the famous British novelist Daphne du Maurier. Units of the division had participated in small-scale, commando-like raids on the coast of occupied France, in Norway and in TORCH. In Tunisia, elements of the division deployed as light infantry had seen some tough combat. In place of helmets, British paratroopers wore maroon berets and, as a consequence, the Germans in Tunisia had nicknamed them "the Red Devils." Like American paratroopers, the Red Devils had been highly publicized (and glamorized) but the division had never participated in a full-scale airborne combat action. About the time Ridgway arrived in North Africa, Browning had turned over command of the division to G. F. (Hoppy) Hopkinson and had been named "airborne adviser" to Eisenhower.[16]

Owing to the shortage of transport aircraft and gliders, the role of the 82nd Airborne Division in Sicily had been sharply limited. The plan was that a single American "parachute combat team" (a regiment reinforced by a battalion of artillery and engineers, medics, etc.) would be dropped inland of Patton's forces on the second day of the invasion, utilizing some of the aircraft that had previously dropped the British 1st Division. In addition, a second American operation, in support of a smaller landing, was planned for the fifth day of the invasion.

On the insistence of naval leaders, it had been decided that the invasion of Sicily should take place at night. The naval planners believed that a nighttime invasion was more apt to achieve surprise and that darkness would provide some protection for the ships from enemy air attacks. This meant that the airborne assault forces would also jump at night. This had not been done before in combat on a large scale, but American paratroopers preferred night

---

* For Sicily operations, the division consisted of the 1st, 2nd and 4th parachute brigades and the glider-borne 1st Airlanding Brigade. A British airborne brigade was roughly the equivalent of an American airborne regiment.

jumping and had trained extensively for this mode of attack. Nighttime airborne assaults presented certain problems, but these were more than offset by the reduced risk of enemy attack during the parachute-descent and ground-assembly phases. It was thus decided to launch the invasion on a night when the paratroopers could jump by moonlight and the rest of the forces could come ashore just after moonset. Since the most favorable moonlight conditions would occur on the night of July 9/10, this date had been chosen as D day.[17]

Ridgway was not happy with these preliminary plans. Theretofore he had been led to believe that the 82nd Division would share equally in the airborne assault on Sicily, that it would be committed in full strength. Now its mission had been reduced to a sideshow which depended on the availability of aircraft *after* the big British airborne assault, and after the element of surprise had been lost. Since these airborne plans had been strongly influenced by Boy Browning, who had Eisenhower's ear, it seemed imperative to Ridgway to have a senior American airborne representative on the scene, who might at least attempt to counteract Browning's considerable weight. With his rank, tact and intelligence, Max Taylor seemed the ideal choice. Ridgway cabled Taylor to leave at once for North Africa with a small staff. His mission was to fight for a larger participation for the 82nd Division in the Sicily invasion.[18]

By this time, Ridgway's classmate Mark Clark, who had ably served Eisenhower in TORCH, had been promoted to the three-star rank of lieutenant general. Eisenhower had offered Clark a job in the Tunisian campaign, but Clark had declined it. His heart was set on commanding nothing less than an army. After Clark had "begged and pleaded" for a considerable period, Eisenhower had created the Fifth Army for Clark. It was largely administrative. Its mission at the time of Ridgway's visit was to train and equip new outfits and individual replacements arriving in North Africa. Eisenhower had assigned Al Gruenther to be Clark's chief of staff in order to give Gruenther more rank and experience so that he would be fully qualified to replace Bedell Smith in case anything should happen to him (Smith had very bad ulcers). Clark had placed Fifth Army headquarters and some training facilities at Oujda, French Morocco, a village close to the Morocco-Algeria border.[19]

Inasmuch as the 82nd Division would be administratively assigned to Clark's Fifth Army on arrival in North Africa, Ridgway paid Clark and Gruenther a visit in Oujda. He was warmly welcomed. Gruenther, a brilliant, high-strung officer (the best bridge player in the Army), was an old friend. They had overlapped two years at West Point and had met again at Fort Benning. It was decided that the 82nd Division should bivouac in the Oujda area—Gavin's and Tucker's parachute regiments at Oujda, Lewis' glider regiment at Marnia, a village nearby. Refurbished French airfields would be used as a base for the troop-carrier units, and a small parachute school would be established to train replacements and new volunteers. In addition to his Sicily planning assignment, Max Taylor would confer with Clark and Gruenther on these matters.[20]

At that time, Clark's chief "airborne adviser" on the nuts-and-bolts level was a young West Pointer (class of 1936) and paratrooper, Charles Billingslea.

Like the Adams boys, Billingslea was tall (6' 3"), handsome and impressive. Before the war, both Adams boys and Billingslea had served together in the same infantry regiment in California, so Hank Adams knew Billingslea quite well and admired him. In fact, Billingslea had probably influenced Hank's decision to become a paratrooper. Learning of this connection, Ridgway asked Hank Adams to stay in North Africa and work with Chuck Billingslea on the planning for the Sicily airborne operation. Adams recalled: "What an experience! For about two weeks I sat in conferences with Generals Eisenhower, Montgomery, Patton, Arthur Tedder, Browning and others. Every now and then one of the generals would stop talking and turn to me and say, 'Well, Lieutenant, what do you think?' "[21]

Before leaving North Africa, Ridgway made a point of investigating a little-known TORCH sideshow which had involved the first use of American paratroopers in combat. It turned out to be a harrowing tale with many lessons for would-be combat paratroopers.

The story began in the spring of 1942, when, as part of the ROUNDUP forces, the War Department sent the 2nd Battalion of Bud Miley's 503rd Parachute Infantry Regiment to England. This independent outfit, comprising about six hundred men, subsequently renamed the 509th Parachute Infantry Battalion, was commanded by Edson D. Raff (West Point, 1933).[22]

While in England, the 509th became closely associated with pioneering British airborne elements, which were eventually organized into Boy Browning's 1st British Airborne Division. In one early TORCH plan, the British 1st Airborne Division was to be employed in the assault. This plan was eventually discarded, but on Mark Clark's urging, smaller British and American airborne units, including Raff's 509th Battalion, were included. Raff's initial mission was to capture two airfields near Oran, at Tafaraoui and La Senia.

The Raff mission was far too ambitious and was grossly handicapped by the inexperience of the troop-carrier pilots. Departing England late in the evening of November 7 in thirty-nine C-47s, the 556-man outfit was to fly fifteen hundred miles nonstop to Oran, where it would either jump into combat or peacefully land—depending on the attitude of the French. En route, the planes ran into foul weather and most got lost over the Mediterranean. Singly or in small groups, the widely scattered planes eventually began to land in Gibraltar, Spanish and French Morocco, some of them hundreds of miles from the target. Only six of the thirty-nine planes managed to fly directly to Oran. Some paratroopers jumped in daylight (including Raff, who broke a rib), and some were attacked by French aircraft and troops, but none managed to play a decisive role in the brief battle for Oran or seize the two airfields. In this confused action, two airmen and eight paratroopers were killed by the French and two dozen or more paratroopers were wounded—all to little avail.

A week later, British and American airborne forces joined in the "race" for Tunisia. One of Boy Browning's battalions jumped into Bône, Algeria, to help capture that seaport (Chuck Billingslea with them). Raff's outfit was assigned a mission similar to the first: capture a French airfield near Tebessa, on the

Tunisian border. Thirty-three C-47s were employed in the hastily organized operation. The Raff force, of some 350 men, jumped directly on or near the field in daylight, only to find themselves zeroed-in in the sights of French weapons. Fortunately neither side fired. Eventually Raff was able to persuade the French to "surrender" the airfield to the Americans without bloodshed. Later the Raff force, deployed as light infantry, aggressively fought the Germans in southern Tunisia.

A third and far smaller airborne mission was carried out in Tunisia in late December. This was more like a commando raid 110 miles inside German lines. Two C-47s dropped thirty of Raff's paratroopers (plus two French paratrooper guides) at night to blow up a bridge near El Djem. Dropped in the wrong place, the group was unable to locate the bridge, and the next day they were discovered by a German patrol. Eight paratroopers escaped and, after hiding out for a month, finally reached Allied lines. The rest were killed or captured.

The operations of the Raff force had earned high praise from Eisenhower and Clark, but they had also brought to light some serious weaknesses in airborne operations. The principal weakness was the difficulty of projecting long-range operations in the dark with green or inept Air Force transport pilots and navigators. These weaknesses had been clearly demonstrated in the Oran and El Djem bridge operations.[23]

While in North Africa, Ridgway met Edson Raff and other officers who had participated in the abortive Oran operation. These included Chuck Billingslea's West Point classmate William P. Yarborough, an innovative pioneer paratrooper also on Mark Clark's staff. Yarborough had accompanied the 509th into Oran as a supernumerary and had participated in Raff's subsequent operations as Mark Clark's observer. Later, in an account of these early airborne operations, Yarborough described Raff, appropriately nicknamed "Little Caesar" as a "superb soldier" and "a tough disciplinarian, fearless, aggressive and tenacious." Offsetting these admirable soldierly qualities, however, were grave personality flaws. Raff was almost intolerably egotistical (he was already writing a quickie book extolling the 509's feats in North Africa, *We Jumped to Fight)* and abrasive to the point of rudeness. Some senior officers who served under Raff did not believe he was a capable combat commander.[24]

Believing his men could profit from the experience of these 509 men, Ridgway considered taking some of them back to the 82nd Airborne Division. But not Little Caesar Raff. Ridgway had no "slot" for a full colonel, however experienced, and he had taken an immediate dislike to Raff. The upshot: Raff returned to the States to a job at the Airborne Training Center, taking along some officers who had been wounded. At Clark's suggestion, Ridgway did take Bill Yarborough and named him to command the 2nd Battalion in Rube Tucker's 504. The bulk of the 509, now commanded by the former Exec Doyle R. Yardley, remained in North Africa, on standby for special assignment.[25]

Yarborough was not happy in his new job. He had hoped to draw an assignment in the 101st Division under his friend and mentor, Bill Lee. Moreover, owing to his detached service in North Africa, he had not been promoted along with his West Point contemporaries. Most of them were now lieutenant colonels; he was still a major. To make matters worse, his boss, Tucker, only a year ahead of him at the Academy, had been recommended for full colonel. But what was most galling to Yarborough was that nobody in the 82nd Airborne Division appeared interested in recognizing his battle expertise. Yarborough recalled: "So, I, in a sort of young man's prima donna way, felt very dumped on . . . My feelings were hurt and I became a sort of spoiled kind of brat who wanted out of that outfit and [to go] some place where people would come up and say, 'Hey, you've been in [combat] parachute operations; tell us how it was . . .' Tucker . . . had been an old friend of mine, but I was so intractable and so impossible that even Reuben Tucker felt that he had a burr under his saddle . . ."[26]

☆IO☆

ALL THE WHILE, at Fort Bragg, the 82nd Airborne Division had been practic-
ing for its baptism of fire. These rehearsals culminated in an exercise staged on
March 24, the day Ridgway got back from North Africa after another grueling
three-day air trip.

A clutch of high brass had come to Bragg for the demonstration. Among
them: George Marshall and Air Force chief Henry H. (Hap) Arnold. Also on
hand were two distinguished Britishers: Foreign Secretary Anthony Eden and
his escort, Field Marshal Sir John Dill, the senior British general on duty in
Washington. Gavin's 505th provided an honor guard. Gavin would never forget that fleeting moment of the war. After Eden had inspected the guard, he
grasped Gavin's hand, looked directly into his eyes and said "with a slight
touch of emotion, 'Good luck.' " The impact of Eden's words "scared" Gavin
"just a bit." Eden knew the 505 would soon jump into Sicily; as yet, Gavin did
not.[1]

The "highlight" of the visit was a small, carefully staged glider assault demonstration put on by Paul Turner's 2nd Battalion. Owing to the acute shortage
of gliders and to training accidents and mechanical breakdowns, the division
then had only twenty-six serviceable gliders that could be spared for the demonstration. Loaded with troops, the twenty-six were cut loose and landed, as
prescribed, on the airfield near the reviewing stand. The troops debarked,
formed up, and conducted a simulated attack on an enemy strongpoint.

Marshall and Arnold were highly displeased at the lack of realism in the
exercise. Arnold criticized Ridgway for bringing the gliders in over "open
ground" exposed to "enemy fire" and for failing to use the momentum of the
landing speed to run the gliders into "cover"—such as trees. Ridgway defended himself in a letter to Arnold the following week. He freely conceded the
demonstration was "not realistic" and promised that in "real battle" he would
do as Arnold advised. He again explained that owing to the shortage of gliders
they could not "risk mishap" in training exercises. Arnold refused to accept
that as an excuse. In response, he wrote: "I feel that training should be pat-
terned more on the anticipated actual practical use of gliders in combat without so much stress on the saving of equipment for the next demonstration."[2]

About a week later, Gavin's 505 made more history of a sort by becoming
the first regiment to jump en masse. This event, which employed about 130
C-47s aimed at three separate DZs near Camden, South Carolina, was on the
whole a smashing success, the 82nd's most notable training achievement. But it
was marred by a new and unforeseen tragedy. As the paratroopers were leap-
ing from the transports in tight formation, one of the oncoming C-47s lost
power on both engines owing to a mechanical failure and dropped precipi-

tously, running into a mass of the descending paratroopers. Three men were rammed in midair and cut to pieces by the propellers before the C-47 finally made a forced landing in a field. One of the paratroopers who was in the sky that day remarked: "This rare and unfortunate accident shook the hell out of everybody."[3]

Tucker's 504 laid on a similar mass jump aimed at DZs near Myrtle Beach, South Carolina. By this time, Tucker had three new battalion commanders: Warren Williams, Bill Yarborough and Charles Kouns. All men boarded the planes in high spirits, but when the planes neared the DZs, a heavy fog rolled in over the coast. In such conditions the drop was ruled "too hazardous" and was canceled. All planes returned to bases with full loads of deeply disappointed paratroopers. For many the landing was a unique experience: they had never been up in a plane except to jump out of it.[4]

All training exercises had to be curtailed about April 1 in order to get the division ready for shipment to North Africa. Ridgway would later say that "no division that left the States for battle . . . had been torn up and put back together so frequently" and none "had less time to train." He would estimate that the 82nd Airborne Division was committed to combat "with about a third" the training given most divisions. Even Gavin was worried. The 505, he judged, "was far from ready for combat."[5]

The weakest outfit in the division was the 325. The men were unhappy at being gliderists, overshadowed by the glamorous (well-paid) paratroopers with their flashy jump boots and parachute badges. The regimental commander, Harry Lewis, remained quixotic and controversial. At the last minute, he astonished his officers by inviting them to submit lists of fellow officers whom they believed would not be reliable in combat. Another purge followed. At about the same time, there was yet another shake-up in the roster of senior commanders.*

There was another problem—a very grave one. Although Ridgway held the commanding officer of the 52nd Troop Carrier Wing, Brigadier General Harold L. (Hal) Clark, in highest esteem, he was dissatisfied with the level of training in Clark's unit. There had simply not been time enough to fully train the pilots in airborne tactics, especially in the precise formation flying and pinpoint navigation required for effective parachute and glider tow operations.

Of particular concern to Ridgway were the abysmally low scores the airmen had received on night operations. Maintaining tight flight formations and finding DZs in complete darkness had proved to be extremely difficult and often impossible for most of the green pilots. Disaster after disaster had ensued in the

---

* The regimental exec, Jean Scott, left the outfit, replaced by the 1st Battalion commander, Herbert G. Sitler, who in turn was temporarily replaced by his exec, Teddy Sanford. The 2nd Battalion commander, Paul Turner, came down with severe ulcers. After Ridgway personally ordered Turner to the hospital, he was replaced by his exec, John Swenson. Later, Scott, commanding the 393rd Regiment of the hard-hit 99th Infantry Division in the Battle of the Bulge won a Silver Star Medal and two Bronze Star Medals for heroism.[6]

night exercises, with the airmen scattering paratroopers all over North Carolina. After close consultations with Hal Clark, Ridgway finally reached the drastic conclusion that night jumps into Sicily were "not practicable" and would be "foolhardy," because "the 52nd Wing was not . . . capable of conducting night operations" and "no one knows this better than Wing Commander Clark."

After making these judgments, Ridgway cabled Max Taylor in North Africa, urging that Taylor undertake to persuade the HUSKY commanders to postpone the timing of the airborne operations to early dawn on D day. This radical suggestion was not warmly received in North Africa.[7]

On April 20, the division moved by train from Bragg to Camp Edwards, Massachusetts, to prepare for embarkation. To disguise the movement, Ridgway ordered his men to remove parachute badges and other signs that they were anything other than a "normal" infantry outfit, but no one was fooled: the jump boots gave the game away. During the week of April 21 to 27, the division moved to Staten Island, New York, and Hoboken, New Jersey, and boarded three transports. Ridgway and the division staff were assigned to the *George Washington.* The ships sailed in convoy early on the morning of April 29.[8]

On May 10, after eleven days at sea, the convoy arrived at Casablanca, where Max Taylor was waiting on the dock. Ridgway formed up the division and then marched it four and a half miles to a "wasteland" staging area south of the city. The division bivouacked there in tents and had a meal of C rations. Doc Eaton recalled turning on the radio the first night ashore and getting Berlin—Axis Sally. "She was just saying, 'Welcome to Africa, Matt Ridgway and your bad boys.' Just that quick. It sort of shocked you."[9]

Two days later, the division set off for Oujda, some four hundred miles east, traveling by truck and train, the latter composed of small, uncomfortable boxcars reminiscent of the French 40/8 (forty men or eight horses) of World War I. The American GI was consigned to many hellholes in North Africa, but the tent cities near Oujda ranked among the most miserable. A division historian described it as the "worst dust bowl in Africa," where every day at mealtimes "a hurricane wind blew sand and dust through the camp." Ridgway, who had chosen the site himself, remembered it as a "fiery furnace, where the hot wind carried a fine dust that clogged the nostrils, burned the eyes, and cut into the throat like an abrasive . . . The wind and terrain were our worst enemies." The men took Atabrine as an antidote to malaria, but dysentery "struck every man."[10]

"We went through a terrible period in this tough, no-man's land," an officer in the 325 recalled.

It was so bad they had to change the training schedule. Every morning we got up and took a pill to stop diarrhea. It sealed us for about eight hours during the day. We trained early in the morning, stayed in our bunks for about two hours during the heat of the day, then trained again in the late afternoon. You'd be lying on your bunk with your butt on one end and your head at the other and you just shot both ways. Unbelievable. The other thing I remember so vividly were the flies. You had to go through the mess line one-handed, fanning flies from your food in the mess kit with the other hand. Then you had to eat in a kind of circular motion; fanning flies, lifting your fork. If you let a fly land on your food, you'd had it. Ten more flies would land while you were trying to pick out the first one.[11]

The division CP "opened for business" on May 12, about two months prior to HUSKY D day. One of its first transactions was not a happy one. Edson Raff's 509th Battalion, which had participated in the early TORCH operations and which was now commanded by Doyle Yardley, was attached administratively to the division. By now the troopers of the 509th were hardened and cocky veterans who had been in North Africa for six months. Accustomed to the good life in the bars and brothels of Algiers, they resented being banished to remote, austere Oujda, taking orders from an outfit that had yet to hear a shot fired in anger. They had also felt a camaraderie with Boy Browning's British paratroopers and—so it seemed to 82nd staffers—had adopted the sneering British view of the average GI. "This outfit was a headache from the minute it arrived," an 82nd Division staffer observed, "and it never did get integrated into the division."[12]

The battle for Tunisia had concluded three days before, on May 9. In its final stages, Omar Bradley, commanding the rejuvenated II Corps directly under Alexander, had conducted a highly successful all-American drive on Bizerte, which earned the corps and Bradley unstinting praise. Marshall gave Bradley a third star and wrote: "Your leadership . . . has inspired the entire War Department and will be greeted by acclaim and delight throughout the Army . . ." Eisenhower, pronouncing Bradley a "godsend," wrote Marshall that Bradley was "about the best rounded, well balanced senior officer we have in the service." Bradley was on his way to the very top.[13]

One result of Bradley's coolly professional job in Tunisia was an important change in the command setup for the Sicily invasion. Eisenhower and Patton decided to substitute Bradley's experienced II Corps headquarters for Mike Dawley's untried VI Corps. The II Corps would consist of Allen's Big Red One and a new division en route from the States, Troy H. Middleton's 45th National Guard. Another newly arrived division, the 3rd Infantry, reinforced to twenty-seven thousand men and commanded by Lucian K. Truscott, Jr., would operate directly under Patton's control.

With scarcely a day's rest, Bradley reported to Patton's headquarters at Mostaganem on about the same day Ridgway's division opened for business in Oujda. Like Eisenhower and everyone else, Ridgway had a high regard for Mike Dawley, but he was pleased to find that he would once again be working in close harness with Bradley. Bradley reciprocated those feelings; the 82nd Division had been his baby and it would always occupy a special place in his heart.[14]

Ridgway soon learned that the planning for Sicily was in utter turmoil. Busy in Tunisia, Montgomery had not had time to give the initial plans careful study. After he had found time, he demanded—and got—radical revisions. Instead of two widely separated landings on the northwest and southeast coasts, Montgomery insisted on consolidating the landings into one massive and contiguous assault along the southeast and south coasts. Montgomery's Eighth Army would assault the beaches on the southeast coast near Syracuse and drive north to Messina; Patton's Seventh Army would assault the south coast near Gela and cover Montgomery's left flank, an operation that was distinctly secondary and not unlike the initial role II Corps had played in Tunisia.[15]

Airborne operations in Sicily were also being revised radically. Max Taylor had not been able to persuade the planners to change the jump from night to dawn, but he had had no trouble persuading Patton to increase the commitment of the 82nd Airborne. By the time Ridgway arrived in Oujda, Patton was insisting that both Gavin's and Tucker's parachute regiments be included in the D-day assault. They would land inland of his invasion beaches to block Axis counterattacks.[16]

All proposed airborne operations were limited by the acute shortage of troop transports and gliders. There would be a total of only about 400 transports (360 American C-47s, 30 British Albemarles and Halifaxes), not nearly enough to meet both Montgomery's and Patton's new D-day requirements for airborne troops. Some 500 Waco gliders had been shipped to North Africa for Sicily operations, but on May 12 there were only 20 available for training and operations.[17]

The reasons for the glider shortage were several. Each glider was packed in knocked-down state in five crates, weighing ten tons in aggregate. Owing to the German U-boat assaults on Allied shipping, it had been difficult to find cargo space for five thousand tons of glider crates. Moreover, the Americans were inexperienced in loading and unloading procedures. Various pieces of gliders wound up at different and widely separated ports, in many instances without vital assembly tools. Glider assembly received only low priority. It was carried out at a leisurely pace by untrained enlisted men who required, on average, almost 250 man-hours to assemble one glider.

The British contribution to the glider force was slight. They earmarked a total of thirty-six gliders for Sicily. These were the Horsa models; big, flimsy, all-plywood vehicles with a payload of 6,900 pounds—nearly twice that of the Waco. These gliders were taken in tow and flown from England to North Africa. Various mishaps occurred along the fifteen-hundred-mile route, and only nineteen Horsas reached North Africa in usable condition.[18]

The aircraft and glider shortages led to a bitter tug-of-war between Ridgway and Browning over allocations of the C-47s. Each naturally wanted the lion's share of aircraft in order to make the greatest impact on the enemy, thus quickly achieving military objectives and saving lives. There was also an element of intramural rivalry: Sicily was to be the first major Allied airborne operation in the war, and each man naturally wanted the largest possible role for his own outfit. In this bureaucratic struggle, Ridgway deeply resented Browning's favored status as Eisenhower's airborne adviser. He stoutly resisted every move Browning made to get a larger share of airplanes and came to believe that Browning was maneuvering to take command of all Allied airborne operations. He was also incensed by Browning's patronizing attitude toward American troops. According to a close Ridgway associate: "Ridgway always thought Boy Browning was a dilettante of the first water and couldn't stand him."[19]

Ridgway, however, remembered Browning as "an exceedingly capable officer both professionally and intellectually. Very keen mind, a man of great gallantry and initiative . . . the sparkplug of the British airborne effort . . . [but] the British tended to look down on us right from the beginning . . . [Montgomery's] Eighth Army had been bloodied and was successful . . . and there is just some natural tendency on the part of a professional soldier to think, 'Well, these guys haven't been blooded yet and they don't know the score and they are second-rate soldiers.' "[20]

He never forgot one early encounter with Browning. Three days after they had first met, Browning appeared at Ridgway's CP in Oujda to discuss airborne operations for Sicily. When Browning laid out his plans, Ridgway was dismayed. It appeared to him, as he wrote Patton's deputy army commander, Geoffrey Keyes, the following day, that Browning had drawn up plans that would put Browning in "command status" of all airborne operations. As such, Browning would have far greater authority to distribute aircraft between the American and British forces and there seemed no doubt the Americans would get the short end of the stick. When Browning asked to see Ridgway's plans, Ridgway warily refused, saying, "I don't have a plan. Not until General Patton, my army commander, has approved . . . do I have a plan." The meeting abruptly ended on that testy note.[21]

Not many days later, the tension between them was intensified by an indiscretion on Browning's part. It was a trivial matter, but one that ruffled Ridgway's feathers. Browning wrote directly to Doyle Yardley, commander of the 509th Battalion, stating that he would be pleased to inspect the unit, that he always considered the battalion "part of us," that he had arranged for the 509th to be "honorary members" of the British airborne forces and was even making an effort to get the members of the 509 British airborne maroon berets. Ridgway, already losing patience with the 509th, was properly annoyed that Browning would curry favor with it in this fashion and propose to "inspect" it without first clearing through him. He forthwith drafted a curt letter to Browning scotching the visit. On the advice of others, Ridgway did not send the letter but managed by oral means to convey his displeasure to Browning, who promptly backed off.[22]

These disputations between Ridgway and Browning soon came to Eisenhower's attention. On one of Ridgway's visits to headquarters, Bedell Smith, no doubt on Eisenhower's instructions, gave Ridgway a royal chewing out. He forcefully reminded Ridgway of Eisenhower's policy of cooperating to the utmost with the British and told Ridgway that if he did not fall in line immediately, Ridgway "might as well start packing up, for he was going home." In turn, Ridgway lost patience and raised "violent objections." He was, he said, "fighting for the needs of my command" and where lives were in the balance, he would not allow his command to be penalized merely for the sake of Allied "harmony."[23]

This altercation became so serious that Ridgway was compelled to call on Patton for help. Patton came through with typical speed and force. Already resentful of the British dominance in the Sicily operation, Patton suspected Boy Browning was maneuvering "to get command of [all] the paratroopers" and backed Ridgway to the hilt. Ridgway later wrote: "I probably would have been sent home, or at least sternly rebuked, if General Patton had not articulately and wholeheartedly approved my actions."[24]

The disputes over the allocation of the C-47s for D day between American and British airborne forces ultimately became so tense that Eisenhower himself had to make the final decisions. In his view, the ruling "favored" the Americans. He allotted them about 250 C-47s and the British about 110. (Counting the Albemarles and Halifaxes, the British total came to about 150 aircraft.) But in Ridgway's eyes, the ruling did not "favor" the Americans. As he saw it, Eisenhower took planes from his forces and "gave them to the British." With an allocation of only 250 C-47s, Ridgway could not deliver both Gavin's and Tucker's regiments on D day, as Patton wanted. The most he could do was deliver one regiment reinforced by a battalion, in all about thirty-four hundred men. The remainder of the division would have to be delivered on follow-up missions by the surviving C-47s of his allocation.

THE FEVERISH HASTE in which the final plans for the British and American airborne assaults on Sicily were formulated led to grave weaknesses in preparations and training, as well as in the plans themselves.

Without consulting with Browning or any of his airborne experts, Hoppy Hopkinson, the commander of the British 1st Airborne Division, gained an interview with Montgomery and laid before him a daunting plan to assist Montgomery in the capture of Syracuse and its fine harbor. Elements of the British 1st Airborne Division would seize a key bridge—Ponte Grande—just south of Syracuse and hold it until Montgomery's amphibious forces could push north. Montgomery welcomed the plan, approved it, and thereafter resisted any attempt to rescind or modify it. Hopkinson is described by one British airborne historian as a man "determined to make a name for himself." He was a "keen" amateur pilot, who considered himself an expert on aviation and airborne matters, but in fact his knowledge of airborne operations was slight.

For example, it was not feasible that lightly armed British paratroopers could seize Ponte Grande against determined opposition. To be certain of success, the British would need some fairly heavy antitank guns (six-pounders) and motorized vehicles (jeeps) to tow the guns to an advantageous position. There was only one way to bring in heavy guns and jeeps, and that was by gliders. But the airborne forces would land by moonlight, and the concept of night landings in gliders had long since been rejected as impossibly dangerous and impracticable.

The more Hopkinson studied the problem, however, the more convinced he became that an all-out night glider assault was the proper solution to seizing the bridge. All his airborne advisers argued against it. Neither the American nor the British glider pilots had had much night flying experience. None had ever flown a glider into combat. To assign them to make their first combat mission at night seemed highly imprudent. Besides that, and no less important, there were not nearly enough gliders. To deliver the necessary British airborne personnel to Sicily would require many, many gliders—perhaps one hundred fifty Wacos—and there were then no more than thirty fully assembled Wacos in the whole of North Africa, and many of them were grounded for various reasons.

Hopkinson was unmoved by these technical considerations. His mind was made up. The initial British airborne effort on Sicily would be all-glider. Gliders must be assembled faster; glider pilots must be trained on a rush schedule.[1]

Following this radical decision, the Army Air Force declared an "extreme emergency" and set up a Waco glider assembly line that would have astonished Detroit. The work was declared top priority—higher even than repairs on P-38 fighters. Hundreds of skilled airmen were thrown into the assembly line, while other men scoured North Africa for glider crates and tools. Within three weeks —by June 13—some 350 Waco gliders had been assembled and delivered.

Owing to its past association with the British in England and North Africa, the American 51st Troop Carrier Wing, commanded by Ray A. Dunn, was assigned to deliver the British airborne forces to Sicily. This turned out to be an ill-advised decision, because Dunn's pilots had had no experience with gliders, whereas Hal Clark's 52nd Troop Carrier Wing had. When the illogic of the wing assignments was realized, a proposal was made to switch them around, but by then it was too late. Dunn's planes had already been modified for British airborne operations and there was no time to modify those of Clark's wing. Thus Dunn's wing, which had combat experience in parachute operations and no experience in glider operations, was assigned the glider mission, and Clark's wing, which had the most experience in glider operations and none in combat parachute missions, was assigned the parachute mission.

In early June, Dunn's wing commenced intensive training exercises. Owing to the shortage of gliders, most of these exercises consisted of regular British parachute drops. Between June 10 and 18, four such parachute exercises were staged—two separate battalion jumps and a full brigade jump, one in late evening and one at night. On June 14, Dunn conducted his first Waco glider exercise, taking aloft fifty-four gliders manned by British pilots. Two days later, all gliders were temporarily grounded for repairs. In the ten-day period between June 20 and June 30, further Waco glider exercises were held, but after that the gliders were again grounded for three days to repair weak tail wiring.

The British staffs believed each glider pilot should receive a minimum of 100 hours flying time training in the Wacos before going into combat. In fact, they managed to accumulate only an average of 4.5 hours and only about a quarter of that (1.2 hours) at night. They had an average of sixteen landings, but almost all of these were "unrealistic" touchdowns on airstrips in daylight. There were no rehearsals of mass glider releases over water at night, simulating the Sicily plan. As D day approached, a British observer wrote bluntly: ". . . practically none of our glider pilots have sufficient training and it is too late to rectify this omission now."

The American D-day airborne mission for Sicily, reduced in scope to a reinforced parachute regiment, was less complicated to plan and train for. Even so, Ridgway encountered many frustrations and setbacks.

Ridgway chose Gavin's 505th for the D-day mission because of Gavin's seniority and the higher state of readiness of his regiment. The plan was this: the 505, reinforced by one infantry battalion from Tucker's 504th, two batteries of the 456th Field Artillery Battalion and some engineers, would jump behind the Gela beachhead to block Axis counterattacks on Allen's Big Red One. Tucker was to be prepared to come across with his other two infantry battalions on D+1 or D+2 and jump into "friendly territory" seized by the 505th.

Assuming the availability of Wacos, Lewis' 325th Glider Infantry Regiment and the glider artillery would come last, on D+3 or D+4, landing on captured enemy airfields—in daylight. Yardley's 509th Battalion would be held in reserve but prepared to jump into combat if called upon.

The first setback Ridgway encountered was a long and unforeseen delay in "mating" with Hal Clark's 52nd Wing. The wing was to be based at a group of airstrips around Oujda. However, the construction of these fields fell far behind schedule because of misplaced equipment and military red tape. The fields were not completed until May 25—two weeks after the arrival of the division. There was a further delay in amassing the various air staffs and the 250 C-47s onto these fields and getting all the aircraft support equipment and ground crews in place. Not until June 1 was the wing ready to embark on an intense training schedule with the division.

On the first day, the training program ran into serious trouble. The area was lashed by high winds unfavorable for parachute jumping—and these winds continued, almost unabated, for days on end. It had been difficult to find "soft" DZs in the area around Oujda; the combination of high winds and hard, rocky ground caused "jump casualties" to soar. For example, on June 5, when two battalions jumped in a mass formation, the winds were blowing over the ground at thirty miles per hour—far greater than the "safe" limit of twenty miles per hour. Of the eleven hundred men who jumped, two were killed and fifty-three suffered fractured ankles or legs.[2]

Jump injuries continued at such a high rate that Ridgway and Gavin were compelled to severely curtail the training program. Ridgway later wrote that so many "key men" were being injured so close to D day "that the advantages of training were overridden by the disadvantages of losing irreplaceable leaders." Only two nighttime jumps were attempted. The first, a mass jump of Gavin's 505th Regiment, was highly unsatisfactory. The men were scattered all over the landscape, suffered many injuries and had a difficult time forming up in darkness. The second, carried out by Tucker's 504th, was, in the words of one official historian, "deceptively successful." To reduce injuries, it was decided that only one or two men in the lead planes would actually jump. Despite a thunderstorm, Hal Clark's pilots accurately delivered the paratroopers to the DZ and the "token" jumps were deemed successful.[3]

These exercises, together with prior exercises in the States, had brought to light a grave weakness in nighttime parachute operations. Despite any number of easily identifiable landmarks, it was extremely difficult for pilots to locate DZs in darkness. To help solve this problem, the "pathfinder" concept evolved. The idea was that several "pathfinders," carried to the DZ by the most expert Air Force navigators, would jump a little ahead of the rest of the formation and mark the DZs with special lights or with electronic equipment on which the other planes could "home." But there was not time enough to perfect the pathfinder system before D day on Sicily.

In all of this, Ridgway's ADC, Bull Keerans, had been little help and something of a problem. Gavin recalled: "We came across [to North Africa] on a different ship than Ridgway's. Keerans was the senior man aboard. He was drunk most of the time. He'd have us do crazy things. It'd just drive you bananas. Soon after that, Ridgway found out about it and he had the idea of relieving him [of command]." According to Doc Eaton, "In North Africa, Keerans was more interested in writing up training manuals than actually being out with the troops. And, of course, that *immediately* put him in the doghouse with Ridgway."[4]

A key officer in Gavin's 505 also got in the "doghouse." He was James A. Gray, commanding the 2nd Battalion. Gavin wrote later that Gray "went AWOL" and that he relieved him of command, replacing Gray with the battalion exec, Mark J. Alexander. Gray later protested that his alleged "AWOL" was actually all a misunderstanding, that on Gavin's instructions he had been out with the 52nd Troop Carrier Wing observing a night drop and its critique at Clark's headquarters. Afterward, at the suggestion of Clark's operations officer, Gray wrote, he had flown to Tunisia to "inspect the area" from which the airborne assault on Sicily would be mounted. When he was unable to reach Gavin by telephone to explain his absence, he left word with Gavin's adjutant, who may have failed to pass on the message. In any case, when Gray returned, he reported immediately to Gavin, who, Gray wrote later, "advised me that I was relieved of command since he had to report to Division that he didn't know where I was." Gavin may have simply used this incident as an excuse to relieve Gray. "He was a nice, personable, genial man," Gavin wrote later, "who liked to play poker, and he didn't belong in the airborne."[5]

When airborne training was curtailed, Gavin's troopers concentrated on ground tactics. By now Gavin had good reconnaissance photos of the target area and was able to lay out a full-size replica of the main objectives: a series of sixteen mutually supporting reinforced-concrete pillboxes and blockhouses which were situated between Gela and Niscemi and which controlled all road traffic into Gela from the north and east. Gavin labeled these strongpoints "X" and "Y." His troopers "realistically rehearsed their combat roles in every detail," Gavin wrote, including mock attacks on the dummy fortifications with live ammunition.[6]

In the meantime, Hal Clark was trying to train his pilots and navigators in night formation flying and navigation. Some of his planes were reinforcements from Eisenhower's command whose pilots had never before engaged in troop-carrier work and had very little formation-flying experience. Clark laid out courses similar to the route his pilots would fly to Sicily and rehearsed these flights to the fullest extent possible. He developed combat flight formations consisting of Vs with one and a half minutes between Vs, which would become standard for troop-carrier operations. But there was simply not enough time. The official troop-carrier historian, John C. Warren, wrote that when the training period concluded, "the wing was still insufficiently trained in formation flying, navigation, and drop-zone location at night."[7]

At Gavin's request, one "realistic" air mission was flown: a trip to Sicily itself in a British plane based at British-held Malta. Gavin and two of his four battalion commanders, plus three of Clark's group commanders, went along. They picked a night—June 9/10—and time when moonlight conditions were close to those they would have on D day. This flight was successful in all respects. It encountered very little antiaircraft fire over Gela. Gavin could clearly see all the navigational check points and terrain features by the moonlight, "exactly as we had memorized them from the photographs."[8]

During the training period, George Patton visited the division at least twice. On each of these visits Ridgway served as Patton's escort. Tucker's S-4, Julian Aaron Cook (West Point, 1940), was astounded by Ridgway's flashy memory for names. "On both occasions," Cook recalled, "Ridgway introduced Patton to every field-grade officer in the division without benefit of name tapes or coaching from an aide."[9]

During these visits, Patton exhorted the paratroopers and gliderists with earthy pep talks. Gavin recalled that Patton began one such talk with an epigram that would become legendary: "Now I want you to remember that no sonuvabitch ever won a war by dying for his country. He won it by making the other poor dumb sonuvabitch die for *his* country." He went on to emphasize several tactical points in language that Gavin found "applicable to sexual relations." So raw was Patton's language that even Gavin—and his "pack of jackals"—were "somewhat embarrassed."[10]

In a final meeting with all his top Sicily commanders, including Ridgway and Max Taylor, Patton was at his theatrical best. "In a grand peroration," Taylor recalled, "he turned on us with a roar and, waving a menacing swaggerstick under our noses, concluded: 'Now we'll break up, and I never want to see you bastards again unless it's at your post on the shores of Sicily.' "[11]

The division training, such as it was, actually concluded about five days earlier than planned, on June 16. That day, Eisenhower, Clark and their retinues arrived for a "final review"—not a jump exercise, but a parade. One of the division members wrote: "There was no cheering crowd, no waving handkerchiefs, just the Division, almost lost in an empty expanse. It was our greatest moment. Sometimes I think that the men who marched there for the last time that day are the real winners, with this, their brief, bittersweet moment of glory."[12]

It had been decided that both the British and the American airborne assaults would be staged from bases as close to Sicily as it was possible to get. The staging area chosen was Kairouan, Tunisia. While the American and British airborne forces were attempting to train in French Morocco and western Algeria, Army engineers constructed eighteen crude air bases (mostly dirt strips six thousand feet long and three hundred feet wide) in the vicinity of Kairouan. Six of the eighteen were designated for the British airborne forces and Ray Dunn's 51st Wing, plus the British Air Group 38, which included the Albemarles and Halifaxes. The remaining twelve bases were assigned to the American airborne forces and Hal Clark's 52nd Wing.[13]

On about June 21, the American and British paratroopers began moving to Tunisia. In order to get a little more training in, many men were transported by aircraft or glider. Most, however, had to go by truck or train, a long and tedious trip. On June 24, Ridgway's CP reopened at an airstrip five miles outside Kairouan, adjacent to Hal Clark's CP.[14]

Living conditions in Tunisia were ghastly, some thought far worse than Oujda. The daytime heat was nearly unbearable. At times the desert siroccos drove the thermometer to 125 to 130 degrees. Ridgway thought those winds were "like the breath of hell." He and his men took refuge in the shade of pear and almond trees, but there was no escape for those staffers who had to work in Quonset huts. To make matters even more unbearable, the food supply lines broke down, and for "one long stretch" the 82nd had nothing to eat but marmalade and Spam. Ridgway recalled that these conditions made his men "so lean and tough, so mean and mad, that they would have jumped into the fires of torment just to get out of Africa."[15]

Nor was that all. The official 504 historian wrote: "Kairouan, the second most holy city for members of the Mohammedan religion, was the site of one of the largest burial grounds in the world. Bodies were interred only two feet below the surface of the ground and each tomb featured an air-conditioning vent that was to serve as an escape route for evil spirits that might have inhabited bodies of the faithful. Unfortunately, and much to the discomfort of those nearby, evil spirits weren't the only elements to escape through the vents and the air constantly reeked with the odor of departed Moslems."[16]

Other paratroopers, however, thought Oujda had been a far more inhospitable base. One of Gavin's men remembered that in Kairouan the 505 had been bivouacked beneath olive and almond trees to camouflage or hide the unit from possible Axis aircraft attacks. "Thus, in contrast to Oujda, a hellhole situated on a huge treeless plain, in Tunisia we at least had shade," he wrote. "Moreover, in the late afternoon and evening a cooling breeze blew in from the Mediterranean. You could sleep at night and sometimes you even needed a blanket."[17]

The heat may have partly unhinged the 325 commander, Harry Lewis. Wayne Pierce described an extraordinary scene:

> Shortly before the invasion of Sicily, we conducted an extensive training exercise. At the critique, all officers of the regiment were present, seated on the ground, hot, dirty, tired and sleepy, having been up all night. Normally these critiques would be where the "junior officers" caught hell . . . no names, just "junior officers." Colonel Lewis went into a tirade about the lack of leadership and mistakes that he believed he had seen. At the height of the condemnation he stopped, completely lost his composure and in a breaking voice said: "And gentlemen, combat is only two weeks away." Then he turned and walked away, visibly sobbing. We felt leaderless and this was the man who was going to lead us into combat.[18]

In the planning for Sicily, Ridgway had early developed a deep concern over the possibility of his troops' being shot down by friendly fire from land or sea. Of particular concern were the follow-up, or reinforcing, airborne missions, which would occur after American troops were ashore and naval vessels were concentrated near the Gela beaches. British naval units that had been operating in the Mediterranean for several years had done so without much friendly air cover and were notoriously trigger-happy, prone to fire at any aircraft approaching their ships. Some American naval forces had not yet seen any combat and might be very anxious. None of the American ground forces earmarked for Sicily had had any training with airborne forces whatsoever.

In early June—before the division moved to Kairouan—Ridgway and Hal Clark had met with Boy Browning and others, including naval commanders, to discuss this problem. Ridgway's solution to the first flights or D-day missions was actually quite simple: have the airborne forces fly a straight course over the sea from Kairouan to Gela (250 miles), then inland 10 miles to the drop zone, and during the period of flight, have *all* naval vessels withhold fire on *any* aircraft passing over or near them. But the Navy could not—or would not—give any such assurances. Such an order would tie their hands should an enemy air attack materialize during the hold-down period. Moreover, while they could exercise tight control over large men-of-war, they could not guarantee control over the many miscellaneous merchant ships and small craft in the various convoys. The Navy insisted, therefore, that all airborne operations must stay clear of naval convoys by at least five miles.[19]

The upshot of all this was that Ridgway ultimately received assurances from the naval commanders that "fire of friendly forces" would be withheld, provided "air transport movements followed certain designated routes." Considering the level of training of the troop-carrier pilots and navigators and the fact that for most it would be the first combat mission, the zigzagging 355-mile air route finally imposed by higher command was nightmarishly complicated. To make it even more difficult, the decision had been made that in order to minimize detection by enemy radar, the planes would fly the course at altitudes of two hundred to seven hundred feet. Ridgway would later write that "at war's end, we still could not have executed that first Sicily mission, as laid on, at night and under like conditions."[20]

Assuring absolute safe passage for the follow-up airborne missions proved to be even more difficult. These would be flown and launched under far more perilous circumstances: directly over friendly troops ashore and in close vicinity to hundreds of naval vessels just offshore. What Ridgway wanted was a "safe corridor" through which the planes could fly, at a certain time, without being fired upon. The Army, of course, gave absolute assurances, but the Navy categorically refused. Upon learning this, Ridgway wrote Patton's deputy, Geoffrey Keyes, that "unless satisfactory assurances were obtained from the Navy, I would recommend against the dispatch of [reinforcing] airborne troop movements." Patton leaped into the bureaucratic battle on Ridgway's side and Ridgway personally brought the matter to the attention of Eisenhower and the American air-force commander for Northwest Africa, Carl Spaatz, when they visited the division on July 2. These combined efforts got results—of sorts. On July 4, Ridgway obtained grudging and somewhat obscure assurances from naval authorities ashore. On July 6, the details of the "safe corridor" were radioed to the commander of the U.S. Navy's Western Task Force, Vice Admiral H. Kent Hewitt, who was already at sea under radio silence and could not reply. In an after-action report, Hewitt stated that "the route selected by the Air Force [for reinforcing missions] was not suitable from a naval standpoint." But it was now too late to modify it.[21]

Even though Ridgway had willing assurances from the Army, he took special precautions to make certain that Army forces clearly understood the dangers inherent in the follow-up missions. He sent special teams dressed in jump uniforms to the 1st, 3rd and 45th divisions to let the GIs see a "live" paratrooper and acquaint the officers and men with probable tactical maneuvers. In addition, he talked personally with the commanding general of the antiaircraft units which would be participating in the invasion. Everywhere, he was reassured: the American Army would not fire on American paratroopers.[22]

So ended the feverish airborne preparations for HUSKY. Seldom in modern warfare had there been such an ill-prepared force on the eve of battle. Against Ridgway's repeated protestations both British and American paratroopers were to go in by night. The British, contrary to all common sense—and airborne doctrine—were to go in at night in gliders, manned by insufficiently trained glider pilots, towed by aircraft pilots with the least experience in glider work and without having practiced an overwater release at night. The Americans, with virtually no night jump training, were to be delivered by pilots with the least experience in combat and who were grossly undertrained in night formation flying and navigation. The troop-carrier pilots would have to navigate and fly a route over water, at night, that was clearly beyond the capability of most, and in the follow-up missions "not suitable" for avoiding friendly naval fire.

The stage was set for military disaster.

ONE QUESTION no one on the Allied side had ever faced was, Where was the
best place for the commanding general of an airborne division to station himself during an operation? About one third of the division—Gavin's force—
would jump into Sicily, while about two thirds of the division remained on call
in Tunisia. Ridgway decided that the best solution would be to join Patton and
his staff on the USS *Monrovia* (APA-31), an attack transport which was the
flagship of Admiral Hewitt. The *Monrovia* had excellent communications facilities, which would enable Ridgway to keep in close touch with division headquarters, relaying orders to the other two regiments as required. On D day, the
ship would anchor off Gela, enabling Ridgway to go ashore and make contact
with Gavin's force within the first few hours of the assault. Since the *Monrovia*
was already crowded with brass (Joe Swing, who had come over to observe
operations, among them), Ridgway was accompanied only by his aide, Don
Faith, and a few staffers.[1]*

The *Monrovia* departed from Algiers in convoy late in the afternoon of July
6, joining the massive flow of Allied shipping bound for Sicily. The blacked-out
convoy, maintaining strict radio silence, followed a devious route—easterly at
first—one of the many "deceptions" designed to fool the Axis into believing the
assault was aimed at some other destination. The meandering voyage was uneventful. Relentless preinvasion Allied air attacks had achieved complete air
supremacy over the central Mediterranean. Axis air power had been driven out
of Sicily to Sardinia and far up the boot of Italy. The convoy was not attacked
by Axis aircraft or submarines.

The various deceptions, however, had not completely fooled Hitler's chief
Mediterranean commander, General Albert Kesselring. Believing Sicily to be
high on the list of Allied targets, in June Kesselring had sent two reconstituted
German divisions (the Hermann Göring Panzer and 15th Panzer Grenadier,
comprising a total of thirty thousand men and about a hundred twenty tanks)
to Sicily to add punch to the Italian garrison of two hundred thousand soldiers.
The Italian commander in Sicily, General Alfredo Guzzoni, convinced that an
Allied attack would most likely come in the Southeast or South (or both),
wanted to deploy both German divisions in that area, but Kesselring overruled
him and ordered that the 15th Panzer Grenadiers be deployed in western Sicily

---

* Other 82nd Division staffers and Ridgway's protégé Hank Adams crossed on the USS
  Ancon (AGC-4), command ship of naval task force commander Rear Admiral Alan
  G. Kirk, on which Omar Bradley and his II Corps staff were embarked. The *Ancon*
  was a "backup" command and communications vessel, in case the *Monrovia* was
  sunk.

to defend against a possible attack on Palermo. The Allies had learned of these movements from breaking some German codes. The top commanders were well aware that the Hermann Göring Panzer Division was poised in the Southeast to repel any invasion force. But to safeguard code-breaking secrets, neither the "straight leg" soldiers nor the paratroopers were told—not even Gavin, whose force would almost certainly meet the Hermann Göring Division face to face.[2]

On July 9, the convoy swung around on a westerly heading, toward the designated landing beaches on the south coast of Sicily. As it did so, it met strong, unseasonal winds blowing from the northwest at twenty-five to thirty-five miles per hour. The winds kicked up heavy seas, which slowed and slewed the landing craft. The winds were very worrisome to Ridgway. They were far too strong for safe parachute operations. Unless they abated, Gavin and his men were certain to face tough going—perhaps disaster—in the jumps and the landing.[3]

That same day, Gavin's force made final preparations to depart.† Each paratrooper was burdened down with about one hundred or more pounds of equipment: main parachute, reserve chest chute, steel helmet, rifle or carbine, bayonet, ammo, hand grenades, rations, canteen, rope, entrenching tool, knife, gas mask, compass, flashlight, and first aid and escape kits. Some men had submachine guns; others had a new lightweight hand-held antitank weapon known as the bazooka. Still others had demolition kits with eighteen quarter-pound blocks of TNT, blasting caps and wire.[5]

The tension was high. This was *it:* the Army's first mass parachute combat operation. Gavin's orders were that every jumper and every piece of equipment would be dropped on Sicily. No one would return by air. He distributed a printed exhortatory note which concluded: "The eyes of the world are upon you. The hopes and prayers of every American go with you . . ."[6]

At about 10 P.M., which was about sunset in Kairouan, the men climbed into the planes. There were about sixteen or eighteen men in each plane. Some planes carried parachute cargo bundles which would be tossed out ahead of the paratroopers. Others had six droppable parachute bundles mounted on racks beneath the fuselages, which would be cut loose by the paratroopers before

---

† The force consisted of the three battalions of the 505, which were the 1st, commanded by Arthur F. Gorham; the 2nd, commanded by Mark Alexander; and the 3rd, commanded by Edward C. Krause; plus the 3rd Battalion of Tucker's 504, commanded by Charles W. Kouns. In addition, there were the 456th Parachute Field Artillery Battalion, commanded by Harrison B. Harden, Jr., and Company B of the 307th Airborne Engineers, plus miscellaneous signal and medical detachments. Gavin's entire staff was included: the executive officer, Herbert F. Batcheller; the S-1, Alfred W. Ireland; the S-2, Charles Paterson; the S-3, Benjamin H. Vandervoort; the S-4, Edward A. Zaj. In all: 3,405 men. The participating groups within Hal Clark's 52nd Troop Carrier Wing were as follows: the 61st, the 64th ("borrowed" from Dunn's 51st Wing), the 313th, the 314th and the 316th. In all: 226 aircraft manned by 904 airmen. The combined Air Force and other Army personnel totaled 4,309 men.[4]

they jumped. The bundles had different-colored parachutes to denote the various types of cargo. The windows of most planes had small ports through which the men could poke machine-gun or rifle barrels if need be.[7]

Many of the paratroopers were still suffering from chronic dysentery, contracted in Oujda or Kairouan. Honey buckets were provided for the afflicted, but using them was extremely difficult. "Imagine if you can," a 505 paratrooper wrote, "trying to take your pants down with all that gear and parachutes hung on you. Some of the worst afflicted simply didn't put their 'chutes on until just before jump time. Others said to hell with it and jumped into Sicily with more in their pants than they started out with . . . Believe me, it was a real problem."[8]

The pilots started engines. The prop blasts churned up huge dust clouds that could be seen five miles away. They were so thick that some pilots had to take off on instruments. The planes lifted off in three-ship elements at thirty-second intervals. Airborne in the fading twilight, they formed into Vs. Fearing detection by enemy radar, they flew "on the deck," some formations below five hundred feet. Droning east over the sea toward Malta, the great streams of Vs re-formed into five air groups, or "serials," ten minutes apart: the 61st Group in the lead, then the 314th, the 313th, the 316th and the 64th. Four of the groups carried a battalion of paratroopers each; the other group, miscellaneous headquarters staff, medics and engineers. The 226 aircraft formed an aerial column about one hundred miles long. The lead pilot of the whole formation was Willis W. Mitchell, commanding the 61st Group. Gavin rode in the lead plane of the fourth group in the line—the 316th. All planes maintained radio silence.

Suddenly it was dark and the pilots found themselves in trouble. The crescent moon gave off very little light. The planes had dim wingtip lights to aid in keeping formation, but these proved to be too hard to see. Unable to keep tight formation and fearing a mid-air collision, pilots began veering out of formation. Some, flying very low—too low—were blinded by salt spray on the windshields. Quite soon, many pilots were lost. They had been briefed on the high winds ("thirty-five miles per hour"), but they had not had enough experience in overwater night flying to compensate properly, and there were no major landmarks along the way to help them. Many of the paratroopers became airsick.

The first landmark was Malta, which would have aerial beacons flashing. After an hour and thirty minutes, Gavin, who had memorized the flight route, began looking anxiously out the window for beacons. He recalled, ". . . there was no sign of Malta"; unbelievably, on this 185-mile easterly overwater leg, they had missed the big island, the main checkpoint on the complicated route. They could not see any of the beacons. Gavin consulted the navigator. They figured the strong northwesterly winds had blown them southeastward. But how far? They turned left to a northerly heading, continuing to look for Malta or Sicily. They were not alone. Dozens of planes had missed Malta and were groping toward pitch-black Sicily in the dark, by various routes.

Staring down fixedly out the window, Gavin suddenly saw a line of ships. It was one of the many invasion convoys. They flew right over it at an altitude of a thousand feet. Gavin held his breath, waiting for a crescendo of antiaircraft fire. Fortunately, there was none. Other serials also flew low over other invasion convoys without being fired upon.

Gavin continued staring anxiously out the starboard windows, looking for a dark land mass that would be Sicily. Within a few minutes the mass appeared —but it appeared in the *port* windows. How could Sicily be on the *left?* This same baffling experience occurred in plane after plane. They had to be too far east—much too far—and hopelessly lost. Individually or in pairs, the scattered formation wheeled around and headed west, now only vaguely approximating the route. Gavin could see no recognizable landmarks, but soon he could see a few scattered searchlights and tracers arcing into the dark sky. Where were they? No one knew.

Far ahead in the lead plane of 61st Group, which was transporting Charles Kouns's 3rd Battalion (of Tucker's 504), the pilot, Willis Mitchell, fared better than most. He found Malta—twelve minutes ahead of schedule—turned left, made a landfall on Sicily and proceeded westward. Two of his straggling planes, however, missed Sicily and flew all the way to the toe of Italy before realizing the error and turning back. When Mitchell located the DZ north of Gela through smoke and haze, he had only nine of his thirty-nine planes with him in formation. He leveled off at eight hundred feet and turned on the green light. The hundred-odd paratroopers in this formation jumped into pitch darkness. By now, the winds had moderated but they still posed a great danger to the jumpers. Most of these troopers landed within two miles of the DZ, but were badly scattered and many were injured. The rest of Mitchell's 61st Group dropped men all over southern Sicily. They landed hard in trees, on rocky crags, in gullies, fields, rivers, streams and roads suffering uncounted injuries. Some came down into or well behind enemy positions. Six sticks, dropped deep in enemy territory, were still "missing" a month later.

The next group in line—the 314th—did fairly well at first. It found Sicily, then Gela, but most of the pilots could not make out the navigational check points leading to the DZ. One pilot did—and dropped the troopers exactly on the DZ. Others turned southward out to sea and made another run in. A few planes dropped the jumpers within three miles of the DZ, but most dropped near Vittoria, fifteen miles east of the DZ.

The next group—the 313th—which was carrying Arthur Gorham's 1st Battalion, was blown far off course very early in the flight. One squadron missed Malta by twenty miles. Another squadron, recovering from the error, found Sicily, then Gela, and dropped Gorham and some men two miles from the DZ. But many planes in this group—twenty-three out of fifty-three—hopelessly lost, dropped their four hundred paratroopers fifty miles east of the DZ, in the British sector near Noto and Avola, two or three miles inland of Montgomery's main assault beaches. Montgomery thus received an unscheduled gift from Patton.

The fourth serial—Group 316—in which Gavin and Hal Clark were riding, fared worst of all. It probably made the landfall on Sicily near Syracuse. Three pilots in the rear of the formation, believing Syracuse to be Gela, jumped their troopers south of Syracuse, sixty-five miles from the intended DZ. Other pilots dumped the paratroopers at random, spilling men in this serial "all over southeastern Sicily." When Gavin hit the ground, he was not even certain he was in Sicily. He was—but about thirty miles southeast of the DZ.

The fifth and last group—the 64th, "borrowed" from Dunn's wing—was the only one of the five that managed to stick together in tight formation for the whole trip. It, too, missed Malta, but found Sicily and the DZ—or so it was believed. By the time this group arrived over Sicily, the enemy was alerted and the planes came under fire. The pilots coolly maintained formation, and the entire battalion—Mark Alexander's 2nd—jumped en masse, exactly as rehearsed. Even so, the troopers came down badly scattered. They were twenty-five miles southeast of the assigned DZ.

The 226 planes now had to find their way home. Eight were lost over Sicily to enemy flak and crashed, but about half the crews bailed out and later reached Allied lines. Ten other planes were slightly damaged, but managed to fly home. Many planes became lost on the way back and landed at whatever fields they could find in North Africa. So far as could be determined, only one C-47 was fired upon by an Allied naval vessel, but it was not hit. Three pilots—violating explicit orders—refused to jump their troopers into unknown territory and brought them back to Kairouan.

The returning troop-carrier pilots were ecstatic. In spite of the navigational nightmare, most claimed they had found their DZs and had properly delivered their troopers. Adding up the rosy reports, the Troop Carrier Command, commanded by Paul L. Williams, proudly informed higher headquarters that, in the words of an Air Force historian, "80% of the paratroopers had been dropped on the designated drop zones." Although no exact accounting could ever be arrived at, the very opposite was nearer the truth. Eighty percent, or more, of the paratroopers were dropped miles from the designated DZs—anywhere from one mile to sixty-five miles or more. So far as can be determined, only one outfit—I Company of Edward Krause's 3rd Battalion—was dropped exactly on its DZ and was able to fight from scratch as a cohesive unit and take its assigned objective. Gavin later estimated that only about 12 percent of his total force (425 men of 3,405) actually landed somewhere in front of Terry Allen's Big Red One beachhead, as planned. Most of the paratroopers could not find their units or commanders and wound up fighting in small guerrilla bands.

That same evening, Ray Dunn's 51st Wing prepared to tow the British 1st Airlanding Brigade to Sicily in gliders. The outfit, led by Hoppy Hopkinson himself, consisted of 2,075 men.‡ In addition to the standard hand-carried weapons and grenades, they were equipped with six jeep-towed six-pounder

‡ The principal units were as follows: 1st Battalion of the Border Regiment; 2nd Battalion of the South Staffordshire Regiment; 9th Field Company, Royal Engineers.

antitank guns, an extra jeep, ten 3-inch mortars, ammo and ammo handcarts and some lightweight motorcycles. Dunn had a total of 144 gliders (136 Wacos and eight Horsas) and an equal number of tow planes—109 C-47s, twenty-eight Albemarles and seven Halifaxes to lift the brigade. The seven 4-engine Halifaxes would tow seven of the heavily laden Horsas; an Albermarle, one. There were American pilots at the controls of nineteen of the Waco gliders—all volunteers.[9]

The tow planes and their gliders began taking off in a swirl of blinding dust. There were some immediate problems. Six Albemarles aborted—five of them because the Waco gliders proved to be unsound or misloaded. Three other planes also returned with glider problems. Two reloaded their cargos into new gliders from the reserves, the third fixed the problem. All three planes took off again and rejoined the flight. One C-47 lost its glider shortly after takeoff. A reserve C-47 and glider took off to replace it. When an improperly loaded jeep came loose in a Waco, its C-47 tow aborted and made an emergency landing in Tunisia. In all, there were seven aborts.

The remaining 137 tows and gliders continued on. The planes flew in four-ship formations, echeloned to the right, at one-minute intervals. The twenty-nine British planes flew "individually" (not in formation), as was their custom at night. All planes remained below 500 feet—the Halifax-Horsas on top, the C-47-Wacos on the bottom, a mere 250 feet above wave tops. Owing to smart navigation, all planes sighted the beacons of Malta and turned left on a north-westerly course for Syracuse. The high winds made for an uncomfortable trip; the towed gliders bounced all over the sky and many men were violently air-sick.

On the final leg to Syracuse, the formation began to encounter navigational problems. At least 14 of the 137 planes were blown well to the east. Four planes became completely lost and returned to North Africa, still towing their gliders. One Waco glider was accidentally released far out over the sea; a Horsa broke loose from its tow ship in the same area. The men in these two gliders forced down at sea were presumably drowned. Approaching Sicily by moonlight, about eighteen pilots became disoriented and prematurely released gliders fifteen miles south of the landing zone (LZ). About a dozen of these gliders also came down in the sea. One pilot overflew Syracuse and released his glider seventeen miles north of the LZ.

Remarkably, a total of about 115 aircraft in the formation made a good landfall near the area of the four LZs just south of Syracuse. But almost immediately all hell broke loose. Syracuse came awake, searchlights sweeping the skies, flak and tracers slamming into the formations. Blinded by the searchlights and antiaircraft smoke, frightened by the flak, the pilots got rattled. Formations broke. Gliders were cut loose willy-nilly. Tow ships and gliders became all mixed up in the deadly whirling melee. Too many gliders were released too far from shore at too low an altitude. At least sixty-nine Wacos,

---

Dunn's wing was composed of the American 60th and 62nd groups and the British 38th Wing.

carrying about eleven hundred men, came down in the water. About two hundred of these troopers drowned. Hoppy Hopkinson was in a Waco that ditched offshore, but he survived—cursing Dunn's pilots for ineptitude and cowardice.

Of the 137 gliders which departed Tunisia, only 54 (49 Wacos and 5 Horsas) landed on Sicilian soil. Of these, only 4—3 Wacos and 1 Horsa—actually landed on the designated LZs. The Horsa and 2 Wacos made perfect landings, but the third Waco hit a tree. The others crash-landed all over the place, ramming into trees, stone walls and canal banks. Most men survived, but the guns and ammo were jammed inside the twisted wreckage. Only about 104 men of the initial force of 2,075—about 5 percent—were able to reach the objective and enter the fight for the Ponte Grande. All 137 tow planes returned to North Africa with no casualties. Dunn's pilots, too, were ecstatic. They claimed the mission had been a complete success, that most gliders were released to LZs as planned.

☆13☆

THE AMPHIBIOUS LANDINGS on Sicily proceeded in pitch darkness in the early hours of July 10. Montgomery's Eighth Army drove ashore with four and a half divisions, Patton and Bradley with three. Montgomery met negligible resistance. Most of the Italians manning coastal defenses surrendered without a fight or fled into the hills. By daylight, Montgomery had the British 5th Division headed north on the highway toward the Ponte Grande and Syracuse.[1]

The Hermann Göring Division, commanded by General Paul Conrath, had been ideally situated to counterattack the American landings. Conrath's headquarters was at Caltagirone, about twenty-two miles directly inland of the Gela-Scoglitti beachheads, far enough back to avoid naval gunfire and yet close enough to dominate the road networks leading toward the beachheads. Gavin later wrote: "If [Conrath] had known the details of the Allies' plans, he could not have picked a better location to assemble his division. As a prudent battle commander should, General Conrath had already made plans for the disposition of his forces in the event of landings on Gela and Scoglitti beaches." When word came of the Allied landings, Conrath promptly sent off two heavy armored battle groups to counterattack. One group went south through Niscemi toward Terry Allen's Big Red One beachhead; the second, south toward Biscari, in the general direction of Troy Middleton's 45th Division beachhead.[2]

That morning, Terry Allen had established his CP to the east of Gela two hundred yards inland from the beach. Soon after daylight, Ridgway and Don Faith climbed off the *Monrovia* into a landing craft, went ashore and found Allen. He had no news of Gavin's paratroopers, had seen neither "hide nor hair of them, and hadn't heard a peep out of them on the radio." Allen's advanced patrols, moving inland, had yet to establish contact with a single paratrooper.[3]

How could this be? Where were Gavin and his men? With a deep sense of unease, Ridgway borrowed an armed bodyguard from Allen and set off to find his paratroopers. The hunt was, Ridgway recalled, "as lonely a walk as ever I hope to take." The little group boldly proceeded through Allen's frontmost positions and kept going, deeper into no-man's-land, then enemy territory. A lone Messerschmitt screamed over, forcing them to hit the dirt, but otherwise they saw no sign of the enemy—or American paratroopers.

Finally, Ridgway found his first paratrooper. He was a 505 company commander—Willard R. Follmer—sitting on the ground, propped against an olive tree. Follmer was in great pain; he had broken his right ankle in the jump. When Ridgway inquired if he could help, Follmer shook his head; he would wait for a medic. Follmer had no idea where the main body of paratroopers might be. Something had gone drastically wrong.[4]

Ridgway and his little party pushed on deeper and deeper into enemy territory. One mile. Then two. Here and there, they began to find small knots of paratroopers; two men, then four, then ten. They were not organized; they were lost. They had no idea where the DZs or their unit commanders or Gavin might be. They had brief hair-raising tales to tell about the fouled-up flight, the jump into the black void and high wind, the futile search on the ground for their units and commanders.

Ridgway ordered these stragglers to join Terry Allen's advance patrols and do what they could to help. Sooner or later, he believed, they would link up with Gavin's main body, which, by then, Ridgway assumed, was pinned down near the DZs farther north. Ridgway returned to Allen's CP to report he had found a few straggling paratroopers. He then got on the radio trying to raise Gavin—or anybody who would answer. No luck. At noon he returned to the *Monrovia,* deeply troubled. He advised Patton to cancel the drop of Tucker's 504, which was scheduled for that evening.

Charles Kouns's 3rd Battalion (of Tucker's 504th Regiment) was the first serial to jump into Sicily. Most of the battalion had been dumped all over southeastern Sicily, and some deep into central Sicily. Many were soon captured, including Kouns. The one hundred-odd troopers of this battalion that Willis Mitchell's lead V dropped near the DZ were badly scattered. After daylight, a band of twenty-four entrenched themselves in Castel Nocera, on a secondary road about two miles east of the DZ and from this position soon repelled a small German force thrusting southward toward Gela. In the following hours—and days—other stragglers who had dropped in that area trickled into the strongpoint, building the total strength to about one hundred men. Although it was not part of the mission, this force denied the enemy this secondary road to Gela and, in so doing, confounded the Axis counterattack.[5]

Another small element of this same Tucker battalion landed two miles northwest of Biscari. In the next hour or so, Lieutenant Peter J. Eaton (no kin to the division chief of staff, Doc Eaton) rounded up about thirty-six troopers and proceeded at a fast pace northwest up the Niscemi-Biscari road toward Niscemi. By dawn, Eaton had collected some stragglers, so his group totaled fifty men. At noon, that group met two Italian vehicles coming down the road from Niscemi, towing antitank weapons. Eaton's men killed the crews, captured the weapons, dug them in, mined the road and waited. Soon a German tank, leading a battalion of German infantry, appeared. Eaton's men destroyed the tank and stopped the battalion, assaulting it from the flanks and dispersing it.

Although most of Arthur Gorham's 1st Battalion dropped sixty-five miles to the east of its DZ, at Noto, in the British sector, Gorham and about two hundred of his paratroopers were scattered only a few miles from the DZ. During the night and dawn twilight, Gorham, who was aptly nicknamed "Hardnose," and his A Company commander, Edwin M. Sayre, met and between them rounded up nearly a hundred paratroopers. They dug into a hillside commanding the main road from Niscemi to Gela. At about 7 A.M., they spotted a German armored column southbound on the road. This was an element of the Hermann Göring Division en route to throw Terry Allen's division back into the sea.

Gorham let the column approach to within a thousand yards or so, then he and his men opened fire. Slaughter ensued. Using bazookas at point-blank range, Gorham's men knocked out two tanks and damaged two others. They then opened up with small arms on two companies of German infantry advancing over an open field, decimating both. Shattered, the Germans began to pull back, then went to the rear in full retreat. Had it not been for Gorham's timely block, this column might well have smashed through to the Gela beachheads, with disastrous consequences.

Without pause, Gorham reorganized his men and moved against the 505's main objective, "Y," the nest of pillboxes along this same road. By 1045 hours, he had overwhelmed the Italian force inside the pillboxes and induced them to surrender. Gorham deployed his men inside the pillboxes just in time to see a second column of four German tanks coming down the road toward Gela. From the protection of the pillboxes, Gorham's men hit the tanks with a hail of bazooka rockets and machine-gun bullets and small-arms fire. The tanks and accompanying infantry turned tail.

An hour and a half later, advance patrols from Terry Allen's 16th Infantry Regiment arrived from the Gela beachheads. After the linkup, Gorham attached his paratroopers to the patrols and put through a call to Ridgway in Allen's CP. He reported what his force had accomplished—that objective "Y" was seized and two separate German tank columns had been destroyed or repelled and that he was moving northward toward Niscemi with the 16th Infantry. In sum, Gorham's little band of about one hundred paratroopers had accomplished all the missions assigned to the entire Gavin force. Gavin would recall: "It was a remarkable performance and I know of nothing like it that occurred at any time later in the war." Ridgway—relieved beyond words to have this good news—would later award Gorham the Distinguished Service Cross for his resourcefulness and courage.[6]

Mark Alexander's 2nd Battalion, which had jumped en masse, landed to the south of the town of Santa Croce Camerina, twenty-five miles southeast of the DZ. They found themselves amid clusters of multistoried pillboxes manned by Italian troops. Alexander was "quite successful" at rounding up "the majority" of his men, got the battalion organized and commenced a systematic and highly effective attack on the pillboxes. After daylight, Alexander found out where he was, ran patrols out to broaden his perimeter and later in the day assaulted and took Santa Croce Camerina, about the time 45th Division troops were approaching. Thus Alexander transformed a wildly misplaced drop into an entirely unforeseen bonus for Troy Middleton's 45th Division.[7]

Thirty miles to the southeast of the DZ, Jim Gavin landed in the darkness with a bone-jarring thud, shucked his parachute and made contact with his S-1, Al Ireland, and his S-3, Ben Vandervoort. Both Gavin and Ireland had leg injuries. They had no idea where they were. They had no radio. In the pitch dark they found several other troopers, then a few more. Finally the little band numbered about twenty men, some of whom had also suffered leg injuries in the jump. On the far northwest horizon, they could see bursting shells, tracers and flares. In a way the sight was reassuring; it led them to believe they were in Sicily. However, they were miles and miles from where they were supposed to be.[8]

Recalling an old West Point maxim, "When in doubt, move toward the sound of the battle," Gavin led his band northwest. Not all the men could keep up the fast pace he set. Six hours later, at dawn, only six men were left in the band. Coming over the crest of a hill, they met a furious burst of small-arms fire. One trooper went down—fatally wounded. The rest hit the dirt and returned fire. Both Gavin's and Vandervoort's carbines jammed. While they silently cursed the weapons and rigged them to fire single-shot, Ireland got an Italian officer with a squirt from his machine gun. They soon realized they had run head on into a major enemy formation—at least a platoon. As mortar fire began to rain down, they carefully withdrew and, later, found a concealed ditch to hide in, feeling "like hunted animals." Gavin said to Vandervoort: "A hell of a place for a regimental commander!"

Outnumbered, weapons jammed, they remained in the ditch until dark. It was the hardest day of Gavin's life. He was dead tired, but couldn't sleep. His mind was torn with anxiety. What had happened to all their carefully laid plans? Where was the regiment? As well as he could judge, the jump had been "an absolute shambles." It appeared the regiment was "scattered like chaff in the wind" and "possibly destroyed," and that he, personally, had "failed." He thought: "Could it be the critics were right—that airborne combat was just so much nonsense?" He cursed the jamming carbines, thinking it was "homicidal" to send men into battle with such unreliable weapons. He was furious and frustrated that they could not move on toward the battle. Gavin later wrote: "Sitting and worrying had been the hardest part of all and I had done a lot of it."

After nightfall, they moved out to the northwest, toward the sounds of battle. In the middle of the night they ran into a 45th Division outpost and, for the first time, were able to accurately determine their position. Gavin was stunned. There was still a good fifteen miles to go. They kept moving to the northwest all through the night—the second night on Sicily—not once stopping to sleep.

These scattered, disorganized paratrooper attacks, carried out by small bands of brave men, many of whom had no idea where they were, and who merely attacked at random, significantly blocked the two armored forces Conrath had sent toward the Gela-Scoglitti beachheads on July 10. Other paratroopers caused confusion and fear in the enemy ranks merely by appearing here and there all over southern Sicily. Conrath had no way of knowing the airdrops had been disastrously disorganized and dispersed. He had to assume the drops had been well executed, that there might well be numerous organized paratrooper battalions within or behind his front and that many more could descend on him at any moment. Neither he nor any other German general had any previous experience in fighting a "vertical envelopment." This was a new dimension of warfare. It was no doubt terribly distracting, perhaps terrifying, both for him and his troops. He was further confounded because American paratroopers, as instructed, cut enemy telephone and land lines wherever they found them.

The upshot was that on that first day, July 10, the counterattack of the Hermann Göring Division was not pressed with utmost vigor, and it failed. Thus the scattered bands of paratroopers bought valuable time for Patton and Bradley, Allen and Middleton. It was a good thing, too. Owing to some confusion on the beachheads, and sporadic enemy air attacks, Allen and Middleton had not been able to get their artillery, armor and antitank weapons ashore on D day as planned. Had Conrath been able to press the counterattack on the beachheads, there could well have been an American catastrophe.

Far to the east, in the British sector near Syracuse, the handful of surviving British gliderists gathered in the pitch dark to assault Ponte Grande. They took the bridge with ease and stripped it of its demolition charges. By dawn, the force, which had been enlarged by a half dozen stragglers (including an American glider pilot), consisted of about eighty-seven officers and men, led by a Lieutenant L. Withers. These men set up defensive positions and, at about 8 A.M., repulsed the first enemy counterattack.[9]

All during the morning, the Axis poured troops south from Syracuse to retake the bridge. Withers and his men, running short of ammo and lacking heavy weapons, nonetheless heroically held the bridge hour after hour, praying that the British 5th Division would hurry up from the south. No such luck. Unaware that so few gliderists had reached the bridge, the 5th Division took its own sweet time. By 3:30, with over three quarters of his eighty-seven men wounded or killed, Withers gave the order to fall back, and the Axis retook the bridge. In the ensuing melee, Withers and his remaining eighteen unwounded men were soon surrounded by a battalion of enemy troops and forced to surrender.

Only minutes later, advance patrols of the British 5th Division appeared on the scene with tanks, motorized vehicles and heavy weapons. Before the enemy could set demolition charges and blow the bridge, the British retook it. As the enemy fled north toward Syracuse, they abandoned most of the glider POWs, who were then rescued.

In one sense, the British glider operation was "successful." A few men had taken the Ponte Grande and held it long enough for the 5th Division regulars to get across. But it was a near thing and the cost was dear. Of the original 2,000 men, nearly 30 percent, or about 600, were casualties—327 killed (some by drowning) another 261 wounded or missing. By any yardstick, that was a heavy price to pay for a single bridge, however great its tactical value.

During the night of July 10/11, Axis airways sizzled with messages about Sicily. Adolf Hitler sent an order to Albert Kesselring in Rome demanding that Allied forces be thrown back into the sea. To assist in this effort, Berlin ordered that two additional German divisions (the 1st Parachute, based in France, and the 29th Panzer Grenadier, based in southern Italy) be rushed to Sicily. Kesselring, in turn, sent an order to General Guzzoni, relaying Hitler's orders. Guzzoni, in turn, ordered the 15th Panzer Grenadier Division, in western Sicily, to immediately rush eastward to help Conrath's Hermann Göring Panzer Division. During the night, Conrath laid plans to renew the attacks on the Gela-Scoglitti beachheads. To assist in this effort, the Luftwaffe would launch nearly five hundred aircraft in daylight raids against the various Allied beachheads.[10]

No American on Sicily would ever forget that day, July 11. Conrath's orders to his subordinate commanders were to throw the Americans back into the sea. His right column crunched toward Gela with renewed fury. This massive attack overran the small, scattered bands of paratroopers trying to block the roads, including Hardnose Gorham's little group from the 1st Battalion. One of Gorham's men described the action laconically: ". . . a battalion of infantry and about twenty tanks hit our position . . . we drove the German infantry off but the tanks managed to get through us." The paratroopers had no antitank weapons; the bazookas were proving to be less than effective against the heavy front armor of German tanks, and the paratroopers soon exhausted the bazooka ammo. (The bazooka shell, Bradley wrote, was "far too small" and "simply bounced harmlessly off the tank.") In a subsequent action against German forces, Gorham, "fearlessly engaging two tanks" with a bazooka, knocked out one but was killed by fire from the other. For his unstinting valor, Ridgway awarded him a second Distinguished Service Cross—both medals and a Purple Heart awarded posthumously.

This German force, supported by relentless Axis air attacks on the beachheads, which blew up some ships and scattered others, pushed right into the outskirts of Gela. By that time the Big Red One was dug in deep. "Fortunately," Gavin later wrote, "it was a veteran division; otherwise, it surely would have broken under the weight and magnitude of the German attack." The Rangers, who had captured Gela, turned some Italian guns against the German tanks. Patton, ashore and carrying on in the front lines like a platoon leader, exhorted the men to ever greater deeds of courage and, in desperation, called for naval shore bombardment. The well-placed naval salvos, Bradley wrote, "saved the day" at Gela. The cruisers and destroyers blasted away at the oncoming tanks with a rain of six- and five-inch shells, while antiaircraft batteries blazed away at swarms of Axis aircraft and often, by mistake, at Allied aircraft as well.

The other German column moved south toward Biscari and Middleton's 45th Division beachhead. The senior German general on Sicily, Fridolin von Senger, who was acting as Guzzoni's "eyes and ears," was with this column. Owing to vigorous actions that day by Mark Alexander's 2nd Battalion paratroopers, Middleton's 45th Division had moved out from its beachhead quickly. Guzzoni, concerned about the 45th's rapid advance toward Vittoria, gave orders for the German column to withdraw. But Von Senger, Gavin wrote, sensed the 45th was too loosely strung out, not dug in. He believed that by turning the German column east he could cut the 45th Division in half and destroy it piecemeal. When the column was a mere two miles from the sea, he gave orders for it to turn left toward a place called Biazza Ridge.

At about that same time, Gavin, having traveled westward during the night of July 10/11, arrived in the vicinity of Biazza Ridge. There, to his astonishment, he found a large segment—perhaps 250 men—of Edward Krause's 3rd Battalion sleeping in foxholes in a tomato field. One of Krause's companies, I, had landed on or close to its DZ and performed its mission well. This larger group, which included Krause, had landed some ten miles to the southeast of the DZ. During the night and the following day, Krause had established a provisional CP, sent out patrols in all directions to make contact with other units, rounded up stragglers and hunted down equipment bundles. Later in the day he had decamped with most of the men and marched toward Vittoria. One group, led by William J. Harris, had negotiated the surrender of Vittoria, which was a 45th Division objective. Other Krause men had established tenuous contact with advance units of the 45th Division coming up from the south.

Why was Krause now holed up, sleeping in a tomato field like this? Gavin demanded. What about the regimental objective, which lay to the west? Why had Krause not at least deployed patrols and perimeter guards? Krause lamely replied, Gavin wrote, "That he had not done anything about it" because there were German forces between him and the objective.

Gavin was baffled. In training exercises Krause, who flourished a swagger stick, had been a tiger who well earned the nickname "Cannonball." "He acted like the toughest commander we had," Gavin said later. "He made his troops shave their heads and carry rifles with fixed bayonets when they went through the chow line." However, as D day had approached, Gavin had begun to be "suspicious" of Krause, suspecting that Krause's bravado was actually shielding a lack of confidence, apprehension and fear. Now this suspicion seemed to be borne out. As a consequence, Gavin considered relieving Krause of command right then, but he changed his mind, believing Krause deserved a second chance. Later he would write that his initial instinct was the correct one and he "regretted" that he had kept Krause in command.[11]

There were many 505ers who thought Gavin's sudden loss of faith in Krause was premature or misplaced. Later—and cooler—investigation by the 505 historian, Allen Langdon, established that during the previous evening, Krause, while moving toward Vittoria, had found the 505's exec, Herbert Batcheller, who had ordered Krause and his band to bivouac for the night in the tomato field, which was four miles west of Vittoria on the road to Gela. Moreover, Langdon insisted, the pause for rest made sense, "because the men had been on their feet for thirty-five to forty hours."[12]

Gavin sensed that the battalion was vulnerable, that Germans were coming their way. He was anxious to reconnoiter westward to ascertain their strength. He drafted a platoon of the 307th Engineers, commanded by Benjamin L. Wechsler, and struck off. Almost at once he ran into a rain of heavy German fire. He had met the main German battle force advancing on Biazza Ridge. Wechsler was hit and went down. Gavin sent word back for Krause to bring up his battalion. "Here was a chance to take his battalion into combat against the toughest opposition we could find," Gavin recalled. But Krause was absent, Gavin went on. "He had gone back to 45th Division headquarters to tell them what was going on. I just couldn't believe it."

The 505 historian doubts that Krause ran from the battle or shirked his duty. He speculates that Krause went to the rear to notify the 45th Division he was pulling out and to bring forward about twenty paratroopers he had left behind at the site of the original battalion CP, south of Vittoria. In any event, Krause's executive officer, William J. Hagan, brought the battalion up in Krause's place. Hagan, too, was soon hit, sustaining a bad thigh wound.[13]

What ensued was one of the most furious and one of the bloodiest battles in Sicily: Gavin and the 250-odd lightly armed paratroopers versus the full weight of the German armored column. Gavin was determined "to stay on the ridge no matter what happened." Soon heavy German artillery and mortar fire were tearing through the paratroopers and blasting the ridge. The Americans returned fire, meanwhile digging shallow foxholes so the German tanks could roll over them "without doing too much damage." When they saw the bazooka shells bouncing off the German tanks, they devised a tactic of going at the softer underbellies as the tanks came over a rise nose up. But they were no match for tanks.

The battle raged on for hours. American casualties were heavy. After a time, Krause appeared. As Gavin remembered it, Krause counseled retreat, saying, Gavin wrote, "that all his battalion was killed, wounded or pinned down and ineffective." Gavin was furious at Krause: "I told him we were going to stay at the top of the ridge with what we had and fight the German infantry that came with the tanks. He said that we didn't have a chance, that we'd be finished if we tried to stay there. He went to the rear."

Why did Krause go to the rear? Again, Langdon's research indicates it was not out of fear, as Gavin believed. "He had sustained a small wound," Langdon wrote. "He went back to have it treated." The wound, Langdon wrote, "was corroborated by the battalion surgeon, Dr. Daniel McIlvoy, who had no love for Krause."[14]

Gavin, in one of the finest, most dogged displays of leadership in all of World War II, held on to Biazza Ridge. As the day wore on he got decisive outside help. Some 75 mm pack howitzers of Harrison Harden's 456th Parachute Artillery arrived. (Harden himself was dropped thirty-two miles from the assigned DZ.) Perhaps as a result of Krause's appeal, a battalion of the 45th Infantry Division, supported by some tanks and artillery, came up. A naval liaison officer made contact with destroyers and cruisers offshore and asked for salvos on enemy positions. As at Gela, the Navy responded quickly and effectively, slamming six- and five-inch shells into the Germans. "From then on,"

Gavin wrote, the battle seemed to change." He could feel a dramatic decrease in the weight of the German attack.

As evening approached, Gavin, who had not had a wink of sleep for sixty hours, felt that the time was ripe for a counterattack to secure the ridge in case the Germans attempted a reinforced attack on the following day. He rounded up everyone in sight—cooks, clerks, truck drivers. They charged over the ridge into the German lines and put them to rout. They "captured" a German Tiger tank, many mortars and other heavy weapons. Gavin wrote: "The attack continued, and all German resistance disappeared, the Germans having fled from the battlefield."

After Gavin "had the situation in hand," one senior 505 officer, who shared Gavin's misgivings about Krause, recalled: "Gavin came across Krause sitting on a roadside curb, head down and sobbing. Krause said, in essence, his troopers would never be as brave again as they had been that day. Krause himself had been brave. He went down into the vineyard in front of the ridge and bounced 2.36-inch bazooka shells off a German tank. There was no effect on the tank and every German gun in the area fired at the spot where they saw the bazooka blast. It was our first real hard-fought battle—with the issue in doubt all afternoon. We were all affected to some degree by first-battle trauma. Somehow, relieving Krause didn't seem the right thing [for Gavin] to do at that moment."[15]

Gavin's stand at Biazza Ridge, for which Ridgway awarded him a DSC, would become a turning point in the invasion of Sicily. Having met a stone wall and sustained heavy losses, Conrath now became gravely concerned about his forces in Gela. The opposition at Biazza Ridge led him to make the decision to break contact with the Americans at Gela and withdraw. That decision, of course, had been influenced to no little extent by the stubborn stand of Patton, the Rangers and Allen's Big Red One, plus the naval fire support at Gela. But the action at Biazza Ridge had played a crucial role in the decision. Thus, as Gavin observed, in this indirect way the paratroopers at Biazza Ridge had helped fulfill the overall regimental mission of protecting the American forces at Gela. Moreover, in making the decision to withdraw, Conrath lost the initiative and he would not get it back. The Americans were on Sicily to stay.[16]

14

ON THE DAY of the Battle of Biazza Ridge—July 11—Patton, facing severe pressure at Gela, ordered Ridgway to bring the rest of Tucker's 504th Regiment to Sicily. Tucker's two remaining battalions were the 1st, commanded by Warren Williams, and the 2nd, commanded by Bill Yarborough. In addition, the 376th Field Artillery Battalion commanded by Wilbur M. Griffith, and a company of engineers would go along. In all, there would be 1,902 men in the jump. The designated DZ was Farello, an abandoned airfield three miles east of Gela, not far from Allen's CP.[1]

The first of Hal Clark's 144 C-47s assigned to this mission began taking off in clouds of dust at 7 P.M., the last group forty-five minutes later. Since this mission took off earlier than the D-day force, it had about an hour of daylight. The weather was excellent. There were no strong winds. After getting airborne, the planes formed up in Vs and proceeded easterly toward Malta. Thinking this would be a "milk run," the air crews concentrated on navigation and formation flying, determined to improve on the D-day mission. In one C-47, violating strict orders to the contrary from Ridgway, there was a senior 82nd Division "observer" along for the ride: the ADC, Bull Keerans.[2]

At first all went well. All planes sighted the beacons of Malta and made the left turn to Sicily. On that leg they flew low (seven hundred to a thousand feet) over some Allied convoys. Some of these convoys opened fire on some of the planes, but no hits were registered. However, as the Air Force historian Warren wrote, it was a "bad omen," which showed that "three days of tension had tightened the trigger fingers of the antiaircraft crews."

This time all planes made the proper landfall on Sicily, near Cape Passero. Here there was a change from the flight plan of the D-day mission. To avoid passing over the many ships off the beachhead at Gela, this mission flew the last leg *inland* to the DZ. As they followed this new route over southern Sicily, the planes encountered cumulus clouds and climbed higher than planned—to one thousand feet—to avoid them. There was a battle haze on the ground, which made landmarks more difficult to pick out. Nonetheless, at 10:40 P.M., five minutes ahead of schedule, the lead group—313—found the DZ at the Farello airfield and dropped its troopers.

Ridgway and his staff were at the field to watch the jump and welcome the reinforcements. He—and Bradley and others—had gone out of their way to alert both Army and Navy forces to this second airborne mission, spreading the word on its routing and times of arrival. Ridgway had personally visited six pairs of antiaircraft crews to make certain they had the word. Five did, one didn't. Thereafter, he was assured that all antiaircraft commanders would spread the word. Thus he was reasonably confident that despite the twenty-three separate Axis air raids Gela had endured that day—the last one only a few minutes past—American gunners would not fire on the C-47s. He watched with satisfaction as the first sticks left the aircraft and slowly descended in the moonlight.[3]

Then suddenly all hell broke loose. It would never be established who fired first—nor did it make much difference—but suddenly a trigger-happy antiaircraft gunner either on land or a ship opened up on the C-47s. This burst triggered a nearly incredible crescendo of sympathetic antiaircraft fire from other weapons. Within a minute it is probable that every antiaircraft weapon afloat and ashore opened up along the entire length of the beachhead. Some gunners believed the C-47s were low-flying Axis bombers. Others thought that a German parachute division was jumping into the beachhead. The firing continued without letup.

Ridgway could do nothing to stop the slaughter. As he watched, horrified, sixty of the 145 C-47s—about 42 percent of the planes—were savagely hit. Twenty-three of these sixty never returned. They crashed into Sicily or the sea —six of them before the paratroopers inside could jump. The ADC, Bull Keerans, was apparently in one of the planes that crashed into the sea. In any event, no trace of him was ever found. The planes broke formation and dumped paratroopers wherever they could. Some troopers came down inside German lines; others, without proper passwords, fell into the 45th Division sector. In the wild melee, hundreds of paratroopers were wounded in the planes or during the parachute descent or on the ground. Four were found dead and six wounded in returning planes. Eight pilots peeled out of formation and headed for home with their 107 paratroopers, rightly convinced that it was suicidal to fly into the DZ.

Reuben Tucker was in the lead aircraft of the third serial. It came in all alone, low over the 1st Division beachhead near Gela. Terrific fire raked the plane; the pilot could not find the DZ in the gun smoke that lay all across the land. Tucker coolly instructed him to fly west until he could find a recognizable landmark. They soon found Licata, wheeled around and made another run over Gela, braving another withering blast of fire. Tucker and his men jumped straight into the hail of fire; his S-4, Julian Aaron Cook, was wounded. When Tucker hit the ground, he released his parachute, ran to a cluster of five American tanks which were firing at the planes with .50 caliber machine guns, and demanded they stop firing. They did. The plane from which Tucker jumped made it home, even though it had sustained "over 1,000" direct hits, a figure that was arrived at by counting the bullet holes.[4]

Tucker's executive officer, Leslie G. Freeman, also survived, although few could understand how. The plane in which he rode was so badly riddled it went out of control and crashed before the fifteen paratroopers inside it could jump. Shocked and stunned, Freeman and the others inside the mangled wreckage realized they were still alive and crawled out, helping one another. When they got free of the wreck, it was discovered that eleven of the fifteen had been wounded.[5]

It was difficult to fix the casualty figures. The best estimate was that the paratroopers suffered about 229 casualties in the drop, the air crews about ninety. There were 81 paratroopers killed, 132 wounded, 16 missing. Probably 60 airmen died and 30 were wounded. No less important than the numbers was the fact that two crack combat outfits—the 504 and the 52nd Troop Carrier Wing—had been cruelly chopped up by friendly fire, and the survivors of each were so shocked and shattered that neither would be fully combat effective for some days to come. Particularly hard hit had been Griffith's 376th Parachute Artillery. His exec, Robert H. Neptune, remembered that about half the planes shot down had been carrying C Battery of the 376th.[6]

The next morning—July 12—all was ready to tow Harry Lewis' 325th Glider Infantry Regiment and the division staff to Sicily. Lewis and many of his men, Bill Moorman recalled, had "shaved their heads" to look meaner. But after the gliders were loaded, higher headquarters canceled the tow "in view of the unfortunate incident last night." Regardless of Patton's need for infantry, there would be no more immediate airborne missions to Sicily. Ridgway's division would remain split up: one third in North Africa; the other, badly decimated two thirds, in Sicily.[7]

In the two American airborne missions, a total of 5,307 paratroopers of the 82nd Division had left North Africa for Sicily. On the morning after the second mission—July 12—Ridgway reported to Patton that he had no "formal element of Combat Team 505 under my control" and that some elements of the 504 were "dribbling in." Among these 400-odd stragglers was Reuben Tucker. Gavin did not reach Ridgway's CP until the following morning, July 13. By then, Gavin had a total of 1,200 men under his control, and by nightfall that same day, some 3,024 of the 5,307 paratroopers had reported in. Three days later, July 16, Ridgway reported he had 3,883 of the 5,307 in his control, leaving 1,424 unaccounted for. These were the dead, the wounded, the missing. The casualty rate was thus about 27 percent.[8]

When Eisenhower received the first reports on the 504 disaster, he was furious. He wrote Patton: "If the cited report is true, the incident could have been occasioned only by inexcusable carelessness and negligence on the part of someone. You will institute within your command an immediate and exhaustive investigation into allegation with a view to fixing responsibility. Report of pertinent facts is desired and if the persons found responsible are serving in your command, I want a statement of the disciplinary action taken by you . . . This will be expedited."

Patton confided to his diary: "As far as I can see if anyone is blamable it must be myself but personally I feel immune to censure . . . Perhaps Ike is looking for an excuse to relieve me . . ."[9]

In response, Boy Browning, the "observer" Joe Swing and Ridgway submitted reports. Browning bluntly laid all the blame on the aviators. ". . . The navigation by the troop-carrier aircrews was bad . . . It is essential both from the operational and morale point of view that energetic steps be taken to improve greatly on the aircrews' performance up to date. Intensive training in low flying navigation by night, especially over coast lines, must be organized and carried on continuously. This must form part of the aircrews' training before they reach a theater of war and the standard set must be very high."

Swing listed five major errors that he believed had been made: insufficient prior planning in outlining and coordinating the air routes with all forces; inability of the airmen to follow given routes, owing partly to the complexity of the route, partly to the low state of training of the navigators; the rigid naval policy of firing at any and all aircraft; the unfortunate timing of the drop on the heels of so many enemy air attacks; the failure of some Army ground commanders to warn all antiaircraft of the impending drop.

Ridgway, cataloguing his many frustrating and fruitless efforts to prevent the disaster that occurred, particularly his attempts to get cooperation from the naval forces, rightly concluded:

> The responsibility for loss of life and material resulting from this operation is so divided, so difficult to fix with impartial justice, and so questionable of ultimate value to the service because of the acrimonious debates which would follow efforts to hold responsible persons or services to account, that disciplinary action is of doubtful wisdom. Deplorable as is the loss of life which occurred, I believe that the lessons now learned could have been driven home in no other way, and that these lessons provide a sound basis for the belief that recurrences can be avoided. The losses are part of the inevitable price of war in human life.[10]*

In the meantime, Montgomery's drive up the east coast of Sicily toward Messina was not moving as rapidly as planned. The Axis had thrown in an armored column to block his path north of Syracuse. Owing to the slowdown, a second British airborne operation, scheduled for July 10, was postponed, then canceled. Another was scheduled for the night of July 13. Its mission was like the first: to capture a key bridge to help speed Montgomery northward. This bridge was the Primosole, spanning the Simeto River just south of Catania.[11]

This airborne mission was designed as a combined parachute-glider operation. Some 116 transports of Ray Dunn's 51st Wing (incorporating the British 38th Wing) would parachute the British 1st Parachute Brigade (1,856 men), commanded by Brigadier General Gerald W. Lathbury, near the bridge. Another 19 transports (C-47s, Albemarles, Halifaxes) would follow two hours behind, towing eight Waco and eleven Horsa gliders containing artillery, jeeps and other heavy gear. In all: 135 transports.

The lead planes with paratroopers took off from North Africa the evening of July 13 at 7:20 P.M. Two transports developed engine trouble before reaching Malta and had to turn back. The remaining 114 flew on at low altitude. The

---

* The American airborne disaster on Sicily was kept secret for about eight months. Knowledge of it first became public in mid-March 1944, via a *Stars and Stripes* reporter on leave in the States. Sketchy accounts appeared in the March 27, 1944, issues of *Time* and *Newsweek*.

weather was good, with minimum wind; the moon was bright. At 10 P.M., the transports towing the nineteen gliders took off. Three glider transports aborted the mission owing to takeoff accidents or control problems. The remaining sixteen had no noteworthy problems. All aircraft found Malta with no difficulty and made the left turn for Sicily.

In view of the American airborne disaster of the night before, extraordinary precautions had been taken to assure safe landing for the British. The flight formations were routed along "safe" lanes; they were not to come closer than six miles to the coast until they had reached the DZ and LZ areas. Despite these precautions, when the formation passed low over a convoy north of Malta, trigger-happy gunners fired on three Albemarles in the rear of the stream. No hits were registered, but the incident set nerves on edge.

All was peaceful again until the 130 planes approached the southeastern tip of Sicily. There the seas were jammed with convoys supporting Montgomery's army. The naval commanders had been fully briefed on the airborne mission—and also on a possible Axis aircraft attack—but inexplicably, the merchant-ship captains had not. As the airborne formation continued north, holding a course at least six miles off the coast, the merchant ships suddenly opened fire. As at Gela, other gunners joined in and a repetition of the American disaster ensued.

The planes broke formation in wild evasive tactics. Two aircraft were immediately shot down. Two others collided, but managed to recover and limp home. Seven other planes, badly damaged or with wounded pilots, as well as six other planes with no appreciable damage, likewise turned tail. The remaining 113 planes (and sixteen gliders) continued on.

North of Syracuse the planes wheeled westward and began the run in toward the DZs and LZs. They met a solid wall of antiaircraft fire. Some of it was friendly, some of it enemy. Nine planes dropping paratroopers were fatally hit. Four of these managed to limp to sea and ditch; the others crashed on land. Three aircraft towing gliders were shot down. Ten transports with paratroopers gave up and went home, making a total of twenty-five (about 20 percent of the whole force) which returned with troops. In all, friendly and enemy antiaircraft fire shot down a total of fourteen of the 130 transports. The sixteen gliders fared little better. One Horsa was accidentally released over the sea; four others were probably shot down.

Remarkably, some eighty-seven planeloads of paratroopers got through the flak. Even more remarkably, of these, nearly half (forty-two) dropped within one mile of the DZ. Some twenty-two more planes dropped within five miles of the DZ and seventeen others within ten or eleven miles. The other four dropped their troopers on the lower slopes of Sicily's legendary landmark, Mount Etna, twenty miles away. Four planes were hit by antiaircraft fire while dropping paratroopers. Some dropped too low. Two parachutists were killed in the jump; many others received serious injuries. Most of the parachute cargo bundles were lost. Of the remaining eleven gliders, three made disastrous crash landings; four came down amid strong enemy emplacements and were neutralized. Three Horsas landed in good shape near the bridge; one came down seven miles south of the LZ.

Earlier that same night, Italian forces holding the Primosole bridge had been reinforced by some three hundred German paratroopers from the 1st Parachute Division, based in France. These Germans had been hastily airlanded or dropped near the bridge on the same DZs or LZs used by the British. They gave the British a hot reception and created "history" of a sort: the first face-to-face encounter of opposing airborne forces. Nonetheless, a group of about fifty British paratroopers attacked and captured the bridge. However, on the following day, during a furious fight (reminiscent of the action at the Ponte Grande), they were unable to hold on, despite gunfire from a British cruiser. At 5 P.M., they retreated, joining a pocket of British paratroopers in the hills nearby. That evening, forward elements of the British ground forces came up from the south, but they were too late to help. They recaptured the bridge in the following days, but by that time the Axis had established a defensive line south of Catania which absolutely blocked Montgomery's northward drive to Messina.

British casualties in this second mission were also heavy: nearly 470, including about 50 among the air crews. In the two British airborne missions combined, a total of 3,856 parachutists and gliderists had left North Africa for Sicily. In total, the two groups had suffered about 900 casualties, a rate of about 23 percent.

In all, the Allies had thrown 9,163 paratroopers and gliderists into the invasion of Sicily. Had they made any substantial contribution?

On the British side, Montgomery thought not. At the time, he summed up his opinions in his diary. The glider operation on D day, he wrote, "failed badly." The parachute operation at the Primosole bridge "also failed." He blamed the failures on the fact that "the pilots of the aircraft were completely untrained in navigation, and were frightened off their job by flak." The "big lesson," he continued, "is that we must not be dependent on American Transport aircraft, with pilots that are inexperienced in operational flying; our airborne troops are too good and too scarce to be wasted." He forthwith canceled all further British airborne operations, and when he heard that Boy Browning was discussing possible further operations with his corps commanders, he sent a "furious signal" to Alexander, demanding that Browning cease and desist.[12]

The American consensus also was that the two British missions had to be counted as failures but that Jim Gavin's mission, despite its erratic character, had made sufficient impact on enemy operations to be regarded as a "qualified success." Some testimony from the American participants in Sicily supports the latter judgments. Both Patton and Bradley believed the contribution of Gavin's 505 had been very worthwhile, particularly the actions led by Arthur Gorham and Jim Gavin. Bradley wrote: "The dispersion that resulted was not wholly without its own reward. For the scattering of U.S. airborne troops throughout that target corner panicked the enemy and caused him greatly to exaggerate our strength. Raiding parties plundered the countryside, demolish-

ing bridges and severing the enemy's communications. Afterward Patton was
to estimate that, despite its miscarriage, the air drop speeded our ground advance inland by as much as forty-eight hours." Both Patton and Bradley would
remain unstinting advocates of airborne operations.[13]

The Germans believed that Gavin's force had been quite useful to the Allies.
Although Albert Kesselring correctly characterized the Allied airborne operations as "weak" and "scattered," in his postwar memoirs he conceded that they
"very considerably impeded the advance of the Hermann Göring Division"
against the American landing forces.[14]

The "observer" Joe Swing, taking a lofty, strategic view, believed that Allied
airborne forces could well have been a decisive factor in the invasion of Sicily
had they been employed in a considerably different manner. His view was that
instead of mounting the four more or less independent regiment-size airborne
operations in what were essentially blocking moves to support the seaborne
invasion or bridge-seizing tactical operations, the Allies should have consolidated all airborne forces into a mass attack into the heartland of Sicily. That is,
well *behind* (or inland of) the Hermann Göring Division. He believed that the
paratroopers could have landed and assembled with little enemy interference
and, maneuvering as a single force, could have aggressively struck the Hermann Göring Division *in the rear* with devastating results, and perhaps
blocked or at least checked the shift of the 15th Panzer Grenadier Division
from western to eastern Sicily.[15]

For Ridgway and his men, the Sicily operation had been a "sobering" experience. It led to much soul-searching within the division staff, and ultimately to a
temporary conceptual split that found Ridgway and Taylor on one side, Gavin
and Tucker on the other.

Nonparatroopers Ridgway and Taylor concluded that since the Air Force
had demonstrated it could not drop paratroopers on DZs at night without
"tremendous improvement in training" and since it had demonstrated an "un-
willingness" to provide "adequate fighter escort" for daylight parachute operations, the paratroopers should be "withdrawn" from the division and reincor-
porated into separate parachute regiments, to be utilized by the theater
commander for special missions of regimental size or smaller. The new "airborne" division, stripped of its parachutists, would become, in effect, an "airlanded" division. It would go into battle in daylight by glider or transport. It
would be composed of three regiments totaling about eleven thousand men. It
would have some heavier artillery and organic transport. Ridgway likened it to
"light infantry," which could be employed, in special situations, against special
enemy objectives "appropriate to its firepower and combat strength," such as
amphibious, mountain or jungle operations or other "ranger-type" missions. In
fact, Taylor wanted to call it an "air ranger" division.

Paratroopers Gavin and Tucker, disagreeing, believed that the parachute
regiments should be retained in divisional formations, more or less as they were
presently organized. However, they proposed several new operational concepts. They suggested that the Air Force, in addition to intensified air crew
training for troop-carrier pilots, explore the feasibility of including large num-

bers of B-17 Flying Fortress bombers in the aerial formations to provide both electronic navigation and firepower against enemy aircraft. They urged the use of paratrooper "pathfinders" to mark the DZs with electronic homing devices and with lights. They also proposed a number of improvements for the C-47: the addition of a rear right-hand door to hasten the exit of paratroopers, armor to protect the aircrews, self-sealing fuel tanks and defensive weapons such as machine guns in turrets.[16]

This conceptual split, which perhaps reflected the old gliderist/parachutist dichotomy, did not officially go beyond the division. When Ridgway sat down to make formal recommendations to Eisenhower, he made no mention of splitting off the parachute elements; to have done so at that time would have shorn the division of two thirds of its manpower. Instead, he stressed that the division should not thenceforth be committed to action piecemeal as it was on Sicily; that there was an obvious and urgent need for many more C-47 transports in order to commit the division as a whole; that (as was now universally believed) the Air Force must greatly intensify training for all forms of airborne operations but especially night operations; that to prevent accidents and other foul-ups, there should be a single commander of airborne operations capable of choosing routes and enforcing safety rules; and the division must have heavier antitank weapons and artillery, prime movers to tow the antitank guns and artillery, and much more ground transport (jeeps and trucks) for moving personnel.

Beyond that, what Ridgway wanted "as soon as possible" was to get the rest of his division (notably the 325th Glider Infantry) to Sicily and commit the division, as a whole, to combat. It was "essential," he wrote, that the division get more "ground battle experience" before the next airborne operation, in order to "conclusively establish the division's ability to accomplish a mission."[17]

There was also much soul-searching on high levels. John P. Lucas (West Point, 1911), who had served as Eisenhower's "eyes and ears" during the Sicily invasion, submitted a report to Eisenhower in which he stated that "the organization of Airborne Troops into [units as large as] divisions is unsound" and doubted that an airborne unit of division size could be landed in an area where a headquarters could exercise control. The Lucas report no doubt influenced Eisenhower, who later wrote Marshall: "I do not believe in the airborne division. I believe that airborne troops should be organized in self-contained units, comprising infantry, artillery, and special services, all of about the strength of a regimental combat team." Back in the States, AGF commander Lesley McNair was ready to pare the airborne units to even smaller size. At a later date he wrote that, after Sicily, "my staff and I had become convinced of the impracticality of handling large airborne units," and McNair "was prepared to recommend to the War Department that airborne divisions be abandoned . . . and that the airborne effort be restricted to parachute units of battalion size or smaller."[18]

Sicily had thrown the entire airborne-division experiment into question.

☆ 15 ☆

In the hectic Allied planning for Sicily, there had been no time to work out a master plan for the conquest of the island. The general idea was that Montgomery's Eighth Army would make a northward dash for Messina; Patton's Seventh Army would move inland on his left flank. More than any other factor, it was Axis reaction to the assault that determined Allied ground strategy on Sicily.[1]

After Conrath failed to throw the Americans back into the sea, but had blocked Montgomery at Catania, the Axis shifted to the defensive. As in Tunisia, the plan was to fight a delaying action for as long as possible, thereby tying down Allied troops, air and naval power which might be used elsewhere. However, unlike Tunisia, Sicily would not be an Axis fight to final destruction. Here the Axis had an escape hole: ultimate withdrawal across the narrow Strait of Messina onto the Italian mainland. Beginning on the day the Allies landed in southern Sicily, Axis planners commenced to make certain the escape hole was never closed. Unfortunately, the Allies, absorbed in the details of the battle itself, failed to reckon properly with this possibility.

Blocked at Catania, Montgomery improvised a new plan. He would circle his troops around the base of Mount Etna in a generally northwesterly direction, then swing around the mountain, northeasterly, to Messina. He launched this plan without even informing Patton or Bradley, imperiously (and dangerously) marching a corps directly across Bradley's front. Only after he had launched the plan did Montgomery inform Alexander of his intention. As laid out, it was to be primarily a British "show." Patton's Seventh Army was reduced to the ignominious role of protecting Eighth Army's left flank and rear.

When they received the details of Montgomery's plan via Alexander, the American generals were absolutely furious. Patton, and others, appealed to Eisenhower and Alexander for a larger and more important role for Seventh Army. Eisenhower remained aloof from the dispute, deferring to Alexander, further enraging the American generals. At first Alexander stuck by Montgomery's plan. But he soon yielded to a scheme Patton proposed: that only Bradley's II Corps (of two divisions, Allen's 1st and Middleton's 45th) would protect Eighth Army's left flank and rear, while Patton, with a newly formed, temporary (or "provisional") corps, made a northwestward dash to Palermo, "conquering" the western half of Sicily and gaining Palermo as a resupply port. Since the Axis had shifted the German 15th Panzer Grenadier Division from western Sicily to eastern Sicily to help in the delaying action, there remained only a few lackluster Italian troops to defend western Sicily.[2]

Patton chose his deputy army commander, Geoffrey Keyes, to command the

Matthew Bunker Ridgway: As a West Point cadet in 1917.

As a major in 1932 and as a major general commanding the 82nd Airborne Division in 1944.

USMA

USAMHI

Training American paratroopers: On the practice towers at Fort Benning, on the ground and in the air from C-47 "Skytrain" troop-carrier aircraft. Five training jumps "qualified" paratroopers, who were awarded this coveted silver insignia.

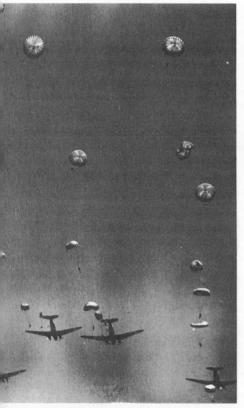

Pioneering Allied paratrooper generals: William C. (Bill) Lee (upper left); British General Frederick A. M. (Boy) Browning (upper right).
Bottom: (left to right) Ridgway, Joseph M. Swing, William N. (Bud) Miley, jumpmaster Warren R. Williams, and Ridgway's aide, Don C. Faith.

Preparing for the invasion of Sicily, July 1943: George S. Patton (left) and Omar N. Bradley inspect the 82nd Airborne Division on June 4, 1943. Ridgway and his artillery commander, Maxwell D. Taylor (right, wearing sunglasses) were the escorts.

REUBEN H TUCKER III
COL

Invading Sicily, July 10, 1943. The 82nd's 505th Regiment commander James M. (Slim Jim) Gavin and 504th Regiment commander Reuben H. (Rube) Tucker jumped with their troopers. The 325th Regiment commander, Harry L. Lewis, and his gliderists remained on standby in North Africa. Ridgway went in by landing craft.

Waco gliders in training exercises: taking on a jeep (top) and a 75 mm pack howitzer artillery piece (middle) or jammed with gliderists (bottom) from the 101st Division.

Ridgway in Sicily. Upper left, conferring with artillery commander Max Taylor and, upper right, with M/Sgt. Frank Morang. Bottom, posing with division staffers after completion of the 82nd Airborne Division mission in western Sicily.

Ridgway in Italy: With Fifth Army commander Mark Wayne Clark and other commanders in the Salerno beachhead (above). Behind Ridgway in jeep: his driver, Staff Sgt. Frank G. Farmer (below).

provisional corps. It consisted of the following major units: the 3rd Infantry Division (which had taken Licata); the 2nd Armored Division (which had been in Patton's "floating reserve"); a regiment of the 9th Infantry Division (just arrived from Patton's army reserve in North Africa); two ranger battalions (which had taken Gela); and Ridgway's two airborne regiments, Tucker's 504 and Gavin's 505, plus the parachute artillery battalions and miscellaneous units.

In preparation for the offensive, on July 16, the rest of the 82nd Division staff (some four hundred men), including Max Taylor, was airlifted to Sicily in fifty-one C-47s. This third and final airlift to Sicily was carried out in daylight, with fighter escort, and came off without a hitch. The addition of the staff brought the division strength on Sicily under Ridgway's control to 4,309 men. Artillery units from Manton Eddy's 9th Division—including the 34th battalion, commanded by William C. Westmoreland—were attached to the 82nd for the western Sicily campaign.[3]

Before embarking on the offensive, Ridgway filled some holes in key command positions. After Bull Keerans was presumed dead, Ridgway named his next-senior officer, Max Taylor, to temporarily replace Keerans as ADC. With the death of Art Gorham and the capture of Charles Kouns, there were two battalion-commander slots vacant, one in the 505th and one in the 504th. In both instances the replacements Ridgway chose were West Point sons of "old Army" officers. Command of Gorham's 1st Battalion, 505, went to the exec, Walter F. Winton, Jr. (like Ridgway, the son of a retired artillery colonel), who would, in time, become one of Ridgway's inner circle. Command of Kouns's 3rd Battalion, 504, went to Ridgway's protégé and Winton's classmate Hank Adams. The selection of two such young men (both twenty-six years old and from the class of 1940) to be battalion commanders, raised eyebrows, but no one questioned their courage or ability.[4]

In these command readjustments, Ridgway named Gavin's S-1, Al Ireland, who had proved himself able and cool in combat, to be Winton's 1st Battalion exec. Ireland recalled that Ridgway, "from our first meeting remembered me and my name and position in the regiment and never forgot it." He felt that although Ridgway's "countenance and posture were warlike," his manner was gentle and most gracious and "he always had a cheerful and friendly greeting." Ireland observed that "under stressful conditions, combat particularly," Ridgway "always seemed cool but determined in his every move and thought." He also noted another of Ridgway's quirks. "[H]e was a pacer. It would be interesting, if possible, to get a surviving close member of his staff to estimate the miles traveled by Ridgway [pacing] in his field headquarters."[5]

The provisional corps commenced the western Sicily campaign at 8 A.M., July 19. Four hours later, new orders arrived from Alexander, canceling the offensive. These orders, drastically changing the American plan, directed that Patton send the full force of Seventh Army due north to the coast, to split the island in two. In other words, Patton's *entire* army would do the job assigned to Bradley's II Corps. Then, later, if conditions were favorable, Patton could conquer western Sicily and take Palermo. When he saw these orders, Patton's chief of staff, Hobart R. (Hap) Gay, was at first dumfounded, then angry. They seemed to him one more effort by the British to diminish the American role on Sicily. On his own, he made the decision to conceal the order from Patton for several days; to let Patton's dash to Palermo proceed as planned. Some months later, when Bedell Smith found out what Gay had done, he persuaded Eisenhower to relieve Gay and demote him to assistant chief of staff.[6]*

Thus, unaware of Alexander's change in orders, Geoffrey Keyes's provisional corps continued on its thrust into western Sicily. Bradley, left behind with only two divisions to fight through the strong and skillfully manned German defenses to the north coast, was scornful of this Patton operation. He called it a "public relations gesture," "great theater" and "meaningless in a strategic sense," since it took the "main weight of Seventh Army off in the wrong direction."[7]

The five-day campaign into western Sicily was a cakewalk; in the words of the official Army historian, "little more than a road march." Ridgway thought it was "more like a maneuver than a shooting war." Gavin found it "a strange affair, unlike anything else I encountered in the war." The Italian and Sicilian troops they met along the way melted away into the hills or surrendered by the thousands. However, many Italians felt the need to fire a volley or blow up a bridge for the sake of "honor" before raising a white flag. These "honor" volleys were infuriating, because, as Gavin wrote, they were "just as likely to cause casualties as a shot fired in anger." The Italians killed one officer and six men and wounded sixteen others in the division. Along the way, the division processed some 23,191 POWs. Lacking "organic" transportation (trucks, jeeps, etc.), these superbly fit paratroopers marched most of the 150 miles on foot, at a speed that astonished corps headquarters.[8]

This was the first opportunity Ridgway had ever had to deploy so much as two regiments of his division in extended cross-country operations. By and large he was disappointed in the performance, particularly at "the caution of the advanced elements." If they came under fire—the "honor volleys"—too often they "would stop to ponder the situation." Ridgway's solution was to go right up front and lead the men himself. The official division historian wrote: "Every phase of the advance . . . was led in person by General Ridgway who kept himself in personal touch with the reconnaissance elements, the point, and the advance guard command." Taylor, Gavin and Tucker were not far from his side.[9]

Ridgway's personal exposure to enemy fire at the extreme point of advance of his troops would become legendary. He would write: "I always felt my place was up where the heaviest action was—not interfering with the commander who was actually doing the fighting, but looking over the situation and helping

---

* Patton resisted the demotion to his utmost, but finally yielded and named another man to be his chief of staff. However, as Gay recalled it, still later, Eisenhower conceded that Bedell Smith had been "dead wrong" in the matter and Gay was repromoted to chief of staff.

him all I could." On Sicily the practice earned him a rebuke from, of all people, George Patton, who was notorious for exposing himself to enemy fire. Coming from Patton, Ridgway considered the rebuke "more of a compliment." However, Ridgway was led to take one precaution. Realizing that a single lucky enemy "honor" volley could wipe out the entire division command, he sternly ordered Max Taylor to the rear: "By God, you're to get back and stay back until I send for you."[10]

Although Patton's style of leadership was not entirely to Ridgway's liking, one facet of it impressed him and he would eventually adopt it. Ridgway noted that Patton "would frequently stop and get out of his car to praise somebody in a very lowly position—maybe he was clearing a ditch along a highway, an engineer or something like that, or maybe an MP at a crossroad directing traffic. That is great stuff . . . and word of that gets around and I'm sure it was sincere on George Patton's part. It wasn't just done for effect."[11]

Jim Gavin had this to say about Ridgway's front-line leadership: "He was a *great* combat commander. Lots of courage. He was right up front every minute. Hard as flint and full of intensity, almost grinding his teeth with intensity; so much so, I thought: that man's going to have a heart attack before it's over. Sometimes it seemed as though it was a personal thing: Ridgway versus the Wehrmacht. He'd stand in the middle of the road and urinate. I'd say, 'Matt, get the hell out of there. You'll get shot.' No! He was defiant. Even with his penis he was defiant."[12]

Later, when Ridgway was asked about this seeming fearlessness in the front line, he replied: "I don't believe there's any man who doesn't feel fear at times. But when you get a job to do and a place to go, you just put it out of your mind. So far as enemy fire is concerned, hell's bells, you never hear what hits you and you never see the guy who's shooting at you."[13]

There was another factor as well. A deep religious faith sustained him. He was not ostentatious or demonstrative about his faith, but it was real. To one colonel who complained that Ridgway's exposure to the enemy drew unnecessary fire and endangered those who were compelled to emulate his "damnfoolish" example, one of Ridgway's staffers explained sincerely: "The general is very religious. He reads the Bible and prays. He firmly believes that God will not permit him to be hit before Germany is totally defeated."[14]

The crowd of nervous, emulating staffers that Ridgway drew to the front sometimes became a tactical annoyance. The Division Engineer, Robert S. Palmer, recalled: "At an after-action critique . . . battalion commander Ed Krause capped his presentation with the statement that he could have deployed his unit and knocked out the opposition in half the time if he had not had to get around half the division staff, including the division commander, on the road in front of him! Ridgway saw his point and said it wouldn't happen again."[15]

As the 82nd marched ever westward in Sicily, Bill Yarborough, the veteran of the 509th Battalion in TORCH operations and now commanding Tucker's 2nd Battalion, was still an unhappy warrior. He had not been invited to participate in the Sicily planning and had been appalled at the outcome. He believed he knew the paratroop game better than the people who were giving him orders and developed a gnawing resentment toward those he believed responsible for the tragedy.

One day, Yarborough's battalion was ambushed by some Italian soldiers with artillery at a place called Tumarilla Pass. Yarborough deployed his troops and cleaned out the Italians, but Ridgway, who soon came up, was unhappy about the delay the ambush had caused and about the fact that Yarborough had allowed his men a pause to eat. "This is no way to do it," Ridgway snapped angrily. "You're vulnerable here. Get your butts out of here and get on the road and let's get going."

The incident led to an irreconcilable break. Yarborough recalled: "Again, my feelings were hurt . . . I felt that he should have patted me on the shoulder and said, 'Say, you guys did a good job here.' " Yarborough let his resentment be known and openly criticized both Ridgway and Tucker for the Sicily fiasco. Shortly thereafter he was relieved of his command. Years later he conceded that his exercise of command of the battalion was "seriously flawed" by his immaturity and "high-spirited stupidity" in challenging Ridgway and Tucker. "You just can't have that kind of thing and I recognized where the deficiency lay. It was with me and not with Ridgway or Tucker."[16]†

Many officers in the division were shocked at the way Ridgway had come down on Yarborough. Some thought it ruthless. Counting TORCH operations, Yarborough had more "combat jumps" than anybody else in the division—and had only barely survived the disastrous 504 jump into Sicily.

The following day, Warren Williams, commanding Tucker's 1st Battalion, also felt the Ridgway lash. Ridgway had confronted Williams and asked if he had guards out on his flanks—to prevent an ambush. Williams did not; he said the flank guards would slow him down and reminded Ridgway that, above all, Ridgway had demanded speed in the advance. Ridgway then asked Williams if he knew what had happened the day before to Yarborough. Williams said, "Yes, sir." Ridgway said, "You better not run into the same thing," and drove off in his jeep.[18]

The 82nd Division's real—and final—objectives were situated on the westernmost tip of Sicily: Trapani and Castellammare. Gavin would take the former, Tucker the latter. Carried forward in borrowed trucks, Gavin's troopers reached the outskirts of Trapani late in the afternoon of July 23. There the cakewalk advance abruptly stopped. The Italian commander of Trapani, Admiral Giuseppe Manfredi, appeared at first to have no intention of surrendering. His troops had blocked the road and sown it with mines. Suddenly, heavy artillery units in the hills overlooking the road let loose with well-aimed salvos. The paratroopers leaped from the trucks and hit the dirt, seeking cover.[19]

† Ridgway sent Yarborough back to Mark Clark's headquarters in Mostaganem. There Yarborough was assigned to Clark's Fifth Army G-3 Section, and became Clark's chief airborne adviser and planner. Ridgway and Tucker chose Yarborough's exec, Daniel W. (Danny) Danielson to replace him.[17]

To counter the artillery fire, Ridgway and Gavin brought up some guns of Harrison Harden's 456th airborne artillery. Seeing this, the Italian artillery zeroed in on the American artillery, sending in a hail of bursting shells that forced one gun crew to run for shelter. Ridgway's G-2, George Lynch, and the G-3, Klemm Boyd, were watching. What happened next was one of the boldest acts Lynch had ever seen, and he would never forget it. "Ridgway calmly strode up to the deserted gun while Italian shells were bursting all around it. His brave example rallied the crew back into action."[20]

The incident did not bode well for Harrison Harden. Later, on Ridgway's order, Max Taylor relieved Harden of command, reduced him in rank and sent him back to the States. Harden, replaced by his exec, Hugh A. Neal, was bitter. He wrote later that he distrusted most infantrymen, whom he found to be "uncooperative, unimaginative and unintelligent." He faulted infantryman Ridgway in particular for "lack of care for his men" and for "bad judgment in the planning of the second jump into Sicily." In the Trapani "battle," Harden thought that Ridgway "seemed to be commanding well and was brave under fire to the point of being exhibitionistic."[21]

As the battle of Trapani reached a climax, Al Ireland, exec of Winton's 1st Battalion, 505, remembered:

> About mid-afternoon, during a lull in the firing, Ridgway decided it might be time to approach the Italian headquarters . . . Being nearby in my jeep and privy to the discussion, I volunteered to ascend the mountain and demand the garrison's surrender. I think I would have even been willing to try a Teddy Roosevelt "charge" up the hill . . . Ridgway assented . . . With white flag attached to the front of the windshield we began to climb through Axis lines, past pillboxes armed with machine guns and dug-in troops. The enemy looked at us with some surprise but—fortunately—all honored the signal of truce. My mission was accomplished without incident. The admiral in command, along with his staff, accompanied me to division headquarters. Here I introduced the admiral to Ridgway.[22]

Admiral Manfredi, outnumbered, outgunned and outgeneraled, yielded Trapani that night, July 23, ceremoniously surrendering its five thousand defenders and presenting Ridgway his sword and binoculars. Tucker took Castellammare the next day. The honor of "capturing" the historic city of Palermo had been reserved for Hugh J. Gaffey's 2nd Armored Division, which had been rumbling along behind the infantry. Although Patton would grandiosely describe the maneuver as "a classic example of the use of tanks," it was less. In fact, elements of the 82nd (and other divisions) had already entered the city unopposed before Gaffey's tanks got there. When the tanks came clanking menacingly into the city, Ridgway later wrote, the paratroopers were "applauding them from the sidewalks, where they had been for hours, cutting the dust from their throats with wine."[23]

Thereafter, the 82nd Division settled down to easy "occupational duty" at Trapani and Castellammare, the troopers bathing in the warm, iridescent Mediterranean waters, consuming countless bottles of wine, and, like all conquering soldiers, making the acquaintance of the young female population, who, owing to the fortunes of war, were without much local male companionship.[24]

The latter pleasure, in fact, became something of a problem. Venereal diseases were not unknown in Sicily; Eisenhower discouraged "fraternization." But Ridgway forthrightly arrived at a solution. Doc Eaton recalled: "He came in one day and said out of the blue that we ought to start a semi-official [whore] house. I almost fell out of my chair—he was such a *moral* man. He said these boys are red-blooded. They'll be messing around. The townspeople might get upset. So we started a [whore] house and put the division Sanitary Officer in charge. (We called him 'The Madam.') The next thing I know, Ridgway came in and said he was going to inspect the house. I argued with him not to, telling him he'd be thoroughly disgusted. He went anyway and *was he disgusted!* 'They're just like animals!' he said."[25]

While in western Sicily, Ridgway made another important change in his senior staff. Klemm Boyd, the division G-3 (head of plans and operations) who, as Boyd conceded later, "had made some mistakes and did not admire Eaton," was replaced. Ridgway sent Boyd to command Harry Lewis' 1st Battalion, displacing the temporary commander, Teddy Sanford. This move caused some anxiety and resentment in the 325, because Boyd was an "outsider" and because Lewis suspected, wrongly, that Ridgway might be grooming Boyd to replace him as commander of the regiment.[26]

To replace Boyd as division G-3, Ridgway chose a dynamo who was commanding the 325's 80th Antiaircraft Battalion, Whitfield Jack. He was a West Point graduate (1928) who had early resigned from active Army service to follow a career in law in his hometown, Shreveport, Louisiana, until his recall to active duty in 1940. Ridgway had not known Jack earlier, but after seeing him in action at Claiborne and Bragg, he was determined to bring him into his high inner circle. One of Jack's assistants remembered him thus: "He was simply a great guy. All keyed up, a bundle of energy, the tightest main spring you can imagine. Everything he did, he did fast. He walked fast, talked fast, he'd have three cigarets going at the same time. His eyes were all over the place. If anybody could stimulate you to action, it was Whit Jack."[27]

The Sicilian campaign continued in the eastern end of the island with savage fury. Montgomery's plan to swing his forces northwesterly around Mount Etna, then northeasterly toward Messina, ran aground on determined German resistance. Despite the addition of an infantry division from its North African reserve, bringing its total strength to six divisions plus, the British Eighth Army ground to a halt. As a consequence, Alexander was compelled to order Patton's Seventh Army to turn about and drive east along the north coast of the island for Messina. Patton was delighted at the idea of "going to Monty's rescue" and became determined to beat him to Messina.[28]

Bradley's II Corps, which had reached the north coast, spearheaded the turnabout and drive on Messina. To relieve Bradley's tiring 1st and 45th divisions, Patton disbanded Keyes's provisional corps and sent Bradley Lucian

Truscott's 3rd and Manton Eddy's 9th infantry divisions. To hasten the advance to Messina, Patton also engineered several minor and unsuccessful amphibious landings along the north coast and gave fleeting thought to a parachute drop. But the rocky, mountainous terrain along the north coast was deemed utterly unsuitable for airborne operations. Nor was the terrain suitable for Hugh Gaffey's 2nd Armored Division tanks.

Facing two Allied armies totaling some ten divisions powerfully supported by Allied air, the four German divisions on Sicily now began to slowly fall back for an evacuation through Messina, skillfully utilizing the rugged terrain and narrow mountain roads to advantage. The evacuation commenced on August 10. A week later, it was completed and the Allies entered Messina—the Americans first, by an hour or so. The four German divisions of some forty thousand men, plus seventy thousand Italian regulars, escaped with about fifty tanks and seventeen thousand tons of supplies. Not many days would pass before the Allies would again feel their sting.

PART III

Italy:

Airborne to the Rescue

☆16☆

ALL DURING THE THIRTY-NINE DAYS of fighting on Sicily, the Allied high command had been debating grand strategy. The Americans were still convinced that the cross-Channel invasion (ROUNDUP, later renamed OVERLORD) was the best way to defeat Hitler, and urged that OVERLORD receive highest priority. The British, still cool to OVERLORD, urged further operations in the Mediterranean aimed at Hitler's "soft underbelly": incursions into Greece, the Balkans, Italy. The last particularly appealed to Churchill. Italy was already tottering. The capture of Rome might well unseat Mussolini's fascist government and knock Italy out of the war. If so, Hitler would be faced with a tough strategic decision: to defend Italy with German forces which were badly needed elsewhere, or yield it to the Allies.

The British view prevailed; Italy would be invaded. But the Americans insisted on an important caveat: the invasion must be carried out with minimum forces. Allied air, ground and sea power in the Mediterranean already earmarked for movement to England for OVERLORD would not be diverted to Italy. The liberation of Rome would be the main objective; if the Axis yielded northern Italy, so much the better.[1]

Where to attack Italy?

Eisenhower already had a limited invasion of Italy in the planning stage: a leap across the Strait of Messina into Calabria, at the toe of the boot. This modest leap (Operation BAYTOWN) was intended merely to clear the toe, so Axis guns could not shell Allied forces in Messina or ships in the Strait. However, inasmuch as a move across the strait could be accomplished with a minimum of landing craft, which were everywhere in short supply, some of Eisenhower's planners advised expanding this crossing into a full-scale assault on Italy. This approach would clearly entail a long, arduous offensive up the mountainous boot, a campaign that would favor the defense. Churchill scotched that plan with the apt comment: "Why crawl up the leg like a harvest bug from the ankle upwards? Let us rather strike at the knee."[2]

The knee was Rome itself, the grand prize, the seat of government. It became the focus of early planning. Rome was some fifteen miles inland up the Tiber River, but there were ideal landing beaches near Rome and good tank country in between: Civitavecchia, Ostia, Anzio. An amphibious landing at Ostia, supported by an airborne assault inland, or even on Rome itself, might gain the prize swiftly.[3]

However, the military planners deemed a strike directly at Rome unfeasible. It was too far from Sicily (250 air miles) for short-legged fighter aircraft to reach and stay long enough to fight. After the experience of Sicily, everybody from Eisenhower to the lowliest private demanded Allied fighter cover over an invasion beachhead. The Combined Chiefs of Staff made available five British aircraft carriers (one light and four escort, or "jeep," carriers) which could accommodate a total of 120 British Seafire fighters, but that kind of slim fighter cover satisfied no one. Such small carriers would be vulnerable to enemy air and submarine attack and did not have sufficient endurance or "staying power" to sustain an air umbrella over the invasion forces.

Having been informed of these limitations, the Combined Chiefs settled on Naples, which was fifty air miles closer to Sicily. On July 23, they instructed Eisenhower "to prepare a plan, as a matter of urgency, for direct attack on Naples, using the resources which have already been made available. . . ." Naples was 125 miles south of Rome by land, but it had at least one impressive plus: a large, deep-water harbor which could be utilized for logistical support. On closer inspection, however, Naples proved to be beyond fighter range, and it, too, had to be rejected.

Almost by default, the planners settled on the Gulf of Salerno, about thirty-five miles south of Naples. The American P-38 fighters based on Sicily could patrol over Salerno for one hour. The British Spitfires (the best of the Allied fighters), equipped with wingtip fuel tanks, could patrol over Salerno for twenty minutes, or if challenged to a dogfight and forced to drop the wingtip tanks, ten minutes. The five British aircraft carriers could provide supplementary air cover at Salerno. Shorter-legged fighters (American P-39s and P-40s) could provide convoy air protection between Sicily and Salerno.

Offsetting these air-power advantages were grave disadvantages. The entire shoreline of the Gulf of Salerno was dominated by a range of hills and cliffs ideal for defense. The beach itself was almost exactly split in half by the Sele River. The river would physically divide an invasion force, making interchange of units and lateral communications difficult. Moreover, the formidable Sorrento mountain range lay athwart the route from Salerno to Naples. An aroused and determined enemy, driven back on Naples, might well destroy the port before yielding it to the Allies. And lying between Naples and the real objective, Rome, was the broad Volturno River, a natural defensive barrier, should the Axis desire to make a stand south of Rome.

Two days after the Combined Chiefs ordered Eisenhower to strike at Naples —July 25—the Allies received astonishing news: Italy's King Victor Emmanuel III had summoned the Grand Council and deposed and arrested Benito Mussolini. The King had replaced Mussolini with the aging Marshal Pietro Badoglio, a fascist who had engineered the rape of Ethiopia years before. Badoglio had publicly reaffirmed support for the "Pact of Steel" which bound Italy and Hitler, but almost immediately thereafter, a high-level Italian emissary, Giuseppe Castellano, made surreptitious contact with the Allies to open negotiations for a separate surrender.

Eisenhower entered into these secret negotiations eagerly but cautiously. He was eager because he believed a neutralized Italy or an Italy turned against Germany could greatly reduce the military risks entailed in the Salerno invasion, which was to be mounted with the slimmest of resources. He was cautious because Castellano might be a Hitler "plant" setting a trap, or a spy collecting information, or a political fanatic acting without authority of Badoglio or of the king. Even when Castellano's *bona fides* had been established, the negotiations remained complicated, because both sides, who wanted the same thing, were trapped by their own propaganda: at Casablanca, the Allies had announced the policy of "unconditional surrender" and "no deals with fascist dictators"; Badoglio had publicly proclaimed continuing loyalty to Hitler. He was negotiating with a noose around his neck. One misstep or premature leak could provoke a swift Nazi takeover of Italy and wholesale executions, the king, Badoglio and Castellano at the top of the list. Moreover, Castellano's preliminary list of conditions was, in Allied eyes, outrageous. Italy wanted to get out of the war with honor and also share in the fruits of victory over Hitler.

The negotiations continued in an atmosphere of mutual suspicion and distrust. The Allied high command continued to insist on unconditional surrender, the terms of which Eisenhower himself considered "unduly harsh." The surrender must be publicly announced before the Allies invaded Italy, to ensure that Italian troops would not fire on the Allies. Before yielding to these demands, Badoglio wanted to be certain that the Allied invasion would be strong and swift enough to preclude a German takeover of Italy. He wanted at least a fifteen-division invasion force to land near Rome and a parachute drop on Rome to ensure the survival of the Italian Government. Eisenhower could not, of course, guarantee either of these conditions.

In the meantime, Hitler was not asleep. Berlin foresaw that Italy might throw in the towel, and began making preparations to counteract treachery. However, Hitler and his top advisers were divided about exactly what to do. Occupy all of Italy? Occupy Rome northward? Withdraw to northern Italy and establish an invincible line at the Po River to block an Allied invasion of Austria or southern France? When Mussolini was overthrown, Hitler's first instinct was to order a *coup d'état* and restore him to power in a Nazi-occupied Italy. But Hitler's advisers counseled other, less drastic, courses. Erwin Rommel, who was brought into the picture and given major responsibility for the Italian military problem, advised a complete withdrawal to the Po River. Albert Kesselring, in Rome, believing the Badoglio government would remain loyal, and (perhaps jealous of Rommel's new authority in his baliwick) advised against withdrawal. He believed that the Badoglio government could be propped up and kept on Hitler's side and that the Axis could repulse an Allied invasion with only minimum reinforcement.

In the end, Kesselring's advice more or less prevailed. Hitler, in effect, made Italy a prisoner. He poised Rommel in the far north with a powerful force (five infantry and two panzer divisions) to dominate the approaches to the Alpine passes and southern France. Some of Rommel's forces quietly edged into northern Italy, much to Badoglio's consternation. Plans were made to withdraw the German 90th Panzer Grenadier Division from Sardinia and a brigade from Corsica to Leghorn to join Rommel's forces.

The most muscular German moves were made in the vicinity of Rome and farther south. Hitler positioned two divisions near Rome: the 3rd Panzer Grenadier and 2nd Parachute divisions, plus an armored element. In all, there were about forty-three thousand Germans in the Rome area. In southern Italy (south of Rome), he created a new army, the Tenth, commanded by Heinrich von Vietinghoff, who reported to Kesselring. This army comprised six divisions, four of them recently withdrawn from Sicily and in process of rest and rehabilitation: 29th Panzer Grenadier, then in Calabria; the 1st parachute, near Brindisi and Bari, in the east-coast district of Apulia; and the Hermann Göring and 15th Panzer Grenadier divisions, in the Naples area. To these were added two new divisions: the 26th Panzer, which had dropped off the armored element in Rome and joined the 29th Panzer Grenadier in Calabria, and the 16th Panzer, deployed along the beaches in the Gulf of Salerno, which Kesselring (who well knew Allied fighter-plane ranges) believed to be the likeliest Allied invasion target. In addition, Kesselring controlled an air force composed of some fifteen hundred planes (including many inferior Italian models), widely dispersed throughout Italy from the Po River south, and on Sardinia and Corsica.[4]

Kesselring's plan was roughly this: If Italy remained loyal to Germany *before* the Allies invaded Italy, the combined German-Italian forces would resist the invasion to the utmost. However, they would not stand in the "toe" (Calabria) or "heel" (Apulia), where logistics and air power favored the Allies. Rather, the three German divisions there would fall back toward the "knee" (the Salerno-Naples-Rome area), where logistics and air power favored the Axis, who could consolidate all ground forces (eight divisions) in the defense. If Italy surrendered *before* an Allied invasion, the Germans would disarm the Italian forces and then commence falling back on Rome. However, as the official U.S. Army historian, Martin Blumenson, points out, there was no German plan to cope with a *simultaneous* Italian surrender and Allied invasion, which was Eisenhower's objective in the secret talks with Castellano.

As final plans were refined on both sides, the Allied moves unwittingly played into the hands of the Axis. The first step in the Allied plan was for Montgomery to make a leap into the toe—Calabria. In that event, the two German divisions there, the 26th Panzer and 29th Panzer Grenadier, were under orders to slowly withdraw northward along Italy's west coast—toward Salerno. Inasmuch as the Salerno invasion was to follow Montgomery's leap by about a week, it meant that those two German divisions would reach the vicinity of the invasion beaches and join the 16th Panzer at Salerno at about the time of the Allied invasion, increasing German beach defenses from one division to three. These three divisions would also be in a position to block a linkup of Montgomery's forces and the Allied forces at Salerno. The two German divisions refitting in the Naples area, the Hermann Göring and 15th Panzer Grenadier, were ideally positioned to join the Salerno beachhead defense, building German opposition to five divisions, and/or to block the Allied advance on Naples.

The German troop dispositions and many of Berlin's orders to Kesselring (and his replies) were intercepted by Allied code breakers. Thus the Allies had a fairly good picture of what they might face at Salerno. Nonetheless, the Allies did not attempt to change either the timing of Montgomery's invasion, which would push the two German divisions northward toward Salerno, or the location of the main assault, which was now clearly pinpointed by the Germans. The hope was that complete tactical surprise could be achieved at Salerno simultaneously with an Italian surrender, thus catching the Germans at an instant of utmost political and military confusion.[5]

As the distinguished British military historian B. H. Liddell Hart has pointed out, in all of the Allied planning, no serious thought was apparently ever given to a landing on the backside of the boot, along the east coast of Italy: Brindisi, Bari, or even as far north in the Adriatic Sea as Pescara. The Apulia district was defended only by the lightly armed German 1st Parachute Division, which had no armor, few vehicles and little ammunition, and in event of trouble, was under orders to fall back on the Axis air complex at Foggia, then Rome. An Allied amphibious landing in Apulia (up the backside of the boot), combined with an airborne assault on the Foggia airfield complex, would have met almost no opposition, immediately delivered the Foggia air-base complex (and perhaps aviation fuel dumps) to the Allies and cut off the 1st Parachute Division at Bari. Kesselring's chief of staff, Siegfried Westphal, told Liddell Hart after the war that the Germans could have done little or nothing to stop an Allied landing at Pescara (one hundred miles east of Rome) or a subsequent Allied drive westward over the mountains to Rome. A successful Allied landing at Pescara and a quick drive on Rome would have cut off all six of Vietinghoff's German divisions to the south of Rome. In neglecting to go at Rome in this bold and unorthodox manner, Liddell Hart observed, the Allies failed to capitalize on their chief asset—amphibious mobility. Instead of "hitting 'em where they ain't," the Allies would hit them where they were—in greatest possible strength. They would pay a high price for this inflexibility and caution.[6]

AVALANCHE, the Salerno invasion, was to be a combined American-British landing, composed of one American corps and one British corps of very nearly equal strength. Since British General Montgomery was leading the leap across the Strait of Messina into Calabria, Eisenhower decreed that an American general should command Salerno. Both operations would be carried forward under the general supervision of Eisenhower's ground commander, Harold Alexander.

Which American general would lead AVALANCHE?

A logical choice would have been Patton or Bradley, or both. They were then managing the final American stages of the battle for Sicily and each, in his very different way, had proved to be an outstanding field commander. Eisenhower might have been well advised to replace them on Sicily with Mark Clark and Mike Dawley, to give Clark and Dawley battle experience, and give the Salerno job to Patton and Bradley. Instead, he elected to give Salerno to Clark's theretofore "administrative" Fifth Army and Mike Dawley's VI Corps, both eager but entirely green.

Owing to Allied commitments on Sicily and for OVERLORD, Clark had a choice of only two American infantry divisions to spearhead the Salerno assault. Both were National Guard divisions. One was the 34th (Minnesota), commanded by Charles W. (Doc) Ryder, a classmate of Eisenhower and Bradley's; the other was the 36th (Texas), commanded by Fred L. Walker. Ryder's 34th Division, which fought in Tunisia, had gotten a bad reputation. At one point the British had insisted that it be withdrawn from the line and retrained. But Bradley, in his all-American drive on Bizerte, had "saved" the division and it had more than proved itself by capturing a key Axis bastion, Hill 609. The 36th was a green division, newly arrived from the States. It stood high with Clark and Dawley because it had done well in training under their tutelage and because Texans had the reputation of being dependable soldiers. Moreover, Fred Walker had worked harmoniously with Clark and Dawley; they had become close. Clark thus chose the green 36th Division to spearhead the Salerno invasion, perhaps in part to prove the soundness of his own training program, perhaps in part because he had a lingering doubt about the 34th.[7]

In the initial plan, the British 10 Corps was to have been commanded by one of Montgomery's outstanding field generals, Brian Horrocks. However, when Horrocks was gravely wounded in Bizerte, he was replaced by Alexander's chief of staff, Richard L. McCreery, a cavalryman who, like Dawley, had never led a corps into combat and about whom Montgomery would say, "I doubt if Dick McCreery understands the Infantry Division." McCreery's assault forces, landing to the north, or left, of Dawley's, would be the British 46th and 56th infantry divisions, plus some British and American commandos.[8]

Both British assault divisions were relatively new to combat. The 46th had arrived in Tunisia the previous February, assigned to Anderson's British First Army. It had fought in the line for about ninety days, but it had not achieved anything outstanding. More recently, its commanding general, H. A. Freeman-Attwood, had been relieved and arrested for a security violation, causing turmoil in the staff and commands. The 56th Division had first entered combat the previous April 29 as a unit of Montgomery's Eighth Army. It had so badly fallen on its face that Montgomery was forced to report that the division had "little fighting value." Neither division had fought in Sicily.[9]*

In sum, the AVALANCHE force was woefully inadequate for the assigned task. It comprised, in total, the equivalent of about nine Allied divisions. Of the four assault infantry divisions, one (American 36th) was entirely green and one (British 56th) was of uncertain quality. The AVALANCHE forces would confront nearly the equivalent number of German divisions, based in Rome and southern Italy. Although the German divisions were widely dispersed and short of tanks and manpower, most were manned by tough veterans of Sicily, the Russian front and other battlefields. Three of the German divisions were panzers. Two were parachute infantry, which, although lightly armed, were

---

* These assault forces were backed up by more experienced troops for the exploitation phase toward Rome. Dawley would get the American 3rd and 45th infantry divisions (then fighting in Sicily) and the veteran 1st Armored Division; McCreery would get the famous British 7th Armored Division (the "Desert Rats"), plus an independent armored brigade.

considered tough and skilled combatants, no less so than American paratroopers. Moreover, Rommel was poised in northern Italy with an additional seven German divisions (two of them panzer) which could be thrown into the battle if Hitler should so decide.

Montgomery was especially displeased with Eisenhower's and Clark's plans for the invasion of Italy. "The whole affair," he wrote, "was haphazard and untidy." He would complain that there was no "master plan . . . no attempt . . . to coordinate my operation [in Calabria] with those of Fifth Army landing at Salerno. . . ." He warned that the Allied AVALANCHE forces were too weak, that Kesselring could concentrate force at the Salerno beachhead faster than Mark Clark could, and reminded Alexander that the Germans had a total of fifteen divisions (including five panzer) in Italy. He did not trust the Italians, did not believe they would fight the Germans or be of any real help to the Allies, and thus believed that Eisenhower's negotiations with them were ill-advised.[10]

At the eleventh hour, Eisenhower made the decision to reinforce Clark with airborne forces. The Allies then had available about three hundred C-47 troop transports and about four hundred Waco gliders in North Africa and Sicily, barely enough to simultaneously lift two airborne regiments with artillery. These aircraft were made available to Clark to utilize as he saw fit. Eisenhower then had to choose between the British 1st Airborne Division and the American 82nd. The 82nd got the assignment.

☆17☆

HAD THERE BEEN a Hollywood screenwriter on the staff of the 82nd Airborne Division, he would have been hard pressed to invent a more incredible or melodramatic scenario than the one the division enacted over the next seven weeks. In a report drafted not long afterward, Doc Eaton aptly described it as "a remarkable series of orders, counter-orders, plans, changes in plans, marches and counter-marches, missions and remissions, by air, water and land." Forty years later, the principal characters involved found it hard to believe that it had happened as it had.[1]

The story began in late July at Ridgway's headquarters in Trapani, Sicily. He was restive. The division was still fragmented—Gavin and Tucker in Sicily, Lewis in Kairouan, along with the Air Force troop-carrier wings. Meanwhile there were rumors that the division might be called upon for another airborne mission. Ridgway believed it was imperative that the division be reassembled into a single body and commence intensive training with the troop-carrier pilots and that if the rumors were true, he be informed as soon as possible about the plans. He conveyed his feelings to his then immediate boss, George Patton. Patton concurred and suggested that Ridgway write a letter directly to Eisenhower. Ridgway did so on July 26.

To expedite matters, three days later, on July 29, Ridgway flew to Eisenhower's headquarters in Algiers and presented the letter to Eisenhower in person. Eisenhower confirmed that Mark Clark wanted to use the division in AVALANCHE and that he had approved, but he did not know the details. He suggested that Ridgway call on Mark Clark. That very same afternoon, Ridgway flew to Clark's headquarters in Oujda and learned exactly what Mark Clark and his chief of staff, Al Gruenther, had in mind. He found that Bill Yarborough, whom Ridgway had relieved of command, was now Clark's chief airborne adviser.[2]

The plan Yarborough had cooked up was breathtaking. Most of the division (both parachute regiments and the glider regiment) was to be committed (in multiple lifts) ahead of the invasion force to capture the towns of Nocera and Sarno, which lay just to the north of the Sorrento mountains. The purpose of the airborne mission was twofold: to block the movement of the Hermann Göring and 15th Panzer Grenadier divisions in the Naples area to prevent their using the Sorrento mountain passes to reach the Salerno beachhead; and to assist McCreery's British 10 Corps breakout from the beachhead toward Naples through those same passes. The plan envisioned the use of both parachutists and glierists plus a "small seaborne task force" (from the division) which would land amphibiously in the Amalfi-Maiori area, link up with the airborne forces, and provide a supply route and a means of evacuating the dead and wounded. It would be a night operation like Sicily, taking advantage of moonset.

After a quick study of the plan, Ridgway concluded that it would be very difficult—and risky—but not impossibly so. However, to pull it off, he believed the division had to train relentlessly with the troop-carrier pilots in night parachute and glider operations, to say nothing of amphibious operations. Eaton wrote that "not one individual in the entire Division, officer or enlisted man, had ever had any experience or instruction in amphibious operations."

Ridgway next flew back to Algiers to confer with Eisenhower's G-3, Lowell W. Rooks, on these problems. He insisted that his division must have a minimum of three weeks of intensive training with the troop-carrier pilots and amphibious forces. This demand presented two serious bureaucratic problems. First, Rooks had to find troops to relieve the Gavin and Tucker regiments of occupation duty on Sicily. Second, he had to find shipping to move the two regiments back from Sicily to Tunisia. All this had to be expedited, because the Air Force troop-carrier forces in Tunisia would soon be moving forward to Sicily to stage for the operation—but not soon enough to carry out the airborne training on Sicily.

Dealing with Eisenhower's vast headquarters was not unlike dealing with the Pentagon. Ridgway came away with written assurances that the division would—just barely—get its necessary three weeks' training in Tunisia. However, to make certain that it would really happen, Ridgway decided to post Max Taylor and a small contingent in Algiers. Ridgway returned to Trapani, and on August 2 Taylor established a beachhead in the St. George's Hotel in Algiers. In addition, Taylor was to serve as division liaison officer with Mark Clark's advanced Fifth Army headquarters in Algiers.[3]

On close inspection, the Nocera-Sarno plan appeared even more difficult than at first glance. The planners had by now accumulated hundreds of excellent detailed aerial photographs of the proposed drop area. These photographs were highly disconcerting on several counts. They showed that the proposed flight path over the coastline (between Mount Vesuvius and the Sorrento mountains) was so infested with enemy antiaircraft batteries as to make it unusable. The only alternative was to fly over the forbidding five-thousand-foot Sorrento mountain range. But that way would compel the pilots to release gliders and parachutists at extremely high altitudes (about six thousand feet and two thousand feet, respectively), which would make for a very long, vulnerable descent in the pitch dark and in the uncertain wind currents generated by mountain masses. Moreover, there were very few suitable DZs and LZs near Nocera and Sarno.

Nonetheless, planning proceeded in feverish haste. In his account of those days, Doc Eaton observed: "The Division Commander flew almost in circles, again and again, from his Division Command Post at Trapani, 600-odd miles to his planning staff at Fifth Army Headquarters, Algiers, thence over 400 miles to his Division Command Post at Kairouan, thence almost 300 miles to his Division Command Post at Trapani."[4]

On Sicily itself, the two parachute regiments were scattered in six separate locations. To keep Gavin and Tucker up to date on the secret planning, Ridgway flew back and forth between them in his own two-place Piper Cub airplane. He had a pilot, but he often took the "front seat" controls. On one of these flights when he had the controls, he very nearly killed himself. As he was taking off in a short field, he saw "piles of scrap" lying in his path. When he swerved to avoid them, a wingtip struck a tall cactus. This skewed the plane off course and directly toward some stone houses. "Perhaps I had no narrower escape during the war," Ridgway recalled. "We cleared the roof of a house on the field by inches." He never again took the controls.[5]

Days flew by. For unaccountable reasons, the promised orders from Lowell Rooks to move the two regiments to Tunisia for training did not materialize. The staff grew nearly frantic with anxiety. The paratroopers on Sicily had nothing but the clothes and weapons they had jumped with. Many weapons and pieces of equipment had been lost or were worn out. All of the men had to be reclothed and reequipped. In addition, there were "better than 1,000" replacements in Tunisia who had to be integrated into the parachute units. Time was running out.

Finally word came on August 12, but it was far from what had been expected. Owing to the extreme difficulties of the Nocera-Sarno operation, Mark Clark had canceled it. Some other objective would be substituted; the division, as Doc Eaton put it, would definitely be "employed, somehow, somewhere." This message evoked further anxiety. The AVALANCHE invasion date had been set for early morning, September 9. That was only twenty-seven days away. The division had no new objective and had not yet received the promised orders to move the two parachute regiments back to Tunisia.[6]

There was more agonizing waiting. Then, on August 18, orders arrived identifying the new objective. The plan was so bold, so risky, that at first few could believe it. It called for committing the division by air and amphibious assault at Capua, a key road hub on the Volturno River, about eighteen miles due *north* of Naples and forty miles from the Salerno beachhead. The mission was to block the movement of German forces from Rome to Naples so that McCreery's 10 Corps could more easily take Naples. The two parachute regiments would jump; some 130 gliders would bring in artillery, antitank weapons and ammunition. Lewis's glider infantry regiment would embark in twenty-five landing craft well beforehand, make an amphibious landing at the mouth of the Volturno and march overland about fifteen miles and link up with the paratroopers in the airhead. After that, the division would fight as a complete unit. McCreery's 46th Division would break through to Capua, it was hoped within five days at the most.

Along with these new orders finally came authorization to move the division headquarters and the two parachute regiments to Tunisia. It was too late to carry out the much-needed three weeks of intensive training, but Ridgway was determined to train as much as possible in the time left. The movement orders specified that Ridgway should work out the transfer with Patton's Seventh Army staff. Accordingly, he sent the division planners to Palermo to confer. The best movement that could be arranged was one that would take days and days: by truck to Palermo, by sea to Bizerte, thence by truck to Kairouan, Tunisia.

Ridgway quite properly viewed the plan as absurd. He flew at once to Algiers and badgered higher-ups into moving the Sicily-based elements of the division by air. On the afternoon of August 19, he flew back to western Sicily to inform Doc Eaton, Gavin and Tucker of the new movement plan and to say that the aircraft would commence arriving the following morning. The ensuing night was frantic. The division had only twenty-five trucks and about fifty jeeps in Sicily with which to round up and deliver the men and equipment to the designated departure airfields at Borizzo and Castelvetrano. And yet the job got done. On August 20 and 21, the Sicily-based elements returned to Tunisia in a shuttle of Hal Clark's and Ray Dunn's C-47s. The division staffers who had been in Palermo working with Patton's headquarters on the complex truck-ship-truck movement plan arrived back just in time to board the last plane for Tunisia. Official orders approving this plan came through three days after all hands had already assembled in Tunisia!

The size and scope of the Volturno mission dictated that both Clark's 52nd and Dunn's 51st troop-carrier wings would be employed. The planes would stage from nine widely separated airfields in Sicily. Due to the complexity of the aircraft restaging from Tunisia to Sicily, this movement had to commence no later than September 1. This left only one week for training with the division. Eaton wrote: "Gone was the opportunity for any real air-ground training. It was impossible to parachute, rescue parachutes and repack them in time for the impending operation." However, Ridgway managed to work in "some four days" of night-jump training "to a fairly satisfactory degree." The actual parachute training was limited mostly to jumpmasters and to replacements who had never made a night jump.

Much of the training that week was devoted to the new concept of using pathfinders to mark the DZs. Four devices had been developed for pathfinder operations: a brilliant battery-operated beacon known as the "Krypton light"; a radio transmitter, the 5G, on which the C-47 transports could home; and a more sophisticated electronic device, the Eureka, a portable radar beacon which transmitted range and bearing to the DZ to a receiver in the aircraft called the Rebecca. The electronics in all aircraft were modified to receive the 5G radio homing signals; sixteen pathfinder aircraft were equipped with Rebeccas to receive the Eureka radar signal.

Tests of this array of gear on the nights of August 28 and 29 brought mixed results. The Krypton light was supposedly visible up to thirty miles. However, it was found that a ground haze or moderate cloud cover greatly diminished the range at which it could be seen. The 5G radio beacon homing test was a complete flop. Interference from a nearby high-frequency radio transmitter blanked out the signals. However, the tests of the Eureka-Rebecca system showed great promise. On the first night, the pathfinder pilots picked up the Eureka signal at ranges of fifteen to twenty miles, and three air groups flew precisely over the DZ. The test on the second night, when token pathfinder parachutists jumped, led to the conclusion that had there been a mass jump, some 90 percent of the paratroopers would have come down within one mile of the DZ.[7]

During that same frantic week, Harry Lewis' glider infantry regiment made hurried preparations to convert itself into an amphibious landing force. The original plan was that the regiment had to load and sail by September 5. On August 25, the regiment moved to Bizerte for amphibious training, but the promised landing craft were not on hand. When these finally arrived, there were only a few days left for "intensive training." Even this crowded schedule was cut short. New orders arrived directing that the regiment had to have all its equipment, ammo and vehicles waterproofed and loaded and be fully prepared to set sail by 4 P.M., September 3.

Ridgway had decided that he, Taylor, Eaton and other key members of the division staff would go with the amphibious force to the Volturno River. They would remain at Kairouan until September 2, working with the airborne elements, then rush to Bizerte and jump aboard a landing craft. Ridgway designated Jim Gavin airborne task force commander and gave him complete responsibility for planning the parachute and glider phase of the operation. To this was added yet another responsibility. Mark Clark, at Bill Yarborough's instigation, added a second, smaller, independent airborne operation: Doyle Yardley's independent 509 Battalion, which was still administratively attached to the 82nd Airborne Division but which had never left Tunisia, would jump at either Nocera, Sarno, Minturno, Battipaglia or Avellino to do whatever damage and blocking it could.[8]

In the meantime, Mark Clark's American naval advisers had been studying the proposed amphibious landing of the glider regiment at the mouth of the Volturno River more closely. Taking a good look at a recent batch of aerial photographs, the naval planners discovered that the mouth was laced with reefs and shoals. It soon became apparent that the plan to land the glider regiment there in LSTs and LCIs was unfeasible. They considered the idea of scaling down the operation to one battalion, then merely one company, but it was decided that not even this could be done. Accordingly, the seaborne element of the Volturno River operation was canceled at the very last minute. Clark intended to use the regiment as part of his general floating reserve at Salerno, but Lewis was not informed of this. He and his troops at Bizerte continued waterproofing and loading weapons and gear and vehicles, preparing for the September 3 departure.

The Navy's decision meant that the Volturno River airborne mission could not be carried out unless Gavin's troops could be supplied ammo, food and other equipment solely by air. Gavin estimated he would need about 175 tons a day to sustain his force. To provide that tonnage, Hal Clark and Ray Dunn would have to use about half of all their C-47s—some 145. These planes would have to fly a set route at night without any escort over territory alive with enemy antiaircraft emplacements and fighters and drop supplies in darkness precisely where Gavin signaled they were most urgently needed. To succeed, Gavin later wrote, would "require an almost incredible amount of good luck."

Indeed so. The more Ridgway thought about the plan the less he liked it. On August 31, when all the AVALANCHE commanders gathered with Eisenhower at Mostaganem for a final briefing, Ridgway had a private talk with Eisenhower's air chief, Arthur Tedder. Ridgway forcibly expressed his reservations, insisting that the Capua plan was "tactically unsound" and would subject his men to an "unreasonable risk." After hearing him out, Tedder replied: "I think you're right. Why don't you tell Clark what you told me?"

Ridgway then privately presented his reservations to Clark, who was disappointed but reasonable. The outcome of these talks was a compromise. A Capua mission would proceed, but in drastically modified form. One reduced regiment (of two battalions) would make the jump. The men would carry enough supplies (ammo, food, etc.) with them to last at least five days, by which time it was believed the major land forces could link up. That same day, Clark issued formal orders modifying the mission.[9]

These decisions dramatically curtailed the role of the 82nd Airborne Division in the invasion of Italy. As of September 2, the plan was that Gavin would jump with two battalions at Capua on the Volturno River; Yardley and the 509th Battalion would probably jump at Avellino. That kept six of Ridgway's eight infantry battalions unemployed in airborne operations, including the whole of Lewis' glider regiment, which had now been vaguely shunted off into the Salerno floating reserve. After all the priming for battle, it was a bitter disappointment.

Eisenhower, meanwhile, had been continuing the secret, complex negotiations with Badoglio's emissary, Giuseppe Castellano. One of the big issues in these talks was the question of ensuring the survival of the king, Badoglio and the other conspirators in Rome, and the city itself. Castellano raised again the possibility of an airborne drop on Rome. There were four or five (one could hope) loyal Italian divisions near Rome. The Germans had stripped these divisions of much ammo and fuel and antitank weapons on various pretexts, but Castellano claimed they still had enough power to support an Allied airborne operation on Rome. They could probably guarantee the safety of four to six airfields in and around Rome, and provide transportation for the paratroopers.[10]

Eisenhower was smitten by this rather nebulous scheme. So was his salty chief naval commander, British Admiral of the Fleet Andrew B. Cunningham. The latter became so enthusiastic, in fact, that he proposed sending landing craft and even destroyers up the Tiber River with ammo and supplies, a maneuver resembling the original Volturno River plan. On September 1, Eisenhower approved the scheme and formally notified the Combined Chiefs and his ground commander, Harold Alexander. From President Roosevelt and Prime Minister Churchill came an enthusiastic endorsement. Since the 82nd Airborne Division was already "integrated with AVALANCHE," Eisenhower's first instinct was to give Hopkinson's 1st Airborne Division the "Rome job," but they were practically on the docks, technically in AVALANCHE reserve but in reality awaiting shipment to Britain. The 82nd Division was deployed on Tunisian airfields. Within a few hours, Eisenhower changed his mind and assigned the "Rome job" to Ridgway.[11]

This momentous news reached the division staff on September 2. The first to learn about it was Max Taylor, still serving as liaison officer at the various higher headquarters. Early that morning he was summoned to Alexander's headquarters in an olive grove at Cassibile, south of Syracuse, Sicily. Later that same day, Alexander called Ridgway to Cassibile. Ridgway set off with his G-3, Whitfield Jack, and a few others. By the time he reached Cassibile, late that day, Taylor had drawn up a rough plan of sorts and set forth the principal problems involved in the operation. The gist of the plan was that the division would commit the maximum force the troop-carrier command could lift. Since Rome was beyond glider tow range, the planes would drop paratroopers and airland Lewis' glider regiment. The troopers would aim for three airfields immediately east and northeast of Rome on the night of September 8, several hours ahead of the Salerno invasion. On successive nights, the rest of the division (including Lewis' glider regiment) would be brought in by air. In "conjunction with Italian forces in the area," the division would defend Rome against a German takeover.

Right from the start, Ridgway had the greatest misgivings about the "Rome job." He thought it was a "hare-brained scheme." In the first place, there was hardly any time left to plan and get it organized. It was now September 2; only six days remained before Rome D day. The two troop-carrier wings were in process of deploying to the nine airfields on Sicily, preparing for the last assigned missions. Once established on Sicily, the planes would have to return to Tunisia and transfer the entire 82nd Division to the Sicily airfields. This movement would now include Lewis' glider regiment, still uninformed about any new plans and still loading aboard landing craft in Bizerte for the original (canceled) Volturno River mission. Once Clark and Dunn were prepared to do so, it would take at least two full days to move the division to Sicily. This would leave almost no time for joint planning with Clark and Dunn. There was not even time for the division to deplane once it reached Sicily. The men would have to combat-load in Kairouan and stay on the planes in Sicily while they refueled and then proceed to Rome. By the time the troops reached Rome, they would be tired and frazzled.[12]

Even if all this could be arranged in time, what lay beyond Sicily was frightening to contemplate.

● First, a long over-water flight in darkness and an uncertain landfall on the Italian coast near Rome. On the HUSKY invasion, the four Air Force missions over water at night had been navigational nightmares. The pilots, diverted to other tasks since then, had not received the recommended—or demanded—further training. There would be no time to rehearse an over-water flight to Rome.

● Second, the transports would have no escorts on the approach to Rome. It lay beyond range of most fighters; even those that could reach it (P-38s) could not stay long enough to provide a meaningful umbrella. Besides that, how many fighters could be spared from AVALANCHE to provide the escort? Every troop-transport aircraft would be easy prey for enemy fighters.

● Third, the route to Rome would take the planes over the area occupied by the German 2nd Parachute Division, which was well equipped with antiaircraft guns. There was seemingly no way to avoid this fire or probable fire from Italian antiaircraft emplacements. It could be a perfect slaughter—like the 504's jump into Sicily.

● Fourth, the whole operation would depend on the cooperation of the Italians. Could they really guarantee the safety of the airfields, and would they provide transportation and then help repulse the Germans? So far as was known, the Italians had not fought with any spirit since the collapse of the Afrika Korps in Tunisia; certainly not in Sicily—unless the Germans had held a gun to their heads. Could the Allies risk the lives of eight thousand men on the word of one Italian general? What if he was lying or overstating the extent of Italian "cooperation"?

● Fifth, the follow-up reinforcing and resupply missions would be extremely dangerous and uncertain. By the second night, the Germans would be on full alert with both fighters and antiaircraft for such missions, and with Rome in the balance, they would no doubt mount a maximum effort. The possibility had to be faced that the D-day paratroopers might be isolated, dependent entirely on the Italians, an uncertain prospect.

● Finally, what if the Germans decided to let Salerno and Naples go and fell back on the Volturno River or Rome with all six divisions then in the South of Italy? The 82nd Division might successfully seize Rome but then find itself trapped behind a stout German line which Mark Clark could not break through with double the force earmarked for AVALANCHE. If so, Rome would be a suicide mission for the 82nd Airborne Division.[13]

Mark Clark arrived at Alexander's headquarters the following day, September 3. He was dismayed and angry that Eisenhower had withdrawn the 82nd Airborne from his slim AVALANCHE forces. He had been counting on Lewis' glider regiment as part of his floating reserve. Lewis was due to sail from Bizerte for the Salerno operation within a few hours. He had now to stop that departure and substitute another regiment. He radioed Lewis to meet him at the Bizerte airfield and took off. He arrived at Bizerte at about 2 P.M., two hours before Lewis was scheduled to sail for what Lewis still believed was the Volturno River operation, long since canceled.[14]

For security reasons, Clark did not mention that Lewis was now scheduled for the Rome operation. Eaton wrote: "Colonel Lewis was instructed that his amphibious mission had been canceled, that all of the assault craft were urgently needed for another mission involving other troops and that all of his troops, supplies, vehicles, etc. now being loaded must be cleared off the craft not later than 1900 [7 P.M.] that afternoon. Back to the amphibious loading area went Colonel Lewis as fast as his jeep would take him. It was a bitter disappointment to all of the officers and men, but in the best tradition of the Division all hands turned to and unloaded and cleared all the craft in record time." Lewis and his men bivouacked on the beach ten miles from Bizerte.

Later that evening, Lewis received orders to move to an airfield at Mateur and prepare to enplane his troops for Sicily. A regiment from Troy Middleton's 45th Division took over the landing craft and became part of Clark's floating reserve.[15]

That same day, September 3, Montgomery made the short leap (Operation BAYTOWN) across the Strait of Messina into Calabria. It was the fourth anniversary of World War II, and the Allies were now back on the European continent. To dramatize the anniversary, Montgomery's crossing was well staged. It was preceded by a massive (and completely unnecessary) artillery bombardment utilizing some six hundred Army and Navy guns, wasting thousands of rounds of valuable artillery shells, and an equally unnecessary aerial bombardment. The British 13 Corps, commanded by Miles Dempsey and composed of the 1st Canadian and 5th British infantry divisions, reinforced by an armored brigade and an infantry brigade and some commando units, met no opposition in the landing.[16]

The crossing proved to be a valuable intelligence for Albert Kesselring. It was a clear signal that the Allies were now moving on Italy. He knew very well that Montgomery's was not the main effort—that with all the amphibious and air power available, the Allies would not stupidly crawl up the leg like a harvest bug. An invasion at Salerno was the next obvious step. As planned, he signaled Tenth Army commander Vietinghoff to order the two German divisions in Calabria, the 26th Panzer and the 29th Panzer Grenadier, to fall back toward Salerno in a delaying action.

In sum, Montgomery's crossing into Calabria divided Allied forces, with no follow-up plan to reunite them; employed valuable landing craft which could have been used to strengthen AVALANCHE; wasted valuable artillery ammunition and air power; tipped off Kesselring that the Allies were moving on Italy, giving him plenty of time to alert his forces and dig in at Salerno; and pushed two German divisions back on Salerno.

☆18☆

RIDGWAY AND HIS RETINUE remained encamped at Alexander's headquarters in Cassibile from September 2 to September 4. On the evening of September 3 —the day of Montgomery's crossing into Calabria—Castellano, acting for the Badoglio government, signed the armistice instrument. As part of the deal, Bedell Smith, who was acting for Eisenhower, unequivocally assured Castellano that an American airborne division would drop on Rome and, in conjunction with Italian forces, prevent a takeover of the city and thus ensure the safety of the king and the Badoglio government.[1]

Ridgway and Taylor were torn. Everything about the Rome mission smelled of disaster. And yet it was tough to oppose Roosevelt, Churchill, Eisenhower, Alexander and Smith, who had enthusiastically endorsed it. It had become a key Allied commitment to the armistice agreement. As Doc Eaton wrote: "American troops *had* to land in Rome. The armistice had been signed, sealed and delivered with that understanding. Only the most unlooked for complications could justify the non-performance of an airborne invasion of Rome."[2]

That evening, Castellano met without interruption for ten and a half hours with Ridgway, Max Taylor, Lowell Rooks, Ray Dunn and other American staff officers to go over the airborne operation. Castellano laid out the exact positions of the major German units in and around Rome and his plans to thwart their movements with four or five Italian divisions. He produced maps showing the location of six small airfields, none then actually occupied by the Germans, which Ridgway could use to parachute and airland the division. He assured Ridgway that these fields could be held by the Italians, that Italian antiaircraft gunners would not fire on Allied planes, that navigational aids would be provided, that the airfields and runways would be lighted and that adequate transportation would be furnished at the airfields, under control of high-ranking Italian officers.

Ridgway and Taylor remained deeply skeptical. They pressed with question after question, particularly with reference to Italian and German antiaircraft emplacements. Under pressure, Castellano conceded that the original proposed air route (along the south bank of the Tiber River) was infested with both German and Italian antiaircraft emplacements and he could not guarantee that he could silence them. He also conceded that the best two of the proposed six airfields lay in the midst of heavy antiaircraft defenses. In a memo for the record, Ridgway later wrote: "During these prolonged conversations the deep-rooted fear of the Italian representatives of German armed forces became more and more apparent. They would give no assurance of their ability to withstand a German attack, or even to guarantee complete elimination of German antiaircraft defenses in the Rome area in the approach corridors by which the airborne forces had to reach the airfields." In his memoir *Soldier*, Ridgway put it this way: "I knew in my heart they could not, and would not, meet the commitments they were making."[3]

As the long night wore on, a new plan took shape, designed principally to avoid German antiaircraft defenses. Rather than drop into the heart of Rome, the spearhead paratroopers of the division would utilize two airfields twenty-five miles to the northwest of Rome and very close to the Mediterranean shoreline. These fields, at Furbara and Cerveteri, were absolutely in Italian hands. There were no German forces in the immediate vicinity. The amphibious force (if there was to be an amphibious force—this was not yet settled) could link up without a heroic, and perhaps suicidal, fight up the Tiber River. The pilots could make a landfall and locate the coastal fields more easily than fields in the dense urban Rome area, and if everything went wrong, as seemed highly possible, the spearhead could conceivably withdraw into a beachhead perimeter with some hope of a Dunkirk-type evacuation carried out at night.

Even this less risky plan did not satisfy Ridgway. On the morning of September 4, when conversation with Castellano was resumed, Ridgway found "Italian fear of the German forces was conspicuous." He and Taylor became unshakably convinced that the division could not rely on Italian promises of help.[4]

Troubled in mind and spirit, Ridgway sought out his old friend Bedell Smith. They sat down beneath an olive tree out of earshot of the others. Ridgway unburdened his soul to him. "I stated," he later wrote in a memo, "that I felt it my responsibility as Division Commander to express my views frankly on the contemplated mission; that within the past few days the Division had been assigned two different missions in a distant area; and that now with only four full days for preparation, two of which would have to be employed for air movement of the Division from Tunisia to Sicily, I was about to receive a mission involving the employment of over three hundred aircraft in a new area. I stated that in my opinion this mission, under these conditions, violated every sound principle we had developed in our training, and that my conscience compelled me to state my strong objections." On reflection, Bedell Smith "supported this view" and suggested Ridgway take up the matter with Alexander himself.[5]

Ridgway well knew that given the high-level enthusiasm for the "Rome job" and the commitment to the Badoglio government, his objections to it would come, as he later wrote, "at the risk of my career." He did not hesitate to lay his career on the line. He went immediately to Alexander and spelled out his objections. Ridgway later wrote that he was "shocked" by Alexander's reaction: "General Alexander treated the whole matter in a cavalier fashion, making light of the enemy situation, apparently giving full faith to the Italian guarantees of full military support, and exhibiting startling ignorance of the logistics of airborne operations . . . [he] stated in substance that the armistice had been agreed to by the Italians solely on the condition that immediately after its announcement Italian troops in the Rome area would be supported by strong allied airborne forces, and that without this condition the Italians would not have signed. For this reason General Alexander stated it was imperative that airborne forces be sent . . ."[6]

Ridgway did, however, score one point. Alexander accepted Ridgway's judgment that a division-size operation on D day would be impossible to work out in the time remaining (four days) and conceded that "a much smaller force would be satisfactory." Ridgway thereupon proposed a D-day force of one parachute regiment (less one battalion), reinforced by parachute artillery, similar to the force Gavin had been priming for the now canceled Volturno River operation. If this force landed without disaster, it would be followed up in successive nights with the other paratroopers and airlanded forces. Ridgway himself would jump with the D-day regiment.[7]

Ridgway would never forget Alexander's last words as he dismissed him: "Don't give this another thought, Ridgway. Contact will be made with your division in three days—five at the most."[8]

Earlier in the discussions, Ridgway had suggested that an American, or several Americans, be smuggled into Rome to conduct a firsthand assessment of the military situation and the firmness of the Italian resolve to help his paratroopers. Fearing it might jeopardize the secrecy of the operation, Alexander had vetoed that idea. Now that the operation was definitely on, Ridgway again proposed the idea, and this time Alexander approved it, provided it was carried out at the very last moment. Max Taylor volunteered to go. He would be accompanied by Colonel William T. Gardiner, the intelligence officer of Ray Dunn's 51st Troop Carrier Wing. Gardiner, a Harvard graduate (1914), was a fifty-three-year-old New York lawyer (and sports pilot) who had been governor of Maine for one term.[9]

Later that day—September 4—Ridgway flew back to the 82nd Airborne Division "advanced CP" in Bizerte. He worked feverishly all the remainder of the day and most of the night on plans for Rome and on plans for moving the division to staging bases in Sicily. The final Rome plan was as follows. Rube Tucker's 504th Regiment (less Adams' 3rd Battalion), reinforced with some artillery or antitank batteries, engineers and medics, etc., would jump into the coastal airfields (Cerveteri and Furbara) early on the evening of September 8 and "push to Rome." On the second night, Gavin's full 505 would jump onto three airfields in the Rome area: Guidonia, Littorio and Centocelle. On the third night, they would airland Lewis' glider regiment at these fields or others.[10]

The proposed airlanding phase of the operation was in many respects the most uncertain and risky. The designated airfields in Rome were not, in fact, first-class bases but, rather, small airstrips with single grass or dirt runways. Under the most ideal training conditions (daylight, good weather, flawless air traffic control, etc.) the airborne forces had never been able to airland more than thirty-six transports (or one battalion of men) per hour. Gavin judged they would be lucky to do half as well in far-off Rome in darkness. That meant that if all went perfectly—a dubious and dangerous assumption—it would take about six hours to airland Lewis' men, plus the equivalent of a battalion of engineers, signal technicians, medics, etc.

There were many unknowns and dangers. How could they exercise the necessary air traffic control in the landings? What if a C-47 broke a landing gear or blew a tire or, worse, cracked up or was shot to pieces on landing and blocked the single runway? How would they remove the wreckage in time so the others, which could not circle for very long, could come in? Gavin concluded that, realistically, they could not count on airlanding more than a "relatively small" number of men each night, and thus the airlanding operation would take several nights. This, in turn, meant a piecemeal commitment of the regiment, the worst possible way to enter battle, and, of course, a delay in total commitment of the full power of the division.[11]

The next day—September 5—Eisenhower's headquarters, which had previously vetoed any amphibious support, now about-faced and authorized a "small seaborne task force" which would land at the mouth of the Tiber River. This "little flotilla" would ultimately consist of one LST and three LCIs. It would land an artillery battalion, three antiaircraft batteries, one company of infantry, and two antitank platoons. Ridgway chose William H. Bertsch, from Taylor's Division Artillery Section, to command this force. It was quickly organized in Bizerte under the supervision of Harry Lewis, who, based on his two weeks' experience in amphibious operations, was now the division's resident expert on such matters.[12]

That same day, Ridgway commenced staging the division to Sicily by air. The movement comprised all major units, including the independent 509th Battalion, which was still tentatively scheduled for an independent drop near Avellino and would also stage from Sicily. This giant shuttle, carried out by the 51st and 52nd troop-carrier wings, required the better part of three days, September 5, 6 and 7. One of the last men to leave North Africa was Harry Lewis, who remained with Bertsch's "little flotilla" in Bizerte until the very last minute. Ridgway established his roving CP on an airfield at Licata, on the south shore of Sicily, where the troop-carrier command was temporarily headquartered. Here, and at a dozen other airfields on Sicily, the 504th, 505th and 325th regiments made last-minute preparations for the Rome operation.[13]

Max Taylor and Bill Gardiner set off on the daring trip to Rome from Palermo at 2 A.M. on September 7. A British PT boat took them forty miles north of Palermo, to the island of Ustica. There they rendezvoused with an Italian corvette, *Ibis,* which took them aboard and carried them the remaining 175 miles to the port of Gaeta. Before debarking, they wet their uniforms to give themselves the appearance of shot-down aviators rescued from the sea. They were escorted by armed Italians, who treated them "roughly" for public consumption. They climbed into an Italian Navy sedan and drove off. On the outskirts of Gaeta they transferred to a military ambulance with frosted windows for the seventy-five-mile drive to Rome along the Appian Way. They passed numerous German patrols but were not challenged. Just after dark they entered Rome and later that evening met with several high-ranking Italian generals. Still later, in the early hours of September 8, they met with Badoglio himself, at his private villa. They conducted the talks in French.[14]

The Italians were unanimously gloomy. The Germans, they said, had recently been increasing their forces around Rome. There were now some twelve thousand paratroopers in the 2nd Division. They were equipped with one hundred 88 mm guns which could be used either as antiaircraft weapons or artillery pieces. The 3rd Panzer Grenadier Division had been beefed up to twenty-four thousand men, with one hundred fifty heavy and fifty light tanks. Moreover, the Germans had sharply cut supplies of gas and ammunition to the Italian divisions. The Italian Motorized Corps, on which the paratroops were counting for transportation, was virtually immobile and had ammo enough for only a few hours of combat. The Italians could not possibly support an Allied airborne assault on Rome. Badoglio renounced the armistice terms Castellano had signed in Cassibile, categorically refusing to publicly announce the armistice that night—September 8—as agreed by Castellano. He needed much more time to get his ducks in a row—days.

One big problem was that, for security reasons, Castellano had not been told the time or place of the Allied amphibious landing, which would take place at Salerno within about twenty-four hours. Unaware of this, Badoglio felt no sense of urgency. He believed the Allied landings were at least some days away and he was not going to announce an armistice well beforehand. That would be suicidal. Although Taylor was under explicit orders not to reveal the time or place of the Salerno landings, he "hinted at the imminence of the invasion and urgency of the armistice in sufficiently clear terms" to convey to Badoglio that "it was a matter of hours rather than days." Hearing this, Badoglio appeared shocked. And yet the news did not noticeably spur him to action. The Italians set little store by an Allied landing so far from Rome as Salerno and in such little strength. What the Italians wanted was a very strong Allied amphibious landing near Rome (Anzio, Ostia or Civitavecchia), *followed up* by an airborne assault on Rome.

The Salerno invasion had been premised on an Italian declaration of surrender immediately beforehand and the "Rome job" on the same declaration, plus Italian cooperation. Now, as Taylor saw, neither would be forthcoming. He attempted to persuade and intimidate Badoglio into carrying out Castellano's commitment, but got nowhere. Thereafter, at 1:21 A.M., September 8, he radioed a message from Badoglio—and a separate one from himself—to Eisenhower through clandestine Italian channels stating that there would be no armistice announcement and that since the Italians could not guarantee the airfields, the airborne operation on Rome was "impossible." Later, at 8:20 A.M., Taylor sent another radio message repeating the substance of the first two messages and adding some further useful intelligence. Fearing that these messages might have been delayed in the encoding and decoding process or perhaps even killed by the Italians, at 11:35 A.M. he sent yet another message on his own portable radio transmitter. The message contained the codeword "innocuous," a prearranged signal that the Rome airdrop was impossible and had to be canceled.

Later in the afternoon, word came from Eisenhower's headquarters for Taylor and Gardiner to return to Algiers immediately, in an Italian aircraft, as previously arranged. They got back into the ambulance and were driven to Rome's Centocelle airfield, where an old trimotor plane awaited. For Taylor, this two-hour flight to North Africa was the most nerve-racking part of the mission. Both the Italian and Allied air forces had been warned to give the plane safe passage, but still, as he wrote, there was a "high probability of error" in such a hastily arranged flight from enemy to friendly skies. However, all went well and Taylor and Gardiner reached the Algiers airport safely at about 7 P.M.

Eisenhower, of course, was furious. On receipt of Taylor's message, he sent a blistering one to Badoglio over the secret radio network. He stated that he intended to proceed with the public announcement of the armistice late that afternoon as agreed and that if the Italians failed to cooperate, "I will publish to the world the full record of this affair." (Thus virtually guaranteeing Badoglio's execution by the Germans.) He "temporarily suspended" the airborne operation on Rome at Badoglio's "earnest representation" but demanded "full information on which to plan earliest airborne operations" against Rome. If Badoglio failed to carry out the obligations Castellano had agreed to, Eisenhower went on, "the most serious consequences for your country" would ensue, including the dissolution of the Italian "government and nation."[15]

Ridgway knew nothing of all this. During September 8, as Taylor was relaying his messages to Eisenhower and Eisenhower was blistering Badoglio, the division prepared to descend on Rome.

The first elements to leave were the three slower LCIs of Bertsch's "little flotilla" in Bizerte. They sailed, as scheduled, on the morning of September 8. Bertsch, in the faster LST, would sail the following morning. He and his naval commanders had sealed orders directing them to point "FF" on an "unknown map." In actuality, "FF" (as Bertsch suspected) was a beach at the mouth of the Tiber River. If no one met him at "FF" they were to proceed to "GG," a point halfway up the Tiber River to Rome.[16]

At the dozen airfields on Sicily, the paratroopers spent the day making final preparations to enplane and depart. Ridgway's "go" signal, expected at about 5:45 P.M., was to be the two public radio broadcasts, first by Eisenhower, then by Badoglio, announcing the Italian armistice. Late that afternoon at Licata, Ridgway, Doc Eaton and some other staffers went over to Ray Dunn and Hal Clark's CP to listen on a special radio receiver. Near the appointed time of the broadcast, the radio set failed. Doc Eaton scurried about and found a small commercial radio. They tuned in and waited.

Fearing a communications breakdown, Eisenhower's headquarters had sent a high-level messenger, Brigadier General Lyman L. Lemnitzer, to Ridgway to notify him the "Rome job" had been "postponed." On the trip from North Africa, the pilot became confused, then lost, and not until Mount Etna loomed up in his windshield did he get his bearings. He swung southwest and set a course for Licata.[17]

In the meantime, two telephone calls came over Air Force lines at the Licata CP, both indicating a drastic change in plans. The first informed them that the

Rome drop had been postponed twenty-four hours. The second said that Lemnitzer would be arriving at five-thirty with detailed instructions. By the time Lemnitzer arrived, sixty-two planes carrying paratroopers for Rome had warmed engines and were preparing to taxi into take-off positions. Ridgway and Dunn raced out on the field to meet Lemnitzer, who outlined the situation —conveyed the essence of Taylor's report that the Rome drop was "impossible"—and said operations were not to be commenced until further orders. Doc Eaton rushed out and personally stopped one group of pathfinders from taking off.

The paratroopers deplaned—an indescribable anticlimax. Ridgway requested that Lemnitzer notify Bertsch's "small flotilla" to abort the seaborne mission to "FF" and/or "GG." Mark Clark diverted the flotilla to Salerno to support the British commandos and American rangers who would land at Maiori. Later that same evening, word came to cancel the Rome drop. It was dead.[18]

At 6:30 P.M., Eisenhower made his broadcast. He said the Italian Government had "surrendered its forces unconditionally," that he had granted "a military armistice," that the Italian Government had bound itself to those terms "without reservation" and that "all Italians who now act to help eject the German aggressor from Italian soil will have the assistance and support of the United Nations." When Badoglio did not come on the air to confirm the deal, Eisenhower authorized the broadcast of the statement Badoglio was to have made. At 7:45 P.M.—one hour late—Badoglio finally came on the air and read the same statement, standing Italy—and the world—on its ear. Since he included no specific instructions for the Italian military forces, they did not know what to do: fight Germans or flee. A somewhat disillusioned Albert Kesselring turned his forces on the noncooperative Italian Army divisions and Air Force units and disarmed them and quickly won Rome. No less important, the German 16th Panzer Division replaced the Italians manning the beach defenses at Salerno. The Italian Navy, however, slipped from its ports and surrendered to the Allies. The king and the Badoglio government escaped to Brindisi, where a government-in-exile was established.[19]

Doc Eaton recalled: "That night, after it was all over, I went back to my tent and sat on my cot. I was trembling, thinking that if Ridgway hadn't fought that thing tooth and nail we'd have gone in and it would have been a disaster. Who should come into my tent but Matt. He was not a drinker—not a drunkard—but of all things he had a bottle of whiskey. We each took a drink—and then he began to cry. And so did I. It was so close and we felt so deeply about it and we were both exhausted. Then he went away. I sat there thinking that I owed him my life."[20]

The Allied handling of the Italian armistice would subsequently evoke a great deal of criticism. In particular, Ridgway and Taylor would be skewered for approaching the Rome airborne operation with such great caution. The distinguished World War II American naval historian Samuel Eliot Morison, for one, wrote: "Here a great opportunity was lost . . . [The Italians] had grossly exaggerated the strength of the Germans near Rome and minimized that of the Italian Army in Rome. An air drop on Rome was what the Germans most feared . . . So spectacular a move as a paratrooper dropping on Rome would have rallied the people, who were only waiting for some gesture to rise against their oppressors . . . General Taylor, an airborne specialist, saw the difficulties only too readily and had neither the wit nor the information to call [the Italian] bluff. We should have resolutely gone ahead with the drop; Badoglio would have not dared not to cooperate, since he knew that if he did not, his government and king would be overthrown."[21]

To buttress his case, Morison paraphrases the memoirs of Kesselring and his chief of staff, Westphal. But Morison, perhaps unwittingly misinterprets those memoirs. As the Germans made clear, it was not an air drop alone on Rome that the Germans most feared. It was a *combined* amphibious landing "in the general area of Rome" (as Westphal put it) or "nearby" Rome (as Kesselring put it) together with the air drop that they feared most. In Kesselring's mind, Allied parachutes over Rome—which he looked for diligently—would be a certain signal of an Allied amphibious landing near Anzio, Ostia or Civitavecchia, designed to link up with the paratroopers. It is clear that both men knew very well that the Allies were unlikely to mount an air drop alone so distant from the amphibious assault at Salerno.[22]

Morison and others have argued that the Germans were poorly deployed, militarily, to repel an Allied air drop. This argument bears closer scrutiny. The German 2nd Parachute Division was deployed very close to Rome, along the south bank of the Tiber River and between the river and the Alban Hills. In addition to the one hundred 88 mm guns, it had some armor and plenty of transportation. It was well situated to cut off a paratrooper dash from the coastal airfields to Rome. The 3rd Panzer Grenadier Division was bivouacked some forty to forty-five miles north of Rome, between Viterbo and Lake Bolsena. Attached to it was an armored force from the 26th Panzer Division. As it was to demonstrate in the next several days, the division was highly mobile. And it, too, was well situated to intercept and cut off a paratrooper dash from the coastal airfields to Rome.[23]

After the war, when Jim Gavin was stationed in Italy, he studied the German after-action reports and the terrain between the proposed coastal airfields and Rome. Later he wrote: "There is no doubt in my mind that the decision to cancel was a proper one . . . There was heavy ack-ack along the Tiber and around many of the airfields . . . To me it was totally unrealistic to believe that the parachutists could have survived all that en route by air and then prevail against any German armored force on the ground . . . German armored units could have held up the parachute forces almost indefinitely."[24]

Taylor wrote: "It was a great personal disappointment to me and I suspect to most of the members of the 82nd Airborne Division . . . that [Rome] had to be called off. What more glorious task could fighting men receive than to liberate and defend the Eternal City while easing the difficulties of our troops at Salerno? But the obstacles, then and now, seemed too great to allow any reasonable hope that the accomplishments of our airborne soldiers, heroic though they might be, could compensate for the losses to be expected . . . They would have landed twenty-five miles from Rome with no trucks, few supplies and limited ammunition . . . The German Air Force would never have allowed further reinforcements to arrive from Sicily by air and our men on the ground would have been on their own with no assurance that the Italian forces would be even friendly to them. What they could have accomplished under these circumstances I certainly do not know, but I have never regretted the decision which spared these elite troops to serve their country with distinction at Salerno, Anzio, Normandy and elsewhere rather than end their useful days in Italian graves or German prisons."[25]

Ridgway wrote: "When the time comes that I must meet my Maker, the source of most humble pride to me will not be accomplishments in battle, but the fact that I was guided to make the decision to oppose this thing . . . right up to the top. There were other operations which I opposed, on similar grounds, but this was the one of greatest magnitude, and I deeply and sincerely believe that by taking the stand I took we saved the lives of thousands of brave men."[26]

In the aftermath, some division staffers commenced to view Eisenhower in a new light. They believed that he had been a little too quick to endorse and promote this "hare-brained scheme" for the sake of getting an armistice of uncertain value. Doc Eaton recalled: "That was the first time I went against Ike. He wouldn't call it off merely because of loss of life. Hell, it wasn't *his* goddamned life. It was somebody else's." For his part, if Eisenhower was disappointed that the Rome mission was aborted or with its chief abortionist, Ridgway, he did not so note in his vast collection of writings. However, there is no doubt that the difficulties involved in mounting the Rome mission reinforced Eisenhower's growing belief that, as he wrote at the time, "the airborne division is too large" and airborne operations should be restricted to "strong regimental combat teams."[27]

☆19☆

MARK CLARK'S AVALANCHE forces closed on the Gulf of Salerno late on the evening of September 8. He commanded an assault force of 170,000 men: 100,000 British in McCreery's 10 Corps; 70,000 Americans in Dawley's VI Corps. By that time the 16th Panzer Division had displaced the Italian troops and was dug in on the hills overlooking the beachhead and on full alert.[1]

The Salerno invasion was at best an ill-conceived, shoestring operation. Mark Clark further imperiled his forces by the following decisions:

● He allowed the news of the Italian surrender to be circulated to the troops in invasion vessels that night, on the eve of battle. Eisenhower's naval chief, Admiral Cunningham, wrote that this news induced a "sense of complacency." Naval historian Morison commented: "Complacency is hardly the word for it; the general impression seemed to be that the war was over. We were landing in Italy, and the Italians had quit, hadn't they?"[2]

● Believing he could achieve tactical surprise as Patton and Bradley had at Gela, he forbade any preliminary naval gunfire to "soften up the beachhead." Morison wrote that this was a "fantastic" assumption. Montgomery's invasion of Calabria had already alerted the Germans that the Allies were coming into Italy; Salerno was the most obvious point to make an entry in force. Every longshoreman in North Africa and Sicily knew the invasion target was Italy. German reconnaissance planes regularly patrolled the Mediterranean; they could hardly miss the AVALANCHE armada.[3]

● He spread his thin assault forces over too much real estate. The main beachhead stretched twenty miles from Salerno to Paestum. A decision to land rangers and commandos at Maiori (to quickly seize the Sorrento mountain passes into Nocera) enlarged the front by some five miles, to a total of twenty-five. There was a seven-mile gap between the main British and American assault forces, a dangerously weak "seam" which lay almost exactly along the Sele River.

There was, of course, no tactical surprise. When the British and Americans commenced moving toward the beaches at about 3 A.M. on September 9, the Germans spotted them at once. They shot brilliant flares into the sky and shouted over loudspeakers: "Come on in and give up. You're covered." Then came a withering storm of artillery, mortar and machine-gun fire. A horde of German aircraft—the largest number ever to appear over an Allied invasion beach in Europe—raked the invading forces with bombs and gunfire. The naval covering forces returned the fire, but they were shooting blind.[4]

Despite this vicious reception and the usual foul-ups on the landing beaches, the assault forces got a toehold on the shore and began inching inland. One regiment of Fred Walker's green 36th Division was pinned down on the beach

Allied Invasion of Italy

and made little progress, but other forces in the division crawled several miles inland, capturing Capaccio and the surrounding high ground. The British advanced inland several miles but, owing to the heavy German fire, failed to capture three crucial D-day objectives: Salerno Harbor, Battipaglia and the Montecorvino airfield.

Neither the British nor the Americans had been able to land much artillery or armor. However, as at Gela, the naval forces produced substitute artillery fire with a high degree of effectiveness. Admiral Hewitt concluded that "without the support of naval gunfire, the assault beaches could not have carried, and the Army could not have remained ashore without the support of naval guns and bombing aircraft." Walker's ADC, Otto F. Lange, seconded that judgment. He radioed the naval forces: "Thank God for the fire of the blue-belly Navy ships. Probably could not [otherwise] have stuck out Blue and Yellow beaches. Brave fellows there; tell them so."[5]

The first two days on Salerno were hellish nightmares. German fire remained intense and never abated. Allied casualties, especially in the 36th Division, were very heavy. No one slept. Clark brought his "floating reserve"—two regiments of Troy Middleton's 45th Division—ashore to plug the weak seam between the British and the Americans and shifted the boundary north of the Sele River. One of these regiments came ashore prematurely and on the wrong beach, causing "untold irritation" and no little confusion. Clark and Dawley fell out. Clark infuriated Dawley by pulling one reinforced battalion out of the VI Corps sector and sending it to reinforce the rangers at Maiori. However, in spite of these command altercations, the desperate shortage of men and unyielding enemy resistance, both the Americans and the British continued to crawl inland, gaining tentative and precarious footholds in Battipaglia, Persano and Altavilla, and Clark began laying plans for the breakout to Naples.[6]

Kesselring, meanwhile, was reinforcing the 16th Panzer Division per plan. Down from the Naples area sped elements of the Hermann Göring Panzer Division and the 15th Panzer Grenadier Division. These were soon joined on the northern end of the beachhead by elements of the 3rd Panzer Grenadier Division from Rome. Up from the "toe" came the 26th Panzer and the 29th Panzer Grenadier, skillfully laying mines and demolishing roads and bridges to delay Montgomery's slowly advancing Eighth Army. On Italy's east coast, in the Apulia district, the German 1st Parachute Division fell back toward the Foggia airfield complex, then crossed the boot toward Salerno. In sum, Kesselring committed major elements of seven of the eight German divisions in southern Italy to Salerno.

Here—fortunately for the Allies—Hitler made a crucial mistake. The Germans were in a dominating position at Salerno. At this point had Hitler authorized Kesselring to "borrow" two or three of Rommel's divisions sitting idle 450 miles away (in northern Italy), beyond any doubt Kesselring could have thrown the Allies back into the sea, with ghastly consequences. But Rommel was still opposed to fighting the Allies in southern Italy and did not volunteer any of his forces.[7]

This mistake was partially offset by one on Eisenhower's part. Late in the Salerno planning, consideration was given, almost as an afterthought, to taking advantage of German weakness in Apulia. Admiral Cunningham came up with the notion of rushing Allied troops into the "heel" at Taranto. Eisenhower heartily endorsed this scheme (as a way of reinforcing Montgomery's "right flank") and chose part of Hopkinson's British 1st Airborne Division, which was still on the docks in Bizerte, to carry out the mission. Having no landing craft, Cunningham hurriedly organized a task force of fourteen men-of-war (two battleships, five cruisers, six destroyers and a minelayer), which picked up and landed an advance force of thirty-six hundred paratroopers (from the 2nd and 4th parachute brigades) in Taranto at dusk on September 9—D day on Salerno.[8]

By that time, Kesselring's 1st Parachute Division was pulling up stakes and falling back on Foggia and Salerno. In the "assault" Hopkinson's men met no opposition whatsoever, although the landing was marred when the new British cruiser *Abdiel* hit a mine and sank, with the loss of 48 sailors and 101 paratroopers. Hopkinson's troops, later reinforced by the rest of the division, struck off northward toward Foggia in pursuit of the retiring Germans. The Germans mounted desultory delaying actions. During one of these—at Castellaneta— Hoppy Hopkinson was hit in the head by a German machine-gun burst and killed. Much later, the British 78th and 8th Indian divisions also landed in the "heel"; these British forces were organized as the 5 Corps, commanded by Charles Allfrey, who fell under Montgomery's command—Eighth Army.[9]

Considering the slimness of the AVALANCHE forces and the obvious difficulties they faced at Salerno, the landing at Taranto was a mistake. Had Eisenhower diverted this thirty-six-hundred-man force to Salerno, rather than Taranto, it could have reached the beachhead no later than September 11. This would have given Clark not only badly needed experienced manpower but also the massive added firepower of two battleships, five cruisers and six destroyers. In violation of sound military maxims to concentrate maximum force at the decisive point, adding the Taranto invasion fragmented Allied forces into three separate noncoordinated entities while Kesselring was concentrating into one.

When the "Rome job" was canceled, Eisenhower returned the 82nd Airborne Division to Mark Clark's control for use in AVALANCHE. The message came down through the chain of command to Alexander's CP (on Sicily), where it was apparently delayed by encoding and decoding, and it did not reach Clark until September 10, the second day of the invasion. Clark was glad to hear the news, and in his initial thinking, he considered the possibility of using the division to help the British break through the Sorrento mountains toward Naples, possibly in conjunction with a British "end run" amphibious operation. But these ideas were not fully developed.[10]

In the meantime Alexander had found nine valuable LCIs standing idle in Licata. These were some of the ships Montgomery had utilized to cross into Calabria. Knowing that Clark was hard-pressed for manpower, Alexander proposed to Clark on September 10 that these nine LCIs be utilized to bring part of the 82nd Airborne Division to Salerno. Clark readily agreed to the idea, but it was not until September 12 that the word trickled down to Ridgway.[11]

The obvious choice for this reinforcing mission was Harry Lewis' 325th Glider Infantry Regiment, which had the most "experience" in amphibious operations. But since the regiment had only two—instead of the conventional three—infantry battalions, the decision was made to add a third battalion. As in the initial Sicily operation, Ridgway chose to add the 3rd Battalion of Tucker's 504th, now commanded by Hank Adams. But Adams himself would not participate: in western Sicily he had come down with a severe case of malaria. His exec, William R. Beall, would take the battalion to Salerno.

No one involved in this hastily conceived amphibious movement was very happy about it. By this time there were about four hundred Waco gliders in Sicily. Lewis' gliderists much preferred to enter combat by air, as they had been trained. The paratroopers of Beall's battalion also preferred to go by air. However, orders were orders, and on September 13 the gliderists and paratroopers assembled at Licata and boarded the LCIs. At 10 P.M. the little flotilla got underway, headed around the western end of Sicily for Palermo, where it would pick up air and sea escort for the remainder of the voyage.[12]

Ridgway, keyed up and anxious about the Salerno beachhead, awaited formal orders from Clark for committing the rest of the division. But no word came. On the afternoon of September 11, Alexander had prodded Clark: "I want to make it clear that you may use [the 82nd] . . . in any manner you deem advisable." His message crossed a long-delayed one from Clark requesting two parachute operations as soon as possible: the 509th Battalion to drop on Avellino and an 82nd regiment to drop "northeast of Naples" near Capua, both for the purpose of blocking enemy movements from the north toward Salerno. If possible, Clark wanted both drops on the night of September 11 or, at the latest, September 12.[13]

Clark's message, relayed through Alexander, also did not reach Ridgway until September 12. Ridgway was ready and eager to move at once, but there were logistical difficulties. The staff could find no suitable DZs "northeast of Naples" and, in any case, the complicated drops could not be mounted on such short notice. The best the division could plan for was a regimental drop on Capua on the night of September 14/15 and a drop on Avellino on September 15/16. That same day, Ridgway relayed this information to Alexander for Clark, who was now studying the possibility of bringing a regiment right into the Salerno beachhead by parachute or, if an airstrip could be built in time, by glider.[14]

All during that day—September 12—German pressure on the Allied beachhead had been mounting steadily. The next day, the Germans attacked in great force at the weak seam between the Americans and the British. The Allied "front" collapsed, units were cut off and decimated. Casualties were ghastly. There were few reserves to throw into the fight. When Clark asked Dawley what he intended to do, Dawley replied, as Clark recalled: "Nothing . . . all I've got is a prayer." Facing what he would describe as a "near disaster," Clark ordered his chief of staff, Al Gruenther, to prepare plans to evacuate the beachhead and/or to move one corps into the other's sector by sea in order to solidify and concentrate his forces. Dawley, Walker, Middleton and the naval chiefs rebelled. They believed any of these moves would lead to catastrophe and refused to seriously entertain them. "Put food and ammunition behind the 45th," Middleton said defiantly. "We are going to stay here."[15]

The Allied situation was soon utterly desperate. No man on the Salerno beachhead that day would ever forget it. While the Allied commanders huddled over evacuation plans, the Germans punched through and advanced toward the beach itself. What saved the day was the awesome valor of a handful of soldiers manning key antitank and artillery positions rallied personally by Clark—and the U.S. Navy. The men-of-war standing offshore laid down a relentless and merciless bombardment on the advancing German tanks and infantry. Von Vietinghoff would recall: "With astonishing precision and freedom of maneuver, these ships shot at every recognized target with very overwhelming effect."[16]

As this grave crisis at Salerno mounted, Eisenhower issued orders for all hands to give Clark every possible assistance. His air chief, Arthur Tedder, sent every aircraft at his command that could help—including heavy strategic bombers. Admiral Cunningham dispatched every available man-of-war, including cruisers and the two battleships and six destroyers that had lifted the British paratroopers to Taranto. Alexander urged Montgomery, who had paused to bring up supplies, to go flat out for Salerno. Eisenhower's staff combed the Mediterranean for LSTs that could be used to rush the U.S. 3rd and 34th infantry divisions (based in Sicily and North Africa, respectively) and the 1st Armored Division (based in North Africa) into the beachhead. They found eighteen LSTs in Oran, en route to India, and commandeered them. Serious consideration was given to moving some of the 3rd Division from Sicily to Salerno in the four hundred gliders spotted on the Sicily airfields.[17]

This was all to the good, but it would take time—many, many days—to get manpower into the Salerno beachhead. Clark was desperate and needed instant help. On that darkest of days—September 13—he and his airborne adviser, Bill Yarborough, hatched a rescue operation: they would try to bring in a regiment of Ridgway's paratroopers that very night. Clark quickly wrote a letter to Ridgway stating that the fight for Salerno had taken a turn for the worst, that it was a touch-and-go affair. "I want you to accept this letter as an order," Clark continued. "I realize the time normally needed to prepare for a drop, but this is an exception. I want you to make a drop within our lines on the beachhead and I want you to make it tonight. This is a must." He added that he hoped the Capua and Avellino drops could go on the next night, September 14/15. Clark then found an Air Force reconnaissance pilot, Jacob R. Hamilton, who had bravely landed on a crude airstrip near Paestum, and told him to fly to Sicily and give the letter to Ridgway "and no one else." Hamilton took off immediately.[18]

Ridgway, grown impatient with the red tape of communicating with Clark through Alexander, had decided to go to the beachhead and talk face to face with Clark on the pending air drops at Capua and Avellino. At about the same time Hamilton took off from Paestum, Ridgway took off from Licata in a C-47 bound for Termini, where he hoped to catch a ship. Hamilton reached Licata at about 1:30 P.M. and went immediately to the 82nd Division CP. He talked with Doc Eaton and Jim Gavin but, as ordered, refused to give them the letter from Clark. Realizing that the letter was a vital matter, Eaton raced to the Licata tower and had the men radio an urgent recall to Ridgway's plane. Ridgway, headed for a battlefield on urgent business, was momentarily tempted to ignore the recall, but a "sixth sense" warned him "that this thing was important."[19]

When Ridgway got back to Licata, the "tired, begrimed" Hamilton turned over the letter and waited for a reply. As Clark remembered, Ridgway's answer was classically brief: "Can do." Hamilton flew back to Salerno, landed on the airstrip, jumped into a jeep and headed for Clark's CP. On the way, eight German planes strafed his jeep, forcing him to dive out of the vehicle into a ditch, a maneuver that probably saved his life but cost him a dislocated shoulder. Exhausted and in no little pain, Hamilton finally got Ridgway's can-do message to Clark.[20]

Since Gavin's 505th was gearing up for the drop on Capua on the night of September 14/15, Ridgway chose Tucker's 504th (less Beall's LCI-embarked 3rd Battalion) to make the emergency drop into Salerno. Never had the 82nd Division staff or the staffs at Troop Carrier Command worked so frenetically to mount a mission. While they did so, Ridgway personally took steps to prevent the friendly-fire disaster that had occurred on the 504th's previous jump into Sicily. Bypassing Alexander, Ridgway radioed Clark direct that *all* Allied ground and naval forces *must* withhold fire at *any* aircraft from 9 P.M. onward until otherwise notified. Well aware of the Sicily disaster, Clark sent Bill Yarborough to order every battery on the VI Corps beachhead to halt fire at the scheduled time. Admiral Hewitt instructed his naval forces to do the same.[21]

On Sicily there was a tremendous reshuffling of troop-transport aircraft. The three groups (61st, 313th, 314th) assigned to fly Tucker's men gathered at Comiso and Trapani airfields. So hurriedly was all this done, troop-carrier historian John Warren wrote, that at Comiso, the troop-carrier pilots had to be briefed "by the light of a few flashlights and maps held against the side of a plane" while Tucker's men were boarding.

About seven hours after Hamilton had brought Clark's message to Licata, the mission commenced. Hal Clark's operations officer, Joel L. Crouch, took off from the Agrigento airfield, leading two other pathfinder aircraft. Two hours and thirty minutes later, the three planes reached the Salerno beachhead without incident. Fortunately, not a single friendly (or enemy) gun fired at them. Moreover, Bill Yarborough had improvised an astounding DZ marker: a "T" of lighted gasoline cans, each leg of the "T" a half mile long! In addition, the men on the beach fired green Very flares and held up flashlights.

The fifty pathfinders jumped with equipment, five minutes after a German air raid, which Clark's men had endured without shooting back. The first group landed squarely on the DZ; the second in a ditch alongside it. The men had 5G "homing" radio transmitters, Eureka radar devices and Krypton lights. One 5G broke loose and smashed in the landing; another was held in reserve and never used, since the men had little faith in the device. The Eureka was set up and operating within three minutes. It proved to be as effective as it had been in the field tests in North Africa.

Behind the pathfinders came the main body of aircraft: eighty-two planes carrying thirteen hundred troops. In the van was 313 Group with Danny Danielson's 2nd Battalion in thirty-six planes. Two planes were forced to abort owing to mechanical difficulties, but the stick in one was transferred to a reserve plane which caught up with the main formation. At 11:26 P.M., homing on the Eureka signals with Rebeccas, the planes reached the well-marked DZ and the men jumped from eight hundred feet altitude. Most men landed within two hundred yards of the DZ, and all within a mile. Neither they nor the planes were shot at by anybody. All thirty-five planes returned safely to Sicily.[22]

The other two air groups, 61 and 314, transporting Warren Williams' 1st Battalion plus the engineers, did not fare so well. Some planes of the 61st were forced to abort before takeoff. Forty-one planes finally got airborne, very late. These did not reach the DZ until 1:30 A.M. Three of the four flights dropped all troops on or within a mile of the DZ, but the other flight (which had no Rebecca to receive the Eureka signals) strayed and dropped a company of men eight to ten miles southeast of the DZ (in friendly territory). In 314 Group, two planes aborted before takeoff. The troops from these two were jammed into the other six planes, which did not get airborne until fifteen minutes after midnight. Homing on the Eureka signals, these six reached the DZ three hours behind the lead group, at about 2:30 A.M., and dropped the men within a mile of the DZ (still marked by the flaming gasoline cans). All forty-seven planes in these two groups returned safely to Sicily. None of the planes or paratroopers was fired on by friendly forces.

On the ground, Tucker assembled his men within one hour, using the brilliant Krypton lights as a rallying point. (The one missing company, dropped far off target, reported in after daylight.) Some seventy-five paratroopers had been injured in the drop, but only one seriously. Tucker immediately reported in person to Clark.

"As soon as you are assembled," Clark said to Tucker, "you are to be placed in the front lines."

"Sir," Tucker replied, "we are assembled and ready now."[23]

The 504 moved immediately to the front in the Monte Soprano area of the 36th Division sector. "They lived up to their fine reputation," Clark wrote. Tucker was "a real fighting soldier." Later that day, September 14, when Von Vietinghoff renewed his drive to split the Allied forces and throw them into the sea, Tucker's thirteen hundred men proved to be a valuable reinforcement and perhaps—there is no way of knowing—a decisive one. Without doubt they gave the Salerno invaders a much-needed psychological shot in the arm, which may have counted for a great deal. Hugh Pond, a British Salerno historian, wrote that when the men on the beach saw the paratroopers floating down they "stood in their trenches cheering themselves hoarse." The arrival of the paratroopers, he went on, "was a welcome fillip to the morale of the troops and provided Mark Clark with sufficient reinforcements to hold the balance against increasing German pressure." Jim Gavin, perhaps not the most unbiased witness, wrote that Tucker's regiment "swung the tide of battle back in favor of the Americans." That judgment would become an article of faith within the 82nd Airborne Division.[24]

Later that same day, September 14, while the beachhead battle was still in doubt, Mark Clark decided that having more manpower on the beachhead would outweigh possible theoretical gains in a drop on distant Capua. Accordingly, he messaged Ridgway to cancel Jim Gavin's drop on Capua that night and redirect the drop—in effect duplicating Tucker's drop.

The drop of Gavin's three-battalion 505 was substantially larger than Tucker's. One hundred thirty-one planes were to carry some twenty-one hundred men. Joel Crouch again led with the pathfinders, who jumped into the exact center of the blazing "T" at 11:38 P.M. Fifty-four planes were to follow with Edward Krause's 3rd Battalion, Jim Gavin and the regimental staff. One plane aborted on takeoff with a blown tire; two planes got lost and returned to Sicily with full loads; the rest reached the DZ at 1:10 A.M. and began dropping squarely on target. Behind this group came Mark Alexander's 2nd Battalion in thirty-eight planes, all of which reached the DZ at about 1:30 A.M. and made nearly perfect drops. The last group, some thirty-eight planes, carrying Walter Winton's 1st Battalion, got a very late start and did not reach the DZ until 3 A.M. Two planes aborted on takeoff; three got lost, found themselves over Naples and hurriedly reversed course. One of these located the DZ and dropped, but the other two returned to Sicily with full loads. Two other planes, whose pilots mixed up signals or got lost, also returned with their loads to Sicily.

Notwithstanding all the care and pains to prevent it, one C-47 was lost to friendly fire, but the troopers and aircrew survived. The 505 historian, Allen Langdon, wrote that this plane carried a stick led by John Tallerday, exec of C Company in Winton's 1st Battalion. As the plane flew over the invasion fleet in Salerno Bay, Langdon wrote, it was far off course, and "some itchy-fingered gunners fired on it, setting the left engine on fire." The stick—and aircrew— bailed out of the flaming plane just as it crossed the beach, all landing in the no-man's-land near Battipaglia, in the British sector. The paratroopers eventually attached themselves to a British unit and rejoined the 505th about two weeks later.

This piecemeal nighttime drop into friendly territory was judged to be the best the 505th had ever made. Of the 127 planes that left Sicily, six had turned back with full loads, one had been destroyed and dropped far off course near Battipaglia, but the other 120, carrying about two thousand men, had dropped on or within a mile and a half of the DZ. There were only a few serious injuries. Forty-five minutes after the last man landed, Gavin had the regiment assembled. Mike Dawley assigned it to VI Corps "reserve," deployed in combat formation—and actively patrolling—on his right flank between Albanella and Agropoli, in the extreme southern end of the beachhead. Dawley drew Gavin into his corps headquarters "for several days" as a senior aide and planner.[25]

That same night, unfortunately and inexplicably, the 509th Battalion proceeded to carry out Clark's still-standing orders for a drop on Avellino. The Avellino mission—the first Allied airborne operation to be launched behind a fixed, active and fully alerted, enemy front—was another nightmare.[26]

Avellino was a key road hub about twenty miles north of Salerno, nestled in a valley surrounded by five-thousand-foot mountains. The air route selected duplicated that of the two Salerno beachhead drops—as far as the Salerno DZ. After that, the planes were to fly twenty miles due north (over German lines) to Montecorvino, then fifteen miles north by northwest to the DZ. In all it was a challenging three-hundred-mile trip, one way, thirty-five miles beyond the Salerno beachhead DZ and the German front lines through a range of mountains.

Ray Dunn's 51st Wing was designated for the mission. Forty planes would carry the 640 paratroopers. After hectic and hurried reshuffling, all assembled at Comiso airfield on Sicily. At 9:25 P.M., a single pathfinder plane with a team of eleven paratroopers took off. They had an unreliable 5G radio transmitter and two narrow-beam Aldis lamps, but no Eureka, because Dunn's 51st Wing was not yet equipped with Rebeccas to receive the Eureka radar signals. The remaining thirty-nine planes followed ten minutes later. The battalion commander, Doyle Yardley, flew in the lead plane of the main formation.

The pathfinder plane passed over the dark Salerno DZ (ahead of Gavin's pathfinders) and the German lines, then climbed well above four thousand feet to cross the mountains. The DZ, selected from aerial photographs, was near a crossroads village, Santa Lucia di Sorino, three miles southeast of Avellino. The moonlight was good. The pilot could clearly distinguish houses on the ground, but they were not distinctive enough to mark a village. The pathfinders jumped from fifteen hundred to twenty-five hundred feet (a long descent) onto a crossroad a mile south of the DZ. Since the main body of planes was only a few minutes behind, there was no time to find the DZ. The pathfinders set up operations where they landed.

Almost everything possible went wrong. The 5G radio transmitters proved to be useless, the narrow-beam Aldis lamps not much better. Few pilots could find the pathfinders or the DZ or Avellino. One squadron took a wrong turn into the mountains, got lost, flew back to the coast and made a second pass. Another squadron, also lost, dropped 175 men at Cassano, ten miles from the DZ. Another dozen planes dropped 180 paratroopers anywhere from eight to twenty-five miles from the DZ. Only fifteen of the forty planes (with 240 paratroopers) managed to place men within four or five miles of the DZ. All planes returned safely to Sicily. The pilots angrily condemned the 5G radio transmitters, but judged the drop itself to be "highly successful."

The paratroopers would not have agreed with that assessment. In fact, they were wildly scattered. By luck, the battalion commander, Doyle Yardley, was in one of ten planes which dropped nearest to the DZ. He rounded up about 160 men and commenced advancing on Avellino. Almost immediately, the group ran into a German tank park and a heavy firefight ensued. Yardley, severely wounded, was soon captured along with some of his men. Elsewhere, his executive officer, William R. Dudley, who was dropped some forty miles (he guessed) from Avellino, concluded it would be suicidal to try to sneak through German lines to the town. He and some sixty men holed up. One officer, William C. Kellogg, and his stick blew a bridge while a German troop convoy was crossing it. This action split the convoy into two confused groups and Kellogg cleverly got them shooting at one another, then pulled out. For this action, Kellogg was later awarded a DSC. Here and there other paratroopers carried out similar random, minor feats of sabotage and harassment, but other than Yardley's brief and futile effort, there was no concentrated attack on Avellino. Ultimately about 520 of the 640 men (including Dudley and Kellogg) who jumped, filtered back to Allied lines or were later overrun by the Allies and rescued.[27]

Whether or not this mission was worth the effort and loss of life remained moot. Although he would never again employ paratroopers in a drop behind enemy lines, Mark Clark wrote that "the outfit did a wonderful job." Jim Gavin agreed. He wrote that "the battalion had accomplished what General Mark Clark had in mind. It disrupted German communications and partly blocked the German supplies and reserves. It also caused the Germans to keep units on anti-parachute missions that otherwise could have been used at the point of their main effort at Salerno." However, the official military historians were less enthusiastic. Troop-carrier historian Warren wrote that "it seems clear that the mission was a failure." Army historian Martin Blumenson wrote that the mission was "too small" and "too dispersed" to be more than a "minor nuisance" to the Germans and concluded that "the battalion had no effect on the battle of the beachhead."[28]

This much seems clear: had the 509th been dropped into the Salerno beachhead that night, rather than at Avellino, its contribution to the crisis at Salerno would have been substantially greater.

In the meantime, Ridgway had flown to Palermo and crossed over to Salerno on an LST. By the morning of September 15, he, Tucker and Gavin were in the beachhead with the 504 and 505. That same morning the little nine-ship flotilla of LCIs transporting Harry Lewis' three-battalion task force left Palermo. That night it reached the battle zone, where it was divided up. The 1st Battalion of the 325, commanded by Klemm Boyd, and the 3rd Battalion of the 504, commanded by William Beall, landed on Red Beach in the 36th Division sector. The 2nd Battalion of the 325th, commanded by John Swenson, landed at Maiori, joining the rangers and the original "Tiber River Task Force," which had left from Bizerte and had been diverted to Maiori on September 11.

That same day—September 15—a bold plan was set in motion to lift the division staff and other headquarters elements into Salerno by glider. This plan, Doc Eaton wrote, "called for an enormous amount of troop shifting, movement of gliders, etc." The gliders were spotted on various airfields and the troops assigned for each. However, Eaton continued, "reconnaissance in the Sele River area failed to disclose suitable glider landing areas." The glider mission to Salerno was therefore scrubbed.[29]

It seemed hard to believe. Merely one week earlier the division had been loaded into planes for a drop on Rome. Now its full infantry fighting strength was deployed at Salerno.

ON SEPTEMBER 16 the Germans made yet another all-out effort to throw the Allies back into the sea. On the left, the British 46th and 56th infantry divisions, reinforced by newly arriving elements of the British 7th Armored Division, held firm. On the right, Troy Middleton's 45th Division—now up to full strength of three regiments—absorbed the attack, inflicting severe casualties on the enemy. Offshore, the massive Allied naval armada continued to rain shells into German positions. Overhead, the sky was crowded with Allied fighters and bombers staging from Sicily and North Africa.[1]

The Allies did not know it yet, but this attack was Von Vietinghoff's swan song. When it failed, he concluded he could not inflict a decisive defeat on the Allies. They had too big an edge in sea and air power, and Montgomery's slowly advancing Eighth Army would soon present a threat to his left flank and rear. He recommended a slow, orderly withdrawal northward and the creation of a defensive line across the boot south of Rome. Hitler and Kesselring, more than pleased with Vietinghoff's "victory" at Salerno, approved the plan, and not long afterward Vietinghoff left for northern Italy to temporarily relieve Rommel, who had suffered an attack of appendicitis. One of Vietinghoff's corps commanders, Hans-Valentine Hube, temporarily assumed command of the Tenth Army and organized the withdrawal.

Ridgway now had all three of his regiments in the Salerno beachhead. It was the first time the division had been committed to combat in full strength. But it was not deployed on a neat single front, the way it was done in paper studies at the Command and General Staff School. Gavin, Tucker and Lewis were filling holes in the front or rear of a line that was by now literally a hodgepodge of battalions and regiments from three infantry divisions. Moreover, Ridgway did not have a division command structure. His staff was still back on Sicily, trying to find transportation. Eisenhower had drafted his acting ADC, Max Taylor, to serve as a member of an Allied liaison group to the exiled Italian Government in Brindisi. (Taylor wrote wryly: "Apparently I qualified for membership on the basis of having become an Italian expert after some twenty-four hours in Rome.")[2]

There were some other command problems in the American sector. Troy Middleton and Fred Walker had performed magnificently. But Walker's ADC, Otto Lange, physically exhausted, was relieved of command, busted to colonel and sent home. More important, Mark Clark had also lost all confidence in his corps commander, Mike Dawley, who was no less exhausted and showing the strain. He appeared extremely nervous; his hands shook and his voice was wavery and uncertain. On a visit to the beachhead on September 15, Alexander, after a briefing by Dawley, concluded that Dawley was (in Walker's phrase) "too unsteady for combat command," thought he should be relieved and recommended that Eisenhower go and have a look for himself.[3]

Actually it was Mark Clark's decision to make. He agreed that Dawley should be relieved but was reluctant to take this drastic, career-destroying step. Clark was still a young commander on trial; he had made his own share of mistakes. Dawley was seven years senior to him by West Point class; he was held in highest regard by Clark's old boss, Lesley McNair. Moreover, Walker and Middleton (also both senior to Clark in age and both combat veterans of World War I) got along well with Dawley and found no fault, as did some of the young colonels.

Jim Gavin, for instance. Gavin wrote: "I do not know that any man could have done more . . . Clark seemed to feel that someone had to be relieved and the axe fell on Dawley . . . I always had a feeling that, unlike General Bradley, Mark Clark really didn't have a true feel for what soldiers could and could not do and how much power it took to accomplish a particular mission. Perhaps it was lack of experience."[4]

That first day—September 16—Clark conferred with Ridgway about Dawley. Ridgway believed (he wrote later) that Dawley had "failed" and should be relieved. Clark was still reluctant to take that drastic step without Eisenhower's approval. Pending a visit from Eisenhower, Clark asked Ridgway if he would serve, temporarily, as deputy corps commander, "so as to help out," as Eisenhower later explained this unusual step to Marshall. Clark informed Eisenhower of Ridgway's appointment, adding that Dawley "should not be continued in his present job. He appears to go to pieces in emergencies."[5]

Decades later Clark recalled: "I tried to save Dawley because he was McNair's dearest friend. It was McNair who rammed him down my throat. I didn't want him. [Before the invasion] I said to Ike one night: 'Ike, I don't want Dawley.' Ike said, 'You're a damn fool if you take him.' I said, 'McNair has radioed me, please accept him, please accept him. I owe so much to McNair I am not going to turn him down.' And so, in combat he broke. No question about it. I had to send Ridgway in as deputy corps commander. I had to have somebody there I could lean on."[6]

On the following day, September 17, Eisenhower boarded a British ship and visited the Salerno beachhead. He met with Clark, Dawley, Walker and Ridgway, among others. After closely watching Dawley in a briefing, Eisenhower agreed with Clark that Dawley should be relieved. He wrote George Marshall: "Dawley is a splendid character, earnest, faithful and well-informed. There is nothing against him except that he can not repeat not exercise high battle command effectively when the going is rough." He busted Dawley to colonel and sent him home. Like Gavin, official Army historian Martin Blumenson was never convinced Dawley's relief had been completely warranted.[7]

Who would replace Dawley? Clark wanted Ridgway: "I asked for Ridgway, whom I already had there. He was a fine commander. He and I had been very, very close at West Point and later. I wanted somebody of my vintage. I never had a corps commander all through the war who wasn't hundreds and hun-

dreds of files and several years ahead of me at West Point. It made it awfully
difficult. But when I asked for Ridgway, it had to go [for approval] through
McNair, whom I admired so much. He offered me Johnny Lucas, another
artilleryman and friend of McNair's. I discussed it with Ike, saying, 'Ike, I'm in
the same boat here, but I'll take him.'"[8]

Apart from a natural desire to help out an old friend, McNair may have had
other reasons for choosing Lucas over Ridgway. Clark's appointment to the
senior position of army commander had been a special case. So far, no member
of the class of 1917 or younger had been appointed to the rank of corps commander. Bradley (class of 1915) had been the youngest corps commander thus
far. Walker and Middleton were senior to Ridgway. So were Lucian Truscott
and Charles Ryder, who were then in the process of rushing their 3rd and 34th
infantry divisions to Salerno to reinforce the beachhead. Clark had found it
"awfully difficult" to command men who were his senior. That awkwardness
could have been compounded had Ridgway been appointed corps commander.
Besides that, Ridgway was the Army's leading airborne expert, and his expertise, as well as his division, were earmarked for OVERLORD.

John Lucas (class of 1911), who had served as Eisenhower's "eyes and ears"
during Sicily, had recently assumed command of II Corps, relieving Bradley,
whom Marshall had ordered to England to begin planning OVERLORD. Lucas came over to Salerno two days later, and on September 20 Ridgway was
released from his brief (four-day) service as deputy commander of VI Corps.
Ridgway agreed with Clark that Lucas was not much of an improvement over
Dawley. He would later state that Lucas (along with Dawley) "failed in World
War II."[9]

Reuben Tucker's 504, which had not seen much real fighting on Sicily, led
the way in Salerno. The performance of the regiment was remarkable, and
Tucker became a legendary battlefield figure overnight. He was, Gavin wrote,
"a tough, superb combat leader . . . probably the best regimental commander
of the war."[10]

Sensing that the Germans were running out of steam, Ridgway and Fred
Walker began laying plans to go on the offensive and push inland. A key
objective was the town of Altavilla, and the high ground surrounding it. They
assigned Tucker this objective. On the afternoon of September 16, Tucker
moved out toward the jump-off line near Albanella, leading two of his three
battalions: Warren Williams' 1st and Danny Danielson's 2nd.[11]

It was a rugged, hot, uphill march. The diarist for Danielson's 2nd Battalion
wrote: "The terrific heat of the day and the steepness of the walk, together with
the excessive weight of equipment, was too much for the men. They could not
keep up with the rate of march, particularly the mortar platoon, several of
whom passed out along the way." An assistant company commander in the
battalion, Louis Hauptfleisch, remembered an encounter with Ridgway:

In a scheduled halt in the line of march to Albanella, I found myself virtually opposite General Ridgway, whose command jeep was parked by the side

of the road. Feeling obliged to acknowledge his unexpected presence in our midst, I dutifully went up to him, saluted and announced my rank, name and command identification, all as prescribed by military protocol. Very calmly he inquired of me: "Lieutenant, is everything O.K.?" To which I replied: "Yes, sir, except for the fact that I don't know where we are or where we are going."

In retrospect, it was a rather sorry admission for which the general would have had good reason to "chew my ass out." Not so. He quietly responded, unbuttoning his map case and spreading an unfolded map on the hood of his jeep. "Lieutenant," he said, "you are at this point [citing same on map] and headed here [pointing to Albanella on the map] and you and your men will then move into the Altavilla area [again pointing out same on the map] to take the high ground in that area." I dutifully saluted, thanked him for his orientation and upon departure preparatory to resuming our difficult march, he threw a "and good luck, Lieutenant" at me . . . The men under my command were impressed, and I believe highly-encouraged by my meeting with their general and being brought up to speed vis-à-vis the combat situation and assignment.[12]

The Germans were not yet out of steam. They saw Tucker advancing and opened up with a murderous machine-gun, mortar and artillery barrage. Tucker's solution to this problem was to try to speed up the advance toward high ground. But even his lionhearted example was not enough. The men were driven to cover in the rocks and ravines. In so doing, they began to lose contact and cohesion, but no man was seen to fall back.

Tucker was in his element. "The little colonel was up to his ears in battle and seemed to be having a hell of a good time," one of Williams' men wrote later. But as the fierce battle raged into the second day, a German force surrounded Tucker's CP. He escaped and established radio contact with Ridgway, but his fragmentary reports were not reassuring. At one point Ridgway and Walker, believing Tucker's force to be on the point of annihilation, considered sending regular troops to rescue him, and suggested he might want to pull back. Tucker's reply: "Hell no! We've got this hill and we are going to keep it. Just send me my other battalion."[13]

He was referring to Beall's 3rd Battalion, which had landed at Red Beach by LCI attached to the 325, and which was then being held in reserve. What Tucker wanted that day, September 17, he got. Ridgway gave the orders. The 3rd Battalion was moved up behind the 1st and the 2nd. In addition, Ridgway persuaded the Navy to deliver a smashing, 350-round barrage on Altavilla. Behind that came a barrage of heavy Army artillery. Altavilla was reduced to rubble—and many civilians were killed—but Tucker's men held.

On September 18 the Germans commenced the general withdrawal. They pulled back from the hills around Altavilla, leaving the body-strewn battlefield and the heap of rubble that had once been the town to Tucker and his exhausted men. Tucker's casualties had been heavy, but one participant declared: "We inflicted eight times the number of casualties we ourselves suffered." For his valor, Tucker was awarded the Distinguished Service Cross (as were two of his men). But the greatest compliment came from Jim Gavin. He now judged the 504 to be "just as tough" as his 505.[14]

Among the 504 wounded was Tucker's exec, Leslie Freeman, who had barely escaped alive in the Sicily drop. He was evacuated to a hospital. To replace him, Ridgway chose Mark Clark's other airborne adviser, Chuck Billingslea, who had jumped as Clark's observer with the British in TORCH and with Gavin's 505 in Sicily and who was anxious to get into a fighting outfit. His pal Hank Adams recalled: "Chuck Billingslea was cold, brilliant, and fearless. He also had a well organized mind. Tucker was very, very weak in administration—paperwork, detailed planning, and so on—so Billingslea became an extremely strong addition to the 504's leadership."[15]

That same day, Ridgway managed to bring the majority of the 82nd Airborne staff into Salerno. Having abandoned the idea of coming in by glider, the staff (and other units left behind in Sicily) had embarked by truck and jeep for Termini, Sicily, to catch a ship. While they were en route to Termini, Ridgway determined that a crude airstrip near Paestum could accommodate a C-47. He made arrangements for fifty C-47s to airlift some eight hundred staffers, who backtracked to Licata and climbed on the planes. Doc Eaton wrote: "The runway [at Paestum] was so short and rough that ten planes crashed on landing. Fortunately, only one person was slightly injured." Most of the remaining artillery, antitank, antiaircraft, engineer and signal units arrived from Termini by ship on September 22 and 23 and the last stragglers on September 30.[16]*

One major element of the division remained behind: the 456th Parachute Artillery, now commanded by Hugh A. Neal. Ridgway and Taylor had soured on the outfit and had replaced its commander, Harrison Harden. For that reason, neither Ridgway nor Taylor nor Andy March pressed to have the 456th included in the Salerno operation. It enplaned in Sicily for North Africa and, owing to an administrative foul-up, was scattered around North African bases. Much later, it regrouped and landed in Italy by ship.[17]

Thanks to the Allied code breakers, Alexander soon had a good intelligence on German plans. Kesselring intended to withdraw his forces slowly back to the Volturno River, holding there until at least October 15. Naples (and its fine harbor) was to be demolished, sparing only the historic shrines, churches and museums. Meanwhile, German engineers were to construct a defensive "winter line"—called the Gustav Line—across the narrowest part of the boot, about midway between Naples and Rome. The overall German plan was to fight a delaying action, denying the Allies Rome for as long as possible.[18]

---

* Paul Wright's 320th Glider Artillery and Wilbur Griffith's 376th Parachute Artillery landed by ship at the Salerno beachhead September 23. When Max Taylor was detached, his exec, Andy March, temporarily took over his duties as division artillery commander. At the same time, the 319th's Glider Artillery commander, Harry Bertsch, became acting exec of division artillery, replaced in the 319th by J. Carter Todd.

Alexander's counterstrategy was, for the moment, to pursue the Germans hard and fast and, if possible, overrun them before the Gustav Line could be completed. Clark's Fifth Army would drive up the western side of the boot and liberate Naples; Montgomery's Eighth Army would drive up the eastern side of the boot and take the Foggia airfield complex. The armies would cross the Volturno River line abreast, and drive north to overrun the Gustav Line.

This strategy placed a heavy burden on Clark's Fifth Army. He faced by far the greater number of German divisions. The liberation of Naples raised the prospect of nightmarish house-to-house fighting. Beyond Naples lay the Volturno River, which (on Clark's end) was paralleled by numerous canals in marshy delta where it flowed to the sea. Every mile of the advance was certain to be covered by German 88s and heavily mined and booby-trapped. He would be lucky to find a single undemolished road or bridge. In sum, the worst had happened: they would have to crawl up the leg like harvest bugs.

Clark's army was in poor shape for a long, arduous race north. The British 46th and 56th divisions and commandos and the American 36th Division in particular had been badly mauled at Salerno. Morale in McCreery's 10 Corps had been undermined by a fantastic, unprecedented mutiny. When some seven hundred veteran British reinforcements from North Africa, who had been led to believe they were homeward bound for England, were landed on Salerno, they promptly sat down on the beach and refused to go farther.† Clark's new VI Corps commander, John Lucas, an artilleryman, was a firm believer in massing artillery for an infantry advance. That view would save lives, but it was bound to slow the pursuit, perhaps literally to a crawl.[19]

There were, however, some positive notes. The British 7th Armored Division—the Desert Rats—fresh and fully equipped, was now ashore. Truscott's 3rd and Ryder's 34th infantry divisions, both fresh and newly equipped, began landing in the beachhead. Ridgway's 82nd Airborne Division and the American rangers (both lacking armor and heavy artillery) could be detailed to take and police Naples, freeing Clark's seven "heavy" divisions for the chase. When Naples was secure, Allied fighters and fighter-bombers could be moved forward from Sicily to stage from its two big airfields, and the harbor could be utilized for logistical support.

So the chase began. Lucas jumped off first, heading northeast in the general direction of Avellino, into the rugged mountains east of Mount Vesuvius. His 3rd and 45th divisions made slow progress in the difficult, rugged terrain. The skilled German soldiers yielded territory only grudgingly. Supplies had to be packed into the mountains by mule or by human porters. Not until September 30, after advance elements of Ryder's 34th Division came up and the Germans had fallen back, did Lucas take Avellino. It was during this advance that most of the men in Yardley's ill-fated 509 Battalion (thought to be "lost") were recovered. Subsequently, Clark appointed his other airborne adviser, Bill Yarborough, to command the bedraggled, leaderless outfit.[20]

---

† McCreery coaxed all but 192 back into battle. The holdouts were court-martialed and sentenced to five to twenty years in prison.

On the west coast, McCreery organized for the drive on Naples. The general plan was to send the American rangers and Lewis' 325th Regiment plus supporting elements through the Sorrento passes leading to Nocera, then punch out onto the plain for the run to Naples with the 7th Armored, 46th and 56th divisions in the lead. The American rangers' commander, William O. Darby, was reinforced for the mission with the independent British 23rd Armored Brigade and Harry Lewis' 325th Glider Regiment. In all, Darby commanded a task force of eighty-five hundred men. He jumped off on September 23 but couldn't break through. The attack failed—an ignominious setback.

Clark sent Ridgway and the rest of the 82nd Division, which was momentarily in army reserve, to the rescue. Ridgway was placed in overall command of the breakout, which would include three regiments of the 82nd, three battalions of Darby's rangers, the British 23rd Armored Brigade, a battalion from Walker's 36th Division (in Army reserve) and supporting artillery units. In all, the Ridgway force numbered about thirteen thousand men—more men than Ridgway had ever commanded. The plan was to punch through Chiunzi Pass to the high ground, then turn the 23rd Armored Brigade loose on Nocera.[21]

Ridgway, as was his custom, led his forces from the front lines. He paid close attention to Harry Lewis' 325th Regiment, which had entered combat for the first time. Ridgway insisted, in spite of the conditions, that his men at all times look neat and soldierly. A company commander in Swenson's 2nd Battalion, Robert L. Dickerson, recalled:

I thought there was no way General Ridgway could be a better division commander. He was most respected but not feared. We welcomed his visits. He never talked down to us, but spoke as though we were on his level. He never used a profane or vulgar word and his tone was always conversational. He could be ruthless but never cruel. His knowledge of infantry weapons was phenomenal. He knew each part and its function. He gained the respect of my people by pointing out our mistakes in a gentlemanly, but firm, manner and he therefore secured instant compliance.

An example . . . occurred on Mt. Saint Angelo . . . where my company had been engaged with elements of the Hermann Göring Division for several days. We were very short of ammunition, food and water. The weather was very warm. I had not shaved in about ten days because of the water shortage and I did not insist that my men do so. Early on a sunny morning, who appears from the valley below but General Ridgway. His first question was, "Why aren't you shaved?" He would not accept the excuse about water, but pointed out that I was the senior officer on that mountain and expected to set the example and that I should shave immediately, then require my men to do so. Then he asked how many casualties we had suffered, complimented me on the performance of Company E, and approved all my weapons and troop dispositions. His last words were, "You and your soldiers have done a fine job." Later he wrote a Letter of Commendation to the Company.[22]

Ridgway's force jumped off at dusk on September 27. Gavin, Tucker, Lewis and Darby led the fight through rugged Chiunzi Pass. By the next morning, Gavin stood atop the crest of the mountains around Sorrento. In the distance, beyond Mount Vesuvius, he could see clouds of black smoke billowing up from Naples, twenty-two miles away. Later, the 504 and the 505, supported by artillery and the British 23rd Armored Brigade, led the way out of the mountains onto the plain. The Germans abandoned Nocera and Naples, and on September 29 the paratroopers hurried by the famous ruins of Pompeii, on the southern slope of Mount Vesuvius.[23]

During this action, Tucker's 3rd Battalion commander, Hank Adams, had recovered sufficiently from his malaria to resume command of the battalion. It was a timely return. Only a few days later, his exec, William Beall, who had ably led the battalion into Salerno, was killed by enemy artillery fire. Beall had taken temporary cover in a cave and was buried alive. His comrades dug him out, but it was too late. "The explosion had infused his lung tissues with fine soil or dust particles, denying him essential oxygen. He succumbed more like drowning . . ." Adams himself was among those who tried to save Beall—by "massaging his heart."

Beall's death was a shock to the 504, not only because of the peculiarly horrible way it occurred, but also because he had been well liked and was the most senior man in the outfit to be killed in combat. His death moved Ridgway deeply. Adams remembered: "When Ridgway came up, I happened to mention that I would write a letter to Beall's wife. He fixed me with that sharp eagle-eyed look that he had when he was displeased and said to me rather sharply, '*I'll* write his wife.' He felt that it was not only *his* obligation, but also *his* privilege to honor such a fine officer."[24]

Ridgway's successful breakthrough sprung McCreery's "heavy" divisions: the 7th Armored and 46th and 56th infantry divisions. These rolled out of the Sorrento mountains and drove slowly north by various roads, the 56th to the east of Vesuvius toward Capua. The mixed Ridgway force clung to the coast road headed directly for Naples, passing through a string of villages. Their movement was soon retarded by the hundreds of Italian civilians who rushed into the streets to hail (and kiss) the liberators, make speeches and present flowers and bottles of wine or stronger spirits. Ridgway was exasperated by this attention but admitted there was little he could do to avoid it: "You just can't run a truck over a delegation that wants to make a speech, or present you with some flowers and I know of no soldier who won't pause for a moment when a pretty girl throws her arms around his neck and offers him a glass of wine."[25]

On October 1, Gavin's lead elements reached the outskirts of Naples. There was no sign of Germans; they had apparently abandoned the city. Gavin, warily on the lookout for treachery or a surprise attack, was thus astonished when John Norton, his young (West Point 1941) operations officer, came up to say that word had come down from Ridgway "to wait until a triumphant entry is organized." Never one to shrink from a publicity opportunity, Mark Clark intended to lead his troops into Naples, Ridgway at his side.[26]

In preparation for the "triumphant entry," Ridgway sent for the chief of police of Naples. He told him to get everybody off the streets of Naples, because the 82nd Airborne Division was "coming fast" and anybody in the way —German or Italian—would "get hurt." Ridgway also made arrangements for a ceremony to be held in Piazza Garibaldi—or so he thought. He gave Gavin the honor of leading the procession and of ensuring Clark's safety. Gavin, in turn, chose Krause's 3rd Battalion to provide the escort.

In late afternoon, the procession formed up. Gavin took the lead position in a jeep—holding a Naples street map—then came Mark Clark and Ridgway standing in an open armored vehicle. Ridgway held his .30-06 Springfield rifle at the ready, searching the windows and rooftops for snipers. Behind them came Krause and his men in trucks. True to his word, the police chief had cleared the streets of Naples. With the exception of a few policemen at intersections, there was not a single soul in sight. They drove along, staring at the rubble and bombed-out houses and twisted steel that was once a great city. As Clark described it: "I felt that I was riding through ghostly streets in a city of ghosts."

When they pulled into Piazza Garibaldi, Gavin was puzzled. There was no official delegation to offer a surrender of the city; in fact, still hardly a soul in sight. Later Gavin learned there had been a colossal mixup. They were supposed to go to Piazza Plebiscito, where "conquerors traditionally had been received," not Garibaldi. At the Piazza Plebiscito an official delegation and "thousands of people" had gathered for the triumphant entry of the Allied generals.[27]

Naples was a complete shambles. The Germans (or Allied bombers) had destroyed all communications, electrical, water and sewage facilities, as well as the waterfront. They had demolished railroads and fuel-storage tanks and even set great mounds of stockpiled coal on fire. The Germans had set booby traps and left delayed-action explosives behind. Half the eight hundred thousand civilian population had fled into the nearby hills. Those who stayed had no food or water or light or heat. Many armed Italians filtered into the streets after dark to hunt down and shoot Nazi collaborators.

While Army engineers cleared up the rubble, put out the fires and cleared the harbor, Ridgway's troops occupied and policed the city. He established a CP in the police chief's headquarters and then divided the city into three zones, assigning one of his regiments to each zone. The men put a stop to revenge killings and ferreted out time bombs and booby traps. But not all the time bombs could be found in time. On October 7, one went off in the main post office, causing seventy casualties, half of them Ridgway's soldiers. On October 11, another went off in a requisitioned Army barracks, killing eighteen of Ridgway's soldiers from the 307th Airborne Engineers and wounding fifty-six. Ridgway himself narrowly escaped being killed or wounded by one of these devices, made of seventeen hundred pounds of TNT. It was discovered—and disarmed—in the basement of the hotel he chose for his living quarters, "all rigged up, fused and ready to go" within a few minutes.[28]

To make matters worse, the Germans launched sporadic air raids against

Naples. During one of these raids, Ridgway had another very close call. Hearing the engines, he stepped through French windows onto his balcony to see what was going on. At almost precisely that instant, a German plane dropped a large bomb on a British antiaircraft-gun emplacement close by. Ridgway wrote: "The blast blew the French window, just behind me, completely out of its frame, blew all my things off my bureau, and left my room a wreck. Yet I didn't feel a thing."[29]

That hotel suite held a Nazi treasure. Doc Eaton recalled: "Ridgway's aide, Don Faith, and I were playing cribbage. A card fell down behind a cabinet. Faith moved the cabinet to get the card and—lo and behold!—there was a secret room behind the cabinet, about ten by twelve feet. The room was stacked to the ceiling with bottles of good wine and brandy. The secret room became a sort of prize exhibit for our VIP visitors. I kept my bottle of bourbon in there and the visitors always took my bourbon—so I took the label off."[30]

Soon Naples became a peaceful backwater, as the war moved northward—toward the Volturno River. "By and large," Ridgway remembered the occupation duty as "a fairly pleasant experience." For the first time in five months—since leaving New York—his men were "able to sleep in a bed, bathe when they wanted to, know again the little pleasures of life as it is lived by civilians." As on Sicily, Ridgway established an official whorehouse—but he did not inspect this one. He left that chore to Doc Eaton. Notwithstanding the temptation of the flesh and grape, Ridgway's soldiers were, as Ridgway put it, "the gentlest of conquerors." During the occupation, only two of his men had to be brought up on court-martial charges.[31]

As the main body of Clark's Fifth Army approached the Volturno River, stoutly defended by Hube's Tenth Army, Clark turned to the 82nd Airborne Division for help in forcing a breach in the German defenses.

Clark's first proposal was a hurried and ill-conceived plan to mount a simultaneous airborne-amphibious "end run" designed to force a breach on the cheap. While Ridgway dropped a regiment of paratroopers at Sessa, Clark would land a regiment at Mondragone. The two forces would then link up behind the German lines, causing panic and forcing a German withdrawal. Fortunately, cooler heads prevailed and this plan was soon abandoned, because, as a Fifth Army historian wrote with unmatched understatement: "Enemy concentration in the areas in question made both plans too risky."[32]

Clark's second—and far more serious—proposal came soon after Fifth Army's two corps drew abreast of the south bank of the river. The plan was that the 82nd would be attached to John Lucas' VI Corps and serve as assault troops to lead the corps across the river. Upon learning of the plan, Ridgway went immediately to the front to inspect the proposed area. He took a perch on the crest of a high hill which overlooked the river. He wrote: "It was about as mean a place to try a river crossing as any I saw during the whole war." The Hermann Göring Panzer Division was dug into a rough semicircle of hills facing the designated crossing point. The plan reminded Ridgway of World War I battles in which thousands of men had been callously sacrificed for an objective, often because a general wanted a little glory. If the crossing were attempted, he concluded, he would lose "much of the 82nd." He would not permit his division to be destroyed.

For the third time in six weeks, Ridgway faced the necessity of killing an ill-advised mission assigned his troops. He first went to see Lucian Truscott, whose judgment he respected. Truscott agreed that Ridgway was right, that the mission would be suicidal. He next called on Lucas and "didn't mince any words" in stating his objections. To make certain the plan went no further, he also saw Mark Clark. He heard nothing more about the plan. The mission finally went to Truscott, whose heavy 3rd Division was reinforced for the crossing.[33]

Paul Turner, the West Pointer who had lost his 2nd Battalion (325) to John Swenson because of bleeding ulcers, was discharged from the hospital and rejoined the division at this time. Ridgway—happy to see him back—had appointed Turner to his G-3 section, and Turner was involved in planning this proposed crossing. "The attack was to be over an extremely wide front," Turner recalled, but then Ridgway "made the decision to have the order rescinded. This was an example of true leadership. He could have said, 'We have our orders—we attack.' Instead, he laid himself on the line by asking that the mission be called off. This was a very serious decision to make."[34]

In the end, however, the 82nd Division was drawn into the Volturno River crossing, albeit in a more modest role. At Mark Clark's request, Ridgway assigned two of Gavin's 505 parachute battalions to put some ginger into Mc-Creery's flagging 10 Corps. These were Walter Winton's 1st and Mark Alexander's 2nd, both attached to the 10 Corps spearhead, the British 23rd Armored Brigade. The paratroopers and armor would lead the 10 Corps across the Volturno near the town of Arnone, in the canal-laced British 46th Division sector in the river's delta. By a curious coincidence, this was the same area which Alexander's battalion had been assigned to capture in the original (canceled) Capua drop. Alexander had never been "even slightly enthusiastic" about that airborne plan, and when he saw his old objective from the ground, he remarked, "Thank God [the Capua drop] was abandoned."[35]

The mission proved to be a tough one. In this sector of the river, which had high levees, there were five canals to cross. Mark Alexander's 2nd Battalion led the way on the night of October 13/14. His men secured two canals that night and the remaining three the following day, October 14, all in the face of murderous enemy fire which inflicted such heavy casualties on his battalion that Winton had to send Alexander two of his three infantry companies to back him up. Alexander said later—no doubt correctly—that "we were the first Allied troops to cross the Volturno River." The fine but costly work of his battalion and Winton's cleared the way for the British 23rd Armored Brigade and, behind it, the British 46th Division.

Although Ridgway's principal mission at this time was the policing of Naples, he spent a great deal of time at the Volturno River front. Despite his stubborn refusal to employ the division in the Volturno River crossing, Lucas continued to hold him in highest esteem. When the 45th Division commander,

Troy Middleton, was laid low with severe arthritis of the knees, Lucas considered appointing Ridgway temporary commander of the 45th, as he recorded in his diary: "If Clark will lend me Ridgway for a while I will send Middleton to the hospital." However, Middleton toughed it out and the temporary change of command was not necessary.[36]

On October 13, Ridgway returned to the Volturno River to watch the main assaults of Fifth Army. Paul Turner recalled:

> We arrived at a river crossing where the engineers, commanded by my classmate [Charles F.] Bill Tank, were building a bridge. Tank briefed us and warned us that we were going to be fired on by a German 88. The warning became a reality and we had to run for cover. Leaving the jeep in the middle of the road, the general and I dived into a ditch; the jeep driver, Frank Farmer, ran down the road several hundred yards, seeking cover. Finally Ridgway said, "Let's make a break for it." I had to urinate, but I jumped in the jeep. No Ridgway. I yelled, "Come on, General, let's go. I'll drive." I looked around and saw him standing in the middle of the road urinating, with the 88 shells crashing all around him. I am sure he did that for my benefit; I honestly don't think that he really knew the meaning of fear. So I jumped out of the jeep and did the same. Then we got in the jeep—the 88 firing at us—and picked up Farmer and got out of there.[37]

By evening of October 14, Clark's Fifth Army was across the Volturno. However, it was all too little and too late. By then, Hube's Tenth Army was skillfully withdrawing into a temporary "winter line" immediately in front of the Gustav Line. When the Gustav Line was finished, the Germans fell back to occupy it. Although Clark pursued the Germans with vigor, there was no hope of rolling over the Gustav Line. Cold, miserable winter rains soon set in, miring his tanks and wheeled vehicles, and disheartening Clark's tired troops. Hitler allotted Kesselring several more divisions; eight long, bitter winter months would pass before Clark would reach Rome.

It would be a controversial campaign which would cost the Allies some 188,000 casualties—32,000 killed. In the aftermath, some military historians—most notably Samuel Eliot Morison—would argue that it was ill-advised. The principal objective of the invasion of Italy—knocking her out of the war—had been obtained before the first shot had been fired at Salerno. The capture of Naples and the Foggia airfield complex satisfied the stated requirements for strategic air bases to attack the German industrial base from the south, where the air defenses were less formidable, and the Romanian oil fields. The Allies should have been satisfied with that, Morison held, and gone over to the defensive at the Volturno River. Advocates of continuing the campaign, who included Churchill, Eisenhower and Alexander, argued that the capture of Rome remained a valuable psychological prize and, furthermore, that Allied offensive operations in Italy drained off substantial German troops and military resources that could otherwise have been utilized on the Russian front or to oppose OVERLORD.[38]

☆21☆

THE CAMPAIGNS in Sicily and Italy had been temporary detours for the 82nd Airborne Division. After the Allies crossed the Volturno River, Ridgway began laying plans to return the division to the task for which it had been conceived: OVERLORD, the invasion of German-occupied France, to be staged from the British Isles.

He ran into unforeseen opposition, however. Mark Clark, believing Ridgway to be "an outstanding battle soldier; brilliant, fearless and loyal," who had "trained and produced one of the finest Fifth Army outfits," did not want to give up either Ridgway or the 82nd. Clark wanted to keep the division for use in airborne-amphibious "end runs" behind German lines along the west coast of Italy. His ideas led to prolonged discussions at the highest levels in North Africa, London and Washington, which resulted in a compromise: Clark would keep Bill Yarborough's 509th Battalion more or less permanently. In addition, Tucker's 504th Regiment, reinforced by Wilbur Griffith's 376th and Hugh Neal's 456th Parachute Artillery (the three constituting a "combat team") would remain in Italy on temporary duty a while longer, but would be returned to Ridgway in plenty of time for OVERLORD. The rest of the 82nd, and most of the British 1st Airborne Division, would be transferred to the British Isles as soon as possible.[1]

The news came as a blow to Ridgway. He expressed his disappointment in a letter to Clark: "This division sees a major part of itself about to be left behind when it moves to another theater. Its officers and men view this separation, temporary as it is promised to be, with live concern. Eighteen months and an untold amount of devoted effort have gone into the building of this team. It has been tested in and out of battle. It has worthily met all those tests. It has developed a spirit and a soul of its own, and no member of the division could view its partition without a sense of personal hurt." Clark responded reassuringly: "My troops are tired. I do not have the strength I need for this show; hence, your Regimental Combat Team is indispensable at the present moment . . . You know I have your interests at heart and I will protect them as though they were mine, and I will see that my staff does likewise."[2]

Taking immediate advantage of the decision, Clark put the 504th Combat Team to work, not as airborne but as regular "light infantry." By that time, there had been yet another change in the command of Tucker's 3rd Battalion. Tucker's former exec, Leslie Freeman, returning from the hospital recovered from his Salerno wounds, found his job now filled by Chuck Billingslea. Tucker made a place for Freeman by reappointing Hank Adams S-3 and naming Freeman to command the 3rd Battalion. Warren Williams and Danny Danielson retained command of the 1st and 2nd battalions, respectively.

Mark Clark assigned the 504th the mission of filling the "gap" between his Fifth Army and Montgomery's Eighth Army in the bleak, rugged mountains of central Italy. The official Army historian, Martin Blumenson, described the terrain in that area as "so difficult that it was necessary often to communicate by carrier pigeon and sometimes to send food and ammunition by overhead trolley strung across deep mountain gorges." For most of the next sixty days the 504 led the Fifth Army's northward drive toward Venafro and Cassino, where, finally, the "chase" bogged down at the "winter" and Gustav lines, in mud and frustration.[3]

This rugged campaign added laurels and luster to the 504th Regiment and its commander, Rube Tucker. Jim Gavin, who visited the regiment several times in the early stages of the campaign, found no letup in Tucker's "extraordinary ability" as a combat leader. VI Corps commander John Lucas, under whose command Tucker fell, expressed his admiration for the regiment in his diary: "The 504th parachutists on the right have never halted in their advance . . . This unit served with great distinction throughout these operations. Being lightly equipped and trained to operate 'on their own,' the paratroopers soon gained a reputation for skillful patrolling and the ability to infiltrate through the German formations in the high mountains . . ."[4]*

As Ridgway made final arrangements for shipping the rest of the division to the British Isles, he also made several important changes in command and staff.

First, and most important, was the selection of a new second-in-command, or ADC. After Bull Keerans had been lost in Sicily, Ridgway had appointed Max Taylor temporary ADC. But Taylor was seldom present. First he had carried out the secret Rome mission, then Eisenhower had named him a temporary emissary to the Italian government-in-exile. Since there was no indication that Taylor would be returning soon, Ridgway decided to choose another man, one who would remain with him permanently. Jim Gavin was Ridgway's choice for the job. On October 10, 1943, at age thirty-six, Gavin was promoted to brigadier general and officially named ADC, thus becoming one of the youngest generals in the U.S. Army.[6]

Gavin's promotion raised a difficult question: Who would command the now famous 505? In a manner of speaking, Gavin would. He found it hard to let go of the regiment and, despite his new responsibilities, was seldom out of touch with the outfit. In title, Gavin was replaced by his executive officer, Herbert F. Batcheller, who had jumped with Gavin in Sicily and Salerno. Batcheller was a West Point classmate of Tucker's, but, as time would show, he was nowhere near Tucker's match as a regimental commander.[7]†

---

* But not without heavy casualties. Among these were Tucker's 2nd Battalion commander, Danny Danielson, who was severely wounded and evacuated, replaced by Melvin S. Blitch, Jr.[5]

† Mark Alexander, 2nd Battalion commander, was promoted to regimental exec, replaced by Ben Vandervoort.[8]

Ironically, Ridgway temporarily "lost" Gavin as well. Like Taylor, Gavin was soon detached to special duty. Marshall wrote Ridgway to say that he "urgently" needed "an able officer with vision and combat experience" to serve as airborne adviser to the OVERLORD planners in England. Ridgway recommended Gavin, cabling Marshall: "He, more than any other [officer] I know in my division or out, has vision, combat experience, professional knowledge and personality for this assignment." However, Ridgway added, "I want him back."[9]

Before Ridgway released Gavin, they had a long talk about the technical and political problems of OVERLORD. One potential political problem in their special field was Boy Browning. Recently Browning had been promoted to lieutenant general, outranking Ridgway by one star and Gavin by two stars. Ridgway was concerned that Browning would attempt, as he had in the Sicily operation, to gain command of all OVERLORD airborne operations. As Gavin later recalled, Ridgway warned him to beware of Browning's "machinations and scheming." Under no circumstances should Gavin knuckle under to any proposal to name Browning overall airborne commander. In conclusion, Ridgway promised that Gavin would be returned to the division in time for the OVERLORD battle. So briefed, Gavin departed Naples on November 16.[10]

The second important personnel change occurred in Ridgway's staff. After Salerno, Mark Clark was in sore need of a regimental commander to help rebuild the shattered 36th Division. Since the job carried the rank of full colonel, Ridgway proposed that Clark take his G-2, George Lynch, whom Ridgway believed deserved a promotion—and a field command. Although Lynch left with tears in his eyes, he was delighted to get the command and would be forever grateful—and admiring—of Ridgway. He was replaced as division G-2 by the chain-smoking G-3, Whitfield Jack, who, in turn, was replaced by his senior assistant, Paul Turner.[11]

Meanwhile, Ridgway completed arrangements for transferring the division (minus the 504 combat team) to the British Isles by ship. He would not accompany it himself. Marshall had ordered him back to the States by air for important airborne conferences. Ridgway named Doc Eaton to serve as "acting commander" of the division in his absence. The convoy sailed from Naples on November 18, stopped a few days in Oran (where the men were granted R & R) and reached Belfast, Ireland, on December 9.[12]

Doc Eaton remembered:

Ridgway gave me three important tasks: 1) Get the division to Ireland; 2) Get his Cadillac staff car—an old rattletrap—to Ireland; 3) Get that wine and brandy cache from the secret room in the Naples hotel suite to Ireland. I loaded the Caddy and the booze, packed under a tarp in a trailer, on board our ship. A high-ranking Army staff officer said, "What the hell is that Caddy doing on this ship!" I said it was Ridgway's staff car. He said, "Well, get it off right now!" So I lost his car. One day off the coast of Ireland there was a great hullaballoo in the Merchant Marine crew. They were all drunk! I thought, "Uh-oh" and rushed down into the hold to the booze trailer. Sure enough, it was completely empty. They had stolen it all. But I got the division there![13]

On the verge of his own departure for the States, Ridgway was still uneasy about leaving the 504 behind. Long experience in the Army had taught him that a "temporary" arrangement often became permanent. Before leaving Italy, he visited the unit at the front and personally assured Tucker and his senior commanders that they would soon rejoin the division. To Mark Clark he wrote: "I know I can count, as you have assured me I may, upon your assistance in securing the prompt return of these troops to Division control as soon as the temporary need for their services in your Army shall have ceased. I therefore bespeak, earnestly, your personal attention in safeguarding the interest of these units and in helping to bring about their early return to their own Division." Clark replied: "I will get it out in time for any airborne mission [e.g. OVERLORD] and I will return it to you in the best shape I can, commensurate with any job they have to do."[14]

Ridgway was still not fully reassured. Nor was he happy about leaving Max Taylor behind in the nebulous liaison job with the exiled Italian Government in Brindisi. He thus conceived, and proposed to Bedell Smith, a plan to have Taylor take overall command of the 504 and supporting units, and make certain that it was returned to the division. This plan was approved, and in December Taylor reported to Mark Clark's headquarters in Caserta, Italy. Taylor recalled that his job was "to keep an eye on Tucker's troops and extricate them from the clutches of . . . Mark Clark just as soon as possible." Taylor kept pressure on Clark and his chief of staff, Al Gruenther, "and thereby made a nuisance of myself," but he got nowhere. At Churchill's insistence, Clark had begun planning a combined airborne-amphibious "end run" at Anzio. Churchill himself made a successful personal appeal to George Marshall and Eisenhower to retain the 504 for the Anzio operation.[15]

By the time Ridgway reached the States, in late November, the controversy over airborne forces, begun in Sicily, had reached the crisis stage. Inside the Army, intense debates were raging everywhere over the size, scope and employment of airborne forces. George Marshall was still a believer in the airborne division and wanted to use several in OVERLORD. But Eisenhower was on record as opposing the airborne division as "too large" and unwieldy, preferring instead "strong regimental combat teams." Lesley McNair, no doubt influenced by the report from his friend John Lucas on the Sicily operation, believed parachute units should be even smaller: battalion-sized at most.[16]

There was considerable justification for the debate. Despite all the glamorous publicity, the truth was that so far airborne combat operations had been disappointing—or worse. The Allies had attempted eight major airborne combat operations in the Mediterranean Theater behind enemy lines: the drops of the independent American 509th Battalion in North Africa and, later, Avellino; the drops of the American 504th and 505th regiments in Sicily; British battal-

ion-size drops at Bône and another deep inside Tunisia; the drops of the British
1st Parachute and 1st Air Landing brigades in Sicily. All eight operations had
been disasters; only Gavin's 505 jump into Sicily had made a worthwhile contribution. Worldwide, there had been only one "successful" major Allied airborne operation: the daylight drop of the independent 503rd American Parachute Regiment in Nadzab, New Guinea, on September 5, 1943, in conjunction
with an Allied amphibious assault on Japanese-held Lae. But even this "success" was open to question. By the time it was launched, the Japanese were
under orders from Tokyo to withdraw from Lae at the first sign of an Allied
threat, and the 503rd had met no real enemy opposition.[17]

Owing to the widespread doubts about the soundness of airborne operations,
Marshall had convened a study panel to evaluate the evidence and weigh the
pros and cons. The panel was chaired by 11th Airborne commander Joe Swing,
who was a firm believer in the airborne division and on whom Marshall could
count to render a verdict which supported his own views. All during the fall of
1943 the "Swing Board" conducted extensive hearings. When Ridgway returned to the States, he gave the Swing Board, as well as Marshall and Mc-
Nair, a number of strong recommendations, based on his combat experiences.[18]

Although he had had some doubts after Sicily, by now Ridgway was an
uncompromising advocate of the airborne division. He believed the airborne
disasters in the Mediterranean Theater had occurred largely because the senior
ground commanders (Eisenhower, Alexander, Montgomery, and Clark) and
their airborne advisers (namely Browning) did not understand how to properly
use airborne forces. He criticized the ground commanders for committing both
the British 1st Airborne and the 82nd Airborne haphazardly and "piecemeal"
in North Africa, Sicily and Italy. "Commanders," he wrote, "must refrain
from assigning airborne missions merely because airborne troops are available,
and commit them only at appropriate times on missions suitable to their capabilities, limitations and available supporting means." This view coincided with
Marshall's, who believed, in the words of his official biographer Forrest C.
Pogue, that "airborne units were being frittered away merely as support troops
instead of being used decisively in an assault."[19]

To prevent future misuse of airborne forces, Ridgway submitted to Marshall,
McNair and the Swing Board a set of written principles which theater commanders should be required to follow when contemplating the use of airborne
forces. He urged close, continuous and detailed coordination between airborne,
air, ground and sea forces; "realistic" appraisals of objectives and enemy capabilities; adequate troop-carrier aircraft, staging airfields, and air escort; and
other commonsense matters. Above all, he urged "realistic" and intensive
training of troops and troop-carrier pilots over "a matter of weeks" before each
operation.

He used his own airborne division to illustrate the weakness in training.
Higher headquarters might think the division and its troop carrier were ready
for extended combat operations, Ridgway wrote; if so, "there could be no
greater nor more dangerous fallacy." In fact, he went on, "grave deficiencies
exist," most of these due to inadequate training with troop-carrier pilots. In

reality, the division was far from ready to carry out either a day or a night parachute or glider operation (especially a *night glider* operation) with any hope of success.[20]

His recommendations for the division were uncompromising. Before the division could be employed in a major airborne operation (e.g. OVERLORD), certain steps had to be taken "without delay": 1) The division had to be withdrawn from other duties and responsibilities and enter into a prolonged period of intense airborne training—two months at an "absolute minimum" in Fort Bragg's favorable terrain and climate or "three months, or even longer" in less favorable terrain and climate (such as that in the British Isles). 2) At the same time, a troop-carrier wing had to be permanently mated with the division with no other duties than training—the logical wing being Hal Clark's 52nd, owing to "the high degree of mutual confidence built up between the two organizations" over the past nine months.

Beyond that, Ridgway urged a significant increase in the makeup, size and power of the airborne division. In effect, he recommended increasing the then approved fighting strength of the airborne division by over one third. He wanted more paratroopers and fewer gliderists. In his view, each division should be composed of two or three parachute regiments and only one glider regiment (of three battalions), plus substantially more artillery, antitank and other supporting units. However, in this recommendation Ridgway met a stone wall. McNair, who was far from convinced that the airborne division was even feasible, stubbornly clung to the concept of a "light" division, comprising primarily gliderists, who did not require expensive and time-consuming parachute training.[21]

Finally, to all the foregoing principles and specific recommendations for his own division, he added two other matters which were of deep concern to him: yet another recommendation for hazardous-duty pay for gliderists; and a recommendation for greater leniency toward those few paratroopers who "froze" at the airplane door and "refused" to jump in combat. Although Ridgway believed prison sentences were necessary "for deterrent effect," he found even reduced punishment too harsh and "not the best solution." He recommended a stricter "weeding out" process to find the "weaklings" in parachute school, together with a provision for resignation before graduation. He further recommended that parachutists be allowed to "resign without prejudice" after one year in combat or eighteen months in Stateside duty.[22]

Out of all these deliberations emerged a proposal for a dramatic, large-scale Stateside "test" of the airborne division to determine if it was a valid concept. Although George Marshall and Joe Swing (as well as Ridgway) were already convinced that the airborne division was a valid concept, a poor showing would almost certainly have been a devastating blow to the advocates of the airborne division. Failure would have provided Eisenhower, McNair and other opponents of the airborne division with powerful arguments to abandon it. For this reason, airborne veterans would look back on the test as a "life or death" milestone for the airborne division.

The test was staged at a site convenient to Fort Bragg. An airport and

surrounding terrain were designated an "enemy stronghold." The "stronghold" was "defended" by a regimental combat team from Bud Miley's 17th
Airborne Division. The "aggressors" would be Joe Swing's 11th Airborne Division, which would jump and glide into the stronghold and—it was hoped—
overwhelm it.

The maneuver was launched on December 6, 1943. On hand to observe were
Under Secretary of War Robert P. Patterson, Lesley McNair, a host of generals
and colonels—and Matt Ridgway. Joe Swing's parachute and glider regiments,
staging from four airfields, were keyed up and well rehearsed. One airborne
historian wrote: "Swing's troops knew they were testifying for or against the
life of their division as well as the lives of all other airborne divisions, so they
put maximum effort into every task . . ."

The maneuver, the historian wrote, was "a huge success for the airborne."
Swing's parachute and glider regiments landed as planned (incurring only a
negligible number of accidents) and "overwhelmed" Bud Miley's airborne defenders. Since the future of Miley's own 17th Airborne Division was also on
the line, whether or not Miley's men mounted the best possible "defense"
remained moot. In any case, the chief opponent of the airborne division, Lesley
McNair, was apparently convinced. Ten days later, December 16, he wrote
Swing: "I congratulate you on the splendid performance of your division in the
Knollwood maneuver . . . The successful performance of your division has
convinced me that we were wrong, and I shall now recommend that we continue our present schedule of activating, training and committing airborne
divisions."[23]

After Christmas, Ridgway flew to Ireland to rejoin his troops. Lying ahead
was the greatest military enterprise in the history of mankind: OVERLORD,
the invasion of Nazi-held Europe. D day was set for May 1, a mere 120 days
away. It would begin with a vast Allied assault in Normandy. There could be
no mistakes or miscalculations this time. Hitler's preeminent general, Erwin
Rommel, was poised in France behind the "Atlantic Wall," waiting to pounce.
If the Allies were thrown back into the sea, it might be years before another
attempt could be made, giving Hitler time to deal with the Russian front and
put into operation his promised "secret weapons," which, if they lived up to
the advance ballyhoo, might win the war for him.

PART IV

England:
Eve of Invasion

☆ 22 ☆

THE ORIGINAL OVERLORD invasion plan had been conceived by British General Frederick E. Morgan, who presided over an Allied staff in London.

The assault phase, NEPTUNE, was modest in scope. A mere three divisions —two British and one American—would spearhead the invasion. The British divisions would land on the left (or east) flank near Caen; the American division on the right (or west) flank near Bayeux. Small contingents of British and American airborne forces would jump or glide (or both), by moonlight, into the Caen and Bayeux areas several hours preceding the dawn landing to blunt German counterattacks on the invasion beaches.[1]

George Marshall had been the chief advocate of the cross-Channel attack. He had finally gained approval for it against British indifference or opposition. Since the Americans would contribute the preponderance of military force after the assault, it was long assumed in American Army circles that the supreme commander of OVERLORD would be an American. Marshall himself was the odds-on favorite for the job. For a long time Marshall assumed the command would be his and he therefore followed the evolution of the OVERLORD plan closely.

He was not happy with the Morgan plan. It was, Marshall believed, an unimaginative frontal assault that would draw German mobile reserves like a magnet. He believed the invasion stood a good chance of bogging down in Normandy, perhaps even turning into ghastly trench warfare of the kind he had seen all too much of in World War I. What was needed, Marshall believed, was a bold, new concept which would capitalize on Allied assets and absolutely foreclose any such possibility. Hap Arnold, Marshall's air counterpart and fellow member of the four-man U.S. Joint Chiefs of Staff, agreed with his views.

In the fall of 1943, Marshall and Arnold, working in utmost secrecy with a small Washington planning staff, devised such a plan. It was, to put it mildly, breathtaking. In effect, it turned the NEPTUNE plan around. Allied airborne forces, striking deep into France, would constitute the primary thrust of the invasion; the amphibious forces would be secondary.[2]

In general, the plan was as follows. A force of four or five Allied airborne divisions would be dropped and airlanded at Évreux (near Paris), where they would establish an airhead. These paratroopers and gliderists would quickly commandeer all vehicles within the airhead. At the same time, they would make contact with forces of the French underground, which would have been clandestinely preassembled in the area. These combined forces would hold the airhead and assist in enlarging it with more airlanded troops while the amphibious forces, freighted with armor and mobile artillery, landed in Normandy and dashed inland to link up with the airborne forces.

Marshall and Arnold believed the plan would so thoroughly stun the Germans that it would succeed before they came to their senses. Marshall later said, "We could build up a force right behind the German lines before they had time to get things together and make it almost impossible for them to do anything but to fight you with small groups . . . [The airborne forces] could have been used with great effect in splitting up the Germans very quickly at the start. And the minute it was a little split up, the whole thing would fall apart because the continued reinforcement [by the Allies] would have been a simple matter."

In October 1943, when Morgan came to Washington for conferences, Marshall and Arnold unveiled their plan. Morgan was thunderstruck and, when he recovered from the shock, highly dubious about the merits of the plan. Finding himself much outranked—eight stars to two—he cabled London to send high-ranking reinforcements to help him knock down the plan. Among these, the principal figure to arrive was Air Chief Marshal Sir Trafford Leigh-Mallory, whom the Combined Chiefs had already appointed to command all tactical air power in OVERLORD, including fighters and troop carriers.[3]

Like most airmen of that era, Leigh-Mallory was a zealot who believed that air power alone could defeat Germany. From his lofty viewpoint, the great air-power tasks were the destruction of the German Air Force, the obliteration of Germany's war-making capacity, transportation and oil refineries, and the demoralization of her people. He thought in terms of vast air battles between opposing fighters and of massive fighter-escorted strategic bombing raids. Near the bottom of his list of priorities were the unglamorous tasks of providing close air support for ground armies and ferrying airborne troops into battle.[4]

Leigh-Mallory threw cold water on the Marshall-Arnold plan. He argued, first, that there were not nearly enough troop-carrier planes to lift so vast a force. At that time, Leigh-Mallory had barely enough aircraft to lift one division. Second, he argued, troop-carrier aircraft—and gliders—were highly vulnerable to German fighters and flak. Flying coffins. In such an operation, he predicted, losses would be catastrophic. Third, he argued, the proposed airhead was much too far from the beachheads to assure a timely linkup. The isolated, lightly armed paratroopers would, in all probability, be cut up and destroyed in detail by German armor and artillery. He considered the plan almost suicidal.[5]

Marshall and Arnold were unmoved by these negatives. All along, Marshall had been "very strong" for airborne operations. Largely on his say-so, the American Army had committed vast resources to the concept, and at Marshall's instruction, the American Army was sending more and more airborne forces to England. In the face of Leigh-Mallory's implacable opposition, Marshall decided that, if necessary, he would carry out the airborne concept "exclusively with American troops."[6]

The buildup of American airborne forces in the ETO was becoming formidable enough for the task. Bill Lee's 101st Division had arrived with its normal complement of one parachute regiment (502) and two glider regiments (327 and 401) plus another parachute regiment (506) temporarily attached. Ridgway's 82nd Division had arrived with one parachute regiment (505) and one glider regiment (325) with another parachute regiment (504, in Italy) to follow. In addition, Marshall had sent over the 2nd Parachute Brigade, composed of two parachute regiments (507, 508) plus another independent parachute regiment (501). (Coming behind these, but on a schedule too late for D day, was Bud Miley's 17th Airborne Division and, behind that, the 13th Airborne Division.) Hap Arnold had sent over nearly fifteen hundred crated Waco gliders, and hundreds more were on the way. British furniture manufacturers were now turning out Horsas by the hundreds.[7]

Once Tucker's 504th arrived, there would be a total of seven American parachute regiments and three fully trained glider regiments in the British Isles. Under McNair's existing table of organization for an airborne division (one parachute regiment, two glider regiments) this was sufficient paratrooper manpower to create seven American airborne divisions—assuming, as McNair did, that additional glider regiments could be easily created from ordinary infantry with merely one or two indoctrination glider flights. If enough planes could be found to fly these divisions deep into France, this was sufficient force to carry out Marshall's invasion plan.*

But Marshall never got the chance to pursue it. President Roosevelt, who was in failing health, had become more and more dependent on him for strategic guidance and management of the war. He declared that when Marshall was out of the country he could not sleep at night. Although Roosevelt and Secretary of War Stimson had assured Marshall he would command OVERLORD, that Marshall would become "the Pershing of the Second World War," in early December, at the Big Three Conference in Teheran, Roosevelt changed his mind. He simply could not spare Marshall from Washington. As a result, the job of OVERLORD Supreme Commander went to Eisenhower.[8]

Before moving on to England, Eisenhower petitioned the Combined Chiefs to transfer his winning team of British land, air and sea commanders from the Mediterranean to lead OVERLORD forces. He did not get his way. Only one, Arthur Tedder, played a significant role in OVERLORD. He was named Deputy Supreme Commander. Leigh-Mallory had already been named tactical air commander; British Admiral Bertram H. Ramsay was designated naval commander. Bernard Montgomery was recalled from Italy to command all Allied ground forces in the assault. These would include the British Second Army, commanded by Miles C. Dempsey, and the American First Army, commanded by Omar Bradley.[9]

The four senior soldiers in this lineup—Eisenhower, Montgomery, Bradley, Dempsey—generally concurred with the Morgan plan for NEPTUNE. They agreed with the time (May 1, 1944) and place (Normandy), but all believed the assault lacked sufficient "wallop." They soon nearly doubled the size of the

---

* There were, in addition, two British airborne divisions: the 1st, redeploying to England from the Mediterranean, and a new one, the 6th, based in England.

assault force from three to five heavily reinforced divisions and expanded the beachhead from about twenty-five miles to nearly fifty to include the Cotentin Peninsula, so that the Allies could quickly capture its big seaport, Cherbourg. Owing to the continuing shortage of landing craft (LSTs in particular) this decision forced a postponement of D day from May 1 to June 1 in order to gain one more month's production of LSTs. The LST shortage in part delayed a controversial subsidiary amphibious landing in southern France known first as ANVIL, then DRAGOON.

The revised invasion plan soon arrived at was as follows: Dempsey's Second Army would land on three beaches (Gold, Juno, Sword) near Caen. On D day, they would seize Caen and the flat terrain southwest of the city, which was needed for tactical airfields. After that, the British would hold in place to absorb the shock of the German counterattacks. Dempsey would be reinforced by the Canadian First Army, commanded by Henry D. G. Crerar. Bradley's First Army would land on two beaches (Omaha and Utah) to the west of Caen at the base of the thumb-like Cotentin Peninsula. The American forces would isolate the Cotentin and capture Cherbourg, which was designated the principal supply port for all Allied armies. Thereafter, George Patton's Third Army would come into the American beachhead to reinforce Bradley, at which time Bradley would be elevated to 12th Army Group commander (on a par with Montgomery), turning over First Army to Courtney H. Hodges. Patton's Third Army would first capture Brittany (and its seaports) then about-face to the east. Then Hodges' First Army and Patton's Third Army would "wheel," with Caen as a "hub." When all four Allied armies were more or less abreast, they would advance easterly to the Seine River, where it was expected that the Germans would make an all-out stand to hold France.

An important part of the OVERLORD plan was an elaborate and ingenious hoax, or military deception, called FORTITUDE. The deception was designed to convince the Germans that the main Allied landings would occur not in Normandy but in Pas de Calais (with a subsidiary landing in Norway) and that the Normandy operations were merely feints. Toward this end, the Allies created a fictional American "1st Army Group," which was "commanded" by George Patton and seemingly poised to strike at Pas de Calais. This army group had "assigned" to it both real and fictional American divisions, including a fictional airborne unit. The army group had a dummy headquarters and masses of dummy tanks and landing craft made of plywood and rubber. Radio operators kept up a steady stream of "messages" between army-group headquarters and the divisions. German spies, who had been captured in England and "turned," fed bogus information on Patton's army group to Berlin. The Allies monitored the progress of the deception through intercepted and decoded German radio traffic.[10]

Of the senior British commanders assigned to OVERLORD, Eisenhower was disappointed in two: Admiral Ramsay and Air Chief Marshal Leigh-Mallory. His three British Mediterranean commanders, Eisenhower tactfully wrote Marshall, had been men of the "broadest possible caliber," but Ramsay and

Leigh-Mallory, "although extremely able, are somewhat ritualistic in outlook and require a great deal more of inoculation."[11]

Of these two senior British commanders, airman Leigh-Mallory would prove to be the more difficult. He was a much-publicized hero of the British Fighter Command and did not wear his fame with easy grace. He talked too much, was high-handed with subordinates and seldom listened to their advice, and his imperious, brusque manner antagonized almost every commander in OVER-LORD. Montgomery confided in his diary that Leigh-Mallory "is definitely above his ceiling . . . and is not good enough for the job we are on." A senior American airman said, "Nobody wanted to be under Leigh-Mallory, even the British . . . He didn't seem to know what he wanted. He couldn't get along with people. He seemed more concerned with preserving his forces than with committing them."[12]

As tactical air boss of OVERLORD, Leigh-Mallory commanded both the British tactical air forces and the much larger American Ninth Air Force, into which all American tactical air had been organized. The Ninth Air Force was, in turn, commanded by Lewis H. (Looie) Brereton, a senior airman who was, oddly enough, a graduate of the U.S. Naval Academy (class of 1911). After being commissioned an ensign in the Navy, Brereton had transferred to the Army's Field Artillery, then to the embryonic Army Air Corps, and had served in France in World War I, where he won a DSC and was wounded and shot down.

In peacetime, Brereton had ably climbed the career ladder and, along the way, had made a favorable impression on Marshall and Arnold. In 1941, they had handpicked him to command the first crisis deployment of the Air Force's most vaunted weapon system, the B-17 Flying Fortress. Brereton took about forty of the bombers to the Philippines to help implement Douglas MacArthur's plan to defend the islands from Japanese attack. But he ran into trouble. On December 8 (Manila time), when the Japanese attacked, Brereton inexplicably lost most of his B-17 force on the ground. MacArthur, thoroughly disillusioned, later asked for a new air general. After that, Brereton had migrated to India, then North Africa, where he had commanded the Middle East Air Force, headquartered in Cairo.[13]

Then fifty-three years old, Brereton was a short (five-six), vain dynamo with a legendary temper, a salty tongue, and an eye for girls. Describing him in a lengthy *Life* magazine profile published in 1942, Clare Boothe (Luce) wrote that Brereton was "tough, hard-boiled, and a terrific driver," with a "rich vocabulary, swearing in three or four languages." He began each day, Boothe wrote, with a "brimstone coverage of staff delinquencies," and seldom used the pronoun I—"preferring to refer to himself as 'Lewis Brereton.' " Married first in 1913, Boothe wrote, Brereton was divorced in 1929 and two years later, at age forty, married a woman sixteen years his junior. One of his senior subordinates, Elwood P. (Pete) Quesada, recently recalled: "He was a doer, who worked hard during the day and played very hard at night. Drank very hard and was a hell-raiser and woman-chaser until he died." The latter proclivity had generated so much gossip that George Marshall had been compelled to send Brereton an extraordinary personal letter of rebuke.[14]

Brereton shared Leigh-Mallory's view that air power alone could defeat Germany. His mind was also preoccupied with vast aerial battles with the German Air Force, since his fighters were then engaged in providing escort for the big strategic bomber raids on Germany. Omar Bradley would later say that Brereton was not "interested" in mundane matters such as close air support for ground forces and "resisted any effort to work together." Bradley wrote that during one important OVERLORD rehearsal, when Brereton's close air support inexplicably failed to appear, the general seemed "strangely unconcerned with the failure of the air mission." One result, Bradley wrote, was that "we went into France almost totally untrained in air-ground operations." Brereton's attitude toward troop-carrier operations was no less cavalier. Doc Eaton's earthy opinion of the Ninth Air Force commander no doubt was shared by many within the airborne forces: "Brereton was a stupid ass."[15]

Among these senior OVERLORD commanders, the airborne forces found few friends. There was, however, one important exception in the American camp: Omar Bradley. Even though the American airborne operations on Sicily had been less than perfect, Bradley had come away convinced that Ridgway's forces had given the Allies a significant edge in that invasion. Bradley's views would make a big difference in the shape of NEPTUNE—and in Ridgway's future.

☆ 23 ☆

WHEN RIDGWAY'S SURROGATE, Jim Gavin, had arrived in London in December 1943, to join Bill Lee as an adviser for NEPTUNE airborne planning, he was dismayed at what he found. Brereton's Troop Carrier Command had only been recently launched with a handful of planes and green pilots fresh from the States. The NEPTUNE airborne plan itself was modest. Only portions of two airborne divisions had been earmarked for the assault, and the plans all too closely resembled those for Sicily. Elements of the new British 6th Airborne Division would drop near Caen to seize or blow bridges and a coastal artillery battery. Elements of Bill Lee's 101st, deployed in battalion strength, would drop near Bayeux, immediately behind the American beachhead Omaha. Although it was now restaging to England, the 82nd Division was not then included in the plan.[1]

Gavin was young and junior—merely a brand-new one-star general—and had to tread his way carefully through the corridors of power. But he had a brilliant mind and combat record and he made a strong and favorable impression. Morgan named him "Senior Airborne Adviser" for OVERLORD planning, a position and title that gave Gavin entrée and influence at all levels of OVERLORD planning.[2]

Before he could even begin to dig in, Gavin became enmeshed in a distracting—and disquieting—political sideshow. As Ridgway had warned him, Boy Browning, recently promoted to the position of head of all British airborne forces, was already making moves aimed at gaining absolute control of all OVERLORD airborne operations. As Gavin divined it, Browning's plan was two-stepped: first to persuade the Allies to create a single (combined) troop-carrier command and second, a single Allied airborne force, both to be commanded by Britishers, the airborne forces by Browning.[3]

In pursuit of these objectives, Browning evidently found it expedient to derogate American airborne operations and leadership. Gavin recalled that at their very first meeting Browning "made a rather unkind remark to me about General Ridgway's not having parachuted into Sicily." In other words, Ridgway was a coward. Gavin coolly but stoutly defended Ridgway's decision to land in Sicily on Patton's command ship and marked Browning as a man to watch even more closely than Ridgway had suggested. If they let down their guard, the Americans might well find themselves serving under Browning, a prospect Gavin did not relish.[4]

As it developed, Browning suffered a reverse in his first big power play. Shortly after his encounter with Gavin, he met with Brereton and others to propose step one: creation of a combined Allied troop-carrier command. Brereton, no political babe-in-the-woods, heard Browning out and then "agreed in principle" to the proposal but added a large caveat: "provided the commander was American." The caveat, Brereton noted in his diary, was "unacceptable to the British." Thereafter, Brereton would squash all further British attempts to gain control of Troop Carrier, arguing that inasmuch as the preponderance of aircraft was American, an American should be in command.[5]

In time, Browning would have better luck. But that would come later—after NEPTUNE. For now, his political meddling—and the gratuitous slur of Ridgway—served only to undermine the tenuous harmony that had been achieved between American and British airborne forces.

Gavin soon set to work analyzing in detail the modest NEPTUNE plans for employment of American airborne forces: the drop of battalion-sized elements from the 101st behind Omaha Beach. He found the DZs suitable, the anticipated flak within acceptable limits, but he took "a rather dim view" of the terrain. Around Bayeux, it was flat and open—"excellent tank country." He feared that German armor would quickly and decisively overrun lightly armed parachute elements operating in that flat, open country. Moreover, the plan itself was so obvious that a schoolboy could have conceived it. Gavin argued strongly against employment of American airborne forces behind Omaha Beach, and the plan was ultimately canceled.[6]*

Seeking alternatives, Gavin called on Omar Bradley, who warmly received him. Bradley had formed a lasting regard for Gavin's courage and ability in the Sicily beachhead and soon won Gavin's trust. In Gavin's estimation, Bradley "had a real feel for what could and what could not be done, and it was always reassuring to plan such operations with him."[8]

Bradley, working closely with Gavin, soon radically altered—and increased—the plans for utilizing American airborne forces in NEPTUNE. Under the newly expanded assault scheme, the responsibility for the quick seizure of the Cotentin Peninsula and Cherbourg was his. Bradley's plan was to cut the Cotentin at its base, then quickly wheel a force north to Cherbourg. Early in this revised planning, Bradley decided he would employ both the 101st and 82nd airborne divisions to help cut the Cotentin and to seize the key road hub, Carentan, and to block German countermoves designed to seal or trap his forces in the Cotentin or throw him off Utah Beach.

Gavin could not have been more pleased. The plan was big and bold and it employed airborne forces not piecemeal in battalions but en masse in division strength—the dream of all airborne-warfare advocates. (Not incidentally, it also gave the 82nd Division a specific D-day mission, theretofore lacking.) Moreover, the Cotentin seemed ideal airborne country. It was pastoral, a checkerboard of small farms, ideal for DZs and LZs. The soil was soft and

---

* Perhaps too hastily, as matters finally developed. Some military authorities, Max Taylor among them, have suggested in hindsight that an airborne force behind Omaha Beach on D day, however exposed and vulnerable, might have alleviated or even prevented the slaughter that occurred there. "If we'd been behind Omaha, there would have been no stopping on the beach," Taylor said.[7]

crosshatched with rivers and canals, which would discourage major enemy armored operations.

In the ensuing weeks, Bradley settled on the forces and the generals who would carry out his invasion plans. His First Army would be composed of three corps: V, VII and XIX. The V and VII corps would be the assault forces —V for Omaha Beach, VII for Utah Beach. The XIX Corps, in reserve, would come behind them. The three corps commanders Bradley inherited were distinguished older men. Ridgway's former boss in War Plans, Gee Gerow, four years Bradley's senior, commanded V Corps. Eisenhower and Bradley's classmate (and cadet captain), Roscoe B. Woodruff, commanded VII Corps. A noted tanker from the class of 1913, Willis D. Crittenberger, commanded XIX Corps, but he was soon sent to Mark Clark's Fifth Army, replaced by his classmate Charles H. (Pete) Corlett, who had commanded a division in combat in the Pacific.

Bradley was not completely happy with the assault corps commanders. Neither Gerow nor Woodruff had had any combat experience in World War II, nor had many of the divisions in their commands. Nothing could be done about Gee Gerow; he was untouchable. He was simply too good, and besides that, he was a Marshall protégé and a close friend of Eisenhower's. However, Bradley did make the decision—a painful one, he admitted—to replace Woodruff with a more seasoned combat veteran. He tried his best to pry Lucian Truscott away from Mark Clark, but Clark refused to release him. The job eventually went to Ridgway's classmate J. Lawton ("Lightning Joe") Collins, who had earned his nickname by doing an outstanding job against the Japanese in the Southwest Pacific with his 25th, "Lightning" Division and who had earlier served with Bradley at the Infantry School and in Marshall's Secretariat.[9]

Inasmuch as the 82nd Airborne Division was now to support the VII Corps assault on Utah Beach, Ridgway found himself subordinated to a West Point classmate for the second time in the war—first Mark Clark, now Joe Collins, who had been tagged one of the "Class Babies."† The Clark appointment could be rationalized. Clark was almost blatantly "political." He had helped Eisenhower in several important ways before the war; Eisenhower had repaid the favors by giving Clark large responsibilities in North Africa and Italy. The Collins appointment must have been more difficult for Ridgway to accept. Lightning Joe had only recently arrived from the Pacific. He was undeniably a well-organized, articulate and charismatic leader, and his association with Bradley in peacetime years had been close. But Collins had not yet fought the Germans. He had missed the trials of North Africa, Sicily and Italy, where American generals had been put to the ultimate test.

If Ridgway was jealous of the Collins appointment, he gave no outward sign of it then or later. But his true feelings may have been reflected by his confi-

† Clark and Collins, both born on May 1, 1896, were the youngest members of the class of 1917.[10]

dant, Doc Eaton, who recalled: "I didn't like Collins and I don't think Matt did either. I thought Collins was a slicker. He was all for Collins. Ridgway never seemed to like anybody who was too ambitious."[11]

The Collins appointment may well have given Ridgway some second thoughts about the course of his own career. Circumstances had led him into becoming a "specialist," a label in the American Army that all too often led to a career dead end. Moreover, his "specialty," however glamorous, had become decidedly controversial, and so had Ridgway himself, as its most doggedly uncompromising advocate. Had Marshall been named OVERLORD commander and had he carried out his massive airborne assault, he would almost certainly have appointed Ridgway an airborne corps commander. But under Eisenhower's leadership, the Marshall airborne plan had been put on the back burner and Joe Collins was now in charge of Utah Beach.

In the weeks of January and early February 1944, the revised NEPTUNE airborne plans were cast, analyzed and recast in a series of tedious and seemingly endless meetings in London. Ridgway and Doc Eaton, flying to and from Ireland, attended most of the meetings. Ridgway did not hesitate to express his views. Eaton recalled: "Bradley and Ridgway were close. They had a high opinion of each other, no question about that. Bradley was a fine man, a quiet man. I loved him. I wondered sometimes why Bradley didn't get provoked with Matt. Matt was always a jump ahead of everybody—and *pushing*."[12]

The plan for Collins' VII Corps, which the airborne would support, was roughly this. The 4th Division would make the assault on Utah Beach, then quickly wheel right (or north) to spearhead the drive on the key objective, Cherbourg. The corps had two more divisions, the 9th and the 90th, plus heavy artillery and some armor, which could be utilized to support the 4th, as required. The 82nd and 101st divisions would be dropped behind Utah Beach and across the base of the Cotentin, to help the 4th Division ashore, to seize the key road hub, Carentan, and link up with Gerow's V Corps forces at Omaha Beach, and to block German counterattacks against the Cotentin. Collins wrote: "My plan was to drive on Cherbourg via the corridor between the sea and the Merderet and upper Douve rivers while blocking possible counterattack with the 82nd and 101st Airborne Divisions along the Douve and at Carentan. If Cherbourg could be seized quickly, it might not be necessary to seal off the peninsula in a time-consuming attack across its base to the west coast."[13]

The specific airborne missions arrived at were as follows. Bill Lee's inexperienced 101 would drop and glide into an area closest to the troops landing at Utah Beach—between Ste. Mère-Église and a wide marshy area behind the beach. Lee's troops would capture four causeways across the marsh to the beach, guaranteeing the amphibious forces exits to the west; capture Ste. Mère-Église and establish roadblocks on the highway north and south of the town; capture the two bridges over the Merderet River west of Ste. Mère-Église and, when all this had been done, prepare to move south and capture the eastern "gateway" city of Carentan. Ridgway's combat-experienced 82nd Division drew a tougher and more perilous job. It would drop much farther west, in the vicinity of St. Sauveur-le-Vicomte. Ridgway's troops would seize the town and set up roadblocks on the main highway north and south of the town; capture the bridge over the Douve River; prepare to move south and capture the town of La Haye-du-Puits, the western "gateway" to the Cotentin.

Throughout these meetings and elsewhere, Leigh-Mallory and his American deputy, Hoyt S. Vandenberg, continued to oppose airborne operations and did not hesitate to express their views. Leigh-Mallory was, in fact, the "strongest opponent" of such operations, as Ridgway wrote. Never too keen for the British airborne operations at Caen, he at first welcomed the shift in emphasis to the American sector in the Cotentin. But, on analysis, he soon objected to the American plan as well. He argued that he did not have sufficient troop-carrier aircraft to deliver so many British and American paratroopers simultaneously, that German fighters and antiaircraft would inflict disastrous losses on the aerial formations, that the Cotentin terrain was ill-suited for glider operations —and so on.[14]

Omar Bradley dug in his heels, insisting that his airborne plan go forward as designed. Bradley went so far as to state flatly that he would not invade Utah Beach without full support from the 82nd and 101st airborne divisions. If there were not enough troop-carrier planes to drop the 101st and the 82nd simultaneously, Bradley argued, then the 82nd could land twenty-four hours later in a second lift. Since the Utah Beach invasion had by then become a vital aspect of NEPTUNE, Eisenhower had either to accept Bradley's demand or relieve him of command. Leigh-Mallory opposed the second lift idea as well, because the element of surprise would have been lost. However, in the end, Eisenhower overruled Leigh-Mallory in favor of Bradley.

In these acrimonious meetings, one issue caused more heat than all others combined: glider operations. The airborne planners believed it was crucial that the glider elements land with the paratroopers or soon after so that the paratroopers would have not only the backup of the glider infantry but also glider-lifted artillery and antitank guns. Inasmuch as it had been decided irrevocably that the paratroopers would jump by moonlight, this demand called for large-scale night glider operations. Citing the British experience in Sicily, Leigh-Mallory predicted that night glider "casualties will not only prove fatal to success of the operation itself but will also jeopardize all future airborne operations."[15]

An impasse ensued. To help break it, the airborne planners yielded somewhat, delaying the time of the proposed glider landings to "dawn" on D day. But a "dawn" landing in Normandy still entailed a hazardous takeoff and a long overwater flight in darkness. Notwithstanding the British experience in Sicily, the airborne planners insisted the enterprise was feasible, and, to "prove" it, staged a "demonstration." Some forty-eight gliders (both Wacos and Horsas) were assembled and the pilots briefed and carefully rehearsed. But the demonstration backfired. One glider sustained a major crash with loss of life; twenty-three others crash-landed, causing many personnel injuries and severe damage to both gliders and the equipment they carried.[16]

This demonstration resolved the glider issue in favor of Leigh-Mallory and the airmen. There would be no mass glider landings at night or dawn in the British or American sectors. However, in a minor concession to the airborne planners, Leigh-Mallory agreed that the British and American forces could utilize about a hundred gliders each to bring in a few antitank guns, ammo and key personnel simultaneously with the paratroopers. However, the major glider reinforcing missions in both the British and the American sectors would not take place until about dusk on D day, with second missions on the morning of D + 1.

This decision also distressed Bradley. He had been counting on the 327th Glider Regiment of Bill Lee's 101st Division to arrive at dawn on D day and prepare to move south against Carentan by noon. Unable to overturn the decision, Bradley, determined to have the 327th for early engagement, ordered that it land amphibiously at Utah Beach with Collins' assault forces. This order came as a sharp blow to George Wear and the gliderists of the 327th, who were now to be denied the mission for which they had so long trained.

The decision to postpone the glider reinforcing missions to daylight hours led to another radical alteration in the American paratroop drops. It created a "surplus" of troop-carrier aircraft—so many, in fact, that it now appeared possible that the 101st and 82nd paratroopers could be dropped simultaneously. Since this would give the 82nd (as well as the 101st) the valuable element of surprise, Ridgway seized upon the idea and pushed it through and the plans were changed accordingly.

The "final" American airborne plan which emerged from these interminable meetings was as follows. Bill Lee's 101st parachute regiments would drop into the eastern Cotentin behind Utah Beach in the early hours preceding H hour, followed by fifty-two gliders bringing antitank guns, ammo and key personnel. Lee's 327th Glider Regiment would come by sea, together with the division's "tail" (trucks, clerks, etc.). At dusk on D day, another thirty-two gliders would bring in more high-priority gear and people. The parachute regiments of Ridgway's 82nd Division, also followed by fifty-two gliders, would come immediately behind the 101st, dropping almost simultaneously in the central Cotentin at St. Sauveur-le-Vicomte. Ridgway's 325th Glider Regiment would land in 177 gliders at dusk on D day. The sea "tail" of the 82nd would land on Utah Beach and link up with the division in due course. Follow-up glider missions of one hundred craft each would reinforce both divisions on D + 1.

Marshall and Arnold were kept abreast of these plans—and remained decidedly unhappy. They still believed NEPTUNE airborne operations were far too conservative, that their concept of a mass drop deep in France would be a more effective and perhaps decisive use of the airborne forces. Although Marshall and Arnold left most NEPTUNE planning to Eisenhower and his staff, they would not let go of this one idea. In February, they sent a team to London to brief Eisenhower on the plan. In addition, in an attempt to convert Eisenhower, Marshall wrote him:

This plan appeals to me because I feel it is a true vertical envelopment and would create such a strategic threat to the Germans that it would call for a major revision of their defensive plans. It should be a complete surprise, an invaluable asset of any such plan. It would directly threaten the crossings of the Seine as well as the city of Paris. It should serve as a rallying point for considerable elements of the French underground. In effect, we would be opening another front in France and your [amphibious] build-up would be tremendously increased in rapidity.

The trouble with this plan is that we have never done anything like this before, and frankly, that reaction makes me tired. Therefore I should like you to give these young men an opportunity to present the matter to you personally before your Staff tears it to ribbons. Please believe that, as usual, I do not want to embarrass you with undue pressure. I merely wish to be certain that you have viewed this possibility on a definite planning basis.[17]

Eisenhower did not take this strong representation from Marshall and Arnold lightly. He consulted Montgomery, Bradley, Tedder, Leigh-Mallory, Brereton, Ridgway, Lee, Gavin and other airborne planners. All unequivocally opposed it for all the reasons Leigh-Mallory had put forward in Washington the previous fall. It was simply too much—too big a bite. When he had heard all the objections, Eisenhower wrote Marshall a long, carefully reasoned and tactful letter knocking down this concept, but assuring Marshall that airborne forces would be more imaginatively used in operations beyond OVERLORD.

Eisenhower said, "I agree thoroughly with the [strategic] conception but disagree with the timing." He had first, he argued, to get a "firm and solid footing" on the continent and capture Cherbourg for use as a supply port. To meet these initial tactical objectives, he said, he intended to use everything at his disposal, "including airborne troops." Beyond doubt the Germans would quickly move forcefully against Allied landings in Normandy. The airborne troops would provide "an important means" of blocking these movements. "I instinctively dislike ever to uphold the conservative as opposed to the bold," Eisenhower wrote. After this "first tactical crisis" had been met, Eisenhower assured Marshall, he would certainly consider future strategic employment of airborne forces. He concluded: "Airborne operations are planned to be as bold and in as large a mass as resources and the air situation then existing will permit."[18]

Marshall did not immediately yield. He replied that he was sorry that Eisenhower did not see his way clear "to commit the airborne effort en masse." As a further goad he enclosed a memo from Hap Arnold, who remained convinced that the Marshall plan was sound. Arnold deplored the idea of a "static beachhead slowly building up before an offensive blow is struck." On the contrary, Arnold wrote, "I like to think of a fluid situation wherein prongs or fingers are constantly and swiftly reaching out, joining and reaching out again. If we have this view the beachhead and the airhead will soon join." Eisenhower held his ground. He replied to Marshall: "Please tell General Arnold that in spite of the glowing prospects he has painted for this particular type of airborne operation,

the ground situation we are facing is one that will yield only to stern fighting
. . . At the very least we are going to have here lively air opposition and a
strong and well organized ground defense. His idea must be applied after the
beachhead forces gain the power to put on a sustained offensive."[19]

That settled the matter of employment of American airborne forces in
OVERLORD. Eisenhower heard no more from Marshall or Arnold on this
subject. OVERLORD airborne operations would proceed as designed in London. However, there is no doubting that Marshall's persistence had made a
strong impression on Eisenhower, who owed Marshall much and who deferred
to Marshall on most matters. Now, in order to live up to his promises to
Marshall and Arnold for airborne operations beyond OVERLORD, Eisenhower had to plan not merely in divisional size, but in multidivisional size. In
sum: an airborne army.

☆24☆

AFTER THE 82ND and 101st airborne divisions had been solidly integrated into NEPTUNE, Ridgway became determined to do informally in the field what he had not been able to do formally in the States: increase the fighting strength of the American airborne divisions. In response to repeated entreaties from Ridgway, supported by Omar Bradley and others, Eisenhower's headquarters authorized two temporary measures for NEPTUNE.[1]

First, the three new American parachute regiments that had recently arrived in the ETO—two of them organized as the 2nd Parachute Brigade—were divided up and temporarily attached to the 82nd and 101st divisions for D day. Bill Lee's 101 was assigned the independent 501st Parachute Regiment, giving his division a total of three parachute regiments: 501, 502, and 506. (The last was also temporarily attached.) Ridgway was temporarily assigned the two parachute regiments of the 2nd Brigade, the 507 and 508, also giving the 82nd Division a total of three parachute regiments: 505, 507 and 508.[2]

The 2nd Brigade commander, Brigadier General George P. Howell, an abrasive pioneer paratrooper, was absorbed into the 82nd Division along with the 507th and 508th regiments. His seniority and rank (and personality) presented Ridgway a problem: What was to be done with him? He was six years senior to Gavin and under ordinary (peacetime) circumstances might well have bumped Gavin out of the ADC job. But the circumstances were far from ordinary and Gavin remained the real ADC. Howell was added to the rolls as a second ADC, but Ridgway assigned him the job of commanding the "seaborne element" of the division—the heavy support forces which would land with the amphibious forces on Utah Beach.[3]

Second, it was decided that the 82nd and 101st divisions would have only one glider regiment each, but that each of these regiments would be beefed up, temporarily, from two battalions to three.

Lee's 101st Division still had its two original glider regiments, George Wear's 327th and Bud Harper's 401st, both of which had been spawned in the States by the 82nd Division. In order to increase Ridgway's 325th and Lee's 327th to three battalions, Bud Harper's less senior 401st was to be "temporarily broken up," one battalion going to Lee, one to Ridgway.

Bud Harper was of course outraged by this decision. He had trained the 401st hard and well. He "objected strongly" to the breakup of his command, pointing out that his 1st Battalion, commanded by Ray C. Allen, had received "the highest rating for combat readiness in the entire division." But Harper could not overturn the decision. This time there was no selfless coin toss; Bill Lee kept Ray Allen's superior 1st Battalion and gave Ridgway the 401's 2nd Battalion, which was commanded by a West Pointer, Charles A. Carrell.

This battalion, as Harper recalled later, had had some command problems. Originally Harper had selected a gung-ho non-West Pointer to command it, but Lee or one of his senior staffers had more or less imposed West Pointer Carrell on non-West Pointer Harper. No one in the 401 was happy with this decision, least of all Harper, who recalled: "Carrell was ordered in and I was told to put him in command. He knew no one in the battalion. He just never seemed to fit in. I believed at times he did not like gliders. He seemed aloof and did not mix well, and I don't believe the men liked him." The higher-ups also tried to impose another West Pointer on Harper to be Carrell's exec, but this time Harper dug in his heels and held out for a non-West Pointer he considered superior, Charles Moore.[4]

Neither of these temporary glider battalion transfers went smoothly. The men of Ray Allen's 1st Battalion, assigned to Wear's 327th, proudly insisted on calling themselves the "401st," perhaps in hopes that their old regiment would someday be reconstituted. The integration of Carrell's 2nd Battalion (401) into Harry Lewis' 325th Regiment was even more difficult. This alien outfit had come from a rival division, and worse, it had never seen combat. The old hands of the 325th, veterans of North Africa, Sicily and Italy, lorded it over Carrell's "greenhorns" and looked down on them, adding to an already difficult problem.[5]*

These two measures gave the 82nd and 101st divisions a temporary strength of three parachute regiments and one glider regiment of three battalions. It increased the infantry fighting strength of the divisions from about six thousand to about nine thousand men: about sixty-six hundred paratroopers and twenty-four hundred glider men.

The beefing up of the airborne divisions with manpower was not accompanied by a commensurate increase in division artillery. There were no "surplus" artillery outfits which could be attached to the divisions in time; moreover, even if there had been, there was not sufficient airlift to accommodate them. Each of the four-regiment airborne divisions would be supported by only three artillery battalions (one parachute, two glider). Since Ridgway's 82nd was to jump deep into the Cotentin Peninsula, it was planned that all of his artillery would come by parachute or glider. Taylor's parachute artillery would come by plane, the glider artillery by ship.

At that time, Ridgway had his two glider artillery battalions but no parachute artillery. Both Wilbur Griffith's 376th and Hugh Neal's 456th were still in Italy with Tucker's 504th. Since it was imperative that Ridgway begin training some parachute artillery (and aircraft pilots) for NEPTUNE, he was finally able to pry loose one 75 mm pack-howitzer battery of Neal's 456th (along with the battalion's numerical designation) and have it shipped to England. Neal was naturally incensed at having his outfit "broken up" and later called it "the rape of a battalion." What was left of the 456th in Italy was thereupon

---

* Harper, bereft of his command, determined to parachute into Normandy and made two practice jumps. But Taylor designated him "beachmaster" for the division's seaborne tail at Utah Beach.[6]

redesignated the 463rd Parachute Artillery Battalion and did not ever rejoin the 82nd Division. When Neal was seriously wounded, his exec, John T. Cooper, took command of the 463rd. Command of the 456 cadre shipped to England was given to an 82nd Division artillery staffer, Wagner J. d'Allessio, who quickly expanded it to a fully manned parachute artillery battalion.[7]†

In this reorganization, Ridgway now had a total of four regimental commanders in the 82nd Division: Herbert Batcheller (505), George V. (Zip) Millett, Jr. (507), Roy E. Lindquist (508) and Harry Lewis (325). Three, all West Pointers, were, in effect, new: Batcheller, Millett and Lindquist.

Herbert Batcheller, a married man, soon committed professional suicide through a romantic indiscretion. His exec, Mark Alexander, explained: "To take over the 505 from Gavin was, to say the least, a pretty tough assignment. Batcheller had a great deal of courage but was not very impressive in demeanor . . . [but] his troubles [really] started when he fell in love with an Irish lass where we were training and he neglected the regiment to be with her almost every afternoon." Gavin, who still kept a close eye on the 505, remembered that "Batcheller really wasn't a good regimental commander—he got in a little trouble and had to be relieved."[8]

Ridgway did not countenance this affair for long. The efficacy of the regiment, and thus lives, were at stake. He fired Batcheller from command of the 505 and drafted Lindquist's exec from the 508, William E. Ekman, a West Pointer, to replace him. Ekman, in turn, was replaced as exec of the 508 by another West Pointer, Harry J. Harrison, who had commanded the 508's 1st Battalion. Perhaps to soften the blow—or to give Batcheller a chance to redeem himself—Ridgway sent Batcheller to command the 508's 1st Battalion, replacing Harrison. Gavin recalled: "Batcheller was lucky to get a command of any kind."[9]

Could the green Bill Ekman fill the large shoes Gavin had left behind at the 505 and that Batcheller had failed to fill? Gavin thought so: "He looked like a physically tough, smart guy, so Ridgway gave him the chance." The 505 historian, Allen Langdon, recalled the challenge Ekman faced:

I doubt that any regimental commander took over a regiment under a greater handicap than Ekman did. The 505 men, with two combat jumps

---

† Final airborne artillery for NEPTUNE: In the 82nd, Carter Todd's 319th Glider (75 mm packs), Paul Wright's 320th Glider (105 mm snub-noses), d'Allessio's 456th Parachute (75 mm packs). Total authorized firepower: twenty-four 75 mm packs, twelve 105 mm snub-noses. The "sea tail" would bring in conventional 105s for the 320th and extra 75 mm packs for the 319 and 456. In the 101st Division, similarly organized, Bill Lee had two glider (321st, 907th) and one parachute (377th) battalions, all equipped with 75 mm pack howitzers. Total firepower: thirty-six 75 mm pack howitzers. In both the 80th and 81st "antiaircraft" battalions, the British 6-pounder antitank gun (57 mm), which had a narrower wheelbase and was thus easier to load in a glider, was substituted for the American 57 mm antitank gun.

and two campaigns to their credit, felt that they were combat heroes and entitled to go home since they had already won the war, so to speak. And then to be handed a noncombatant commander was the absolute pits. Batcheller had let us run a little wild after we got to Ireland . . . and I suppose the boss figured we needed a disciplinarian to shake us up, so we got Ekman. He tightened the screws a little bit but did it in such a sensible manner that I think everyone had begun to respect him by the time of Normandy—and certainly we did thereafter.[10]

Paratrooper Gavin, taking the measure of the two other new parachute regimental commanders, Zip Millett (507) and Roy Lindquist (508), was not overjoyed. He thought Millett, who was his West Point classmate, was "way overweight" and "not in shape, physically and mentally, for what he was going into." He thought Roy Lindquist was "a hell of a good administrator" who "kept records like I've never seen before" but, when it came to leadership, "was the very opposite of Rube Tucker." But neither man was replaced. "It was hard to find commanders of parachute regiments at that time," Gavin said.[11]

Of the two, Zip Millett was by far the more controversial. Even his own officers were divided in their opinions of him. One battalion commander thought "Zip Millett was a 'laid back guy' and 'good ole boy,' who was totally addicted to sports. The regiment had outstanding basketball and boxing teams and excellent intramural programs in all sports. We seldom saw him in the field checking the quality and effectiveness of training. Fortunately for the regiment, Millett had outstandingly capable subordinates who took up the slack. I believed Zip lacked the leadership and dedication to professional soldiering so necessary in developing a well-disciplined and combat-effective unit."[12]

Another officer, Chester B. McCoid, viewed him more positively: "My impression was that he was a bright, somewhat overweight oldster for a paratrooper . . . He was a bit of a hedonist, partial to ladies at home and abroad, and insisted that his mess go first rate, including a well-stocked bar . . . He seemed to have a surer touch as an administrator than as a trainer of troops; we rarely encountered him as we trained. In the beginning he tended to wrongheadedness in his treatment of senior officers. They arrived and departed in a dizzying procession, the axe falling on reservists and regulars alike . . . But once he had his chosen command team, he was unfailingly loyal to it . . . To Millett's credit stands the fact that he raised the 507th, molded and trained it, and readied it for battle—and we *were* battleworthy."[13]

A new candidate for parachute regimental commander appeared on the scene one day: Edson Raff, former commander of the independent 509th Battalion, now a full colonel and, thanks in part to his own book *We Jumped to Fight,* a paratrooper celebrity.

Since departing North Africa, Raff had had a hard time finding a niche that suited him. Previously, in the States, both Ridgway and Lee had declined to take Raff as a regimental commander, but Lee had agreed to use him as an "advance man" to find billeting for the 101st Division in England. Thereafter,

Raff had gravitated to an airborne planning job on Omar Bradley's staff in London. Raff, dissatisfied in his staff position, even volunteered to go into Normandy as a "spare" colonel in a regular infantry division. Hearing this, Bradley resolved the problem by literally forcing Raff on Ridgway.[14]

When Raff reported to the 82nd Division, he met a frosty reception. Ridgway, Raff recalled, "had no use for me at all." For his part, Raff found Ridgway to be a "conceited, self-centered, narcissistic man" and a "disgrace to the airborne," whom Raff "could never loyally serve." He thought Ridgway's staff were amateurs (peacetime "schoolteachers or reserve officers") and "sycophants who loved to praise Ridgway."[15]

Raff still hungered for a regimental command and hoped he might get the 505, since he was senior to Bill Ekman. But Ridgway would not then give Raff the 505 or any other regiment. Instead, he assigned Raff a less glamorous (for a famous airborne colonel) D-day task. Raff would command a special sea-landed armored "task force" composed of twenty-one Sherman medium tanks, two armored cars and ninety gliderists from the 325. This task force would land at Utah Beach and "break through" overland to the 82nd Division, to provide it with added firepower.[16]

There were also some important changes and additions in the division and Ridgway's personal staff. The highly promising new G-3, Paul Turner, still suffering from ulcers, had a relapse and had to be evacuated to the States for medical treatment. Turner was replaced by the G-4, Bob Wienecke, who in turn was replaced by Bennie A. Zinn. Wienecke's G-3 section was strengthened by the reassignment of Walter Winton, commander of the 1st Battalion, 505. While playing football with his men, he badly acerbated a knee injury incurred in the Sicily jump and was "grounded."[17]‡

Ridgway recruited two new men for his personal staff. The first was a new orderly, James A. Casey, a tough veteran paratrooper from Tucker's 504 who had been wounded in Italy. He would serve more as bodyguard than orderly. The second was a new but temporary aide-de-camp. Ridgway wanted to give his regular aide, Don Faith (who was married), a promotion from captain to major, so, for the Normandy operation, he appointed him headquarters commandant, which carried the rank of major. Faith's replacement, recommended by the G-2, Whitfield Jack, was gliderist Arthur G. Kroos, who was serving in Jack's old outfit, the 80th Antiaircraft Battalion. Kroos had also qualified as a parachutist at a temporary school in North Africa, making five jumps (including one night jump) in the hard, rocky terrain. Kroos had vivid memories of his first days on his new job:

I reported to Doc Eaton, the Chief of Staff, scared to death, and sat at attention. Eaton was a wonderful, understanding, brilliant man. We chatted a while, Doc carefully looking me over, then Doc led me in to meet the

‡ Winton was replaced as 1st Battalion commander by his exec, West Pointer Francis Caesar Augustus Kellam.

general. Ridgway was very precise, absolutely military all the way through. Stiff backbone. He said he'd like to have me join him, then he took me to a country estate to have tea with the owners. I balanced a tea cup on my knee and did not speak unless spoken to. If this was an aide's test, I guess I passed and a few days later I became aide de camp and was soon promoted to captain.

It was a very demanding, but interesting, job. Ridgway was hard to talk to— little small talk, never any letdown in discipline. No warm spirits. Everything was business—war business. He was always very courteous and seldom raised his voice—at least not to me. When he did raise his voice to someone, boy, he was dead from that time on.

I held him in awe. He was very brilliant and intense. Intense all the time. I think he slept that way. I never saw him cross his legs. Unbelievable! He sat up straight—no slouching—and no matter how soft his chair might be, the goddamned chair stiffened when he sat in it. He was very determined. He knew what he wanted and wouldn't tolerate anything that was not right up to perfection. When things were not to his liking, his expression told you everything. He didn't have to speak. His facial expressions, his use of eyes— perhaps raising his eyebrows—said one hell of a lot more than any words he could have used.

He would walk in a room and he would create a presence by being in that room. He didn't have to say anything. Just the way he walked, the way he looked. When his eyes would go over a room, everyone was instantly drawn to him, just like that. He didn't have to say a word. But when he spoke, he had a commanding voice. He was just a remarkable person—determined to get what he wanted and absolutely fearless.

Early in my duty we attended a meeting. When it broke up he scooted out of there and headed for his plane without bothering to say a word to me. Actually, I should have been three paces behind him, but I was new on the job—and left alone. I didn't have a car. I flagged down an Englishman on a motorcycle and he rushed me out to the airport. Ridgway's plane was taxiing to take off. I told the Englishman to drive in front of the plane—toward the propellers. That forced the plane to stop and they took me aboard. All Ridgway did was smile at me. Didn't say a word like, "Where were you?" After that, I seldom let him out of my sight. When he said we're leaving at 6:02 A.M., he meant just that: 6:02. And I was there at 5:45 to make damn sure.[18]

Bill Lee, who had not been 100 percent since his parachute accident in late 1941, had developed a heart problem. He concealed it for a time, but on February 8, while in the field with Bud Harper, Lee suddenly turned to Harper and said, "Bud, I can't go any farther; I have a terrible pain in my chest." Harper flagged down a passing Army truck and sent Lee to the hospital, where doctors diagnosed "a severe heart attack." He would be returned to the States for close medical care. There was not a chance that he could recover to lead the

101st into battle. The men of the division, who idolized Lee, were profoundly shocked and grieved.[19]

The ADC, Don Pratt, took temporary command of the division, but not for long. The command was a plum which Pratt was not, in Eisenhower's or Bradley's eyes, ready for. Instead, Eisenhower and Bradley unhesitatingly chose Max Taylor (still in Italy) for the job. Taylor flew from Italy and informally took command of the division on March 8 and was officially installed on March 14.[20]

Taylor's appointment to command the 101st lifted many eyebrows in the airborne force. He was not only an "outsider" who had had no connection with the 101st Division since its inception, but his combat command experience in the Mediterranean had been limited. Taylor did not pretend to be a paratrooper—so far he had made only one jump—yet he had served with airborne forces for nearly two years and had shown himself to be a brilliant officer with great potential. He had helped nurse the 82nd Division through its growing pains, been an advance man for the deployment of the division to North Africa, and later had served as senior airborne planning officer in Eisenhower's and Clark's headquarters. Almost certainly Taylor's daunting clandestine trip to Rome had saved the division from disaster and spared Eisenhower a painful personal reverse. It is likely that at the moment of Bill Lee's cruel stroke of fortune, Eisenhower was looking for a more responsible—and higher-ranking —job for Taylor. As Taylor later put it: "I became the beneficiary of a stroke of good fortune with a most unfortunate cause."[21]

At the time of this appointment, Taylor was still being carried on the rolls of the 82nd as artillery commander. With this promotion, his exec, Francis (Andy) March III, was officially named artillery commander (a job he had already been filling). William Bertsch, erstwhile commander of the "Tiber River Task Force," who had served in Sicily and Italy, was advanced to be March's exec.

After all these comings and goings, the 82nd Division command team for NEPTUNE was set, and remained unchanged. Ridgway designated the ADC, Jim Gavin, commander of Task Force A, which comprised the three parachute regiments (505, Ekman; 507, Millett; 508, Lindquist) and gave him responsibility for all parachute training. Ridgway would command Task Force B, comprising all glider infantry and artillery and support elements. George Howell commanded Task Force C, the seaborne "tail," of which the Raff force was a key element.*

---

* The execs and battalion commanders of the infantry regiments were as follows: 505, Mark Alexander, Fred Kellam (1st), Ben Vandervoort (2nd), Ed Krause (3rd); 507, Arthur A. Maloney, Edwin J. Ostberg (1st), Charles J. Timmes (2nd), William A. Kuhn (3rd); 508, Harry Harrison, Herbert Batcheller (1st), Thomas J. B. Shanley (2nd), Louis G. Mendez (3rd); 325, Herbert Sitler, Klemm Boyd (1st), John Swenson (2nd), Charles Carrell (2nd—ex-401).[22]

☆ 25 ☆

FOR ALL TOO LONG, Ridgway's 82nd Airborne Division marked time in the wrong place: Northern Ireland. The division was waiting for the embryonic IX Troop Carrier Command of Brereton's Ninth Air Force to get organized and settled into air bases in England. When that had been done, the division would move from Ireland to England, bivouacking close by the appropriate air bases.

Lacking troop-carrier planes in Ireland, Ridgway and Gavin concentrated on combat indoctrination, ground tactics and physical fitness. They sent hardened combat veterans of the 505 to live with the men of the 507 and 508 to teach them things that were not in the training manuals.

The 508 official historian wrote: "If any man who was with the Regiment in Ireland were questioned on what was the most valuable training he got there, he would undoubtedly answer that it was the knowledge and confidence acquired from battle veterans of the 82nd Airborne Division . . . They explained what they knew of war and gave many helpful hints about fighting the Germans."[1]

Gavin, delegated responsibility for training, was, as usual, merciless:

All maneuvers in which decisions were required were preceded by a long, grueling physical test, usually an overnight march of about eighteen to twenty miles with full combat equipment. Then when the men expected a rest, they were presented with difficult combat situations. After an all-day maneuver, when they were tired and hungry, a night march was ordered. After a couple of hours of marching, at about midnight, they would be ordered to halt and go into a dispersed bivouac, in anticipation of a night's rest. After about an hour of sleep, which was just enough to cause them to lose their sense of orientation to events and environment, unit commanders were suddenly awakened and given a new set of orders requiring immediate movement. They marched until daylight, when a new situation was given to them, usually a final attack order . . . It was exacting training, but it gave me an opportunity to get to know a lot about them and for them to learn much about themselves . . .

Even so, Gavin was not satisfied. "Rarely could the training be exacting enough to compare to the shock of battle itself," he later wrote, "and the paratrooper unfortunately meets the shock head on in seconds, rather than via the gradual approach to battle on foot, as so often is the situation with our other troops." He would berate himself for not being tougher, later writing an airborne cohort: "I should have trained the 507 and 508 much harder than I did."[2]

Slowly—all too slowly—the IX Troop Carrier Command got itself organized. On February 25, 1944, a mere ninety days before D day, Brereton finally put the right man in command. He was Paul L. Williams, a veteran of Mediterranean airborne operations whom Ridgway knew well and respected. Williams brought in a staff who were the "cream" of the Mediterranean troop-carrier operators and established his headquarters in The Midlands near Leicester. But it was very late in the game and, owing in large part to Brereton's indifference, all too little had been accomplished.[3]

In its final form the IX Troop Carrier Command comprised Hal Clark's veteran 52nd, which came from the Mediterranean, and two brand new wings: the 50th and the 53rd, which came from the States. (The veteran 51st Wing was held in the Mediterranean for possible airborne operations in Italy and elsewhere.) Although all three wings were supposed to be qualified in both parachute and glider missions, eventually the D-day glider missions were assigned exclusively to the 50th and 53rd wings, and Hal Clark's wing was restricted exclusively to parachute operations. Accordingly, the 50th and 53rd wings (mated to the 101 for training) established themselves at bases in southern and southwestern England (between Reading and Bristol) so that the glider runs to France would be as short as possible. Hal Clark's 52nd Wing took over seven air bases in The Midlands, where, as Ridgway had urged, it mated with the 82nd Division.

Of the three wings, Hal Clark's 52nd was by far the most experienced. It arrived from the Mediterranean in early March with four veteran air groups in the command: the 61, 313, 314 and 316. The pilots in these groups had accumulated an average fifteen hundred hours of flying time; most crews had participated in airborne combat missions. A fifth group, the 315, was added in England. It was made up of some planes and crews with combat experience in the Mediterranean and some that had been engaged in routine transport work. The 315 thus needed much work in formations and night flying and navigation. A sixth group, the 442nd (from the 50th Wing), which had arrived directly from the States and was utterly green and short of aircraft, was temporarily attached to the 52nd Wing for training, but remained to fly with the 52nd on D day.

In all, there were fourteen troop-carrier groups. At first each group was composed of fifty-two C-47 aircraft. During the spring of 1944, as the airborne missions and the division force levels were expanded, the strength of each group was increased from fifty-two to seventy-three aircraft, nine of these considered in "reserve." Thus, by March 1, Williams had a total of 845 planes; by May 1, 1,062, and by June 1, with the addition of yet more spares and reserves rushed from the States, 1,207. By D day, in fact, Williams had about 100 more aircraft than he had crews. The official troop-carrier historian, John Warren, wrote that about 20 percent of the air crews for D day were "inexperienced filler personnel who had been overseas less than two months." Moreover, there was a "grave" shortage of ground crews, but since most of the planes were new and the ground crews were "enthusiastic," they proved to be adequate for the task.[4]

At first there was an acute shortage of gliders. Hap Arnold had shipped nearly 1,500 crated Waco gliders to England and continued to ship more gliders all through the fall and winter of 1943/1944. By February 1944, there were 2,100 Wacos in England. However, when civilian workmen began assembling the gliders, there ensued a debacle almost exactly duplicating the glider assembly debacle in North Africa. Of the first 62 gliders assembled, 51 were "unflyable," so the Air Force had to take over the job. By the end of 1943, its "inexperienced, ill-equipped and undermanned" assembly units had barely managed to put together 200 gliders and half of these, inadequately tied down on airfields, were badly damaged by storms. By April 1, 1944—sixty-one days prior to D day—Paul Williams still had fewer than 300 Wacos, and the attrition rate in training exercises was eating up gliders almost as fast as they could be assembled. The upshot was that another "crash" glider assembly program had to be decreed. Following the edict, in April alone, the technicians turned out an astonishing 910 flyable gliders. By June 1, Williams had 1,118 operational gliders in his command, including 288 retrofitted with a "Ludington-Griswold nose"—a spider web of aluminum bars in front of the windshield designed to protect the pilots in crash landings.

In addition, the British furniture manufacturers were building gliders at a fast pace. These were the big Horsas and the monstrous Hamilcars, which could carry a payload of 17,500 pounds—over twice that of a Horsa and four times that of a Waco. (The Hamilcar was designed to lift a light tank or two armored scout cars or forty troops with gear into battle.) The British gave Williams 301 Horsas for D day (increasing the American glider force to a total of 1,419 craft), but the Horsa, to say the least, was not popular with the American gliderists. Its frame was made entirely of wood (plywood glued to wooden ribs) and was considered "fragile" or, more derisively, "a bundle of matchsticks" certain to self-destruct in the inevitable crash-landing. (Each was equipped with saws so the men could cut their way out of the wreckage.) Being larger and heavier, the Horsas were harder and more tiring to fly and far more difficult to land in short fields, even with their huge air-speed brakes (flaps) and wheel brakes.

Each glider, Waco or Horsa, had a crew of two: pilot and copilot. At first it was believed that there were more than enough American glider pilots. By April 1, there were two-man crews for 618 gliders. However, as the airborne planners drew increasingly ambitious plans for follow-up operations, a shortage of glider pilots was foreseen and "drastic steps" had to be taken to rush glider pilots to England. Another 600 pilots and copilots arrived during April and May. Many of these had been rushed through glider schools or drafted from other Air Force outfits. The additions gave Williams sufficient two-man crews for 951 of his 1,419 gliders. As it turned out, this was more than enough for American glider missions in NEPTUNE, but not nearly enough for future operations. Despite a steady inflow of glider pilots to the

ETO, there would be an acute shortage of American glider pilots for the rest of the war.[5]

The separate and independent British Troop Carrier Command was likewise hard-pressed for aircraft. It was launched in the fall of 1943 with the British 38th Wing, veterans of the Mediterranean operations.* The 38th Wing was soon built up into a group, consisting of ten squadrons of about twenty-two planes each. A second group, 48, equipped with about 175 C-47s (which the British called Dakotas) borrowed for D day from the RAF Transport Command, was added in January 1944. In total, the British Troop Carrier Command could call on about 400–450 aircraft, but until D day many of the glider-towing bombers of 38 Group were employed on bombing missions. However, there was no shortage of gliders or glider pilots, even after giving the Americans 301 Horsas; the British had almost eleven hundred Horsas available for D day, plus about twenty-five Hamilcars.[6]

This was not nearly enough aircraft to lift a full division, so British NEP-TUNE airborne operations had to be scaled down accordingly. In the end, it was decided that only two of the three brigades (regiments) of the 6th Airborne Division would be utilized in the initial assault; the third brigade (regiment) would be brought in by glider in a second lift at dusk on D day. Moreover, since Leigh-Mallory was now forecasting a possible 50 percent loss rate for aircraft in the initial assault, plans were made to draw on the American IX Troop Carrier Command reserve aircraft, if necessary, to reinforce the 6th Division and, if conditions made it imperative, to bring in the British 1st Airborne Division. These contingency plans, in turn, generated a need for "joint" American-British parachute and glider training. But there was never enough time or equipment to properly carry it out.

In mid-February, Ridgway received orders to move the 82nd Airborne Division from Ireland to England. It would go by rail and ship and be bivouacked in the Leicester-Nottingham area in The Midlands, near Paul Williams' troop carrier command headquarters and Hal Clark's 52nd Wing air bases. Ridgway opened the division CP on February 14 at Braunstone Parke, in Leicester. The division followed, unit by unit, a complicated movement that was not completed until March 10, when the last regiment, Roy Lindquist's 508, settled in at Wollaton Park, near Nottingham.[7]

The change of geography did not go altogether smoothly. Theretofore the Leicester-Nottingham area had been the exclusive preserve of all-black American Army service units. These men, Ridgway recalled, "had established themselves socially with the friendly folk of England" and "many of them had made pleasant liaisons with some of the young women of the towns." On the first night, the blacks and the paratroopers clashed and a paratrooper was badly knifed. A false rumor spread that he had been killed, and Ridgway's paratroopers plotted revenge. Sensing big trouble, Ridgway personally moved to

---

* Confusingly, a British air wing was about the equivalent in size of an American group. A British group was the equivalent of an American wing.

prevent it. He visited every one of his units to warn his officers of what was afoot—and why they should take stern measures to prevent it—and doubled the MPs on the streets. He "personally spent the early hours of the next few evenings riding and walking the streets" to see his orders were carried out. He thus prevented a certain, and perhaps deadly, confrontation. The grateful city authorities in Leicester and Nottingham later presented the division "beautiful little antique salvers of Irish silver" and a "silver tray" in appreciation of the "good relations" Ridgway had established between his soldiers and the citizenry.[8]

These "good relations" grew ever more intimate, so much so that Ridgway became concerned that there might be repetitions of the Batcheller affair and that the division might lose its keen fighting edge. Eaton recalled:

This was my second time in England during a war. In the First World War, the British women were snobbish. In the Second World War they were free. Ridgway came to me one day and said, "Doc, our people are getting mixed up sexually with British women." I said, "Right, Matt. We're probably the only two virgins left in the 82nd!" But he was dead serious. So I called the staff in as a group and told them: "Your personal life is yours. But I don't like it. If you get mixed up with a woman and it comes to me officially, I'll crucify you!" That satisfied Ridgway.[9]

By about mid-March, the division was at last ready to commence the long-delayed intensive airborne training Ridgway had deemed vital. It was now more crucial than ever. The 505, for example, had not jumped for six months —since Salerno. The regiment now included hundreds of replacements from parachute school who had never made a jump with an organized combat unit. The men of the 507 and the 508 were fully qualified Stateside parachutists who had jumped in regimental exercises, but they had not jumped as a unit for some time (the 508 since October 5) and they needed to rehearse the new techniques they had learned from the veterans of the 505. Besides that, of course, it was vital to give the new troop-carrier groups jump experience.

Regrettably, it did not work out as planned. The short daylight hours in The Midlands greatly restricted day operations. Most of the time the weather was foul—cold, rainy, foggy. As it developed, two thirds of Hal Clark's wing was unable to conduct joint exercises. The veteran 313 and 314 groups could not, owing to a delay in construction of their airfields, which dragged on all through March. The newly formed 315 and 442 groups could not, because the green pilots had to concentrate on basics (formation and night flying and navigation) to such an extent that neither of these groups could make drops during March and April. That left mainly the veteran 61 and 316 groups, which severely limited parachuting and glider training. As in North Africa and Ireland, most divisional training had to be confined to ground operations, launched from simulated DZs and LZs.[10]

By April, four of Hal Clark's air groups were available, and the tempo of airborne training increased and the division concentrated on battalion-size jumps. However, the official troop-carrier historian wrote, "time and time again, in big and little exercises . . . wind and low visibility, particularly at night . . . scattered troop formations, twisted them off course or spoiled their drops." Ridgway recalled a visit with a battalion commander after one such jump. He was "quite bitter," Ridgway said, because the airmen had "scattered us all over—dropped us in deep forests and everything else."[11]

The danger of bad weather was never more vividly demonstrated than in late April, when Ridgway and Hal Clark, drawing on all their combined resources, conducted a full division-size rehearsal of the D-day mission. Foul weather turned it into a fiasco. Gavin recalled: "The takeoff was normal, we got most of the division into the air and then found that we could not get it down. Fog and bad weather closed in on us, the drop zones could not be located, and close troop carrier formations could not be flown. A few drops were made but most of the troops had to be airlanded at airdromes scattered all over England." The 508 historian wrote of the exercise: "The weather was unfavorable, the regiment staged at the airport for more than a week waiting for an opportunity to take off. When the planes did finally take off the weather was still unfavorable. After a fifteen minute flight, word was received from the air bases to return. However, heavy clouds prevented the visual signals from the lead planes from being seen in most cases. Over the DZ confusion reigned as planes approached from all angles at different altitudes. Most had become lost from their formation and had found the DZ on their own. Here . . . was a premonition of what was to happen later in Normandy."[12]

Max Taylor's 101st planned a similar exercise for May 10 and 11, code-named EAGLE. Since by that time the 82nd Division's D-day drop had been moved forward to coincide with that of the 101, and the troop-carrier forces badly needed realistic training, EAGLE was expanded to include "token" jumpers from the 82nd Division. EAGLE went off in nearly perfect weather. The 50th and 53rd wings dropped all three of Taylor's parachute regiments (over 6,000 men) from 432 aircraft and, in addition, towed in 55 gliders. Hal Clark's 52nd Wing, mounting 369 aircraft, dropped two 82nd men per plane, for a total of about 638.

On the whole, EAGLE was judged to be highly successful. In the 101st, the official historian reported, an astonishing 75 percent of the parachutists landed on or close to the proper DZs. (Twenty-eight planes of 440 Group with 529 parachutists got lost and returned to base; eight other planes mistakenly dropped about 130 parachutists into the town of Ramsbury, nine miles from the DZ.) Forty-four of the fifty-five gliders, landing at dawn, found the proper LZ and made "good" touchdowns. (Four gliders aborted; seven landed on the wrong LZs.)

However, the 52nd Wing—and Ridgway's men—did not fare nearly as well. The pilots of the green 315 Group got fouled up and did not drop at all. Only sixteen of forty-five planes of the green 442 Group found the DZ; the rest tried again by the light of dawn only to drop ten miles off target. Nine planes of the veteran 314 Group also gave up and came home; another nine from the group dropped far off target. The rest of 314 Group and most of the planes of the veteran 313, 316 and 61 groups made fair-to-good drops. In sum, 226 of Ridgway's 638 paratroopers—almost one third—either did not jump or jumped far from the DZ.[13]

Based on data compiled on the 101 drop, EAGLE induced a mood of heady optimism throughout the ranks of troop-carrier and airborne forces. Paul Williams was giddily led to predict that 90–100 percent of airborne forces would be delivered to proper DZs and LZs on D day. Although Leigh-Mallory remained fundamentally skeptical of all airborne operations, even he professed to be "highly impressed." However, as the official troop-carrier historian pointed out, the optimism was premature and would lead to a grave and tragic error in the actual combat operations to follow. The weather during EAGLE, he wrote, had been so "halcyon" that the previous training fiascos caused by bad weather seemed to have been forgotten, ignored or pushed into the background. The result was that the D-day operational orders failed to include "full and specific precautions against bad weather," a lapse that was to prove costly indeed.[14]

Missing from all this training was Rube Tucker's 504 Regimental Combat Team. Despite the assurances of Mark Clark and the needling of Max Taylor (and a Ridgway appeal direct to George Marshall), the 504 and the 376th Parachute Artillery remained in Italy for a very long time.[15]

After giving the regiment a respite over the Christmas holidays, Clark, as Churchill had insisted, had scheduled it and Yarborough's 509th Battalion for a parachute operation in SHINGLE, the amphibious "end run" at Anzio. On reflection, Clark had canceled the parachute drop but had landed the 504 and the 509th Battalion at Anzio on January 22, 1944, to fight as "light infantry." Like AVALANCHE, SHINGLE had been hastily and ineptly conceived, and plagued with command problems, and it very nearly failed. In a decision reminiscent of the Dawley affair at Salerno, Clark had relieved VI Corps commander John Lucas, replacing him with Lucian Truscott. The 504 and the 509 had fought gallantly in the "bloody Anzio" beachhead for almost sixty days— until March 23.[16]†

Tucker's 504 Combat Team finally arrived in England on April 22, one month after it was pulled out of Anzio. Two of the three battalion commanders (Blitch of the 2nd and Freeman of the 3rd) had been rotated to the States and replaced, but otherwise the senior command was in good shape and Tucker was eager to participate in NEPTUNE. The regiment had incurred about 25 percent casualties (590 dead, wounded or missing) at Anzio, but there were plenty of replacements available in England. Gavin, who judged the regiment to be "in fine spirits and good shape," urged that the 504 be substituted for the green

---

† During Anzio the 504 got a nickname which became legendary: "Devils in Baggy Pants." It was derived from the captured diary of a German officer who opposed the 504. He wrote: "American parachutists—devils in baggy pants—are less than 100 meters from my outpost line. I can't sleep at night; they pop up from nowhere and we never know when or how they will strike next. Seems like the black-hearted devils are everywhere . . ."[17]

The supreme command for OVERLORD, the invasion of Normandy. (Seated left to right) Air Chief Marshal Sir Arthur Tedder, Eisenhower, land commander British General Sir Bernard L. Montgomery. (Standing left to right) Omar N. Bradley, British Admiral Sir Bertram H. Ramsay, Air Chief Marshal Sir Trafford Leigh-Mallory, and Eisenhower's chief of staff, Walter Bedell Smith.

Airborne planning for OVERLORD. (Left to right) Don F. Pratt, assistant commander, 101st Airborne Division; Omar Bradley's chief of staff, Leven C. Allen; Bernard Montgomery; and the 101st commander, Bill Lee.

The 82nd Airborne Division staff for Normandy: Front row (left to right) assistant division commander Gavin, Ridgway, chief of staff Ralph P. (Doc) Eaton. Back row (left to right): Ridgway's aide for Normandy Arthur G. Kroos, Jr.; G-3 Robert H. Wienecke; G-1 Frederick M. Schellhammer; G-4 Bennie A. Zinn; G-2 Whitfield Jack.

USAMH

Maxwell D. Taylor, named commander of the 101st in March 1944, following Bill Lee's heart attack, escorts Prime Minister Winston Churchill on an inspection of his division.

Waco gliders lining up on the runway for takeoff with C-47 tows and lifting off.

Rehearsal in England. Some 1,500 paratroopers of the 101st Airborne Division stage a mock invasion of Normandy on a clear day in late March 1944.

Paratroopers of the 101st prepare to enplane for Normandy. Battalion commander Robert L. Wolverton, killed in Normandy on D day, inspects the gear of his fellow officer.

Some paratroopers shaved their heads and daubed their faces to resemble fierce American Indian braves.

A few hours before takeoff, Eisenhower paid a visit to the 101st and remained until the last man was airborne.

Airborne troopers load and depart for Normandy. (Top) Americans (wearing Mae West life vests) line up to board a British Horsa glider.

(Center left) paratrooper climbing into a C-47, burdened like a medieval knight.
(Center right) one paratrooper's burden on display.
(Below) One paratrooper "stick," as seen inside a C-47.

A panoramic view of Omaha Beach, as erected in this striking montage.

507 or 508, taking replacements from one or the other regiments. However, Ridgway said no, later explaining that the 504 was "so badly battered, so riddled with casualties . . . that they could not be made ready for combat in time to jump with us."[18]

Ridgway's decision to exclude the 504 and the 376th Parachute Artillery from this greatest of all military ventures and his public reasons for doing so did not sit well either with Gavin or with Tucker. Gavin felt that "the 504th was one of the very best and very much a part of the 82nd." So, of course, did Tucker. Gavin later wrote (in understatement) that he was "surprised" by Ridgway's decision and felt that the inclusion of the 504 in NEPTUNE "would have made a tremendous difference to the division." Gavin was never fully satisfied with Ridgway's "riddled with casualties" explanation. He speculated that Ridgway must have had a firm administrative cutoff date in his mind and that Clark had returned the 504 "too late" to meet that cutoff.[19]

However, most paratroopers who were in a position to judge agreed with Ridgway: the 504 had sustained brutal casualties in Italy and was neither mentally nor physically prepared to take on a formidable job like NEPTUNE. Allen Langdon remembered: "I agree with Ridgway that the 504 was in no condition to go into Normandy. I was on the detail that readied their camp near Leicester and I saw them when they arrived. I have never seen a more beat-up bunch of men."[20]

Even so, the 504 was represented in NEPTUNE. When Gavin sought "volunteers" for the pathfinder groups and for other special missions, perhaps fifty 504 men stepped forward. Among them were four senior officers. One was Tucker's exec, Chuck Billingslea. Another was Ridgway's protégé Hank Adams, who had relieved Mel Blitch as commander of Tucker's 2nd Battalion in Anzio. (Adams was attached to the 82nd's G-3 section.) Another was Willard E. Harrison, highly recommended by Tucker for his courage and resourcefulness. (Harrison became a sort of field assistant to Gavin.) In addition, Ridgway's artillery commander, the burly Andy March, drafted Robert H. Neptune, exec of Griffith's 376th Parachute Artillery, to serve as exec of d'Allessio's hastily organized, mostly green 456th Parachute Artillery. Neptune, a "nonprofessional" Army officer, probably represented the majority view in the 504:

March said he was offering me the "honor" of going into Normandy with the 456. "They need your experience," he said. Maybe so, but I didn't want to go. I'd been through the hell of Sicily—where the 376th had been devastated in the drop by Allied antiaircraft—and the hell of Italy—the mountains campaign, then Anzio. Our table of organization called for thirty officers and we'd gone through at least one hundred. I'd had many close calls, but I was the only officer in the 376 who had not been killed, wounded or hospitalized. Most of d'Allessio's 456 (ten of twelve pack howitzers) were to come by ship to Utah Beach, but Gavin wanted two howitzers—and me—in the air assault. I figured that in Normandy my number would come up—but of course I went. Reluctantly.[21]

☆26☆

ALL THIS TIME, Allied intelligence had been keeping a close watch on German defensive preparations in Normandy by means of decoded German radio intercepts, photoreconnaissance and reports from the French underground and other sources. The decoded radio intercepts, in particular, were invaluable. They revealed in utmost detail the German chain of command, troop dispositions and strategy.[1]

The top German commander in France was Field Marshal Gerd von Rundstedt. Immediately beneath him was Erwin Rommel, who commanded Army Group B, which comprised the Fifteenth Army, in the Pas de Calais area, and the Seventh Army, in the Normandy-Brittany area. Rundstedt and Rommel disagreed over how to repel the inevitable Allied invasion. Rundstedt preferred to hold reserves inland and fight a war of maneuver. Rommel, believing Allied air supremacy made a war of maneuver impossible, preferred to meet the Allies directly at the beachheads (as in Sicily and Salerno). The result was bureaucratic infighting and compromise which satisfied neither German commander and would ultimately work to the advantage of the Allies.

Hitler, who had at first swallowed the lures in the Allied deception FORTITUDE, had a sudden and uncanny intuition that the landings would actually take place in Normandy. Accordingly, in the spring of 1944, he ordered Rundstedt and Rommel to greatly strengthen the so-called Atlantic Wall, which stretched more or less from Cherbourg to Calais. This chore—launched belatedly—fell to Rommel. He ordered that the beaches be mined and made impassable with landing-craft and tank obstacles. Above the beaches, in the dunes and high ground, Rommel had his men build thick concrete pillboxes, many with big guns and mortars with interlocking trenches and fields of fire. In addition—as if reading the Allied minds—he ordered that the Normandy farmers implant tall, heavy poles in the open fields and pastures to obstruct parachute and glider landings. Seeing aerial photos of these alarming poles, the Allied airborne forces tagged them *Rommelspargel* (Rommel's asparagus).

The real German problem was manpower. By the spring of 1944, German operations on the Russian front had severely bled Germany. The decision to hold the line in Italy had further drained army resources. Von Rundstedt had fifty-odd divisions under his command, but all too many of these were static coastal divisions or fought-out divisions from the Russian front sent to him for rest and rehabilitation, or brand-new divisions just organizing. Moreover, owing to the manpower shortage, most of his first-line infantry and panzer divisions had recently been substantially reduced in size and strength (generally from seventeen thousand to thirteen thousand men). The panzer and panzer grenadier divisions were short of tanks. All units were short of armored vehicles, trucks and ammunition. Relentless Allied air attacks made it difficult for the first-line German divisions to move in daylight, thus greatly reducing their mobility.

In the spring of 1944, there were in the proposed Allied landing sector five organized divisions, plus miscellaneous units amounting in numbers to another division, for a total of six. Two of these were coastal divisions, made up of second-rate German soldiers and many disaffected Russians and East Europeans. One, the 716 (six battalions), manned the beach fortifications in the British sector. Another, the 709 (eleven battalions), manned the beach fortifications in the American sector. Behind the 716, in the Caen area, was the first-line 77th Infantry Division. Behind the 709, in the Bayeux area, was another first-line infantry division, the 352nd. On the west coast of the Cotentin, near La Haye-du-Puits, was the 243rd Division, originally a static coastal division but then under orders to reorganize into a first-line attack division.

In late spring, also in response to Hitler's intuition, the Germans took steps to increase army power in Normandy and Brittany. The most formidable change was the substitution of the 21st Panzer Division for the 77th Infantry Division at Caen. (The 77th went to Brittany.) Some additional special battalions, and the 6th Parachute Regiment (thirty-five hundred tough young soldiers), of the 2nd Parachute Division, which had been withdrawn from Rome, came into the Cotentin. In addition, Rommel reinforced some of the static coastal divisions and tried—vainly—to motorize some units. The first-line 352nd Division was inched forward toward the beach and semiintegrated with the 709; its division artillery took positions overlooking what the Americans called Omaha Beach.

Allied intelligence detected most, but not all, of these reinforcements and shifts. The most notable failure occurred with the 352nd Division. Its existence had been detected, but its location was unknown until a few days before D day, too late to change plans for the Omaha Beach assault. Offsetting this failure was a notable *coup:* in mid-May, Allied code breakers discovered that the first-line 91st (Airlanding) Division, en route from Germany to Nantes (in Brittany), had been diverted at the last minute to the Cotentin—specifically to St. Sauveur-le-Vicomte, backing up the 243 Coastal Division and nearly on top of the DZs and LZs of the 82nd Airborne Division. It was also learned that the 6th Parachute Regiment (at Périers-Lessay) had been attached to the 91st Division, greatly increasing its strength. The specific mission of the 91st and the 6th Parachute Regiment (and several other units as well) was to repel possible Allied airborne operations.[2]

The news of the redeployment of the 91st Division, its increase in strength and its specific antiairborne mission reached the Allied camp on May 25, causing panic. It appeared that the Germans knew the exact Allied airborne plan. Eisenhower, Tedder, Montgomery, Bradley, Leigh-Mallory, Brereton and others conferred long and earnestly.[3]

From the outset, Leigh-Mallory took the position that American airborne operations in the Cotentin were now simply out of the question. He categorically predicted that 50 percent of the parachutists and 75 percent of the gliderists would be wiped out even before they hit the ground. Thus shattered, he argued, the 82nd and 101st would be powerless to carry out their missions. Implied but unstated were the ensuing consequences: the Utah Beach landings and the follow-up capture of Cherbourg would fail. All of OVERLORD might turn into a disaster.[4]

After conferring with Ridgway and Taylor, Bradley dug in his heels and overnight produced a new airborne plan. The drop of the 82nd at St. Sauveur-le-Vicomte would be canceled. The DZs would be moved about ten miles eastward to the vicinity of Ste. Mère-Église, directly adjacent to the 101 DZs. The 82nd would take over the 101's mission of capturing the town and the two bridges over the Merderet River. Bradley would move the 101 DZs slightly east and south, the better to block any movement of the 6th Parachute Regiment out of Carentan. In sum, all six parachute regiments—some thirteen thousand men—would be massed into the area around Ste. Mère-Église, within four miles of Utah Beach.

Despite the influx of German reinforcements and the new stress on antiairborne tactics, Ridgway, Taylor and Gavin were unalterably convinced that Bradley's revised plan would succeed. Ridgway later commented: "The drop was a great gamble, we admitted. The whole great operation was a desperate gamble . . . Both General Bradley and I argued strongly that these were risks that we would have to take, and we were willing to take them . . . General Bradley and I argued that despite the hazards, which we recognized clearly, the divisions could carry out the missions assigned to them . . . The 52nd Troop Carrier [Wing] could get us there without disastrous loss either to enemy fighters or ground fire. And once on the ground, we could take care of ourselves."

The revised plan did not find approval from Leigh-Mallory. On May 27, he declared in a meeting with Tedder, Bradley and others, that "if you do this operation, you are throwing away two airborne divisions." Bradley, still stubbornly holding to his position responded flatly that he "would not land on the Utah Beach without the support of the U.S. 82nd Airborne Division." Montgomery's chief of staff, Francis de Guingand, backed Bradley, and on May 29, in Eisenhower's absence, Tedder ruled that the 82nd would be landed in the new DZs Bradley had proposed.

The next day, May 30, Leigh-Mallory, still determined to do all in his power to kill the American airborne missions, called on Eisenhower and protested the "futile slaughter" of "two fine divisions." As Eisenhower wrote: "It would be difficult to conceive of a more soul-racking problem." He went on: "If my technical expert was correct, then the planned operation was worse than stubborn folly . . . if he was right, it appeared that the attack on Utah Beach was probably hopeless, and this meant that the whole operation suddenly acquired a degree of risk, even foolhardiness, that presaged a gigantic failure, possibly Allied defeat in Europe."

Eisenhower withdrew to his "tent" alone to sit down and weigh the matter. He worried that he might carry to his grave "the unbearable burden of a conscience justly accusing me of the stupid, blind sacrifice of thousands of the flower of our youth." On the other hand, as he later reflected, "Leigh-Mallory's estimate was just that, an estimate, nothing more . . . Bradley, with Ridgway and other airborne commanders, had always supported me and the staff in the matter." In the end, Eisenhower concluded "that Leigh-Mallory was wrong" and telephoned him to say the American airborne forces would go as Bradley wished. Later Eisenhower would say that this decision was more difficult for him than his decision to launch D day, already postponed by inclement and uncertain weather, on June 6.

For Ridgway, Taylor, Gavin and many other airborne leaders, it had been a very close call, and it would lead to an irrevocable—and intolerable—break between the airborne forces and Leigh-Mallory. Thirty-four years later, in his memoir *On to Berlin,* Gavin wrote: "Even today . . . I feel fury rise in me when I realize that Leigh-Mallory was going to have us left behind . . ."[5]

PART V

Normandy:
The Stuff of Instant Legend

☆ 27 ☆

As D DAY DREW ever closer, Ridgway maintained a physically punishing fourteen-hour workday. Much of the time he was on the move—by staff car or airplane—visiting his far-flung troop units or attending planning meetings in London and elsewhere. On one of the field outings, while "vaulting" a fence, his foot hit a patch of ice and he slipped. His trick back went out and, as he put it, "the old pain shot through me."[1]

In the field, he divided his time between the paratroopers and the gliderists, teaching and exhorting. He made two more parachute jumps (his third and fourth), leaving only one more before he formally qualified as a bona fide paratrooper. He survived both jumps without serious injury or back pain. He also took "several more" rides in gliders. One of these was exotic and dangerous. The airmen had developed a new technique (called "snatching") for retrieving gliders in fields too small for C-47s to negotiate. They flew low over the field at 140 miles per hour with a hook trailing from the tail to "snatch" the glider towrope, which was raised on an H frame called a "clothesline." Ridgway, Paul Williams and the 439th Group commander, Charles H. Young, rode in the first fully loaded glider snatch in England, "to see if this thing would work," Ridgway airily recalled. Fortunately, it did, and snatching soon would become an approved—although never popular—procedure.[2]

One day as Ridgway was making his rounds, he developed a high fever and became weaker and weaker. He saw a doctor, who diagnosed the illness as malaria. It was a disease he had first incurred in the 1920s while on one of his Latin American missions. Previously he had had several recurring bouts, but nothing so severe as this. He went straightaway to his quarters in Leicester, went to bed and stayed there, absolutely determined to get well before D day.[3]

It had always been assumed that Ridgway would go into Normandy by glider with the division staff. But as D day approached, he made a sudden decision to jump with the paratroopers, much to Doc Eaton's relief:

> The Americans had never made a glider landing at night in combat and our rehearsals had not been too encouraging. The British experience with night glider landings in Sicily had been disastrous. Leigh-Mallory was predicting seventy percent losses in our glider forces in Normandy. Nobody believed that, yet the odds seemed high that Ridgway might, at least, get badly hurt and that, of course, would end his career. I urged him not to go in a glider—fought it tooth and nail. And, in the end, I won. I kept him from going in the glider.[4]

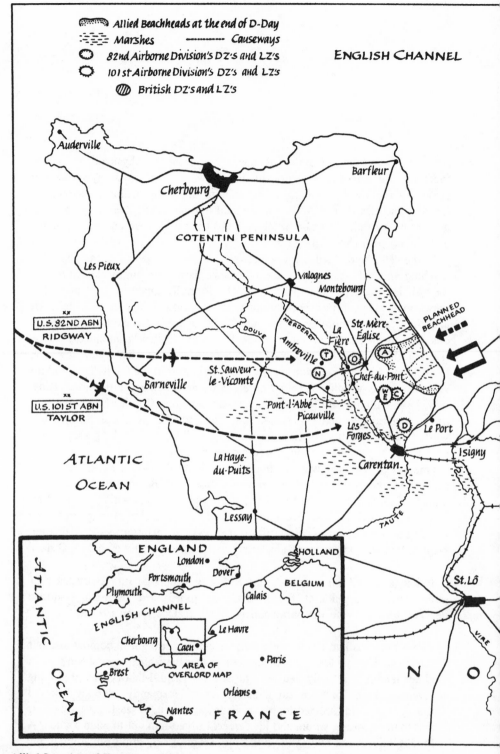

Allied Invasion of France

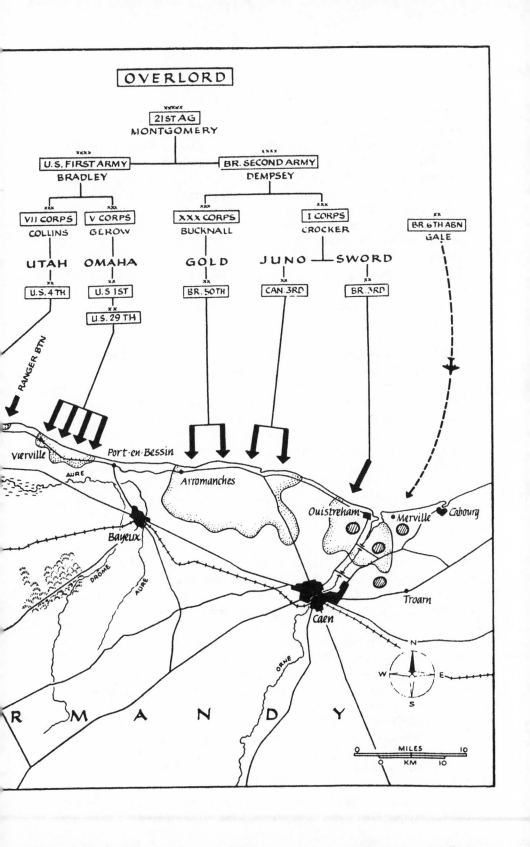

OVERLORD

21ST AG
MONTGOMERY

U.S. FIRST ARMY
BRADLEY

BR. SECOND ARMY
DEMPSEY

VII CORPS
COLLINS

V CORPS
GEROW

XXX CORPS
BUCKNALL

I CORPS
CROCKER

BR. 6TH ABN
GALE

UTAH

OMAHA

GOLD

JUNO — SWORD

U.S. 4TH

U.S 1ST

BR. 50TH

CAN. 3RD

BR. 3RD

U.S. 29 TH

RANGER BTN

Vierville

AURE

Port-en-Bessin

Arromanches

Ouistreham

Merville

Cabourg

Bayeux

DROME

AURE

Caen

Troarn

ORNE

N

W   E

S

R   M   A   N   D   Y

MILES
0   10

0   KM   10

Ridgway's new aide, Arthur Kroos, had his own story, however, about Ridgway's decision:

> Ridgway asked me how I would prefer going—jump or glider. I said jump. He called [Paul] Williams at Troop Carrier Command and said, "I want the best plane, the best pilot, the best navigator, the best crew. I want no screw-ups on this thing." Williams said, "You will go exactly where you want to go." I'm sure Ridgway never really seriously considered going in by glider. That would have been an ego destroyer for him. It wouldn't be the symbol he was creating. He would have been ashamed to have gone to a meeting with other generals and said, "I went in by glider."
> We got him a parachute and took it back to the house in Leicester. We fitted him out in the privacy of his quarters because he didn't want anybody else to see this. We made sure all the straps were exactly right and everything properly taped down.[5]

Ridgway chose to jump with his most experienced outfit: Bill Ekman's 505. Mark Alexander, Ekman's exec, picked a plane for him "flying on the far right side of the formation where they had the best chance of seeing the beacon lights on the ground from our pathfinder unit."[6] Mark Alexander delegated the task of briefing Ridgway and his stick and putting the plane in the proper slot to Talton W. (Woody) Long, who had entered the Army a private in 1941, won a commission and now commanded the 505's headquarters company. Long found the jump briefing for Normandy "a rather demanding experience for a young captain. However, I recall that General Ridgway sat there intently following every detail of my briefing. I don't think those piercing eyes left me once. Afterwards, he graciously thanked me and made some comment about seeing me on the ground."[7]

In the first days of June the airborne forces moved to sealed airfields in central and southern England for final briefings and preparations. The weather was terrible—cold, rainy, foggy—and everybody was on edge. Eisenhower postponed D day to June 5, then—in his famous agonizing decision—to June 6.

Eisenhower had located his advance CP at Portsmouth, a seaport on the southern coast of England. He spent the evening before D day with Taylor's 101st Division, at Newbury, forty miles north of Portsmouth. This was Eisenhower's second visit to the 101st; he had inspected it earlier in March with Churchill and others.* He had dinner with Taylor and his staff and then toured some of the airfields to wish the paratroopers and airmen well. Earlier that day, Taylor, who would also jump with his paratroopers, had badly injured his leg playing squash. "I could hardly walk," he recalled, and the leg would "torture" him for a full week.[9]

---

* By D day, Eisenhower had inspected most British and American divisions in NEPTUNE, except the 82nd Airborne. Montgomery had visited the 82nd in mid-January.[8]

Still deeply concerned about Leigh-Mallory's grim casualty forecasts, Eisenhower was heartened by this visit. He wrote: "I found the men in fine fettle, many of them joshingly admonishing me that I had no cause for worry since the 101st was on the job and everything would be taken care of in fine shape." According to Taylor, "The men glowed with pride that the Supreme Commander himself had come to see them off." Eisenhower, watching from a rooftop, would remain with the 101 until the last plane had taken off.[10]

At 10 P.M. (British Double Summer Time) that night, June 5, about one hour before dark, the special pathfinder groups of both divisions took off in twenty aircraft. Each plane carried about thirteen men, a total force of about two hundred sixty. The teams were equipped with Eureka electronic beacons and marker lights and panels. Their mission was to mark the six DZs and one LZ. Airman Joel Crouch, who had led the pathfinders into Salerno, flew the lead plane. To avoid detection by German radar, the planes flew "on the deck." They employed a British electronic navigation system called "Gee."[11]

These planes followed a precise and complicated route to the Cotentin. The route had been selected to avoid the invasion forces in the Channel and to maximize surprise. It took the planes to the west of the Cotentin Peninsula, then southeast near the islands of Guernsey and Jersey, then due east to the Cotentin. In effect, the airborne forces entered the Cotentin via the "back door," on the opposite side of the peninsula from Utah Beach. The Channel route was well marked with ships equipped with electronic and visual navigational beacons. No serious problems were encountered over the water save one: One plane carrying a 101st team had to ditch. The men were later saved.[12]

Rising over the coastline of the Cotentin, the pilots encountered unexpected and serious trouble. There was a heavy layer of low, turbulent clouds stretching from Barneville eastward toward Utah Beach and a "brisk" northwest wind. Some pilots climbed above the clouds, some flew below, some bored straight through. The precise formations began to break up. Some of these handpicked, highly trained pilots became disoriented and, despite Gee, strayed slightly off course. Since there were no provisions in the orders for dealing with bad weather and all planes were under orders to maintain strict radio silence, they could not—and did not—notify the main body of airborne forces behind them of this unfavorable cloud layer in the western Cotentin.

The nineteen surviving pathfinder planes achieved complete surprise. Some at the tail end of the formation encountered light, scattered flak, but nothing serious enough to warrant evasive action or panic. The courageous pathfinders —the first Allied forces to land in France—began jumping about fifteen minutes after midnight, June 6. Despite Gee and much visual checking, the drops did not come off with the pinpoint accuracy achieved in rehearsals. Only two of the seven teams came down in precisely the right place. Owing to navigational and other errors, some pathfinders were dropped as far as two miles off target, errors that would have grave consequences.

Some of these pathfinders, operating in darkness, were the first to discover a major intelligence failure. The Merderet River was not, as believed from close analysis of reconnaissance photos, a tidy, well-contained stream with dry, abutting meadows. The Germans, utilizing water locks near Carentan, had dammed the flow of Douve River, and unknown to the Allies, this had caused its tributary, the Merderet, to overrun its banks, creating large marshes or deep swamps. These marshes grew flora which had misled the photo interpreters. As Ridgway explained: "The area near [bordering] the Merderet banks looked like a grassy, flat pasture. Actually it was very heavy vegetation . . . [covering] five or six feet of water, [in some areas] but there was not enough water [showing] to get a reflection."[13]

As a result, some pathfinders, weighted down with gear, splashed down in water in the marshes and drowned. The survivors, fighting shock and confusion, had to slog through sucking mud to dry land. But which way? Some believed they had been wildly misdropped far to the south toward Carentan, where it was known the Germans had dammed and flooded the Douve River banks. Those who realized they had landed in the Merderet could do nothing to warn the thousands of paratroopers coming behind them.[14]

There was also another shock for the paratroopers. Normandy, which looked so inviting in the photographs, with its checkerboard of small farms and leas, proved to be a pastoral nightmare. Each plot on the board was boxed by what the Americans called "hedgerows." A hedgerow was an embankment of dense, often impenetrable, hedges or trees or stone walls or all three. To move cross-country, the soldiers had to navigate through or around these hedgerows, which might outline a square or rectangle or trapezoid, or some other unnamed and confusing geometric shape. The hedgerows and stone walls not only offered the Germans concealment and ideal defensive positions, but also made it difficult for the scattered paratroopers to find one another and link up. It was not unlike being caught in a maze. Unable to move smartly over open country following compasses, the men soon became narrowly focused on negotiating small and dangerous and seemingly endless little plots of isolated, hostile terrain in pitch darkness. A few men, scared out of their wits at being alone in German-occupied territory and drained by the tension and terror of the flight or dopey from the Dramamine they had taken to prevent airsickness, simply gave up and crawled into the hedges and went to sleep.[15]

Thirty minutes behind the pathfinders came Max Taylor, his three parachute regiments (501, 502, 506) and fifty-two gliders. They were flown and towed by three air groups of the 50th Wing (439, 440, 441) and four of the 53rd Wing (434, 435, 436, 438). In all, the formation comprised about 485 aircraft. Some 433 of these planes carried about 6,900 paratroopers. The fifty-two gliders (all Wacos) were loaded with sixteen 57 mm antitank guns, twenty-five jeeps, a small bulldozer, 155 men (mostly from the 81st Antiaircraft Battalion), ammo, and other gear. The legendary stunt pilot Mike Murphy flew the lead Waco. In his craft was the most senior American officer in NEPTUNE to go in by glider: the 101 ADC, Don Pratt.

The paratroopers were weighted down like medieval knights in armor. They wore jumpsuits (impregnated with a malodorous chemical to resist gas) with large patch pockets in the trousers. These pockets were crammed with ammo, grenades (fragmentation, smoke and antitank Gammons), and K and D rations (for two days). Over the jumpsuits, they wore pistol belts, supported by suspenders, to which were attached ammo clips, canteens, shovels, first-aid kits, .45 caliber pistols, bayonets, compasses and musette bags containing extra socks, cigarets, ammo and, usually, a ten-pound antitank mine. They strapped gas masks and trench knives to their legs or boots. Some men carried bandoliers of ammo slung over their shoulders; others had binoculars or radios. Some had extra "leg packs" of TNT and ammo, designed to be released on a line in the descent and hit the ground first. Then came the main parachute and its integral harness, which included a wide "belly band," designed to hold the backpack snug. Weapons (M-1 rifles or carbines) were jammed inside the "belly band" butt upward at the shoulder, either in one piece or broken down and stored in Griswold containers. Next—for the overwater flight—came a Mae West inflatable life preserver. Lastly came the reserve chest parachute, which was snapped on to two D rings on the main-parachute chest harness, and a steel helmet, held in place by a chin strap and cup.

In all, the average paratrooper carried between 125 and 150 pounds of gear tightly strapped on his body. This made it difficult—or impossible—to walk upright or climb into the planes. Men helped one another through the plane doors. Inside the cabin, many found they could not sit in the bucket seats. They simply knelt in the aisles in a praying position, with the bulk of the equipment resting in the seat.[16]

The enormous weight of this gear made it all the more important that the jump speed be as nearly perfect as possible. A jump above the recommended "safe" speed of 120 miles per hour would inflict proportionately stronger parachute-opening shocks on the men, which could tear away vital equipment required for combat on the ground, or "blow out" the nylon parachute panels, resulting in a disastrously fast descent.

The mighty aerial armada carrying the 101 flew the same complicated course the pathfinders had flown. Crossing the western coast of the Cotentin at fifteen hundred feet, it encountered the heavy, turbulent clouds which lay between eleven hundred and two thousand feet. Had there been a provision in the orders for coping with inclement weather, the pilots could have adjusted in formation, flying over or under the clouds. But there was no such provision and the pilots bored into the clouds, holding at fifteen hundred feet. Some of the lead planes were fired at from the ground, but the flak was sporadic and ineffective.[17]

Inside the clouds, most of the tight V formations did not hold together for long. It was impossible to see the dim wingtip lights of the adjacent planes in the V, let alone the squadron leaders flying ahead with Gee and Rebecca electronic devices. Some pilots, fearing a midair collision, became panicky. Against orders, they broke formation and climbed above the clouds or descended below them. Only a few Vs maintained a steady, tight flight pattern.

The cloud strata was not wide—about fifteen miles. Those planes that did not deviate from their course broke into the clear west of the Merderet River in

220 ★ RIDGWAY'S PARATROOPERS

about four or five minutes. However, the many that climbed or descended faced new flight problems. Those that were high had to dive quickly to get back down to the proper drop altitude of six hundred feet and the dive increased the plane's momentum beyond the safe bailout speed of 120 miles per hour. Those that had descended were, in many cases, too low to pick out landmarks, and since only two planes in five had navigators, many pilots completely lost their bearings.

The four lead serials of the formation—about 177 planes of 436 and 438 groups—carried twenty-five hundred men. These were George Van Horn Moseley's 502nd Regiment and Benjamin Weisberg's 377th Parachute Artillery Battalion, whose twelve 75 mm pack howitzers were carried in droppable bundles beneath the wings of the planes. They were all bound for DZ "A," directly behind Utah Beach and close to the four causeway exits over the swamps behind the beach. The 502's mission was to seize the causeways. At about 12:45 A.M., when the green light went on, the first paratroopers went out the door shouting, in honor of their founder, "Bill Lee!"[18]

No pathfinders had marked DZ "A," and the drop was, on the whole, poor or worse. The worst was the serial carrying the 377th Parachute Artillery. Its pilots dropped the men—and pack howitzers and ammo—anywhere from three to twenty miles off target. One 377 veteran, Everett G. Andrews, later said: "The outfit only got one of its twelve howitzers in action in Normandy—and it took twelve days to do so." Later, the 377th commander, Ben Weisberg, was sacked for a security indiscretion. "He was a hell of a fine and courageous man," the 101's deputy artillery commander, Thomas L. Sherburne, said, "but he did a really stupid thing. After the battle, he mailed his father all the OVERLORD plans to keep for a souvenir. The censors intercepted the plans—and of course Weisberg went to limbo."[19]

A 101 survivor recalled: "Men landed in pastures, plowed fields, grain fields, orchards, and hedgerows. They landed at the base of anti-glider poles (Rommel's asparagus), in tall trees and small trees. They landed on roof tops, in cemeteries, town squares, backyards, paved roads, and in roadside ditches. They landed in canals, rivers, bogs and flooded areas."[20]

All too many drops were too fast. As a result, many men were knocked cold or injured by the severe opening shocks. Much gear was torn away and it fell on Normandy, a rain of lethal steel. Many men sustained severe injuries when they hit the ground. A few were killed.[21]

Among the injured in this first group, the most notable was the regimental commander, George Moseley, who broke his leg. He fashioned a cane and commandeered a wheelbarrow from which he directed his troops, but Moseley (son of a famous Army general) had a more serious affliction, according to his exec, John H. (Mike) Michaelis, who later became a four-star general:

> He was crazy. He twice pulled a pistol on me in combat—things like that. He was a superb, tough trainer—accepted no excuses. He could strike terror in the heart of God. Exactly what you needed for preparation for combat. Let me put it this way: he wasn't popular, but he gave the outfit a damned

fine discipline. All you had to do was whisper and the men would come on the run. But he was not a good tactician. In Normandy he was in a wheel-barrow—his orderly pushing him—and he told me to send a patrol to Carentan. I said, "There's no need to, sir, we know where the enemy is, just five hundred yards from us. The patrol would all be killed." This started him. He said, "I'm in command here and I'm telling you what to do." I said, "Not me, sir. If you want that, you'd better relieve me." He pulled his [.45 caliber] pistol on me and I had to dive . . . to keep from getting shot.

Soon after this incident, Max Taylor relieved Moseley of command of the regiment and gave it to Michaelis. Moseley was evacuated and hospitalized, and did not return to the division.[22]

The next three serials—about 126 planes of 435 and 439 groups—carried some two thousand paratroopers. These were mainly Robert F. Sink's 506 Regiment. Max Taylor, his bodyguards, his aide and some staffers flew in the lead aircraft of 435 Group, piloted by the group commander, Frank J. MacNees. The 101st's artillery commander, Tony McAuliffe, and others flew in the second plane of that group. Bob Sink was in the lead plane of the 439th Group, flown by its commander, Charles Young. These serials were bound for DZ "C," about three miles south of DZ "A." The mission of the 506 was to help seize the causeways.

Once again the neat flying formation came apart in the clouds. When the planes broke into the clear—just west of the Merderet River—the Germans were on full alert and firing. Six planes—three from each group—were shot down; many were damaged. Taylor recalled: "It was a thrilling sight to see; the sky ablaze with rockets, burning aircraft on the ground, and the antiaircraft fire rising on all sides." Taylor, shouting "Bill Lee!" went out the door at five hundred feet. It was only his second parachute jump. He came down "with a bang," all alone, in a lea enclosed by hedgerows, amidst "a circle of curious Norman cows," who eyed him "disapprovingly." He cut away his harness with a knife, discarded a bottle of Scotch he had brought along, and limped off on his bad leg in the darkness to find his companions. He had made airborne history of a sort: he was the first American general to parachute into combat. Immediately behind him was Tony McAuliffe, who became the second.[23]

The drops of these three serials were likewise imperfect. MacNees did well. He put Taylor and McAuliffe and the others within a mile and a half of the DZ. Young made one of the best drops in NEPTUNE. However, many pilots became disoriented and simply dropped men all over the eastern Cotentin. Some troopers came down near or on 82nd Division DZs; others in Ste. Mère-Église. Eight planes dropped 128 men eight miles southwest of the DZ—on the south side of the Douve River. One utterly bewildered pilot of 435 Group returned his load to England.

The last three parachute serials—about 135 planes of 440 and 441 groups—carried some twenty-two hundred men. These were mainly Howard R. (Skeets) Johnson's 501st Regiment. Johnson flew in the lead plane of 441 Group, piloted by the group commander, Theodore Kershaw. The three serials were bound for DZ "D," about a mile or two south of DZ "C", where Taylor and McAuliffe had landed. In the original airborne plan, conceived before the German 91st Division moved in and the 82nd had been shifted eastward, the 501's mission had been to seize Ste. Mère-Église. The new D-day mission was to face south toward Carentan, along the Douve River, and prepare the way for George Wear's seaborne 327th Glider Regiment to move on Carentan by seizing or destroying the bridges over the Douve.

Drop Zone "D" was only three miles from the heavy German concentrations in Carentan, and by now they were on full alert. These last parachute serials ran into "very intense flak" and automatic-weapons fire. The pilots were further bedeviled and harassed by searchlights and flares. The two groups lost five planes; a sixth was compelled to make a forced landing. Many, many were damaged. The drops were poor, among the worst in NEPTUNE, and as a result, Johnson's men were scattered far and wide. By a fluke—a bundle jammed in the doorway delaying the exit—Johnson's stick landed squarely on the DZ.

The fifty-two gliders in the armada brought up the rear. They were bound for LZ "E," which overlapped the west side of DZ "C", where Taylor and McAuliffe had landed. One glider—containing the 101st Division's main radio —broke loose over England and aborted, a serious loss. One plane and glider were shot down over the Cotentin. One plane got lost and released its glider south of Carentan. The other forty-nine tows found the LZ by moonlight and released. All but one glider landed within two miles of the DZ. Six hit it on the nose, fifteen were within a half mile, ten landed tightly bunched at les Forges, one and a half miles off. The other eighteen were close but widely scattered.

The glider landings were hair-raising. Most ended in crashes, destroying the gliders beyond repair. The gliders hit trees, stone walls, houses, hedges, ditches. Almost miraculously, most pilots and men survived. Five airborne men were killed, seventeen injured and seven missing. The gliders were so badly mangled that it was difficult to pry out the guns and vehicles. However, when the job was finally done, Taylor warmly welcomed the 57 mm antitank guns, the jeeps, ammo and other supplies he received.

Among the five glider casualties was the ADC, Don Pratt, the first American general to land in combat in a glider and the first to die. Pratt's glider pilot, Mike Murphy, recalled that he made a good landing on a thousand-foot field, locked the wheel brakes and stood the glider on its nose skid. Even so, he said, "We slid for over 800 feet on wet grass and smashed into trees at 50 m.p.h." Murphy broke both legs; his copilot was killed. Behind him in the crumpled wreckage, Pratt had been crushed to death by a jeep and other gear which had broken loose.[24]

When news of this tragedy reached him, Taylor, somewhat impulsively, named his young chief of staff, Gerry Higgins, ADC. Thoughtfully looking back years later, Taylor said, "Whether I was right in making him ADC, I don't know. I know I got a damn good one." But the battlefield appointment, which carried a promotion to one star, blocked Taylor from promoting equally deserving and more senior colonels in the 101. "Bob Sink, for example," Taylor recalled with a note of regret. "He was among the bravest, most able men I knew—exposed himself to enemy fire more than anyone in the division—but he never got promoted in the war." Taylor chose another West Pointer, Raymond D. Millener, an old associate, who had jumped for the first time ever into Normandy, to replace Higgins as his chief of staff.[25]

The smaller British airborne operations for NEPTUNE were timed to coincide with the drop of the 101. The task had been assigned to the new British 6th Airborne Division, commanded by Richard N. Gale. Owing to the shortage of troop-carrier aircraft, and other factors, Gale could utilize only two of his three brigades (regiments) in the initial assault. These were the 3rd, commanded by James Hill, and the 5th, commanded by Nigel Poett. The total assault force, comprising some forty-eight hundred men (the majority of them paratroopers), was to be lifted to battle in 264 aircraft of 39th and 46th groups (wings) and ninety-eight towed gliders. At dusk on D day, the division's third brigade (the 6th Airlanding) would be brought across in a second lift of 256 gliders.[26]

The general mission of the British airborne forces was to protect the left (or east) flank of Sword Beach. This was to be achieved by seizing key points in a five-mile-wide swath of territory lying between the Orne and Dives rivers (east of Caen) and extending about seven miles inland (south) to the Caen-Troarn highway. Some bridges were to be captured or blown and certain terrain firmly occupied.

All objectives were vital, but none drew greater attention than two closely situated bridges on the west side of the sector between Caen and Sword Beach. One was the bridge at Ranville over the Orne River; the other was the bridge at Bénouville over the Caen Canal, a man-made waterway running parallel to the Orne River. Two special commando teams of Poett's 5th Brigade, commanded by John Howard, were to be brought over in six Horsas and ghost down and crash-land adjacent to the two bridges and seize them in a *coup de main.* Thereafter, Poett's parachute brigade would drop just east of Ranville. One of its three battalions, the 7th, would dash west to the bridges to reinforce the commando teams until the amphibious forces pushed inland to link up.

This much-rehearsed and very tricky operation succeeded as designed. Five of the six Horsas, unhampered by clouds like those which blanketed the western Cotentin, hit literally within yards of their targets, and the commandos seized the bridges and stripped them of demolitions before the shocked German guards could come to their senses. (The sixth Horsa, misreleased, went astray.) Poett's 5th Brigade, likewise blessed with clear weather, jumped from 124 planes of 38 Group. Owing to a pathfinder foul-up, flak and some minor navigational errors, many paratroopers of the three battalions (7th, 12th and 13th) were, in the words of the official British historian, "dispersed and had to search the darkness for both equipment-containers and for the rendezvous." However, the American troop-carrier historian John Warren, wrote that the British drops, all blessed with clear skies, "were unquestionably more accurate than those of IX Troop Carrier Command." The 5th Brigade DZ was soon reinforced by sixty-eight Horsas and four giant Hamilcars carrying 57 mm antitank guns, vehicles, ammo and other gear. In spite of the flak, the gliders also did well. About fifty of the sixty-eight Horsas landed on or near the DZ. In one of these was the division commander, Richard Gale, the highest-ranking officer to land by glider in Normandy.

The other brigade, Hill's 3rd, was assigned a number of special tasks in widely separated locations. One task was to mount a complex glider-paratrooper assault on a heavily fortified and manned coast-artillery battery at Merville, which was believed to pose a grave threat to the British invasion fleet. The brigade's 9th Battalion would capture the Merville battery. The 1st Canadian Parachute Battalion was to land southeast of Merville at Varaville and blow the bridge over the Dives River at Robehomme and a tributary bridge at Varaville. The 8th Battalion was to land much farther to the south near Touffreville and destroy the bridges over the Dives River at Troarn and Bures.

The drop of the 3rd Brigade, by 46 Group in clear weather, was on the whole poorer than the drop of the 5th. Nonetheless, the brigade managed to carry out all its principal missions. The 9th Battalion, much reduced owing to dispersal in the drops, assisted by two Horsas (a third was lost) brimming with commandos, assaulted and took the Merville coastal battery in a remarkable and bloody *coup de main*—only to find that the size of the guns had been greatly exaggerated and posed no serious threat to the invasion forces. The Canadian battalion, also reduced in strength, blew the bridges at Varaville and Robehomme. The 8th Battalion blew the Dives River bridges at Troarn and Bures. In addition, the brigade forces, often under heavy German attack, seized and held assigned terrain.

In sum, the forty-eight hundred men of 5th and 3rd British parachute brigades, despite a misdrop of some pathfinders, heavy flak which shot down seven planes, glider mishaps or aborts, minor (and a few major) navigational errors, and misdropped or lost equipment, did remarkably well in the few hours of darkness between drop time and daylight on June 6. They captured the Orne River and Caen Canal bridges—and would hold them until the amphibious forces linked up. They captured the Merville battery. They blew four key bridges over the Dives River. They occupied key ground in the airhead and threw the Germans, who had been caught unawares, into general panic and confusion.

☆28☆

FACING THE UNKNOWNS and dangers of Normandy, Ridgway was fatalistic and sentimental. He had written a message on a photograph of himself, to be read should he not return: "To the members of the 82nd Airborne Division, with everlasting affection and appreciation of life shared with them in the service of our country. May their incomparable courage, fidelity, soldierly conduct and fighting spirit keep for this Division a place second to none in our Army." In his wallet he carried a memento: a stained, faded photo of a soldier's monument in Edinburgh, Scotland. The soldier, Ridgway wrote, "sits, head up, rifle across his knees, as if for a moment there had come a lull in the battle." The inscription beneath the soldier was one Ridgway had "perhaps unconsciously" woven into "the fabric of my own philosophy: 'If it be Life that waits, I shall live forever unconquered; if Death, I shall die at last, strong in my pride and free.' " He also carried a small GI prayer book—familiar quotations from the Old and New Testaments—into which he had pressed several four-leaf clovers, collected in Sicily, Italy, England and elsewhere.[1]

On June 4, Ridgway had reported to his takeoff field, Spanhoe, the base for the 315th Group of Hal Clark's 52nd Wing. There he had waited for Eisenhower's "go" signal. When Eisenhower postponed D day, Ridgway returned to his quarters in Leicester for the night. The next day, June 5, he returned to Spanhoe to wait again. During the afternoon, killing time, he played softball with some of the men. While at bat, he took a healthy swing at the ball; then, with a jolt, he remembered a trick-back attack while playing baseball with Omar Bradley at Fort Benning. Fearing that another attack might occur, incapacitating him for "the great adventure," Ridgway dropped the bat and walked off the field.[2]

That night Ridgway, heavily burdened with gear, boarded his plane. His "soul was at peace, my heart was light, my spirits almost gay." There were two distinctive features to his jump outfit. One was a hand grenade taped to his right chest harness. The other was a first-aid kit taped to the left chest harness. He would continue to wear the harness, grenade and first-aid kit in battle and, in time, these would become a personal cachet, like Patton's bone-handled pistols. Often the first-aid kit was mistaken for another grenade, and because of this and Ridgway's intense and steely battlefield demeanor, some GIs would call him "Old Iron Tits." It was a nickname that did not stick the way "Old Blood and Guts" stuck to Patton.

The slot to which Mark Alexander and Woody Long had assigned Ridgway's plane was one in the 505's swollen third and last serial. This serial initially had been composed of the normal thirty-six aircraft to lift Fred Kellam's 1st Battalion. To it had been added the 505th Regimental Headquarters

(Ekman, Alexander and senior staffers) in nine planes, and a platoon of the 307th Airborne Engineers, jammed into three planes. Ridgway's plane brought the total in the serial to forty-nine.[3]

Paul Williams had handpicked the aircraft and aircrew for Ridgway. The plane, piloted by Chester A. Baucke was equipped with Rebecca and also carried a navigator. In all, it had a crew of six.

Considering the shortage of planes, the jump stick was small and would later cause some negative comment: eleven men, including Ridgway. The other ten men were five officers and five enlisted men, all more or less Ridgway's attendants. The officers were the jumpmaster, Dean L. Garber; the division signals officer, Bill Moorman; an interpreter, Peter Schouvaloff; the newly appointed Division Headquarters commandant, Don Faith, and the aide, Art Kroos. The enlisted men were the orderly, Jim Casey, and four handpicked members of the division CP reconnaissance (or defense) platoon, who were, in effect, bodyguards. Ridgway's driver, Frank Farmer, rode in a glider with his jeep.[4]

The loading at Spanhoe was marred by a horrifying accident—the first of its kind. A paratrooper accidentally exploded a powerful antitank Gammon grenade in his pocket. This, in turn, exploded other ammo and set fire to the plane. Three paratroopers were killed outright, eight others were severely wounded, one fatally. A lone, uninjured paratrooper from this plane elbowed his way aboard another plane, only to be killed later in Normandy. The accident reduced the swollen third serial from forty-nine to forty-eight aircraft.[5]

The lead serials of the 82nd Division began taking off about thirty minutes behind the lead serials of the 101st Division. The 82nd forces comprised about sixty-four hundred men from the three parachute regiments (505, 507, 508), two howitzers from d'Allessio's 456th Parachute Artillery Battalion and the few engineers. They were flown by six air groups of Hal Clark's 52nd Wing (61, 313, 314, 315, 316 and the temporarily attached 442), in a total of about 377 aircraft. The formation would be joined by fifty-two Waco gliders which would take off from Ramsbury, in southern England, towed by planes of the 437 Group, 53rd Wing.[6]

The great aerial armada formed up smartly over England and proceeded toward the Cotentin on the same complicated "back door" route. Bill Ekman's 505 led the way—twenty-one hundred men in one hundred twenty planes of 315 and 316 groups, arranged in three serials. In the lead serial was Ben Vandervoort's 2nd Battalion in thirty-six planes. Next came Ed Krause's 3rd Battalion (with the handful of parachuting artillerymen of the 456th) in another thirty-six planes. In the last serial, of forty-eight planes, were Fred Kellam's 1st Battalion, the platoon of engineers, the 505 regimental headquarters group and Ridgway.

The destination of the 505 was DZ "O," which lay between Ste. Mère-Église and the Merderet River. The 505's principal missions in the revised airborne plan were to capture Ste. Mère-Église and secure the two bridges over the Merderet, one at La Fière and one at Chef-du-Pont and to establish a blocking line north and northeast of Ste. Mère-Église at the towns of Neuville-au-Plain and Beuzeville-au-Plain. While pursuing these missions, the 505 would link up eastward with Taylor's forces, which would be (in theory) concentrated between Ste. Mère-Église and Utah Beach and southward toward Carentan.

Following the aerial path blazed by the pathfinders and the 101, these three closely packed lead serials had an uneventful flight until they reached the western shore of the Cotentin. There they encountered the turbulent clouds. Ridgway recalled, "The plane began to yaw and plunge, and in my mind's eye I could see other pilots, fighting to hold course, knowing how great was the danger of collision in the air." Many planes climbed above the clouds to about fifteen hundred feet and stayed there. Vandervoort recalled, "The pilot I had was extremely reluctant to come down to the correct jumping altitude. We came in at 1400 feet and our speed was excessive." However, the clouds hid the planes from antiaircraft weapons; flak was light and erratic.[7]

The planes abruptly broke out of the clouds, many flying too high and fast and with too little time to readjust altitude and speed. Vandervoort's pilot mistook the Douve for the Merderet River and turned on the green jump light. Fortunately, Vandervoort, who was looking out the door, saw the error and coolly ordered the light turned off. But the plane was still too high and moving too fast. Vandervoort, watching the landscape, passed word to the crew chief to "slow down." The pathfinders had marked the DZ with Ts of green lights and Eureka. When the pilot saw the Merderet River and the DZ lights, he once more turned on the green light. At about 0200 hours, the stick went out, high and fast. When he hit the ground, Vandervoort broke his left tibia (leg) "one inch or so above the ankle." In pain, he watched the rest of his battalion jump. "They were well spread out," he recalled. "The ships being too high and too fast." Some fell into the Merderet marshes, some into the town of Ste. Mère-Église.[8]

Behind Vandervoort's 2nd Battalion, came Ed Krause and his 3rd Battalion in thirty-six planes of 316 Group. When his serial hit the clouds, great confusion ensued in the formation. Krause recalled:

We tried to keep our formation but ships constantly overran each other. The pilot called for evasive action and we split up. Some went high, some went lower, others right and left. This split our formation. An element of three ships was directly below us, not more than thirty feet. One came up from under and passed miraculously between my ship and the left wing ship . . . In the next three minutes I came as close to being crashed in the air as I ever hope to. Just about two or three minutes before drop time we saw this green T [on the DZ]. It was a Godsend and I felt like I had found the Holy Grail. I would say that I dropped from over 2,000 feet. It was the longest ride I have had in over fifty jumps. While descending, four ships passed under me and I really sweated that out. Just after I landed, a mine bundle hit about eighty yards away from me without a parachute and exploded.[9]

Bringing up the 505 rear came Fred Kellam's 1st Battalion, the 505 commander, Bill Ekman, his exec, Mark Alexander, and the regimental staff and Ridgway. When the serial entered the clouds, it also climbed, then abruptly broke out, flying too high and too fast. Ekman reported, "I bailed out at about 0204 hours, according to my watch. I had a very hard opening because we were going at least 150 miles per hour. I do not remember the landing because I was pretty dazed . . . [only that] I landed in the midst of a field of cattle. No other personnel were present . . . I wandered around, still dazed, for about two hours." Ekman had received a very poor drop, landing a long two miles north of the DZ, near Fresville. Mark Alexander's drop was even worse. He landed three to four miles northeast of Ste. Mère-Église.[10]

No one was certain of the position Ridgway's plane now flew. It was somewhere among the hodgepodge of the third serial, a few minutes behind the first and second serials. His aircrew was coolly professional and soon picked up a good signal on the Rebecca from the Eureka on DZ "O." The pilot, Chester Baucke, then saw the lighted "T," made a few minor corrections, descended to six hundred feet and decreased speed to 120 miles per hour or less. At exactly the proper moment, he turned on the green light and rang the bail-out bell. The jumpmaster, Dean Garber, standing in the open door, cried, "Let's go!" and leaped into the night, leading what may well have been the most perfectly dropped stick in NEPTUNE.[11]

Ridgway—making his fifth parachute jump—went out the door behind Garber. After his chute cracked open ("the most comforting of all sights"), he got a brief glimpse of Garber's canopy, then he could see nothing. "I was alone in the sky," he recalled. The descent was fast, but luckily he hit hard "in a nice, soft, grassy field." He rolled, spilled the air from his canopy, shucked his harness and grabbed for his .45 pistol, but it slipped from his grasp and fell into the grass. As he was pawing the ground for the weapon, his eye caught a movement. He turned and spoke the password: "Flash." He waited for the countersign: "Thunder."* There was no reply. With vast relief, Ridgway realized the movement was that of a cow. "I could have kissed her," he recalled. The sight of the cow indicated the pasture was not mined or booby-trapped.[13]

The stick got out without accident, but not according to plan. It was scattered. James Casey thought that happened because the six officers, who jumped first, had been a little slow in getting out of the plane: "In training, the enlisted men had been taught to jump almost on top of one another's back. So when the officers jumped, there might have been a pause of a second, or whatever, between jumps. Kroos was the last officer out, and we [five enlisted men] came out right behind him, close together. Kroos was the first officer I met on the ground." As Kroos remembered it, "The stick was supposed to 'roll up' on me on the ground. Those who jumped first would come back to me; those who jumped last would come forward to me. We landed beautifully, right on the

* Some accounts, and the film *The Longest Day*, depict the 82nd paratroopers as being equipped with toy "crickets" for recognition purposes. The 101st troopers used such crickets, but most of the 82nd veterans did not.[12]

damned nose, only a couple of hundred yards from where we would put the division CP. The enlisted men rolled up on me—but there was no sign of Ridgway!"[14]

Ridgway had landed alone in a pasture girded by hedgerows. Pistol in hand, he slowly moved off and tried to get his bearings. "I felt a great exhilaration at being here alone in the dark on this greatest of adventures," he recalled. Like every paratrooper who jumped into Normandy, he was awed by the spectacle. "By now, all over the countryside around us the Germans were beginning to rouse and shoot. The finest fireworks display I ever saw was going on around me. Rockets and tracers were streaking through the air and big explosions were going off everywhere."

His eye caught another movement in the shadows at a hedgerow. He whipped his pistol around and spoke the password. This time he received a proper countersign. To Ridgway's utter astonishment this first paratrooper he found on Normandy turned out to be the first paratrooper he had found in Sicily: Company commander Willard Follmer, who had broken his right ankle in the Sicily jump. In both the Salerno and the Normandy jumps, Follmer "favored" his right leg, in Normandy perhaps too much so. In the landing, he had broken his right hip. Scarcely able to believe this amazing coincidence, Ridgway tried to cheer Follmer with feeble humor: "I guess you hope to God you never see *me* again."[15]

Leaving Follmer to the medics, Ridgway moved on to locate the division CP area. Pistol drawn, he walked carefully and slowly, all alone, through the hedgerows, until he came upon Vandervoort's S-2, Eugene A. Doerfler, who led him to Vandervoort's CP. By now a doctor had looked at Vandervoort's tibia and had diagnosed a broken ankle. Unfazed, Vandervoort had tightly laced his boot and was using his rifle for a crutch. He and Ridgway consulted a map by flashlight, talked briefly, then Ridgway went on to the division CP area close by. Everybody was relieved to see him, but none more so than Kroos and Casey.[16]

Ridgway was all business from the moment he reached the CP. He was now armed with the .45 pistol and his trusty .30-06 Springfield rifle, which he considered more reliable than a carbine and which he would always carry in combat during the rest of the war in Europe. Bill Moorman, who was third out of the plane after Ridgway, had a memorable encounter with him on the ground. "I lost my helmet in the jump. I landed in a pasture next to a cow, wandered around and found a jumpmaster at the T. We almost hit it. I was talking to the jumpmaster when a fellow came up and said, 'I'm looking for Frank W. Moorman. General Ridgway wants to see him right away.' I said, 'That's me.' I was feeling all teary-eyed because Ridgway was worried about me and had sent someone to find me. I went up to him all gushing sentiment and saluted. Noting I had no helmet, he said, 'Where's your equipment?' So he was all right."[17]

On the whole, the drop of the 505, like those of Taylor's 501, 502 and 506, had been confused and disorganized. And yet the 505 was lucky. The official Air Force historian wrote that the 505 drop was "the best" of the six parachute drops in the Cotentin. Of the 118 sticks in the regiment, thirty-one landed on or very close to DZ "O." Some twenty-nine sticks landed within a mile of the DZ and twenty within two miles. About twenty sticks fell beyond a five-mile radius of the DZ, three of these about fourteen miles to the north. The historian could not account for the others. At least half of the 505 (eleven hundred men) landed on or within one mile of the DZ; another three hundred fifty men within two miles. The remaining six hundred (including Ekman and Alexander) were widely, and in too many cases wildly, scattered.

Thirty of the twenty-one hundred paratroopers in the 505 returned to England that same night on their planes. Flak had hit one 315 Group aircraft, injuring seven paratroopers and blocking the rest in the stick. Six men had lost courage and "refused." These refusees no longer necessarily faced a court martial and minimum ten-year prison sentences. Ridgway's earlier recommendations for softer penalties had been approved. The refusees would be drummed out of the airborne, but "disciplinary action" would consist of that which the unit commander saw fit to administer, taking into account "mental conditions." If a court-martial and sentence ensued, "reviewing authorities" could consider suspending the sentence "in order to provide the man an opportunity to make good with a ground combat unit within the theater."[18]

Next in line came Roy Lindquist's 508th Regiment, about twenty-two hundred men, carried in four serials comprising 132 planes of 313 and 314 groups. Jim Gavin flew in one of these serials. His stick totaled nineteen men, including the temporarily assigned Willard Harrison from the 504; Gavin's aide, Hugo V. Olson; and two other officers. There was also a brave outsider: *Time* magazine war correspondent William Walton, who in later years would become an intimate friend of John F. and Jacqueline Kennedy, a Camelot insider, *bon vivant* and artist.[19]

The destination of the 508 was DZ "N," on the west side of the Merderet River, about equidistant from the La Fière and Chef-du-Pont bridges. Its missions, generally, were to hold the southern and southwestern sectors of the airhead (west of the Merderet) and, in the process, to secure the bridges over the Merderet at Chef-du-Pont and the Douve at Pont-l'Abbé and Beuzeville-la-Bastille. Meanwhile, unknown to Allied intelligence, German General Wilhelm Falley had moved the headquarters of the recently arrived 91st Airlanding Division to the hamlet of Picauville, about one-half mile south of the DZ. The German headquarters was protected by numerous first-class German troops. These troops—and others—had prevented the pathfinders from reaching the DZ.[20]

When the 508 serials entered the dense cloud layers over the western Cotentin, the formations came apart. Some encountered "intense flak." The clouds were so thick that Gavin "could not see the wingtips of our plane, and of course, I could not see any other planes. Since we had been flying in close formation, it was quite dangerous."[21]

The division engineer, Robert S. Palmer, and one platoon of the 307th Engineer Battalion were flying with Lindquist's serials. As Palmer's plane passed near the division's original objective (St. Sauveur-le-Vicomte), nearly twenty miles west of the new DZ, the confused pilot turned on the green light at twenty-five hundred feet. Palmer and his stick obediently dived out into the night. They landed more or less intact, but after daylight, while trying to infiltrate eastward, Palmer and most of his stick were captured.[22]

When the other serials broke into the clear, flying high and fast, Gavin, looking out the door, saw a river, but he did not know if it was the Douve or the Merderet. He could also see much flak and small-arms fire. The green light went on and out he went at six hundred feet. At about the same time and place, Roy Lindquist and his stick jumped from about twelve hundred feet.

Gavin and Lindquist had been dumped out a long two miles north of DZ "N." Like Taylor and Ridgway, Gavin landed "with a pretty loud thud" among grazing cows. The stick rolled up smartly and Gavin set about finding his bearings. Almost immediately he ran into "a vast expanse of water." This was the marshes west of the Merderet. Lindquist made a "soft landing" in the marshes in about two and a half feet of water, to the east of Gavin but well beyond Gavin's sight or contact. "All of our equipment," Lindquist recalled, "went into the water and went out of sight." When Gavin and Lindquist finally got their bearings, they were angry and shocked at the way they had been dropped.

With good reason. The drop of the 508 was a shambles—so badly dispersed that the men were seldom able to organize into platoons and companies, let alone battalions. Many landed to the north of the DZ (near Gavin and Lindquist); many others fell among the German forces at Picauville. All too many dropped into the Merderet marshes or the marshes farther south along the Douve and drowned or exhausted themselves trying to slog out of the mud. Some, Gavin recalled, were dumped into the English Channel, beyond Utah Beach. One full company landed almost completely intact eight miles east of the DZ on Utah Beach and had a ringside seat for the invasion.[23]

All three of Lindquist's battalion commanders—and hundreds of men—were dropped south of the DZ in the vicinity of Picauville, where strong German forces were concentrated. Louis G. Mendez, commanding the 3rd Battalion, jumped from twenty-one hundred feet, which was, he recalled, "too much of a ride." As a result, he encountered intense small-arms fire in the descent; three bullets hit his field bag, and he "ran into a lot of trouble" as soon as he landed. He was pinned down by Germans and "did not see my battalion or anybody else except a messenger for five days." Herbert Batcheller, commanding the 1st Battalion, and his exec, Shields Warren, Jr., survived "a hell of a lot of flak" and landed near the Douve River below Picauville. Later that day, when Batcheller was shot in the neck and killed, Warren assumed command of the battalion. He rounded up about fifty paratroopers and headed north toward higher ground near Haut Gueuteville.

Thomas J. B. Shanley, commanding the 2nd Battalion, was the only one of the three who was dropped passably close to the DZ. He collected a band of about thirty-five paratroopers but, owing to German pressure, had to abandon the mission of blowing bridges on the Douve. Instead he struck for a key piece of "high" ground—Hill 30, so-called for thirty meters—just west of the Merderet River about midway between the roads leading west from the La Fière and Chef-du-Pont bridges. Shanley made radio contact with Shields Warren, who eventually was able to bring his small forces to join Shanley on Hill 30.[24]

Five paratroopers of the 508 returned to England on their planes. One had been wounded too severely to jump; two had fouled parachutes inside the cabin and could not jump; two had "refused."

Next came Zip Millett's 507th Regiment, some 1,937 men, in three serials comprising 117 aircraft of the veteran 61 Group and the green 442 Group. The destination was DZ "T," west of the Merderet River about half a mile north of Amfreville. The mission of the 507 was to capture Amfreville, seize the La Fière bridge by attacking from the west and establish blocking lines in the western, northwestern and northern sectors of the division airhead west of the Merderet. Pathfinders had reached the vicinity of the DZ and set up one Eureka, but, owing to heavy German fire, they had been unable to set up a lighted "T."

This drop was another shambles. The veteran 61 Group held together fairly well in the cloud layers, but the green 442nd broke up, dispersed, and was badly harassed by flak. When the planes came out of the clouds, they were flying too high and fast. Only two or three sticks hit the DZ. Many pilots overshot the DZ by a thousand to two thousand yards and dropped their sticks into the Merderet marshes, where some were drowned. Too many others who survived the marshes, the Air Force troop-carrier historian wrote, "were in a sorry state to start a battle." Not a few came down on the east bank of the Merderet in the 505 Sector. One man refused to jump.[25]

George Millett and about forty men landed squarely on the DZ near Amfreville. Of the division's three regimental commanders, he was the most exposed—closest to the bulk of the German 91st Division forces in St. Sauveur-le-Vicomte. A considerable number of 507 sticks fell into this area, and in time Millett was able to round up the largest single force west of the Merderet: at one time some 425 paratroopers. On D day he attacked Amfreville. However, the Germans fell on Millett in strength and soon isolated his force. Millett's isolation, a 507 officer recalled, "cut the guts out of the regiment."[26]

The battalion commanders of the 507, like those of the 508, were widely scattered and unable to find their men and organize them into cohesive fighting units. None came down near Millett and his force. Edwin J. Ostberg, a West Pointer, commanding 1st Battalion, landed near Gavin's group. He made contact with the 507's exec, Arthur A. Maloney. They rounded up a mixed group of about a hundred fifty men from the 507 and 508 and in time linked up with Gavin. William A. Kuhn, commanding the 3rd Battalion, was wildly misdropped near Fresville, where Ekman had landed. Kuhn was compelled to bail out at high speed. He later reported that he had never had such a "hard" parachute opening. The shock dislocated his collarbone, and as soon as it became possible, he was evacuated to England, where he recovered. He was temporarily replaced in command of the 3rd Battalion by his exec, West

Pointer John T. Davis.† Charles J. Timmes, commanding the 2nd Battalion, got the "best" drop of the three battalion commanders. He came down in the marshes about a mile southeast of the DZ, climbing out to the west, realized he could not attack toward Amfreville, but he was in good position to move against the west end of La Fière bridge. He rounded up all the men he could find—about fifty—and moved toward the bridge but Germans soon hemmed him in.[27]

Gavin soon found his bearings—he was on the west bank of the Merderet River about two miles north of the La Fière bridge—and made his way southward, under intense and growing enemy small-arms fire, toward the west end of the crossing. When Maloney and Ostberg and the band of a hundred to a hundred fifty men of the 507 (and some 508) joined him, Gavin believed at first that he had a force large enough "to accomplish a lot." (That is, capture the west end of the La Fière crossing.) But he was soon disappointed. "To my utter frustration, I found them completely disorganized, lacking unit organization and even unit leadership." All the 507 men had covered the insignia on their helmets and no one could distinguish the officers and noncoms from the privates. They were "milling about" and diving for cover in the hedgerows and "it was impossible to get them organized in any rational way." Gavin exposed himself to increasingly intense enemy fire, "trying to stir the troopers to react, with little success."[28]

A former paratrooper later attempted to shed light on the behavior of these men:

It is likely that these 507 men were suffering from a little-known phenomenon experienced by enlisted men, more so than by senior officers in first-time combat jumps. A parachute jump and in particular a combat jump (if you survived it) was so exhilarating that first-timers were apt to forget the real reason they were there—to kill Germans. The feeling was: "We've made the jump, now the Germans should roll over and play dead." In every regiment it seemed to take one combat jump to instill the idea that jumping was only a means of transportation. Another phenomenon noted for airborne troopers (and of which much has been written) was the shock of the quick transition from a peaceful, no-shooting situation to a war zone. Because of it, troopers were oft times reluctant to shoot. Usually, hostile fire soon corrected both these lapses.[29]

In what his critics believe was a serious tactical error, Gavin gave up his plan to capture the west end of the La Fière crossing. He led the group—under fire—eastward through the shoulder-deep marshes to a railway line, which ran

† About one quarter of Kuhn's 3rd Battalion—some one hundred sixty men—got the worst drop in NEPTUNE. Ten errant planes of the veteran 61 Group dumped them eighteen miles southeast of the DZ near Isigny, where most were promptly overwhelmed and captured.

along a dirt embankment several feet above the marsh. Knowing that these tracks crossed the Merderet and passed close to the east end of the La Fière bridge, Gavin set off at about first light in that direction. He did not know it then, but Roy Lindquist, who had gathered about a hundred men from the 507 and 508, had preceded him southward along those same tracks about an hour earlier, also bound for the La Fière bridge.[30]

Time magazine correspondent Bill Walton would never forget that experience:

> The fields were very bright but the hedgerows were like tunnels, and in the woods there was sort of a half light. Gavin gathered up a group . . . and took us across a wide marsh with the Germans shooting at us from behind. We plunged into the water overladened beyond belief, wearing those godawful anti-gas suits that let water in but didn't let it out. A number of men drowned in the marsh, and I saw Gavin go under once. I threw away two horribly expensive movie cameras that I was carrying for a Signal Corps captain. He let out a low moan when he saw me do it.[31]

Last came the serial of fifty-two gliders. They were to land on the 505's DZ "O." They carried two batteries of Raymond E. (Tex) Singleton's 80th Antiaircraft Battalion, equipped with the jeep-towed British 57 mm antitank guns. There were sixteen such guns and jeeps in the gliders, plus five jeeps with loaded ammo trailers, and one extra jeep with a command radio. Some division staffers rode in these gliders, including the division artillery commander, Andy March, who was (after Pratt) the second-most-senior American officer to land by glider, and the chief of staff, Doc Eaton. Ridgway had specifically assigned the 505's Al Ireland the vital responsibility for delivering the 57 mm guns to the men of the 505.[32]

The glider mission was, to put it mildly, harrowing. Shortly after takeoff, one of the 437 Group planes "lost" its glider and returned to base to pick up a reserve. When the other fifty-one planes flew into the turbulent clouds, chaos ensued. The glider pilots could not even see the tow planes. Seven gliders broke (or cut themselves) loose in the clouds. (Two were later found in western Normandy, but a month after D day the other five were still "missing.") After breaking out of the clouds, another seven gliders were prematurely released and crash-landed on the west side of the Merderet, some in the marshes. (Gavin had paused to retrieve a 57 mm gun from one of these, but he was driven off by German fire.) One tow plane was shot down, others were damaged. Some gliders were hit by flak, which wounded some men, but no gliders were shot out of the sky.

At about 0415 hours—an hour and fifteen minutes before first light—thirty-seven gliders crossed the Merderet and cut loose for DZ "O." They came down badly disorganized in ones and twos, many under German fire. Only about twenty-three crash-landed on or close to the DZ. Nine others, including two which crashed into Ste. Mère-Église, were within two miles of the DZ. (Three came down on the 101 LZ "E.") These glider landings were also disastrous.

They hit trees, stone walls, even a herd of cattle, but most of all they hit "Rommel's asparagus," which caused about half the crack-ups. Twenty-two of the gliders were utterly destroyed, most others too badly smashed to salvage. Three soldiers were killed and twenty-three were injured in the crashes. Andy March's glider landed in a tree, but, other than scratches and bruises, he emerged in "good shape." Half the guns (eight) and jeeps (eleven) were lost or found unusable. The division radio was gone. The commander of the medical company, William H. Houston, was killed.

Among the badly injured was the division chief of staff, Doc Eaton, who remembered:

> I rode in the lead glider. With me was the G-3, Bob Wienecke, the G-2, Whitfield Jack, the division surgeon, Doc [Wolcott L.] Etienne and some others. We were cut loose miles from Ste. Mère-Église. The pilot had no choice but to pick a small rectangular field from which German machine-guns were firing. Fortunately they did not see us until the last minute. I was hit in the head by a machinegun bullet—or Wienecke's helmet—and knocked unconscious with a big gash in my forehead. The landing impact was so hard my seat belt broke and I fell forward into the aisle. As they rushed out, the men trampled over me. Ridgway's driver, Frank Farmer, dragged me out of the glider, put me on a stretcher and hid me in some tall weeds, looking for help. Doc Etienne was wounded and ultimately evacuated. A patrol of the 501 happened by and took me to the regimental CP from which I was eventually carried to the 101st CP, where a surgeon taped up my chest (three broken ribs) and both legs (badly bruised tendons) from mid-thigh to ankle. I tried to beg, borrow or steal a jeep to reach the 82nd CP but when a doctor saw me fall on my face—I couldn't walk—he evacuated me to England.[33]‡

Whatever could be salvaged from the glider wreckage was welcomed, especially the 57 mm antitank guns. Al Ireland delivered eight such guns to the 505; within a short time at least six were in action. The 505's 2nd Battalion commander, Ben Vandervoort, was lucky enough to commandeer one of the jeeps and was able to keep on moving and fighting despite his broken ankle. Reflecting on his harrowing glider ride to Normandy, paratrooper Ireland said: "Those guys don't get paid enough."[35]

So concluded the delivery of Allied airborne assault troops into Normandy. In numbers, it was an impressive feat. In the American sector, some 816 troop-carrier aircraft and about 100 gliders and tows had delivered about 13,100 paratroopers and 375 gliderists. In the British sector, 264 troop-carrier aircraft

‡ A few days later, Eaton, with Ridgway's approval, went "AWOL" from the hospital and rejoined the division CP in Normandy. When he tumbled off a cot during a close artillery barrage and could not get back onto the cot, Ridgway sent him back to the hospital in England.[34]

and about 100 gliders and tows had delivered 4,800 paratroopers and gliderists. Thus by first light on D day there were about 18,250 Allied paratroopers and gliderists behind the Atlantic Wall, including nine generals (six American, three British), one of them, Don Pratt, killed in the landing. Ridgway was the most senior of this starry constellation.

The delivery operations in the American sector had been, on the whole, poor or worse. Of the six parachute regiments dropped, only Ekman's 505 achieved a passable degree of accuracy. By first light on D day, the 505 was the only one of the six regiments that was able to function as a cohesive, three-battalion force with most of its commanders (but only half the men) in place. The drops of Ridgway's 507 and 508 regiments west of the Merderet had been disastrously poor. Only about one third of the men in these regiments (1,350) had landed in the assigned operational area. Neither regiment was able to achieve any degree of organization west of the Merderet as planned. Most of the 508 missions—to secure bridges on the Douve—were soon abandoned as impossible. The principal organized forces west of the Merderet were small enclaves of paratroopers under Millett, Shanley, Warren and Timmes, all but Millett close by the west bank of the Merderet. However, these forces and roving or static bands of lightly armed paratroopers in the west sector—beyond the Merderet —would considerably impair German troop movements toward the La Fière and Chef-du-Pont bridges.

The poor American drops were due, principally, to lack of vigorous training in the American troop-carrier command. The buildup of IX Troop Carrier Command aircraft and glider forces had been too slow and casual. Bad weather, short daylight hours and other factors had impeded training in March and April, but even so, the airborne forces believed it had never been pursued with a real sense of urgency. In the mission itself, provisions should have been made for possible bad weather; at best an advance "weather plane" to test the skies and radio back an encoded report to Troop Carrier Headquarters. At least there should have been a provision for the pathfinders or lead serials to break radio silence in order to warn those planes coming behind. To allow some nine hundred planes, manned by undertrained crews (20 percent of them completely green) and all too few navigators to fly completely unwarned into bad weather suggests incompetence and stupidity. The resulting loss in life, injuries and wounds and the utter disorganization created within the 82nd and 101st divisions was nothing short of scandalous. Brereton would soon pay a high price for so neglecting the foot soldier.

There had also been too many problems in locating the DZs. Not enough American planes had been equipped with Gee and other electronic navigation devices, and the few crews who had such gear were not sufficiently trained in its use. The result was that many pilots, disoriented and dispersed by the turbulent clouds, were never able to regain their bearings. Without Rebecca electronics to receive Eureka signals from the pathfinders, too many American planes were left to find the DZs "by guess and by God." In addition, the DZ marker lights and panels put in operation by the pathfinders proved to be inadequate.

In spite of this, Leigh-Mallory's grim forecasts of airborne, troop-carrier and glider losses proved to be wildly unfounded. He had predicted that at least 50 percent of the troop-carrier aircraft and 75 percent of the gliders would be shot down. Out of the total of about 1,250 aircraft employed in the combined American and British airborne operations, only about 29 were lost, a rate of a little over 2 percent. Out of the total of about two hundred gliders employed by both American and British airborne forces, only five or fewer were actually shot down, a rate of at most 2.5 percent.

When these slight losses were tallied up, Leigh-Mallory was quick to concede error. Eisenhower wrote: "He was the first to call me to voice his delight and to express his regret that he had found it necessary to add to my personal burdens during the final tense days before D day."[36]

Ridgway would be forever grateful on several counts. His decision to jump, rather than glide, into Normandy had proved to be the correct one. He was on the ground and uninjured; his trick back had not gone out. His decision to jump with the 505 had likewise proved correct. It had put him exactly where he should be at H hour, June 6: at the center of action in the fight for the division's prime objectives, Ste. Mère-Église and the Merderet bridges.

☆29☆

THE MOST IMPORTANT ASSIGNMENT of Max Taylor's 101st Airborne Division was to seize and hold the four causeways spanning the marshes behind Utah Beach. This assignment was carried out by bands of paratroopers clicking toy crickets who met in the darkness and proceeded with the job, no matter what their original assigned tasks may have been.[1]

On the left (south) flank of the beachhead, Max Taylor himself organized a band of about ninety men and proceeded toward Exit 1, at Pouppeville. His group included Tony McAuliffe; the division's new ADC, Gerry Higgins; and Julian Ewell, who had supervised Taylor's first jump at Fort Bragg and who now commanded the 3rd Battalion in Skeets Johnson's 501. Ewell, who was in division reserve, served as tactical leader of this group, which was so rank-heavy that Taylor was led to joke, "Never were so few led by so many."[2]

A little to the north of this group, the apparently fearless Bob Sink began collecting all the misdropped and disorganized paratroopers he could find. The mission of his 506 Regiment was to secure the two southern causeways, Exit 1 and Exit 2. He soon sent a group led by his 1st Battalion commander, William L. Turner, toward Exit 1 at Pouppeville. Neither Sink nor Turner was aware that the Taylor force was moving on the same objective. Also unknown to Sink, his 2nd Battalion commander, Robert L. Strayer, who had been mis-dropped far to the north, had rounded up about two hundred men (including twenty from Lindquist's 508) and was moving rapidly toward Exit 2.

Still farther north, the Moseley/Michaelis 502nd Regiment was to seize Exits 3 and 4 and the coast artillery battery dominating Exit 4. Fortunately the 502 was blessed with three first-rate battalion commanders: Patrick F. Cassidy (1st), Steve A. Chappuis (2nd) and Robert G. Cole (3rd). These four rounded up all the men they could find (including some from the 505 and 508) and carried out the regimental objectives. Cole took the unguarded west end of Exit 3 without a fight and moved part of his force to help at Exit 4, where Michaelis and Cassidy were encountering heavy fighting. Chappuis, who also suffered a leg injury in the jump, captured the threatening coast artillery battery. It turned out to be another false alarm: the guns had been removed.

These attacks against the four causeways would prove to be of enormous help to the amphibious forces landing on Utah Beach. Only one—Exit 3—was seized in a clear-cut *coup de main;* the other three were more difficult. These holds (some gained very late in the day), wherever established, were at best tenuous and unsupported by airborne artillery, but the bands of American paratroopers, coming up behind the Germans in their beachhead pillboxes, were decisively distracting. They caused panic and confusion, cut lines of com-

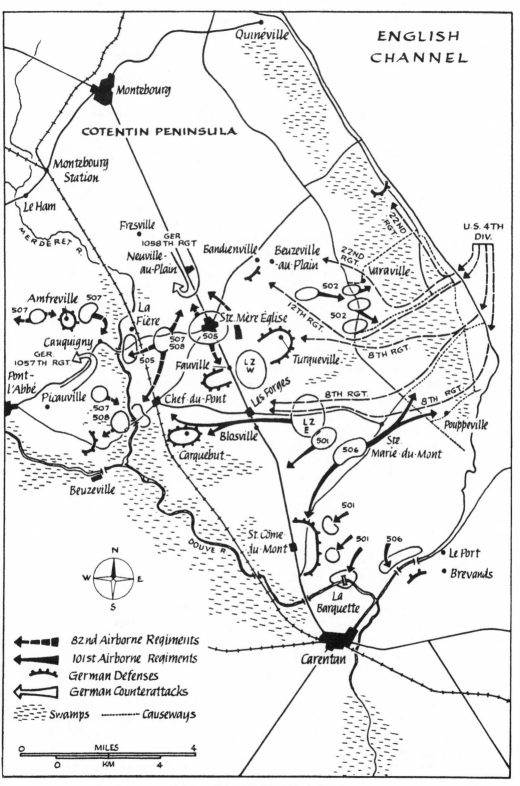

Airborne Forces Behind Utah Beach

munications and blocked reinforcements to the beach units as well as lines of retreat.

The other important mission of the 101—to block the lower Douve River above Carentan—was less successful due to the poor, flak-harassed drop of Skeets Johnson's 501 and other units as well as to the well-organized local German reaction to the assault. Johnson's 1st Battalion commander, Robert C. Carroll, was killed in the jump and his men were wildly scattered. Sink's 3rd Battalion (temporarily attached to the 501) was also hit hard. The commander, Robert L. Wolverton, and the exec, George S. Grant, were both killed.

Skeets Johnson was an unforgettable character, as Max Taylor remembered with some awe: "He was tough, very, very tough. He'd begun his military service with two years at the Naval Academy [in the class of 1927] then resigned to take a commission in the Army. He was an All-American collegiate boxer. He'd made I don't know how many parachute jumps—over one hundred, I think. He wanted his 501 to win the war all by itself and worked his troops awfully hard. If the 501 had been just an ordinary regiment, half the men would have been muttering about the 'brutal treatment' by the commanding officer, but they were airborne . . ."[3]

Despite all the setbacks, Johnson managed to get a toehold across the Douve at La Barquette and roadblocks established at the bridges near Brevands and Le Port. However, his 2nd Battalion, commanded by Robert A. Ballard, was isolated and unable to reach the Douve bridges on the main Carentan–Ste. Mère-Église highway. This left a vital "doorway" into the Cotentin wide open. The commander of the German 6th Parachute Regiment at Carentan, at first disbelieving that the invasion was real, belatedly sent two battalions north along this road to St. Côme-du-Mont and Ste. Marie-du-Mont. These German forces would further impede Johnson's work.

Omar Bradley had hoped that Carentan could be seized on D+1, a plan that was probably optimistic. Part of that plan called for reinforcing Johnson's 501 with George Wear's sea-landed 327th Glider Infantry Regiment and the sea-landed 321st and 907th glider artillery battalions. The 1st Battalion, 327, landed as planned but, inexplicably, the other two battalions remained offshore until the afternoon of D+1. There was also a problem with the glider artillery, which embarked on two ships. One of these ships struck a mine and sank; the other (with most of the guns and ammo) remained offshore for two days.[4]

George Wear's leadership was called into question. The 327 exec, Curtis Renfro, recalled: "When we waded ashore we went into an assembly area to wait until General Taylor wanted to commit the regiment to combat. Two of the battalions went into action. Sitting there, George Wear showed no concern for what his battalions might be doing. I said to him, 'General Taylor wants to push the attack to reach the Douve River before nightfall. You should go up to the front with the battalions. If you don't, I am.' He got up and went away and soon came back and said to me, 'I'm sure glad you told me to go up front because General Taylor was there raising Cain and wondering where the hell I was.' "[5]

Because of these foul-ups, Taylor decided to commit Bob Sink's 506 (with

Wear's 3rd Battalion attached) in support of Johnson's 501. Sink jumped off during the early hours of D + 1, for the moment without Wear's 3rd Battalion, which, as the 101 historian wrote, "had not appeared." Sink boldly attacked toward St. Côme-du-Mont with all the forces he could gather and promptly ran into heavy fighting—the German paratroopers who had come up from Carentan. During the fighting, Sink's 1st Battalion commander, Bill Turner, was killed. He was replaced by the exec, Franklin E. Foster, who was wounded later in the day and temporarily replaced by Lloyd E. Patch. Eventually, Wear's lagging 3rd Battalion—making slow progress against some resistance—caught up with Sink, and Sink captured Ste. Marie-du-Mont and linked up with all of Johnson's widely scattered forces. But Taylor was not able to cross the Douve bridges and causeways in force and capture Carentan.[6]

After these initial airborne operations came the vast armada carrying the American amphibious forces to Utah and Omaha beaches. H hour was 0630. At first light the air forces attempted to bomb the German beach defenses, and on the heels of that, at about 0530, the naval vessels commenced a withering bombardment. Owing in part to the cloudy weather, in part to lack of skill, the air force bombing was ineffectual, but the naval bombardment, though all too brief, was telling.[7]

At Utah Beach, the green 4th Infantry Division, commanded by Raymond O. (Tubby) Barton, led the amphibious assault. In the van was his 8th Infantry Regiment, commanded by a classmate of Eisenhower and Bradley, James A. Van Fleet. By mistake, the naval landing craft put Van Fleet's battalions ashore one mile south of the proper landing zone. This proved to be a lucky error, as this landing place was less heavily defended than the initial objective, and Van Fleet's men were quickly able to overwhelm the defenders. They soon found the causeways and commenced moving inland, cheered along by the small bands of paratroopers at the exits. Behind them came the follow-up waves of landing craft bringing the rest of the division, the support troops and advance men from Joe Collins' VII Corps headquarters. In all, twenty thousand men and seventeen hundred vehicles came ashore at Utah Beach on D day. The Utah Beach D-day casualties were gratifyingly light: 197, and 60 of these were lost at sea. Omar Bradley wrote: "Utah Beach was a piece of cake."

Not so Omaha Beach, farther east. The assault elements of the green 29th and the veteran 1st divisions ran head on into the vicious guns of the 709th Static Coastal Defense Division, plus the added firepower of the 352nd Division—discovered too late to change Allied plans. Omaha Beach, Bradley wrote, "was a nightmare." No exact accounting was ever made, but Bradley estimated that in storming Omaha Beach, Gee Gerow's V Corps suffered twenty-five hundred casualties on D day. At one point that morning, Bradley came very close to the drastic step of withdrawing V Corps and relanding it on Utah or one of the British beaches.

To the east of Omaha Beach, Miles Dempsey's British Second Army went ashore at Gold, Juno and Sword beaches, opposite Caen. There were three divisions in the attack: the British 50th and 3rd Infantry and the Canadian 3rd

Infantry. Owing to the tides, Dempsey's forces landed an hour and a half behind the Americans. This "gift of time," as Bradley put it, enabled British air and naval forces to deliver far more punishing and effective attacks on the beach defenses. The British amphibious forces, encountering only light-to-moderate resistance, pushed inland with comparative ease. They then, as the official British Army historian put it, "displayed little evidence of the urgency" required to reach the D-day objective: Caen. However, a special task force did link up with Poett's paratroopers at the Orne River and Caen Canal bridges, about halfway to Caen.[8]

Notwithstanding the horror of Omaha Beach, the landings had been a success. The Allies had come in force, determined to stay. They enjoyed absolute air-and-sea supremacy and could reinforce the assault units almost indefinitely. The Germans, still half believing these operations were merely feints—that the main attack would come in the Pas de Calais area—generally reacted sluggishly and slowly to the threat in Normandy and thereby threw away whatever chance they had to decisively defeat the Allies at the beaches.

Meanwhile, men of Ridgway's 82nd Airborne Division had been gathering in the darkness, unaware that they were about to launch one of the most famous battles in the history of the American Army.[9]

Ridgway's CP had been established in an apple orchard about twelve hundred yards west of Ste. Mère-Église. Not much of the staff showed up; many were lost or out of action: Doc Eaton, badly injured; the surgeon, Etienne, wounded (replaced by William C. Lindstrom); the engineer, Palmer, captured (replaced by Edwin A. Bedell); the ordnance officer, Joshua A. Finkel, wounded (replaced by William B. McGuire). The G-2, Whitfield Jack, and the G-3, Bob Wienecke, who had come by glider, did not appear until late on D day. The G-1, Fred Schellhammer, badly landed, did not arrive until late on D+1. The G-4, Bennie Zinn, who had come on the first glider mission, got hit. Ridgway named the signal officer, Bill Moorman, to take his place; Robert E. Furman replaced Moorman.[10]

Moorman recalled:

There was no CP as such—no tent. Just a place under a tree and not much to do. Mostly what we did at the CP was sit around and wait. Every now and then a stray bullet would come. That's how Bennie Zinn got hit. Poor fellow. He already had one bad eye and the bullet hit him in the other eye. It was one of those tricks of fate. We were standing on the same spot, talking, and I had to run a personal errand. When I got back he had been hit in the eye and gone—not blinded but out of the war. Ridgway had nobody else to be G-4. I was all he had, so I was made G-4 right there.[11]

It was soon clear to Ridgway that—as on Sicily—the drop of the division and the gliders had been disastrously poor and, owing to that fact, the division might well be in grave trouble. How grave, he could not judge, because most units had lost short-range radios and could not report to him. Moreover, the good long-range radios had been lost in the marshes or glider crashes. He could not raise Taylor or Van Fleet or Barton or Collins or Bradley or England—or anybody. He did not even know if the great invasion had taken place. Rumors were flying that, for some reason, it again had been postponed because of bad weather or had been repulsed.[12]

The official Army historian, S. L. A. Marshall, later wrote in his privately published book *Night Drop:* "Seldom, if ever, has an American division commander been placed in a more futile position than was Ridgway's throughout D day. Amid battle, his personal isolation was nigh complete. As a soldier, he was doing his part nobly; as a chief, he was almost devoid of power to direct anything, because of the collapse of communications." Ridgway conceded: "There was little I could do during that first day toward exercising division control. I could only be where the fighting seemed the hottest, to exercise whatever personal influence I could on the battalion commanders . . ."[13]

Foremost on the agenda of the 505 was the capture of Ste. Mère-Église. Sitting astride the Carentan–Cherbourg highway, this small town with its great Norman cathedral was the key piece of real estate behind Utah Beach. In Allied hands it would, like a citadel of yore, dominate the highway down which Germans would come from north and south and the terrain toward the sea. It would provide Taylor a firm bastion in his rear and Collins' amphibious forces coming ashore a clearly recognizable objective. From it, assaults could be mounted to the west.

Ed Krause, the abrasive, flamboyant yet experienced commander of Ekman's 3rd Battalion, drew the job of capturing Ste. Mère-Église. By 0300, he had collected one hundred fifty men plus a tipsy French guide. The guide revealed the good news that the town was lightly held, by less than fifty Germans who were manning some antiaircraft guns. A larger contingent of Germans had earlier fled to the woods in the south. Led by the drunken Frenchman, Krause's force stealthily approached the town by a circuitous route. Despite the din of the night's airdrops, there was no sign of an organized German defense.

Krause seized this almost unbelievable chance and rushed into town, guns blazing. The stunned Germans—perhaps forty men—were quickly overwhelmed. Ten died in the exchange, another thirty came out of buildings, hands held high in surrender. To celebrate this triumph, Krause theatrically raised an American flag which had first flown over Naples, the city his battalion also had been first to enter. Of more importance, he then cut the telephone cable linking Carentan and Cherbourg and established roadblocks at the obvious points. At 0600 hours, he reported the town "secure."

For some paratroopers the town had been an unlucky place. Earlier in the evening an incendiary bullet had set a house on fire. Twenty-odd men of the 505 and 506 had been misdropped inside the town, many coming down in a park near the square, where townspeople were fighting the fire. (This sudden onslaught may have caused the bulk of the German garrison to flee to the woods south of town.) One 505 paratrooper had fallen into the embers of the burning house and had been shot to death as he scrambled out. Another had snagged on the cathedral spire but had survived by playing dead. Perhaps ten others had been shot during the descent or after landing in trees. Some of the casualties were from Vandervoort's 2nd Battalion.[14]

The mission of Ben Vandervoort's 2nd Battalion was to help secure Ste. Mère-Église by blocking the Carentan–Cherbourg highway, two miles to the north, at the village of Neuville-au-Plain. In theory his flanks would also fan east toward Utah Beach and link up with men of the 101. At about 0530 hours, Vandervoort addressed his men quietly: "Let's go."

So far, Vandervoort, one of the few commanders with a radio, had heard nothing from his regimental commander, Bill Ekman, or the 505 G-3, John Norton, who were then, in fact, making their way south toward the regimental CP after a very bad drop. Ridgway, who was more or less acting as 505 regimental commander in Ekman's place, soon had second thoughts about Vandervoort's mission. He was worried that Krause's band might not be able to hold Ste. Mère-Église against a strong German counterattack and might need help. Therefore, soon after Vandervoort set out, Ridgway radioed him to hold in place before he became engaged in action from which it might be difficult to withdraw.

Bill Ekman and John Norton, making their way south, came upon Vandervoort's halted force at about 0700. They sized up the situation, then hurried south to the regimental CP on the DZ, arriving about 0800. There Ekman took complete charge of his regiment. Also worried about the security of Ste. Mère-Église, Ekman tried to raise Krause on his radio. When he could not, he assumed (wrongly) that Krause might be in deep trouble and, at about 0810, he radioed Vandervoort to turn around and go back to Ste. Mère-Église.[15]

Vandervoort instinctively felt these orders were not quite right, that something should be done at Neuville-au-Plain. Accordingly, on his own initiative, he made what Gavin described as "one of the best tactical decisions in the battle of Normandy." He detached a platoon, commanded by Turner B. Turnbull, and told Turnbull to do his best to carry out the original battalion objective. Then Vandervoort, reversing his march as ordered, went to Ste. Mère-Église with most of his men. He arrived just a few minutes after a German force of about two hundred men attacked the town from the woods in the south. These were the Germans who had only recently evacuated Ste. Mère-Église, and now they wanted it back. Krause's men, facing south, had repelled them—sent them reeling back to the woods, where most remained for the rest of the day, posing no further threat.

In these furious actions, Ed Krause had incurred three wounds. First a shell fragment had hit his right lower leg, breaking the skin and causing pain. Later that day he was nicked a second time, and still later, a bullet went clean through his left calf. Turning over the battalion to his exec, William Hagan, Krause checked in at a temporary aid station. He was in the blackest possible frame of mind, convinced—at least momentarily—that disaster was upon them.[16]

Krause's withdrawal to the aid station and sudden onset of pessimism would become intensely controversial. A senior 505 officer who was present in Ste. Mère-Église, later described Krause's wounds as "superficial" and said his pessimism demonstrated "a lack of aggressiveness such as to incapacitate the man for combat command." When he heard about it, Gavin was contemptuous. Agreeing that the wounds were superficial, he wrote that when Krause checked into the aid station, "that finished Krause" as far as he, Gavin, was concerned. He regretted he had not relieved Krause of command in Sicily during the battle of Biazza Ridge. Some of the many men who disliked Krause shared these views.[17]

On the other hand, many, including some who disliked him personally, would defend Krause. His battalion had been given the most important mission in Normandy—the capture of Ste. Mère-Église—and Krause had accomplished the mission with a mere one hundred fifty men. In the process, he had incurred three wounds. They were indeed superficial wounds, but he had not turned himself in until the third wound, which was the most serious of the three. Perhaps being hit three times in one day momentarily unhinged Krause psychologically. If so, it was forgivable. The 505 historian Allen Langdon, for one, concluded that Gavin and others were too quick to condemn Krause for his conduct at Ste. Mère-Église (as well as Biazza Ridge) and that notwithstanding Krause's abrasiveness and excessive flamboyance, which engendered a "love-hate" relationship for him in the 3rd Battalion, Krause "was a good (if not great) battalion commander." Ridgway refused to be drawn into the controversy; however, he gave an indication of his view of Krause when he approved the award of Krause's Distinguished Service Cross for his valor in Normandy.[18]

The greatest German threat to Ste. Mère-Église that morning was developing not in the south, but in the north, Vandervoort's sector. Elements of the German 91st Division's 1058th Regiment and other hastily attached units (comprising three or four battalions, as was later assessed) rumbled south out of Montbourg to recapture Ste. Mère-Église. They first ran into Turnbull's platoon at Neuville-au-Plain at about 1 P.M. By that time, Turnbull had one of the glider-landed 57 mm antitank guns. For about three hours Turnbull and his men mounted a savage and heroic defense, suffering heavy casualties but inflicting a perfect slaughter on the Germans. At about 4 P.M., Vandervoort (now riding in a jeep) sensed that Turnbull was in trouble and sent a platoon to help him and his men withdraw to the stronger defenses Vandervoort had established on the northern outskirts of Ste. Mère-Église. Facing this massive German onslaught, maneuvering with difficulty on a broken ankle, Vandervoort was (in contrast to Krause) a mountain of calm optimism. Ridgway would later write that Vandervoort was "one of the bravest, toughest battle commanders I ever knew." Vandervoort's men stood their ground, raking the approaching Germans with small-arms fire. Later in the evening, Vandervoort was significantly assisted by naval gunfire from the battleship *Nevada* and other vessels, whose fire was directed by a naval liaison officer who had jumped with the 505.[19]*

The battle to hold Ste. Mère-Église rightly absorbed most of Ridgway's energies on D day. But, as matters developed, he soon had to worry about his rear as well. Owing to the disastrously poor drops of the 507th and 508th, the securing of the bridges over the Merderet River at La Fière and Chef-du-Pont had not proceeded according to plan. Moreover, a serious threat to the airhead was soon posed in that area by elements of the German 91st Division's 1057th Regiment, supported by tanks, which rushed east toward the La Fière bridge from St. Sauveur-le-Vicomte.[21]

The terrain at La Fière bridge and that two miles farther south at the Chef-du-Pont bridge are similar. In that region in June, the Merderet River is usually no more than a creek. Both bridges are small stone structures, somewhat like fancy culverts. However, the terrain to the west of both bridges is low-lying and often floods in the rainy season. For that reason, both bridges have raised, open "causeways" running about five hundred yards across the low ground to the high ground to the west. Since the Germans had closed the locks on the Douve River, deliberately backing up the Merderet, the low-lying area to the west of the bridges, through which the causeways ran, was flooded. Thus the mission of "securing" the bridges, also included securing the causeways.

The detailed plan for securing the bridges and causeways was as follows. Zip Millett's 507th, to be dropped into DZ "T," west of the La Fière area, would send a force east to the hamlet of Cauquigny, on the west end of the La Fière causeway. This 507 force would establish a "beachhead" in Cauquigny, then rush across the long causeway to the small La Fière bridge. At the same time, 505 commander Bill Ekman would send a force from his DZ, "O," west to the La Fière bridge to clean out any defenders and prevent demolition of the bridge. Two miles south, Roy Lindquist's 508th, landing west of the Chef-du-Pont causeway on DZ "N," would send a force east to establish a "bridge-head" and seize that causeway. Ekman would send a combat patrol from DZ "O" to the Chef-du-Pont bridge to clean out defenders and prevent demolition. In sum: 505 and 507 forces would link up at La Fière bridge; 505 and 508 forces would link up at the Chef-du-Pont bridge.

The 507 and 508 forces assigned to these bridge-causeway missions, having been wildly misdropped, were unable to carry out the plan as designed. The sole effort on the west side of the Merderet was made by the 507's 2nd Battalion commander, Charles Timmes, whose group had gathered not far from the west end of the La Fière causeway. However, Timmes was soon hemmed in by Germans and he was able to send only a small patrol, led by Louis Levy. It made its way to Cauquigny at the west end of the causeway, where Levy found another small group of 507 men led by Joseph Kormylo. These two disparate and improvised 507 groups numbered about thirty men, all green to combat.

---

* A World War I behemoth, damaged and beached during the attack on Pearl Harbor and later salvaged and refitted, *Nevada* had ten 14-inch and twenty-one 5-inch guns.[20]

This was probably sufficient force to "rush" the La Fière causeway and link up with the 505 men assigned to secure the bridge itself, but Levy and Kormylo could see no 505 paratroopers at the bridge, so they elected to dig in at Cauquigny to secure the west bank bridgehead and await developments.

In the 505th, special units of Fred Kellam's 1st Battalion, with attached engineers, had been assigned to secure the La Fière and Chef-du-Pont bridges (but not the causeways) from the east side. Kellam's A Company, commanded by John J. Dolan, would take La Fière; Kellam's C Company would assist A Company. Dolan's A Company got one of the best drops in Normandy and quickly assembled for the La Fière mission. However, C Company and the engineers were misdropped, and considerable time elapsed before they could assemble. Dolan was unable to find Kellam on the DZ, but Kellam's exec, James P. McGinity, gave Dolan his marching orders and, on second thought, decided to accompany Dolan to the La Fière bridge. Less than two hours after the initial drop, McGinity and Dolan were on the way.

Unknown to the Allies, the Germans, for the first time, had stationed about thirty men at the La Fière bridge-causeway on June 5, the day before. The Germans established a CP in a group of stone farm buildings—Le Manoir La Fière—on the east bank of the Merderet, close to the La Fière bridge. They then set up three machine-gun nests: one near the houses covering the approach to the bridge from Ste. Mère-Église and two out on the causeway itself, with a clear field of fire east or west. Some of the Germans scouted out likely sniper positions around the farmhouse grounds. Hearing the aircraft and gunfire in the early hours of June 6, the Germans at La Fière went on full alert.

Dolan's task force soon reached the La Fière bridge. The men inspected the bridge for demolition charges and found none. They looked across the long causeway for the expected 507 task force, but saw nothing. (The Levy-Kormylo groups were dug in at Cauquigny, out of sight.) Then Dolan's force was hit by sudden fire from the well-concealed Germans. Within a matter of minutes, four of Dolan's men (two officers, two enlisted men) were killed or mortally wounded. Moments later, Kellam's exec, McGinity, was killed by a sniper. In the face of these sudden and grievous losses, Dolan and his men ducked for cover.

In the meantime, a hodgepodge of miscellaneous paratroopers was converging on La Fière bridge. Many of these were misdropped 507 and 508 men (most from the marshes), who were following the raised railway track south to the bridge. Their intent was to cross the La Fière causeway to join their units in the west. First came a 507 company commander, F. V. (Ben) Schwartzwalder, and one of his platoon leaders, John W. Marr, leading a group of about one hundred men. Next came the 508's commander, Roy Lindquist, and his growing group, which was now being led by a 507 intelligence officer, John H. Wisner. Next came the 505's C Company, backing up the 505's A Company. Next came the misdropped engineers, bringing a 57 mm antitank gun salvaged from the wreckage of a glider. Next came Jim Gavin, leading the group of 507 men he had gathered in the marshes. In total, there were soon six or seven hundred paratroopers at La Fière.

The first of these newly arriving groups also came under fire and several more men were wounded. In response, Dolan's 505 force and the Schwartzwalder-Marr 507 force commenced separate and uncoordinated attacks on the Le Manoir farmhouses. One of Dolan's platoons, led by William R. Oakley, shot a sniper out of a tree, then rushed the house with machine guns and grenades. Almost simultaneously, the Schwartzwalder-Marr force knocked out the machine-gun nest covering the road to Ste. Mère-Église. In the face of these attacks, which incurred further paratrooper casualties, twenty-odd Germans came out of the farmhouse, arms raised in surrender. So ended the "Battle of Le Manoir La Fière."[22]

Gavin, surveying this scene at La Fière bridge, was well pleased. He wrote that he talked with the troopers and found them "in great shape." What now concerned him most was the other bridge—Chef-du-Pont. There had been no sound of gunfire from that direction, nor any indication that Chef-du-Pont was secured. Feeling a need to see for himself, Gavin commenced organizing a pickup force which he would lead to Chef-du-Pont.[23]

In hindsight, some historians believe this was another tactical error on Gavin's part. Although the Germans in Le Manoir had been routed, and there were hundreds of paratroopers gathered, the situation at La Fière bridge was still fluid. There had been no linkup of 505 and 507 forces, as planned. No one had yet crossed the causeway. The senior officer after Gavin, Roy Lindquist, was utterly green to combat, as were the bulk of the men gathered at La Fière. These historians assert that Gavin should have first directed a crossing of the La Fière causeway, established a strong bridgehead in Cauquigny, *then* gone on to Chef-du-Pont.[24]

Gavin's pickup force for the Chef-du-Pont operation consisted of about two hundred men of the 507, including the 507 regimental exec, Art Maloney, and the 507's 1st Battalion commander, Ed Ostberg. He divided the group in two, placing Maloney in command of one group, Ostberg in command of the other. Overseen by Gavin, the two groups marched on Chef-du-Pont by closely parallel but different routes along the east bank of the Merderet. When Gavin reached the hamlet at Chef-du-Pont, he encountered a situation similar to that at La Fière: newly arrived Germans had established machine-gun positions in and around the hamlet near the bridge.

After sizing up the situation, Gavin attacked the hamlet. In this action, Ed Ostberg was severely wounded by machine-gun fire (and won a DSC for his valor). The Maloney force came at the hamlet from a different angle. The combined Ostberg-Maloney forces flushed the Germans from the hamlet, but these Germans did not surrender. They withdrew, with machine guns, out onto the causeway. There they dug in with a clear field of fire at the Chef-du-Pont bridge. To rush these well-concealed Germans across the open causeway would have been suicidal. Thus the Germans retained control of the Chef-du-Pont causeway. There was no sign of help from 508 men on the west bank.

Back at La Fière bridge, 507 officers Ben Schwartzwalder and John Marr were growing impatient. They were still on the east side of the Merderet; their mission lay on the west side, with Zip Millett, Timmes and the rest of the outfit. Forming up a force of about eighty 507 men, Schwartzwalder and Marr decided to cross the La Fière causeway. As they started out, the lead scout drew rifle fire from a foxhole on the causeway. In response, the scout threw a grenade at and emptied his M-1 rifle into the foxhole. This action flushed two Germans, who emerged with hands held high in surrender. Then, suddenly, five other Germans came out of another foxhole with hands up. Inspecting these foxholes, Schwartzwalder and Marr saw they were two machine-gun nests. Why the Germans had surrendered, they never knew.

Reaching Cauquigny, Schwartzwalder and Marr found the Levy-Kormylo groups dug in at the church. This was the first "linkup" at La Fière. But Schwartzwalder and Marr did not stay. They were still impatient to join Millett and Timmes and get on with their assigned mission. They exchanged a few words with Levy and Kormylo, reporting that the causeway and bridge were clear of Germans and they believed Roy Lindquist was sending across some men to reinforce the bridgehead. They found out from Levy where the Timmes group was and proceeded onward to join it. Some of the Levy-Kormylo groups joined them, dangerously thinning the Cauquigny bridgehead.

Levy then left the churchyard at Cauquigny and ran across the causeway to confer with Lindquist. No doubt Levy described the weakness of the force in the bridgehead. In any event, by that time Lindquist had organized a force of about fifty of his 508 men (grandly labeled "Company B") and Lindquist himself led them across the causeway to Cauquigny. Levy, who welcomed the reinforcements, returned to his position in the churchyard. Apparently satisfied with the setup, Lindquist returned to Le Manoir to establish a provisional 508 CP.

These various decisions and actions early on D day had, in effect, turned the original Merderet plans topsy-turvy. As things now stood, the senior 508 commander, Roy Lindquist, was in charge of the La Fière operation, originally a 507 objective, and the senior 507 officer present, the exec Art Maloney, was in charge of the Chef-du-Pont operation, originally a 508 objective.

At about this time, the 505 commander, Bill Ekman, until recently Lindquist's exec, and like Lindquist green to combat, arrived at La Fière bridge. By then almost the whole of Kellam's 1st Battalion, 505, had assembled there. Counting the 505 men and the strays from the 507 and 508, there were still about five or six hundred paratroopers at or near La Fière bridge. They were not actively engaged. They were milling around or lying down trying to catch some sleep—all awaiting orders. In due course, Ekman returned to DZ "O" to see how the rest of his regiment was faring.

Some critics of the campaign would assert with hindsight that at this time Lindquist or Ekman, or both, also made a grave tactical error. Lindquist had "reinforced" the Levy-Kormylo group in the Cauquigny bridgehead with about fifty men ("Company B"). Yet it should have been obvious to Ekman and Lindquist—both West Pointers and longtime Army professionals—that this was far from sufficient. The Cauquigny bridgehead was still very, very weak, held by utterly green troops. The critics assert that right then it should have been further—and heavily—reinforced with the idle combat veterans of the 505's 1st Battalion plus the scores of green strays of the 507 and 508. Had this been done, it would have probably been possible to establish firm contact with the isolated Timmes group, drawing it into Cauquigny, further strengthening the bridgehead. The failure to properly reinforce the Cauquigny bridgehead would not only prove to be costly for the 82nd Division, but it would also change the shape of the battle for the Cotentin Peninsula.

Fred Kellam, perhaps alerted by some sixth sense, sent a runner across the causeway, ostensibly to round up any stray 505ers on the west bank. The runner scouted the road past Cauquigny until he heard the "unmistakable sound" of approaching tracked vehicles. These were the leading elements of the German 1057th Regiment, 91st Division. The runner tore back through Cauquigny, alerted the Levy-Kormylo groups and Lindquist's "reinforcements," then ran across the causeway to report to Kellam. With this advance warning, Kellam deployed his 1st Battalion "in depth" at La Fière bridge, with Dolan's A Company on a narrow front at the bridge. Some of Dolan's men pushed an old truck out on the bridge to block the passage and strung land mines from the truck. Two bazooka teams found a spot that overlooked the bridge, and others zeroed in the single 57 mm antitank gun.

The Germans reached Cauquigny, easily overran the weak Levy-Kormylo group dug in at the church and routed Lindquist's "Company B," which ran pell-mell back across the causeway. They then advanced onto the causeway itself, letting loose a murderous barrage of artillery, mortar and machine-gun fire. Two French Renault light tanks led a large procession of German infantry. The lead tank almost immediately knocked out the crew of the 505's 57 mm antitank gun. But the two 505 bazooka teams let loose a fusillade of rockets which disabled one tank and set the other on fire. (Later, all four enlisted bazooka men received DSCs.) Meantime, other paratroopers slaughtered the German troops on the open, exposed causeway with small-arms fire. The German survivors dived for cover or withdrew.

The artillery—German 88s—continued pounding the 1st Battalion savagely. One of these deadly bursts hit Fred Kellam, his S-3, Dale A. Roysden, and Kellam's runner. Kellam was killed, Roysden mortally wounded and the runner seriously wounded. Kellam was the second of Ridgway's battalion commanders to die in Normandy, after Batcheller. Learning of Kellam's death, and knowing that the 1st Battalion exec, McGinity, had been killed earlier, the 505 exec, Mark Alexander, hurried down to La Fière to take command of the 1st Battalion.

At Chef-du-Pont, Jim Gavin received erroneous word that the La Fière bridge-causeway had been "lost." Leaving a group of thirty-five 507 men under command of Roy E. Creek to hold the east bank of Chef-du-Pont, Gavin, Maloney and the other 507 men raced back to La Fière to reinforce the 505's 1st Battalion. By that time the battalion, under Alexander, had decisively repulsed the German attack and had a firm hold at La Fière bridge. Alexander asked Gavin if he should counterattack across the causeway to Cauquigny, but

Gavin told him to stay put on the east bank and build up his defenses to meet what was certain to be a renewed German attack the following day.†

These German reactions on D day had the effect of squeezing Ridgway into an airhead roughly the shape of an equilateral triangle the sides of which were about two miles long. The points of the triangle were Ste. Mère-Église, the La Fière bridge and Chef-du-Pont. One German regiment—the 1058th—was pressing hard at Ste. Mère-Église from the north. Another—the 1057th—was pressing hard against La Fière from the west. A battalion of the 6th Parachute Regiment, belatedly moving north from Carentan, had passed through St. Côme-du-Mont and reached Blosville, three miles south of Ste. Mère-Église. Had this battalion driven harder, it might have linked up with the Germans in the woods south of Ste. Mère-Église to press hard on the town from the south. But, fortunately for Ridgway and his paratroopers, the attack was too little and too late, and the Germans in the woods remained isolated.

The situation within the airhead was precarious. Ridgway had control of only about twenty-five hundred men, mostly from the 505, plus the strays from the 507 and 508 under Roy Lindquist in "reserve." Of the 505 battalion commanders, Fred Kellam had been killed, Vandervoort had a broken ankle and Krause was temporarily out of action at the aid station. Of the 507 commanders, Zip Millett was isolated near Amfreville, Charles Timmes was hemmed in on the west bank of the Merderet, Ed Ostberg had been severely wounded at Chef-du-Pont and Ed Kuhn had been badly injured on the jump. Nothing was known of the three 508 battalion commanders: Batcheller (already killed), Shanley (isolated with Shields Warren west of the Merderet opposite Chef-du-Pont) and Mendez. Ridgway had only six 57 mm antitank guns and precious little ammo of any kind. He had no communications with the world outside his besieged triangle.

Few American generals in World War II would experience such a hellish nightmare. And yet Ridgway, according to many who were present, did not once falter, did not yield to pessimism, doubt or fear; or if he did, he gave no outward sign of it. His "worst-case" plan was to hold Ste. Mère-Église, whatever the cost and even if he had to yield the bridge at La Fière. He had utmost faith in his elite airborne fighters and the surviving senior combat leaders still in action: Gavin, Ekman, Maloney, Alexander, Vandervoort and ten dozen of lesser rank.[25]

Besides that, Ridgway knew, unless the invasion had been postponed or canceled, substantial help must arrive soon. Van Fleet's 8th Infantry was scheduled to drive due west from Utah Beach to Les Forges, two miles south of

† That evening, the stray 507 and 508 troops at La Fière were pulled out of the line and formed into a division "reserve," which could be used to reinforce either Ste. Mère-Église, La Fière or Chef-du-Pont. This planned withdrawal of 507 and 508 troopers led to a false rumor—and later to an erroneous published report—that the Germans had forced the 505 from La Fière bridge. The 505, Langdon reports, did not yield an inch at La Fière.

Ste. Mère-Église on the Carentan–Cherbourg highway. Immediately behind Van Fleet would come Edson Raff with a sea-landed task force of Sherman tanks whose specific mission was to break through to Ste. Mère-Église and support Ridgway. A large, reinforcing glider mission crammed with artillery, antitank guns, ammo, medical supplies, radios and vehicles, as well as some twelve hundred artillerymen, was due in two flights, at 9 and 11 P.M.

☆30☆

JOE COLLINS, an eternal optimist and a hard driver, was more than satisfied by the ease of the Utah Beach attack and gratifyingly light casualties. Unaware of the disastrous drops of the airborne divisions—especially that of the 82nd—or the defensive advantages the hedgerows provided the Germans, or the quick reactions of the local German commanders which had led to Ridgway's grave situation in the Ste. Mère-Église triangle, Collins gave the "go" signal for the dash to Cherbourg. The three regiments of Tubby Barton's green 4th Division would pivot north and attack toward Cherbourg in the corridor between the Merderet River and the English Channel. The 101st and the 82nd would anchor the VII Corps base along the Douve River at Carentan and St. Sauveur-le-Vicomte, respectively.

When this order was issued, Van Fleet's 8th Infantry was going ashore through Utah Exits 1 and 2 and inching inland toward Les Forges. On D+1 he was supposed to pivot north and attack up the highway through Ste. Mère-Église. Thereafter the 8th Infantry would link up, line abreast, with the 12th and 22nd Infantry and the three regiments would then go flat out for Cherbourg. It was hoped they would reach the hilly outskirts of the port in two or three days—before the Germans had time to organize a stout defense.[1]

The twenty-one Sherman tanks of the Raff force came ashore at Utah Beach at 1:30 P.M. behind Van Fleet's 8th Infantry. They met "absolutely no opposition," as Raff put it. The force proceeded on its mission to dash to Ste. Mère-Église and link up with Ridgway's forces "as quickly as possible" and, in addition, ensure that LZ "W," near Fauville, was clear for the 9 and 11 P.M. glider landings on D day.[2]

Raff, riding in a lead jeep, followed Van Fleet's forces westward over a road toward Les Forges. He encountered no enemy fire, little sign of opposition at all. For a while it was like a peaceful outing in the pastoral Norman countryside. Raff pulled ahead of the Van Fleet forces, reached Les Forges, double-checked his bearings, then swung right (or north) on the Carentan–Cherbourg highway. Ste. Mère-Église lay a mere two miles to the north. Unaware that Ridgway's situation was tight, Raff proceeded on the final leg of his "dash" with proper military caution.[3]

Minutes later he ran into grave difficulty. The Germans who had fled Ste. Mère-Église and holed up in the woods to the south of the town opened fire with 88s which had been zeroed in on the road. These accurate salvos hit and destroyed an armored reconnaissance vehicle and three Sherman tanks and inflicted numerous casualties. Raff was thus temporarily blocked at Les Forges, unable to move north, either to secure LZ "W" (one mile north) or reach

Ridgway (two miles north). Raff realized with mounting concern that the Germans in the woods overlooked and dominated LZ "W," but he was virtually powerless to do anything about it. His tanks were no match for the deadly 88s. None of Van Fleet's heavier forces were close enough to call on for direct help, but they did provide one valuable service: they blocked the northward advance of the battalion of the 6th Parachute Regiment that was approaching Les Forges from St. Côme-du-Mont.

The American glider reinforcing missions for dusk on D day were organized into three echelons. The first small mission, composed of 32 Horsas, was earmarked for Taylor's 101. The second and third, composed of 177 gliders (140 Horsas, 37 Wacos) were earmarked for the 82nd Division. The 434 Group towed the 101 gliders; the 437th and 438th groups towed the 82nd gliders. The two LZs, "E" and "W," were so close together—"E" a mile to the east of "W" at Turqueville—that they were virtually abutting. The 172 Horsas and 37 Wacos were heavily laden with troops (1,200 from the 82nd Division, mostly artillerymen), vehicles (163), artillery (more 57 mm antitank guns and twenty-four snub-nose 105 mm howitzers), 300,000 pounds of ammo and other gear.[4]

The lead planes in the first echelon took off at 6:30 P.M., heavily escorted by fighters. They were to fly in the "front door" of the Cotentin, directly over Utah Beach. The weather was good, navigation a breeze. No German fighters appeared. At 8:53 P.M. the lead serial—the first daylight Allied glider mission —approached LZ "E" seven minutes ahead of schedule.

These thirty-two gliders for Taylor—all Horsas—cut loose, circled steeply toward the ground, and came in. Fortunately, most had been erroneously cut loose short of LZ "E." Nineteen made good landings two to three miles northeast of the LZ beyond the range of the Germans in the woods. Only five landed on the LZ itself. These five immediately came under heavy fire. Of the 157 troops in this serial, 14 were killed by gunfire or in the crashes, 30 others were wounded or injured, 10 were "missing." All in all, the landings had gone remarkably well and Taylor welcomed the supplies the gliders carried.

The lead elements of the next two echelons—177 gliders for Ridgway— followed the first group by about thirty minutes. They carried badly needed guns: those of the rest of Tex Singleton's 80th Antiaircraft Battalion and of two full airborne artillery battalions, James Todd's 319th and Paul Wright's 320th. Two gliders aborted, but the remaining 175 flew "serenely" over the English Channel to Utah Beach. By this time, Ridgway, guessing LZ "W" was dominated by German weapons, had set in motion a plan to redirect the gliders to the 505's DZ "O," inside the besieged triangle. His men marked DZ "O" with a green T, green smoke and a Eureka beacon. However, he was not able to get word of the change in plans to the outside world and could only hope the tow pilots would see, or detect, the change.

The first group, of seventy-five gliders, did not detect the change and headed straight for LZ "W." The tows released the lead gliders at 9:04 P.M. Watching from the ground, Raff detonated orange smoke grenades in an effort to draw the gliders away from the Germans in the woods and toward his position. It was futile. The gliders flew straight into a hail of German fire and crashed all over the countryside. Those men who survived the crash had to run from the gliders to avoid being killed or wounded by German artillery fire.

An observer with Raff wrote:

> It was too small a landing ground for so many gliders under any conditions. Only a few of them were able to make it. For desperate seconds they beat the air over our heads like monstrous birds. Then they crashed into trees and hedgerows on each side of us. They pancaked down on the road. They skidded crazily, and stopped . . . All our tanks began firing at once and everyone with a rifle shot it off, trying to get some lead into the woods where the Germans were and so slow up the fire on the helpless gliders. Men were scrambling from the wrecks of the gliders, running about as if in a daze.[5]

Two hours behind these came the second, larger, group, of a hundred gliders for Ridgway. The lead tows picked up the Eureka on DZ "O" and headed in that direction. The change in course took the tows over the German concentrations north and northeast of Ste. Mère-Église. The ground fire was heavy and frightening. Just at sunset, 11:05 P.M. British Double Summer Time, the lead gliders cut loose. According to the troop-carrier historian:

> Once again the small fields and enemy fire played havoc with the glider landings. The fire in some places was intense, and many men were killed or wounded in the one or two minutes before their gliders reached the ground. Some pilots, despite strict orders for a slow landing, slammed their Horsas into the landing fields at 100 miles an hour. Since the fields were short, some being only 100 yards long, and since the twilight made a precise approach over the hedgerows increasingly difficult, even the most careful pilots were lucky to escape a crash . . . Once again the occupants of most gliders had to take cover immediately after landing, and unloading was postponed until after dark.[6]

The 175 gliders earmarked for the 82nd Division in these two echelons crashed all over the place. Only a very few came down on LZ "W," a few on LZ "O" and a few on LZ "E." Most crashed outside the LZs in pastures, roads, ditches; many behind German lines. Most of the fragile Horsas disintegrated on these rough landings; the Wacos held together far better. Only eight of the 175 gliders made perfect, undamaged landings. The troops in the 139 Horsas suffered 142 casualties; the troops in the 36 Wacos, 15. In all, 33 troopers were killed, 124 were wounded or injured.*

---

* That same evening, at about the same time, 256 aircraft of the British 38 and 46 groups (wings) delivered the 6th Airlanding (Glider) Brigade (Regiment) into the British sector—three battalions and support units, comprising some 4,000 men. One or two gliders were shot down and some strayed, but an astonishing 246 gliders— which included some Hamilcars carrying Tetrarch light tanks—landed "on or very

The exec of the 320th Glider Artillery Battalion, William S. Lancey, remembered:

The 320th was lifted to France in Horsa gliders. Our commanding officer, Paul Wright, came down miles and miles from the LZs—we didn't see him for several days. My Horsa came down—crashed—right in the middle of Ste. Mère-Église. Hell of a mess; we were lucky to get out alive. At first light I set up our "artillery" right at Ste. Mère-Église where we crashed. This consisted of one M-3 105 snub-nose, which had survived the crash-landing, and one [of the two] 75 mm pack howitzer from [d'Allessio's] 456th. The pack had a broken wheel, so I used a tree stump to lay it on. That was our so-called "divisional artillery."[8]

At Les Forges, Raff and his men helped the glider troopers and pilots, who had landed close by, to safety. Since he had no medics in his party, he could do little for the wounded and injured. He did not feel it prudent to make a dash through the German fire to Ste. Mère-Église. Thereafter, he called it a day. Like the pioneers in the American West, he circled his tanks, and his men encamped inside the circle for the six hours of darkness and fell into the deep sleep of tired soldiers.

Raff's decision to halt and sleep the night would later cause a minor controversy. With hindsight, some of Ridgway's troopers inside the besieged triangle believed that if Raff had launched a northward attack in darkness, he could have broken through the thin crust of Germans in the woods, many of whom began withdrawing under cover of darkness, trying to reach either the 1057th Regiment, west of the Merderet, or the 1058th Regiment, north of Ste. Mère-Église. At the very least, Ridgway's troopers believed, Raff could have sent a small patrol—or even a runner—to reassure Ridgway that he was close by and would make an all-out effort to reach Ste. Mère-Église after daylight. Raff's response was that he did not know, and as one historian put it, "couldn't even conceive" that Ridgway had no communications and was unaware that Raff was so close by.[9]

Inside the besieged triangle, Ridgway and his men soon heard that the glider missions from which they expected vital artillery and antitank gun support were fiascos. After dark, men raced out to the nearby crashes to retrieve the wounded and injured and salvage whatever guns, ammo and vehicles they could pry from the wreckage. The supplies were "manna from heaven," but it was not nearly enough to provide the kind of artillery and antitank backup Ridgway would need to stave off the two German regiments hammering at his north and west gates.

For many of Ridgway's men, this was the spiritual nadir. There was no sign

near their zones," in what was aptly described as a "highly successful" operation. These D-day Allied glider missions raised the total number of Allied paratrooper/ glider troops in France to about 23,000.[7]

of or word from the Raff force. The big glider mission was apparently a shambles. And yet Ridgway remained cool and steady, buoyed by the timely receipt of important news. He now knew, from two sources, that the invasion had actually taken place and that in at least one area Barton's forces had moved well inland from Utah Beach. One source was the rescued glider pilots and troopers who had crashed close by. The other was a Vandervoort patrol. Earlier in the evening, it had met a patrol of the 12th Infantry, 4th Division, near Beuzeville-au-Plain, about two miles northeast of Ste. Mère-Église and nearly four miles inland from Utah Beach.

Ridgway received some disquieting news as well: the German 1058th Regiment, pressing Ste. Mère-Église from the north, was said to have been reinforced by armor—many tanks. This information would later prove to be false; the 1058th had been significantly reinforced by two heavy motorized artillery battalions and an antitank battalion with self-propelled guns that looked like tanks.[10]

Unaware of the true situation—which was bad enough—Ridgway decided to try to get a messenger through to Tubby Barton urgently requesting antitank guns, tanks, artillery and medical supplies. He chose the assistant G-3, Walter Winton, to carry the message. Winton recalled:

> He called me over and told me to take the patrol that had met the 4th Division patrol and go back and find Ray Barton's CP and brief them on our situation, try to make arrangements for some artillery support and get information about Raff and so on. By that time I'd been on my feet for about forty-eight hours and I didn't know if I could move my frame. Bill Moorman gave me some stuff—Benzedrine, I think—and off I floated.

Winton found the Vandervoort patrol and set off for Beuzeville-au-Plain in the dark. The men in the patrol were dead tired and Winton soon left them far behind. He reached Barton's CP about midnight and briefed the general. This was the first authoritative news Barton had received about the 82nd Airborne Division's grim situation: the disastrous drop of the 507 and 508, the intense German pressure from the west and north, the fouled-up glider mission. Barton promised Winton he would send help—tank destroyers and other forces— at first light. He then notified Joe Collins and VII Corps Headquarters, still aboard ship off Utah Beach, that word had at last been received from Ridgway. Having successfully completed his mission, Winton lay down and fell into exhausted sleep.[11]

Back at his CP, Ridgway was feeling similar fatigue. He, too, had not slept for about forty-eight hours. "I was in fine physical shape," Ridgway recalled, "but never in all my life have I been so weary as I was at the end of that first day in Normandy." He found a cargo parachute, wrapped himself inside it, flopped down in a ditch and was instantly fast asleep, oblivious to the German artillery which crashed on all through the night.[12]

Not far away, Jim Gavin had established his CP near the La Fière bridge. He now had a jeep, an interpreter, and a telephone by which he established contact with the division CP. Like Ridgway, he was dead on his feet and crawled into a ditch, wrapped in a camouflage net, and went to sleep.[13]

A few minutes later, Gavin's aide, Hugo Olson, shook him awake. Ridgway wanted him, Olson said. At first Gavin could not believe it, because he knew that Ridgway "always went forward to see his officers in combat rather than take them away from their tactical commands." Wearily he got up and checked. The message appeared authentic. Gavin and Olson then set off for the division CP in bright moonlight. It was Gavin's first visit to the "rear."

Gavin later discovered that he and Olson either just missed or walked right through a throng of Germans. These were some of the troops who had taken refuge in the woods south of Ste. Mère-Église and were now withdrawing. They were creeping northward through the night to join the 1058th Regiment, and, on the way, they passed between Ridgway's and Gavin's CPs. They had captured Gavin's translator, who escaped several days later and told Gavin the story. Gavin had probably missed capture—or death—by the slimmest of margins.

Gavin found Ridgway sleeping in the ditch and shook him awake to report. Gavin recalled: "He didn't seem too happy about it and said he had nothing for me and didn't need me" and went back to sleep. Recalling the same event in his memoirs, Ridgway wrote that "a messenger" had shaken him awake to announce that the Germans were "counterattacking in strength" across the La Fière causeway. "I couldn't see what the hell I could do about that single-handed," Ridgway wrote, "so I sent back word that the battalion was to hold if it could. If this was impossible, then it could pull back."[14]

It had all been a mistake, probably due to the misguided zeal of a harassed staff officer sending messages in Ridgway's name. Such things often happen in battle and Gavin did not resent the mixup. But having been rudely awakened to embark on what later proved to have been a risky trip, he did resent Ridgway's curtness, and later was nettled by the way Ridgway recalled the incident in his memoirs. Ridgway's account contained the clear inference that the "messenger" (actually Gavin) had come in panic to ask for Ridgway's help. This was far from accurate and Gavin would take it as a slur on his courage and professional ability. Thus this silly little mixup would be the beginning of what would eventually become a major rift between these two strong-minded airborne commanders.†

When Joe Collins came ashore, early on D+1, he went straight to Tubby Barton's CP. There he found out in detail about the plight of the 82nd and its

---

† In his oral history, Ridgway, identifying Gavin as the "messenger," continued to insist that Gavin had come in distress for help or permission to withdraw from the La Fière bridge. Ridgway recalled that Gavin woke him and said, "I think the Germans are going to get through this time." Ridgway said he replied, "Well, you're in command down there, Jim. You have full authority to pull back." Then Ridgway added, "I rolled over and went to sleep. You've got to get some sleep or you're no good to anybody."[15]

urgent request for help. Over Barton's objections, Collins ordered that a reserve 4th Division tank battalion, the 746th, commanded by D. G. Hupfer and encamped at Reuville, be sent at once to break through to Ste. Mère-Église.[16]

At Les Forges that same morning, Edson Raff awoke and appraised his situation. Unaware that many of the Germans in the woods between his force and Ste. Mère-Église had slipped away during the night, he was still cautious about launching a northward attack on his own to relieve Ridgway. While he went off to confer with Van Fleet on a joint assault, a staff officer attached to the Raff force attempted to flank the woods with a reluctant, ragtag group of glider pilots, some of whom had to be coaxed into the assault at pistol point. About half the glider pilots "bugged out" for Utah Beach, and the attack failed.[17]

In the meantime, Van Fleet had already redeployed his 8th Infantry Regiment for the planned D + 1 attack northward. His three infantry battalions, supported by tanks and artillery, soon moved north out of Les Forges toward the German emplacement in the woods. The remaining Germans did not readily yield, but the weight of Van Fleet's advance soon overwhelmed most of them. Thereafter, only lightly scattered pockets of Germans lay between Van Fleet and Ste. Mère-Église. However, these were sufficient to slow the advance of this green outfit to a crawl, and Van Fleet, for all his personal heroism and undeniable leadership (Bradley wrote that he was "earning about three DSCs a day"), could not immediately reach Ste. Mère-Église.[18]‡

One of the first men from Barton's 4th Division to reach the 82nd Division CP was none other than Brigadier General Theodore Roosevelt, Jr., son of the twenty-sixth President. The fifty-seven-year old Roosevelt, a reservist and a strong Army advocate, had had a checkered combat career. He had gone to North Africa with the 1st Division, then commanded by Terry de la Mesa Allen. He was a frail man who had severe arthritis and had to use a cane, but he proved to be an inspiring leader who was absolutely fearless in combat. Nonetheless, in Sicily, Omar Bradley, believing the 1st Division to be undisciplined and poorly led, had sacked both Allen and Roosevelt. Allen was given command of a new division organizing in the States; Bradley had subsequently appointed Roosevelt understudy ADC of the 4th, because he believed Roosevelt's famous presence with the Utah Beach assault forces "would be an inspiration" to the GIs."[20]

It was. Roosevelt had landed with the first assault wave, helped organize the attack inland and then led it, sitting in the rear of a jeep, grandly waving his cane. (His son, Quentin, had landed on Omaha Beach with the 1st Division.) He rolled into the 82nd CP on the morning of D + 1, Ridgway recalled, "as if the bullet that could kill him had not been made." Ridgway's aide, Art Kroos, was astonished: "Somehow he, by jeep, went through a no-man's area to get to Ste. Mère-Église. He certainly didn't look like a soldier, but he was a *man.*

‡ Gavin later wrote with derision that Van Fleet's attack north was "held up . . . for a couple of hours so the troops could be issued cigarettes."[19]

Very thin. Had a cane. No weapon. Helmet pushed back on his head, sort of casually saying, 'Fellows, where's the picnic?' "[21]

Ridgway and Roosevelt were "warm, close friends." In the early thirties, when Ridgway was posted to the Philippines for a tour, he had served Roosevelt, then Governor-General of the Philippines, as a military adviser. In 1933, Roosevelt (and Roosevelt's good friend the distinguished soldier-diplomat Frank McCoy, under whom Ridgway had also served) had played a large hand in getting Ridgway an appointment to the Command and General Staff School. Now, eleven years later, on the battlefield, Roosevelt, as Ridgway put it, had come "to offer to us all the help, in guns and ammunition, that we would need." For this act of bravery, and others, in Normandy, Roosevelt was awarded the Medal of Honor.[22]

The sight of Ted Roosevelt in the flesh was reassuring for Ridgway and his men, but Roosevelt did not have so much as a single round of ammo to give them, and whatever help he could summon would obviously take time. Ridgway's most immediate hope for help lay in the giant D + 1 glider reinforcing mission for the 82nd. The plan called for some 200 gliders (50 Horsas, 150 Wacos), in two echelons, two hours apart, to bring in the three battalions of Harry Lewis' 325th Infantry Regiment, plus ammo and supplies to LZs "E" and "W." Lewis had orders to advance west from the LZs to the Merderet River near Chef-du-Pont. Ridgway could hope that higher authority had changed those orders to an advance on Ste. Mère-Église.[23]

The first echelon, consisting of about 100 gliders, took off from bases in England at 4:30 A.M. It was towed by 434 and 437 groups. In the gliders was Klemm Boyd's 1st Battalion plus some engineers and artillerymen—717 troops in all. At 7:00 A.M., this echelon arrived over the Cotentin headed for LZ "E." The formation was raked by German ground fire. All gliders were released too far east and too low—most at 200 to 300 feet. The gliders crashed far and wide —none on LZ "E." Seventeen troopers were killed in Horsa crashes; ninety-eight others in Horsa and Waco crashes were injured.

Among the injured was Klemm Boyd. He was soon evacuated to a hospital in England and did not ever lead his battalion in Normandy combat. Nor did he return to the division. Command of the 1st Battalion went to his exec, Teddy H. Sanford. Boyd was the sixth of twelve infantry battalion commanders lost to the 82nd Division during the first thirty hours in Normandy.[24]

The second echelon, of 100 gliders, leaving England two hours after the first, was towed by 439 and 411 groups. These gliders carried John Swenson's 2nd Battalion and Charles Carrell's 2nd Battalion (ex-401), in all about 1,330 troops, the majority (800) in Horsas. The lead planes reached the Cotentin at about 9 A.M. and released the gliders for the besieged LZ "W," one mile to the north of the Raff force and in the path of Van Fleet's advancing 8th Infantry. These gliders, too, crashed all over the landscape. Those that came down on the northern end of LZ "W" were hard hit by German fire. In all, about sixteen troopers were killed in the crashes and seventy-four were injured.

The 200 gliders in this mission had brought a total of about 2,000 troops into

Normandy. The troop-carrier historian calculated that total delivery casualties (killed, injured, missing) were about 7.5 percent. That meant that 92.5 percent made it. Many troopers were in shock from this rude introduction to battle, but physically unscathed and more or less ready for combat. Thus the mission was deemed successful, with one exception: the Horsas were declared unacceptable. No American combat unit would ever go into battle again in a Horsa glider.*

Remarkably, Harry Lewis was able to assemble most of the far-flung elements of the 325th Regiment within several hours—by about 11 A.M. But he had received no change in orders from higher authority to advance on Ste. Mère-Église. Following the original tactical plan, the three battalions moved, more or less in cohesion, westward from the Les Forges area toward the Merderet River; Carrell's 2nd Battalion (ex-401) was ordered to detour through Carquebut, which proved to be devoid of Germans. The regiment stopped in the vicinity of Chef-du-Pont and bivouacked, for the time being held in division reserve. The Raff force followed in the path of the 325, going first to Chef-du-Pont, then northwest toward Ste. Mère-Église.

Inside the besieged Ste. Mère-Église triangle, Ridgway thus had little "outside" help on D + 1. The most significant was a smattering of artillery, pried from the gliders which had wrecked nearby the evening before. Carter Todd had salvaged six 75 mm pack howitzers of his 319th; Lancey had his 105 mm snub-nose howitzer and the broken 75 mm pack. (The remainder of the 456th reached Utah Beach on D + 1 but did not land as scheduled.) This gave Ridgway a total artillery firepower of about seven 75 mm pack howitzers and one or two 105 mm snub-nose howitzers.

As expected, on D + 1, the Germans renewed the attack, hitting Ridgway's forces on two fronts. Early that morning, the reinforced German 1058th Regiment attacked Ste. Mère-Église from the north at about the same time the 1057th attacked La Fière from the west. It fell to Bill Ekman's 505 to repulse these attacks. Vandervoort, reinforced by a miscellany of 507 and 508 men, commanded the defenses at Ste. Mère-Église; Mark Alexander commanded the defenses at La Fière under the supervision of Jim Gavin. Ridgway raced back and forth between the two fronts.

The German attack that morning on Ste. Mère-Église was strong and relentless. First came a prolonged artillery barrage, then swarms of infantry supported by the self-propelled artillery. Vandervoort's men stood like rocks, kill-

---

* The arrival of these last 2,000 men raised the total number of Allied paratroopers and gliderists brought into Normandy solely by air to about 25,500. That same day, two large parachute resupply missions were mounted. The first, consisting of 208 planes from the 52nd Wing, carrying 234 tons of supplies (half of it ammo), set off for the 82nd Division DZs. The second, consisting of 126 planes from the 50th Wing, set off for 101st DZs. Both missions, bedeviled by poor weather, interdicted by enemy flak and unable to locate DZs, were failures. Many planes aborted or were damaged or shot down. Much of the dropped supplies fell into German hands.

ing and wounding scores of Germans, withdrawing only to find better cover or fields of fire or to evacuate wounded.

One man in Vandervoort's fine battalion stood above all others that day: First Lieutenant Waverly W. Wray, a devoutly religious Mississippi woodsman with the courage and rifle skill of Sergeant Alvin C. York. Armed with an M-1 rifle, a .45 pistol, a .38 revolver and pocketsful of grenades, he embarked on a stealthy one-man flanking patrol through the hedgerows. He found the headquarters of the German 1st Battalion, 1058th Regiment, leveled his M-1 at the commanding officer and seven staffers and ordered them to surrender. When one German attempted to draw his pistol, Wray shot him. Hearing the fire, two Germans in a nearby slit trench rose up and nicked Wray in the ear with bursts from Schmeisser machine pistols. Disregarding this fire, Wray shot the seven other men in the headquarters group, reloaded his M-1, then killed the two Germans in the slit trench with one shot apiece. Later Wray directed the close-in placement of 60 mm mortars, which routed hordes of Germans from cover in consternation and confusion. Finding no command structure, these hundreds of Germans fled north. "Wray shattered the battalion," Vandervoort said later. "He was nominated for the Congressional Medal of Honor, but the recommendation was downgraded to a DSC. Sad to say, he was killed about three months later."[25]

This sound and savage defense once more saved Ste. Mère-Église from being overrun. After it, Van Fleet's 8th Infantry filtered into the southern outskirts of the town. Not long afterward, Hupfer and his 746th Tank Battalion came from the east. After Hupfer came the Raff force, and a little after that Joe Collins and Van Fleet, tightly buttoned up in an armored car, drove into Ste. Mère-Église amid a German artillery barrage. They found Ridgway at the division CP west of town. Collins recalled that Ridgway was in "fine" spirits and thanked him for sending Hupfer's tank battalion.[26]

With scarcely a pause for amenities, Ridgway and Van Fleet launched a coordinated attack to overwhelm the remaining Germans to the north of the town. Since Van Fleet's troops were slow in coming forward to regroup, the attack was mounted principally by Ekman's 505—Vandervoort's men—and the Sherman tanks Raff had brought. By lucky happenstance, Hupfer's Shermans rumbled into the attack unannounced and without plan or coordination. At first awestruck by the appearance of all this heavy Allied armor, Vandervoort's men soon took advantage of it and continued surging northward. This attack routed the surviving Germans, who had conducted the bloody attack on Ste. Mère-Église earlier in the day. The German units, battered but still defiant, withdrew to positions north of Neuville-au-Plain and dug in.[27]

These actions and the arrival of Van Fleet's 8th Infantry and the heavy artillery and armor ended forever the German threat to Ste. Mère-Église. Ekman and Vandervoort and others in the 505 had saved this important citadel, which now anchored the left flank of the invasion force. Ridgway awarded Vandervoort a DSC for his cool and magnificent performance.[28]

That same morning, D + 1, the German 1057th Regiment launched a savage attack eastward across the Merderet causeway toward La Fière. It was led by four more French Renault tanks. By this time, Mark Alexander's men had mined and partially blocked the road with the wreckage of several vehicles and again zeroed in a single 57 mm antitank gun and two bazooka teams. At about 9 A.M., the Renaults clanked eastward, followed by truckloads of infantry.[29]

Alexander's men hit the first tank, blocking the road. While the other tanks backed off, the German infantry swarmed forward, using the wreckage and the disabled tank and other vehicles for cover. The fiercely determined Germans surged toward Alexander's positions on the east bank. Another 1st Battalion officer, William Oakley, was killed, but the 505 again held, and the German infantry momentarily fell back. Then the Germans resumed shelling the east bank with 88s and 120 mm mortars. One of the men, Sergeant William D. Owens, recalled:

> They really clobbered us . . . The artillery shells and mortars were coming in like machinegun fire. I don't know how it was possible to live through it. Then the infantry came again and we gave them everything we had. The machinegun I had was so hot it quit firing. I took . . . a BAR [Browning Automatic Rifle] and I fired until I ran out of ammunition. I then took a machinegun [from two paratroopers who had been killed] and rested it across a pile of dirt . . . with this and one other machinegun and a 60 mm mortar we stopped them. But they had gotten to within twenty-five yards of us. I really thought we'd had it.[30]

Then, eerily, the Germans quit. They raised a Red Cross flag, a signal for a truce to recover casualties. Shifting to a vantage point, Owens watched warily as the Germans removed some two hundred dead or wounded to the west end of the causeway. Shortly thereafter, the 88s and mortars resumed firing. But the Germans did not again attempt to send infantry across the causeway.

The 1st Battalion, 505, assisted by a miscellany of men from the 507 and 508, had first captured, then held the La Fière bridge. The cost in commanders had been great: Kellam, McGinity, Roysden, Oakley and two other officers of the battalion were dead. Nearly half of "A" Company (sixty-six men) had been killed or severely wounded; another twenty-three were walking wounded, still in the fight.[31]

A less aggressive division commander might well have called it a day. The key objective, Ste. Mère-Église, was secure. The La Fière bridge had been saved, extending the left flank of the invasion forces to the Merderet River. With the arrival of the tanks, artillery and regular infantry that afternoon, Ridgway could have dug in on the east bank of the Merderet, established an impregnable defense, and sat back to lick his wounds until relieved by the regular infantry reserves coming ashore at Utah Beach. Ridgway himself had recommended in his November statement of "principles" that airborne forces be relieved of combat duties after about forty-eight hours.

However, such a passive course now seemed unthinkable to Ridgway. The situation had dramatically changed; the division was no longer isolated and cut off and in danger of decimation. Part of the division's mission had been to occupy and hold the territory west from the Merderet to the Douve and southward toward Pont-l'Abbé. Owing to the bad drops of the 507 and 508, this mission had not been carried out. Moreover, there were desperate pockets of isolated paratroopers—Millett, Shanley-Warren, Timmes, among others—west of the Merderet that he felt he must rescue.

Beyond that, Joe Collins had requested help on another front. The northward dash of Tubby Barton's three green regiments (8th, 12th, 22nd) had, by the end of D+1, run into the dug-in and heavily reinforced German 1058th Regiment and bogged down. Believing the addition of the elite 505 to this attack would help inspire and thus spring Barton's green GIs, Collins proposed that the 505 link up with Van Fleet's 8th Infantry for a joint attack toward Montebourg, six miles north of Ste. Mère-Église. The 505 would take the left flank of the attack, advancing up the east bank of the Merderet River to Le Ham and Montebourg Station. Ridgway readily agreed to this proposal.[32]

In sum: On the following morning, June 8 (D+2), Ridgway's 82nd Division would attack out of the Ste. Mère-Église triangle in two directions—west over the Merderet on its original mission, and north toward Montebourg on an added mission.

These plans and movements required formal staffing. By the end of D+1, most of the key division staffers had reported in: Fred Schellhammer (G-1); Whitfield Jack (G-2); Bob Wienecke (G-3); assisted by Walter Winton and Ridgway's protégé Hank Adams who had parachuted in that day; and the newly appointed G-4, Bill Moorman. To temporarily replace the injured Eaton, Ridgway chose Edson Raff, who no longer had a job.

The division staff still had no love for Raff and once again received him frostily. For his part, Raff "was not impressed" with any of the staff, and he still believed that they were "sycophants"—all except the new G-4, Bill Moorman, who, Raff wrote, "was not afraid to argue with Ridgway." Raff also remained unimpressed with Ridgway, later writing that "I never saw General Ridgway do anything outstandingly brave in battle." Ridgway, on the other hand, had revised his opinion of Raff, at least for the moment. Later, on D+4 (June 10), he wrote Eaton to explain that Raff was "temporarily" filling his shoes, adding that he was "much pleased" with Raff's work.[33]

The new attack plans envisioned a large role for Harry Lewis' 325th Glider Regiment, which had not yet seen action. The most experienced 325 units, Teddy Sanford's 1st Battalion and John Swenson's 2nd Battalion, would be committed to combat, with Charles Carrell's 2nd Battalion (ex-401) held in reserve. Sanford would go west across the Merderet. Swenson, attached to the badly depleted 505, would join the northern attack.

The attack west was the more complicated of the two. Rather than a frontal assault across the Merderet causeway into the teeth of the 1057th Regiment, Sanford would attempt an encircling maneuver. He would cross the Merderet at a recently discovered ford north of the La Fière causeway, link up with the besieged Timmes group, then advance on Cauquigny village from the north. At the same time, Millett's group (isolated but now in radio contact), of 250-odd men, would attack eastward to join the combined Sanford-Timmes force. Carrell's 2nd Battalion (ex-401) would be poised near La Fière to rush across the causeway into the Merderet bridgehead which Sanford and Timmes would establish at Cauquigny. At the same time, Lindquist, with a scratch force of miscellaneous 508 and 507 paratroopers, would attack west over Chef-du-Pont to rescue the Shanley-Warren group.[34]

The officer-observer attached to the Raff force had returned to Utah Beach on the afternoon of D+1 to bring Ridgway two truckloads of badly needed ammo. That evening he arrived at Ridgway's CP, which had now been equipped with a powerful radio for transmitting and receiving. He was shocked to find the CP under heavy fire from German 88s. When some shells ripped through nearby trees, he—along with others—dived into a ditch for cover. Later, he drew this portrait of Ridgway:

> In the field we had left so suddenly there was now only one man standing and that was the General. He was standing there quite alone, bareheaded, and looking down at his staff and his visitors. What he said quite calmly was "I *thought* they were ranging on that radio. You know, I think we ought to tell them to move it. The radio operator might get hurt over there . . ." It was obviously a crazy thing for the commanding general to do—to stand there without even a helmet on and let the 88 fire break around his head. But it was one of the things he had to do, and it was superbly right to do it, and Ridgway did it with grace and dignity—and great courage.[35]

31

THE NORTHWARD OFFENSIVE of Joe Collins' VII Corps jumped off at 8 A.M. on the morning of D+2 (June 8). The corps comprised four regiments, including Ekman's depleted 505th, which was to be reinforced by Swenson's 2nd Battalion of the 325th. The 505, on the extreme left (west) flank of this formation, more or less hugged the Merderet River. Vandervoort's 2nd Battalion and the 3rd Battalion, with Ed Krause back in command, spearheaded the 505 attack. Alexander's 1st Battalion remained in reserve; Swenson's 2nd Battalion (325) was still moving up. In the initial push, Vandervoort and Krause took Fresville. On the following day, D+3, Krause's 3rd Battalion was placed in "reserve" (but covering the 505's left flank), while Vandervoort, Alexander and Swenson led the onward attack toward Montebourg Station and Le Ham.

On the whole, the offensive was disappointing. The Germans were numerous, deeply dug in, and backed by heavy artillery including railway guns. Hitler had given direct orders that Cherbourg be held at all costs. Elements of the German 243rd and the 77th Infantry divisions (rushed from Brittany up the west coast of the Cotentin) were thrown into the battle. The 505 advanced steadily toward its objectives, taking heavy losses, but the green 8th, 12th and 22nd regiments bogged down in the face of determined and well-organized German resistance. The fighting took a heavy toll of 4th Division commanders. The ADC, Harry A. Barber, and the commander of the 22nd Infantry, Harvey A. Tribolet, burned themselves out and had to be replaced—Barber by his understudy Ted Roosevelt. The commander of the 12th Infantry, Ridgway's good friend Russell P. (Red) Reeder, Jr., who won a DSC, was severely wounded and evacuated. Among Barton's regimental commanders, only Van Fleet, who also won a DSC, survived the ordeal. Collins brought up a reserve regiment—the 39th, from Manton Eddy's 9th Division—but even so the offensive ground to a halt.[1]

The gliderists of the 2nd Battalion, 325, joining the Normandy fighting for the first time, had performed exceptionally well, but circumstances led to a difficult command situation. The battalion commander, John Swenson, awarded a DSC for heroism, was gravely wounded in the attack on Le Ham. When he was evacuated, his exec, West Pointer Osmund A. (Oz) Leahy, unofficially took command and ably led the battalion in the capture of Le Ham.[2]

The officers of the battalion assumed that Leahy's performance that day had earned him a permanent job as their battalion commander. However, before official orders were cut, an unfortunate incident denied Leahy that promotion. A battalion officer who was present, H. C. (Tom) Slaughter, explained:

Ridgway was a good—or great—commander. But he was impulsive. After we took Le Ham, Ridgway came steaming into the battalion headquarters area in his jeep. We'd done all we were supposed to do: cleaned the area of Germans, posted guards, etcetera. But some dumb soldier said, "Watch out, General, there's a German sniper out there." [In the church belfrey.] Well, it was the wrong thing to say to Ridgway—it was not even correct—and Ridgway marched right in and relieved Leahy of command. This was a terrible injustice to Leahy, who had only just [temporarily] taken over and done an outstanding job in taking Le Ham.[3]

Ridgway chose Roscoe Roy to permanently replace Swenson and sent Leahy to 325 headquarters. Perhaps in part because of the relief of Leahy, Roy was heartily disliked in the battalion, "a pain in the ass," Slaughter recalled. Few mourned when Roy was killed in action several days later. To replace Roy, Ridgway chose the 325's S-4, Charles (Tad) Major, who was soon well liked and who brought stability to the battalion. Even so, Slaughter remembered, the battalion officers, feeling a great injustice had been done Leahy, democratically drew up and signed a petition to Harry Lewis requesting that Oz Leahy be made a battalion commander. Harry Lewis, and then Ridgway, were deeply moved by this highly unusual political action and in time responded to it favorably.[4]

The 82nd Division's attack to the west of the Merderet River, supervised by Gavin and launched on the same day (June 8) as Collins' northward offensive, was less swiftly and expertly executed and far costlier. Of its bloody culminating battle, Ridgway would say, "I think that fight was as hot a single battle as any U.S. troops had, at any time, during the war in Europe."[5]

The first attempt that day was scheduled to go in the southern sector, at Chef-du-Pont, where Lindquist's 508 men had relieved the 507 force under Roy Creek, which had valiantly held Chef-du-Pont incurring heavy losses. The purpose was to secure the causeway and rescue the Shanley-Warren group on Hill 30, on the west bank. By that time, Roy Lindquist had assembled sizable forces. Mostly they were his own 508 men, but they also included misdropped strays of the 507th Regiment and paratroopers from the 101st Division. Lindquist established contact with Shanley by radio and runner, and told him that if he, Shanley, could clear the road (leading southwest from the causeway to Pont-l'Abbé), he, Lindquist, would send a rescue convoy across the causeway. Shanley complied with this plan. A group of twenty-three men led by two daring officers, Lloyd L. Pollette, Jr., and Woodrow W. Millsaps, cleared the road of all Germans and then triumphantly fought east across the causeway and reported to Lindquist. However, by this time the causeway was under fire from German artillery situated south of the Douve, and Lindquist canceled the rescue convoy, nullifying the good work of the Pollette-Millsaps patrol. The Shanley-Warren group thus remained unhappily isolated and under intense German fire and desperately in need of medical supplies.[6]

Lindquist's failure to more aggressively attack the Chef-du-Pont causeway and relieve the Shanley-Warren group on Hill 30 was unfortunate. The failure would be disguised in the 508 regimental history, although Pollette and Millsaps were singled out for praise: "The action of this patrol has been recognized by the Theater Historian as one of the outstanding feats of the period of instability in Normandy . . . Lieutenants Pollette and Millsaps, later to be acclaimed as two of the really outstanding combat men in the Regiment, showed their love for a fight by aggressively engaging the enemy and personally routing many of them . . . in some of the fiercest fighting yet seen on the hill . . ."*

Late that same day, June 8, Ridgway, Gavin and Lewis launched the encircling attack to capture the La Fière causeway. Shortly after sunset, at 11 P.M., Teddy Sanford led his 1st Battalion over the ford to dry land on the west bank and made contact with the Timmes force.[8]

In the meantime, the 250-man Millett force started east toward the Merderet, encumbered by ninety-six German POWs who had been captured in the previous two days. Millett had been joined by the badly misdropped exec of Lindquist's 508, Harry J. Harrison, and Ben F. Pearson, exec of the 507's 2nd Battalion. In the darkness, the Millett force, owing to the carelessness of a soldier, became separated, dividing the force into two independent groups. Leading the first group, of a hundred men, Millett unwittingly walked straight into a German bivouac. He was captured, and most of his group, except Harrison and Pearson, were captured or killed. When Ridgway learned this, he appointed Arthur Maloney commander of the 507th.

Command of the second group, of a hundred fifty men and ninety POWs, temporarily devolved to a 507 company commander, Paul F. Smith, who continued east toward the Merderet, maintaining radio contact with Arthur Maloney, who gave Smith specific orders to stay on the west side of the river and try to link up with the Timmes or the Shanley-Warren groups. Having just escaped capture with Millett, the 508's exec, Harry Harrison, joined the Smith group and, being senior to Smith, took command. Contrary to the instructions from Maloney, Harrison ordered Smith and the others in the group to move across the Merderet marshes and river to the east bank. Smith strongly protested these orders, but Harrison insisted, and eventually this group—and Ben Pearson, independently—reached La Fière. Ridgway, displeased on learning of the Harrison withdrawal, ordered an official investigation. It would not turn out well for Harrison.[9]

The combined Sanford-Timmes force moved on Cauquigny in darkness from the north, but the attack failed. The Germans were deeply dug in and refused to yield a foot. They inflicted heavy casualties on the Americans. Reluctantly Sanford reported by radio to Ridgway and Gavin that the attack had not carried, that he was withdrawing to the Timmes enclave and digging in to meet a certain counterattack. One man, PFC Charles N. DeGlopper, stood up in plain sight of the enemy with a BAR, covering the withdrawal until he was gunned down, dead. He was later awarded the Medal of Honor, the only man

* During the ETO fighting Pollette won the DSC and two Silver Stars; Millsaps won two Silver Stars and a Bronze Star.[7]

in the 82nd Division to be so honored for the Normandy combat. Of Sanford's operation, Gavin commented: "It was a great deal to ask of a battalion that had not been in combat . . . The Germans counter-attacked violently and by sheer numbers overwhelmed the inexperienced glidermen."[10]†

In all of this, one of the most astonishing developments was the sudden fearlessness and bravado of Harry Lewis. One of his officers, Leonard F. Fleck, recalled:

> I disliked him when he berated the junior officers [prior to combat] but in combat he was something else . . . the perfect old soldier . . . rough, tough and, I thought, very brave. I remember an incident in Normandy. We were pinned down on both sides of the road by artillery fire. He came walking up the middle of the road as though nothing was happening. Someone yelled for him to take cover. Lewis said, "If they can hit a little guy like me, you big guys had better watch out."
>
> Another time we had driven a bunch of Germans into an old stone building. Lewis came up and took charge, brought up the anti-tank guns and a section of .50 caliber machine guns, which had been following us . . . doing nothing. Lewis had the anti-tank guns fire at the building and, as the Germans came out, they were hit by the .50 caliber machine guns. Not one escaped and we didn't lose a man.

This view of Lewis in combat was shared by another 325 officer, Wayne Pierce:

> He showed courage but was not fearless or foolhardy. I was near him when small arms fire broke out around us and the zip of bullets was clearly audible. Most of us in the party hit the ground but Lewis did not move. Another time some incoming artillery shells screamed overhead and crashed nearby. Lewis did not move and I held my ground that time. However, Teddy Sanford was flat on the ground. Lewis said, 'What's the matter with you, Sanford?' Sanford stood up and looking sheepish, said, "I guess I'm getting jumpy, Colonel."[11]

The failure of the Sanford-Timmes attack was awkward for more than one reason. That same day, Omar Bradley, aware from decoded radio dispatches that the Germans were routing the 77th Infantry Division and other units into the Cotentin through St. Sauveur-le-Vicomte, decided Collins must send in regular forces to cut the Cotentin at its base. Bradley directed Collins to pass one of his reserve infantry divisions, the green 90th, commanded by Jay W. MacKelvie, through the 82nd Division sector—and the La Fière bridgehead— and have it attack toward St. Sauveur-le-Vicomte. The 90th was even then

---

† Sanford's 1st Battalion had seen about two weeks of frontline combat in Italy, but perhaps in Gavin's memory that experience had been so inconsequential that it did not count.

unloading at Utah Beach. It was ordered to cross the La Fière causeway late on June 9.[12]

The pressures on Ridgway were intense. His men had captured the La Fière causeway on D day, only to give it back and heroically repulse, at great cost, a German attack on the La Fière bridge itself. The lackluster attempt to frontally force Chef-du-Pont and rescue the Shanley-Warren group had failed. The clever plan to encircle the La Fière causeway and rescue Millett and Timmes had failed as well. Having endured these failures, Ridgway was now asked to stand aside and permit the green but heavily equipped 90th Division to make a power crossing of the causeway, rescue his men, and carry out what had origi-nally been an 82nd Division mission.

The fact was, Ridgway's own views of airborne warfare more or less recom-mended that procedure. Airborne forces were not equipped for power crossings of heavily defended rivers. Ridgway himself had rejected just such a mission in Italy—the Volturno crossing. But this case was different. To stand aside in favor of a new, green division would be, at the very least, humiliating for him personally and might possibly taint the division's proud history.

There was also the possibility that the 90th itself might fail. It would jump off into the face of concentrated enemy fire and might well become so demoral-ized that it would collapse as a fighting unit. If so, Collins would have lost his principal means of cutting the Cotentin and blocking the German reinforce-ments streaming up the west coast to Cherbourg. If allowed to pass, these reinforcements would further retard the already slow advance of Barton's rein-forced 4th Division, further delaying the attack on Cherbourg, which was the most vital objective of VII Corps. A failure to take Cherbourg promptly could drastically impede the entire Allied invasion.

These factors led Ridgway to conclude early that morning—June 9—that the 82nd Airborne Division had to force a crossing of the La Fière causeway. That is, a frontal assault into the teeth of the German defenses. Moreover, it had to be done promptly, regardless of the cost. He would brook no delay. Gavin, who agreed entirely with the decision, would command the attack.[13]

There was only one organized outfit available for this arduous task: Charles Carrell's 2nd Battalion (ex-401). Carrell's glider outfit had not yet been spiritu-ally integrated into the 325. Carrell still did not admire Lewis; he scarcely knew Ridgway and Gavin, except by name. Carrell felt the mission was sui-cidal and that he had drawn it because he and his men were outsiders, or "orphans" who would be sacrificed, like cannon fodder, with scant regret. His negative attitude soon swept through his battalion, which moved forward to the jump-off position in a sour mood.[14]

Ridgway and Gavin, meanwhile, had been making preparations for artillery and tank support. By this time, Andy March's division artillery was in some-what better shape. James Todd's 319th Glider Artillery now had seven 75 mm pack howitzers facing Chef-du-Pont, and Paul Wright's 320th Glider Artillery had eight 105 mm snub-nose howitzers near the La Fière bridge. Word had reached Ridgway that the ten other 75 mm packs of d'Allessio's 456th Para-chute Artillery would unload that afternoon at Utah Beach.

But this was not sufficient artillery firepower to support a frontal assault across the Merderet River. Fortunately, by this time, the commander of the 90th Division Artillery, John M. Devine, who was a West Point classmate of Collins' and Ridgway's, had come ashore and was deploying two of his field-artillery battalions (the 344th and the 345th), one equipped with twelve big, 155 mm howitzers. Devine very willingly—and somewhat hastily—zeroed these guns in on the German emplacements in Cauquigny. In addition, Hupfer brought elements of his 746th Tank Battalion forward and zeroed the turret guns in on the west bank.[15]

The commander of Devine's 345th Field Artillery Battalion, West Pointer Frank W. Norris, entering combat for the first time, was profoundly impressed by Ridgway and Gavin and the challenges they faced. Norris said later:

> Devine and I and my exec, Lloyd R. Salisbury, went down to look over the situation. The 82nd had an appalling mission that day—to seize the Merderet crossing across that long, single causeway. Two well-defended [German] machine guns could have denied that crossing to a regiment.
>
> Ridgway told us the plan and asked if we could help. I only had five 155 mm howitzers ready right then. I told him if he could wait about an hour, I'd have all twelve of my howitzers ready. Although Ridgway had Collins and his staff breathing down his neck, he immediately turned to Gavin and his officers and said: "The attack is delayed." Then he said to Gavin: "Take these officers"—Salisbury and me—"down to the bridge and show them what you want to hit."
>
> So Gavin took us down to the bridge. He had a very fine foxhole just to one side of the bridge. The Germans were firing hot and heavy. Gavin stood by the foxhole and said: "You two get in there and I'll show you what we want to hit." I said: "General, that's *your* foxhole." He said: "You look like you need it more than I do, and besides, I want you to do the shooting."
>
> So we got in the foxhole and Salisbury began zeroing in our batteries, using one howitzer from each. Two things about Ridgway had greatly impressed me: first his instantaneous decision to delay the attack in spite of all the high-level pressure on him and second, sending a general—Gavin—to make certain his orders were carried out and that we were shown every possible courtesy.[16]

The 507's new commander, West Pointer Art Maloney, was a huge and impressive figure: six feet, four inches, about 240 pounds. He was extremely tough. One of his officers remembered that he had a "grizzled look and a voice to match," but that "behind his gruffness," there was a "real helper to the inexperienced." He might "gore you and toss you in the air a bit when you screwed up," the officer wrote, "but if he felt you had any redeeming worth, he would save you . . . Only the backward and foolhardy crossed him deliberately. The troops thought he was great. So did I."[17]

Artilleryman Norris (Maloney's West Point classmate) continued his story:

While we were preparing for the attack, there was a terrific explosion. I looked around and there was Art Maloney, flat on his back, with a lot of blood coming out of his head. I thought we'd lost him. We went over and I saw his eyes start fluttering, then he was conscious. A hell of a big shell fragment had gone through his helmet and gave him a big flesh wound in the head that bled like hell but wasn't . . . dangerous. They took him off a few yards, propped him up against a tree, then a medic put a big bandage on his head. Maloney put his helmet back on and stood up again, ready to go. Pretty terrific.[18]

The 82nd now had formidable artillery and tank reinforcements: twelve 155 mm howitzers plus Hupfer's Shermans. Even so, Carrell was still less than enthusiastic. Gavin, at a loss to understand why a fellow West Pointer like Carrell was not eager to gallantly ride into this valley of death, tried to reassure him. The causeway, Gavin asserted, would be completely blanketed by artificially generated smoke, to follow a sustained, thunderous artillery barrage that would knock the Germans senseless. The attack would not be easy but it was by no means suicidal.[19]

Unsure that Carrell and his men would prevail, Gavin began privately arranging a backup. He turned to two 507 paratroopers who had proved themselves to be fearlessly aggressive: Art Maloney and one of the 507 company commanders, Robert D. Rae. Maloney, Gavin wrote, "was an impressive sight —a tough burly trooper wearing three days' red beard streaked with dry blood." Rae, no less impressive, had emerged as a powerful fighter during the seventy-two hours of combat at La Fière. Gavin told Maloney and Rae to gather a force of 507 paratroopers and stand by. He said, "These glidermen are probably going to hesitate at some point when their losses are heavy and the shock hits them. At that instant I'm going to wave at you. I want you to jump up with all your men yelling their heads off and go right through them and take them with you."[20]

According to the regimental S-2, John H. Wisner, these orders were not received by the 507 men with overwhelming enthusiasm:

Maloney, commanding a rump of the 507 PIR had an officers' meeting . . . to give us the order for the attack. When what he was asking for became plain, every man there turned pale. Silence. Then one officer spoke up: "Colonel, it will be a slaughter! They can fire on us from three sides for 500 yards." Maloney said, "I know, but Timmes is over there and we must go to his help." Silence once more . . . Timmes was on the other side being methodically cut to pieces by the Germans. A great deal of the regiment and even the division were embarrassed . . . I looked carefully from face to face for a man to make a counter argument. No one could . . . No one could deny that we owed it to Timmes no matter how thick the bullets on the causeway. I had been contemplating the Merderet for three days and I could not think of any other way to get across . . .[21]

At ten-thirty, the artillery barrage commenced. As Gavin remembered:

We poured everything we had right on top of the German positions. It was just hair-raising. The noise, the unbelievable shrieking of the shrapnel, the screeching of the German horses—they had a lot of horse-drawn artillery and stuff—the cries of the men who were hit, the tank guns, machineguns, mortars, BARs, carbines, rifles. It was like the modern-day "mad minute" demonstrations at Fort Benning when they fire off everything they've got simultaneously and continuously to impress the visiting firemen. Soon Germans in a bad state of shock, their faces covered with dust, and blood trickling from their mouths, began coming across the causeway with their hands up.[22]

Now it was time for Carrell to charge. However, the promised smoke cover was nowhere to be seen. That part of the plan had miscarried; the causeway was starkly visible. Moreover, the Germans were now answering the American artillery barrage in kind. Shells screeched over the La Fière bridge; German machine-gun fire "beat like hail" on the stone walls and roads by the bridge. The force and intensity of the German fire was simply not to be believed.[23]

Carrell waited—and waited too long. Gavin was fast losing patience; valuable time was slipping away. As Gavin recalled, the two men had a terse conversation something like this:

"Go! Go! Go!" Gavin shouted.

"I don't think I can do it," Carrell shouted back.

"Why not?"

"I'm sick," Carrell replied.

"Okay, you're through," Gavin said, making his first command relief in the heat of combat. He did not relish it. "Carrell had never been in combat," Gavin recalled. "Never been in a position like that. But I had to do it. The whole battle was hanging by a thread."[24]

Ridgway fully concurred in Carrell's relief. Later he wrote Doc Eaton to transfer Carrell out of the division, stating Carrell was not battalion-commander "material" and "I will not permit him to command one." Carrell was transferred to MacKelvie's 90th Division, which he had earlier helped mobilize and train. The powers there viewed his case differently. Named to command a regular infantry battalion, Carrell won a Combat Infantry Badge and a Purple Heart for severe wounds. But, as Gavin put it, Carrell's professional career had been irretrievably ruined. He retired as a captain in 1947. Recently Carrell commented: "This incident was and has been very painful to me. The way it was done. No chain of command and no consideration . . . This was rather precipitous and brutal since we were recently attached to the 82nd. I was treated very badly. It was unfair to all of us."[25]

The logical man to succeed Carrell was his exec, Charles Moore, who was well liked and respected by his men. But Harry Lewis did not know Charles Moore, and in this tense moment Lewis turned to one of his own men, the 325's S-3, Arthur W. Gardner, to lead the battalion across the causeway. This may have been a mistake. Gardner was a complete stranger to the men he was now called upon to lead.[26]

When Gardner shouted, "Go! Go! Go!" only a few brave men rushed over the La Fière bridge onto the causeway. As one historian wrote, the failure of the smoke screen to materialize became an excuse for some: "To the soldiers' mind, a contract had been defaulted. The strong sulked; the weak saw an excuse for funking out."[27]

A few men followed Gardner. One, a lieutenant, tried loyally to move the others with shouts of "Follow me!" and "Let's go kill the sons of bitches!" Some men came behind him, but most of them were hit. When Gavin sent a tank to clear the old wreckage from the causeway so that other tanks could follow, it hit an American mine and was partially disabled. The blow-back of the explosion wounded seven men. The ditches on the sides of the causeway, a historian wrote, soon "filled with malingerers and the wounded."[28]

Ridgway remembered the moment:

The fire was so intense that the men were physically recoiling. We just grabbed our men and walked them out. The physical force of that fire pouring in was such that they just stopped and started back—not from cowardice at all. We just grabbed them by the shoulders and led them down into this thing and pushed them. We were right there too. This is where your personal presence makes a hell of a lot of difference. I haven't the slightest doubt that if Gavin and I and the battalion commanders had not been there that crossing of the causeway would not have succeeded. The men would not have gone.[29]

Artilleryman Norris, who was directing his howitzers from Gavin's foxhole, was awed by this first closeup of combat and the leadership he witnessed. "The most memorable sight that day was Ridgway, Gavin and Maloney standing right there where it was the hottest. The point is that every soldier who hit that causeway saw every general officer and the regimental and battalion commanders right there. It was a truly inspirational effort. And to top it all off, Ridgway, with all the problems he faced, had the courtesy to go out of his way to thank me for our artillery support."[30]

Watching tensely, Gavin soon saw the attack was failing. He waited a little longer to be sure, then shouted to the 507 paratroopers Maloney and Rae: "All right, go ahead! You've *got* to go!" Maloney and Rae jumped up and led about ninety men out onto the causeway. They got as far as the ruined wreckage and the partially disabled American tank before they paused. These and the pile of dead bodies and the crowd of malingerers were blocking the road. Maloney and Rae grabbed men by the collars and shook them and screamed at them and kicked them in the butt. Soon the logjam broke and they, and others no less valorous, were able to run on to the west, seemingly oblivious to fear and German fire, Rae in the lead. Many more men fell dead or wounded. However, the Rae charge, which earned him a DSC, carried the survivors to the west bank, where the men fanned out left and right seeking cover.[31]

In the midst of this slaughter, Matt Ridgway appeared on the causeway carrying his .30-06 rifle. He and Gavin and Lewis and Maloney "personally by word of mouth, by gesture and by actually taking hold of individuals" (as Ridgway later put it) reversed the backward flow of men and sent them running after Rae. Ridgway then turned his personal attention to the wreckage. It was obvious that for the charge to fully succeed, the junk had to be cleared away. Otherwise, American tanks could not pass. Amid falling German mortar and artillery shells, Ridgway began rigging the towing cable on the partially disabled American tank.

A German mortar shell fell ten feet from him. It killed one man, wounded four severely and bloodied five others. One of the severely wounded was Lieutenant Joe L. Shealy, who was hit by steel fragments in his skull, arm and leg. But Ridgway's example inspired Shealy to keep going. "I had to go on," he said later. "The steel in Ridgway offset the steel in my body." Leading a small group, Shealy reached the west bank and collapsed from loss of blood. He survived, was evacuated and patched up and eventually returned to the battalion (to be wounded twice again). Meanwhile Ridgway, with the help of several GIs, succeeded in getting the wreckage off the causeway.[32]

While Ridgway cleared the wreckage and shoved the men onward, Gavin returned to lead the rest of the tanks over the causeway. When they rumbled into view, they had to pause while the American dead and wounded were cleared off the road. Gavin recalled that men "were stretched head to foot along the causeway; one had to move with care in running across to avoid stepping on them." No one had time—or the inclination—to make a count of the dead and wounded; they probably numbered above two hundred.[33]

The carnage was not yet over. The men had only a tenuous footing in Cauquigny; the Germans were showing no signs of yielding. Grim hand-to-hand fighting ensued as Gavin, Maloney, Rae and others rooted the Germans out of their trenches and gun emplacements. Behind them, Harry Lewis trotted across the causeway with his exec, Herb Sitler, and the regimental staff, prepared to establish a CP in Cauquigny. Lewis now had two battalions (including Sanford's 1st, merged with the Timmes group) across the Merderet, and the opportunity for fame and glory lay before him.

But in this moment of crisis, tough old Harry Lewis failed. Exactly what happened is not clearly recorded or remembered. "Combat fatigue" and "burnout" have been suggested. He was "too old," 325 officers recall. "The war was out of his reach," said one. Perhaps the shock of threading through his dead and wounded momentarily snapped his mind. Or perhaps his body—fighting the cancer—simply gave way. Gavin recalled, "That afternoon, Lewis was in pretty bad shape. The doctors gave him a shot of some kind and put him to bed for twenty-four hours. Very sad story." The exec, Herb Sitler, temporarily took over the regiment.[34]

Lewis, evacuated to Utah Beach and England, would not return to the division. Not all mourned his departure, but one who did was Ridgway. In his eyes, Lewis was a "gallant" officer who had fallen in the hottest—and bloodiest—tactical fight Ridgway would ever experience. Ridgway did not recommend

Lewis for a DSC (nor, for that matter, did he so honor any of his original regimental commanders), but later he would strongly recommend that the War Department promote Lewis to brigadier general. This recommendation was not followed. Within eight months Lewis would be dead of cancer.[35]‡

Amid this chaos, Herb Sitler took temporary command of the 325th Regiment. He hastily set up a CP of sorts near the Cauquigny church. By that time the Germans were plastering the area with artillery, and communications were decidedly uncertain. A patrol reached the Sanford-Timmes group a half mile to the north, tenuously "linking up" the regimental CP with Sanford's 1st Battalion. However, Arthur Gardner's battered 2nd Battalion (ex-401) forces were in utter disarray. Gardner himself, one historian wrote, was "highly elusive," lost touch with the flow of battle, and when he did appear, gave the wrong orders.[37]

Later that afternoon, the Germans launched a brutal counterattack against the 325. Under heavy pressure, the disarrayed glidermen began to fall back. Herb Sitler first deployed his headquarters staff for a last-ditch stand. Then, on second thought, prepared to withdraw across the causeway. Hearing that "the bridgehead was breaking," Gavin raced to the 325 CP, where Sitler told Gavin he could not hold.[38]

Gavin was livid. It was unthinkable that after all the effort and slaughter they would once more surrender the causeway. To Gavin the solution was clear: counterattack with every resource available. He told Sitler that anybody who could carry a rifle—including Sitler—would join the counterattack. Sitler, who "blanched a bit" and "seemed rather startled," nonetheless mobilized his clerks and staff officers. Meanwhile, Gavin posted two formidable officer-guards at the west end of the causeway: Arthur Maloney and Willard Harrison, the tough 504 officer Tucker had "loaned" Gavin for Normandy. Gavin told them: "We're going to attack. I want you to stand on this bridge and don't let any man by. Turn them around." Maloney, holding a stout tree limb, nodded silently, as did Harrison.[39]

Gavin, making contact with Robert Rae, who was still on his feet and leading valorously, hurriedly laid out the attack plan. They would surge west down the fields and hedgerows toward the high ground at the next town, Le Motey, just short of Amfreville, which was believed to be the German assembling point. John Devine's long-range 155 mm howitzers would provide support. On the right, Teddy Sanford and Charles Timmes would attack in the same direction. On the left, the Shanley-Warren group, still isolated on Hill 30, was to hold in place, "anchoring" that flank, until reinforcements could be spared.

‡ After the heat of battle, Lewis apparently took his relief philosophically and felt no bitterness toward Ridgway. Two months later, he wrote Ridgway from Walter Reed Army Hospital (where he was operated on September 4, 1944) that "in spite of what appeared at the time severe blows, I could not do otherwise than admit your decision as well as your selection of key personnel have never been other than the best." He thought Ridgway was "the best division commander in the United States Army and a wonderful man" and would "like to serve with him in any capacity." In reply, Ridgway praised Lewis to the heavens for his contribution to the 325th Regiment.[36]

The counterattack was not a model of perfection. In the confusion of battle, many units and individuals became disoriented and reacted wrongly to rumors or misinformation. Some advance units reached Le Motey, only to be heavily shelled by Devine's howitzers, which compelled a withdrawal. Even so, the counterattack carried, Maloney did not have to use his tree limb (or more lethal weapons), and by nightfall the 325 had reoccupied Le Motey and established a reasonably coherent front, with Gardner's men and the Sanford-Timmes forces more or less joined.

When this had been done, and the hamlet of Cauquigny declared secure, Ridgway ordered Roy Lindquist to rescue and reinforce the Shanley-Warren group on Hill 30. In anticipation, Lindquist had marched his 508 men north from Chef-du-Pont to La Fière. They crossed the bloody causeway, then pushed southward down the road to Gueutteville. Late that evening Lindquist routed scattered groups of Germans that had isolated Hill 30 and "linked up" with the Shanley-Warren group, which had been holding out for nearly four full days. Later that night, the 508 CP moved across the now-"liberated" Chef-du-Pont causeway and bivouacked on Hill 30, strengthening the left flank of the bridgehead. Subsequently Lindquist located his many strays, including Louis Mendez, commander of the 3rd Battalion, and named Shields Warren to command his 1st Battalion, replacing the dead Herbert Batcheller.[40]

It was discovered that, soon after reaching French soil, one of the 508 strays, Malcolm D. Brannen, commander of Mendez's Headquarters Company, had ambushed and killed the commander of the German 91st Division, Wilhelm Falley, near Picauville. When Brannen related his coup to Ridgway "with great glee," Ridgway responded: "Well, in our present situation killing division commanders does not strike me as being particularly hilarious. But I congratulate you. I'm glad it was a German division commander you got."[41]

The strays included the 507's Charles Timmes, who, like Shanley, was highly praised (and awarded a DSC) for his prolonged, dogged stand on the west bank of the Merderet River. Timmes had been slightly wounded twice. Gavin later said, "It's a strange thing. You can't ever predict how people will act in combat. Take Timmes. He was as quiet as a mouse. And yet he proved to be a terror in combat. He'd go right into the enemy position and get behind them and come daylight, there he'd be, dug in. He scared the Germans to death."[42]

For Timmes and his group of strays, Ridgway relaxed some of his rigid rules about being cleanly shaved and neatly and completely turned out in regulation gear. Timmes recalled:

On Saturday, June 10, 1944, the small group I commanded was relieved and ordered to assemble to mount trucks to take up a new position . . . While awaiting the arrival of the trucks, contrary to all the rules of the 82nd, I sprawled out on the ground in the open field without my helmet and unshaved. I woke up to have none other than General Ridgway gazing into my face. Needless to say, I was most embarrassed and expected the worst. [But] he showed genuine consideration and compassion for our exhausted condition. He greeted me with a smile and congratulations and told me to keep up the good work.[43]

While the epic crossing of the Merderet was taking place, Max Taylor was giving his full attention to a vital but delayed 101 objective: the capture of the "gateway" city of Carentan. The operation had been delayed, because of the poor drop of Skeets Johnson's 501, the movement of the two battalions of the German 6th Parachute Regiment northward into the 101's sector, the foul-up in landing the glider artillery, the ineptitude of George Wear's leadership of the 327 and other factors. Bradley had too optimistically planned that the 101 would capture Carentan by June 7. It was June 9 and the Germans still held the city.

Taylor's plan for the attack on Carentan, revised and modified in Normandy, was as follows. Mike Michaelis' 502nd Regiment would attack southeast down the Carentan-Cherbourg highway, crossing the Douve and the flooded marshes around it over a long, exposed series of bridges and causeways. George Wear's 327th Glider Regiment would cross the Douve at the Brevands bridgehead, circle the city, and simultaneously attack it from the east.[44]

The 502 jumped off first, early on the morning of June 10. Robert Cole, leading his (depleted) 3rd Battalion, spearheaded the attack. German resistance was intense on the open causeways and bridges; some of the bridges were blown or blocked. In spite of a heroic try, including an authentic bayonet charge (which earned Cole the Medal of Honor), the battalion could not break through the maze of open waterways. Later in the day, Patrick Cassidy came forward with his (depleted) 1st Battalion to assist, and still later Michaelis committed his reserves—Steve Chappuis' (depleted) 3rd Battalion. This combined force, backed by heavy artillery, broke down the German defenses, but the 502nd Regiment was too exhausted to fight on into Carentan. At the end of this long, bloody day, Michaelis was forced to request relief, and Taylor sent Bob Sink's 506 forward.

That same day, George Wear's 327th Glider Infantry crossed the Douve downstream at the Brevands bridgehead. One unit pushed eastward to Auville-sur-le-Vey, making a tenuous link with a unit of the 29th Division from Omaha Beach, while the bulk of the regiment moved toward Carentan from the east. George Wear so badly botched this attack that Taylor relieved him of command. "He just went to pieces," Taylor recalled. Ironically, command of the 327 went to Bud Harper, whose 401st Glider Regiment had been broken up to reinforce Wear's 327 and Lewis' 325, and who was then serving as the 101st's beachmaster. Harper promoted the 2nd Battalion commander, Tom Rouzie, to be his exec; Rouzie was replaced by Roy L. Inman.[45]

Eisenhower, Montgomery and Bradley were deeply concerned over the delay in taking Carentan. It was not only the gateway to the Cotentin but also the place where Collins' VII Corps and Gee Gerow's V Corps (from Omaha Beach) were to join. Until Carentan was taken, a gap would exist between VII and V Corps and such gaps historically invited enemy attacks. Accordingly, on

June 11, Bradley sent his understudy, Courtney H. Hodges, to confer with Collins and Taylor on Carentan. On Bradley's order, Hodges was to take charge of the 101 attack, freeing Collins to give his full attention to cutting the Cotentin and capturing Cherbourg.[46]

The final plan which evolved was as follows. Three of the 101st regiments, the 327th Glider and the depleted 501 and 506 Parachute, would participate. Bud Harper's 327, backed by Johnson's 501, would attack from the northeast and east, while Sink's 506 pushed down from the northwest. The division artillery commander, Tony McAuliffe, appointed task-force commander, would direct the attack. The general plan was to more or less encircle the city with infantry, pulverize it with naval gunfire and heavy artillery, then seize it.

The final attack was launched on the night of June 11/12. After the punishing naval and artillery barrages, Harper's 327 pushed southwest toward the city, while Johnson's 501, crossing the Douve at Brevands, came around from the east. Under Harper's new, driving leadership, the three 327 battalion commanders, Hartford F. Salee (1st), Ray C. Allen (1st, ex-401) and Roy Inman (2nd) performed far, far better, carrying the burden of the assault. Salee was wounded, temporarily replaced by George P. Nichols. Bob Sink's (depleted) 506 joined the encirclement as planned. Early on the morning of June 12, the city, having been abandoned by the German 6th Parachute Regiment, fell to the 101st, and the long-sought linkup of VII and V Corps was soon achieved.[47]

However, this thin seam was immediately threatened. Allied code breakers intercepted word that a large German armored-infantry force—most of the 17th SS Panzer Grenadier Division, from Tours—had joined the 6th Parachute Regiment for a powerful counterattack. Forewarned by the code breakers, Bradley rushed a strong force from his Omaha Beach bridgehead—tanks from the 2nd Armored Division and some heavy artillery—to backstop Taylor and McAuliffe, while the latter brought Mike Michaelis' depleted 502nd Parachute Regiment into the city. These combined forces proved sufficient to repulse the German counterattack, and by the following day, June 14, Carentan was in Allied hands and the linkup of VII and V Corps had been solidly achieved.[48]

ON JUNE 10, after Ridgway had secured the Merderet bridgehead, Joe Collins ordered MacKelvie's 90th Division to proceed west at top speed to cut the Cotentin Peninsula. Two of its three infantry regiments were committed: the 357th, commanded by Phillip H. Ginder, and the 358th, commanded by James V. Thompson. The third regiment, the 359th, which had been held in VII Corps reserve for the drive on Cherbourg, remained in that status temporarily —one of its battalions relieving the 505 for the occupation of Le Ham. Ginder's 357 crossed the Merderet at La Fière, Thompson's 358 at Chef-du-Pont.[1]

Striking off for Amfreville and Pont-l'Abbé, the 90th Division passed through the tired, begrimed paratroopers and gliderists with a discernible case of what Gavin termed "jitteriness." When the 90th first encountered German fire it very nearly halted in its tracks. Over the next several days it advanced slowly and uncertainly. To give it more punch, Joe Collins brought up its third regiment, the 359th, commanded by Ridgway's classmate Clarke K. Fales, and inserted it between the 357 and the 358. The reinforcements did not help much; the division seemed virtually paralyzed.[2]

Gavin visited some of the commanders in the 358th to see what was happening. Two of the senior officers were his classmates William L. (Spike) Nave and Christian H. Clarke. Both Nave and the 358 commander, James Thompson, had been wounded on June 11. Clarke, the next-most-senior officer, had temporarily taken over, but Nave had refused to stay hospitalized and had returned to become acting commander of the 358 on the day of Gavin's visit.[3]

Nave had been a famous football player at the Academy and Gavin admired his spunk: "Spike had been hit twice—had a big white bandage around his stomach—but he wouldn't stay in the hospital," Gavin remembered. "He said, 'Jim, how in hell do you make these guys fight in the face of fortifications and machineguns? If I don't go through first, the troops won't go with me. So I've got to go through and take them with me.' I said, 'Spike, it's the only thing to do. But you might try it at night when you have a better chance of making it. Nobody's a Napoleon the first time in combat. It's hard to make green troops fight.' In the next day or so, Spike was killed leading his men in an attack." (And was posthumously awarded a DSC.)[4]

About this same time, Joe Collins went forward on foot to find out why the division was not moving. He could find no sign of fighting or artillery firing, and he encountered some men who were obviously malingering. MacKelvie, Collins wrote, "seemed at a loss as to what to do about the lack of fight in the division." When Collins got back to his CP, he called Bradley and told him the division was inadequately trained and lacked leadership. He blamed not

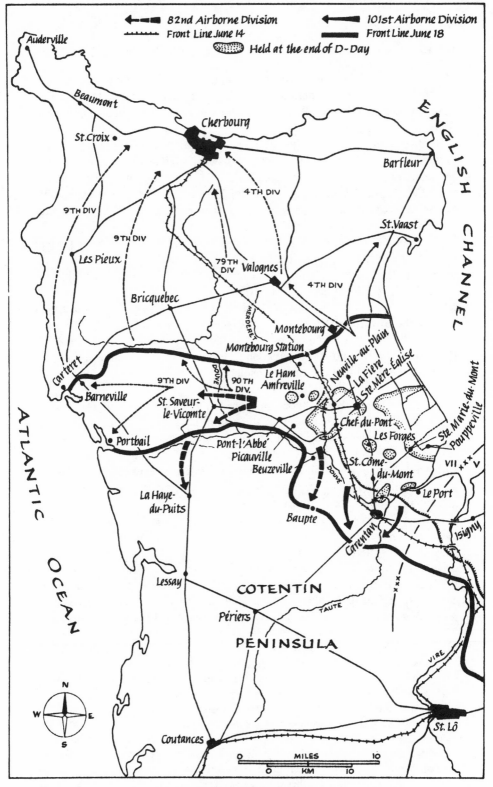

Auderville

Beaumont

Cherbourg

ENGLISH CHANNEL

St.Croix

Barfleur

4TH DIV

9TH DIV

St.Vaast

9TH DIV

Les Pieux

79TH DIV

Valognes

4TH DIV

Bricquebec

MERDERET

Montebourg

Montebourg Station

Le Ham

Amfreville

Neuville-au-Plain

La Fière

Ste.Mère-Église

Carteret

9TH DIV

90TH DIV.

DOUVE

Ste.Marie-du-Mont

Barneville

St.Saveur-le-Vicomte

Chef-du-Pont

Les Forges

Pouppeville

Portbail

Pont-l'Abbé

Picauville

Beuzeville

St.Côme-du-Mont

VII ×××V

La Haye-du-Puits

DOUVE

Le Port

Baupte

Carentan

Isigny

×××

Lessay

COTENTIN

TAUTE

Périers

PENINSULA

VIRE

ATLANTIC OCEAN

N
W E
S

Coutances

St.Lô

0 — MILES — 10
0 — KM — 10

Cutting the Cotentin

MacKelvie (an artilleryman who had commanded the division for only five months) but its "former commander." That was Henry Terrell, Jr., who had served with distinction in World War I and whom Marshall had promoted to command a corps in the States.[5]

Bradley soon agreed that the 90th Division was "one of the worst-trained [outfits] to arrive in the ETO." Joe Collins swept a big broom through the top command of the division. He relieved MacKelvie ("without prejudice") but left the ADC, Samuel Williams, a veteran of World War I, in place. Eugene M. Landrum (like Collins, a Pacific veteran), then serving as VII Corps deputy commander, replaced MacKelvie.*

The failure of the 90th Division had immediate and important consequences in the battle of the Cotentin. It forced Collins to bring in yet another division to help cut the peninsula. This was the corps reserve, Manton Eddy's 9th. One consequence of this decision was that Eddy's 39th Regiment, which had been temporarily attached to Barton's 4th Division for the drive on Cherbourg, had to be withdrawn from that task and reattached to the 9th Division. The reassignment of the 39th Regiment as well as the new task for the rest of the 9th Division meant that no all-out drive on Cherbourg could be mounted until the 9th (and the 90th) had cut the peninsula.

Under existing airborne "doctrine"—primitive as it was—Ridgway's 82nd Division had fulfilled its mission to the best of its ability by June 10, when it secured the Merderet bridgehead. It had suffered grievous losses in lives and equipment; it had no heavy artillery, armor or transport. According to Ridgway's "principles," the division should then have been withdrawn to England to refit and train for the next airborne operation, leaving the heavy ground slogging to the conventional divisions.

But Joe Collins—like Patton on Sicily and Clark in Italy—was reluctant to part with such fine and aggressive infantry in the face of such heavy German resistance. He therefore prevailed on Bradley to let him add the 82nd to the drive west across the Cotentin. Owing to the failure of the 90th Division and to the increasing toughness of the German defenses and the need for speed in cutting the peninsula, Bradley agreed. There is no evidence that Ridgway protested these orders; indeed, it is likely that he welcomed the new challenge. It

---

* Other important changes: Collins relieved Ginder of command of the 357th Regiment, but when Ginder's replacement was killed the next day, Collins brought in an "outsider," George B. Barth (then serving as chief of staff of Manton Eddy's 9th Division) and Barth gave the 357th the leadership it badly needed. The acting commander of the 358th, Chris Clarke, was replaced by another "outsider," Richard C. Partridge, but he was soon severely wounded, evacuated, and later named chief of staff of VII Corps. Clarke, again elevated to acting commander of the 358th, was soon replaced by Clarkson D. McNary, but he lasted "only a few days" before being relieved. For the fourth time, Clarke was named 358th commander—and stayed commander, ultimately winning a DSC and other decorations. The commander of the 359th, Clarke Fales, was replaced by the division chief of staff, Robert L. Bacon.[6]

would provide the division an opportunity to fulfill to completion its originally assigned mission (of occupying the Cotentin westward to the Douve) and to help destroy the hated German 91st Division, which had killed (and often murdered in cold blood) and severely wounded so many of his paratroopers and glidermen.

The revised plan for cutting the peninsula was as follows. Ridgway's 82nd would regroup, pass through the 90th Division and attack southwestward on the left flank along the lower Douve River from Pont-l'Abbé to St. Sauveur-le-Vicomte. Manton Eddy's 9th Division (to also include the 359th Regiment of the 90th Division) would pass through the 90th Division sector and attack due west toward Ste. Colombe, abreast of the 82nd. The other two regiments of Landrum's 90th Division—the newly commanded 357th and the 358th—would pivot north and take positions on the right flank to hold a defensive line between Le Ham and Terre-de-Beauval. The attack, which involved considerable shifting of forces, would proceed as quickly as possible, with full power expected to be attained by June 14 or 15.[7]

When this plan was finalized, Ridgway's greatly depleted regiments were scattered. Ekman's 505, detached from the 4th Division, was in process of withdrawing from Le Ham to the rear. Arthur Maloney's 507 was reorganizing in the bridgehead. Roy Lindquist's 508, reinforced by the 319th Glider Field Artillery and other units, was in process of attacking due south from Picauville across the lower Douve toward Beuzeville-la-Bastille in order to establish a bridgehead over the lower Douve and link up with the 101st Division forces expanding westward from Carentan.[8]

This 508 drive southward over the lower Douve, June 11 to June 13, had been the first time the regiment had fought as a cohesive (though depleted) whole. Lindquist and the exec, Harry Harrison (still under official investigation), had regrouped the 1st, 2nd and 3rd battalions under Shields Warren, Tom Shanley and Louis Mendez, respectively. On June 13, at the height of the attack, Ridgway jeeped down to inspect the battle. Shields Warren remembered the visit:

After we crossed the Douve, my objective was to occupy the area around Coigny. We came upon the largest clearing I had seen in Normandy. Two hundred yards into the clearing, between us and our objective, were five Renault tanks, eight other tanks armed with low-powered 40 mm guns and one machine gun. While these tanks were not too significant a threat, we had no anti-tank weapons other than our bazookas, which were ineffective at that range. The tanks were getting air bursts in the trees [near us] with the 40 mms and dusting the hedgerows with the machine guns. I was getting quite frustrated when an artillery liaison officer suggested using 155 mm howitzers [from the 90th Division artillery]. One round destroyed one tank with a near miss; the others fled.

I was watching all this through field glasses in a hedgerow nearest the tanks. As the tanks disappeared down the road, a familiar voice at my elbow said, "Well, Shields, how are things going?" I was quite aghast that Ridgway was that far forward and could have been hit by the hot lead and steel flying around. I explained why we had been held up and told him we'd be on our objective and have the area cleared in one hour. He expressed satisfaction with that schedule and asked what I'd been shooting at the tanks. I explained. He said, "Well, that's fine, but be careful how you use that heavy stuff." They were having trouble getting ammo over Utah Beach. As he turned to leave, he added, "Besides, isn't that sorta like swatting a fly with a sledge hammer?" I had no rejoinder to that.

The point of the story is that no one ever had to tell General Ridgway what his assault troops were doing. He knew from personal observations.[9]

The 508 attack southward of the Douve achieved its limited objectives. Some units of the regiment pushed as far south as Baupte, then dug in. Elements of Taylor's 101 fought west from Carentan, linking up with these 508 spearheads. In order to hold this thin front, Ridgway left some small units of the 508 in place, but he brought the bulk of the depleted regiment back across the Douve to support the drive west through the Cotentin.

The 82nd Division jumped off on its westward push on the morning of June 14. Maloney's vastly depleted 507 and Sitler's 325 spearheaded the attack. They moved west from Pont-l'Abbé, passing through the 358th Regiment, of the 90th Division, which then pivoted north. The 60th Regiment, of Manton Eddy's 9th Division, spearheaded that division's attack on the right, lagging considerably behind the 82nd Division. Ekman's 505 and Lindquist's 508 (regrouping from its southerly minicampaign) were held in reserve at Pont-l'Abbé.[10]

The battalions of the 507th and 325th regiments, moving forward, both used the same road, and this resulted in "confusion and delay." The Germans, seeing the mixup, took advantage of it and heavily shelled both units. Nonetheless, the 507 continued on with "vigor and speed," so much so that it left the 325 and the 9th division units far behind. The backup American artillery was "very encouraging," but it was not "sufficiently flexible" to keep up with the 507 advance, and unfortunately a heavy barrage fell on Timmes's 2nd Battalion, which was leading the westward drive. One 507 historian wrote that this friendly fire was "heavier than any German barrage [the 507] had been subjected to throughout the campaign." The same unfortunate mishap occurred on the following day. This second barrage of friendly fire on the 507 "inflicted casualties, stopped the advance, and upset the men's feelings," the historian wrote. It took "some time" to stop the [American] artillery and "more" time to "get the men back in an aggressive frame of mind." In the meantime, the Germans had time to set up a "line of resistance" beyond which the 507 could not pass. Thus, the 507 historian wrote, "this bitter and bloody fight ended indecisively." The 507 had lost 192 more men in two days.[11]

Ridgway was not satisfied with the speed of the 82nd's advance. As in Sicily and Italy, he was out front all the way, cajoling and exhorting the battalion commanders. The aide, Art Kroos, recalled:

Whenever there was a trouble spot, a place where things were bad or not moving, that's where we'd go. One of our battalions bogged down in a hedgerow alongside the road. Ridgway was quite concerned. We went up and he said to the battalion commander, "Let's get this damn thing going." But he didn't get too much action. This was still the dry period; the roads were dusty. Ridgway then ordered his jeep driver, Frank Farmer, to run down the road as fast as he could go for several hundred yards. This raised one hell of a cloud of dust. The GIs in the ditches yelled at Farmer, "Cut it out, you son of a bitch—you're raising too much dust, you'll draw fire." Ridgway shouted back defiantly: "That's exactly what I want. You won't know where the enemy is until they start shooting and we're going to get them shooting." And zip, off we went.[12]

One "trouble spot" was the 325's 2nd Battalion (ex-401), command of which had been given to Arthur Gardner during its legendary assault on the Merderet causeway. Gardner had not yet taken firm hold of his unit when, on about June 14, he was killed in action. The exec was still the well-liked Charles Moore, but at about the time of Gardner's death, Moore was shot in the neck. Refusing evacuation, Moore began to behave in a "strange" manner, as one officer put it, spending his time on "scouting or patrolling missions" and even—so rumor had it—serving as an ammo carrier for a mortar squad. Eventually, an officer recalled, Moore was again hit, and evacuated.[13]

This battalion quite clearly demanded firm (and empathetic) leadership. Breaking precedent, Ridgway chose a veteran paratrooper to temporarily command these gliderists. He was Ridgway's troubleshooter Al Ireland, who had come into Normandy by glider on his special mission to deliver the antitank guns. Ireland temporarily commanded the battalion during the drive to St. Sauveur-le-Vicomte. Some gliderists interpreted paratrooper Ireland's appointment as the first move in a Gavin "plot" to convert the 325 gliderists to parachutists, a concept Gavin actually had under consideration.[14]

Edson Raff was still "acting" chief of staff of the division when the westward attack was launched. But his relationship with Ridgway and the staff deteriorated and, during the early stages of the attack, Raff was relieved of this temporary job. One reason, he later wrote, was probably his refusal to sign a staff-generated recommendation for a DSC for Ridgway. Far more important was Raff's middle-of-the-night approval of a change in a 325 attack plan. The original plan had been approved by Ridgway; however, Raff did not feel it necessary to wake Ridgway to clear the change. That oversight, Raff wrote, was "an error of judgment on my part" which he believed to be the *"coup de grâce."* The G-3, Bob Wienecke, replaced Raff as temporary chief of staff; Wienecke's G-3 job was temporarily filled by his assistants, Walter Winton and Hank Adams.[15]

What to do with Raff?

There was one possible solution. The 507 was a badly shattered outfit, much in need of reorganization, remanning, and in Gavin's view at least, tough training. The probability was that after Normandy, the 507 would not remain with the division. It would probably go elsewhere, replaced by Tucker's 504. It was still (temporarily) commanded by Art Maloney, who had proved to be an inspiring and fearless leader but who was quite junior in rank (West Point, 1938), perhaps the most junior regimental commander in the ETO. Assigning Raff, who was five years senior to Maloney and a notoriously tough trainer, to command the 507 seemed an ideal solution to a number of problems.

On June 15, Ridgway named Raff permanent commanding officer of the 507 and placed the regiment in reserve. Art Maloney was, in effect, "demoted" or "bumped" and was given command of the 507's 3rd Battalion, formerly commanded by William Kuhn, who had been hospitalized with jump injuries. At the same time, Ben Pearson officially replaced the badly wounded DSC winner Ed Ostberg as commander of the 1st Battalion. DSC winner Charles Timmes remained in command of the 2nd Battalion. Raff was delighted. The regimental command, he wrote, "was really what I had been looking for in the war."[16]

The sudden change of command caused a trauma for the 507. By that time, the senior staff had come to admire Arthur Maloney. One officer recalled that "Art Maloney was a thoroughly professional, straight-arrow, courageous soldier who preferred working with troops in the field to desk duty. He was an outstanding leader in every respect. It was the consensus of the junior officers that Maloney was destined to be a general—if he didn't get himself killed." When the "abrasive" and "egotistical" outsider Raff bumped Maloney, there were many cries of dismay. Raff was tough as nails and at first not a few 507 men hated him. He bluntly let it be known that he considered the 507 to be "poorly trained" and "poorly led" and manned by personnel in "pitiful physical condition." He looked upon the regiment as "confused, defeated, demoralized and floundering." He saw his mission as one of "saving" it from further disgrace. Raff spared no feelings in pursuit of this role.[17]

On the other hand, some among the senior staff believed, in retrospect, that at that moment in its history, Edson Raff was exactly what the regiment needed. Charles Timmes, conceding that Raff was "received coolly" and "disliked," thought that "firm command" was imperative, that Raff did a "good job" and that on the battlefield Raff was "a highly competent combat commander." Chester McCoid recalled that in "staff matters," Raff was a "miserable monster" who seemed to "relish savaging his subordinates," but "despite his queer quirks of character," on the battlefield he was "a *terrific* combat leader."[18]

On the afternoon of June 15, Ridgway committed Ekman's 505 to spearhead the final drive on St. Sauveur-le-Vicomte. Mark Alexander's 1st Battalion took the right flank, Ben Vandervoort's 2nd the left flank; Ed Krause's 3rd came behind in reserve. Moving up, Alexander passed close to some men of the 9th Division's 60th Regiment on the right. There were many green replacements in the regiment, which probably explained why it had lagged on the drive. Alexander described these replacements: "What a sad lot! . . . They were lying in rows along the hedgerow and getting their asses shot off with mortar fire . . .

Obviously they would have had far less casualties if they had moved forward." The dash of the 505 inspired these greenhorns. The official Army historian wrote: "The success of the 82nd Airborne Division gave such impetus to the 9th Division's attack that it gathered a momentum which carried it swiftly across the peninsula."[19]

At noon on June 16, the 82nd Division, moving at high speed and backed by plenty of tanks and trailed by fifteen batteries of artillery, reached the east bank of the Douve, overlooking St. Sauveur-le-Vicomte. By this time Sitler's 325 was on the left, Ekman's 505 on the right. The town had been nearly pulverized by Allied aircraft, and Ridgway could see that the Germans were pulling out. He formally requested permission from Joe Collins to cross the Douve, but even before the okay came back from Collins, Ridgway ordered the 505 to cross the river and seize the town. That evening, he brought up Lindquist's 508 to help establish a defensive perimeter extending southward to a vast marsh, Prairies Marécageuses, lying athwart the highway leading south to La Haye-du-Puits.[20]

Bradley's First Army understudy, Courtney Hodges, visited the 82nd Division CP to talk with Ridgway and Gavin. Hodges' aide, William C. Sylvan, was keeping a diary. That day he made some grim notes: "The 82nd has apparently found that the Boche have slit the throats of several of their boys, and are asking for no quarter and giving none . . . All along the roads in this area were smashed gliders, some stripped of their clothing [fabric], others completely burned out, hung and draped against trees and hedges. How the men came out alive to fight as they have fought is something of a miracle."[21]

While savoring the triumph of the 82nd Division, Mark Alexander, who was still officially exec of the 505, received a visit from Ridgway. The general, who would later characterize Alexander as "one of the finest battle leaders I know," had yet another special assignment for him: Harry Harrison, of Lindquist's 508, had not survived the official investigation and had been transferred out of the division. Ridgway wanted Alexander to temporarily fill that slot. In later years, Gavin told Alexander that Ridgway did not think the 508 was "sufficiently aggressive" and that Alexander would add the needed pepper.[22]†

Alexander did not show it, but he was not happy with his new assignment. He did not want to leave the 505. In the earlier action, he had already formed doubts about Lindquist, who would be his commanding officer. Alexander later wrote that Lindquist was "probably the best administrator in the division," but he was a "poor combat leader" who "experienced unnecessary casualties" and was "less effective" because he "often gave orders from his command post without full knowledge of the terrain and objective."[24]

Another important personnel change about this time evoked considerable comment. Al Ireland, temporarily commanding the 325's 2nd Battalion (ex-

---

† The temporary division assistant G-3, Walter Winton, would replace Alexander as exec of the 505. Ed Krause's 3rd Battalion exec, Bill Hagen, would replace Alexander in command of the 505's 1st Battalion. West Pointer Harry Harrison, later assigned to the 28th Infantry Division, won a Bronze Star for heroism and was killed in action in November 1944.[23]

401), reinjured his knee—first damaged in the Sicily jump—and had to be replaced. Responding to the written petition from the officers of the 325's 2nd Battalion, Ridgway and Harry Lewis chose Oz Leahy, then regimental S-3, for the job, and Leahy retained it for the rest of the war. Eventually, this battalion was redesignated the 3rd Battalion, 325, thus losing all identity with its origins in the 401, and under Leahy's leadership, it became one of the division's best.[25]

The 82nd's quick seizure of St. Sauveur-le-Vicomte opened the door for a final dash to the Atlantic Ocean, the severing of the remaining roads and the "sealing off" of the Cotentin. The final westward dash was made on June 17 and 18 by the 47th and 60th regiments of Eddy's 9th Division. At 0500 on June 18, elements of the 60th Regiment reached the high ground overlooking Barneville and the vast, gray Atlantic Ocean, and a few hours later this major task was finished.

The drive west had mauled or trapped many German units inside the Cotentin. The hated 91st Airlanding Division, which had caused the 82nd so much grief, was, the official Army historian wrote, "so badly decimated that it could scarcely be counted as a division at all." The 77th Infantry Division, newly arrived from Brittany, had been badly chewed up; some elements of it escaped to the south, but most were trapped in the Cotentin. These and the surviving elements of the 243rd and 709th divisions, plus other, miscellaneous units, established an east-west line above Le Ham and prepared for an orderly withdrawal toward Cherbourg, which Hitler still wanted held at all cost.[26]

With the Cotentin now "sealed off," Joe Collins, with scarcely a pause, prepared to relaunch the northward offensive for Cherbourg. But Bradley, who had code-breaking intelligence indicating it would be a tougher fight than Collins thought, delayed the offensive until it could be reinforced. The new plan that evolved increased the attacking force to three full divisions: Barton's 4th, Eddy's 9th and a newly arrived one, the 79th, commanded by Ira T. (Billy) Wyche, an older West Pointer (1911). Collins jumped off in the early hours of June 19, the very day that a prolonged and devastating Channel storm raked the Allied invasion beaches. The storm lent added urgency to the attack; more than ever, the Allies needed a large, protected port. In a swift, brilliant campaign, heavily supported by Allied air and naval forces, Collins captured Cherbourg on June 26.[27]

While the Cherbourg campaign was being launched, Bradley brought in yet another corps headquarters, Troy Middleton's VIII, to assume responsibility for holding the line across the lower Cotentin—Carentan to Barneville. Middleton, who had performed so ably as commander of the 45th Division in Sicily and Italy, was still suffering from severe arthritis, but George Marshall had insisted that Middleton be given a corps, wryly observing he'd rather have a man with arthritis of the knees than a man with arthritis of the brain. Middleton's VIII Corps would incorporate Taylor's 101st, Ridgway's 82nd and some units of Landrum's 90th.[28]

Before the 82nd was officially transferred from VII to VIII Corps, on June

19, Collins gave it one final assignment: to reinforce the bridgehead over the lower Douve (south of Pont-l'Abbé) near Baupte, where some 507 and 508 units had linked up with the 101 and were holding a tenuous line. The plan called for a new bridgehead over the lower Douve directly south of Pont-l'Abbé. A stronger force in that area would not only strengthen the linkup but also be well situated for a southwestward attack on La Haye-du-Puits or to strike the flank of any German force attempting a northward attack on St. Sauveur-le-Vicomte.[29]

Ridgway created a mixed force for this task: Herb Sitler's 325th Glider Regiment in the lead, backed up by Louis Mendez's 3rd Battalion of the 508 plus some engineers and other units. By the time the force was in place, June 18, the Pont-l'Abbé bridge had been blown and new German forces had moved to the vicinity of the south bank of the Douve. The 325 was assigned to force the crossing on the night of June 18/19.[30]

Ridgway, Gavin and aides were present for this imposing task. Art Kroos recalled:

> It was a tough assignment. Heavy enemy artillery was falling on the bridge —and into our positions on the north bank. Standing beside Ridgway, I suddenly felt this wetness down my leg. I thought, My God, I'm hit. But I was all right. A piece of shrapnel had hit my canteen and it was leaking down my leg.
> The 325 was supposed to go over the bridge. The engineers were doing a damn good job trying to repair the bridge, and the artillery shells were dropping in the water. But the lead companies of the 325 had stopped cold. They were just petrified and wouldn't go. Ridgway went out on the bridge all by himself—with shells falling all around him—just to prove that if an artillery shell landed in the water it wouldn't throw shrapnel, that it had to be a direct hit. He made his point, but the 325 still hung back.[31]

Art Kroos himself played a key role in making the bridge passable, and for that Ridgway awarded him a Bronze Star Medal. The citation, in part, stated that while forcing a crossing of the Douve, "it was found impossible to bridge the demolished span as planned and the recommended substitute involved considerable delay, necessitating the halting of the leading battalion under considerable hostile artillery fire. On his own initiative, Captain Kroos suggested an alternate plan involving the floating of a span into the gap between the two fallen steel trusses and personally entered water 15 feet deep where he worked for a half hour helping to bridge the gap. His suggestion and assistance materially increased the rate of reinforcement and contributed to the success of the river crossing."[32]

In these and other actions, Tom Slaughter of the 325 was impressed by Ridgway's eye for small professional details:

> We got across the river and captured this little French village. Ridgway came right behind me in his jeep—crossed the bridge—and asked me the usual

questions: How many casualties had we sustained? How many Germans had we captured? and so on. Then—to my astonishment—he pointed out a tiny flaw in the operation. We were using some 81 mm mortars in the attack. The mortar has three basic pieces: base plate, bipod and tube. He said, "You know one of your mortars back there is missing a base plate?" I did not know and I said, "Yes, sir" and got right on it. But just how Ridgway was able to spot that little flaw with all he had on his mind was beyond me.[33]

This southward attack over the Douve, led by Ridgway and Gavin, took them into strange open country where there was no clearly definable front and the strength of the opposing forces, just digging in, had not been established. According to Kroos, moving about in such country could be hazardous.

We were always out there in the jeep, with the wonderful freckle-faced kid, Frank Farmer, who never said a word, at the wheel. One day Ridgway pointed to a spot on a map and said, "I want to go there." (Down a certain road to a turnoff) We jumped into the jeep and off we tore at 50 miles an hour, me trying to give directions to Farmer as we bounced along. Finally I was completely lost—had no idea where the turnoff was—but I said, "Farmer, keep going." Pretty soon we ran straight onto a German road-block. We got within twenty yards of it before Farmer could stop. Fortunately the Germans were so astonished they didn't shoot. Farmer did a quick 180 turn and we got out of there unharmed. That really scared hell out of me. But it didn't seem to faze Ridgway. I was waiting for him to say, "Dummy, look what almost happened to us!" But he didn't say a thing.[34]

The force advanced as far south as Pretot. There it met strong resistance and dug in. Units of Raff's 507 came out of reserve and relieved Mendez's 3rd Battalion, which then rejoined the 508 in the rear. The front was extended to the east (more firmly linking with the 101st) and slightly to the southwest toward La Haye-du-Puits, but no farther advance south was attempted at this time and the division went over to the defensive, now assigned to Middleton's VIII Corps.[35]

While the fight for the Cotentin had been in progress, Montgomery and Bradley had gradually enlarged their beachheads. Montgomery, confronted with ever-mounting German pressure, was not able to take his D-day objective, Caen, but Dempsey's right-flank forces had pushed inland several miles beyond Bayeux and had linked up with Gee Gerow's V Corps at Caumont. Bradley had brought ashore yet another corps, the XIX, commanded by Charles H. (Pete) Corlett.[36]

Every yard of advance in France had been difficult and costly. While the Germans still half believed the Allied operations in Normandy were feints— that the main attack would come in Pas-de-Calais—they had thrown division after division into the defense of Normandy. These included about seven panzer and two infantry divisions in front of Montgomery and Dempsey in the

Caen area. Moreover, the Allies had grossly underestimated the difficulties of the hedgerow terrain in the American sector and had not yet learned how to cope with it. As a result, OVERLORD forces were falling far behind the planned timetable and facing the possibility of a ghastly stalemate.[37]

Bradley was frustrated at the slow, bloody slogging on all fronts in the American sector. While Collins was capturing Cherbourg, he conceived a plan for a massive breakout using all the forces at his command. In outline, the plan was as follows. All four of his corps (about twelve divisions) would attack southward in a giant wheeling movement, pivoting on Gerow's V Corps at Caumont. From west to east: Middleton's VIII Corps would attack south from St. Sauveur-le-Vicomte through La Haye-du-Puits to Coutances. East of Middleton, near Carentan, Collins's VII Corps would drive south toward Périers, then angle toward Coutances. East of Collins, Corlett's XIX Corps would drive directly at St. Lô. East of Corlett, Gerow's V Corps would serve as the hub of the pivot. The offensive would go as soon as Collins could redeploy VII Corps from Cherbourg to Carentan.[38]

The tactical situation Bradley confronted presented an opportunity for utilizing airborne forces for another disrupting strike behind enemy lines. However, there is no evidence that he gave this idea serious thought. Neither the 101st nor the 82nd was in any shape for an airborne operation. Both had been badly chewed up. Before they could engage in another full-scale airborne attack, they would have to return to England for refitting and restaffing, and that would take too long.‡ Besides that, Bradley had hit upon what he believed to be a more immediately valuable mission for Paul Williams' IX Troop Carrier Wing. The storm which wrecked the landing beaches had, in part, contributed to a grave ammunition shortage. The thousand troop-carrier planes had been urgently pressed into service to haul ammo to Normandy.[40]

Middleton's VIII Corps was completely reorganized for the breakout offensive. Taylor's 101st was withdrawn from the Carentan sector and redeployed to Cherbourg for policing and occupational duties. Billy Wyche's 79th and Landrum's 90th divisions were assigned to VIII Corps along with a brand-new one, the 8th, commanded by Ridgway's West Point classmate (and Mark Clark's roommate), William C. McMahon. Inasmuch as all the units were relatively green and did not yet have Bradley's full confidence, the decision was made to keep the 82nd Division in the corps to add some well-seasoned troops

---

‡ The British 6th Airborne, still engaged in fighting near Caen, was likewise badly chewed up and in no condition for airborne operations. The British 1st Airborne was still in reserve in England and eager to join the Normandy fight. On June 10, Montgomery had requested it be dropped into his sector to assist in the capture of Caen, but Leigh-Mallory refused on the grounds that an airborne operation near Caen would be, in the words of one Normandy historian, "far too hazardous for his air crews." Montgomery, furious, wrote London that Leigh-Mallory was "obviously a gutless bugger who refuses to take a chance and plays for safety on all occasions. I have no use for him." Other plans for dropping the 1st Airborne Division in the British sector were conceived and similarly discarded.[39]

to the initial assault. After the offensive got rolling full steam, the 82nd would be withdrawn and returned to England with the 101st. The VIII Corps divisions were deployed facing south, thusly: 79th on the right (western) flank, 82nd in the center and 90th on the left (east) flank, abutting the VII Corps sector. The 8th Division, in reserve, would move up after the initial assault and replace the 82nd.[41]

Now a great—and lasting—controversy arose in the 82nd Division. Apparently two of the three parachute regimental commanders, Roy Lindquist (508) and Edson Raff (507) protested this plan for yet another offensive, making their case orally to higher headquarters. Jim Gavin recalled that Roy Lindquist came to him and pointed out that his rifle companies had been "decimated" (in some instances, down from 190 to 50 men) and that another attack might incur so many casualties that Lindquist would not be able to reconstitute the regiment for another airborne operation for a long time to come. In fact, Gavin later wrote, Lindquist "wanted to have his regiment pulled out of the line because of the shortage of troops." Raff remembered that he made a similar case to Gavin: "If we attack any more we won't have a cadre to make a regiment when we get back to England. I think we ought to be withdrawn." However, Gavin did not recall Raff's visit.[42]

These protests soon reached Ridgway. He wrote later that it was Jim Gavin who brought them to him and that, in effect, Gavin concurred. Gavin, however, remembered it was Lindquist who took the protest to Ridgway and that when he did so, thereafter Ridgway "had little regard for him as a combat infantryman." Raff recalled that after he protested to Gavin, he was sent on to Ridgway with his demurral, and that Ridgway at first appeared somewhat sympathetic. However, Ridgway later insisted that he did not talk to either Lindquist or Raff on this matter—only to Gavin.[43]

Without referring to Gavin by name, Ridgway recalled the controversy this way in his memoir *Soldier:* "Late in the campaign one of my senior officers came to me and told me that the division couldn't make another attack. If it did, he said, it would be so impaired in effectiveness that it would take us months to get ready for another major action. It was an honest estimate by a gallant battle leader. It deserved soul-searching thought. I was well aware of the brutal punishment the division had taken. But I had spent most of every day of the campaign up with the forward battalions. I knew that, though they were weak in numbers, their fighting spirit was still unimpaired . . ."

Ridgway's final decision was to make one more attack. Whether or not Gavin took the protest to Ridgway, as Ridgway remembered it, Gavin disapproved of the decision. He said later: "Ridgway grew up in the World War I tradition that an infantryman can always take one more step, fire one more shot. That isn't so, but he wanted to believe it . . ." Raff also disapproved. He recollected bitterly: "I had exercised the prerogative of a commander, which is to protect his men from generals who, for their glory, want to expend them. Such a glory-seeker was General Ridgway—he didn't give a damn about the men fighting for him, me included. I had decided earlier I would never die for him . . . My motto was: I never gave a damn for any damned man who didn't give a damn for me."[44]

Middleton's VIII Corps led the offensive, jumping off at dawn on July 3 in terrible weather: heavy squalls and fog. The tactical plan was for all three divisions to mount a power drive on the first major objective, La Haye-du-Puits. On the right, the 79th would angle in from the west. On the left, the 90th would angle in from the east. The 82nd would advance in the center until it reached the outskirts of the city (Hill 95), where it would be "pinched out" by the converging flank divisions which were to take the city. Thereafter McMahon's 8th Division would replace the 82nd for the continued southerly push to the next major objective, Lessay.[45]

The 82nd Division, coiled into the new bridgehead south of Pont-l'Abbé, jumped off at 0630, July 3. Ekman's 505, Lindquist's 508, Sitler's 325 and Timmes's 2nd Battalion of the 507 spearheaded the drive. The rest of Raff's 507 was committed the following day. Despite the weather, the 82nd made astonishing speed in the attack. By this time, Ekman had proved to be an outstanding regimental commander and his 505 performed spectacularly. By nightfall on the first day, the division, with the 505 in the lead reached the outskirts of La Haye-du-Puits. A First Army historian wrote: "The aggressive spirit of the airborne fighters carried them to startling successes. They [the 505] took Hill 131 on the very morning of the jumpoff and captured La Poterie Ridge before dark. They complained that only the corps order prevented them from entering La Haye-du-Puits." On the following morning, July 4, the 505 helped the 508 take Hill 95, overlooking the city, and the division went over to the defensive as per the tactical plan.[46]

The attack, unfortunately, tended to bear out Lindquist's lugubrious forecast. Two of the ablest commanders in the 508 fell in a single twenty-four-hour period. First to be hit was the 2nd Battalion commander, Tom Shanley. As he remembered it: "I was watching a German machinegun firing at our men. I tripped over a red telephone wire. Too late, I realized it was a booby trap. It blew and I flew through the air. I had several pieces of shrapnel in me—one in the neck. I was pretty badly crippled but I bandaged myself and kept going." But not for long. Lindquist sent his new exec, the division pinch hitter Mark Alexander, to temporarily replace Shanley. In the early hours of the following morning, while talking on a field telephone to Lindquist, Alexander was hit by a German mortar and severely wounded (two fragments of steel in his left lung). Thereafter the regimental S-3, Otho E. Holmes, took command of the 2nd Battalion.[47]

Both wounded men were hospitalized, Shanley for ten days, Alexander for well over two months. When Shanley returned to the regiment, he replaced Alexander as exec, a job he had for the rest of the war. Holmes remained in command of the 2nd Battalion for the duration. Alexander would return to the division at a later date, but owing to continued physical weakness (extreme loss of weight and lung hemorrhages), he was limited to staff duties.[48]

There were also severe losses in the 507. On July 5, Louis Levy was killed and John W. Marr was wounded. On July 7, 3rd Battalion commander Art

Maloney was severely wounded and evacuated, and did not return to the division. His battalion exec, John T. Davis, replaced him. (Two years later Maloney retired, disabled, from the Army.) That same day, the 1st Battalion commander, Ben Pearson, was also wounded, but stayed at his post. Since D day, the 507 had lost nearly half its strength (840 men) killed, wounded, captured or missing, and four of its five original commanders: Millett (captured); Ostberg (severely injured); Kuhn (injured in drop); and now Maloney. For a time, the lone survivor of the original leaders in Normandy was the "mouse" who was a "terror in combat," Charles Timmes, but William Kuhn would soon rejoin, to become regimental exec.[49]

Despite the promising start the 82nd Airborne Division had given VIII Corps, the massive breakout offensive failed. The failure, a "crushing disappointment" to Bradley, was ascribed by him to several causes: bad weather and unseasonal heavy rains which mired the armor and vehicles and grounded close air support; the unanticipated difficulties of fighting in the hedgerow and marshy terrain; determined German resistance (by the regrouped 6th Parachute Regiment and the newly arrived 17 SS Panzer Grenadier and the Panzer Lehr divisions, plus other units), which mounted strong counterattacks; insufficient time for Collins to properly regroup for the attack; and poor leadership in all too many of the divisions.[50]

The poor divisional leadership was nowhere more evident than in Middleton's VIII Corps. Eugene Landrum, commanding the wobbly 90th Division, failed to take hold. When he complained that his ADC, Sam Williams, was "trying to take my division away from me," Bradley fired them both. Bradley chose Theodore Roosevelt to command the division, but before Roosevelt could report for duty, he died of a heart attack. The top job then went to Middleton's former 45th Division artillery commander Raymond S. McLain (an Oklahoma City banker and National Guardsman), who proved to be an extraordinarily stable—and able—commander. McLain got West Pointer (1912) William G. ("Wild Bill") Weaver, a hero of World War I, for his ADC and retained Barth, Clarke and Bacon as his regimental commanders. These men ultimately turned the division into one of the best in the ETO. Ridgway's classmate William McMahon, commanding the 8th Division, which replaced the 82nd at La Haye-du-Puits, likewise failed and was relieved by Bradley and sent to Mark Clark's staff. McMahon was replaced by Manton Eddy's ADC, Donald A. Stroh, a tough veteran of the North Africa, Sicily and Italian-mainland campaigns. Finally, although Bradley was not initially impressed with Billy Wyche, who commanded the 79th Division, he kept Wyche on the job and eventually that division also became one of the best.[51]

The 82nd Airborne Division, officially relieved of combat duties on July 8 after thirty-three days in action, became the stuff of instant legend. Its record in Normandy may well have been the most remarkable of any division in Army history. It had been poorly dropped and instantly surrounded and threatened with annihilation, squeezed into the small Ste. Mère-Église triangle. It had held a determined and far larger enemy at bay for thirty-six desperate hours without tanks and little or no artillery and with very little ammunition. When relieved at noon on D+1 by Van Fleet's 8th Infantry, it had unhesitatingly joined in the general VII Corps attack north to Le Ham and Montebourg Station. Simultaneously, it had attacked west, forcing a bloody crossing of the Merderet River, opening the way to cut the peninsula. Still without respite, it gained a bridgehead south of the lower Douve, then regrouped and joined the general attack to cut the Cotentin, outrunning the fresh and fully manned 9th and 90th divisions to the Douve River. Although it had been reduced by casualties to about half strength, it regrouped again into its lower Douve bridgehead to spearhead Bradley's July 3 "breakout" offensive, achieving all its objectives with remarkable speed. In all of this, it had inflicted savage losses on the German 77th and 91st divisions and attached units.

It was the kind of performance generals dream about but seldom achieve. Under Ridgway and Gavin's frontline, personal leadership, most of the paratroopers—and ultimately most of the gliderists—had performed magnificently. A few leaders had caved in, some (in comparison to others) had been less aggressive. But even these "weak" commanders stood like giants when compared to many commanders in the 4th, 8th, 9th, 90th and 79th divisions of VII and VIII Corps. In truth, the 82nd Division emerged from Normandy with the reputation of being—in Eaton's phrase—a pack of jackals; the toughest, most resourceful and bloodthirsty infantry in the ETO.

The cost had been frightful. Of the nearly 12,000 men of the 82nd Division committed in Normandy, about 46 percent (5,245) were listed as casualties—killed, wounded or missing. Of these, 1,282 were killed and 2,373 had suffered wounds or injuries severe enough to warrant evacuation. When the division embarked for England on landing craft at Utah Beach, there were only 6,545 officers and men.[52]

The toll among the senior infantry commanders had been especially severe. Two of the four regimental commanders had been lost: Harry Lewis to battle fatigue, George Millett captured. The toll of infantry battalion commanders may have been the heaviest for any division in a single campaign in the war. Of the twelve battalion commanders who landed in Normandy, eight did not last the full course: two (Batcheller, Kellam) were killed; two (Ostberg, Swenson) were severely wounded; one (Shanley) was seriously wounded; two (Kuhn, Boyd) were incapacitated on landing; and one (Carrell) was relieved. Of the four in this original group who lasted the full course, two (Krause, Timmes) were slightly wounded, and one (Vandervoort) was injured on landing. Only one (Mendez) escaped without reportable injuries or wounds. Of the twelve replacement battalion commanders, two (Roscoe Roy, Arthur Gardner) were killed and four (Alexander, Davis, Pearson, Maloney) were wounded. Six replacement battalion commanders (Hagan, Holmes, Leahy, Major, Sanford, Shields) escaped without reportable wounds or injuries. In sum, of the twenty-four men who commanded 82nd Division battalions in Normandy, four were killed; two were incapacitated on landing and had to be replaced; seven were wounded. This was a casualty rate of about 50 percent.[53]

Ridgway felt the losses deeply—as though these men were his sons. In subsequent weeks, he sent signed letters to the families of all the dead and missing division soldiers, a tremendous undertaking that overwhelmed the clerical staff. In addition, he directed that all unit commanders write personal letters to their wounded hospitalized in France or England in order to lift their spirits and increase their desire to hurry back to their units. Beyond all that, Ridgway wrote personal letters to the wives and loved ones of his surviving staffers, to say they were safe and had done a splendid job in Normandy. Doc Eaton recalled: "All this tended to create a 'family feeling' about the division that was unique in the ETO."[54]

Max Taylor's 101 had been baptized by fire and, despite an equally bad drop, had acquitted itself with distinction. It had carried out its vital D-day mission of seizing the four causeways and, somewhat belatedly, the capture of Carentan, an objective Bradley had seriously underrated.

The cost to the 101 had also been frightful, although not as severe as the 82nd's. In Normandy, the 101 suffered a total of 4,670 casualties. Among these was the highest-ranking American airborne officer to be killed in Normandy: the ADC, Brigadier General Don Pratt. Like Ridgway, Taylor had lost two of his four regimental commanders (Moseley, broken leg and irrational behavior; Wear, relieved), but Taylor's loss of infantry battalion commanders, by comparison, had been far less severe. Three (Carroll, Turner, Wolverton) had been killed, and one (Salee) wounded; one replacement battalion commander (Foster) had been wounded.[55]

A rain of compliments from on high flowed to Ridgway. Omar Bradley, in passing along a congratulatory message from George Marshall to Ridgway, added his own: "I cannot express too strongly my appreciation for the very fine work done by your division. You did a magnificent job in this show and I am sure you will do the same in any future operation in which you are committed. As you know I will always have a very strong feeling for the 82nd Division." Joe Collins, who awarded Ridgway a DSC, sent his congratulations and appreciation, stating (in part), "The battle across the Merderet River . . . was one of the toughest operations during the campaign and called for the highest order of valor . . . [also] to the 82nd Division must go credit for having broken the back of the German resistance in the Cherbourg Peninsula when . . . these divisions drove through German resistance . . . and seized bridgeheads west of the Douve. This breakthrough insured the cutting off of the Cotentin Peninsula and sealed the fate of Cherbourg. VII Corps looks forward to the day when they can serve with the 82nd again." Troy Middleton wrote (in part): "The [82nd] Division has fulfilled in an admirable manner every requirement asked of it. Furthermore, during the current campaign the division has acquitted itself in a manner such as to mark it as one of the outstanding units of the United States Army. The personnel of this excellent division should feel proud of its achievement. Those of us who have watched her work have been proud to have been associated with you."[56]

Perhaps more important to Ridgway was the reputation he had established among his men. He had been relentless, demanding, unyielding and in the heat of battle, seemingly indifferent to the brutal casualties. He had lopped off a few heads, sometimes impulsively and wrongly. And yet the majority of the men who survived this ordeal revered and loved him and would continue to do so. They had been awed by his unflinching courage, his coolness and clearheadedness, his nearly flawless leadership in tight corners, and when it was done, his compassion for those who had fallen. Gavin, who did not lightly bestow praise, wrote: "His great courage, integrity, and aggressiveness in combat all made a lasting impression on everyone in the division . . ."[57]

Max Taylor once reflected that Ridgway had one flaw in his character: an intense possessiveness coupled with blind adoration of his possessions: "Anything Ridgway had or owned was priceless—just perfect—and he wanted the world to know that. You couldn't say anything negative about it. He had a wrist watch—a Longines. That was the best watch in the world. And his second wife—Peggy. The best wife in the world. Wrote her every day. The 82nd was his baby—the best in the world."[58]

It was natural that Ridgway would want to brag about the performance of "his baby." He therefore drafted a flowery personal letter for George Marshall, which imprudently compared the 82nd Division's record to other American divisions in the invasion. Perhaps to be certain that Eisenhower also got the message, Ridgway first sent it to his good friend and Eisenhower's chief of staff, Bedell Smith, for "comment." A few days later, Eisenhower's G-3, Harold R. (Pink) Bull, replying for Smith, wrote Ridgway that although the letter was a personal one and "you must be the sole judge," he and Smith thought it would not be wise to send it. "Better to let the division's fine record speak for itself," Bull advised, suggesting Ridgway's "just pride" in the division would be "more effective" with a brief statement. Bull concluded: "While we are all justly proud of the outstanding accomplishments of the 82nd, I question the wisdom of suggesting a comparison on the basis of merit with other divisions which have spent such long periods in the line." Upon receipt of this note, Ridgway prudently filed the letter away and settled for a "brief statement" which said, in part: "No ground gained was ever relinquished and no advance ever halted except on the orders of Corps or Army."[59]*

No congratulatory letter came from Eisenhower. However, in connection with another matter, Eisenhower stated his opinion of Ridgway's performance in a letter to Hap Arnold when he told Arnold that Ridgway "has commanded in combat with great distinction." Still later, Eisenhower wrote Marshall that Ridgway was "one of the finest soldiers this war has produced."[60]

More to the point, Eisenhower rewarded Ridgway with an immediate promotion: command of an American airborne corps into which the 82nd, 101st and soon-to-arrive 17th airborne divisions would be organized.

---

* In composing this "statement," which became a famous 82nd Airborne Division slogan, Ridgway apparently did not consider the La Fière causeway and the Cauquigny "bridgehead" technically "gained" on D day.

⭐33⭐

GEORGE MARSHALL and Hap Arnold had never abandoned the idea of massive and decisive airborne operations deep in enemy territory. Even before D day they resumed prodding Eisenhower, suggesting (as Boy Browning had earlier) that to better mount such operations, American and British airborne troops and the troop-carrier aircraft be merged into a single outfit headed by a sort of mini-Allied supreme commander. On May 20, Eisenhower assured Marshall and Arnold that he was thinking along the same lines. He had already had some preliminary talks with Montgomery and Bradley. Montgomery (perhaps influenced by Browning) had approved the idea, but Bradley opposed it.[1]

Bradley's view, beyond doubt influenced by those of Ridgway, Lee, Gavin and others, was that the American ground commander should retain tight control over American airborne forces. Like Ridgway, Lee and Gavin, he believed that American airborne forces should be organized into a corps which would report directly to the Army commander in whose sector airborne operations were contemplated; he was as concerned as they were that the British might get command of the combined airborne force and swallow up or misuse American airborne forces.[2]

By this time, Bradley had become Eisenhower's most trusted lieutenant, and in most matters Eisenhower followed his counsel. In this instance, he did not. The pressures from Marshall and Arnold were strong. A combined Allied airborne force seemed logical and tidy, despite the fact that the British contribution would be substantially less than the American and that a clumsy "command layer" would be inserted between the American ground commander and the American airborne forces. In any case, Eisenhower relished creating such "joint commands" and, in the interest of Allied harmony, saw no harm in appointing British generals (and admirals) to inflated command positions out of proportion to the British contribution in men and machines.

Eisenhower soon reduced his ideas to a concrete proposal. The combined outfit would be called First Allied Airborne Army (FAAA). An American airman would command it, with a British general as his deputy commander. It would consist of two corps, the American XVIII Airborne Corps, comprising the 82nd, the 101st and the arriving 17th airborne divisions, and the British 1st Airborne Corps, comprising the British 1st and 6th airborne divisions, plus a Polish airborne brigade and other miscellaneous non-American Allied airborne units. The American IX Troop Carrier Command (50th, 52nd and 53rd wings) and the British Troop Carrier Command (38th and 46th groups) would be absorbed into FAAA, reporting directly to its commander. The FAAA would be "activated" after Eisenhower established his headquarters in France and took command of all ground forces, and it would report directly to him.[3]

Few were pleased with Eisenhower's proposal. The British were particularly unhappy. The British chiefs of staff "felt strongly" that the commander of FAAA should be British—specifically Boy Browning. Browning did nothing to discourage the campaign in his behalf and was bitterly disappointed when Eisenhower chose an American airman. Leigh-Mallory, who favored the general idea, objected strongly to removing the American IX Troop Carrier Command from his tactical air forces, and the RAF resented losing sovereignty over 38th and 46th groups. Bradley, Ridgway and other American senior airborne officers had misgivings about the added and unwieldy "command layer" and considered the appointment of an airman to command the airborne infantry ill-advised.[4]

Which American airman would command the First Allied Airborne Army? Eisenhower soon had a candidate: Hoyt S. Vandenberg, the young (West Point, 1923), handsome, brilliant American airman who was then serving as deputy to Leigh-Mallory. In a memo to Bedell Smith on June 23, Eisenhower proposed Vandenberg, adding, "He is imaginative and energetic." Marshall agreed with this choice, but it was later decided that Vandenberg was too young, too junior and lacking in public prestige. For a time, Marshall, Arnold and Eisenhower considered a more senior airman, John Cannon, but in the end it was decided the job would go to Lewis Brereton, who had the necessary age, seniority and public recognition. Vandenberg would replace Brereton as commander of the Ninth Air Force.[5]

Omar Bradley probably had an indirect hand in Brereton's reassignment. Bradley, already down on Brereton, had been incensed by the disastrous drop of the 82nd and 101st into Normandy and by the ineffective close air support his First Army troops were receiving in Normandy. He blamed these failures on Brereton, whose mind was still apparently fixed on the great air battles with the German Air Force over Germany. Bradley's comment on Brereton's departure from command of Ninth Air Force was "Thank goodness."[6]

To Brereton, the appointment was a kick in the teeth and a great comedown. From commanding great fleets of glamorous fighters, he was reduced to commanding fleets of mundane troop carriers and the GIs who would ride in them, a dead end for his career if there ever was one. When he got the bad news, he wrote in his diary, "I 'took a dim view' of this new assignment."[7]

To help smooth the ruffled British feathers, Eisenhower appointed Boy Browning deputy commander of the FAAA. Browning was disappointed in being slotted into second place and disliked serving a man—an airman at that—who was, by date of rank, four months his junior. Since neither man was overjoyed with his assignment, their relationship was not harmonious. Browning maintained his power base by wearing two hats: he retained command of British 1 Airborne Corps.[8]

The key day-to-day administrator in this new outfit would be the chief of staff. Eisenhower had decreed that this job, too, would go to an American. He suggested Al Gruenther, Bedell Smith's understudy, whom Eisenhower had "loaned out" to Mark Clark, or as a second choice, Lyman Lemnitzer, also serving in Italy. But Marshall was loath to rob the Italian campaign of either of these outstanding men and proposed instead Ridgway's old friend Floyd Parks, who was then serving as ADC of the 69th Division in the States. Parks, a genial conciliator and salesman who knew nothing about airborne operations, would spend much of his time trying to reduce the friction between Brereton and Browning.[9]

There was never any question or doubt about who would command FAAA's most powerful combat arm, the American XVIII Airborne Corps. Eisenhower had only one nominee: Matt Ridgway. Ridgway later wrote that his appointment was a "tremendous honor," and despite his misgivings about the structure of FAAA and his personal reservations about Brereton and Browning, he gave "no serious thought to the idea of refusal."[10]

Indeed not. The appointment brought Ridgway into an elite military group. The dozen American corps commanders who fought under Eisenhower and Bradley would be the key battlefield managers in the victory. The corps commander is, as Ridgway put it, "the highest commander in the military hierarchy who is solely a battle leader, a tactical commander . . ." After Gee Gerow, Joe Collins, Troy Middleton and Pete Corlett, Ridgway was the fifth of these dozen in the firing line and, save Middleton, the most experienced at fighting the Germans. The appointment carried great prestige and ordinarily a promotion to three stars (which would have put Ridgway on an equal rank footing with Boy Browning), but Marshall was notoriously stingy about promotions. Bradley, commanding an army, still wore only three stars, and all of Eisenhower's corps commanders had to wait for promotion until Marshall was good and ready.[11]

Ridgway's promotion raised a serious problem: Who would command the now legendary 82nd Airborne Division? Would it, like the 101, go to an "outsider," or would the job be filled from within?

Ridgway's early and unwavering view, which carried much weight in the final decision, was that the job should go to Jim Gavin. In forwarding the proposal to Bedell Smith for Eisenhower, together with a recommendation for Gavin's promotion to major general, Ridgway wrote: "Brigadier General Gavin possesses to a superior degree self-possession regardless of pressure in and out of battle, loyalty, initiative, zeal, sound judgment and common sense. His personal appearance and dignity of demeanor are in keeping with these high qualities, and to them he adds great charm of manner. He is a proved battle leader of the highest type, and in my opinion will make a superior airborne division commander."

Gavin, however, was only thirty-seven (six years younger than Taylor) and had been a general officer for a mere nine months. Ridgway took note of these factors in his recommendation: "The relative rank of this officer has been considered, and to the best of my knowledge and belief he is the best fitted officer available in this command for the grade and position for which promotion is recommended."

Eisenhower and Smith apparently accepted Ridgway's recommendations without reservations. Gavin would thus become the youngest American two-star general to command a division since the Civil War.[12]

Who would be Gavin's ADC?

That proved to be a more vexing question. Ridgway did not want an "outsider"—someone with no connection to the division. The senior combat commanders in the 82nd were Tucker (504), Ekman (505), Raff (507), Lindquist (508) and the temporary-acting Sitler (325). Ridgway and Gavin agreed that at that time only one of these men deserved serious consideration for promotion to one-star general: Tucker. He was Gavin's initial candidate, but Ridgway demurred. Tucker was a combat commander without peer but, as Gavin later put it, "he didn't give a damn about administration and paperwork. In fact," as Gavin admitted, "he was famous for screwing up everything having to do with administration. One story going around was that when Tucker left Italy he had an orange crate full of official charges against his soldiers and he just threw the whole crate into the ocean. Ridgway and I talked about it and we decided we just couldn't promote Tucker."[13]

This decision forced Ridgway to search for someone else with some sort of connection to the division. He soon turned up a candidate. He was Stuart Cutler, who had ably commanded the division's original 326th Regiment, then supervised its conversion to a glider outfit, and thus had a "connection" with the division. But Cutler (VMI, 1917), who had been ADC of the 13th Airborne Division and more recently an airborne adviser to various ETO high commands and was then deputy to Floyd Parks at FAAA, was far too senior for Gavin's taste, and more to the point, he lacked combat experience. Ridgway's next idea was to draft the division's former G-2, George Lynch, who had left in Italy to command the 142nd Infantry Regiment of the 36th Division and who had, by all reports, done a splendid job in combat. To Ridgway's chagrin, Lynch turned down the job—and the promotion to general. Lynch wrote Ridgway that he had been in combat so long he had lost the "bounce and freshness" required of an airborne officer. Later he said that he was "in love" with his own outfit, which had been "very successful," and despite the one star offered him, he considered the proposed ADC assignment to be a "secondary, somewhat irresponsible job" compared to that of regimental commander. As the search continued, the ADC job was left vacant for some months.[14]

Next Ridgway and Gavin had to deal with a very important question about the makeup of the division. Tucker's 504 was now restaffed and ready to be reintegrated. This meant that either the 507 or the 508 had to be transferred out. There was little debate. Gavin was still down on the 507; Raff was eager to leave the 82nd. Accordingly, Raff's 507 was transferred to Bud Miley's newly arrived 17th Airborne Division. This decision satisfied Raff, but in the lower ranks it caused "great bitterness," one of the junior officers, Paul Smith, recalled. The 507 had fought as an element of the 82nd Airborne Division in an epic campaign, and most 507 men felt they "belonged" to the division as much as the men of the 504 (or 508), or perhaps even more so, since in their view the 82nd's Mediterranean campaigns had been, by comparison to Normandy, far less significant.[15]

Next they had to deal with several important command problems. The most pressing was finding a replacement for Harry Lewis in the 325th. Gavin then had in mind a plan to toughen up the regiment by sending every man in it to parachute school. This plan (which fell by the wayside) may have influenced in part his choice of commander: Tucker's exec, paratrooper Charles Billingslea, who also had an extensive combat record, including Anzio, and who had jumped into Normandy as an observer. Ridgway approved Billingslea; Herb Sitler reverted to exec.[16]*

The contrast between Lewis and Billingslea could not have been more striking. Lewis was short, aloof and blustery; Billingslea was tall and taciturn. A 325 company commander, Lee Travelstead, recalled:

The first day he reported in Leicester, Billingslea was riding a motorcycle behind the Studebaker staff car I believe Colonel Lewis used. It seemed a good sign to us since Colonel Lewis had been so far removed from us. At breakfast at our officers' mess, he walked in, some six feet, three inches. Most of us had never seen him before. He put his cap on the open ceiling rafters that none of us could reach except a Lieutenant Smith in the antitank outfit, who followed him and put his cap right beside Billingslea's—for a good laugh by all.

Billingslea was rather non-communicative at all times other than in command situations, where he was most positive and highly competent. He was a strict disciplinarian and "all business." When he spoke at meetings, and otherwise, it was almost in a whisper, causing all to strain to hear what he was saying, and someone was always asking me, "What did he say?" Whether by design or natural, it accomplished good results in that people were quiet so as to hear what he said, whereas at many other kinds of meetings they were so noisy that no one knew what anyone said without repeating.

In short, he was a good combat leader, who worked more by example and conduct than words. I never heard of or saw his competence even questioned. Although he was tough, he was highly respected.[18]

Ridgway next presented Gavin with a list of staffers and personal aides that he intended to take with him to the XVIII Corps. It was a modest list which

---

* Other changes: In the 504, Billingslea was replaced as exec by the 1st Battalion commander, Warren Williams, who was replaced by Gavin's "assistant" in Normandy, Willard Harrison, who had won a DSC. Hank Adams, who had assisted Ridgway in Normandy, had a severe recurrence of his malaria and was hospitalized. He was replaced as 2nd Battalion commander by his exec, Edward N. Wellems. (Julian Aaron Cook, who had replaced Freeman in command of the 3rd Battalion after Anzio, remained in place.) In the 505, Ed Krause (who won a second DSC for Normandy) was promoted to exec. His 3rd Battalion went to James L. Kaiser, the regimental S-2 in Normandy. Bill Hagan, commanding the 1st Battalion, broke a foot in a motorcycle accident and was grounded, replaced by Talton (Woody) Long.[17]

cleared the way for Gavin to promote some of his own people to his staff. Ridgway would take the chief of staff, Doc Eaton; the G-1, Fred Schellhammer; the G-2, Whitfield Jack; the G-4, Bill Moorman; the division surgeon, Wolcott Etienne; his aide, Don Faith (his other aide, Art Kroos, returned to his old outfit in the 325); his driver, Frank Farmer; his orderly, Jim Casey.[19]

Gavin now had the pleasure of picking his own divisional staff. His choices, effective August 28, were without exception courageous combat veterans, most of them alumni of the 505. Bob Wienecke, who had been Ridgway's acting chief of staff, remained permanently in that position. The Normandy troubleshooter, Al Ireland, was named G-1. Walter Winton was named G-2, replacing Whitfield Jack. The 505's young (West Point, 1941), able S-3, John Norton, was named G-3. Albert G. Marin became the G-4. All would remain in place until the end of the war.

After these 82nd Division matters were settled, Ridgway then focused his attention on his new headquarters. Before its designation as airborne, the XVIII Corps, comprising some five hundred men, had been organized earlier in the States and had been commanded by William H. H. Morris, a distinguished older West Pointer (1911), who had won a DSC in France in World War I. When the corps was chosen for conversion to airborne, Marshall transferred Morris to command the 10th Armored Division, then in training. An "advance man," the corps G-3, Alexander Day Surles, Jr., had come to England to observe the NEPTUNE operation. Like Don Faith, Walt Winton, Hank Adams, and Bill Moorman, Surles was the young son of an "old Army" officer, and thus a prime candidate for the inner circle. His father, a West Point general (1911), was Marshall's top public relations man, and the younger Surles was married to the daughter of Marshall's former deputy chief of staff for operations, General William Bryden. In his first meeting with Ridgway, Surles felt an instant chemistry:

> I was awestruck. I knew from reading reports what the division had done in Normandy. But his physical presence was so imposing that he struck you dumb right off. He scared me to death. You know the old cliché about the "look of eagles"? He was one who had it.
> I was with him about fifteen minutes. He knew my father. They were not what you call close; my father was a cavalryman. Ridgway won me right over. I felt that his first impression of me was not bad and that he was interested in me. He was my man from that moment on.
> We talked about people in XVIII Corps. He told me he was not bringing over the principal staff officers of the corps because he wanted to move up some people from the 82nd Division who had combat experience. The one exception was the G-3, Bob Wienecke, who would remain as Gavin's chief of staff. So he told me I could hang on to the corps G-3 job until he could find an airborne G-3 to replace me. I was young and full of beans and a quick study and wanted to know all about the airborne business and wanted to

succeed with him and tried my best to do it. In the end, owing to some lucky things, he didn't replace me; I kept the job.[20]

In addition to Surles, Ridgway kept only three key officers of the old XVIII Corps. These were the deputy chief of staff, James B. Quill, a classmate of Gavin's who brought the corps headquarters to England; the commander of the corps artillery, Theodore E. Buechler; and the corps engineer, Benjamin S. Shute. The other key corps staffers were those he brought from the 82nd. Ridgway named Eaton XVIII Corps chief of staff (and got him promoted to brigadier general). Schellhammer was appointed G-1; Whitfield Jack, G-2; Bill Moorman, G-4. At this time, when the 2nd Airborne Brigade headquarters was dissolved, Ridgway declined to have the dislocated George Howell in the corps; Howell eventually wound up in the nebulous job of liaison officer between FAAA and Omar Bradley's 12th Army Group.[21]†

The decision was made that the XVIII Airborne Corps headquarters would go into combat by glider. Surles recalled: "They took us to an airfield for a glider demonstration. One broke up right over the airfield and dumped sixteen people on the ground. Not very pleasant. Several of my boys said they didn't want to be in this outfit at all. I tried to get Ridgway to let me go to [parachute school for] jump training but he said no. If we had to jump, he said, he'd just push me out the door ahead of him and it would be no problem."[23]‡

Ridgway's departure from the 82nd Division commenced officially in August. On August 10, Eisenhower visited the 101st at Newbury for the third time. Later that same day, he came to the 82nd at Leicester for the first time. The 82nd, now fully rested and brought back to war strength with some six thousand parachute- and glider-school replacements, paraded at full strength, along with Hal Clark's 52nd Wing airmen. Eisenhower made a speech extolling the airborne contributions to NEPTUNE and pinned on some DSCs and other medals. Ridgway found these ceremonies deeply moving:

I suppose a prouder division commander never lived than I was as I watched that magnificent division swing past the reviewing stand . . . I had fought by their side in Sicily and Italy, and I had jumped with them in Normandy.

† Among the newcomers assigned to XVIII Airborne Corps was Colonel Harry P. Cain, who served as "civil affairs" officer (sometimes called G-5), responsible for reestablishing civil government in liberated or occupied countries and cities. After the war, Republican Cain was appointed to fill out a Senate term, and in November 1947, he ran and was elected for a full six-year term. Eisenhower, who lunched with him in February 1947, wrote of Cain in his diary: "Energetic, logical, friendly. He ought to make a fine Senator."[22]

‡ The curse of being a gliderist was ameliorated somewhat by several important policy decisions reached—on Ridgway's insistence—after Normandy. First, the Americans would never again attempt a nighttime glider landing. Second, the Americans would never again be assigned to ride into combat in the flimsy British Horsas. Third, gliderists would receive hazardous-duty pay commensurate with paratrooper pay: one hundred dollars per month extra for officers, fifty dollars a month for enlisted men.[24]

They had done all I had asked of them, and more. And I felt for them that deep love, respect and admiration which a soldier feels for the comrades whose dangers he has shared . . . [but] the great pride that welled up in me . . . was tempered by a deep sense of sorrow and regret. For I knew what the division did not yet know—that this was good-by.[25]

Or was it? Some believe that Ridgway, at least spiritually, never cut the cord to the 82nd. Max Taylor recalled, "He never gave up command of the 82nd. Ask Jim Gavin. I could see it. I used to thank God I didn't get the 82nd. I couldn't have lived under that. I'd have been fired."[26]

PART VI
Holland:
Disaster at Arnhem

☆34☆

THE ALLIES REMAINED virtually stalemated in Normandy, incurring ghastly casualties. By July 10, the total had passed fifty thousand. Tempers frayed in the Allied high command. Eisenhower, under great pressure from Washington and London, tactfully exhorted Montgomery and Bradley to get moving. They, in turn, conceived a one-two punch with a brand-new feature: the use of mass bombing attacks on a narrow front to blast a corridor in the enemy lines. Montgomery would strike first at Caen as a diversion; Bradley would strike second with all the forces he could mass from an area near the recently captured St. Lô.

Montgomery massed Dempsey's Second Army and jumped off on July 18. Some two thousand Allied heavy and medium bombers dropped eight thousand tons of bombs into the German front lines. It was a shattering blow, and Dempsey at first advanced smartly, capturing his D-day objective, Caen. But by the second day he had slowed to a crawl, then stopped, obstructed by the many bomb craters and determined German resistance; heavy rains had turned the battlefield into a quagmire. The diversion at Caen had been costly. Montgomery incurred four thousand casualties and lost a third of his fifteen hundred tanks and not a little prestige.[1]

Bradley was primed to jump off on the second day of Montgomery's offensive, July 19, but foul weather grounded the bombers and delayed Bradley's attack until July 24. Bad weather continued to haunt Bradley, and the attack had to be delayed another agonizing twenty-four hours to July 25. That day, in clear weather, 2,430 heavy and medium bombers and fighter-bombers dropped four thousand tons of bombs into a five-mile-square area immediately in front of Collins' reinforced VII Corps, which Bradley had designated to spearhead the breakout. Owing to a misguided Air Force attack plan and poor execution, many bombs fell short into friendly lines, killing 111 soldiers and wounding 490. Among the dead was General Lesley McNair, whose body was thrown sixty feet in the air and mangled beyond recognition.[2]

The Army's anger at the Air Force for this botched job—and the killing of the revered Lesley McNair—was unrestrained. Most of the anger—and blame —focused on Leigh-Mallory, who was already heartily disliked throughout most of the American Army (notwithstanding Eisenhower's continuing defense of him). Bradley, and others, could scarcely wait for implementation of a prearranged plan that would abolish the OVERLORD tactical air command (SHAEF would thenceforth directly command tactical air) and force Leigh-Mallory's reassignment. Brereton was also harshly criticized. Many would construe his "demotion" to commander of FAAA as punishment for the foul-up, but, in fact, Eisenhower had appointed Brereton to FAAA on July 16—nine days earlier.[3]*

Despite the fouled-up bombing attack, Bradley achieved his punch-through, which would go down in history as "the St. Lô breakout." Joe Collins and his VII Corps led the way, breaking the costly seven-week stalemate and earning a famous niche in Army history. Behind Collins, George Patton activated his Third Army, absorbing Middleton's VIII Corps, which promptly swung around into Brittany, now nearly devoid of regular German forces except for those which were withdrawing into the ports of Brest, St. Malo, Lorient and St. Nazaire for last-ditch stands. The American Army had, at last, gotten out of the hedgerows and trenches and commenced the wide-open mechanized warfare for which it had been structured and trained. As planned, Eisenhower moved his SHAEF headquarters to France. Bradley, elevated to command 12th Army Group, which consisted of Courtney Hodges' First Army, Patton's Third Army and Simpson's soon-to-arrive Ninth Army, was now on a par with Montgomery.

The Allies had assumed that once a breakout had been achieved in Normandy, Hitler would commence withdrawing his forces and make a firm defensive stand at the Seine River. The Allied counterplan was thus to race at top speed for the Seine and grab bridgeheads on the east bank before the Germans could get defenses organized. Along the way, the Allied armies would encircle and annihilate whatever retreating Germans they could.

That was the textbook solution. But Hitler took personal charge of the western front. On August 6, he ordered his weary, understrength divisions to launch an unorthodox counterattack on Hodges' First Army at Mortain. Alerted to this attack at the last minute by the code breakers, Bradley, in a brilliant series of maneuvers, easily absorbed it and countered with an opportunistic, short enveloping plan designed to trap the Germans near Argentan/Falaise between his own and Montgomery's forces. Owing to the slow advance of Crerar's First Canadian Army, and other factors, the Allies were not able to close the jaws of the trap, and about fifty thousand German stragglers escaped through the "Falaise gap" to reach the Seine and beyond. Even so, the Allies inflicted such a crushing and decisive defeat on the Germans in Normandy that Hitler was unable to mount a textbook defense at the Seine. France lay wide open, all the way to the German border.[5]

In the wake of this unanticipated victory in Normandy, the Allied high command fell into serious dispute about the next step. All agreed that the Germans should be pursued as rapidly and forcefully as logistical support would permit, but there was a deep difference of opinion about exactly how this should be done.[6]

The original OVERLORD plan had envisioned a stop at the Seine, a long buildup, then a hard slugging march through France to Germany. In that plan, Montgomery's two armies (Dempsey's Second British and Crerar's First Cana-

* After his command was dissolved, Leigh-Mallory was killed in a plane crash on the way to a new assignment, in India.[4]

dian) would drive toward Germany, staying north of the vast, nearly impenetrable terrain known as the Ardennes, while Bradley's two armies (Hodges' First and Patton's Third) would drive south of the Ardennes toward the Saar and Frankfurt. After punching into Germany, Bradley's forces would then circle north to the Ruhr area and join Montgomery's forces for a climactic annihilation of the German armies.

Montgomery now demanded a sweeping change in the strategy. He proposed that all four Allied armies be placed under his command for a single narrow "full-blooded" thrust into Germany via a route considerably north of the Ardennes. This plan would concentrate Allied force and resources, Montgomery argued, and at the same time accomplish two new, urgent missions: eliminate the new, threatening German V-2 ballistic-missile sites on the North Sea coast and gain Antwerp for an Allied supply port.

Bradley agreed on the need to knock out the V-2 sites and gain Antwerp, but he strongly disagreed with Montgomery's concept of a "single thrust" into Germany itself. Bradley thought the plan technically "crazy." Nor did he believe the American public would tolerate a British general in exclusive control of all ground forces when American troops so greatly outnumbered the British. He agreed that Montgomery should be provided additional forces but insisted that the second thrust, to the south of the Ardennes, be kept in the plan, even if on a reduced scale.

It fell to Eisenhower to make the choice. Basically he was in agreement with Bradley, but to mollify Montgomery he produced a compromise which satisfied neither general. In fact, his decision infuriated Montgomery and led to a serious fissure in the high command. Eisenhower rejected Montgomery's "full-blooded" thrust concept but decreed that Montgomery, who would be granted priority for gasoline and ammo, would go farther north of the Ardennes than originally contemplated, in order to knock out the V-2s and capture Antwerp. To assist Montgomery's expanded mission, Hodges' First Army would be routed north, rather than south of the Ardennes (but not under Montgomery's absolute operational control). At the same time, Patton's Third Army, restricted to a lower priority on resources, would drive south of the Ardennes toward the Saar, according to the original OVERLORD plan.

During the Normandy stalemate, the St. Lô breakout, the battle to close the "Falaise gap," and the debate over strategy, the Allies did not mount further airborne operations in Normandy. The reasons were several.

● Bradley's decision to prolong the utilization of the 101st Division and the 82nd Division in Normandy. When the two shattered divisions reached England in mid-July, it was estimated that it would take seventy-five days to restaff them for combat. Owing to a little-known parachute-glider replacement center Ridgway and Taylor had established in England in advance of Normandy, the restaffing time was cut in half. Even so, neither division was fully ready for combat operations before mid-August.

● Montgomery's similar decision to prolong the utilization of the British 6th Airborne Division in his sector. The 6th Division was not released and returned to England until late August. By then, it was also shattered and, owing to limited British manpower and training facilities, it would take several months to restaff it for combat.

● The decision of the Combined Chiefs to temporarily shift about one third of all IX Troop Carrier Command aircraft to Italy for airborne operations in support of DRAGOON, the controversial subsidiary Allied landing in southern France on August 15.

● Bradley's decision to continue utilizing IX Troop Carrier Command aircraft for emergency hauling of gasoline and ammo to the front lines in France and evacuating the wounded.

In spite of these restrictions, requests and demands for airborne operations in support of OVERLORD continued through the summer. The G-3s at all levels churned out mountains of plans. In all, about a half-dozen major airborne operations were conceived, only to be canceled for one reason or another.

The first airborne operation to receive serious consideration after NEPTUNE was a proposed attack on one of several seaports—Quiberon Bay, St. Malo or Brest—in Brittany. Apparently this plan was conceived by Eisenhower himself during the Normandy stalemate, when he was desperately seeking any idea, however rash. St. Malo seemed the best bet for a breakout. Eisenhower knew from code breaking that the Germans had "thinned out" the area. His plan was to drop all the available airborne reserves (the British 1st Airborne Division and perhaps the Polish Airborne Brigade) on St. Malo in coordination with an amphibious landing of an American infantry division. He believed such an Allied force could envelop St. Malo (providing the Allies an additional seaport), then advance toward the German rear at Avranches, possibly creating a breakthrough on Bradley's right flank.

The St. Malo idea—like the "Rome job"—was freighted with risk. The British 1st Airborne Division had been reconstituted on arrival from the Mediterranean. The majority of its personnel had not seen combat; the Polish Brigade had no combat experience whatsoever. St. Malo was deep behind German lines. Should the drop or the amphibious landing miscarry in some manner (as seemed highly possible, based on the Normandy experience), it would be difficult to rescue the scattered paratroopers. Logistical support of a combined British-American operation utilizing differing weapons and ammo would have presented formidable difficulties. An attack at the German rear could well have invited instant encirclement and piecemeal annihilation. Nonetheless, the planning for the proposed Brittany operations progressed far enough to warrant code names: HANDS UP for Quiberon Bay; BENEFICIARY for the likeliest target, St. Malo; SWORDHILT for Brest. Perhaps fortunately, the plans were discarded when Joe Collins broke through at St. Lô.[7]

The second airborne operation of the summer—support of DRAGOON—was the only operation that proceeded as planned, but it heavily drained FAAA of resources. On July 13, Paul Williams and a small planning staff left for Italy to lay the groundwork. Eventually Williams was assigned 413 troop-carrier aircraft (most of the 50th and 53rd wings) and about six hundred glider pilots from FAAA. These joined forces in Italy with the 51st Wing, which had been retained in the Mediterranean, giving Williams a total force of 526 airplanes and some 450 Waco and about 50 Horsa gliders.[8]

Owing in part to this large commitment of FAAA resources, the DRAGOON airborne operation was followed closely by Ridgway and other ETO airborne commanders. In an indirect way, Ridgway had a considerable stake in DRAGOON. A heavy loss of the loaned aircraft could seriously restrict contemplated ETO airborne operations. Another botched drop might tarnish the reputation of the airborne forces and discourage further use of such troops in the ETO.

DRAGOON was to be carried out by Patton's old outfit, the U.S. Seventh Army, now commanded by Alexander M. (Sandy) Patch, a West Pointer and veteran of the Pacific. His principal striking force was to be the VI Corps (3rd, 36th and 45th infantry divisions), commanded by the able Lucian Truscott, to be followed up by six French divisions (one of them armored), later to be organized as the First French Army. The two armies would subsequently be assigned to the American 6th Army Group, commanded by Jacob L. (Jake) Devers, and they would strike northeastward through the Rhone Valley toward the Saar.

The Seventh Army would come ashore on the rugged, mountainous Côte d'Azur, between Toulon and Cannes. This exotic resort area was held by the German Nineteenth Army, composed of eight divisions—seven infantry and one panzer. On paper, that appeared to be formidable opposition, but the Allies knew from code breaking that these divisions were woefully undermanned and probably unreliable, composed in part of Russian and East European defectors and other non-Reich personnel. There was little or no air opposition. By now Bradley had broken out at St. Lô and the Allies were trying to close the "Falaise gap." The code breakers indicated that Hitler would not fight for southern France. When Sandy Patch struck the Riviera, the likelihood was that the Germans would withdraw toward the homeland, that the invasion would quickly turn into a long chase up the Rhone Valley.[9]

The airborne operations in DRAGOON, like those in Sicily and Normandy, were principally designed to block counterattacks against the landing forces on the beach. For this purpose, Sandy Patch pulled together a motley collection of miscellaneous Allied airborne forces in the Mediterranean which in aggregate amounted to a full airborne division. These were the British 2nd Parachute Brigade (left behind when the 1st British Airborne Division moved to England); the American 517 Parachute Infantry Regiment (which had come independently to Italy more or less to replace Tucker's 504); and three American airborne battalions: Bill Yarborough's 509th; the 550th Glider Battalion and the 551st Parachute Battalion. The British brigade and Yarborough's 509 were hardened combat veterans. The 517 had been baptized with several weeks of ground combat while attached to the 36th Division in Italy. The 550th and 551st, which had recently arrived independently in Italy, were green. In all, there were nine battalions of airborne infantry, plus artillery and other units, comprising about nine thousand men—sixty-five hundred paratroopers and twenty-five hundred gliderists.[10]

The American paratroopers would be supported by only two artillery outfits, both parachute. One was the 463rd, commanded by John Cooper, which had been created from Ridgway's old 456th. It had fought long and hard at Cassino and Anzio, and had spearheaded the Anzio breakout and the liberation of Rome. The other was the 460th, commanded by Raymond L. Cato, which had recently arrived in Italy, "mated" with the 517th Parachute Regiment, and had seen only limited combat.[11]

Command of this potpourri, christened the 1st Airborne Task Force, was given to an extraordinary soldier from outside the "airborne establishment." He was Brigadier General Robert T. Frederick (West Point, 1928), until then head of the joint American-Canadian 1st Special Service Force, a commando-like outfit which had engaged in numerous hair-raising "special operations," including some parachute drops and, more recently, the battles at Anzio and Rome.†[13]

Launched by moonlight in the early hours before the invasion, on August 15, DRAGOON airborne operations were directed at three DZs in the vicinity of Le Muy, a road and rail hub in rugged terrain ten miles behind the invasion beach. The first assault—396 aircraft—carried fifty-six hundred American and British paratroopers and towed a token force of seventy gliders. Yarborough's 509th, mated with Cooper's 463rd Parachute Artillery, led the assault. Next came the 517th Regiment, commanded by Rupert D. Graves (West Point, 1924), mated with Ray Cato's 460th Parachute Artillery. Last came the British 2nd Airborne Brigade, commanded by Brigadier C. H. V. Pritchard.[14]

There was little or no enemy opposition, but, once again, bad flying weather wrecked the enterprise. The nine planeloads of pathfinders arrived to find the Riviera densely shrouded in fog. Only one of three teams managed to find a DZ and set up a Eureka. The oncoming armada of troop-carrier aircraft, mostly dropping blind, dumped paratroopers into the fog all over the Riviera from Toulon to Cannes. Despite some lucky drops, the troop-carrier historian calculated that 60 percent of the American and 40 percent of the British paratroopers landed too far from the DZs for the drops to be considered "successful." Thus, on the whole, he wrote, the paratrooper assault was only "fifty percent successful." Half the gliders (thirty-five Horsas) were ordered back; the thirty-five C-47s tugging Wacos circled, waiting for the fog to lift, then cut their

† Later in the war, when Frederick was named commander of the 45th Infantry Division, some war correspondents would mistakenly describe him as the "youngest major general to command a division since the Civil War." In fact, he was merely a close runner-up to Jim Gavin, who was born about one week earlier than Frederick but was named to command the 82nd some months before Frederick commanded the 45th. He may well have established another record, however. During World War II he received a total of eight Purple Hearts as a result of eight separate, reportable and verifiable battle wounds.[12]

gliders loose at about 9:30 A.M. Most found the LZ, but the landings were disastrous.

Later in the afternoon of D day, there was a second airborne assault. By that time the fog had cleared. The 551st Parachute Battalion, commanded by Wood G. Joerg (West Point, 1937), made a nearly perfect drop at 6 P.M. This was the first American combat parachute drop in Europe to be carried out in daylight, and although it was conducted against slight enemy opposition, its success would reinforce the case for daylight parachute drops in the ETO. Next came 370 gliders, including the thirty-five Horsas that had turned back that morning. In the Wacos was the reinforced 551st Glider Infantry Battalion, commanded by Edward I. Sachs (West Point, 1930). Owing to several operational foul-ups, all 370 gliders arrived at the two LZs at almost exactly the same time and another great glider fiasco ensued. All but a few crashed into houses, walls, trees, ditches or "Rommel's asparagus." Eleven glider pilots were killed and many were injured; one hundred glider troopers were severely injured but, almost miraculously, none were killed. Later, fewer than thirty gliders were found to be salvageable. Fortunately, in all these D-day airborne operations, only one C-47 was lost.[15]

The DRAGOON airborne operation was yet another fiasco. Although landing injuries had been gratifyingly slight, the initial main paratrooper drops in DRAGOON and the late-afternoon D-day glider missions were disastrously poor. Had there been significant enemy opposition in the air or on land, a major catastrophe might well have ensued. However, the Air Force managed to artfully "cover up" these disasters. Paul Williams, for example, entered an official report claiming the parachute drops were "85 to 90 percent accurate." His estimate was accepted as gospel for at least eleven years.‡ Thus, by this Air Force sleight of hand, DRAGOON encouraged rather than discouraged further airborne operations in the ETO, and the final outcome proved a salubrious one for Ridgway (and FAAA), who did not learn the real story for months.[17]

After a few stiff engagements which cost the American and British paratrooper units a few dead and some wounded, the Germans collapsed and retreated, and the long Seventh Army chase began. The American elements of Frederick's 1st Airborne Task Force (517, 509, 550, 551 and artillery battalions) were left behind to occupy the Riviera and to establish a defensive line in the mountains behind Monaco to block attacks by German forces based in northern Italy. The paratrooper missions were not unduly arduous or bloody and the men jokingly dubbed their war "the Champagne Campaign." There were two senior airborne command casualties in DRAGOON and the aftermath. In the jump, the 463rd artillery commander, John Cooper, broke his leg

‡ The official Air Force history, published in 1951, asserted that the pathfinders had been dropped "with great accuracy on the DZs as well as the LZs" and that, as a result, the main body of aircraft "effectively overcame the adverse weather conditions" and "only twenty aircraft missed their DZs by an appreciable distance," resulting in a "well-executed" operation. The historian commented: "Airborne operations had come a long way since those unhappy days on Sicily."[16]

and was temporarily replaced by his exec, Stuart M. Seaton. In a battle after the jump, Yarborough's new exec, John H. Apperson, was killed by a land mine and replaced by a veteran 509 officer, Edmund J. Tomasik. In mid-October, when Yarborough left the battalion to attend an abbreviated course at the Command and General Staff School, Tomasik became the 509's commander.*

After Bradley broke out at St. Lô on July 25, and before Hitler ordered the disastrous counterattack at Mortain on August 6, which led to Bradley's short envelopment at Argentan-Falaise, Bradley had been thinking of a long envelopment that would reach beyond the Seine. His rough idea was that an American armored force (six divisions) led by Patton's Third Army would drive east to the Seine, wheel east of Paris, then veer northwest to the English Channel at Dieppe. Bradley believed this stroke would be a "war-winning drive."[19]

As he planned it, the maneuver would leave a seventy-five-mile gap between Orléans and Paris through which the Germans might retreat or counterattack. Bradley wanted the FAAA to plug that gap with all available paratroopers, who would seize roads and bridges and help Patton's tanks along. The proposed airborne operation was code-named TRANSFIGURE. Eisenhower agreed with Bradley that, in the words of the troop-carrier historian, the envelopment could be "the blow most likely to end the war in Europe."[20]

Planning for TRANSFIGURE commenced in earnest on about August 6. It was decided that Browning's 1 Airborne Corps would be employed, consisting mostly of British-Canadian forces: the British 1st Airborne Division, the Polish Airborne Brigade, the 52nd Scottish Division (to be airlanded in the airhead), plus a miscellany of British support forces. One American airborne division would be added. Since, on August 6, Taylor's 101st was farther along in restaffing, and Ridgway was in process of turning the 82nd over to Gavin, the 101st was chosen for the mission, on Ridgway's recommendation. Owing to the shortage of troop-carrier aircraft (DRAGOON had reduced FAAA to about 870 C-47s), two lifts would be required. The 101st and the 52nd Scottish Division would go on the first; the British 1st Airborne and the Polish Brigade and other units on the second.[21]

FAAA proceeded with TRANSFIGURE planning at a feverish pace. By August 13, all troops had been moved to airfields and "sealed in." By that time, however, Bradley had improvised the short envelopment to trap the Germans in the Carentan-Falaise pocket and TRANSFIGURE was put on hold to await the outcome. (FAAA conceived several airborne operations to assist Bradley in trapping the Germans in the short envelopment, but these were not utilized.) In the ensuing battle, Bradley sent Patton's armored forces wheeling east toward Orléans, Chartres and Dreux. These forces, facing scant or no opposition,

---

* Yarborough later returned to the Mediterranean Theater to command the nonairborne 473rd Regimental Combat Team in the fight to clear northern Italy. In the postwar years, he was a founder of the Army's Special Forces (Green Berets) and rose to the rank of three-star general.[18]

made astonishing speed, and by August 16 had overrun the proposed DZs and LZs for TRANSFIGURE; the next day, the airborne operation was canceled.

Then another problem arose: a shortage of gasoline and ammo. The Germans had demolished the docks in Cherbourg. Army engineers, working a twenty-four-hour schedule, were clearing the wreckage, but it would take time to make the port usable. Bradley was still relying on Utah and Omaha beaches for his supply lines. The laying of the cross-Channel gasoline pipeline ("PLUTO") had been delayed by the June 21 storm and other factors. Bradley urgently needed gasoline and ammo. He asked that they be brought from England by air, and Eisenhower approved the request. On August 12, SHAEF ordered that one thousand tons a day be airlifted to Bradley. Two days later, August 14, SHAEF raised the quota to two thousand tons a day.[22]

These requests landed on FAAA like bombshells. Since an (overloaded) C-47 could carry only two tons, Bradley's two-thousand-ton daily quota would require one thousand C-47 missions a day. This meant that at least five hundred of FAAA's eight hundred seventy available C-47s would have to be diverted for the purpose—each flying two daily missions. Therefore, until the 412 aircraft loaned out for DRAGOON were returned (on about August 25), it would not be possible to mount a significant airborne operation; nor would there be sufficient C-47s available to conduct vital airborne training.

FAAA's chief of staff, Floyd Parks, flew to Bradley's 12th Army Group headquarters to discuss this conflict. Until then, Bradley had been the best high-level friend the airborne forces had, but now, faced with a choice of supplies or paratroopers, Bradley opted for supplies. The "Falaise gap" operation had created a gasoline-and-ammo emergency that Bradley could not solve without an airlift. Parks sought a compromise: some airborne operations, some supply operations. But Bradley was only reluctantly willing to listen. He complained that the C-47s were diverted for too long to prepare and mount airborne operations; that the planes often stood idle for days. Parks assured Bradley that in the present emergency they might be able to conduct an airborne operation in three days at most, then return the planes to supply missions. He also suggested that other planes—bombers—might be substituted for the supply missions during that time. Bradley was understandably skeptical. He did not slam the door on all airborne operations, but he held to his position that he must have two thousand tons a day during the emergency. If Parks could find a way to supply his quota and also mount airborne operations, Bradley would welcome them.[23]

After Eisenhower had compromised the bitter dispute between Montgomery and Bradley over how best to pursue the Germans beyond the Seine, all four Allied armies drew abreast of the river on or about August 25. Montgomery, with Dempsey's Second Army and Crerar's First, would go flat out for Antwerp, supported on the right flank by Hodges' First Army, which would now go north of the Ardennes. Patton's Third Army, reduced to the lowest priority on supplies, would go south of the Ardennes.[24]

Montgomery requested airborne operations in support of his dash from the

Seine to Antwerp. FAAA first proposed a drop near Calais at Boulogne (operation BOXER) to seal off the German Fifteenth Army, but Montgomery rejected it on August 26 as too far off his main line of drive. FAAA then proposed a bigger bite: a drop at Tournai, Belgium (operation LINNET), then believed to be well in advance of Montgomery's and Hodges' fast-moving armies. Montgomery (and Eisenhower) approved LINNET, and D day was set for September 3. Eisenhower ordered that most of the C-47s supplying Patton with gasoline be reassigned to LINNET, together with the 50th and 53rd wings, now returned from DRAGOON.[25]

LINNET would be by far the largest single airborne operation of the war. Three airborne divisions and the Polish Brigade were placed on alert to carry it out. These were Gavin's 82nd, Taylor's 101st and the British 1st, now commanded by Robert L. (Roy) Urquhart. Urquhart had taken over the division from Eric Down, an experienced paratrooper, in early January 1944, when Down was sent to the Far East to raise an Indian airborne division. Urquhart was a distinguished ground soldier, but he knew little of airborne operations and was prone to airsickness. He had asked Boy Browning for time off to take parachute training, but Browning cavalierly denied the request, saying Urquhart was "too big" and too old for parachuting. (He was forty-two.)[26]

Ridgway had assumed that since two of the three divisions in LINNET would be American, he and his XVIII Airborne Corps would command the operation. He was wrong. The job went to Boy Browning and his 1 Airborne Corps. There were probably two principal reasons for the choice. First, since the operation was conceived mainly to support Montgomery's British forces, a British airborne commander seemed logical. Second, Browning was senior to Ridgway in job (deputy commander of FAAA) and rank (lieutenant general) and may have insisted on the job. A third reason may have been that Ridgway had antagonized Brereton. Ridgway later wrote: "I felt in my heart that we could do a better job of commanding that operation than could anyone else, and I imagine I expressed those views, in private, with some fervor." After he was informed that Browning would command, Ridgway, as he wrote later, "harbored a sense of deep disappointment, if not of resentment."[27]

It was not wounded vanity that led to Ridgway's "resentment." The Americans were deeply concerned over Browning's appointment, first because in spite of all they had done to prevent it, the British were "taking over" American troops, and secondly, because they had real doubts about Browning's battlefield competence. Browning had risen high in the British airborne establishment, but he had not ever commanded major airborne forces in combat. In North Africa, after TORCH, he had become a staff adviser to Eisenhower; Hoppy Hopkinson had commanded the British 1st Airborne Division in Sicily and on the Italian mainland until he was killed in action. Richard Gale had commanded the British 6th Airborne Division in Normandy. LINNET would, in effect, be Browning's first major command in combat and, notwithstanding his elegance, charm, intelligence and fame, there was a possibility that he would cave in under pressure. Moreover, the Americans were not impressed by Browning's 1 Airborne Corps staff. They had a feeling that in contrast to

Ridgway's combat-hardened XVIII Airborne Corps staff, Browning's staff was "pickup" and "makeshift."[28]

When Bradley got wind of LINNET and learned that his airlift would be curtailed to support it, he was furious. By that time, Hodges' First Army (on Montgomery's right) was bearing down on Tournai at high speed. Bradley telephoned Eisenhower to request that LINNET be canceled (and the C-47s returned to supply missions), because, as Bradley said, "we'll be there before you can pull it." But Eisenhower, committed to giving greater support to Montgomery's sector, turned Bradley's plea aside. In the end, Bradley proved to be right. On the evening of September 2, Hodges' forces, slightly leading Dempsey's, reached the outskirts of Tournai. At 10:24 P.M., Montgomery ordered Brereton to cancel LINNET. Bradley later angrily complained that the canceled LINNET operation had cost him at least five thousand tons of supplies.[29]†

Having anticipated a cancellation of LINNET, Brereton had an alternate plan ready—LINNET II—which could be executed virtually on a moment's notice with no change in forces. This was a drop in front of Hodges' First Army near Aachen. Although LINNET II had been hastily conceived and was an alternate plan, it was in reality one of the great intuitive ideas for winning the war. The Germans had been routed in Normandy, and the chase through France had been spectacularly fast and easy. Montgomery, with uncustomary speed, was closing on Antwerp, his principal objective. On his right, Hodges' First Army, moving with equal speed and ease, was approaching Liège. South of the Ardennes, Patton's Third Army, which had captured one million gallons of German gasoline, was blazing toward Nancy, Metz . . . and the Saar. On Patton's lower right flank, Jake Devers' 6th Army Group, spearheaded by Patch's Seventh Army, was dashing up the Rhone Valley, aiming generally for Strasbourg.[31]

Eisenhower now believed that the climactic moment of the war was at hand, that with the correct Allied moves Germany could be defeated in a matter of mere weeks. Much influenced by Bradley, Eisenhower believed that the correct moves were now to de-emphasize Montgomery's northerly thrust, since he had reached Antwerp, and to throw the mass of power behind Hodges' First Army and Patton's Third Army. Thus, Hodges could smash through the "Aachen gap," to the north of the Ardennes, and Patton could smash through the "Metz gap," to the south of the Ardennes.[32]

One way to put greater power into Hodges' First Army drive was to approve LINNET II, with Ridgway and his XVIII Airborne Corps in command of the

---

† In his war memoir *A Soldier's Story,* Bradley grumbled that FAAA "showed an astonishing faculty for devising missions that were never needed." Moreover, he was furious over Brereton's inclination to appoint Browning to command these proposed operations. Referring to Browning's appointment to command an airborne operation earlier that summer, Bradley's aide, Chester B. Hansen, who mirrored Bradley's thinking, angrily wrote in his diary: "Christ, why don't they use Ridgway [as the commander]? He's a fighter and knows more about airborne than all of them."[30]

proposed drop of three airborne divisions (82nd, 101st, British 1st). These fresh, strong, elite forces might seize or crack through the Siegfried Line at Aachen, giving Hodges' tiring troops a tremendous psychological lift and opening the door for a First Army dash (possibly led by the 82nd and 101st divisions) to the Rhine River at Cologne. They might also create a fortified airhead into which C-47s could bring gasoline and ammo for the First Army, which, despite the higher priority, was now low on both, owing to the speed of the advance. A First Army dash into Cologne, in turn, might well unhinge the growing German resistance in front of Patton's Third Army, enabling him to punch through the Siegfried Line in the Saar and advance to Frankfurt.‡

At first Eisenhower decided to launch LINNET II in support of Hodges. But when Montgomery heard about it from Bradley in a meeting at Dempsey's CP at Amiens on the afternoon of September 3, he flew into a rage so towering that it threatened to wreck the Allied high command. In a blistering, tactless, nearly insubordinate cable to Eisenhower, Montgomery said, in effect, that Eisenhower was welching on his earlier promises to support his northeasterly drive to the fullest; that it would be a terrible mistake to throw further support behind Hodges and Patton; that to win the war the mass of resources should be placed behind him for a single thrust into Germany from his sector.[34]

Beyond doubt, news of Montgomery's forceful rebellion soon reached Boy Browning. Brereton had already ordered Browning to launch LINNET II on the following day, September 4. But now Browning began to balk and cavil, arguing for a postponement which would have worked in Montgomery's favor. He argued that LINNET II was being mounted in too great a rush, that there were not sufficient reconnaissance photos and maps of the Aachen area. Brereton, perhaps goaded by SHAEF, insisted nonetheless that LINNET II go as ordered. Browning, firmly holding his ground, threatened the greatest possible bureaucratic reprisal: he and "his division commanders" would protest in writing.[35]

Brereton, now in a towering rage himself, telephoned Ridgway and briefed him on Browning's attitude. He asked Ridgway if it were true that Gavin and Taylor would protest LINNET II in writing. Ridgway, Brereton later wrote, felt certain they would not, that they would carry out whatever orders they received. Brereton then informed Ridgway to stand by to assume command of LINNET II, that he was relieving Browning of command. Learning of this, and perhaps believing a dramatic stroke on his part would further help Montgomery, Browning submitted his resignation.[36]

Eisenhower now faced a grave command decision. Although LINNET II was not the direct cause of the crisis (the causes were far deeper), the campaign

---

‡ FAAA generated four other plans for supporting Hodges: NAPLES I, a drop east of the Siegfried Line; NAPLES II, a bridgehead over the Rhine at Cologne; MILAN I, an attack on the Siegfried Line at Trier; MILAN II, a Rhine bridgehead near Coblenz. In addition, FAAA generated at least two plans to support Patton: CHOKER I, a breach of the Siegfried Line at Saarbrücken; CHOKER II, a Rhine bridgehead near Worms.[33]

would become a cause célèbre. If Eisenhower approved LINNET II over Montgomery's objections, it would amount to a direct slap in Montgomery's face and could possibly precipitate a complete breakdown in the Allied high command. Determined to avoid that dire consequence, Eisenhower waffled and at nearly the eleventh hour (9:25 P.M., September 3), he canceled LINNET II. Afterward, in a tense face-to-face talk with Montgomery, Eisenhower explained his new strategy. Greater resources would now be placed behind the Hodges and Patton drives on Aachen and Metz; under no circumstances could Montgomery expect to have all Allied resources placed behind his northerly drive.[37]

In the aftermath of this crisis, Brereton and Browning, both apparently bending with the political winds, had an amicable chat. Browning withdrew his resignation, whereupon Brereton named him to command a smaller airborne operation, COMET, to be conducted by Roy Urquhart's 1st Airborne Division and the Polish Parachute Brigade, commanded by Stanislaw Sosabowski. The purpose of COMET was to secure a bridge across the Rhine River near Arnhem on the afternoon of September 6 or the morning of the 7th, opening the way for Dempsey's Second Army, which was now driving through Antwerp, to establish a bridgehead over the Rhine north of the Ruhr. Since Browning's 1 Airborne Corps staff had already carried out studies of the approaches to Arnhem, and COMET was designed to be in direct support of Montgomery, Browning now offered no objections. Nor did Ridgway, whose troops were not initially involved.[38]

Thus, after a long, hot, frustrating summer which had seen one mission after another canceled for this reason or that, FAAA at last had an assignment that might become reality. It would quickly grow in size and scope and would turn into one of the greatest Allied disasters of World War II.

☆35☆

THE VICTORY IN NORMANDY and the spectacularly easy dash from the Seine to Antwerp had created a dangerous optimism in the Allied high command. The sense of urgency was slipping away. There was a universal feeling that the war had been won, that Germany would probably collapse at any hour. Against this possibility, FAAA even produced a plan for an airborne operation, TALISMAN (later renamed ECLIPSE) to quickly seize airfields in the Berlin area should the Nazi government unconditionally surrender or fly apart. Ridgway would be Commanding General, Berlin.[1]

Overly confident and perhaps too preoccupied with command politics, Montgomery now made what Bradley, and many military historians, considered to be two of the greatest tactical errors of the war:

● On September 4, Montgomery stopped the forward drive of Dempsey's 30 Corps at Antwerp. At that time the Rhine River—Arnhem—lay only about a hundred miles away and there were then no significant German forces between Antwerp and Arnhem. Montgomery had ample stocks of gasoline and ammo. Brian Horrocks, 30 Corps commander, later wrote that if Montgomery had not stopped him, he would have "smashed through" to Arnhem and crossed the Rhine, "and the whole course of the war in Europe might have been changed." The pause, which gradually slipped into a prolonged delay, gave the Germans time to throw troops into the path of 30 Corps and to strengthen defenses at Arnhem.

● Montgomery also failed to properly exploit the capture of Antwerp. The city lies some sixty miles inland from the North Sea. Between the city docks and the open sea is the Scheldt, an estuary cluttered with a maze of islands through which the shipping channels thread. On September 4, the Scheldt was held by German forces. That day, Montgomery had sufficient forces at Antwerp to both quickly clear the Scheldt and also speed Horrocks' 30 Corps to Arnhem. But Montgomery did not clear the estuary. His failure to do so enabled large elements of the German Fifteenth Army (boxed in at Calais, Dunkirk and other Channel ports by the Canadian First Army) to evacuate and move by boat and barge to the Scheldt and to reinforce the thin German forces there, especially those on the large island of Walcheren. It would take a major campaign to dislodge them. "Because of this blunder," Bradley wrote, "Antwerp, captured on September 4 as a matter of highest strategic priority, would not become available to us until three months later—November 28."[2]●

---

* Later, when the error was realized, Montgomery proposed a subsidiary airborne assault (INFATUATE) on Walcheren. However, FAAA opposed the operation, because the Walcheren Island terrain was unsuitable for glider landings and also because FAAA feared that an unacceptable number of paratroopers and gliderists would be accidentally dropped into the water.[3]

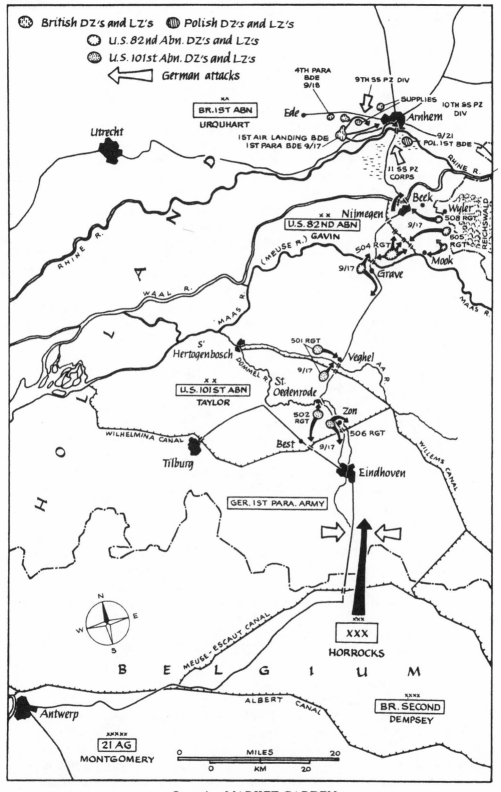

Operation MARKET-GARDEN

The long, easy chase was over. The badly mangled German divisions that had escaped Normandy were halting short of the Rhine River, regrouping and refitting to defend the homeland. Inside the Third Reich, old men and young boys and even sailors and airmen were rushing forward to fill the depleted ranks of the divisions. Whatever tanks and artillery could be spared from the Reich reserves, or from the constricting Russian front, were turned around to face the Allied armies pressing from the west.

The Germans foresaw that Montgomery's next drive would be mounted toward Arnhem and even guessed it might include paratroopers. They sought desperately to stop him with a hasty buildup of strength between Antwerp and Arnhem. Field Marshal Walter Model, commanding Army Group B, established his headquarters in Arnhem. Two armies were assigned him: the retreating Fifteenth, digging into the Scheldt or slipping by into Holland; and a new one, the First Parachute, commanded by Kurt Student. The latter, created overnight, was initially composed of two static coastal divisions long based in Holland, the 719th and the 176th. These units were manned, in part, by old men, semi-invalids and convalescents, most of whom had never been in a fight. But within twenty-four hours, Student moved the 6th Parachute Regiment (which had escaped from Normandy) into southern Holland to help block the Antwerp–Arnhem road. Augmenting Student in this area was the II SS Panzer Corps, which had only recently retreated from Normandy to Holland. The corps had been assigned the remnants of four badly mauled—but hurriedly refitted—panzer divisions: the 2nd, the 116th, the 9th SS and the 10th SS. In addition, a battered but spirited retreating infantry division, the 85th, decided on its own to halt on the west side of the Albert Canal.[4]

During this period, the Allied commanders were the beneficiaries of a heavy flow of decoded German messages. As a result, they could see the German buildup in southern Holland on their order-of-battle maps. However, much of the German "threat" was discounted. The two "coastal divisions" would certainly present no problem; the panzer divisions were believed to be shorn of tanks and motorized vehicles and artillery. (There was little or no information on Student's newly improvised First Parachute Army, nor did the code breakers know that elements of the Fifteenth Army were slipping through the Scheldt into Holland.) Besides that, who could believe the Germans would make a stand in southern Holland against the victorious Allied juggernaut? Most likely, intelligence reported, at the first sign of an Allied push toward Arnhem, the Germans would fall back behind the Rhine.[5]

This general attitude may also have led Montgomery to discount the formidable terrain obstacles he faced. There was only one main highway between Antwerp and Arnhem, a sort of raised causeway running through the low, wet, coastal marshland. The road crossed at least seven canals or rivers. If the bridges across these waterways were heavily defended or blown, it would be difficult for 30 Corps to proceed without laborious and time-consuming bridge building. In sum, as Patton tartly observed, the route was one where Horrocks' tanks—on which much depended—were "practically useless" because of the terrain.[6]

Despite these factors, the original Arnhem airborne operation, COMET, proceeded. By September 7, all plans were completed, the British and Polish troops sealed in at airfields and the pilots briefed for a September 8 takeoff. However, forecasts of bad weather forced a postponement to September 9. On September 8, when the strength of the German buildup before Horrocks began to sink home in Montgomery's headquarters, COMET was postponed another twenty-four hours. On September 10, it was officially canceled.[7]

In its place sprang the far more ambitious MARKET-GARDEN. In essence, MARKET was LINNET II overlaid on COMET. As in COMET, the British 1st Airborne Division and the Polish Airborne Brigade would seize the Rhine River bridge at Arnhem, but as in LINNET II, Gavin's 82nd and Taylor's 101st airborne divisions would be added. The Americans would lay what Montgomery called a "carpet" of airborne troops along the Antwerp–Arnhem highway to defend the road and to seize and hold key bridges for the dash of the ground forces.†

Formal planning for MARKET-GARDEN commenced in a fever on September 10. Originally FAAA believed D day would be September 14, but in the face of the German buildup, Montgomery and Dempsey almost immediately increased the scope and strength of the ground phase, which forced a postponement to September 17. The new ground plan, GARDEN, was as follows: Horrocks' 30 Corps would spearhead the drive up the Antwerp–Arnhem road, as originally planned, but now his flanks were to be protected by the British 12 Corps (on the left) and the 8 Corps (on the right). The British 8 Corps had been stripped of its transport and left behind in Normandy in order to fully motorize Montgomery's dash to Antwerp. Before GARDEN could be launched, 8 Corps had to be brought forward, together with thousands of tons of extra gasoline and supplies.[8]

Omar Bradley was not officially notified of MARKET-GARDEN. When he found out about its swelling size and scope, he was livid and at once called Eisenhower to lodge what he later described as a "violent protest." Bradley believed that the grandiose MARKET-GARDEN was, in reality, a clever scheme designed to draw even greater resources to Montgomery's sector at his expense—ultimately so much force would be committed that Eisenhower would be compelled to adopt Montgomery's "single-thrust" strategy simply because the force was already there and moving. Beyond that, Bradley argued, owing to the unfavorable terrain and to the strong and rapid German buildup, the mission was tactically unsound; among other dangers, it could lead to a "gap" between Dempsey's and Hodges' armies, which the Germans could exploit. He urged Eisenhower to cancel MARKET-GARDEN and order Montgomery to concentrate on clearing the Scheldt so that Antwerp could be opened up as an Allied supply port and the escape of the German Fifteenth Army troops into Holland could be cut off.[9]

† The airborne assault was called MARKET; the British ground attack, GARDEN.

Montgomery, however, had another psychological factor working in his favor. On the evening of September 8, the first German V-2 ballistic missiles fell on London. By that time, London had learned to cope with the German V-1 missiles (primitive pilotless drones, the forerunner of today's cruise missiles) by intercepting and shooting them down. However, the new V-2s came in at terrific speed and with no warning and there was no way to intercept and destroy them. The V-2s had not caused much physical damage, but they had terrorized London and the British Government. Churchill had urgently requested that Eisenhower direct Montgomery's armies to "rope off" the V-2 launching areas near Rotterdam and Amsterdam. A strong drive at Arnhem—and beyond—would achieve this new and what was deemed urgent mission.[10]

There was still another important consideration involved. Eisenhower had long before assured Marshall and Arnold that he would employ his expensive, elite airborne army at the first opportunity. Owing mainly to the unexpected speed of the Allied drive through France and Belgium, the opportunities had evaporated one after the other. Now the good summer flying weather was slipping away and the Germans were crumbling. If left entirely to Bradley, who had made it abundantly clear that he preferred airlifted supplies to airlifted troops, there might never be an opportunity to utilize the airborne army.

MARKET-GARDEN provided Eisenhower with what might well be the last opportunity to carry out his promises to Marshall and Arnold. Dismissing Bradley's objections, he gave the operation unstinting support, including the allocation of an extra thousand tons of supplies a day to Montgomery, which was sent forward in trucks stripped from three of Bradley's newly arrived divisions in Normandy (temporarily immobilizing these reinforcements). Bradley later wrote that Eisenhower's decision to give Montgomery all-out support for MARKET-GARDEN was "his gravest tactical error of the war"; that it launched "a massive assault *in the wrong direction* at what was probably the most crucial moment on the German front." (Bradley's italics)[11]

The Arnhem operation grew by leaps and bounds. The final airborne plan, MARKET, envisioned the deployment of a total of nearly forty-five thousand men—about twenty thousand parachutists, fifteen thousand gliderists, and ten thousand airlanded regular infantry, plus massive and continuing airdrops of supplies. The overall plan was this. Urquhart's 1st Airborne Division, reinforced by Sosabowski's Polish Parachute Brigade,‡ would seize Arnhem and the Rhine River bridges there and prepare airstrips to land the British 52nd (Lowlanders) Airlanding Division. Gavin's 82nd Division would land south of Arnhem near Nijmegen and seize key highway bridges in that area. Taylor's 101st Division would land still farther south near Eindhoven, seizing key highway bridges over waterways in that area. While this was being done, the ground phase, GARDEN, would proceed. Horrocks' 30 Corps would spear-

‡ In effect, beefing up the 1st Airborne Division to American airborne divisional strength of four regiments.

head the ground drive up the Antwerp–Arnhem highway to Eindhoven, Nijmegen, then Arnhem, utilizing the key bridges seized by the airborne forces.

There were several weaknesses in the plan. The first and most important one was familiar: an acute shortage of troop-carrier aircraft. The Allies, still basing troop-carrier aircraft at ever more distant bases in England, had nowhere near enough planes to land 45,000 men on D day. At most they could only slightly exceed the NEPTUNE D-day lift of about 18,300 men. Because Brereton ruled that no air crew should fly more than one mission per day, the aircraft shortage thus imposed a requirement for multiple lifts to be carried out over several successive days. Successful follow-up lifts would depend, to a great extent, on continuing good flying weather—a risky assumption in September.

In addition, serious questions were raised about the ground tactics. Boy Browning thought Montgomery might be asking for too big a bite, or as he put it (in a phrase that would become famous), they might be going "a bridge too far." He and Urquhart wanted to drop or glide the British troops close to the Rhine River bridge in Arnhem. But the RAF balked at that, arguing that the flak near the bridge was too heavy and the terrain unsuitable for glider landings. The upshot was that the DZs and LZs were situated six to eight miles west of the Arnhem bridge. When Urquhart told Gavin this, he was appalled and later exclaimed to his G-3, John Norton: "My God, he can't mean it!" Moreover, owing to the shortage of aircraft, Urquhart could land less than half of his division at Arnhem on D day; about half of one glider regiment and all of one parachute regiment, comprising about fifty-one hundred men. The plan was that the glider regiment would be restricted to protecting the airhead, leaving only the parachute regiment for the long dash through the city to the bridge. Inasmuch as the parachute regiment had not been in combat for a very long time and was composed of many green replacements, the Americans in particular worried that the Arnhem force was too slight and too inexperienced for the assigned D-day tasks.[12]

Nor were the American airborne planners satisfied with Montgomery's plan for the deployment of the two American divisions. According to the FAAA deputy chief of staff, Stuart Cutler: "Boy Browning phoned Brereton and gave him the outline of the operation, which he said Montgomery had requested. Brereton called a staff meeting to discuss the plan. The British plan proposed that we break all the battalions of the . . . 101st Division into battalion units and lay a carpet of airborne battalions along the roads that 30 Corps was to advance over. Brereton asked if any of us had an opinion about the plan. I replied—offering strenuous objections to the breaking up of the American divisions into small battalion units, which was a violation of War Department doctrine for airborne forces. Brereton was a pompous 'little' man. He became very angry. He pounded his desk and exclaimed, 'We'll do it the way Montgomery wants it or I'll get new division commanders.' "[13]

Later, having second thoughts in the privacy of his office, Brereton, who was "still angry," asked Cutler to elaborate on his objections. After Cutler had done so, Brereton, backing down, ordered him to get in an airplane and fetch Ridgway and Taylor for the purpose of critiquing the plan. Ridgway and

Taylor "backed me up," Cutler recalled, "so Brereton ordered us to go to my office and draw up an alternate plan." That plan—ultimately approved by Montgomery—resulted in a far more compact drop of the 101st Division and may very well have averted another airborne catastrophe.[14]

Owing to the disastrous parachute drops, glider mishaps and shipping losses or confusion, the airborne artillery of both the 82nd and the 101st in Normandy had been of scant help in the early stages of the battle. In preparation for MARKET-GARDEN, artillery training was intensified and some changes were made in organization, command, weaponry and tactics. Wilbur Griffith's 376th Parachute Artillery was integrated into the 82nd (along with Tucker's 504), giving Gavin two parachute (376 and d'Allessio's 456) and two glider (Todd's 319 and Wright's 320) artillery battalions, a total of four, or one to support each of his four regiments. Taylor would have only what he had had in Normandy: one parachute (the 377th, now commanded by Harry W. Elkins) and two glider (Edward L. Carmichael's 321 and Clarence F. Nelson's 907) battalions. However, Nelson's 907 was converted from 75 mm pack howitzers to 105 mm snub-nose howitzers.

Parachute artillery was subjected to an intense reevaluation. Ever since Sicily, where Taylor and Gavin had had bad luck with both the 456th (wildly scattered) and the 376th (badly mauled by friendly fire), they had tended to view parachute artillery skeptically. In Normandy, Gavin had parachuted in only two pack howitzers of the 456th; Taylor's 377th had received the worst drop in Normandy, so bad that the unit was virtually useless for the first two weeks. Inasmuch as MARKET-GARDEN would be a daylight operation, the odds for a successful artillery drop were better and it would be far easier for the artillerymen to locate the nine separate pieces of their howitzers on the DZs. Even so, Taylor and Gavin still had some strong doubts.

The upshot of the reevaluation was as follows. In Gavin's 82nd, which would jump "deeper" into Holland, Wilbur Griffith's battle-hardened 376th would parachute on D day with the assault paratroopers. D'Allessio's less experienced 456th would come by glider (with pack howitzers fully assembled) on D+1 with the two glider artillery battalions (319, 320). In the 101, which would jump closest to the British 30 Corps and was scheduled to link up on D day, the need for artillery was thought to be less pressing and was scaled back accordingly. Elkins' 377th Parachute Artillery would mostly come by glider, with fully assembled pack howitzers: three batteries (Headquarters, A and C) on D day with the assault forces; one battery (B) by parachute on D+1. The remainder of Taylor's artillery (the 321st and the 907th) would come by glider on D+2.[15]

At the last minute, the 82nd artillery commander, Andy March, had to make an important command change. His exec, Harry Bertsch, a West Pointer, turned up with a medical chit recommending that he not go into Holland. Bertsch had previously won a Silver Star Medal for heroism, but this chit indicated he wanted out and, as one senior artilleryman remembered, it caused a "good bit of ugly scuttlebutt." In any case, it finished Bertsch with the division and he left immediately. March decided that after the jump into Holland, the 376 commander, Wilbur Griffith, would become his new exec, and Robert H. Neptune—who despite his misgivings had survived Normandy without a scratch—would replace Griffith.[16]

Not least among the questions about MARKET was, who would command this largest of all airborne operations? Since the great preponderance of the assault forces would be American, Ridgway again believed an American commander—namely himself—would be appropriate. However, Brereton apparently viewed MARKET as an extension of LINNET and kept Browning in command—with one difference: after all three airborne divisions and the British 52nd Airlanding Division had entered combat, the four-division force would be broken into two airborne corps: the British (and Polish) forces under Browning's 1 Airborne Corps and the two American divisions under Ridgway's XVIII Airborne Corps. Ridgway realized that his role in MARKET would be largely honorary, that his corps would probably enter combat much too late to influence the course of battle. But since his views had already been well advertised, he made no further objections.[17]

Owing to the difficulties of moving the British 8 Corps and the extra supplies for Dempsey forward from Normandy, Montgomery again postponed MARKET-GARDEN D day—to September 23 or (as he said) "possibly" September 26. Eisenhower refused to countenance such a long delay. He sent Bedell Smith to Montgomery's headquarters to insist that MARKET-GARDEN go on time, September 17. While conferring with Montgomery, Smith called attention to the decoded German intercepts indicating that the 9th and 10th SS panzer divisions were locating near Arnhem and urged Montgomery to greatly strengthen the airborne force proposed for the area. However, British intelligence continued to discount these forces and, as Smith recalled it, "Montgomery ridiculed my idea" and "waved my objections airily aside."[18]

Sunday, September 17, was a beautiful fall day, perfect flying weather for airborne operations. That morning, while the vast MARKET aerial armada was preparing for takeoff at twenty-four airfields in England, Ridgway joined the men of Gavin's 82nd Airborne Division, to see them off and wish them well. He "felt a great sense of loss—a deep regret that for the first time this gallant division was going into battle without me."[19]

Not quite. Ridgway had made arrangements to observe the operation from the air in a B-17 bomber flying two hundred feet or so above the troop-carrier serials. Over Holland the weather was good and there was no sign of the German Air Force. What was left of it was held at bay by hundreds of Allied fighter escorts sweeping ahead of the serials. A wave of bombers had also gone ahead to hit flak installations, but there was plenty of flak and it worried the crew of the B-17. They were not used to flying at a mere thousand feet over enemy territory at nearly minimum speed.[20]

Nearly all the lead serials in the airborne assault had left England at about 10 A.M. The pathfinder teams had gone ahead by about a half hour. One C-47, carrying pathfinders for the 101st Division, was shot down, but all other American and British pathfinder teams landed exactly on target and set up Eurekas and other markers. Behind the pathfinders came the parachute and the glider serials, which flew in different air lanes: the British and Gavin's 82nd Division on the "northern route" and Taylor's 101st on the "southern route." In all, there were about 1,550 troop-carrier aircraft, nearly 500 of these towing Waco, Horsa or Hamilcar gliders.

The British, disdaining the American tactic of paratroopers first, gliders second, led with gliders, as the Germans had on Crete. In the van of the British formation were 320 of them towed by planes of 38th and 46th groups carrying about half (1,500 men) of the reinforced 1st Airlanding Brigade (plus artillery), commanded by Philip H. W. (Pips) Hicks. Urquhart and the division staff flew with this group. En route, 39 gliders aborted and cut loose, but the rest made remarkably good landings with a high degree of accuracy at about 1 P.M. Urquhart, Hicks and staffs landed unhurt. Injuries to the gliderists were slight. Astonishingly, no incoming planes or gliders were lost to flak.[21]

Next in line came the 2,283 men of the British 1st Parachute Brigade, commanded by Gerald W. Lathbury. They were lifted by 143 aircraft of Hal Clark's 52nd Wing. En route, 5 planes were damaged by flak, but none was shot down. Guided by Gee—and by Eurekas in the DZs—Clark's pilots made a nearly perfect flight and, between 1:30 and 2 P.M., dropped Lathbury and his men squarely on the DZs. This drop was the largest and most successful single combat parachute drop in the ETO to date, and those who had urged daylight parachute drops over night drops were completely vindicated.

Next in the long stream in the northern route came 7,250 parachutists of Gavin's 82nd Division. Bill Ekman's 505 (with Gavin) was in the van, followed by (in order) Edwin Bedell's 307th Engineer Battalion (jumping as a complete unit for the first time); Rube Tucker's 504; Roy Lindquist's 508; and lastly, Wilbur Griffith's 376th Parachute Artillery. They were lifted in 480 aircraft from the 50th and 52nd wings. En route, one plane was shot down, but the other 479 reached the drop area. The troopers jumped at about 1 P.M. into three DZs about four miles southeast and southwest of Nijmegen. Although there were a few foul-ups, on the whole the drops were, as Gavin put it, "unusually successful." For the first time in any American airborne operation, the parachuting field artillery (a dozen 75 mm pack howitzers, ammo and 544 artillerymen) landed exactly where they were supposed to, with guns soon in action.[22]

Behind the 82nd Division parachute formations came a flight of 88 gliders. The first 50 gliders (all Wacos) bore elements of Tex Singleton's 80th Antiaircraft Battalion (with eight 57 mm antitank guns), the nonparachuting division staff and miscellaneous special units and personnel. The next 38 gliders (32 Horsas and 6 Wacos, towed by British Stirling aircraft) carried Boy Browning and the British 1 Airborne Corps staff. Owing to the acute shortage of glider pilots, few of the Wacos in the American formation had copilots. In most cases, a trooper sat in the copilot's seat, leading Gavin to comment: "Fortunately, the [Waco] is not too hard to fly or land. But having to do it for the first time in combat is a chastening experience; it gives a man religion." Three American Wacos aborted. Two Horsas aborted, and one went astray. The tow of one

Waco in the American group was shot down over Schouwen Island. In the glider, which cut loose, was Ridgway's former aide, Art Kroos. The glider came down on German-occupied Schouwen. Kroos and the rest played hide-and-seek with the Germans for three full days, but finally they were captured and spent the rest of the war in a POW camp.[23]

The rest of the gliders continued on to LZ "N," adjacent to the town of Groesbeek, arriving at about 1:45 P.M. The American group cut loose too soon and, as a result, only six Wacos landed on the LZ. About forty others came down a mile to the west of it, and one elsewhere. Two Wacos were destroyed and fourteen damaged on landing, but only seven troopers were injured, and all the antiaircraft guns came through intact. Astonishingly, the British glider pilots landed twenty-eight of the twenty-nine Horsas precisely on the LZ. As planned, Boy Browning and his 1 Airborne Corps staff established the corps CP in the woods on the north edge of LZ "N."

Simultaneously with these operations, Max Taylor's 101st Division came by the southern route. In the van were 6,695 parachutists of Skeets Johnson's 501st, Mike Michaelis' 502nd, and Bob Sink's 506th regiments. They were lifted in 424 aircraft of the 53rd Wing. En route to the DZs, the flak was intense. Many planes were hit. Four troop-carrier pilots heroically remained at the controls of burning aircraft to ensure that the paratroopers got out and, although sixteen planes in all were shot down, all 424 sticks did, in fact, get out. The troopers, including Max Taylor, making his third (and last) parachute jump, landed at about 1 P.M. on three DZs north of Eindhoven (two near Zon and one near Veghel). One battalion at Veghel got a poor drop, but the other eight battalions (and Taylor) were put down almost precisely on target. The division historian wrote that it was "the most successful landing that the division had ever had, in either training or combat."[24]

Behind Taylor's parachutists came a flight of seventy aircraft towing Waco gliders. These carried the three batteries of Elkins' 377th Parachute Artillery and other men and gear. Six of the gliders aborted en route. The remaining sixty-four encountered intense flak and had hair-raising journeys. Six tow planes were shot down, forty-six were damaged (six so badly they were scrapped), and some gliders were cut loose prematurely. Three gliders crash-landed on the LZ, but the fifty-three surviving gliders landed safely on the LZ, one piloted by a soldier who took over from the wounded pilot. A young United Press reporter, Walter Cronkite, on board one of the gliders, landed without injury.[25]

Ridgway's B-17 circled at an altitude of about a thousand feet between Eindhoven and Nijmegen. Those aboard could see for miles in all directions. The sight of so many aircraft, gliders and parachutes—especially the thousands upon thousands of parachutes—was simply awesome. There had never been anything like it in daylight—seven parachute regiments jumping almost simultaneously with thousands of varicolored parachute supply bundles—and the sight was unforgettable. For the first time, Allied photographers were able to take pictures of an airborne combat operation, but none was able to capture the stunning scope of the scene.

By about 2 P.M. on that lovely September Sunday afternoon, all Allied para-troopers and gliderists in MARKET had been delivered into Holland. The total numbers in the assault force exceeded the NEPTUNE D-day airborne forces by about one thousand: about 16,200 parachutists and about 3,200 gliderists, for a grand total of about 19,400 men. The great majority of the parachutists (14,000) were American; the great majority of the gliderists (1,700) were British. In addition, nearly five hundred tons of cargo had been parachuted or glider-landed. Of the twenty-four battalions of infantry, only two (both American) had been misdropped, and these were able to recover quickly and move into proper positions. The others had hit right on or very close to the DZs and LZs and, in most cases, had formed up into cohesive units and had made contact with higher headquarters within one hour. Refusals had been few and injuries slight. For the first time in combat, American division commanders were in a position to fight their outfits as a complete force.[26]

There were, in fact, only two sour notes on that September afternoon, both arising from the British sectors at the opposite poles of the operation. In Arn-hem, Urquhart's paratroopers, hampered by inadequate or malfunctioning ra-dios, untrained in urban fighting and meeting unexpectedly heavy German resistance, bogged down in the long race through the city to the bridge. At the opposite pole, Horrocks' 30 Corps, also meeting unexpectedly heavy German resistance, got off to a very slow start up the narrow, vulnerable Arnhem highway.

Unaware of these setbacks, Ridgway flew back to troop-carrier headquarters in England to follow the operation by radio. There he encountered unre-strained euphoria. The IX Troop Carrier Command had, for the first time ever, pulled off a truly successful parachute mission. "The drop was beautiful," Ridgway later wrote. "The best we'd ever done." On top of it all, troop-carrier aircraft losses had been slight—far below the most optimistic forecasts.[27]

That night when Ridgway went to bed in England, he had every reason to believe the MARKET plan would proceed as designed, despite his original misgivings about the weaknesses in the tactical plan and the command. On the morrow a second lift would deliver massive airborne reinforcements: the day after, a third lift would continue the buildup. Accompanied by Brereton, he would leave the following morning for Holland to position himself to take command of the 82nd and 101st divisions when the order came down from Montgomery or Dempsey to break the airborne force into two corps.

☆36☆

ON D+1, SEPTEMBER 18, Ridgway departed England in a C-47 for Antwerp. With him were his aide, Don Faith, his orderly, Jim Casey, his driver, Frank Farmer, who had loaded Ridgway's jeep and two others into the plane, and several bodyguards.

The weather was deteriorating rapidly. Many air bases in England had been closed by fog. There were low rain clouds over the English Channel and the North Sea. The bad weather that morning had compelled Brereton to postpone the D+1 airborne reinforcing missions from morning until afternoon.

Ridgway's pilot arrived over Antwerp to find it completely socked in. There was no way to land. Communications were difficult; the best option seemed to be to return to England and try again when the weather improved.[1]

At the troop-carrier CP in England that day, reports from Holland were maddeningly fragmentary. There was no word whatsoever from Urquhart, in Arnhem, and very little solid news of the division from Browning's 1 Airborne Corps. Ridgway could empathize with Urquhart; he himself had been without communications for all too long in Normandy. But the lack of news from Browning was more puzzling. His corps headquarters was supposed to be a marvel of modern communications. Recently it had been heavily staffed with communication encoders and decoders. Later, it was found that these British and American communicators were green and ill-trained, that there had not been enough time to sort out proper radio networks, frequencies, call signs and other technical details. The result was that Browning was not in contact with Urquhart or Taylor. He was more or less in the dark and, in the words of one British airborne historian, "totally incapable of managing the battlefront."[2]

The troop-carrier CP was thus unaware that after the promising D-day start, MARKET was now heading into grave difficulties. Supposedly within several hours after the landings, the Germans had found the complete Allied battle plan for MARKET-GARDEN in a glider that crashed inside their lines.* Whether through this priceless intelligence, or simply typical German efficiency the senior German commanders, Walter Model, Kurt Student and the II SS Panzer Corps commander, Wilhelm Bittrich, moved to smash MARKET-GARDEN to smithereens. Within hours, they had mobilized every single German combat unit in southern Holland and beefed up each one with whatever Germans they could find here and there—even sailors and airmen on furlough at the spas.[3]

---

* Much doubt has been cast on this story. No authoritative historian has been able to document it.

Model—forced to abandon his CP—struck first and most tellingly against the weakest link: the British force in Arnhem. One of Lathbury's 1st Airborne Brigade's battalions—John D. Frost's 2nd—had raced to the Arnhem bridge more or less according to plan and anchored itself on the northern end in downtown Arnhem. But the follow-up 1st and 3rd battalions had been cut off en route and pinned down in difficult urban fighting, for which the men had not been adequately trained. Other German forces pressed hard against the men of Hicks's 1st Airlanding Brigade, who were left behind to protect the DZs and LZs so that reinforcements could arrive safely. Owing to inadequate or malfunctioning radios, Urquhart lost contact with his three parachute battalions and, while attempting to find them, was himself isolated within the city by a German force for thirty-six crucial hours.

Fifteen miles to the south, in Gavin's 82nd sector, the situation seemed to be far better. The three tough, battle-hardened parachute regiments had carried out all assigned D-day missions with commendable efficiency. Rube Tucker's 504 had captured a big and important bridge over the Maas River at Grave and several canal bridges as well. Bill Ekman's 505 and Roy Lindquist's 508, straddling the town of Groesbeek, had occupied the important heights in the area and had established a strong defensive line facing west into the Reichswald. This dense woods, which actually lay inside the German border, was believed to be an important marshaling ground for German troops (concealed from Allied air) and thus presented the greatest threat to Gavin's sector. Moreover, it abutted the LZs into which the rest of the 82nd's artillery and Charles Billingslea's 325th Glider Regiment were to land on D+1 and D+2. Thus it was vital to repel any German forces that might have gathered in the Reichswald.

At the apex (or north point) of Gavin's sector lay Nijmegen, where two huge bridges (one railroad, one vehicular) crossed the wide Waal River. The Nijmegen bridges were, in fact, Gavin's prime objective. However, Browning had decided that Gavin should carry out his secondary objectives before seizing them. He believed it would be futile—even foolhardy—to seize the main bridges before the bridges in the southern end of his sector had been secured and the supposed German threat from the Reichswald contained.

Gavin fully concurred with Browning's tactical plan but, with Browning's approval, had also devised an alternate, opportunistic scheme. If he found the situation favorable, he would speed a battalion from Lindquist's 508 (closest to Nijmegen) to quickly grab the Waal bridges. As the operation unfolded on D day, Gavin decided the situation was indeed favorable, and that evening Lindquist ordered elements of Shields Warren's 1st Battalion to seize the vehicular or the railroad bridge or both. Gavin had told Lindquist to instruct his troops to avoid the city itself: to circle in the countryside around from the east and north. However, a Dutch guide (ostensibly a member of the underground but perhaps a double agent) led Warren's men straight into the city, and the paratroopers soon became bogged down in house-to-house fighting inside Nijmegen, and the mission failed.

When Gavin heard what had happened in Nijmegen, his "heart sank." He knew the Germans would also consider the Waal bridges a prime objective; now that the element of surprise had been lost, they would take steps to reinforce them. He was right. Kurt Student, delegated tactical responsibility for destroying the paratroopers wherever they might be found, decided the Nijmegen bridges must be held—or blown—whatever the price. He directed one SS panzer battalion to converge on the bridges and hold them and other units to strike into Gavin's airhead from every possible direction.

Long after these D-day operations, Gavin would admit that he had made a mistake in assigning the vital mission of seizing the Nijmegen bridges to Lindquist. The mission had not been pursued aggressively or intelligently. One reason was that Lindquist had too many assignments—too broad a front to cover—and could not spare enough time and men to get the Nijmegen job done properly. Unaware of what had happened to Warren, Lindquist compounded the error by sending elements of Louis Mendez's 3rd Battalion to help in Nijmegen, dangerously thinning out the defenses facing east toward the Reichswald. However, Gavin took full blame for the botched job, writing that it should have "been obvious" to him that Tucker's 504 was "much better prepared" and in a better position to seize the Nijmegen bridges than was Lindquist's 508.[4]

In the meanwhile still further south, near Zon and Eindhoven, the situation in Max Taylor's sector also initially seemed rosy. Taylor's three battle-hardened parachute regiments had likewise carried out all assigned D-day missions with commendable efficiency. Skeets Johnson's 501, landing on two DZs at Veghel, captured two key bridges over the Aa River and the Willems Canal and sent a force south toward St. Oedenrode. Mike Michaelis' 502, landing to the south of Johnson, near Zon on the main division DZs, set up a defense of the DZs and LZs and sent one force north to link with Johnson's troops at St. Oedenrode and one force south to capture a bridge over the Wilhelmina Canal near Best. Bob Sink's 506, landing just south of the 502, overran Zon and sent a force south to capture Eindhoven. There was only one serious setback: before Sink could seize it, the Germans demolished a key bridge over the Wilhelmina Canal at Zon. The engineers of 30 Corps (well stocked with Bailey bridges) would have to build a temporary replacement.

At the extreme southern end of the salient, however, the situation was still disquieting. Horrocks and 30 Corps were moving north all too slowly. On D day the 30-Corps spearhead, the Guards Armoured Division, had been stopped at the jump-off by a hastily organized German force which included elements of the 6th Parachute Regiment, veterans of Normandy. The GARDEN plan called for 30 Corps to reach Eindhoven on D day, Nijmegen on D+1 and Arnhem on D+2. On D day the Guards Armoured had advanced only about halfway to Eindhoven—a mere eight miles—and they now faced the task of building a bridge at Zon.

On the afternoon of D+1, the weather cleared and Brereton was able to mount the delayed morning missions. These were a regimental parachute drop, three large glider missions and three aerial resupply drops. Ridgway monitored these missions from the troop-carrier CP.[5]

All these missions were urgent, but none more so than the British manpower reinforcements at Arnhem. They consisted of about four thousand men: twenty-two hundred troopers of the 4th Parachute Brigade, commanded by John (Shan) Hackett, and the other half of Hicks's 1st Airlanding Brigade, all of which came on the "northern route." The 4th Brigade was lifted in 126 C-47s of Hal Clark's 52nd Wing. The paratroopers jumped at about 2:15 P.M., onto the Arnhem DZs amid intense flak and ground fire. Even so, the drop was judged "highly successful": about 90 percent of the troops came down "slap in the right place." The glider mission, bringing in the rest of Hicks's men (some eighteen hundred), consisted of 295 Horsas and Hamilcars towed by 38th and 46th groups. It was yet another hair-raising glider flight. About 25 Horsas aborted or broke loose en route; the remaining 270 landed on the LZs accurately but in heavy flak and ground fire.

Next came the glider mission for Gavin's 82nd Division: 454 Wacos towed by planes of the 50th and 52nd wings on the "northern route". These gliders were crammed with guns, ammo and 1,899 artillerymen of the 319th and 320th Glider Field Artillery battalions, the 456th Parachute Field Artillery Battalion and the other half of the 80th Antiaircraft Battalion. Seven gliders aborted or were cut loose over England or the water. Ten tow planes were shot down over Holland, but the gliders survived to land here and there. In all, some 385 gliders made it to the 82nd sector, about 240 of them reasonably close to the LZs, the rest scattered all over.

The gliders came down through a hail of enemy ground fire from the Reichswald and other German enclaves. Gavin had tried to devise a way to divert them to an alternate LZ, but he was not successful, and he watched the gliders landing under fire with "a terrible feeling of helplessness." However, Gavin later judged the mission to be a "highly creditable performance" and one that he "never would have thought possible." Of the total thirty-six howitzers carried by the three field-artillery battalions, thirty were delivered. In addition— and equally important—all eight 57 mm antitank guns arrived safely.[6]

Paul Wright's 320th Glider Artillery had the worst landing. The exec, William Lancey, recalled that the unit was simply "scattered all over hell." Division records bear him out. Battery A (six 105 mm snub-nosed howitzers) hit the LZ on the mark, but the Headquarters Battery and Battery B (six 105 mm snub-noses) were wildly scattered. Thirteen gliders of Battery B were listed as "missing." It was later determined that these had overflown the LZ and crash-landed somewhere in German territory. Later, some of the men from these gliders managed to sneak back through enemy lines to the division area, but most were captured. Lancey, wildly mislanded with elements of the headquarters group, rounded up sixty strays and, under cover of darkness that night, reached the LZ.[7]

At about the same time, came 450 Wacos towed by 53rd Wing, destined for LZs in Taylor's sector, plus a flight of C-47s bringing the last battery (B) of the 377th Parachute Artillery. These gliders, which followed the southern route, carried Tony McAuliffe, Bud Harper and the 2nd and 3rd battalions of Harper's 327th Glider Infantry Regiment plus engineers and medics—a total of 2,656 troops. Ten gliders aborted, broke loose or ditched. One was hit by flak and disintegrated, two others cut loose when their tow planes were hit. In all, however, 428 gliders—and the 377th battery, which jumped—reached the LZ or DZ safely, and the mission was judged to be "95% successful."

In sum, these three D+1 parachute and glider missions delivered about 9,000 more paratroopers and glider infantry to Holland. This brought the total number of airborne forces on the ground in MARKET to about 28,400—some 3,000 more than the manpower deployed by air for NEPTUNE. Thus MARKET would become the "largest airborne operation in history." The majority of the new arrivals had gone to Urquhart, in Arnhem, raising his hard-pressed force to about 9,000 men, about the same number as commanded by Gavin and Taylor.

Later that afternoon, Brereton dispatched the three aerial resupply missions. These were all carried out by British or American bombers which had been modified for the job—the American planes hastily and imperfectly. Thirty-five Stirlings of 38 Group flew eighty-seven tons of supplies to Arnhem. Most of the bundles fell into German lines; the British recovered only twelve tons. Two Stirlings were lost in the action. Some 125 B-24 Liberator bombers flew about 250 tons of supplies to Gavin's sector; a like number flew similar tonnage to Taylor. These drops, by completely inexperienced bomber crews who had had only the sketchiest of briefings, were also wildly inaccurate. Most of Gavin's bundles fell into no-man's-land, but after dark his men resourcefully recovered about 80 percent. Taylor's men succeeded in recovering only about 20 percent of the 250 tons earmarked for them, and the division soon felt the pinch. In these missions, eight B-24 bombers were shot down; four others, riddled to shreds by enemy flak, crash-landed in England.

On the following day, September 19 (D+2), Ridgway, accompanied by Brereton, made a second attempt to enter the battle. The weather was even worse than the day before, but Ridgway's pilot found a clearing over Antwerp and got the plane down. Brereton borrowed a truck at the airport; Ridgway's men unloaded the jeeps. The two generals and their small staffs drove in convoy to Montgomery's headquarters, near Brussels, where Montgomery's chief of staff, Francis de Guingand, loaned Brereton a more appropriate vehicle, a staff car. The convoy followed a circuitous route until they found Dempsey's Second Army, then, farther north, Horrocks' 30 Corps, whose thin spearhead had inched beyond Eindhoven that day, linking up with the 101st Division.[8]

By this time the Germans were mounting savage ground attacks along the entire length of the salient. Horrocks' tanks and vehicles were squeezed onto the narrow two-lane road. Taylor's airborne forces were bravely protecting the road from counterattack and holding the bridges they had seized. The situation reminded Taylor of the defense of the western railroads against Indian raids after the American Civil War: "We were forced to spread along the highway, garrisoning key towns with the hope of being able to move rapidly to meet hostile thrusts before they could become dangerous . . . The slowness of the British in coming up and taking over responsibility made it most difficult to maintain tactically sound dispositions." Taylor had divided his sector into three subcommands, one commanded by him, one by the ADC, Gerry Higgins, the third by Tony McAuliffe. The D+1 action had cost Taylor a fine battalion commander: Robert Cole, who had won the Medal of Honor in Normandy for his bayonet charge near Carentan.[9]

The road north was one long, massive traffic jam. Ridgway and Brereton could not move much faster than the British lorries. Halfway to Eindhoven a German infantry force attacked the road, bringing all traffic to an abrupt halt. Ridgway and Brereton, growing impatient, threw caution to the wind, pulled around the lorries and drove on toward Eindhoven.[10]

The weather that day was again foul, disastrously disrupting the D+2 MARKET missions. The most serious setback was the proposed drop of Sosabowski's Polish Parachute Brigade at Arnhem to reinforce Urquhart. The mission had to be canceled, denying Urquhart desperately needed manpower. Two resupply missions were sent to Arnhem—thirty-five towed Horsa gliders plus 163 planes with droppable bundles—but both failed. Twelve of the gliders aborted or cut loose; most of the rest came down on heavily besieged or enemy-held LZs. The 163 planes dropped 388 tons of supplies—most of it into German lines—of which Urquhart managed to recover only twenty-one tons.[11]

The Americans fared only slightly better. A proposed glider mission to bring in Billingslea's 325th Glider Regiment had to be canceled, a serious loss inasmuch as Gavin was counting on the 325 to relieve Tucker's 504 for an assault on the Nijmegen bridges. A resupply mission of 167 planes bringing in 265 tons to Gavin also utterly failed for one reason or another, leaving Gavin desperately short of ammo. A glider mission for Max Taylor, 385 Wacos loaded with the men and guns of the other artillery battalions (321, 907), part of the 81st Antiaircraft Battalion, and the 1st Battalion of Bud Harper's 327th Glider Infantry Regiment (a total of 2,310 troops) turned into a shambles. Dozens of gliders broke loose or were cut loose in bad weather or were ordered back. At least five crashed and seventeen were forced to ditch in the Channel. Seventeen tow planes were shot down over Holland. Only 209 gliders made it safely to the LZ. These brought in about half the troopers (1,341) and forty of the total sixty-eight artillery pieces.

Clarence Nelson, the 907 commander, remembered:

The problem was fog over the continent. In my glider I was flying co-pilot, with [our new] 105 snub-nose's bell sticking into the cockpit. When we hit the fog, the visibility fell almost to zero. You couldn't see anything except the tow rope, and maybe only about thirty to forty feet of that. The formations began to break up and scatter in the fog. When my glider broke out of the fog over Belgium, we were alone. We found two others and hit the LZ okay, but most of my battalion turned back to England and two or three gliders went down in the English Channel. Later we drew more weapons and got everybody over to Holland.[12]

The 81st Antiaircraft Battalion contingent, commanded by X. B. Cox, Jr., later recorded this harrowing journey in a monograph. Some 282 men and twenty-four 57 mm antitank guns had been crammed into eighty-one Wacos. In the fog over the Channel, seven Wacos, nearly out of control, cut loose and ditched. Over Belgium, still in dense fog, fourteen more Wacos were forced to cut loose and crash-land, killing five men. Eleven other Wacos became lost in fog and turned back to England, rather than risk a landing. Two gliders—listed as "missing"—were never accounted for. Only forty-seven of the eighty-one gliders—and 157 of the 282 men—reached the LZ near Zon with fourteen of twenty-four antitank guns.[13]

At his 1 Airborne Corps CP at Groesbeek, Boy Browning and his staff remained virtually useless. Owing to the foul-up in his communications section, for a long while Browning was unable to make contact with the British 1st and American 101st airborne divisions, and he had no idea what was going on in those two divisional sectors. One airborne historian wrote that when the commander of the British 52nd Airlanding Division offered to rush one of his brigades to Arnhem by glider, Browning replied: ". . . offer not repeat not required as situation better than you think." The American troop-carrier historian wrote that Browning's first news from Arnhem was not received until 8 A.M. on D+2 (September 19).[14]

Ridgway and Brereton finally reached Eindhoven about dusk that day. Their arrival coincided with a decision by Hitler to release about four hundred planes of the shattered Luftwaffe for attacks against the Allied salient. About half this force—some two hundred Stukas and JU-88 dive bombers—were directed against Eindhoven. When the first two planes appeared overhead dropping flares, Ridgway shouted to Brereton, "Let's get the hell out of here." They had gone but two blocks when, as Ridgway put it, "the whole world exploded."

The generals and aides dived out of the cars and jeeps, raced for a small city park and lay flat on the ground. The dive bombers tore Eindhoven apart. Neither general was scratched, but in the dive from the jeep, Ridgway's trick back went out, causing searing pain. In the ensuing confusion and darkness, the parties became separated. Brereton withdrew three miles to the south of Eindhoven and spent the night with some British MPs. Ridgway, Faith, Casey and Farmer climbed back into the jeep and drove north toward Zon. They found their way blocked by burning and exploding ammo trucks and gasoline tankers, so they pulled off, crawled into a ditch and went to sleep.[15]

The next morning, September 20 (D+3), Ridgway, who was still in great pain and his party proceeded northward toward Zon and the 101st CP. They soon came upon some advance elements of the Guards Armoured Division, which had halted owing to alleged enemy fire sweeping the road. A young officer told Ridgway he and his party could not proceed farther until the enemy had been dealt with. Ridgway (having no command authority) sat restlessly in his jeep for forty minutes. He saw no enemy fire, nor were the British shooting or attempting to outflank the "enemy."

Finally growing impatient with this "overcaution," Ridgway decided to press onward. He and Faith and Casey, leaving Farmer behind with the jeep, headed up the road on foot, weapons ready. They covered a mile and a half and drew no fire. On signal from Ridgway, Farmer came forward with the jeep and they climbed in and went on to Taylor's CP, which had moved that morning from Zon to Wolfswinkel. The British armored column, crossing the new bridge at Zon, eventually came along behind them, still moving with utmost caution.

Ridgway was infuriated by the slow motion of 30 Corps. Later he described it in his war memoir as "inexcusable" and said that "more vigorous command supervision from the top" could have pushed 30 Corps right through to Arn-hem on schedule. In later years he speculated that perhaps it was the "British characteristic" to be "overcautious." He went on: "I certainly would have chewed out any unit commander of mine . . . that had . . . said there was resistance along that road."[16]

Ridgway had little time to confer with Taylor. By that time, Brereton had arrived at Bob Sink's 506 CP near Eindhoven and had radioed that *he* wished to confer with Taylor. This was an unconscionable imposition on Taylor, who was desperately busy and had to leave his battlefront and travel south six miles through dangerous country, principally to assuage Brereton's ego. Demon-strating his well-developed diplomatic talents, Taylor, in his war memoir, did not allude to the meeting or the risk it had put him to.[17]

Ridgway proceeded northward to Gavin's sector, crossing the bridge over the Maas River at Grave immediately behind advance elements of the creeping Guards Armoured Division. From there, he made his way to Gavin's CP near Groesbeek, where he was astonished to find the 82nd Airborne Division in a desperate struggle. That day—September 20—would rival the most difficult hours of the 82nd Division in Normandy and add a stirring chapter to its history.[18]

The Nijmegen bridges were still held by the Germans, who had substantially reinforced their positions. This was now the last important water crossing between the slow-moving 30 Corps and Arnhem. For three days Gavin had been trying to take the bridge. Now he knew he must make a do-or-die effort or 30 Corps would stall at Nijmegen and never get to Arnhem in time.

Gavin had conceived a new scheme to seize the bridges. Simply put, he would attack them from both ends simultaneously with the two most aggres-sive and competent commanders in the division: Tucker and Vandervoort. Tucker's 504, supported by British armor and concealed by a smoke screen, would cross to the north bank of the Waal River in assault boats, root out the Germans on the bank, then attack the bridges from the north. At the same time, Ben Vandervoort's 2nd Battalion (505), reinforced by tank-supported British regular troops (the Grenadier Guards) would assault the south end of the bridges, attacking through the city. Browning and Horrocks had approved this plan and Horrocks had ordered assault boats brought forward for the river crossing. Tucker had chosen Julian Aaron Cook's 3rd Battalion for the assault. In spite of the nonarrival of Billingslea's 325th Glider Regiment (on D + 2 and again on D + 3), Gavin was proceeding with the plan when Ridgway reached the 82nd sector.[19]

That same day, while Gavin was on the riverbank with Tucker overseeing preparations for the assault crossing, Kurt Student attacked the 82nd Division sector in divisional strength. Two heavy German combat teams broke into the perimeter, one in the eastern part of the airhead at Beek and Wyler, thinly held by Lindquist's 508; one in the southwestern part of the airhead at Mook, thinly held by Ekman's 505. Gavin's chief of staff, Bob Wienecke, frantically radioed Gavin at Tucker's CP to report the attacks and to warn that if emergency measures were not taken immediately, the division CP (and Boy Browning's corps CP) might be overrun and the vital bridge at Mook lost, thereby isolating the Allied forces in and around Nijmegen.

Gavin left the river crossing in Tucker's hands and raced back to the division CP. There, in the midst of this grave crisis, whom should he find but the visiting fireman Matt Ridgway and his aides. Gavin had no time for amenities. He brusquely turned Ridgway over to his G-2, Walter Winton, and hurried off to Mook, where he thought the German attacks posed the greatest danger.

Ridgway had arrived at Jim Gavin's CP in a foul temper. As he later mildly put it, he was "much dissatisfied with the apathy and lack of aggressiveness of the British forces" he had seen on the highway, and still resented the appointment of Boy Browning. He was also still in severe pain from his back. That he was cavalierly dismissed by Gavin and turned over to Walter Winton on his first visit in combat to the division served to increase his irritation. Later, in calm reflection, Ridgway would write that, given the gravity of the situation he faced, "Gavin had plenty of justification for his brusqueness toward me." But right then he was a very angry and frustrated visiting corps commander, a warrior in a crisis with no command responsibility.

As the 82nd sector came under intense enemy pressure that afternoon, Gavin was like a one-man fire brigade. He first raced to Mook to assess the situation and to put backbone in the weakening 505 by a personal show of courage, firing at the oncoming hordes of Germans like a squad leader. After reinforcing Ekman with his only reserves—a battalion of Coldstream Guards and a scratch force of some 300 idle glider pilots—and being reassured by Ekman that the 505 could hold, he raced to Beek. There he found Lindquist's 508—Louis Mendez's 3rd Battalion in particular—in "a very shaky condition," having retreated out of Beek in the face of another horde of Germans. Crawling on his belly across a road under intense fire, Gavin "joined the infantrymen," who were "anxiously digging in." He assured them "they had nothing to worry about," but owing to the nonarrival of the 325, he had no reserves to give Lindquist. Nonetheless, the 508 held.[20]

About this same time, the British assault boats—delayed in arrival—were delivered to Tucker on the south bank of the Waal. They turned out to be flimsy folding canvas craft which offered no protection whatsoever to the occupants. Cook did not hesitate. In what was indisputably one of the most heroic actions of the war, Cook led his assault wave across to the north bank of the river, straight into the teeth of withering German fire. Casualties were very heavy.

While the boats returned for more men, Cook and the assault force, who would not be denied that day, seized the opposite bank and began rooting out the stubborn German defenders. As more and more men crossed, the Germans gave way, and by dusk, Tucker had seized the north end of the vehicular bridge. For this action, Cook was awarded a DSC.

While Cook was crossing the Waal and rooting out the Germans, Ben Vandervoort, leading his 2nd Battalion (reinforced by the Grenadier Guards with tanks) through Nijmegen, hit the German positions at the south end of both bridges. Vandervoort, who was very good, was at his absolute best that day. (He would receive a second DSC for the action.) After a very tough fight, his men routed the German defenders at the vehicular bridge, and the Grenadier Guards sent four tanks across the bridge to link up with Tucker's men, who were firmly encamped at the north end. At the last minute, the Germans attempted to blow the vehicular bridge, but the detonator mysteriously failed and a Nijmegen bridge over the Waal—at last—was secured.[21]†

In later years, Gavin would look back with some awe on the day of Ridgway's visit. It was a day, he recalled, "unprecedented in the division's combat history. Each of the three [parachute] regiments had fought a critical battle in its own area and had won over heavy odds." The battles at Beek and Mook, while vital, were defensive actions and thus less well remembered and noted. The seizure of the Nijmegen bridge by Cook and Vandervoort, Gavin thought, was "brilliant and spectacular." Browning agreed: "I have never seen a more gallant action."[22]‡

A great anticlimax ensued that evening. Additional British forces crossed the Nijmegen bridge, but Horrocks was reluctant to crash the eleven miles to Arnhem. The terrain was flat, the single road a raised causeway-like structure on which his armor would be sitting ducks. Gavin, crossing the bridge the next morning at first light to congratulate Tucker, recalled: "Tucker was livid. I had never seen him so angry . . . His first question to me was, 'What in the hell are they doing? We have been in this position for twelve hours and all they seem to be doing is brewing tea. Why in hell don't they get to Arnhem?' I did not have an answer for him."[23]

In any event, it was already too late. That very same day, September 21, John Frost and the survivors of his riddled 2nd Battalion, still holding on gamely at the north end of the Arnhem bridge, were overwhelmed and cap-

† The railroad bridge was also seized, but with the capture of the vehicular bridge, it lost its importance.

‡ The crossing of the Waal by Cook and his men was vividly depicted in the film *A Bridge Too Far*, based on the book of the same title by Cornelius Ryan. Robert Redford played the role of Cook.

tured. It was a bitter climax to one of the most heroic—and futile—actions of the war. By that time, Urquhart and the rest of his brave and dwindling band had been isolated, squeezed into a small perimeter at Oosterbeek, backs to the Rhine. They clung tenaciously to this ever-shrinking bridgehead, but they also were doomed.

Realizing that his presence was an awkward burden to Gavin, Ridgway left the 82nd sector on September 20 and made his way southward. He stopped again at Taylor's CP, now situated in St. Oedenrode, to spend the night. There he learned that strong and determined German forces had attacked Taylor that day from several directions, cutting the road in several places. The three parachute regiments, reinforced by two battalions of Bud Harper's 327, had fought back tenaciously, resecuring the road and inflicting heavy casualties on the Germans. The 101st was now in the process of integrating its operations with Dempsey's two flanking corps, the 8 and the 12, and was no longer in any serious peril.[24]

By this time word was seeping through that the British 1st Airborne Division had failed at Arnhem. There was no hope that it could be decisively reinforced by the Poles or the 52nd Airlanding Division. Horrocks was still reluctant to crack north on the ground from Nijmegen. The Allies were soon forced to concede defeat at Arnhem.

It would prove to be a costly setback to the Allies for several reasons. First, it dashed any hope that Montgomery could quickly cross the Rhine and "rope off" the V-2 launching sites and encircle the Ruhr from the north. Second, the action had given the Germans time to further strengthen their positions all through the Scheldt in Montgomery's rear, denying the Allies Antwerp for many weeks to come. The nonavailability of Antwerp would force the Allies to continue to rely on cumbersome supply lines reaching all the way back to Normandy and would significantly impede offensive operations all across the western front. Third, the defeat gave the German Army a tremendous psychological uplift. If the Allies had won, it is not inconceivable that the dispirited German Army in the west might have disintegrated. But Model's victory at Arnhem demonstrated that the Allied juggernaut could be repulsed, even by a weak, motley and hurriedly organized force such as he was able to throw together on the spur of the moment. In the ensuing days, the German Army showed renewed vigor across the entire western front.

MARKET had been FAAA's first ETO operation and the first time that a full airborne corps (three divisions) had ever been deployed in battle by either the Axis or the Allies. The Americans had won their part of the battle, but the British had failed at the decisive point, Arnhem, and therefore the entire operation had to be judged a failure. Military analysts would blame the failure on many factors, including the bad weather, which impeded the post-D-day reinforcing missions, the underestimation of German strength and morale, inadequate Allied close air support, the lack of aggressiveness in 30 Corps and the decision to send its armor up a single, narrow, exposed road.

These were indeed major factors in the defeat, but the main fault was the airborne plan itself. In a cursory look, Bedell Smith had put his finger on the fatal weakness: insufficient force committed on D day at the principal objective, Arnhem. As Smith had suggested to Montgomery, a full airborne division, or perhaps even two, would have been a prudent force at Arnhem on D day. In fact, Urquhart had only a single parachute brigade for the assault, and it was landed much too far from the objective. The rest of his D-day force had to guard the DZs and LZs for the D + 1 and D + 2 reinforcements. Smith's observation could also be applied to a lesser extent to operations in Gavin's and Taylor's sectors. They each had a little too much to do and, owing to the necessity of tying down forces to guard the DZs and LZs for the follow-up missions, not enough men to properly carry out the assigned tasks.

The major flaw in the plan—force weakness on D day and piecemeal commitments thereafter—could have been eliminated beforehand, perhaps ensuring success. Brereton had rather too casually ruled that the aircrews would not fly two missions on D day, believing that two missions would overtire the aircrews and the shorthanded ground crews, deny them sufficient time to properly service and load aircraft between missions and, owing to the diminishing daylight hours, probably compel some night flying. Browning had accepted this line of reasoning, apparently without challenge.

In fact, the line of reasoning was wide open to challenge. Only one month earlier, in DRAGOON, Paul Williams had committed his troop-carrier aircraft to dual D-day missions in southern France. From the troop-carrier standpoint, the operation had been a complete success. The aircrews may have been fatigued, but no accidents were attributed to that cause and the planes had been serviced and reloaded for second missions with an absolute bare minimum of ground crews.

A flight plan for dual missions in MARKET would have been no tougher than those in DRAGOON. It was about 250 miles from the troop-carrier bases in England to Arnhem, or about 500 miles round-trip. In flying time, a round-trip took about five hours, about the same as the round-trip flying time in DRAGOON. The first mission could have been launched from England at 5 A.M., returning at 11 A.M. Allowing a full three hours for crew rest and servicing planes, the second mission could have been launched at 2 P.M., arriving over Holland at 5 P.M. The returning planes of the second mission would have arrived in England in darkness, but their landing fields could have been lighted to receive them.

If two missions had been flown on D day, the important additional forces could have been delivered at Arnhem: the British 4th Parachute Brigade and the Polish Parachute Brigade (in 260 aircraft) and the other half of the British 1st Airlanding Brigade (in 300 gliders). This would have given Urquhart his full division (an additional five thousand men) by dusk on D day, and it would have eliminated the need to tie down large numbers of men after D day to guard the DZs and LZs. In addition, it is even possible that the remaining 600-plus troop-carrier aircraft could have delivered the 52nd Airlanding Division at Arnhem on this same second D-day mission.

Had this dual mission schedule been followed on D day, then on D + 1, while the weather was still favorable, most of the rest of the American forces could have been delivered in a single massive glider mission. That is: Billingslea's 325th Glider Regiment (450 gliders), Harper's 327th Glider Regiment (450 gliders) and the 82nd Division artillery (450 gliders). This would have left behind on D + 1 only Taylor's artillery, which was not ever considered to be a vital necessity.

In sum: by flying two missions on D day and one mission on D + 1, as many as forty thousand airborne or airlanded infantry and artillerymen could have been delivered to Holland. This would have put a more prudent and probably decisive force into Arnhem (one, possibly two, divisions) and a much more powerful force in Nijmegen (an extra regiment, plus artillery) and Eindhoven (an extra regiment). Given the beautiful flying weather everywhere on D day, the acceptable flying weather on the afternoon of D + 1 (when about fourteen hundred troop-carrier missions were actually flown) and the absence of the Luftwaffe on those days, such a plan probably could have been carried out without undue strain or losses.

There were other ways to increase D-day deliveries, none apparently given adequate consideration. By that time, "double-towing" of Waco gliders (one C-47 towing two gliders) had been declared acceptable procedure. Double-towing sharply decreased the range of a C-47 (to 315 miles), but that problem could have been solved by installing extra gasoline tanks in the tows and/or by arranging refueling stops at Allied airfields in France or Belgium. The Americans might also have reconsidered Ridgway's ban on the use of the Horsa glider, which had twice the payload of a Waco. The more favorable terrain in Holland greatly decreased the odds of a disastrous Horsa crash on landing.

The ultimate blame for the failure of the airborne plan, MARKET, must be placed on Brereton. His first and most egregious error was his appointment of Boy Browning, rather than Ridgway, to plan and command the operation. His second grave error was his decision to limit aircrews to a single D-day mission, thus committing FAAA to a piecemeal operation during a period of uncertain weather. His third error was in approving Browning's weak and too-distant D-day drop at Arnhem. Had Ridgway and his more experienced XVIII Airborne Corps staff been in charge of the operation, it is likely that the major flaws in the airborne plan would have been detected in advance and corrected —even if Ridgway had to lay his career on the line, as he had done on several occasions in the Mediterranean Theater. Moreover, had Ridgway been in command of airborne forces on the battlefield, he certainly would not have tolerated the slow, cautious advance of the British 30 Corps. Rather than a disaster, MARKET might well have been a smashing triumph, with incalculable gains for the Allies.

☆37☆

On September 21 (D+4), as Ridgway made his way south toward Antwerp, Brereton, unaware that the game was lost, continued with plans to send more manpower to Urquhart and Gavin: the Polish Parachute Brigade and Billingslea's 325th Glider Regiment. But the weather was still terrible—much too foul for airborne operations. The glider lift of the 325 had to be canceled once more, denying Gavin sorely needed reinforcements. The Polish parachute drop, now considered vital, went despite the weather. A force of 114 aircraft of Hal Clark's 52nd Wing bravely took off with 1,511 men. The ambitious plan was that the outfit would drop into a newly-designated DZ on the south bank of the Rhine opposite Urquhart's shrunken bridgehead. Nearly half of the troop-carrier planes got lost in the bad weather and/or were forced to turn back. Five planes were shot down. The rest found the DZ and dropped 998 Polish paratroopers, 750 close to the DZ. Although the drop was judged "50% successful," the mission was futile—too little, too late. The Poles were not able to cross the river in force, but they were helpful in evacuating the elements of Urquhart's force—some 2,500 men.[1]

The British also attempted to resupply Urquhart by air that day. Some 117 Stirlings and Dakotas bravely took off into pea-soup fog with 271 tons of supplies for Arnhem. Unfortunately, the weather had grounded most of their fighter escorts. Luftwaffe fighters attacked in force and shot down 23 of the 117 planes. The rest, harassed by fighters and flak, dumped their loads where they presumed Urquhart to be. Urquhart, who had run out of luck, recovered only 11 tons.

Foul weather would continue to force postponement of air missions in MARKET. However, during a brief break in the clouds on D+6 (September 23), Brereton was able to dispatch another 4,300 men over the southern route. Chuck Billingslea's 325th Glider Infantry Regiment and Tex Singleton's 80th Antiaircraft Battalion (3,385 men) finally set off for the 82nd sector in 406 Wacos. It was yet another fouled-up, flak-harassed journey. En route, 58 gliders went astray or were shot down. Only 348 gliders (with 2,900 men) reached the LZs. (Other men straggled in later.) That same day, an 84-glider misson brought another 400 men to Taylor, and the remaining 560 paratroopers of the Polish Brigade jumped onto one of Gavin's DZs. The arrival of these 4,000 men—the last reinforcements to arrive by air—brought the total number of air-delivered troops in MARKET to about 35,000. (The 10,000 men of the British 52nd Airlanding Division were never delivered.)[2]

From Antwerp, Ridgway traveled to Courtney Hodges' First Army advanced headquarters near Verviers, Belgium, which was a mere twenty miles from Aachen and the Siegfried Line. He had two purposes for this visit. Plans were in the works to permanently transfer the American airborne divisions to the Continent in order to be closer to the combat zone. The 82nd and the 101st would be the first to be based there. They were expected to be withdrawn from Holland within a day or so. Ridgway wanted to bivouac them in the rear of Hodges' First Army area so that the divisions could rely on First Army for transportation and supply. These discussions would lead, ultimately, to a decision to base the two divisions near Rheims, France; the 82nd split between the towns of Suippes and Sissonne, the 101st at the town of Mourmelon.[3]

The second purpose of Ridgway's visit was more urgent. Hodges was thirsting to crash through Aachen to Cologne and cross the Rhine River, a thrust that could unhinge German defenses at Arnhem, perhaps making it possible for Montgomery to move forward, encircling the Ruhr from the north, while Hodges encircled it from the south. Hodges wanted Ridgway to lead an airborne drop of two divisions at Cologne (Operation NAPLES II) to seize a bridgehead on the east bank of the Rhine. Ridgway, who favored the plan, remained overnight with Hodges and spent most of the next day, September 22, closeted with Hodges and staffers, going over details.[4]

That same day, Eisenhower convened a strategy meeting of his top commanders at his new headquarters in Versailles. Montgomery, believing he was "not popular" with the Americans and that his presence might work against him, sent a letter by his chief of staff, De Guingand, who would speak for him. The meeting revealed that Bradley and Montgomery still held opposing views on strategy. Bradley believed that the move into Germany itself should be made in "great depth," engaging the enemy simultaneously "on a very wide front." His plan was for Patton to go through the Saar to Frankfurt, thence north, linking up with Hodges, who would punch through Aachen (and the difficult Hürtgen Forest) to Cologne. Meanwhile, Montgomery, having first cleaned up the Scheldt and opened Antwerp, would continue pushing north in the Arnhem area. Montgomery's plan was to stop Patton right where he was and put the major weight behind himself and Hodges (operating under Montgomery's command). They would close pincers around the Ruhr from their present positions at Arnhem and Aachen.

Eisenhower once more ruled in favor of Montgomery's strategy. Patton would temporarily go on the defensive while Montgomery simultaneously cleared the Scheldt and launched a northward offensive in conjunction with a renewed Hodges offensive toward Cologne. Crerar's Canadian First Army would clear the Scheldt; Dempsey's British Second Army would continue driving north through Arnhem. To assist Dempsey, the 82nd and 101st airborne divisions, deployed as regular infantry, would remain in his command. Hodges' First Army would be beefed up by two additional divisions, one infantry and one armored, but the "loan" of the 82nd and 101st to Dempsey closed out any immediate consideration of an airborne operation at Cologne.

Bradley was again disappointed. He wrote: "This was yet another poor decision . . . stopping Patton, a proven ground gainer, to favor Monty, who wasn't, simply did not make any sense at all." While Patton stopped, the Germans would gain time to improve defenses in front of him. Bradley worried that Montgomery, in his eagerness to encircle the Ruhr, would not give sufficient weight to clearing the Scheldt, further delaying the opening of Antwerp. Even with the addition of the 82nd and 101st divisions, he doubted that Dempsey had sufficient power to make a decisive push north.[5]

Events would soon prove Bradley correct on all counts. The Canadian army was to be incapable of rooting the Germans out of the Scheldt, and finally Montgomery was forced to divert Dempsey's 12 Corps to help them. Thus hobbled, Dempsey got nowhere on his northward drive. He bogged down in a static and inconclusive battle on the south bank of the Rhine below Arnhem and on his right flank in the Peel marshes. Bradley lent Dempsey another American division, the 7th Armored, to help out, but that was not enough to make the difference. Hodges, encountering ever-stiffening German resistance at the German border, took Aachen and advanced to the Siegfried Line. However, the Germans, feeling no real pressure from Dempsey and little or none from Patton, were able to put sufficient force in front of Hodges to firmly block him.

The 82nd and 101st divisions were the real losers in these futile operations in Dempsey's sector. They remained on the static Arnhem front, under Dempsey's control, seemingly engaged forever in indecisive patrol actions. Cold, hard rains lashed the area, turning the battlefield into a quagmire and slit trenches into inhospitable mudholes, reminiscent of World War I. The men were short of cold- and wet-weather clothing; the food was wretched. Many fell ill with fever or suffered from trench foot. Gavin and Taylor remained resolutely upbeat and did everything possible to make life more bearable for their men, but morale began to sag badly.

Ridgway visited the American divisions on several occasions to discuss future plans with Gavin and Taylor and cheer up the men. On one such trip he brought good news to Gavin: on the recommendation of Dempsey, Horrocks and Browning (and with the hearty concurrence of Brereton and Ridgway), Gavin had been given a battlefield promotion to major general. This promotion made Gavin "the youngest two-star general in the American Army since the Civil War." On one of Ridgway's visits, Gavin thought the corps commander unnecessarily exposed himself to enemy fire and worried about his safety. "We got some tree bursts—very dangerous. Ridgway just stood there. I told him you don't just stand there looking at tree bursts, you'd get full of holes. I told him to go be a hero someplace else."[6]

On these visits, Ridgway, as was his custom, usually headed directly for the front lines to confer with the battalion or company commanders. He was deeply concerned about the low spirits of his elite troops. Many of them were no longer taking pride in their personal appearances. Too many looked like the sloppy, bearded GIs, Willie and Joe, in Bill Mauldin's *Stars and Stripes* cartoons. The commander of the 3rd Battalion, 505, James Kaiser, recalled:

Near the end of the Holland campaign, we had taken up positions to defend Nijmegen. After very heavy casualties from combat and wet weather, the 505 was in poor condition. Defensive positions were without shelter in mud and water. General Ridgway came along and said to me in the pouring rain one morning, "Do you know I saw two men on post back there who had not shaved?" I thought that he was being funny since I had not shaved for two days. But at second glance, I saw he was dead serious.[7]

Ridgway's trips into wet, cold Holland may well have triggered another attack of malaria. By October 22 he was confined to bed in his quarters in England. In response to a get-well letter from Brereton, Ridgway cheerfully dismissed his illness: "It takes more than malaria to get an airborne trooper down. This is my fourth and, I hope, last bout with that particular germ." In any event, he said, "It is not nearly so bad as [the attack] just before Normandy."[8]

Days dragged into weeks. Montgomery and Dempsey, like Patton, Clark, Bradley, Collins and Middleton before them, were reluctant to let go of such fine infantry. Dempsey, according to Brereton, thought the 82nd was "the greatest division in the world today." Everybody in the American camp from Eisenhower on down became highly annoyed at Montgomery for hanging on to the airborne divisions for so long. The angriest were the men in the 82nd and 101st, who felt they were being wasted in futile ground fighting for which they had not been designed. Brereton complained repeatedly to SHAEF and noted angrily in his diary: "Keeping airborne soldiers in the front lines as infantry is a violation of the cardinal rules of airborne employment." Finally Bedell Smith at SHAEF brought tactful pressure to bear. On Armistice Day, November 11, the 82nd, having served fifty-six days in continuous action, was at last released. The 101st was held about two weeks longer. In keeping with the plans Ridgway had worked out with Hodges, both divisions were bivouacked by late November near Rheims. Close by, at Épernay, Ridgway had established Doc Eaton and others in an "advanced" XVIII Airborne Corps headquarters.[9]

The three airborne divisions had paid a heavy price in MARKET and the follow-up battles in Holland. Urquhart's British 1st Airborne Division (including the Polish Brigade) lost about 7,500 men out of the 10,000 sent into battle. Gavin's 82nd suffered a total of 3,400 casualties; Taylor's 101, 3,792. All told, the airborne casualties in Holland were about 14,700, about half British, half American.[10]

On the senior command level in Gavin's 82nd Division, casualties were fortunately light. Remarkably, in the three parachute regiments, Gavin had no losses, nor did he relieve any senior commanders for failure to perform. Only Billingslea's 325th Glider Regiment incurred casualties in the senior command, all in the 2nd Battalion but fortunately none was killed.* Administratively,

---

* The 2nd Battalion commander, Tad Major, his exec, David R. Stokely, and the next-senior officer, Tom Slaughter, were all severely wounded and evacuated. (Major and

Billingslea replaced his exec, Herb Sitler, with the 1st Battalion commander, Teddy Sanford, who in turn was replaced by Richard E. Gerard.[11]

Taylor was less fortunate. He lost a slew of senior leaders, including two regimental commanders. The 501's flamboyant commander, Skeets Johnson, was killed and replaced by battalion commander Julian Ewell. The 502's cool and able commander, Mike Michaelis, was severely wounded in the arm, leg and stomach by a tree burst and had to be evacuated and hospitalized. He was replaced by battalion commander Steve Chappuis. This same tree burst severely wounded the 101st G-3, Harold W. Hannah, who was evacuated and replaced by 501 Battalion commander Harry Kinnard. Taylor himself had a close call. On November 9, while visiting frontline positions, an exploding German shell knocked him off his feet, and what he described as "an embarrassingly small" shell fragment lodged in his *"Sitzplatz."* He was an outpatient at a Rheims hospital for a week or so and earned a Purple Heart for the wound.[12]†

After the Arnhem disaster, the British airborne command underwent a shake-up. Boy Browning was relieved of his two hats at FAAA and sent to India to serve as chief of staff to the Supreme Commander, Southeast Asia Command, Admiral Louis F. A. Mountbatten. His departure evoked few tears in American quarters. Browning was replaced as deputy commander of FAAA and commander of the British 1 Airborne Corps by the far more popular and capable veteran of Normandy Richard N. Gale, who turned over command of his 6th Airborne Division to Eric L. Bols. Urquhart would attempt to rebuild the shattered 1st British Airborne Division, but neither it nor the Polish Brigade would again see combat. The force gap left at FAAA would be filled in part by the American 13th Airborne Division, which was en route to England.[14]

Stokely would later return to the regiment.) Major was temporarily replaced by Leahy's 3rd-Battalion exec, Samuel Ogden, then permanently by Richard M. Gibson.
† Other casualties and changes: In the 501, Ewell was replaced as 3rd Battalion commander by the regimental exec, George N. Griswold; the 2nd Battalion commander, Robert A. Ballard, became regimental exec, replaced by Sammie N. Homan. Harry Kinnard was replaced as 1st Battalion commander by Raymond V. Bottomly. In the 502, Chappuis was replaced as commander of the 2nd Battalion by Thomas F. Sutliffe. The 3rd Battalion commander, Robert Cole, who was killed, was replaced by John P. Stopka. Patrick Cassidy, slightly wounded, replaced the regimental exec, Allen W. Ginder, who was wounded; Cassidy was replaced as 1st Battalion commander by John D. Hanlon. In the 506, 3rd Battalion commander Oliver M. Horton was killed, replaced temporarily by Robert F. Harwick, then permanently by 1st Battalion commander Lloyd E. Patch, who was replaced by James L. LaPrade. The division ordnance officer, Roger W. Parkinson, was killed, replaced by Carl E. Anderson.[13]

PART VII

Bulge I:
The German Attack

☆38☆

WHEN MONTGOMERY BOGGED DOWN in the north, Omar Bradley, fearing stalemate and the dreaded prospect of a winter war, proposed a new offensive in the center and south—that is, a massive, simultaneous attack, by Hodges' First Army and Patton's Third Army, designed to break into Germany at Cologne and Mainz, respectively. Since Montgomery was at last preoccupied with clearing the Scheldt in order to open up Antwerp, and any pause or relenting of Allied pressure would give Hitler additional time to prepare defenses, draft and train new troops and, possibly, deploy new secret weapons, Eisenhower unhesitatingly approved Bradley's proposal.[1]

As a preliminary to this offensive, Hodges had first to deal with two troublesome and overlapping tactical problems. The first was to secure the high ground on his right flank overlooking (or south of) the forbidding, nearly impenetrable Hürtgen Forest, where the Germans might conceal troops and vehicles for an attack into First Army's flank. The second was to capture a network of seven dams along the upper Roer River. The Roer lay between Hodges and the Rhine. The dams were so situated (in the rugged high ground in the southern end of the Hürtgen Forest) that the Germans could utilize them to slowly flood the north-flowing Roer, making the Allied crossing of the river even more difficult and perilous.

Hodges grossly underestimated the challenge presented by these two overlapping tactical problems. The rugged terrain, which was unsuitable for armor or armored vehicles, greatly favored the defense. The value of the dams to the Germans was only belatedly realized. Even then, First Army failed to appreciate that the Germans might tenaciously defend them. Accordingly, First Army casually gave this formidable task to an able—but tired and understrength—infantry division, the 9th, now commanded by Louis A. Craig, who had only two regiments available for the task. The Germans, skillfully utilizing the terrain to advantage, literally chewed Craig's two regiments to pieces, inflicting 4,500 casualties. When the attack had clearly failed, Hodges withdrew the 9th and optimistically and imprudently merely substituted the 28th Infantry Division, now commanded by a hero of Omaha Beach, Norman D. (Dutch) Cota. In an appallingly bloody defeat which was more the fault of higher headquarters than his, Cota incurred slightly over 6,000 casualties, 2,000 of these in his 112th Infantry Regiment. The final cost of these fruitless operations, in both 9th and 28th divisions, was about 10,500 casualties.[2]

Meanwhile, Bradley's planned offensive grew enormously in size and scope. To bolster his forces, he brought Bill Simpson's new Ninth Army headquarters forward, inserted it to the north of Hodges, and assigned it two corps: the XIX, now commanded by Ray McLain (partly as a reward for the fine job he had

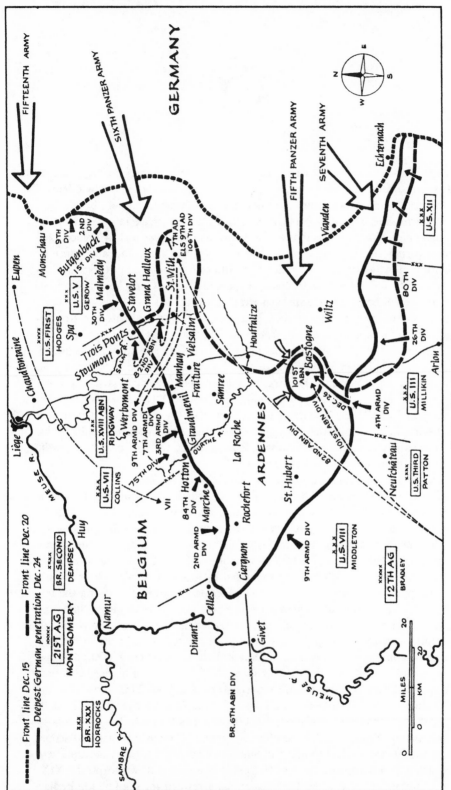

Legend:
- ▪▪▪ Front line Dec. 15
- ▪▪▪ Front line Dec. 20
- ▬▬ Deepest German penetration Dec. 24

Battle of the Bulge

GERMANY

FIFTEENTH ARMY

SIXTH PANZER ARMY

FIFTH PANZER ARMY

SEVENTH ARMY

BELGIUM

ARDENNES

Eupen
Chaudfontaine
Liège
Namur
Huy
Dinant
Givet
Celles
Ciergnon
Rochefort
La Roche
St. Hubert
Marche
Hotton
Grandménil
Manhay
Samree
Fraiture
Vielsalm
Werbomont
Stoumont
Trois Ponts
Spa
Stavelot
Grand Halleux
St. Vith
Malmédy
Butgenbach
Monschau
Houffalize
Bastogne
Wiltz
Vianden
Echternach
Arlon
Neufchâteau

MEUSE R.
SAMBRE R.
OURTHE R.
SALM R.

9TH DIV
2ND DIV
1ST DIV
U.S. V GEROW
30TH DIV
U.S. FIRST HODGES
82ND ABN DIV
8TH ARMD DIV
U.S. XVIII ABN RIDGWAY
9TH DIV
7TH ARMD DIV
3RD ARMD DIV
75TH DIV
U.S. VII COLLINS
VII
84TH DIV
2ND ARMD DIV
7TH AD
9TH AD
ELS 9TH AD
106TH DIV
82ND ABN DIV
101ST ABN DIV
101ST ABN DEC. 26
4TH ARMD DIV
9TH ARMD DIV
U.S. VIII MIDDLETON
U.S. III MILLIKIN
U.S. THIRD PATTON
80TH DIV
26TH DIV
U.S. XII
12TH AG BRADLEY
21ST A.G. MONTGOMERY
BR. SECOND DEMPSEY
BR. XXX HORROCKS
BR. 6TH ABN DIV

MILES
KM
0   20

N E S W

done in rescuing the 90th Division), and a new corps, the XIII, commanded by Alvan C. Gillem. Hodges also had two corps: Gee Gerow's V and Collins' VII (beefed up to the equivalent of five divisions), which would spearhead the main attack. South of the Ardennes, Patton had two corps: the XII, commanded by former 9th-Division commander Manton Eddy, and XX, commanded by Walton H. Walker, each swollen to about five divisions. In all, there were some twenty-two divisions, plus supporting units, comprising about five hundred thousand men.[3]

The offensive got off to a wobbly, uncoordinated start. As planned, Patton jumped off first, on November 8. But the northern thrust (Hodges and Simpson) was delayed by foul weather and did not go until November 16. Both thrusts ran head on into astonishing—and punishing—German resistance. Patton, hampered by cold, rain and cresting rivers, bulled his way east forty miles to the Saar River, but was stopped dead at the Siegfried Line after incurring twenty-seven thousand casualties in three weeks. In the same period, Hodges, also fighting in miserable weather through the dreaded Hürtgen Forest, and Simpson, in more favorable terrain, both punched through the Siegfried Line to reach the Roer River, but the cost was ghastly—about thirty-five thousand casualties—and the Germans still maintained control of the vital Roer dams. In total, the offensive cost sixty-two thousand American casualties; another seventy thousand fell from disease, exposure, fatigue and trench foot.[4]

Bradley's offensive had punished the Germans severely, but, as he later wrote, it had actually failed. His three armies had drawn abreast of the Roer and the Saar rivers—poised at gateways into Germany—but, as Bradley wrote, "a determined enemy held every foot of ground and would not yield." The Allied armies from Nijmegen to the Saar were mired in a ghastly war of attrition and winter was upon them. Eisenhower, in an overly gloomy mood, concluded that it would probably be impossible to launch further offensive actions until after the spring thaws—on or about May 1, 1945.[5]

The failure to win the war by Christmas was a bitter disappointment to the Allied high command (not to mention the GIs), and it touched off another round of sharp political infighting. Montgomery privately denounced Eisenhower (and Bradley) to London, forcefully renewing his demand at SHAEF that he be named overall Allied ground commander and again urging that the Allied front be narrowed and all resources be placed behind his proposed northern "full-blooded" thrust into Germany. Although Eisenhower was angry at Montgomery—and rebuked him in harsh terms—he agreed, finally, that when the time came for a major new offensive to be mounted, Montgomery would once more receive highest priority on resources, including command of Simpson's adjacent Ninth Army, some ten American divisions.[6]

The Allied front thus prepared for a miserable, prolonged winter stalemate. The now static armies were disposed as follows, north to south: Canadian First, British Second, Simpson's Ninth, Hodges' First and (south of the Ardennes) Patton's Third. The line, chewed up by Bradley's November offensive, was everywhere thin and lacking proper reserves, but by far the thinnest sector was a seventy-five-mile stretch facing the Ardennes. This was considered a "quiet" area, a place to refit battered divisions and indoctrinate green ones, and the one least likely to be attacked.[7]

Tactically, the Ardennes front was held by Troy Middleton's VIII Corps, now attached to Hodges' First Army. It was manned by four divisions (north to south): the brand-new 106th Division, commanded by Alan W. Jones; Dutch Cota's 28th Division and Tubby Barton's 4th Division, which had both been badly chewed up and were now refitting and remanning (both had been in continuous action since Normandy); and the new 9th Armored Division, commanded by John W. Leonard, a classmate of Eisenhower's and Bradley's.*

The weakest link on the VIII Corps Ardennes front was the green 106th ("Golden Lions") Infantry Division. Its commander, fifty-year-old Alan Jones, was not a West Pointer, but he was a respected career Army infantry officer who had been commissioned in World War I and who was a graduate of the Infantry School, the Command and General Staff School and the Army War College. Ridgway knew Jones well; they had been classmates at the Infantry School in 1924–25 and again in 1929–30. During its eighteen months of Stateside training, the division had been heavily raided of key personnel for ETO replacements. In fact, half its men had been lost between April and August 1944, replaced by fillers, including some twelve hundred from deactivated Army college programs. The division arrived in France on December 2 and moved to the Ardennes front on December 11, without the benefit of a combat baptism in the company of more experienced troops.[8]

Bradley had not imprudently or rashly thinned out the Ardennes front; he later described his decision as a "calculated risk." Eisenhower elaborated: "At the worst it was a reasonable sector in which to take a risk and [owing to the shortage of divisions] risks had to be taken somewhere." It was believed that the German Ardennes front was also a "quiet" sector, or training ground, manned by inferior *Volksgrenadier* divisions (composed of sailors and airmen and new recruits, many of them hastily trained old men and young boys), which were not believed to be capable of offensive operations. Even so, the weak Ardennes sector was a matter of constant concern to Eisenhower, Bradley, Hodges, Patton—and the man in direct charge, Troy Middleton, who had established his VIII Corps CP twenty miles behind the front at Bastogne, Belgium.[9]

Allied intelligence, which now relied heavily—perhaps too much so—on breaking German military codes, was optimistic in the first weeks of December. The code breakers had no positive information to indicate any danger to the Allies, and all else seemed to favor the Allies for the long haul. On Decem-

---

* Most American armored divisions were composed of three combat commands, A and B and Reserve (CCA, CCB and CCR). Often these commands, which had infantry attached, operated as separate armored battle groups, alone or in conjunction with other infantry units, or were further subdivided into armored task forces. Some 9th Armored infantry held a thin slice of the front (three miles) in the seam between the 28th and the 4th divisions, but its CCA, CCB and CCR were widely deployed some distance behind the frontline infantry divisions.

ber 12, Bradley's G-2 wrote: "It is now certain that attrition is steadily sapping the strength of the German forces on the Western Front and that the crust of defenses is thinner, more brittle and more vulnerable than it appears on our G-2 maps or to the troops in the line . . . With continued Allied pressure in the south and in the north, the breaking point may develop suddenly and without warning." Montgomery's G-2 was even more sanguine. On December 16 he wrote: "The enemy is in a bad way; he has had a tremendous battering and has lost heavily in men and equipment . . . [He is] at present fighting a defensive campaign on all fronts; his situation is such that he cannot stage a major offensive operation."[10]

Ostensibly, Gerd von Rundstedt commanded all German forces on the western front, and the Allies expected that he would continue to fight a conventional, textbook defensive war. In reality, Hitler, operating behind a strict cloak of secrecy, had again taken personal command of the western front, and his demented mind had hatched a wild scheme similar to his Mortain counteroffensive in August, but much larger in scale. He would launch a massive counterattack out of the Ardennes, the aim of which was to split the Allied front wide open and recapture Antwerp, a blow that would buy him time to deal with his equally pressing Russian front. In utmost secrecy and radio silence, Hitler began amassing the forces: a planned thirty divisions backed by fifteen hundred tanks, nineteen hundred artillery pieces and fifteen hundred Luftwaffe aircraft (including a hundred new jet fighters). When Hitler unveiled the plan, Von Rundstedt was shocked and appalled, as was his chief field commander, Walter Model, whom Hitler designated to lead the offensive. Both professionals believed the offensive would be suicidal—certain to fail. "This damned thing hasn't a leg to stand on," Model confided privately to Von Rundstedt.[11]

Hitler's tactical plan was as follows. The Sixth Panzer Army (four SS panzer divisions and five infantry divisions), commanded by Hitler's Nazi crony Josef (Sepp) Dietrich, would strike west out of the Ardennes with eight hundred tanks and assault guns and drive through Bütgenbach-Malmédy-Spa to the Meuse River, crossing between Liège and Huy, then turn northwest to encircle Antwerp. Simultaneously the Fifth Panzer Army (three-plus panzer and two infantry divisions) commanded by Hasso Eccard von Manteuffel, on Dietrich's left, would also strike west out of the Ardennes and drive through St. Vith, Houffalize and Bastogne, crossing the Meuse at Namur, then turn northwest toward Brussels. The German Fifteenth Army, positioned opposite the Allied front at Aachen, would support the right flank of the Dietrich-Manteuffel panzer assault; the German Seventh Army, opposite Luxembourg, would support the left flank. Speed was essential. The panzer armies were to crack through to the Meuse on the first day, Antwerp on the second or third.[12]

Two special outfits were organized to assist Sepp Dietrich. One was a parachute "battalion" of about twelve hundred men, commanded by Colonel Friedrich A. von der Heydte, which was to jump at night near Monschau, just ahead of the main attack. Conceived at the eleventh hour, this ragtag group was cadred by two hundred fifty men of the veteran 6th Parachute Regiment, plus a hundred men each from the other parachute regiments. There was no time for training; many of the paratroopers were green, and troop-carrier aircraft were hard to find. The other special outfit was a commando or saboteur brigade, led by an extraordinary German intelligence agent, Otto Skorzeny. The men of this brigade, wearing Allied uniforms and equipped with captured Allied tanks and other vehicles, were to go with the main panzer force to sow confusion behind Allied lines, seize bridges over the Meuse River and (so the legend arose) assassinate Allied generals. Skorzeny's outfit was also hastily and imperfectly organized.[13]

The Fifth and Sixth panzer armies had for some time presented the greatest potential threat to Allied ground forces on the western front. For that reason, Allied intelligence had kept a continuous, wary eye on both. The Allies knew from code breaking that both armies were being refitted with tanks and beefed up and were capable of launching "spoiling attacks" and might do so at any time. However, Hodges' G-2—reflecting the majority of G-2 opinion—guessed that the panzer armies were most likely being groomed for attacks *after* the Allies crossed the Roer River into the good tank country between the Roer and the Rhine. That would be a textbook solution to the Germans' problem. Although Patton's G-2—and Patton himself—pointed to the situation with alarm, no one in the Allied camp had any positive information that these armies would be launched out of the Ardennes on a mission to capture Antwerp. As Bradley put it: "At no time did anyone present me with unequivocal or convincing evidence that a massive German attack through the Ardennes at VIII Corps was imminent."[14]

The Germans struck at dawn on December 16 along a sixty-mile front. It was a bitterly cold, foggy, overcast day, ideal conditions for the Germans, who had hoped for such weather to neutralize Allied air. First came a massive artillery barrage, then swarms of infantry, then tanks. The Americans ran out of their warm huts and cellars and sandbagged trenches and stared in stunned disbelief as screeching artillery and chattering small-arms fire kicked up the snow around them.

Some green American troops, meeting panzers for the first time, fled in fear. On the whole, however, considering the massive weight of the attack, the Americans fought valiantly and resourcefully. Many units were isolated and surrounded, communications with higher headquarters cut off. Even so, the tough veterans were not completely intimidated. Whole units of infantry and artillery and bands of engineers pulled back to better defensive positions and to crossroads and bridges, where they quickly set up strong enclaves of resistance.

The main weight of the Sixth Panzer Army simultaneously hit the southern sector of Gee Gerow's V Corps and the northern sector of Middleton's VIII Corps. Gerow's southern sector was held by the newly arrived 99th Infantry Division, commanded by Walter E. Lauer. Like the 106th, this division had been repeatedly raided for replacements and was now composed of many men from deactivated college programs. It had been in the line for about five weeks, but it had seen no really hard action. In the initial assault, it began to give way. As it happened, the crack 2nd Infantry Division, ably commanded since Normandy by Walter M. Robertson, had just launched yet another attack toward the Roer River dams on the 99th's left flank. In a remarkable series of maneuvers, Robertson broke off his Roer dam attack, redeployed into the 99th's sector and more or less commingled his units with Lauer's, to form a kind of superdivision, composed of both veterans and green troops. The amalgamated 99th and 2nd infantry units, fighting like tigers, managed to establish a strong hold on the critical "north shoulder" of the German penetration near Bütgenbach and Elsenborn. This action would prove to be a decisive setback to the German plan, knocking the German timetable askew and causing immense traffic jams in the German rear.

The two special outfits which were to assist Sepp Dietrich's Sixth Panzer Army, the parachute battalion and Skorzeny's saboteurs (impersonating Allied personnel) contributed little in the initial assault. By D day, only four hundred of the twelve hundred paratroopers had assembled, and the operation had to be postponed. Skorzeny's brigade, caught up in the massive traffic jam, could not break out for the planned dash behind enemy lines to sow confusion and seize a Meuse River bridge (and possibly assassinate Allied generals). However, a copy of Skorzeny's operational order was obtained by the Allies from a captured German. The order probably caused greater panic than Skorzeny's troops themselves could have achieved. Word of the order led to extraordinary confusion—and distrust—in the Allied camp and to stringent security measures.[15]

Then, ready or not, the parachute battalion was ordered to jump near Monschau on the night of December 16. All twelve hundred paratroopers had finally arrived at Paderborn; the Luftwaffe had found 112 Junkers transports to lift them. When Von der Heydte talked to the pilots, he was appalled: only one of the 112 had ever dropped paratroopers. Nonetheless, by midnight the formation was airborne, flying very low, following a path of sky-beamed searchlights toward the front. Near the Monschau DZ, Von der Heydte (who had recently broken his arm) jumped first—and was knocked unconscious in the landing. Eventually Von der Heydte assembled about three hundred of his paratroopers, but they never could get organized for an attack, and ultimately Von der Heydte surrendered in despair. His other nine hundred paratroopers, wildly scattered behind Allied lines, caused further disquiet and more stringent Allied security measures, but did no real damage.[16]

Immediately to the south, in Middleton's thin VIII Corps sector, the Germans made better progress, although not as much as planned. Generally, the whole VIII Corps front caved in under the weight of the German attack. However, there, too, many American soldiers fought back with astonishing vigor, courage and resourcefulness. When the Germans hit Alan Jones's green 106th Division, which had relieved Robertson's 2nd Division for the Roer River dam attack and had been in the front lines only five days, it came apart at the seams. Even so, the two regiments in the front lines (422 and 423), cut off and surrounded, held out for two full days before they were compelled to

360 ★   RIDGWAY'S PARATROOPERS

surrender—the worst defeat in the American Army's war with Germany. The 106's other regiment (424) fell back on St. Vith more or less intact, along with some of the division's artillery and CCB of the green 9th Armored Division. To the south of the 106, Dutch Cota's 28th Division, also massively hit, likewise came apart. The 112th Regiment, which had been hard-hit in the Hürtgen Forest and which was composed of many green replacements, fell back on St. Vith. The more southerly placed regiments, 110 and 109, along with CCR, 9th Armored Division, fought valiantly, but the 110 was badly chewed up, the 109 forced to the southwest, while CCR fell back on Bastogne. Farthest south, Barton's 4th Division and the CCA of the 9th Armored Division likewise gave way and bent around to the southwest above Luxembourg City, forming what would become the "southern shoulder."†

Bradley, Hodges and Patton had made contingency plans in the unlikely event the Germans attacked Middleton's VIII Corps. The key factors of the plan were two powerful reinforcements. In event of a "spoiling attack," Simpson would send his reserve 7th Armored Division, commanded by Robert W. Hasbrouck, to backstop Middleton. Patton would send his newly arrived 10th Armored Division, commanded by William Morris (the original commander of Ridgway's XVIII Airborne Corps). Twenty-four hours after the Germans attacked, both divisions were on the move, albeit sluggishly, into the besieged VIII Corps sector: the 10th up from the south, the 7th down from the north. These reinforcements gave Middleton six divisions, three armored (7th, 9th, 10th) and three infantry (106th, 28th, 4th).[18]

At his headquarters in Versailles, Eisenhower was among the first to realize that the German attack was no minor "spoiling attack" but, rather, a massive offensive led by the Sixth and Fifth panzer armies, and that its aim was the Meuse River and beyond to Antwerp. The German armies, no longer under radio silence, soon provided the code breakers with abundant evidence that Eisenhower's intuition was right. Reading the fragmentary and alarming reports from the front, Eisenhower began to doubt that the Allies could hold for long and soon launched a series of steps to reinforce the front and to build a strong defensive line to block the German juggernaut at the Meuse River.

There was very little reserve force to call upon. SHAEF's principal reserve then consisted of the 82nd and 101st airborne divisions, based near Rheims. But Bradley and Hodges had asked for these two divisions to help fill the yawning "gap" torn in the front between V and VIII Corps. Reluctantly, Eisenhower yielded the two airborne divisions to Bradley. At about the same time, he issued orders that the 11th Armored Division, newly arrived in Normandy, and the two airborne divisions in England—Bud Miley's 17th and Eric

---

† A little-known but interesting sidelight in the VIII Corps defense was the first large-scale employment of Negro field-artillery units in World War II. There were a total of nine Negro field-artillery battalions in VIII Corps. Four of seven VIII Corps artillery units (333, 559, 578 and 740) supporting the 106th Division were black. Some of these units broke, but others, fighting bravely, fell back on St. Vith, others on Bastogne and elsewhere.[17]

Bols's 6th—be rushed forward to take positions behind the Meuse, the 17th by air, the 6th by ship. In addition, SHAEF mobilized every available outfit—engineers, artillery, etc.—not actually at the front, to take up positions at the key Meuse River bridges. To reinforce the Meuse Line, Montgomery ordered Horrocks' 30 Corps to positions behind the river between Liège and Huy.

In all of these early Allied reactions, two very different views about how to cope with the situation arose. Montgomery, who had never had much confidence in Eisenhower, Bradley or Hodges, believed that the threat was of utmost gravity and would grow even more dire as the Germans committed reserves to widen the gap. He had no faith in the ability of the American generals to deal with it and felt he should be placed in full command of the Allied front. His tactical plan was to "roll with the punch," hoping to stop the Germans at the Meuse while holding the northern and southern shoulders. He would then "tidy up the battlefield" and at some distant, indefinite date, lead a massive single counterattack into Germany from the north. Eisenhower, Bradley, Hodges and Patton believed that the German offensive was rash, ill-advised and bound to fail and that it had presented the Allies with a golden opportunity to destroy the principal German forces on the western front by a quick and decisive counterattack. Their tactical plan was to simultaneously contain the forward thrust and powerfully attack the "bulge" on its flanks at the earliest possible moment. These differing views would lead to the most tempestuous infighting the Allied generals had yet engaged in, a dispute so bitter that it would very nearly wreck the Allied high command.

Eisenhower's decision to release the 82nd and 101st divisions to Bradley did not at first include Ridgway and the XVIII Airborne Corps. One plan was that the airborne divisions would be assigned to a newly arrived (and green) corps headquarters, XVI, commanded by John B. Anderson. Later this proposed plan would give rise to speculation that Bradley had temporarily "soured" on Ridgway for various reasons. A more likely explanation is that, in the crisis, Bradley initially reached for a corps trained for ground battles, rather than a corps trained for airborne operations. In any case, at the specific request of Courtney Hodges, the plan was soon abandoned and Ridgway and the XVIII Airborne Corps were ordered to lead the airborne divisions into battle. Thus Ridgway would make his combat debut as corps commander on the ground, not in the air.[19]

The orders were telephoned to XVIII Airborne Corps at about 7:30 P.M. on December 17—a long thirty-six hours after the Germans commenced the attack. Owing in part to the sense of complacency in the Allied camp and the approaching Christmas season, not many senior airborne officers were present. Ridgway was in England at XVIII Airborne Corps "rear" headquarters, overseeing some readiness tests in Bud Miley's 17th Airborne Division. Max Taylor, on Ridgway's instructions, was in Washington making yet another try at persuading the War Department to officially authorize an increase in the strength of airborne divisions. The 101's ADC, Gerry Higgins, and five senior 101 commanders were in England conducting a critique on MARKET. (Some

101 senior staffers were investigating the recent and shocking suicide of the 101 chief of staff, Bud Millener, who had killed himself with his pistol.) Other senior commanders of both divisions were on furloughs or junkets in Paris and elsewhere.[20]

The most senior officers present were Major General Jim Gavin, commanding the 82nd, his brand-new ADC, Colonel Ira P. (I.P.) Swift (who was in line for a promotion to brigadier general), the 101's artillery commander, Brigadier General Tony McAuliffe, and Brigadier General Doc Eaton, chief of staff of the XVIII Airborne Corps. Pending Ridgway's arrival from England, Gavin temporarily assumed command of the corps, as well as of his own division, and with Eaton's concurrence, named Tony McAuliffe temporary commander of the 101 and McAuliffe's exec, Thomas Sherburne, temporary 101 artillery commander.[21]‡

Luckily, XVIII Airborne Corps now had additional combat-hardened airborne resources upon whom it could call in this crisis. These were four of the five independent American parachute units that had participated in DRAGOON and then in "the Champagne Campaign" on the Riviera. They had arrived by train and truck only a few days earlier. These were Rupert Graves's 517 Parachute Regiment, the independent 509th Parachute Battalion, commanded by Edmund Tomasik, and the independent 551st Parachute Battalion, commanded by Wood Joerg. (The fifth DRAGOON infantry unit, the independent 550th Glider Battalion, had been sent to England to be incorporated into Miley's 17th Airborne Division.) In all, there were five experienced battalions —about four thousand paratroopers. They were reinforced by two experienced parachute-field-artillery battalions: Raymond L. Cato's 460 and John Cooper's 463, both of which had also participated in DRAGOON and "the Champagne Campaign."[22]

Cooper's 463rd, originally constituted in Italy from cadres of the 82nd's 456th Parachute Artillery, was assigned to the 101st, where it was welcomed. The outfit had fought at Cassino and Anzio and had helped liberate Rome before DRAGOON. Cooper remembered: "We'd only been there five days. We were supposed to be assigned to the 13th Airborne Division, I think. But Tony McAuliffe said: 'How soon can you move out [with the 101st]?' We hadn't even unloaded our trucks yet, so I said: 'Forty-five minutes, but I don't have any orders.' 'To hell with that, go see Bud Harper in the 327th.' I said to Harper, 'Do you need me?' He said, 'You're goddamned right!' So, in this way, we joined the 101st as support for the 327, and stayed with the 101 to the end of the war."[23]

‡ "I.P." Swift was a highly competent and courageous officer but a curious choice to fill the long-vacant 82nd ADC job. A West Pointer (1918), eleven years senior to Gavin, Swift was not a paratrooper, nor had he had any connection with the division. He was a tanker and a Bradley protégé who had only two months of combat experience, as commander of a tank outfit in the 2nd Armored Division. Most likely, Bradley and/or Hodges named Swift to the vacant 82nd ADC job in order to get him a well-deserved promotion. He had reported to the division on December 10.

Gavin assembled the staffs and commanders in the war room at 8 P.M. He was cool, crisp and ready to fight. The initial SHAEF orders were to prepare both the 82nd and the 101st for movement "toward Bastogne" at dawn on December 19. But, at 9:30 P.M., a new SHAEF order arrived directing that both divisions move "without delay in the direction of Bastogne." Gavin decreed that the 82nd would leave first—one hour after daylight the following morning, December 18; the 101, which had remained in Holland longer and was thus less well prepared, would follow at about 2 P.M., the independent units later. The local Army area commander would provide every truck he could lay his hands on. All troopers on pass would be rounded up and brought in; emergency measures would be initiated to find and recall divisional officers from Paris, London, or wherever they might be.[24]

Having set this vast movement in train, Gavin, accompanied by his G-1, Al Ireland, and his aide, Hugo Olson, got in a jeep at 11:30 P.M. and headed for Hodges' First Army headquarters at Spa. It was a long, "wickedly miserable" night's drive in cold rain and fog through territory that was possibly infiltrated by German saboteurs and paratroopers. They arrived cold but unharmed the next morning at nine o'clock. Gavin found First Army headquarters in turmoil —preparing to evacuate rearward to Chaudfontaine, outside Liège—the battle situation "rather vague." However, by this time, Hodges had firmed up his plans for the airborne forces. Gavin's 82nd Division and the independent units would be attached to Gerow's V Corps and take position on the north "front" near Werbomont, a crossroads twenty miles northwest of St. Vith. The 101st would be attached to Middleton's VIII Corps and remain at Bastogne.

For most of that day—December 18—Gavin was on the move by jeep. He first drove south and established the 82nd CP at Werbomont. He then scouted briefly eastward to the village of Habiemont, where he found some engineers preparing a bridge for demolition. Everyone he encountered was "excited." False rumors had it that the German panzers were nearly at the doorstep of Werbomont. Finding no signs of Germans, Gavin drove back to Bastogne to confer with Troy Middleton and Tony McAuliffe, who was assembling the 101st into Bastogne, as per the original instructions Gavin had issued. Gavin gave McAuliffe verbal orders assigning the 101st to Middleton's VIII Corps, then set off again for his CP at Werbomont.

Later, a legend would arise—and get into print—that the 101st went to Bastogne more or less by happenstance. According to this story, the 101st was actually on the way to Werbomont to join the 82nd when McAuliffe, running ahead of the main body of his division, detoured into Bastogne to confer with Middleton. While he was in conference, so the story goes, the acting division artillery chief, Tom Sherburne, leading the main body of the division, learned from an MP on the road that McAuliffe had gone to Bastogne and, "acting on a hunch," led the 101st into the city. However, Gavin's after-action report, written in 1945, makes it clear that the 101st was destined for Bastogne right from the beginning.[25]

What was truly legendary in all this was that both airborne divisions had moved with all their fighting gear from their comfortable rear-area bases to their frontline positions within a mere twenty-four hours, and were ready to fight.

☆39☆

AT ABOUT 0215 on December 18, Ridgway received word that the XVIII Airborne Corps was to be deployed into battle. Most of the corps headquarters personnel were with him at Marlborough. During the early-morning hours of that day he arranged with Paul Williams to have the corps headquarters flown to Rheims. At 0830, Ridgway and the corps personnel (and strays from the 82nd and 101st) took off in fifty-five IX Troop Carrier planes. In spite of the terrible weather, all planes landed safely in Rheims between 1100 and 1300.[1]

Later that day, FAAA received advance word from SHAEF to prepare to move the 17th and the 6th airborne divisions to France by air and ship, respectively. By the time the official movement orders reached Bud Miley's headquarters the next day, the weather had grown far worse and IX Troop Carrier Command was grounded. It would remain grounded for three days. Subsequently, its aircraft would be diverted to emergency resupply missions, delaying Miley's movement several more days. As it would turn out, Eric Bols's 6th Division, moving by ship, arrived in France on about the same day as the 17th Division: about one week after the movement orders arrived, too late to play a significant role in the early Bulge fighting.[2]

After landing at Rheims, Ridgway hurried to the advanced XVIII Corps CP in Épernay, where Doc Eaton was holding the fort, swamped by urgent messages and phone calls.

The first telephone call Ridgway took was from Hodges' chief of staff, William B. (Captain Bligh) Kean. First Army was anxious; Ridgway was to do all in his power to move the two airborne divisions forward to Werbomont and Bastogne. He was to establish XVIII Airborne Corps on the north shoulder near the 82nd Division CP at Werbomont.[3]

There was nothing more Ridgway could do to rush the paratroopers forward. The 82nd had already begun its movement; the 101st and the independent units were now moving out as fast as trucks could be found. Ridgway waited until the last battalion of the 101 had left, then jumped into a staff car and set off in the drizzle and fog to establish the XVIII Airborne Corps CP at Werbomont. The narrow roads were jammed with traffic going and coming.

On the way, Ridgway stopped for the night at Middleton's corps CP in Bastogne. The city was crowded with tired, begrimed and confused survivors of the divisions that had been overrun by the German assault forces. No one seemed to have any solid information on the situation; communications with forward units had been lost. Gloom and fear were in the air; many men had "bug-out fever." Ridgway heard a soldier say, "We better get the hell out of here." Another rejoined, "We can't. They've got us surrounded."[4]

For the fourth time in the war, Ridgway found himself in a crisis in which the outlook appeared very dark for the Americans. On first glance from Bastogne, the German bulge appeared to be a far more desperate situation than Sicily, Salerno or Normandy.

Ridgway seemed to thrive in such crises. While others around him grew ever more frantic and disorganized, he became increasingly cool, deliberate and methodical, as though some magically soothing potion had been released into his blood. The more dire the threat, the calmer he appeared to be. In the bulge, he would become a rock to which many senior commanders would cling.

Notwithstanding the defeatism and panic in Bastogne, Ridgway, like Eisenhower, Bradley and Hodges, was already thinking *offensively*. The Allies had banged on the bloody door to the German lair for three solid months without being able to enter. Now, astonishingly, the Germans had rushed out of the lair swinging like maniacs. The proper response, Ridgway believed, was to first absorb and check the penetration, then close hard on its flanks before the Germans could pull back into the lair. Later, he put it this way: "If a man hits you a surprise blow and knocks you sprawling, you've got to get up off the ground at once, and flatten him, or you are beaten."[5]

From Middleton, Ridgway learned for the first time that the 101st was to remain in Bastogne under VIII Corps control. This news did not sit well. Ridgway had left England with the expectation that his XVIII Airborne Corps would be "all airborne," composed of the 82nd, the 101st and—when it arrived —the 17th. "I felt a keen regret," Ridgway wrote. "The 82nd and 101st were brothers in the blood. They had fought side by side in Normandy and they knew and trusted each other. Now they were to be separated . . ." Later, he was equally disappointed to learn that Miley's 17th Division, which contained many "blood brothers" in Raff's 507 Regiment, would not be joining XVIII Airborne Corps either.[6]

The next day, December 19, Ridgway left Bastogne at first light to establish the XVIII Airborne Corps CP at Werbomont. The shortest route was more or less due north, through Houffalize and Manhay, a trip of about forty miles. Some sixth sense—"God's guidance," he said later—warned him that the Germans might be in Houffalize, so he took a longer way around, angling northwest to Marche, then northeast to Manhay. That morning, spearheads of the 116th Panzer Division overran Houffalize.[7]

Ridgway paused at the Werbomont crossroads briefly, to choose a site for the XVIII Airborne Corps CP (a two-story farmhouse), then continued due north about fifteen miles to Chaudfontaine, outside Liège, where Hodges had relocated First Army headquarters. He arrived "early in the morning," the headquarters diarist William C. Sylvan wrote, "with his two customary hand grenades strapped to his shoulders." (Actually, one grenade, one first-aid kit.) Ridgway immediately went into a lengthy conference with Hodges and his chief of staff, Bill Kean.[8]

Within the small professional infantry branch of the American Army, Georgia-born Courtney Hodges was almost universally revered. In Bradley's words, Hodges was "an august figure like Marshall, the quintessential 'Georgia gentleman' and the most modest man I had ever met." He had begun his Army career at West Point with the class of 1908 but had washed out owing to a weak background in mathematics. He had then enlisted in the Army as a private, won a commission in 1909 (one year behind his classmates) and became a hero (DSC) in World War I. During the peacetime years, Hodges, like Bradley, had been a Marshall protégé and had advanced quietly, steadily and competently through the ranks to command of the Infantry School, then chief of infantry. First Army had fought hard and well (often better than any other), but owing to his innate shyness, modesty and dour personality, Hodges had not made flaming headlines, like Montgomery and Patton.[9]

He was perhaps not the best leader for the battlefield crisis the Allies now confronted. "Even in the most optimistic circumstances," Bradley wrote, "he had an air of caution. Now [on December 19] Hodges was sounding more and more depressed at a time when we needed Pattonesque bravado." He was older than most—nearly fifty-eight—and not in good physical condition. He had not slept much in the past three nights. In addition to all else, he had just undergone the personal trauma and humiliation of moving his CP to the rear.[10]

Ridgway held Courtney Hodges in highest esteem and felt a close kinship with First Army. Hodges' senior staffers were alumni of the II Corps in North Africa and Sicily and had more combat experience than any other American Army staff in the ETO. First Army, in turn, had highest respect for Ridgway and his legendary 82nd Airborne Division and were very glad to have XVIII Airborne Corps in the command. Exuding confidence, optimism and aggressiveness, Ridgway was like a tonic to Hodges and his harassed staff.[11]

That morning, the Battle of the Bulge was three days old and the situation was becoming clearer. First Army had taken a terrific wallop, the German penetration was deep and wide, but there was now some encouraging news. The critical north shoulder near Bütgenbach and Elsenborn was holding. Hodges had reinforced the 2nd and 99th infantry divisions with the combat-hardened 1st Infantry Division, and another veteran infantry division, the 9th, was on the way toward that area, along with massive artillery support. St. Vith was also holding. The horseshoe-shaped defensive perimeter there, manned by two infantry regiments (112, 424), CCB of the 9th Armored Division, and considerable artillery, were being augmented by most of Hasbrouck's 7th Armored Division. These actions had channeled four-plus divisions of Sixth Panzer Army into a narrow (ten-mile) corridor between Bütgenbach and St. Vith, severely limiting maneuver and creating further monumental traffic jams. As a result, Sixth Panzer Army was moving sluggishly and falling far behind schedule. Farther south in the gap, Bastogne, now reinforced by elements of the 10th Armored Division and the entire 101st, was holding, impeding the progress of the much faster-moving Fifth Panzer Army, which could ill afford to leave a strong Allied enclave at Bastogne in its rear.[12]

The greatest danger that morning, as Hodges saw it, was a breakthrough on his front west of Bütgenbach. That danger was posed by a powerful armored force of the 1st SS Panzer Division, Kampfgruppe Peiper, commanded by a Hitler favorite, twenty-nine-year-old SS officer Joachim Peiper, which was spearheading the Sixth Panzer Army. Peiper's force was falling far behind schedule, but it had already passed near Malmédy (where some of Peiper's men massacred eighty-six GIs), and it had reached Stavelot and Stoumont, where Peiper hoped to seize a bridge or bridges to cross the Amblève River, giving him a direct northwest route to Liège and Antwerp.

The principal reason for positioning Ridgway's XVIII Airborne Corps, and the 82nd Airborne Division, at Werbomont was to block Peiper and the Sixth Panzer Army forces coming behind him. To help in this task, Hodges had also brought down from the north the veteran 30th Infantry Division, commanded by Leland S. Hobbs, and the veteran 3rd Armored Division, commanded by Maurice Rose, was on its way down to lend additional support. The three regiments of Hobbs's 30th Division (117, 119, 120) had already deployed at Malmédy (120th), Stavelot (117th) and Stoumont (119th). The 82nd Airborne Division would deploy east from Werbomont, to link on the north with Hobbs's 119th Regiment near Stoumont and Trois Ponts and form a north-south line behind the Salm River between Trois Ponts and Vielsalm and establish a line of communication with the St. Vith forces through Vielsalm.*

The most urgent tasks were thus mainly defensive: to block Peiper and establish a link with the St. Vith forces. But Hodges was already formulating plans for a massive counterattack to trap the Germans outside the lair and had been discussing these plans with Bradley by telephone. (The day before, December 18, Bradley had made half a dozen telephone calls to First Army CP.) The general plan taking shape was a short envelopment: a simultaneous attack on the base of the salient from both north and south, aiming at a linkup near Houffalize. It was to be launched, if possible, within several days.[14]

That same day—December 19—Eisenhower and most of his chief commanders, including Bradley and Patton, met at Bradley's main headquarters, in Verdun, to draw plans for dealing with the crisis. Bradley urged an immediate counterattack on the base of the German salient from the south and, when Hodges stabilized his front, an attack from the north as well. Bradley viewed the bulge as another Mortain (albeit on a larger scale). This time he was absolutely determined there would be no mistakes—no "Falaise gap" through which the Germans could escape. The jaws would clamp shut quickly and firmly at Houffalize. All who were present at the meeting fully agreed with this plan.[15]

When the Germans had struck First Army, Patton's Third Army had been attacking eastward into the Saar. Despite his earlier warnings about the vulnerability of the VIII Corps sector, at first Patton had dismissed the German

* Ridgway's XVIII Airborne Corps would initially command, in addition to the 82nd Airborne Division, the 119th Regiment of Hobbs's 30th Division and all the forces believed to be in St. Vith: the 106th Division, the 7th Armored Division, CCB of the 9th Armored Division, and the 112th Regiment of the 28th Infantry Division. The plan was that after the front had stabilized, the XVIII Airborne Corps was also to command all of the 30th Division and Rose's 3rd Armored Division.[13]

attack as of small consequence and had complained when Bradley took away his 10th Armored Division and stopped his eastward drive. But he had soon realized the gravity of the attack. The day before the meeting with Eisenhower at Verdun, Bradley and Patton had begun making plans for Patton to counterattack the German salient from the south. By the time of the meeting, Patton had already begun alerting some of his forces (organized under a new corps, III) to be prepared to move northward and had established his headquarters in Luxembourg, adjacent to Bradley's.

Thus when Eisenhower asked Patton when he could attack, Patton was able to reply with an answer that became legendary: "On December 22, with three divisions." Unaware that Bradley and Patton had already taken many preliminary steps for such an attack, Eisenhower replied tartly, "Don't be fatuous." But Patton would make good his boast, and III Corps, commanded by a newcomer to the ETO, John Millikin, and consisting of the 4th Armored Division and the 26th and 80th infantry divisions, would jump off on December 22, to be followed shortly by Manton Eddy's XII Corps.[16]

At his headquarters near Brussels that same day, Montgomery, far removed from the scene of battle, unhesitatingly seized upon the American misfortune to renew his political campaign to gain control of all ground forces. He cabled London that the situation in the American area was "not repeat not good," that there was "great confusion" and a "definite lack of grip and control" and "great pessimism" and that the Allied command setup, which had always been "very faulty," was "now quite futile." He proposed that Eisenhower be given "a direct order" to place him—Montgomery—in command of all ground forces north of the bulge, including the American First and Ninth armies. Later that day, he made an identical suggestion to Eisenhower's assistant G-3, British General John F. M. Whitely. Both Winston Churchill and Whitely, acting independently, carried Montgomery's proposal to Eisenhower.[17]

In what was probably Eisenhower's most controversial command decision in the European war, he acceded to Montgomery's suggestion and put all American forces north of the bulge under his control. Eisenhower's reasons were four. First, he believed that Bradley, in Luxembourg, was losing touch with Hodges and Simpson and could not properly manage the battlefield. Second, although he had the authority to order Montgomery to commit British forces to help Hodges, he had hesitated to do so. Eisenhower hoped that by placing Montgomery in charge in the north, Montgomery would be quicker to commit his own forces—most particularly Horrocks' strong 30 Corps, which was an ideal force for launching the counterattack from the north. Third, relieving Bradley of responsibility for northern operations would leave him free to closely oversee Patton's vital northward counterattack, on which the hope of cutting the German salient to pieces now greatly depended. Four, SHAEF had begun to doubt that Hodges had the personality to inspire his soldiers sufficiently to meet the crisis. Montgomery had the necessary battlefield flair that was now required.

When Bradley was informed of the decision, he was shocked and outraged. He perceived it as a slap in the face to him, to Hodges and to every GI in his vast command. He also worried that the media would trumpet the decision as "Monty coming to the rescue of the fumbling American generals." He protested that his telephonic communications with Hodges' CP were excellent and volunteered to move his own CP to Namur to improve them. He doubted that the appointment would encourage Montgomery to commit 30 Corps to battle. Moreover, he well knew that First Army staff had despised Montgomery since North Africa and Sicily days, and he doubted that it would work in harmony with him. Above all else, Bradley worried about Montgomery's professional competence. Bradley believed Montgomery was a mediocre glory hound who lacked aggressiveness and probably would throw away this golden opportunity to annihilate the German Army.[18]

The decision to place Hodges' First Army under Montgomery was made only a few hours after Ridgway opened XVIII Airborne Corps for business at Werbomont. It had no immediate impact on Ridgway's operations. But quite soon Montgomery's views, which conflicted with those of Hodges and Ridgway, would dominate Allied tactics in the north and significantly alter the shape and direction of the battle.

After he had conferred with Hodges at First Army on December 19, Ridgway returned to XVIII Airborne CP at Werbomont. For him and his soldiers it was an eerie and nerve-wracking time. The rumors had spread about the German paratroopers and Skorzeny's saboteurs. The Americans could not be certain who was friend or foe. Everyone was tense and trigger-happy.

"It was quite a challenge," recalled Ridgway, "taking over our sixty-five-mile front in that critical stage of the Ardennes. The visibility was such that at seventy-five yards you couldn't see the bulk of a 2½ ton truck. It was right down to the ground. And those black pine woods on both sides of the road—it was just like night. No one knew where anyone else was . . ."[19]

The XVIII Airborne Corps headquarters, a major staff command, had never yet been deployed in combat. The Bulge was its baptism of fire. Most of the key men—Eaton, Schellhammer, Jack, Moorman—had seen plenty of combat, from Sicily onward, but not the new, young G-3, Day Surles: "I had never been in combat before. At first it didn't seem all that bad, but it soon became so. I wasn't wise enough in the ways of combat to know how bad it really was. Hodges assigned us various and sundry units—divisions, artillery battalions, anybody he could lay hands on. Ridgway and I decided which way they'd go. They'd report to our little CP and I'd draw a circle on the map and say that's where you go. We didn't know if the Germans had got there or not. We just told them to go prepared to fight their way into positions."[20]

When Ridgway was present, the atmosphere in the CP was serene and businesslike. One officer, Richard J. Seitz, remembered being summoned to headquarters on an official assignment:

It was night, dark; the situation was still fluid. People everywhere were on edge; MPs challenging, still lots of confusion, etc. However, when I walked into the CP, there sat General Ridgway in a calm discussion with General

Eaton, looking at a large situation map on the wall, and just completely at ease and in complete control of himself and the corps. To this day the calm that existed in that CP impresses me. Before reporting to the corps, everywhere else seemed confusion, march and countermarch. And then, where there really should have been people running around shouting, etc., everything was calm, low key and organized.[21]

Ridgway, however, would rarely be in his CP. As in previous combat situations, he believed his proper place was at the front. "You must have this close personal relationship with each of your key staff officers," he said later, "as well as with each of your unit commanders, so that they know you and they know your thinking. That way you can listen to any belly-aching they have got and give them an opportunity to talk so you are accessible to them, mentally as well as physically."[22]

This method of operating close to the front—unusual for a corps commander—placed a heavy burden on Ridgway's chief of staff, Doc Eaton. But they had been together so long that, as Ridgway put it, they had virtually a "dual personality" and the "highest degree of mutual respect and confidence." Ridgway would telephone Eaton frequently during the day to relay instructions, talking in code: "I made it clear down through all channels in the corps, [that] any instructions that came from my chief of staff were coming from me. And so Doc ran the staff and kept house at home and I spent all the days out with the troops—where I wanted to be anyway." When Ridgway returned to the CP at night he cleared away "considerable paperwork . . . before getting into his sleeping bag."[23]

By late that same day, December 19, Gavin's 82nd Division was deploying. From Werbomont, Rube Tucker's 504 moved northeasterly toward Stoumont and La Gleize, where Hobbs's 119th Infantry and other elements were blocking Peiper's *Kampfgruppe*. Tucker got as far as Rahier. Bill Ekman's 505 moved more or less due east toward Trois Ponts, where the Amblève and Salm Rivers merge, and where the 1st SS Panzer Division was moving to force a crossing of the Salm. Ekman got to Haute Bodeux. Lindquist's 508 moved out southeasterly in the direction of Vielsalm. His lead elements got as far as Bra. Most of Billingslea's 325 remained near Werbomont in reserve, but some patrols pushed west to Barvaux.[24]

On the next day, December 20, Tucker's 504 had a bloody encounter with the Germans. Scouting northeast from Rahier, Tucker learned that a strong German force from Peiper's command was in Cheneux, a few miles northeast. A bridge over the Amblève led to Cheneux. If left in German hands it could afford Peiper a route west to Werbomont. Gavin, who came on the scene, ordered Tucker to attack Cheneux, destroy the German forces and capture the bridge. Tucker committed two battalions to the attack: Willard Harrison's 1st and Julian Aaron Cook's 3rd. The leading companies of Harrison's battalion attacked across open ground without artillery support into the teeth of a well-organized German defense, which included barbed-wire fences. In two days of bitter fighting, Tucker lost 225 men, dead and wounded, but he took Cheneux —and the bridge—and forced the Germans to flee. Tucker and the 504th were "proud" of that battle, Gavin wrote, but at least one military historian, Charles B. MacDonald, judged that while the frontal assault was "incredibly heroic," it was "ill-conceived and senseless."[25]

Gavin had appointed his new ADC, "I.P." Swift, to oversee the easterly drive of Ekman's 505. Advancing on Trois Ponts on December 20, Swift and Ekman were astonished to learn that a group of American engineers, commanded by Robert B. Yates, still held the major portion of the town on the west bank of the Salm. Moreover, Yates and his men had blown the three main bridges in Trois Ponts, an action which had blocked Peiper and forced him to go northwestward to Stoumont. Yates said laconically, "I'll bet you guys are glad we are here."[26]

Swift and Ekman, taking advantage of this good work, began expanding the Salm River defenses in this sector to ensure an entrapment of Peiper. They ordered 2nd Battalion commander Ben Vandervoort to send two companies (E, F) across the Salm River into "eastern" Trois Ponts. They dispatched the other two battalions (Woody Long's 1st, Kaiser's 3rd) south along the Salm River to La Veuville and Petit-Halleux to demolish bridges in those places and establish defenses on the east-bank there and farther south. Crossing over the ruins of a demolished bridge, Vandervoort's two companies in "east" Trois Ponts were hit by armored elements of the 1st SS Panzer Division, which had come up to help spring Peiper. On Swift's order, Vandervoort reluctantly gave up the "east" Trois Ponts "bridgehead" and withdrew his two companies back across the Salm to the main part of town on the west bank. There, Vandervoort coolly assured Gavin he could hold off the 1st SS Panzer Division—and he did. South of Trois Ponts, Long's and Kaiser's thinly dispersed battalions repulsed 1st SS Panzer Division troops crossing the river, or slaughtered those few who got across.[27]

These early fights of the 504 and 505 were the first the paratroopers had ever had with Hitler's SS forces. The SS soldiers proved to be formidable. They were healthy, young, fanatical (and brutal) Nazis, dedicated to Hitler and the Third Reich. They believed they were embarked on a "holy task" to throw the Allies back into the sea and save the Fatherland. In their own way, they were also like a "pack of jackals," far superior in fighting spirit to the troops of the normal panzer or *Volksgrenadier* divisions.[28]

Roy Lindquist's 508, meanwhile, continued southeastly toward Vielsalm. His task force included Carter Todd's 319th Glider Field Artillery Battalion, which now had 105 mm snub-nose howitzers. Owing to a shortage of trucks, most of the infantry traveled into the unknown on foot. During the late evening and night, the force, having met no enemy, arrived at Goronne, where Lindquist established his CP. His troopers continued south a half mile to occupy Thier-du-Mont Ridge, and east to the small town of Rencheux, which overlooked Vielsalm and the Salm River. At Rencheux his troops established tenuous links with Woody Long's 1st Battalion, 505. Lindquist's position was ten miles due west of the back side of the St. Vith horseshoe.[29]

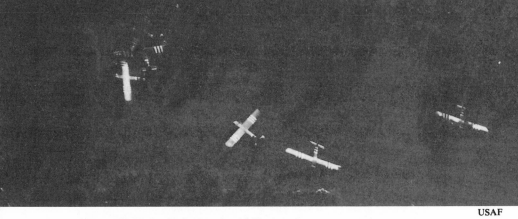

Glider crashes in the hedgerows of Normandy.

A British Horsa (right) and an American Waco crashed side by side.

The 101st regimental commanders in Normandy: (Top) Howard R. (Skeets) Johnson, 501st, shown here, before takeoff, conferring with Ninth Air Force commander Lewis H. Brereton.

(Left to right mug shots): John H. (Mike) Michaelis, who replaced George V. H. Moseley in the 502nd on D+1. Robert F. Sink, 506th. Joseph H. Harper, 327th.

New regimental commanders in the 82nd Airborne Division during Normandy, or later: William E. Ekman, 505.

Edson D. Raff, 507, replacing George V. Millett, Jr., who was captured.

Charles Billingslea, 325th, replacing Harry L. Lewis, who was relieved.

After Normandy, Eisenhower created the First Allied Airborne Army. Its principal fighting strength was the American XVIII Airborne Corps. Posed here are the key staff officers of the XVIII Airborne Corps, less the chief of staff, Ralph P. (Doc) Eaton. (Left to right) Frank W. Moorman, G-4; Whitfield Jack, G-2; Frederick M. Schellhammer, G-1; James B. Quill, deputy chief of staff; A. Day Surles, G-3; Jay G. Brown, air officer; Harry P. Cain (later a U.S. senator), G-5.

The airborne division
commanders for Holland:
Robert E. Urquhart, British
1st Airborne.

James M. Gavin, 82nd
Airborne.

Maxwell D. Taylor, 101st
Airborne.

Gavin with his principal division staffers and regimental commanders prepare for the jump into Holland. (Standing, left to right) Walter F. Winton, Jr., G-2; Rube Tucker, CO, 504; Alfred W. Ireland, G-1; Francis A. March III, commander, division artillery; Albert G. Marin, G-4; Gavin (pointing at map); Charles Billingslea, CO, 325th; John Norton, G-3. (Seated on benches, left to right) William Ekman, CO, 505; Robert Wienecke, chief of staff. Missing: Roy E. Lindquist, CO, 508th.

Paratroopers of the 82nd Airborne Division load for the jump into Holland.

Holland, near Grave. American Waco gliders on the ground, more paratroopers in the sky.

When all this had been done, the 82nd Airborne Division occupied a horse-shoe-shaped area about eighty square miles in area. The "closed end" of the horseshoe faced east on the Salm River from Trois Ponts to just short of Salmchâteau. The northern part curved back through Trois Ponts and Cheneux to Werbomont. The southern part curved back from Vielsalm across Thier-du-Mont toward Manhay. The "open end" of the horseshoe was the area between Manhay and Werbomont. The three parachute regiments manned the "closed end" of the horseshoe: Tucker's 504 from Cheneux to Trois Ponts, Ekman's 505 from Trois Ponts to Rencheux, and Lindquist's 508 from Rencheux through Thier-du-Mont.[30]†

On December 20, after the 82nd had made its deployments, Hodges attached Hobbs's full 30th Infantry Division and major elements of Rose's 3rd Armored Division to XVIII Airborne Corps. Leland Hobbs was a classmate of Eisenhower's and Bradley's, a star athlete at West Point and Bradley's old and good friend. Bradley observed: "At West Point he had a big strong jaw and stubborn streak a mile wide. Nobody could get by him on the football field. His division was a perfect expression of his character." The 30th had landed early at Omaha Beach and fought through the hedgerows to St. Lô. During Hitler's Mortain counterattack in early August, it had absorbed the weight of the blow and held. Now, in a similar defensive mission, it was again reflecting Hobbs's stubborn streak. Ridgway had overlapped at West Point with Hobbs and knew him well. At first, however, the two commanders clashed. Surles remembered: "Hobbs was not flashy, but he was solid. He was not attacking with the kind of vigor Ridgway usually demanded, and, at first Ridgway was very impatient with him. And I don't think Hobbs liked Ridgway either in the beginning. But later, that changed."[32]

Maurice Rose was a rare bird in the American Army: a non-West Point general of Jewish background, son of a rabbi. Joe Collins (a devout Catholic) admired Rose unreservedly, describing him later as "tall, handsome, always dressed immaculately, even in combat," and a "commanding figure" who claimed instant respect and was "somewhat stern" and "not given to easy comradeship." Perhaps because of his Jewish origins, Collins wrote, Rose was "wholly dedicated to defeating Nazis." Ever since Normandy, Rose's 3rd Armored Division, which had operated primarily with Collins' VII Corps, had performed with superb aggressiveness. Patton and his tankers notwithstanding, Collins believed that Maurice Rose "was the top armored commander in the Army." Ridgway agreed. He thought Rose was "one of the most gallant soldiers" he had ever known.[33]

When Ridgway absorbed Hobbs and Rose into XVIII Airborne Corps, their divisions were disposed as follows. The 30th was still holding a south-facing

---

† On December 21, the southern line of the horseshoe was reinforced. Ridgway sent Chuck Billingslea's 325th Glider Regiment south to man a thin line stretching more or less from the 508's position on the high ground at Thier-du-Mont west through Hébronval to Regne and Fraiture.[31]

defensive line from Malmédy west to Stoumont, and its 119th Infantry Regiment at the latter place had linked, tenuously, with Tucker's 504. Unlike most armored divisions, Rose's had no CCR, but his CCA and CCB were very powerful. His CCB, commanded by Truman E. Boudinot, had deployed with the 30th Division, blocking Peiper. His CCA, commanded by Doyle O. Hickey, was in First Army reserve, at Eupen, behind Gerow's V Corps.

At that time Ridgway was quite concerned about the "void" south and west of Werbomont; that is, Gavin's right (or west) flank. There were indications that the Germans, bypassing St. Vith to the south, might swing northwest into that area. He could not persuade Hodges to release Hickey's CCA to fill the "void," but Rose had some armored "reserves," which he detailed to the task. These reserves were divided up into little "task forces" (named for their commanders: Hogan, Kane and Orr), and they staged south and southeast out of the Werbomont area toward La Roche, Samrée and Fraiture.[34]

By that time, the ex-DRAGOON airborne forces were arriving at Werbomont. These five battalions, comprising about four thousand men, gave Ridgway a substantial pool of infantry. He used part of the pool to provide manpower for Rose's thin units at Soy and for the little armored task forces probing south and southeast. Rose got Edmund Tomasik's independent 509th Parachute Battalion and the 1st Battalion of Ralph Graves's 517th Parachute Regiment, commanded by William J. Boyle. In addition, he gave Wood Joerg's independent 551st Parachute Battalion to Leland Hobbs. He kept Graves's two other parachute battalions (2nd, 3rd) in XVIII Airborne Corps reserve near Werbomont.[35]

Ridgway was anywhere and everywhere, jeeping from one unit to the next all day long, heedless of his own safety. On one of these jaunts, while looking for one of Hobbs's battalion commanders somewhere deep in a woods, he dismounted from his jeep, carrying his .30-06 Springfield rifle, which was loaded with armor-piercing cartridges, and went ahead alone on foot. Suddenly he heard a "tremendous clatter." He looked behind him and saw what he thought was a German tank. He spun and fired five quick shots at the swastika on the side. As he did so, he realized that it was not a tank, but a big armored, self-propelled German gun. The vehicle veered crazily and ground to a halt. Fortunately, the entire crew was dead. Later, thanking God for his trusty Springfield, Ridgway said aptly, "It was just lucky that I wasn't picked up by the Germans" on one of these outings.[36]

IN THE AFTERMATH of the Battle of the Bulge, the tenacious and heroic stand of Tony McAuliffe and the 101st Airborne Division at Bastogne would capture the public imagination. Less well known, but no less important, was a similar tenacious and heroic stand of the American forces at St. Vith, which had now been placed under Ridgway's command. Some historians—and senior German commanders—believe the American stand at St. Vith was *more* important than the stand in Bastogne. Years later Gavin said with only slight exaggeration, "A lot of people make the mistake of believing that the Battle of the Bulge was resolved at Bastogne. Actually, that was very much of a sideshow."[1]

St. Vith, an important road hub, lay about midway between Bütgenbach and Bastogne and only a few miles back from (or west of) the original American front. Under Hitler's plan, Manteuffel's Fifth Panzer Army was to overrun both St. Vith and Bastogne in a matter of hours; St. Vith first, then Bastogne. But that plan did not work out. The American forces held at St. Vith for six full days. It became, in the words of one historian, a thumb jammed down the German throat, dividing and channelizing the two German panzer armies, intensifying the traffic jams on the roads in the rear, slowing down everything.

When the Germans first struck the American front, St. Vith (with its many roads) became a sort of collecting point for miscellaneous Allied units which were being pushed back. First came the 14th Cavalry Group, commanded by Mark A. Devine (soon replaced), which had been overrun and mauled in the thinly held Losheim Gap between the 99th and 106th divisions. Next came the headquarters and artillery of Alan Jones's 106th Division, and after that, the 106th's 424th Infantry Regiment, commanded by Alexander D. Reid, an older West Pointer (1923). Next came CCB of Leonard's 9th Armored Division, commanded by William M. Hoge, an able West Point engineer (1916) who, earlier in the war, had built the Alcan Highway, to Alaska. Next came the 112th Infantry Regiment of Dutch Cota's 28th Division, also commanded by an older West Pointer, Gustin M. Nelson (1921). Finally came the full 7th Armored Division, ordered down from the north by Bradley when the Germans broke through.[2]

Of all these forces, by far the most powerful was the 7th Armored Division, which until then had had a somewhat checkered history. Commanded by tanker Lindsey McD. Silvester, it had early entered ETO action in XX Corps of Patton's Third Army. It had done well until Patton ran into heavy German resistance crossing the Moselle River at Metz. There the division had suffered heavy casualties, and Silvester, under pressure from Patton, had perhaps too hastily sacked too many of his senior commanders. (CCA had four commanders in a month; CCR, eight.) In October the division had been transferred from Patton to Montgomery, on "loan" for Montgomery's erstwhile northern offensive, and subsequently, when it bogged down in inconclusive fighting in the Peel marshes, Bradley lost confidence in Silvester and, on October 30, relieved him of command.

Who would now command the division? At that time, the two senior commanders were Robert W. Hasbrouck (CCB) and Dwight A. Rosebaum (CCA). Hasbrouck was a West Pointer (1917) who was described by one of his senior commanders as a "tall, well-built, emotionless, classically handsome man who gave me the impression that, stabbed, he would bleed ice water." He had come to the ETO as an artillery battalion commander in the 4th Armored Division but had later been transferred to a staff job in Bradley's 12th Army Group, where, in a few months, he earned a promotion to brigadier general. He had only recently joined the 7th Armored Division, but he was chosen to command since he was senior to Rosebaum (West Point, 1920) and a Bradley protégé as well.

Immediately after Hasbrouck was named the new commander, the division had been withdrawn from British control and assigned to Ninth Army reserve for refitting. During this period, a colorful, combat-experienced officer from Patton's 4th Armored Division, Bruce C. Clarke, arrived to fill Hasbrouck's former slot as commander CCB. Clarke had not been pleased to leave the 4th Armored and had accepted the new assignment only reluctantly, even though on December 7 he was promoted to brigadier general. St. Vith would thus be the first major test of the division under its new leadership, Hasbrouck and Clarke.[3]

Alan Jones, a major general, was the senior officer present at St. Vith, and while he had almost no combat experience, he initially assumed command and organized a horseshoe-shaped perimeter defense, with the closed end facing due east. He placed Bill Hoge's CCB, Reid's 424 and Nelson's 112 on the right (or south) side of the horseshoe. As Hasbrouck's 7th Armored Division arrived piecemeal from the north, Jones placed it on the left (or north) side of the horseshoe—first (on December 17) Clarke's CCB, later Rosebaum's CCA, and lastly CCR, commanded by Frederick M. Warren.

At first, the 106th's Alan Jones had been outwardly indefatigable and optimistic. Greatly underestimating the strength of the German attack, he had expected that Clarke's CCB would quickly attack east and rescue his surrounded and cut-off 422nd and 423rd regiments. Jones's son, Alan, Jr. (who had stood fourteenth in the swollen, wartime West Point Class of 1943), was serving with the 423rd. But when Jones realized that there was no hope of rescuing the two regiments—and his son—he broke down in despair and asked Clarke, who had been a brigadier general only ten days and was far junior to Hoge, to take tactical command of the defense of St. Vith. Then Jones withdrew his CP rearward to Vielsalm.

When Bob Hasbrouck arrived at St. Vith on December 19 with 7th Armored Division headquarters, he established his CP adjacent to Jones's in Vielsalm. Although he commanded a full armored division, Hasbrouck was still wearing the single star of brigadier general. He was junior in rank to Jones and, owing to that fact, had not been placed by Hodges in overall command of St. Vith forces. Hodges had merely said, "You two carry the ball up there for me," in effect establishing a somewhat murky, joint command: Jones and Hasbrouck. In effect, Hasbrouck, junior to both Jones and Hoge, became *de facto* commander of the St. Vith forces.[4]

After a quick tour of the horseshoe, Bob Hasbrouck became gravely concerned. The forces at hand were not nearly so formidable as the unit designation indicated. He judged that "both infantry regiments are in bad shape"; the 424, for example, he deemed, was only about "twenty percent effective." He felt he was highly vulnerable on his right (or south) flank, where the 424 and 112 were positioned, and he guessed (correctly, it developed) that the Fifth Panzer Army would soon swing a corps northwest and attempt to seize St. Vith and get the thumb out of the German throat.[5]

On the day after he arrived, December 20, Hasbrouck drafted a letter to Hodges' chief of staff, Bill Kean, and sent it off by officer courier. He outlined the weak condition of his infantry forces and predicted a Fifth Panzer Army attack in force on his right (or south) flank, where that infantry was disposed. He stated that *"maybe"* he could delay that attack the rest of that day— December 20—but he would be "cut off by tomorrow." He understood that the 82nd Airborne was coming up on his north flank and stressed that "north flank is not critical." He would hold, as ordered, he said, "but need help," especially close air support. Unaware that the situation in Bastogne was not unlike his own, he proposed an VIII Corps attack out of Bastogne to cut "the bastards" (i.e., Fifth Panzer Army) off in the rear.[6]

Hodges summoned Ridgway to his CP at about the same time that Hasbrouck's letter arrived—the morning of December 20—to discuss options and plans. Ridgway had not even been on the job twenty-four hours, and yet he came bearing a bold and aggressive plan to relieve the situation at St. Vith. His plan was, in a word, *attack*. Hobbs's 30th, Gavin's 82nd and a combat command of Rose's 3rd Armored, positioned on the left (or east) at Malmédy, would attack "vigorously" to the southeast and east "three divisions abreast" and "destroy or drive back all enemy forces in the zone," reestablish contact with the St. Vith forces and "be prepared for further offensive action." Hodges "approved" Ridgway's plan without hesitation, and they agreed that one man —Hasbrouck, who had the preponderance of forces—should be in command at St. Vith.[7]

Ridgway left immediately for his CP, to confer with his division commanders, Hobbs, Rose and Gavin, to lay out the plan. Hodges, meanwhile, got off an encouraging message to Hasbrouck which also named him overall St. Vith commander: "Ridgway with armor and infantry is moving from west to gain contact with you. When communication is established you come under command of Ridgway. You retain under your command following units: 106 Inf Div, RCT 112, and CCB 9th Armed Div . . ."[8]

Upon receipt of this message, Bob Hasbrouck got one off to Ridgway. In a letter similar to the one he had sent Hodges the day before, he outlined his forces in detail and estimated their combat capability. The 424th and 112th had been "roughly handled"; the 424 was "in poor shape." The combat value of the mauled and leaderless 14th Cavalry Group was "uncertain." Hasbrouck may have been skeptical of the rescue plan; however, he gave no hint of it. Nor was there any talk of retreat. However, he cautioned Ridgway that one combat command of the 3rd Armored Division might not be "strong enough to accomplish the mission" and suggested that Hobbs's 30th Division attack without delay. He also asked again for close air support.[9]

At the end of this letter, Hasbrouck raised a point of protocol about his appointment as overall St. Vith commander. "Major General Alan Jones, the Commanding General and his Division Headquarters are in Vielsalm, with my tactical headquarters. He is a Major General, I am a Brigadier so it is probably not legal to attach him to me. Possibly [First] Army didn't realize he and his Headquarters are present. I most definitely do *not* want to be attached to him and suggest he be directed to cooperate with me in holding our present positions which I know he will do. We have been getting along on that basis alright [sic]."[10]

That same day—December 21—Hasbrouck wrote a similar letter to Bill Kean at First Army. Again he expressed concern about his appointment over Jones. He made a point of reminding Kean that Jones was in St. Vith and that Jones "has control of his command and he and I have been cooperating and getting along alright [sic]." He added: "General Jones is a Major General and I am a Brigadier. His being attached to me makes it look as though he had failed in some respect and I want to put myself on record as saying he is in the saddle in control of his outfit and that we are cooperating in the best possible way. If my note [of yesterday] gave any other impression, I want to correct it at once before an injustice is done."[11]

These letters were perhaps merely window dressing, written for the record and designed to absolve Hasbrouck of any possible official (or unofficial) blame for the relief of Jones, who was his superior. Years later, Hasbrouck expressed his candid opinion: "Jones should have been relieved immediately. He had lost half his division (and his son was in one of the surrendered regiments). He was a very disturbed and confused man, incapable of making decisions." Gavin, who visited Jones's CP that same day, confirmed that estimate of Jones. He wrote that Jones "was the picture of dejection . . . and was depressed by the loss of his two infantry regiments . . . I felt sorry for him."[12]

On December 20, Montgomery arrived at Hodges' CP to take command of the northern operations and First Army. Montgomery was apparently incapable of humility and he made an unfortunate, tactless first impression. His attitude, one British officer wrote, was "like Christ come to cleanse the temple." Hodges' G-2 noted in his journal, with understatement, that "Monty's cocky mannerisms and his orders in cricket terms, like 'Hit him for a boundary,' and 'See him off with a clean bowl,' were apt to rouse the old South Boston Irish in us."[13]

After looking at the battle maps and talking awhile, Montgomery expressed

dissatisfaction with the general picture and Ridgway's aggressive plan to relieve St. Vith. He thought it urgent that they "sort out the battlefield and tidy
up the lines." He proposed that St. Vith be abandoned and that those forces
and the 82nd and 3rd Armored divisions be pulled back to a battle line running
more or less due west from Trois Ponts. "After all, gentlemen," Montgomery
said, "you can't win a big victory without a tidy show."[14]

Hodges and his staff looked at Montgomery in stunned disbelief, "as if he
had proposed to strip them of their ranks," one American Army historian
wrote. Give up St. Vith? Pull back the 82nd Division after its remarkably
aggressive deployment merely for the sake of a "tidy battlefield"? It was unthinkable, and Hodges, with unusual forthrightness, declared it so. If the Allies
voluntarily yielded St. Vith at this juncture, it would be like opening up a six-
lane *Autobahn* to Liège. Montgomery backed down, but, as it would develop,
only temporarily.[15]

The discussion next turned to the larger scheme of the Allied counteroffensive to cut off the German salient. By then, Patton was already pivoting his III
Corps north, and his XII Corps was preparing to join it. To increase the impact
and effectiveness of the offensive, Hodges (as he had discussed with Bradley)
was anxious to strike south with a strong corps. The First Army's rough plan
was to assemble a corps in the Eupen area, attack due south through St. Vith,
linking up Ridgway's XVIII Airborne Corps forces, then continuing south
until a juncture was achieved with Third Army. If successful, this would trap
both panzer armies outside the lair and open the way for a massive eastward
drive into Germany. Hodges—spurred on by Bradley—believed it was vital to
launch the offensive quickly—no later than December 23.

Montgomery appeared to endorse this plan and specifically requested that
Joe Collins and his VII Corps lead it. At that time, Collins was far to the
north, engaged in an attack eastward toward Düren, on the Roer River. Arrangements were set in motion to withdraw VII Corps headquarters from this
area secretly (turning its troops over to Ray McLain's XIX Corps) and to
move it south surreptitiously for the counteroffensive. The VII Corps would be
allotted all new forces: Ernest N. Harmon's ("Hell on Wheels") 2nd Armored
Division and two infantry divisions—Fay B. Prickett's 75th and Alexander R.
Bolling's 84th, the latter then moving down from the north into Ridgway's
XVIII Airborne Corps sector.[16]

However, Montgomery soon insisted on a radical change in the concept of
the offensive. The change, Bradley later wrote, "actually crippled it." Rather
than attack due south toward St. Vith, Montgomery insisted that Collins assemble his corps far to the west, behind Marche, and, rather than hit the
German flank, attack eastward straight into the teeth of the westward-moving
panzers. Montgomery's idea, Bradley wrote, was "ill-advised and timid" and
"the wrong way to do it" and "would take far too much time."[17]

Montgomery's reasoning was apparently based on the belief that the Ger-
mans were far stronger than the Americans perceived them to be, that the
Germans were still capable of breaking through to Liège and perhaps beyond.
That day—December 20—Ridgway had only just established a front with a

single full division—the 82nd. The territory to Ridgway's right (or west), where the 3rd Armored task forces were probing, was very weak. To Montgomery, both St. Vith and Bastogne appeared to be in dire jeopardy. Assuming they fell, the Fifth Panzer Army would have a clear northwest path through Marche to the Meuse. There was nothing to stop them. By placing Collins' corps in Marche, ostensibly for an offensive, Montgomery would have a defensive blocking force to hold west of Ridgway's XVIII Airborne Corps. In sum, Montgomery's purpose in redeploying Collins to Marche appeared to be in retrospect not so much to mount an offensive as it was to play a defensive role: to build up and extend the north front westward of Ridgway.

Montgomery's American critics have enumerated several reasons for his "timid" approach. First, he was innately cautious. Second, he did not have much faith in American generalship or the fighting qualities of the American GI. Third, placing Collins at Marche reduced the probability that he would have to call on Horrocks' 30 Corps, incurring further British casualties and disrupting his plans for his offensive in the north. Fourth, if the Americans succeeded in joining forces at Houffalize and then turned east on a power drive (commanded by Bradley) into Germany, this might very well destroy the German Army and cancel the need for Montgomery's northern offensive and Montgomery would thus be denied a triumphant entry into Germany.

Hodges was not happy with the new plan—nor were Joe Collins and Matt Ridgway. Collins recalled in his autobiography: "Monty came every other day to my CP, where Matt Ridgway would join us for a review of the situation. More than once I told Monty that I should be positioned farther east opposite St. Vith and that a counterattack near the point of the German salient would force the enemy out of the Bulge—as he had done in the Falaise Pocket— rather than cutting off escape near its base. Ridgway agreed." But Collins and Ridgway were not able to change Montgomery's mind, and Montgomery's "timid" plan remained in force. Hodges, apparently relieved that Montgomery would consider an offensive from any direction, reconciled himself to the modified plan.[18]

Shifting VII Corps headquarters from the Düren area to Marche was a complicated maneuver, but "Lightning Joe" Collins carried it out with typical swiftness and efficiency. Within mere hours, advance men for VII Corps were on the way. Harmon's 2nd Armored Division began moving south shortly afterward, to join Prickett's 75th and Bolling's 84th infantry divisions, which arrived first in the Marche area, on Ridgway's right. Pending formal assignment to VII Corps, Hodges held the 75th in First Army reserve, but on the afternoon of December 20, Bolling's 84th was temporarily attached to XVIII Airborne Corps, deployed in the military emptiness to the right (or west) of Rose's slim 3rd Armored forces, with the mission of "screening" the assembly of VII Corps. Bolling—a non-West Pointer and formerly McNair's G-1 at AGF—was well known to and admired by Ridgway and was a welcome addition to XVIII Airborne Corps. Collins wrote that Bolling had an air of "calm confidence," and he admired "his courage and quiet acceptance of responsibility."[19]

Collins was pleased to be united in battle again with Matt Ridgway, whom he had not seen since the Normandy campaign. He believed that Ridgway was "one of the very top senior commanders" in the ETO. When he visited Ridgway at his CP in Werbomont, he found him "in fine fettle, as dynamic as ever." Collins was "glad" to have his corps on his left flank, he later said, because "I always felt my left flank was secure."[20]

Both Collins and Ridgway, however, remained displeased at the change in strategy Montgomery had imposed on the north front. Ridgway's greatest disappointment was Montgomery's cavalier attitude toward St. Vith. Montgomery seemed not to appreciate its value as a thumb jammed in the German throat. He had not only summarily dismissed Ridgway's immediate aggressive three-division attack plan to relieve St. Vith, but also suggested a withdrawal from there merely to "tidy up the battlefield." Although Montgomery had backed off the latter proposal for the moment, it was obvious from his orders to position Collins far to the west that he had no real intent to "save" St. Vith and that circumstances would ultimately force a withdrawal.

And what of that other thumb in the German throat—Bastogne?

The 101st Airborne Division had arrived there, unit by unit, on December 18 and 19. When Middleton decamped with his VIII Corps headquarters on the nineteenth, his orders to McAuliffe were classically terse: "Hold Bastogne."[21]

Like St. Vith, Bastogne was a road hub and had become something of a collecting point for units falling back from the broken American front. The first major unit to arrive was the badly shattered CCR of Leonard's 9th Armored Division, commanded by Colonel Joseph H. Gilbreth (West Point, 1927). Next came a horde of artillery, antitank, engineer and other miscellaneous units, plus hundreds of stray infantrymen from Cota's 28th Division. Last came heavy armor reinforcements, ordered there by Bradley: CCB of Morris' 10th Armored Division, commanded by a much older West Pointer (1913), William L. Roberts, who was still a colonel.[22]*

Unlike St. Vith, there was no murky command problem at Bastogne. Tony McAuliffe, a brigadier general, outranked Gilbreth and Roberts. McAuliffe remained overall commander, even though the 101st ADC, Gerry Higgins, arrived in due course. But it required some little time for the armor and the

---

* The artillery and antitank forces which gathered at Bastogne were formidable. The 101st had four artillery battalions: Elkins' 377th Parachute, Carmichael's 321st Glider, Nelson's 907th Glider (105 mm snub-noses) and Cooper's hastily attached 463rd Parachute. The two armored commands had two artillery battalions, 73rd and 420th. Six other artillery battalions were in or had fallen back on Bastogne: the 109th, the 969th and the 755th (all with 155 mm howitzers) and the 333rd, 771st and 687th. In all: twelve artillery battalions, with a force of 130 guns. In addition, there were two antitank battalions: the 101's 81st, commanded by X. B. Cox, and the 705th Tank Destroyer Battalion. The 333rd and 969th field artillery battalions were manned by blacks.[23]

paratroopers to achieve cohesion in operations. Both were "strange and new to each other," the 101 historian wrote, and there was not time, at first, to work out coordinated plans.[24]

Bastogne lay in the path of Manteuffel's Fifth Panzer Army. That army had been initially delayed on its westward drive to the Meuse by Dutch Cota's 109th and 110th regiments and other forces. In the days following, Bastogne was attacked by detached armored elements of Manteuffel's Panzer Lehr Division and the 2nd Panzer Division, which were driving around Bastogne aiming for the Meuse, and infantry of the 26th Volksgrenadier Division. The Germans soon realized that Bastogne, like St. Vith, was causing an awkward split in their forces and traffic jams in the rear of the Fifth Army. By December 20, they decided it must be taken, but they made the mistake of trying to do it with too little force: one armored regiment of the Panzer Lehr Division and the 26th Volksgrenadier Division.

After his four regiments of paratroopers had reached Bastogne, McAuliffe had deployed them in a classic circular airborne "airhead" around Bastogne, about seven miles in diameter. Julian Ewell's 501 and Bob Sink's 506 took positions facing more or less east in the circle, confronting the main weight of the initial German assaults. Steve Chappuis' 502 faced northeast and north, where the pressure, at least for the time being, was not as great. Bud Harper's 327th Glider Regiment was thinly deployed into the area of least pressure—northwest, west and south. The tanks and the light airborne artillery and anti-tank units were intermixed with the paratroopers; the heavier artillery was situated closer to the center of the circle. McAuliffe and Roberts established their CPs in Bastogne itself.[25]

The 101 paratroopers, supported by the tankers, tank destroyers and artillery fought fiercely and heroically. In the initial actions, McAuliffe incurred heavy casualties. Among those killed was West Pointer (1939) James L. LaPrade, commander of Sink's 1st Battalion. He was replaced by Robert Harwick. Among the wounded was Roy L. Inman, commanding Bud Harper's 2nd Battalion; he was temporarily replaced by Robert B. Galbraith. Under relentless pressure, little by little, McAuliffe was forced to shrink the circle inward toward Bastogne itself. But as the circle shrunk it became less difficult to defend.[26]

On December 20, Fifth Panzer Army commander Manteuffel directed his forces to surround Bastogne. This task was carried out on December 21, and on the following morning, December 22, a four-man German delegation under a white flag found Bud Harper's 327th CP and presented Harper with a written demand for the surrender of Bastogne. Harper carried the letter to McAuliffe, who looked at it incredulously and guffawed, "Aw, nuts!" Believing the situation required a written reply, McAuliffe picked up a pencil and pondered a suitable response. Bud Harper, the acting chief of staff, Ned D. Moore, and the Gs gathered around, all trying to think of a defiant refusal. The G-3, Harry Kinnard, finally said to McAuliffe: "That first remark of yours would be hard to beat." McAuliffe did not understand him. "You said, 'Nuts,'" Kinnard reminded him. McAuliffe and all present agreed that was the appropriate response: NUTS!

McAuliffe wrote out the one word on a piece of paper and Harper carried it back to the German delegation waiting in his sector. "If you don't understand what 'Nuts' means," Harper explained to the senior German officer, "it is the same as 'Go to Hell!' "[27]

McAuliffe's note—the most famous American cry of defiance in World War II—infuriated the Germans. They responded with a devastating air attack and intense new pressure around the entire perimeter. Although Manteuffel recognized that Bastogne was drawing strength away from his main objective, the Meuse, he was now determined to seize the city. However, he once again underestimated the force required and the determination and skill of the defenders.

For McAuliffe and his men, those days and the ones that followed were a hellish nightmare. They would continue to fight like tigers, yielding ground only reluctantly, and they would become justly famous as "the Battered Bastards of Bastogne." But at no time during the German drive to the Meuse was the pressure on Bastogne ever close to that exerted by the SS divisions on Gee Gerow's and Matt Ridgway's sectors in the north.

☆ 41 ☆

BY DECEMBER 21, the sixth day of the German offensive, it was becoming clear to Walter Model and his army commanders, Sepp Dietrich and Hasso Manteuffel, that Hitler's grandiose plan was going to fail. There were many reasons. Not least was the gallant spirit and skill of American soldiers still firmly holding at Bütgenbach, Elsenborn, St. Vith, Malmédy, Stoumont, Bastogne and elsewhere. And yet Model continued to do all in his power to make the plan succeed.

On that day, Ridgway's XVIII Airborne Corps sector was under intense German pressure everywhere along its long and irregular front, facing the equivalent of about seven German divisions. This was the situation:[1]

● At St. Vith, the Germans, doggedly determined to overrun the American garrison, regrouped for a new and decisive attack. It would be carried out by the 18th and 62nd Volksgrenadier divisions, supported by a newly committed and powerful SS armored force, the Führer Begleit Brigade, commanded by another Hitler favorite, Otto Remer.

● At Stoumont and La Gleize, Peiper's *Kampfgruppe* was blocked and under heavy attack from the north by Hobbs's 30th Infantry Division, supported by Rose's CCB and, from the southwest, by Tucker's 504th Parachute Regiment. But Peiper was fighting savagely, repulsing counterattacks by Hobbs. Although the *Kampfgruppe* was being whittled away, Peiper remained a major threat.

● At Trois Ponts and south along the Salm River to Rencheux, the 1st SS Panzer Division, held at bay by Ekman's 505th Parachute Regiment, was still attempting to smash west over the Salm toward Werbomont. To reinforce this effort, Dietrich had committed the 9th SS Panzer Division for an attack southwesterly toward Rencheux and Vielsalm.

● In the "void" south and west of Werbomont, where Rose's little task forces were probing, two new German divisions, the 116th Panzer and the 560th Volksgrenadier, suddenly appeared on the attack. Originally bound west to cross the Meuse at Namur, they had been ordered by Model to swing northwest, along the east bank of the Ourthe River toward Hotton and Liège.

The real crisis that day on Ridgway's front came at St. Vith. Having held St. Vith for six days in the face of relentless pressure, the motley American garrison was exhausted and short of ammo, and some men were beginning to despair. The new German attack that day was well coordinated and punishing. At the easternmost rim of the horseshoe, Bruce Clarke, commanding CCB of Hasbrouck's 7th Armored Division, was compelled to order a hurried withdrawal to a new position behind St. Vith, yielding the town. The retreat stranded nine hundred of his men, most of whom were captured. The withdrawal also temporarily uncovered the left flank of Bill Hoge's CCB, 9th Armored Division, but Hoge was able to readjust his lines and establish a tenuous contact with Clarke on the left and the weak 424th and 112th infantry regiments curving around to his right.[2]

As the fighting that day around St. Vith progressed, the grave extent of the threat to the garrison became clearer to Hasbrouck and Ridgway. Hasbrouck was not only facing two Volksgrenadier divisions and the Führer Begleit but, intelligence indicated, possibly yet another division, the 2nd SS Panzer, which German POWs said was coming up to attack St. Vith (or Vielsalm) from the southeast. In sum: three full German divisions (one of them an SS Panzer) plus the Führer Begleit appeared to have been committed to taking St. Vith.[3]

That night—December 21—Ridgway had a guarded telephone talk with First Army chief of staff Bill Kean. As yet unaware of the impending attack of the 9th SS Panzer on Vielsalm, Ridgway, basing his judgment on reports from Hasbrouck, believed that Hasbrouck could contain the attack on the northern sector, but he was deeply concerned over the likelihood of an attack by the 2nd SS Panzer Division in the southern sector. He told Kean he seriously doubted that Bill Hoge's CCB and the depleted 424th and 112th infantry regiments could hold and that he had no reinforcements to help them. They discussed possible close air support to delay and disorganize the 2nd SS Panzer Division, but Ridgway doubted that would be "sufficient to save the people." He requested Kean's permission to withdraw those elements on the southern rim of the horseshoe, subject to Hasbrouck's concurrence, and Kean promptly authorized it. Kean told Ridgway First Army had made it clear to Hasbrouck that "he was not expected to sacrifice his command out there."[4]

These discussions led to an authorization for Hasbrouck to further constrict the perimeter, but Ridgway was not yet ready to withdraw the entire garrison, as Montgomery had proposed. During that night—perhaps in desperation—he conceived a novel idea that might enable Hasbrouck to hold until Ridgway or Collins could get some kind of counteroffensive moving. He believed that Hasbrouck might be able to consolidate his forces inside a "fortified goose egg" between St. Vith and Vielsalm, not unlike that which Tony McAuliffe had created in Bastogne. If so, all St. Vith forces inside the goose egg could become mutually supporting. The weather forecasters were predicting a period of clear skies for December 23 and thereafter. The goose egg could be resupplied by air until such time as XVIII Airborne Corps could link up.[5]

During the night, Ridgway suggested this plan to Hasbrouck. It was not cheerfully received at 7th Armored Division. Hasbrouck's CCB commander, Bruce Clarke, scoffed that the plan would most likely result in "Custer's Last Stand." Clarke's biographers wrote: "Ridgway's paratroopers held him in awe, but tankers didn't . . . While the 82nd was a good outfit, the men of the 7th Armored had to wonder if General Ridgeway [sic] understood the logistics of supplying tanks and the tactics of using them." As the tankers saw it, the goose-egg plan had several grave weaknesses. The terrain inside the proposed goose egg was not favorable for rapidly shifting forces to counter enemy attacks on the periphery. It was heavily wooded, and the few roads available were deep quagmires of mud. Even if the weather cleared—and that seemed dubious—it would take a steady stream of aerial armadas for ammo resupply alone. Moreover, tankers were not accustomed to fighting while surrounded.[6]

During that same night—December 21/22—Ridgway finally reached the conclusion that the situation at St. Vith was probably hopeless. Owing to the bog-down of Hobbs's 30th Infantry Division and the dispersion of Rose's 3rd Armored Division, he could not get an offensive going toward St. Vith. Intelligence now confirmed the increase of pressure on the St. Vith perimeter. The weather was still foul; there was really no hope for air supply of a goose-egg defense. And besides that, the tankers had rejected that scheme as impracticable. His G-3, Day Surles, recalled: "They were almost surrounded and Ridgway felt that if they stayed another day they couldn't get out."[7]

But this was a decision best made by the man on the scene. At 1 A.M., December 22, Ridgway telephoned Hasbrouck again and told him it was up to him to decide what to do. The staff followed up with a written order: "Confirming phone message to you, decision is yours. Will approve whatever you decide. Inform Jones he is to conform." To this written confirmation, Ridgway or someone on the staff appended an unfortunately worded second paragraph that would lead to one of the most heated Ridgway controversies of the war: "In addition to his force, Major General A. W. Jones will command the Seventh Armored Division effective receipt of this message."[8]

Some historians would place an erroneous interpretation on this second paragraph: that Ridgway, in a fit of pique in the middle of the night "fired" Hasbrouck because Hasbrouck was defeatist, and reinstated Jones as overall St. Vith commander. This interpretation is absurd on the face of it. The first paragraph, referring to the Ridgway/Hasbrouck telephone conversation about withdrawal, clearly expresses Ridgway's confidence in Hasbrouck's judgment and, by implication ("Inform Jones he is to conform" to Hasbrouck's decision), gives tactical control of the operation to Hasbrouck. Ridgway—in his telephone talk with Kean—had already reconciled himself to the possibility of —and obtained permission for—a withdrawal.[9]

What, then, did Ridgway mean by the second paragraph? He would later write that he added the paragraph because he believed that in the event of a withdrawal all elements in St. Vith should be placed "under command of the senior officer present." That is, inasmuch as a major troop movement, involving many disparate commands, was contemplated, it was proper to place them all under a senior commander, even if the command would be largely honorary. It was "not true" that he fired Hasbrouck, he wrote; he "never contemplated his relief, much less issued an order to that effect."

Upon receipt of the message, Hasbrouck found it "vague" and puzzling, but he did not interpret it as a relief from command. He later wrote that any such suggestion was "nonsense" and that he ultimately interpreted the order exactly as Ridgway had intended: that Jones would "exercise overall command of the troops in the salient exactly as a corps commander would command the troops in his corps." Day Surles recalled: "Ridgway did *not* relieve Hasbrouck. He just put Jones, the senior man, over him."[10]

The next morning—December 22—Ridgway sent his corps deputy chief of staff, James Quill, to Vielsalm to talk with Jones and Hasbrouck and assess the situation. At 11:35 A.M., Quill reported in with an upbeat message. He said (in part): "Situation good at 0855 until 1045 . . ." Two German attacks had then been launched, "foot troops only; no armor mentioned." Clarke's CCB and Hoge's CCB were "cooperating to stop the attack." "Orders placing MajGen A.W. Jones (CG 106th Div) in command of whole operation received about 0900 . . . Attitude of commanders: 106th [Jones] alarmed; 7th AD [Hasbrouck] steady . . . My own estimate [is that the] situation in hand . . . Ammunition situation is okay . . . Weather up here overcast, low ceiling, ground fog . . ." Air support missions were impossible.[11]

This was encouraging news, but fifteen minutes after Quill's report, Ridgway received a hand-delivered written report from Hasbrouck that was utterly pessimistic. Hasbrouck wrote that "unless assistance is promptly forthcoming I believe our position may become very serious." He listed his reasons, then added an alarming PS: "A strong attack has just developed against Clarke again. He is being outflanked and is retiring west another 2,000 yards refusing both flanks. I am throwing in my last chips to halt him. Hoge has just reported an attack. In my opinion if we don't get out of here and up north of the 82nd before night, we will not have a 7th Armored Division left."[12]

That message decided the fate of the St. Vith garrison. Thirty-five minutes later, at 12:25 P.M., Ridgway radioed Jones, giving Hasbrouck permission to withdraw: "Request of CG 7th Armored received in writing at 1150 approved . . . Inform me of plans . . . Destroy all gasoline where necessary to prevent capture." An hour and a half later, at 2 P.M., Kean called from First Army to say that Hodges had directed the withdrawal of the St. Vith forces and that Montgomery, who was "present," had "approved." Hasbrouck, Clarke and some historians would claim that Montgomery first gave the order to withdraw the St. Vith forces, but this was not true. Orders for the withdrawal, on Ridgway's instigation, had already been sent by the time Hodges' (or Montgomery's) orders were received at XVIII Airborne Corps. The G-3, Day Surles, said, "It was Ridgway's decision to withdraw from St. Vith. He may have cleared it with Hodges, but it was his decision alone."[13]

In the early afternoon of December 22, Ridgway left his corps CP to visit the St. Vith perimeter. He would have a firsthand look and reassure the defenders that he would get them out in one piece. As CCB commander Clarke had painfully learned, a withdrawal under fire was an extremely hazardous undertaking, especially for armor and artillery, which were cumbersome and difficult to cover in retreat. Moreover, an attacking enemy, detecting withdrawal, was usually emboldened. There was real danger that if the St. Vith withdrawal were not carried out with utmost professional skill, the troops might panic and break and be overrun by a fired-up enemy.

Ridgway and his party arrived in Vielsalm before dark. Alan Jones, he wrote later, had a "strange attitude" toward the situation. "He appeared to be casual, almost indifferent" and "little interested in the fact that that night we were going to bring his people out of the trap." That attitude convinced Ridgway that Jones was simply not capable of commanding the St. Vith withdrawal, and he decided to give the job to Hasbrouck.[14]

With Hasbrouck in tow, Ridgway went forward into the perimeter to talk to —and inspire—the men. "It was a gloomy picture," Ridgway later wrote. The men had held St. Vith for seven full days, but now they were dispirited and wanted out badly. It was not going to be easy. German artillery and infantry pressure was mounting all around the perimeter; the Allied tanks and vehicles were mired in mud; it was miserably cold. Bill Hoge and Bruce Clarke, numbed with exhaustion, expressed strong doubt that a successful withdrawal could be achieved. Ridgway assured them it would be done. He looked his old friend Hoge in the eye and said, "Bill, we *can* and we *will.*"[15]

After Ridgway had toured the perimeter, impressing on one and all the need for calm and skill in the withdrawal, he returned to Jones's CP in Vielsalm at 7:55 P.M. Clearing everyone from the room except Hasbrouck and James Quill, he dictated to Quill several orders realigning the command structure. First, he formally relieved Jones of command of the 106th Division and placed all 106 troops under command of Hasbrouck's 7th Armored Division. Temporarily, Jones would be assigned as "assistant to the corps commander"; his ADC, Herbert T. Perrin, would command what was left of the 106th Division. Second, he promoted Bill Hoge to be deputy commander of the 7th Armored Division. Since Hasbrouck had no ADC until then, if anything had happened to Hasbrouck, Bruce Clarke would have assumed temporary command of the 7th Armored Division. This new order put Hoge (senior to Clarke) in the direct line of succession to Hasbrouck, even though he and his CCB were technically still part of Leonard's 9th Armored Division.[16]

Gavin was quite upset with Ridgway that day for the relief of Jones, whose helpless, green 106th Division had caught the full fury of the unpredicted German attack. Gavin later wrote: "Summarily relieving . . . those who do not appear to measure up in the first shock of battle is not only a luxury that we cannot afford—it is very damaging to the Army as a whole . . . [it makes other senior officers] pusillanimous and indeed discourages other potential combat leaders from seeking high command."[17]

For Alan Jones, who now knew his son had been captured or killed, the strain was evidently more than he could withstand, mentally and physically. Shortly after his meeting with Ridgway, he collapsed on the floor, felled by a major heart attack (coronary occlusion). He was placed in an ambulance and evacuated to a rear-area hospital, where, ironically, he was wounded by a V-1 attack on the hospital. He survived both the wound and the heart attack, was transferred to Stateside hospitals and in October 1945 was medically retired from the Army.* Ridgway later wrote that Jones had "failed" as a division commander.[19]

---

* His son, Alan, Jr., liberated at war's end from a POW camp, fought in the Korean War, winning a Bronze Star Medal and a Purple Heart, and retired a colonel in 1973.[18]

Ridgway had hoped to withdraw the St. Vith force quickly—that night, under cover of darkness. But this proved to be an impossibly optimistic schedule. In the early hours of December 23, a few units evacuated through Vielsalm (protected by Roy Lindquist's 508), but the majority went out during daylight later in the day. They were aided by what Clarke described as "a miracle," a sudden drop in temperature, which froze the muddy roads, enabling the tanks and vehicles to operate more efficiently. A cold front had moved through, bringing clear skies that day, and for the first time in a week, Allied fighters and bombers could see the ground. They provided some timely protection for Hasbrouck and his men.[20]

Owing to the loss of records and the polyglot nature of the St. Vith force, Army historians were never able to accurately determine how many men were lost or saved at St. Vith. Ridgway later guessed that he had evacuated some fifteen thousand soldiers and about a hundred tanks. "We brought them out without the loss of a man, with all their equipment," he wrote with justifiable pride. In addition, seven valuable 155 mm howitzers with prime movers, previously abandoned in the area by retreating artillerymen, were retrieved.[21]

However, neither Hasbrouck nor Clarke was happy with Ridgway for his conduct of the St. Vith operation. They remained convinced that he and his forces had been saved only by Montgomery's intervention, that Montgomery had ordered Hodges to order Ridgway to order him to withdraw. Hasbrouck later wrote: "Ridgway was a very courageous man with great determination and drive. Unfortunately his common sense and good judgment were not always the best. Notably poor was his decision [plan] to leave the 7th Armored Division and its many attached troops to be surrounded in a heavily wooded area just east of Vielsalm . . . as an island [the goose egg] for him to fight back to . . . Fortunately Field Marshal Montgomery canceled Ridgway's orders soon after being apprised of them."[22]

Owing to the withdrawal and to the muddled and shifting command situation, the St. Vith operation would remain highly controversial among historians. On analysis, Hasbrouck's and Clarke's criticisms of Ridgway seem overly harsh, if not ill founded. Ridgway's initial plan was to reinforce St. Vith by conventionally attacking with a three-division force (one armored, two infantry). When that could not be organized for various reasons outside Ridgway's control, he soon realized the situation was hopeless. By the time Hasbrouck recommended withdrawal, Ridgway was fully reconciled to that course and, before Montgomery and Hodges could act, Ridgway instantly approved it. Thereafter the withdrawal was carried out with commendable efficiency, no panic, and almost no losses. Hasbrouck, Clarke and the historians would make too much of Ridgway's goose-egg concept, which was merely a fleeting, middle-of-the-night suggestion—never an order—and one that Ridgway had discarded immediately after he realized it was impractical.

☆42☆

THE SECOND MAJOR CRISIS in Ridgway's XVIII Airborne Corps sector arose during the final stages in the defense of St. Vith. It came in his western zone, the "void" where Rose's little task forces had been probing. It was initially caused by Model's decision to redirect the 116th Panzer and the 560th Volksgrenadier northwest toward Hotton and Liège. It was greatly intensified when Model ordered the 2nd SS Panzer Division, which Ridgway and Hasbrouck thought would attack St. Vith from the southwest, to continue westward beyond St. Vith and then swing northwest toward Liège, on the right flank of the 116th and 560th divisions.[1]

Probing the "void," Rose's task forces, some reinforced by parachute infantry, had found little enclaves of lonely Americans here and there, bravely guarding or blocking crossroads and bridges and holding some key ground. But it was all very thinly held. When the 116th Panzer and 560th Volksgrenadier divisions turned northwest toward Hotton along the east bank of the Ourthe River, the tankers and pickup American forces were soon engaged in fierce, bloody battles at Marcouray, Samrée, Dochamps and other places.[2]

When the extent of this new threat became apparent, Courtney Hodges gave Ridgway Rose's powerful CCA, which had been in First Army reserve at Eupen. It arrived in the Hotton and Soy areas on Ridgway's right (or west) flank on December 22, just in time to check spearheads of the 116th Panzer and 560th Volksgrenadier divisions. On the following day, December 23, First Army ordered Rose's powerful CCB to detach from Hobbs's 30th Division and move to the Hotton area. In the fierce and bloody engagements near Soy, the two parachute battalions attached to 3rd Armored Division (Tomasik's 509th and Boyle's 1st of the 517th) fought little-known but heroic and costly battles, which significantly helped Rose contain the German attacks.[3]

Meanwhile, the 2nd SS Panzer Division bypassed St. Vith to the south and continued driving west along a road on the southern arc of Gavin's horseshoe front, seeking a northwest road to Liège. It passed in front of Roy Lindquist's 508 positions in the high ground at Thier-du-Mont, then struck Billingslea's thin 325th positions at Joubieval, where a road led northwest. Billingslea's gliderists fought tenaciously, but were forced back toward Lierneux and, in the process, failed to blow a key bridge. Later in the night, a small force led by West Pointer John C. H. Lee, Jr. (son of Eisenhower's chief ETO supply officer), sneaked back and blew the bridge while German vehicles were crossing it, thereby denying the Germans that road.[4]

Sensing the intent of the 2nd SS Panzer Division, and later confirming it through captured documents, Gavin realized that his right flank, tenuously held by Billingslea's 325th, was in grave danger. Accordingly he detached a battalion (Wellems' 2nd) from Tucker's 504 at Cheneux and rushed it to Lierneux to backstop Billingslea. In addition, he deployed Billingslea's reserve 2nd Battalion, commanded by Richard Gibson, southwest toward Fraiture. As he was doing so, the 2nd SS Panzer, still moving west, took Regne from the 325th. Rushing to the scene, Gavin ordered Billingslea to retake the town, and the 325 troops soon did so, with what Gavin later described as "unusual gallantry."

It was now clear to Gavin that the next attempt of the 2nd SS Panzer to turn northwest would come just west of Regne at a crossroads, Baraque de Fraiture, where a major road—N-15—leads due north to Manhay, Werbomont and Liège. This crossroads was held by a motley collection of American forces, nowhere near strong enough to repulse an SS panzer division. Accordingly, Gavin ordered Gibson to reinforce the crossroads with a company and any other forces that could be brought to bear. Meanwhile, he sent out urgent calls for support to Rose's 3rd Armored Division, which was, in theory, supporting Gavin's right flank.

On the morning of December 23, lead elements of the 2nd SS Panzer Division simultaneously struck Gibson's F Company at the Baraque de Fraiture crossroads and his 2nd Battalion CP, to the northeast. Gibson reacted quickly and organized a counterattack, but F Company, commanded by Junior R. Woodruff, came under savage attack—and got no help from Rose's 3rd Armored Division. Woodruff's men fought heroically, but the German pressure was simply overwhelming. When Woodruff had lost forty-five of his one hundred sixteen men, he requested permission to withdraw. Reluctantly, Billingslea approved.

Gavin was furious, both because his right flank had been ruptured and because he was not getting the help from Rose that he had expected. In his memoirs, he excoriated Rose: "The 3rd Armored Division, which should have been protecting my right flank, had disappeared into thin air." On the battlefield, he told Ed Wellems to move his 2nd Battalion east toward Malempré (near Manhay), where Gavin intended to build as strong a defense as possible. He then called Tucker and told him to rush another battalion of the 504 to Malempré (leaving only one battalion at Cheneux) and take over the defense of the division's right flank.

The failure of the 3rd Armored Division to provide Gavin support was due mainly to two factors. The first was that the division was under heavy attack at Soy and Hotton by the 116th and 560th divisions, and in some places its elements were desperately fighting for survival. The second was that on that same day—before the threat of the 2nd SS Panzer Division was clear to First Army—the division had been transferred to Joe Collins' VII Corps, which was still assembling for the big counterattack east. In the confusion and fog of battle, a communications foul-up had occurred, and Rose had begun shifting his center of gravity (and CP) westward, uncovering Gavin's right flank at a decidedly inopportune moment.[5]

Realizing the gravity of the threat posed by the 2nd SS Panzer Division not only to his own division but to the whole northern front, Gavin jeeped to

Ridgway's CP at Werbomont to emphasize the threat in person and to seek armor to help him blunt the attack. As usual, Ridgway was not there, and Gavin apparently got no satisfaction from Doc Eaton. Gavin also excoriated Eaton in his memoirs: "To my amazement, the corps chief of staff showed no reaction whatever. I asked him what I should do, and he told me it was up to me. I asked him if he could commit more troops, particularly armor, in the area, and he said that they had none." This criticism of XVIII Airborne Corps staff was unkindly echoed by Eisenhower's son John in his account of the bulge, *The Bitter Woods:* "Ridgway's positive, powerful personality was somewhat detrimental to his effectiveness in commanding his corps, for his relatively inexperienced XVIII Airborne Corps staff held him in such awe that when he was absent from his command post—which was frequently—they tended to become immobilized. Even routine decisions had to await the return of the general."[6]

There may have been more to the Gavin-Eaton confrontation. The personal rift between Ridgway and Gavin had grown a little wider since that day in Holland when Gavin was "brusque" with Ridgway, and more recently when Ridgway had relieved Alan Jones. Eaton was not in a mood to try to repair the rift. He was becoming resentful of Gavin. He had concluded, as he said later, that Gavin was "a goddamned Black Irishman, looking out for number one." That is, overly ambitious, independent, not sufficiently beholden to Ridgway, who had, in Eaton's words, "fought" to get Gavin command of the 82nd. There may also have been an element of jealousy. Gavin was a handsome, fearless, young, bright commander with enormous appeal to the war correspondents. Gavin and the 82nd Division made good copy and got a lot of it; Eaton believed that Gavin unnecessarily courted publicity and was deliberately upstaging Ridgway.[7]

Notwithstanding Gavin's later recollections, the XVIII Airborne Corps promptly reacted to the emergency. Early that evening—December 23—Ridgway took the drastic step of ordering all the forces withdrawing from St. Vith to immediately regroup on his southern front near Manhay. Hasbrouck's full 7th Armored Division, plus the 424th Infantry Regiment, would block the highway at Manhay. Bill Hoge's CCB, plus the 112th Infantry Regiment, would be attached directly to Gavin's 82nd Division at Malempré, where Gavin had now redeployed two thirds of Tucker's 504th. In addition, Ridgway ordered his corps artillery commander, Theodore Buechler, to mass corps artillery to cover Manhay.[8]

The forces withdrawing from St. Vith, utterly exhausted, did not welcome this new assignment. Bruce Clarke, in particular, did not. By then, he was punchdrunk. He recalled that when he got his CCB out of St. Vith to safety a surgeon gave him a "drug" which knocked him asleep like a "sack of sand." During the night of December 23, Ridgway sent for him to give him his new orders. But when Clarke was shaken awake and told that Ridgway wanted to see him, he mumbled groggily, "The hell with it," rolled over and went back to sleep.[9]

Ridgway was apparently furious. As Clarke recalled it, when he finally reported to Ridgway the next day, the confrontation was stormy. In Clarke's version, Ridgway did not offer him a chair and began the meeting by saying, "I'm not used to having brigadiers tell me they won't report to me," and he didn't want it to happen again. Still standing, Clarke explained the circumstances—his exhaustion, the drug he had been given—and, in return, "got a lecture on Army discipline." Clarke, no shrinking violet, interrupted Ridgway with vehemence: "General, I came to this command against my wishes. I got nine decorations for bravery in my old outfit. I've got a record in Third Army that I can go back there tomorrow morning and General Patton will be glad to see me . . . I've done my job up here. History will give our unit credit for the job we did at St. Vith. I'd like your permission to leave."

At about that same time, Ridgway had a similar encounter with another of his brigadier generals, the corps artillery commander, Theodore Buechler. He, too, was apparently not reacting to the emergency with sufficient ardor. As Ridgway put it in his memoir (without naming Buechler), there was "little meeting of the minds between him and me." Ridgway simply could not get from Buechler "that degree of conspicuously superior and instant response" that he "regarded as essential." Ridgway made up his mind that when the crisis was over he would replace Buechler.[10]

Back at their headquarters, both Montgomery and Hodges eyed the 2nd SS Panzer drive on Manhay and the drives of the 116th Panzer and 520 Volksgrenadier divisions on Hotton (now Joe Collins' responsibility) with no little apprehension. However, Ridgway, having set all these defensive moves in train, was unflinchingly optimistic. On the evening of December 23, he reported to Montgomery and Hodges that "the situation in the corps sector was entirely satisfactory" and that in his opinion, "it was beyond the enemy's capabilities to penetrate through XVIII Airborne Corps."[11]

Gavin was not so sanguine. As he later wrote, he had "a profound feeling of foreboding." And no wonder. His division, however lionhearted, was spread all over the landscape, under heavy siege by no less than three-plus SS panzer divisions. At Stoumont, Peiper's *Kampfgruppe* had not yet been wiped out; it was still possibly a threat to Tucker's single battalion at Cheneux. The 1st and 9th SS panzer divisions were still assaulting his left flank on the "Salm River line." The 2nd SS Panzer Division had seriously breached his right flank, forcing him to fall back on Malempré. Hoge's CCB had moved to Malempré, but Hoge warned Gavin that his outfit was "absolutely exhausted" and "not capable of any kind of sustained combat." Roy Lindquist's 508, still in place on the high ground west of Vielsalm, was dangerously exposed.[12]

On the morning of December 24—Christmas Eve and the ninth day of the Battle of the Bulge—Ridgway coolly faced the 2nd SS Panzer Division driving north on Highway N-15 at Manhay and Malempré. He exhorted his staff and, by phone, his division commanders with these words, recorded in the headquarters diary: "The enemy has thrown in all his mobile reserves and this is his last major offensive effort in the West in this war—the last dying gasp of the German Army. He is putting everything he has into this fight. This corps will

halt that effort; then attack and smash him. This command is the command
that will smash the German offensive spirit for this war. I have utter confidence
in the results of this battle and in the troops and leaders fighting it."[13]

The 2nd SS Panzer struck Manhay and Malempré an unexpectedly hard
blow. Counterattacking the Germans from the east, Hoge's and Tucker's forces
treated the enemy "roughly." In the midst of this initial battle, Montgomery
arrived at Ridgway's CP. He "commended" Ridgway "on the conduct of his
command," stating that "the corps had fought with distinction," but expressed
deep concern about the renewed German drive. He also had information—or
believed—that Model had even greater reserves at his disposal. The 82nd Division was then under attack by three-plus SS panzer divisions and the 7th
Armored was in danger of being overrun at Manhay. The XVIII Airborne
Corps, Montgomery said, "could now withdraw with honor to itself and its
units." That is, "tidy up" the battlefield by pulling back Gavin's 82nd and
Hasbrouck's 7th Armored to a defensive line along the high ground running
between Trois Ponts and Hotton.[14]

Given the limited forces at Hodges' disposal and Montgomery's earlier decision to withdraw from St. Vith, this decision was almost inevitable. But Ridgway liked it no better than the decision to withdraw from St. Vith—especially
the order to withdraw the 82nd. He had unbounded faith in the 82nd; he
believed it was a wall of steel that would hold no matter what the Germans
threw at it. Moreover, Montgomery's withdrawal order would contravene the
82nd legend that "no ground gained was ever relinquished," possibly with a
serious adverse impact on morale.

There was an alternative option available to Montgomery: he could have
committed Horrocks' 30 Corps into Ridgway's hard-pressed sector (as Eisenhower, Bradley and Hodges had hoped he might). Many, including Horrocks,
wondered why he did not. On December 23, the First Army headquarters
diarist, William Sylvan, wrote: "General Horrocks said that the Americans
had fought magnificently, that the 82nd was the best division he had ever seen
in action and only regretted that his corps, standing in reserve behind the
Meuse with five divisions, was not yet able to get into the fray; that it was
unfair for the Americans to take the sole brunt of this blow."[15]

Ridgway recalled: "The main criticisms of Montgomery have been both his
thirst for publicity and prestige and his overcautiousness . . . He was criticized severely because he ordered me to pull the 82nd Division back after it
had taken a very prominent, key terrain feature along a ridge . . . with great
skill and very little loss. And they hated like hell the order to give it up. But
Montgomery wouldn't hear anything else but that I contract that position, as
he was expecting a very heavy German blow—which never fell."[16]

Given the tactical situation, the possibility that Model was supposedly capable of throwing in yet more forces, and Montgomery's refusal to commit Horrocks' 30 Corps, Ridgway and Gavin, although they disliked the withdrawal
order, did not contest it. Later, Ridgway conceded the decision was "all right"
and Gavin went further to say that "a withdrawal order was very much in
order." It would shorten his front by "about fifty percent" and give him "far

superior" defensive positions "in terms of field of fire and cover." Like Ridgway, he felt mainly concerned with the adverse impact a withdrawal would have on the morale of his paratroopers. "Rather than withdraw," Gavin wrote, "if the troopers had had their way, they would have much preferred to attack."[17]*

During that night—Christmas Eve—the 82nd Division withdrew as ordered, blowing bridges and sowing mines. Bill Ekman's 505 pulled back and dug in on high ground westward of Trois Ponts, linking (on the left) with Hobbs's 30th Division. Roy Lindquist's 508—skillfully fighting off several aggressive 9th SS Panzer Division armored task forces—pulled back to take position on Ekman's right. Tucker established his 504 at Bra, on Lindquist's right. Billingslea's 325 anchored the division's right flank at Tri-le-Cheslaing. Gavin later wrote that "in all the operations in which we have participated . . . I have never seen a better-executed operation than the withdrawal," but "it did not make any of us feel one mite better."[18]

One of the most unusual episodes of the Battle of the Bulge occurred that night. Peiper, whose *Kampfgruppe* had finally been shattered by Hobbs, chose that same night to escape from his cul-de-sac. Abandoning all his vehicles, Peiper led the survivors of his force (eight hundred of about fifty-eight hundred men) southward on foot. As Gavin's men were withdrawing northward, the hostile groups passed one another in the dark woods. One of the last of Ekman's platoons to withdraw from the Salm River ran into Peiper's force, and a heavy small-arms firefight ensued. During this fight, Peiper's senior American POW, Major Hal D. McCown, who had commanded the 2nd Battalion of Hobbs's 119th Infantry, escaped and was rescued by Gavin's men.[19]

In stark contrast to the 82nd, the withdrawal of Rosebaum's CCA, 7th Armored Division, plus attached infantry, was a perfect mess. Rosebaum, too, was unhappy about the order. He thought the terrain south of Manhay would be better defensively than the terrain north of Manhay and could not see the point of conducting a difficult nighttime retrograde movement to occupy an inferior position. In addition, the orders for the withdrawal, which was to be closely coordinated with the withdrawal of Hoge's CCB (on his left) and Doyle Hickey's CCA, 3rd Armored Division (on his right), somehow went astray and did not arrive until Hoge and Hickey had already pulled out.

The upshot was that Rosebaum's CCA was still in its forward positions when the 2nd SS Panzer Division hit it, late in the day, and the belated withdrawal had to be conducted under punishing German fire. Rosebaum's forward elements, in the words of the official Army historian, "broke" and were overrun. A second roadblock, manned by ten tanks, also gave way, with the loss of all the tanks. The tankers and infantrymen scarcely paused in Manhay in their flight to the rear, leaving Manhay wide open for the Germans, who quickly seized it and the adjoining village of Grandmenil.[20]

Bob Hasbrouck felt Ridgway should have shared the blame: "His orders for

---

* Perhaps Gavin did, but one of his veteran troopers commented: "What a lot of BS! The proposed new defensive line was the best I saw in the whole war."

a withdrawal were issued so late in the day that there was no time for a daylight reconnaissance. Units moved around dusk into positions they had never seen. None knew who his neighbor was. Furthermore, no provision was made for liaison with the [adjacent] 3rd Armored Division. Consequently . . . when a column of tanks moved out of a nearby village formerly occupied by the 3rd Armored Division (they had evacuated with no notice to our forces) everybody thought it was the 3rd Armored. Actually, it was a number of American tanks occupied and manned by Germans. They naturally created havoc and completely dissipated CCA to the winds."[21]

Ridgway, who was furious at this debacle, later ordered an official investigation. The upshot was that Hasbrouck relieved Rosebaum of command of CCA, "more for his failure," as Hasbrouck put it, "to make any effort to get his troops assembled again than anything else. He simply sank into a morose state and did nothing." Rosebaum's relief was William S. Triplet:

> Hasbrouck sent me down to take over CCA, leaving me the impression that the commander—whom he did not name—had already left. I went into the CP and there was my old friend Rosebaum who I'd soldiered with in the 67th Infantry when we were lieutenants. There was a short period of utter confusion. Rosebaum had no inkling that he was being relieved. On the contrary, he'd been cited for a Silver Star [Medal]. He phoned Hasbrouck and had a heated conversation . . . I felt terrible about it.

Tanker Triplet, moving into a difficult job at a tense time, formed a view of Ridgway far different from that of Hasbrouck and Clarke. "Of all the general officers I have known," Triplet wrote later, "I rate him Number One . . . He was a fighter, the best I've known . . . Clarke's statement that Ridgway knew nothing of armored warfare still irks me. I will venture that Ridgway knew as much—or more—than Clarke . . . *My tankers* liked Ridgway and his paratroops."[22]

As the Germans probed northward from Manhay, they approached the XVIII Airborne Corps CP. Late on Christmas Eve, Day Surles woke Ridgway with the news that the 7th Armored Division G-3 had called and said three Tiger tanks had burst through the lines and were headed up the road toward the CP. According to Surles the following exchange took place: "Ridgway said, 'How many tanks does 7th Armored have?' I said, 'About 150.' He said, 'You call that G-3 back and tell him to tell his division commander that if his 150 tanks can't stop three Tiger tanks, we're going to have to look for a new division commander.' "[23]†

Ridgway recalled that incident differently: "Somebody came in and said, 'German tanks are coming down the road.' I said, 'Fine, let's get all the bazookas out. That's what we're here for. They can't do anything in the dark.' One fellow grabbed his bed roll and was half out the door. He was going to get the

---

† Hasbrouck, of course, did not have 150 tanks deployed at Manhay, not even half that number; those that were left were in disarray.

hell out of there. I said, 'Put that thing back where you got it. Here's a bazooka; get yourself a tank.' "[24]

The corps headquarters was doing more than that, of course. When it was
clear that Rosebaum's CCA had broken, Ridgway ordered Hasbrouck to rush
Bruce Clarke's CCB forward from its reserve position. The response, however,
was (as noted in the official corps headquarters journal) "slow and inefficient"
due to the "extreme fatigue" of Clarke and his men. They had not yet recovered from the bludgeoning they'd taken at St. Vith.[25]

When Manhay fell, there was panic at Hodges' First Army headquarters, a
mere twenty-five miles to the north. The official Army historian wrote: "General Hodges sent message after message to the XVIII Airborne Corps insisting
that Manhay must be retaken, for it was all too clear that if the Sixth Panzer
Army could reinforce the Manhay salient, Liège and the Meuse bridgehead
would be in grave danger."[26]

This day—Christmas—may well have been the most trying moment of the
war for Ridgway. He had assured Montgomery and Hodges that the Germans
could not crack his front. Almost before the words were out of his mouth, they
had cracked it. Hasbrouck's 7th CCA had been badly mauled. Its attached
dispirited infantry was all but worthless. Alexander Reid's 424th, Ridgway
reported to Bill Kean on Christmas, was "miserably trained and miserably
led." Both it and Gustin Nelson's 112 had to be retrained.[27]

Owing to these factors, Ridgway asked Hodges to commit First Army's only
reserve—Fay Prickett's 75th Infantry Division, even though it was utterly
green, having seen no combat. In response, Hodges released two regiments
(289, 290) of the division, sending the 289th, commanded by Douglas B.
Smith, to the Manhay-Grandmenil area; the 290th to the Hotton and Soy area.
Technically, the 75th division was assigned to Collins' VII Corps to operate in
conjunction with 3rd Armored Division, but owing to the width of his front
and the need to coordinate Smith's 289th moves with adjoining XVIII Airborne Corps forces, Ridgway informally absorbed the 289th. The regiment had
gone into the line on Christmas Eve.[28]

Ridgway had already had some dealings with Fay Prickett. He later wrote
Hodges that he had been "shocked" at their first meeting because of Prickett's
"undisguised lack of confidence in his division and himself." Prickett, Ridgway
wrote, "made no attempt to conceal either, but discussed them freely with me."
Ridgway had done everything within his power "to dispel this lack of confidence, and to replace it with positive, aggressive and confident leadership." But
he had made little or no progress and he knew beforehand that the 289th,
entering combat for the first time and without backing from its division commander, might have serious problems.[29]

Ridgway and Collins, conferring by telephone, hastily drew a plan to retake
Manhay and Grandmenil. Doyle Hickey's CCA, 3rd Armored Division, working with Smith's 289th Regiment, would seize Grandmenil. Hasbrouck's battered 7th Armored Division, with attached infantry, would seize Manhay.
Ridgway's orders to Hasbrouck were unequivocal: retake Manhay whatever
the cost.

Ridgway's maneuvers required closest coordination with Smith's adjacent 289th Regiment. Before the counterattack, Ridgway jeeped over to have a look at Smith's nearest unit, the 3rd Battalion. The battalion headquarters staff, entering battle for the first time, was absolutely astonished at the sight of a begrimed corps commander running around like a platoon leader with a rifle in his hand and "grenades" taped to a chest harness.

This visit led to a famous Ridgway legend: that because he was dissatisfied with the battalion's speed of advance toward Grandmenil, Ridgway (bypassing the division and regimental commanders) gave a direct order to the battalion commander: "Take the next ridge in thirty minutes or you are relieved of command." This story, according to the battalion exec, who was present, was not true. Ridgway was displeased with the battalion's slow progress and plan of attack, but he properly issued corrective measures through the regimental commander, Smith. However, the fact that Ridgway had appeared out of nowhere, unaccompanied by Smith, and had spoken directly to the battalion commander, indisputably "shook up" this green, chain-of-command-conscious outfit, and the staffers would grumble that "it was a hell of a way to run a railroad."[10]

When Hasbrouck launched his counterattack on Manhay, Ridgway was in the front lines to lead and to inspire. It was like Normandy all over again. The German counterfire was intense and terrifying. "Fragments whizzed everywhere," Ridgway recalled. "One struck an artillery observer, who was standing by me, in the leg, and another punctured the tank of his jeep." When an infantry sergeant lost control and threw himself into a ditch, raving and cringing in terror, Ridgway went to him and tried to calm him down. Unable to do so, he then told his driver, Frank Farmer, to march the slacker to the rear under guard and see that he was turned over to his commander for court-martialing. If he tried to run, Ridgway told Farmer, "shoot him without hesitation." With Patton-like scorn, Ridgway later wrote, "He was an object of abject cowardice, and the sight of him would have a terrible effect on any American soldier who might see him."[31]

When a lieutenant leading about a dozen men came up out of the woods from Manhay "headed toward the rear," Ridgway stopped him to ask where he was going. The lieutenant said the German machine-gun fire at Manhay was "too hot for them." Ridgway recalled: "I relieved him of his command on the spot. I told him that he was a disgrace to his country and his uniform and that I was ashamed of him . . ." When Ridgway asked the group if anyone else was prepared to take over, a sergeant smartly stepped forward and led the patrol back toward Manhay.[32]

The battle raged for a full twenty-four hours. The 2nd SS Panzer clung to Grandmenil and Manhay, but gradually it lost "much of its bite and dash." An element of it lashed blindly to the east into Gavin's sector near Tri-le-Cheslaing, but Billingslea's glidermen pushed it back with a severe mauling. By nightfall on December 26, Smith's 3rd Battalion, powerfully assisted by Hickey's CCA, pushed into Grandmenil. But in spite of Ridgway's on-the-scene cajoling, Hasbrouck's attack on Manhay had failed.[33]

Ridgway decided that in order to retake Manhay he must have more—and better—infantry; specifically paratroopers. Gavin could spare none. The fresh 9th SS Panzer Division, which had driven through Vielsalm and then followed the 82nd as it pulled back, was attacking in force at many points along Gavin's front. Informed of this, Ridgway chose the 3rd Battalion of Graves's 517, commanded by Forrest S. Paxton, which was then in corps reserve.

Paxton rushed his battalion to the Manhay front on December 26. A 517 historian wrote, with understatement, that this was one of the regiment's "most important assignments" of the war. Ridgway, the historian wrote, ordered Paxton to "take Manhay at any cost." To ensure that the attack would not again fail, Ridgway ordered Theodore Buechler to pulverize the Germans in Manhay with artillery shells. Buechler zeroed in eight battalions of artillery (the 517 historian thought it was fifteen battalions), which, according to the 517 historian, proceeded to lob eighty-six hundred shells into the town. Following this, Paxton led his men into the ruins and recaptured what had once been Manhay.[34]

With the recapture of Manhay and the realignment of the XVIII Airborne Corps divisions on a "tidy" line, this crisis in Ridgway's sector was over. As he had assured Montgomery and Hodges, his front had held. There would be no further crises.

☆ 43 ☆

BY SUNSET on December 26, it was clear to both the German and the American ground commanders that Hitler's grand scheme to take Antwerp and destroy the Allied armies was a disastrous failure. However, Model's benumbed and shattered German forces continued the futile slaughter, with several more sputtering attacks, some of which proved to be bloody.[1]

● On the "north shoulder" at Elsenborn, where Gee Gerow's V Corps (1st, 2nd, 9th and 99th infantry divisions) had made its magnificent, decisive stand, Sepp Dietrich threw in yet another division, the 246th Volksgrenadier, in a last, futile attempt to crack the shoulder. Like the 12th SS Panzer, the 3rd Panzer Grenadier and the 12th and 277th Volksgrenadier divisions before it, the 246th was slaughtered by Gerow's soldiers with massed artillery, mortar and small-arms fire.

● West of Elsenborn on Matt Ridgway's realigned front, the XVIII Airborne Corps (30th infantry, 82nd airborne and 7th armored divisions), having destroyed Peiper's *Kampfgruppe*, decisively repulsed renewed attacks by the 1st SS and 2nd SS panzer divisions and the fresh, fanatical 9th SS Panzer Division. Holding on its new line and backed by massed, well-coordinated corps and division artillery, Gavin's 82nd Airborne Division dealt the 9th SS Panzer a particularly savage blow.

● West of Manhay, Joe Collins' VII Corps (75th and 84th infantry divisions, 2nd and 3rd armored divisions), whose big counterattack was still on hold, repulsed attacks by elements of about five German divisions, which were still probing west in a dying gasp to reach the Meuse River. Near Soy, Rose's 3rd Armored Division (with the independent paratrooper units still attached) and Prickett's 75th Division repulsed a final strong attack by a battle group of the 2nd SS Panzer Division linked to battered elements of the 560th Volksgrenadier Division. Farther west, near Hotton, Marche and Rochefort, Alex Bolling's 84th Division beat back attacks by the Führer Begleit Brigade and battle groups of the shattered 116th Panzer Division and the fresh Panzer Lehr Division. Still farther west, near Celles, short of the Meuse, Ernie Harmon's 2nd Armored Division, in a classic battle, utterly destroyed the lead groups of the 2nd Panzer Division, plus another battle group of the Panzer Lehr Division. Harmon's victory at Celles was what Collins termed the "high water mark" of the Battle of the Bulge. No German division reached the Meuse.

● At Bastogne, Tony McAuliffe's battered bastards repulsed one final, "desperate" German effort to take the city.

By this time, the "sideshow" at Bastogne, with McAuliffe's defiant cry of "Nuts!" had become an enthralling spectacle. There is inherent drama in "surrounded" or "doomed" or "lost" military forces fighting heroically. Bastogne would assume a hallowed niche in American historical legend, alongside the Battle of the Alamo, Custer's Last Stand at the Little Big Horn and the battles of Wake Island, Bataan and Corregidor. That a flamboyant old cavalryman, George Patton, was "coming to the rescue" heightened the drama.

From the beginning, Bastogne had presented Manteuffel with a tactical dilemma. He believed it was imperative to take the city, but to allot the proper forces required to overcome McAuliffe's battered bastards would weaken his more important objective, the drive to the Meuse. Thus his solution to seizing Bastogne had been a compromise: various armored battle groups had been temporarily "dropped off" to reinforce the 26th Volksgrenadier Division. The compromise had not worked.

As the siege went on, McAuliffe's problems were several. Foremost was a grave shortage of ammo, especially ammo for his twelve artillery battalions. By December 22, his four parachute and glider artillery units were down to about two hundred shells each and strict rationing had to be imposed. There was also an acute shortage of doctors, medics and medicine. The growing numbers of wounded could not be given proper care, and many were in terrible pain and dying from their wounds. These crises were alleviated somewhat when the "Russian high" cleared out the bad weather on December 23. That day and the next, FAAA mounted about four hundred C-47 sorties, dropping a total of about 236 tons of supplies into Bastogne. In addition, eleven gliders, crammed with doctors, medics and medical supplies, came through fog and crash-landed inside the perimeter on Christmas Day.[2]

The clear weather also helped McAuliffe in another way. It enabled the Air Force to support him with fighters and fighter-bombers. The 101 historian wrote that on December 23, 24 and 26, the Air Force mounted a total of one thousand close-air-support missions directly at Bastogne. Air-ground coordination during these close-air-support missions reached nearly perfectionist levels. "It was not unusual," the 101 historian wrote, ". . . to have an infantryman call in that five tanks were coming at him and then see six P-47s diving at the tanks within twenty minutes."[3]

The most perilous battles at Bastogne coincided in time with the most perilous battles in Ridgway's sector: Christmas Eve and Christmas Day. By then, McAuliffe had constricted his bastion into a rough circle with a circumference of sixteen miles. Inside it, he had tightly interlocked his infantry, armor and artillery into battle teams. Compared to the forces in the north, the Germans encircling Bastogne were still not strong. On Christmas Eve, however, the besiegers were reinforced by another armored regiment from the newly arriving 15th Panzer Grenadier Division. This force provided fresh power for a final, all-out assault.[4]

It began in the early hours of Christmas Day in the northwestern and western sectors of the circle near the seam between Steve Chappuis' 502nd and Bud Harper's 327th regiments. As the Germans knew well from previous probes, this was the weakest sector on the rim of the circle. They came on with thundering artillery and tanks painted white to blend with the snow. Since the fog that day grounded Allied fighters and fighter-bombers, German armor

achieved substantial break-ins at three towns: Champs, Flamizoulle and Se-
nonchamps, two of the three in Harper's 327 sector.[5]

For a while, the situation appeared to be grave. McAuliffe and his paratroopers were fatigued, still low on artillery ammo and all too thinly spread. But
there was no shortage of élan; also, the men were aided by another air resupply
drop: on December 26, 289 planes delivered 173 tons. The paratroopers struck
back with impressive strength and resolve, and the final, all-out German attack
failed. On the next day, a second effort, later described as "desperate" by the
German commander, likewise failed, and the Germans were compelled to pull
back to regroup.[6]

But where were George Patton and his rescue team?

The main team was the new, hastily formed III Corps (26th and 80th infantry divisions and 4th Armored Division), commanded by John Millikin, who
was making his debut in combat. It had started from Arlon north for Bastogne
on December 22, as Patton had promised, spearheaded by the 4th Armored
Division, commanded by Hugh J. Gaffey. On Millikin's right, the XII Corps
(5th Infantry Division, CCAs of the 9th and 10th armored divisions), commanded by Manton Eddy, jumped off on December 23 to provide flank support.[7]

It was a mere twenty-five miles from Arlon to Bastogne, but these proved to
be very tough miles for John Millikin and Hugh Gaffey. By then the German
Seventh Army had pushed a salient west between Arlon and Bastogne. The
salient in the III Corps sector was lightly held by second- or third-rate German
units: the German 5th Parachute Division and the 352nd Volksgrenadier Division plus advance elements of the green and ill-equipped Führer Grenadier
Brigade. (Another green and ill-equipped division, the 79th Volksgrenadier,
was moving up slowly to reinforce the salient.) These German units, hastily
and imperfectly deployed, somehow managed to slow III Corps to a crawl and,
in some areas, stopped it cold or threw it back.

Patton was furious at everybody, but especially Millikin. He all but accused
Millikin of cowardice and told him to get up to the front lines and "hear" the
bullets and shells. On December 23, in cold but clear weather, the corps advanced only two to five miles. On December 24—another day of clear weather
—the corps stalled—and in some areas was thrown back. Patton noted in his
diary: "This has been a very bad Christmas Eve. All along our line we have
received violent counterattacks, one of which forced . . . the 4th Armored
back some miles with the loss of ten tanks." On Christmas Day, the corps
managed to inch ahead only a few thousand yards.[8]

Patton came forward to personally goad III Corps. As a result, late on the
afternoon of December 26 (shortly after McAuliffe had repulsed the last "desperate" German attack on the Bastogne perimeter) Patton managed to force a
thin armored column into the city, commanded by Creighton W. Abrams.

Max Taylor, who had departed Washington Christmas Eve on a cargo plane
which got him to Paris on December 26, had asked SHAEF to parachute him
into Bastogne, but Bedell Smith vetoed that daring scheme. Instead, Taylor

had to drive from Paris to Luxembourg to Arlon to Bastogne, arriving in the late afternoon on December 27 in a jeep about twenty-four hours behind Abrams. That night, he and McAuliffe and his staff had a well-lubricated and "hilarious" reunion.[9]

Patton would garner much publicity for "saving" the Bastogne garrison, but it was mostly fiction. The truth was that by the time Abrams' men got to Bastogne the Germans had all but given up trying to take the city as a part of the general offensive aimed at the Meuse and Antwerp. It is possible that with continuing close air support and air resupply drops, and no greater commitment of German forces, McAuliffe could have held out for many more days. As Taylor later wrote, McAuliffe and his men were "indignant when they learned that they had been 'rescued.' " It all made good media copy, but the performance of Millikin's III Corps had been lackluster—or worse—and Millikin was in Patton's doghouse.*

Notwithstanding the legend of Bastogne, the decisive factors in containing and defeating the German Ardennes offensive were the iron-like defense of the north shoulder and at the stand at St. Vith, and later the defenses mounted along the westward extension of the northern front. For this feat of arms, much internal credit would be given the self-effacing Courtney Hodges, his battlewise First Army staff and, in particular, his V Corps commander, Gee Gerow. The V Corps had absorbed the blows of five German divisions (one SS panzer, four infantry) on the Bütgenbach-Elsenborn front, and after the remarkably quick realignment of the 2nd Infantry Division, did not yield significant ground. The 2nd, 99th, 1st and later the 9th infantry divisions had held like rocks, forcing the Sixth Panzer Army to go west around this corner into the narrow channel between Bütgenbach and St. Vith.[10]

The defenders of St. Vith were a ragtag group composed of disparate commands which did not ever fully cohere. A few were cowardly and ran to the rear. But most—Bill Hoge for one—stood staunchly at assigned posts, facing a terrible and powerful onslaught of Germans for seven days. They did not withdraw until the situation was deemed utterly hopeless and the withdrawal itself was remarkably well carried out. After the war, Fifth Panzer Army commander Hasso von Manteuffel wrote that the Allied defense of St. Vith was "brilliant and outstanding" and proved to be "of greatest consequences," even "decisive," in destroying the momentum of the German offensive. Principally because of St. Vith, he said, on December 24 he had recommended to Berlin that "the German Army give up the attack and return to the West Wall."[11]

Only slightly less important was the contribution of Matt Ridgway's green XVIII Airborne Corps. When the German offensive commenced, part of it was in Épernay, part of it was 350 miles away in England. Within thirty-four hours, XVIII Airborne Corps was in operation on the north front at Werbomont, a

---

* Patton's Bulge publicity reached its zenith in the hit film *Patton,* starring George C. Scott. The film was a superb character portrayal of Patton, but it was often historically inaccurate or incomplete.

remarkable feat all by itself. No less remarkable, Gavin's 82nd had deployed from Épernay to the north shoulder in a mere twenty-four hours, in time to give Hobbs's 30th Division valuable backup in blunting Peiper's *Kampfgruppe* and the rest of the 1st SS Panzer Division in the Cheneux and Trois Ponts area, blocking 1st SS Panzer along the Salm River south to Vielsalm, and opening a line of communications to the St. Vith forces. These early moves not only gave heart to the forces at St. Vith, but also significantly impeded the westward assault of the Sixth Panzer Army. The subsequent successful defensive stand of XVIII Airborne Corps in the realigned front from Trois Ponts to Manhay decisively checked the northwestward drive of the 2nd SS and the 9th SS panzer divisions.

The contribution of Joe Collins and his VII Corps during this defensive phase was undeniably important, but not nearly so decisive as that of V and XVIII Airborne corps. Initially brought to the north front to spearhead a counteroffensive, Collins was subsequently assigned a defensive role, extending the north front westward from Manhay to Celles. His VII Corps aggressively repulsed elements of five panzer divisions which were driving for the Meuse, but these German forces were tired, overextended and low on fuel and ammo, and when the weather cleared, on December 23, they were further weakened by Allied air attack. However, Ernest Harmon's classic destruction of the lead elements of the 2nd Panzer Division before the Meuse River was a victory with profound psychological consequences on both sides. It utterly deflated the German drive and gave the Allies a great shot in the arm.

Although Ridgway's personal contribution to the Battle of the Bulge received scant publicity, it was well recognized and appreciated among the professionals.

Montgomery wrote Bradley to say that "Gerow, Ridgway and Collins" had been "quite magnificent" and that "it must be most exceptional to find such a good lot of corps commanders gathered in one Army." Hodges awarded Ridgway a Bronze Star Medal for heroism and in an official Letter of Commendation, endorsed "with pleasure" by Bradley, wrote: "Your tactical ability, inspiring leadership and personal courage won the respect of all who observed your actions as you moved among the forward elements of your command, always appearing at the critical spot at the time when your presence was most needed." Eisenhower, writing Marshall, said, "I think you would like to know that three of our corps commanders, Gerow, Collins and Ridgway, have added in this battle to their former high reputations. Without exception they are universally regarded as three of the finest officers we have and if any vacancies ever occur here in Army command these three men should be selected in the order named above." Jim Gavin, speaking specifically of Ridgway's performance in the Bulge, said, "Wherever Ridgway is, he makes a difference. That's part of being Ridgway. He did a hell of a good job." In his war memoir *On to*

Berlin, Gavin wrote that Ridgway was "undoubtedly the best combat corps commander in the American Army in World War II."[12]†

Later, when the time came to single out certain units for special awards for this defensive phase of the Bulge, the hypnotic aura of Bastogne still prevailed. One result was that Eisenhower, perhaps too hastily, made the decision to recommend the entire 101st Airborne Division, plus attached units (including the black 969th Field Artillery Battalion) for a Presidential Unit Citation, a special honor usually reserved for small military units which performed beyond the call of duty. When Ridgway found out about this proposal, he was hurt that the 82nd Airborne Division was not to be similarly honored. He complained to SHAEF staffers that the 82nd was being "slighted," that its battle actions had been "equally meritorious," but he got nowhere. He was informed that Eisenhower had "personally" made the decision and would himself present the award to the division and that Ridgway would be well advised to keep his counsel.[14]‡

The competition between the 82nd and the 101st divisions was intense. The publicity given Bastogne and the award of this special presidential honor for the 101st angered everyone in the 82nd from Gavin down to the lowliest private and may have precipitated a rift between Taylor and Gavin. Like Ridgway, the 82nd troopers believed they had been unfairly overlooked. Much later, Eisenhower, conceding that he may have been overly influenced by Bastogne publicity, gave the 82nd its due. He wrote: "While it is true that the 101st Division received a Unit Citation for the Bastogne operation, it is equally true . . . that this honor came to the 101st partially because of the spectacular nature of its position in that particular battle and not because it exhibited greater fighting courage and durability and effectiveness than did a number of others. Among these others the 82nd rendered equally valuable service . . ."[16]

Eisenhower probably did not realize it at the time, but he added further insult to the 82nd's injury by his choice of several units which fought on the north front for award of the Presidential Unit Citation. Within XVIII Airborne Corps these special honors went to the two parachute battalions which had suffered appalling casualties while operating with Rose's 3rd Armored Division: Tomasik's 509th and William Boyle's 1st Battalion, 517. In addition, Eisenhower gave a Presidential Unit Citation to Bruce Clarke's CCB, 7th Ar-

† Gerow, the most senior of the three cited corps commanders, was promoted to the three-star rank of lieutenant general on January 1, 1945, and shortly afterward was named to command a new (largely administrative) army, the Fifteenth. He was replaced as V Corps commander by 1st Division commander Ralph Huebner, the "comer" who had been lunching with Ridgway at Fort Bragg when the Japanese attacked Pearl Harbor.[13]

‡ Eisenhower made the presentation—a "first" for a full Army division—on March 15, 1945. The entire division paraded for this well-publicized event, which added official luster to the legend of Bastogne.[15]

mored Division, for its "masterful and grimly determined" stand—and its heavy losses—at St. Vith.[17]*

Ridgway, Gavin and Taylor could be grateful for one blessing: apart from the detached ex-DRAGOON forces, casualties among the paratroopers in the defensive phase of the Battle of the Bulge had not been as heavy as they had feared they might be. At Bastogne, Taylor lost about sixteen hundred men dead, wounded and missing. On the north front, Gavin's casualties were about the same. Remarkably, among the senior commanders in the two airborne divisions, only one, James LaPrade (commanding Bob Sink's 1st Battalion), had been killed, and only one (Roy Inman, commanding Bud Harper's 2nd Battalion) had been seriously wounded. On December 27, although battle weary, both divisions were adequately staffed for airborne operations, should any be required.[19]

---

* Clarke had won a DSC, three Silver Stars, two Bronze Stars and an Air Medal during his combat service under Patton. He was awarded a third Bronze Star Medal for "heroic service" in St. Vith. His fawning biographers wrote, perhaps overenthusiastically and erroneously, that Clarke "refused a higher decoration for St. Vith because he felt that many of his officers and men had no opportunity to have their great deeds recorded."[18]

PART VIII

Bulge II:
The Allied Counterattack

☆ 44 ☆

CORRECTLY SENSING that the Bulge crisis was over, Omar Bradley renewed his efforts to convince the Allied high command to mount a massive counterattack. His general goal was still the same: to cut the German salient at the "waist" near Houffalize and Vielsalm. To achieve this goal, Patton would drive northward through Bastogne almost without pause; Hodges would attack southeast at the earliest possible moment. Bradley controlled Patton's Third Army and could give him orders. But Montgomery still controlled Hodges' First Army and showed no inclination to mount an early counterattack.

In order to persuade Montgomery to get moving, Bradley flew to his headquarters on Christmas Day. The meeting was brief and acrimonious. Montgomery treated Bradley rudely, scolded him like a schoolboy for having invited the German offensive, and categorically refused to consider launching a counteroffensive. Hodges' First Army, Montgomery asserted, was "too weak" to do anything but hold; it would be *three months* before it was ready for significant offensive operations. Patton's counterattack was "futile" and should be stopped; Patton should withdraw to defensive positions in the Saar.

Bradley returned to his headquarters in Luxembourg that same day in a rage. Up to then, he had accepted the temporary loss of First Army to Montgomery with good grace. But now he began to raise Cain. He wrote a private (unofficial) letter to Hodges, urging him to prepare plans to "seize the initiative" as quickly as possible. In a telephone call to Bedell Smith, he *demanded* that Eisenhower personally intervene and order Montgomery to go on the offensive. Bradley's uncharacteristic vehemence so rattled SHAEF that Eisenhower immediately called for a strategy session, and this time Bradley won hands down. Eisenhower ordered Montgomery to launch a counteroffensive in coordination with Bradley's as soon as possible.

At that time, Montgomery had his mind on larger, personal goals. Having, in his view, "saved" the Americans in the Bulge, he thought the time was propitious to reassert his campaign to gain control of all Allied land forces. He made such a proposal to Eisenhower in an arrogant and insulting message that so dismayed and enraged Eisenhower that he made the momentous decision to sack Montgomery. Learning of this proposed drastic step, Montgomery's able and well-liked chief of staff, Francis de Guingand, flew to Versailles to persuade Eisenhower and Smith otherwise. In a truly adroit piece of diplomacy, De Guingand convinced Eisenhower he should keep Montgomery on the team and, in return, elicited a letter of apology from Montgomery to Eisenhower. After this close call, Montgomery made no further attempts to gain control of the land forces, and he began laying plans for a counteroffensive.[1]

Bradley's detailed plan for the counterattack on the German "waist" was as follows. Patton's Third Army, having "rescued" the Bastogne garrison, would, in effect, keep right on moving northeast toward Houffalize, St. Vith and Bitburg. Third Army would continue the attack with three corps, line abreast: Troy Middleton's VIII Corps (to be reconstituted with three new divisions from SHAEF reserve) on the left (or west) of Bastogne; John Millikin's III Corps in the center; and Manton Eddy's XII Corps on the right (or east) of Bastogne. In Hodges' First Army, Collins' VII Corps (to be replaced in the Hotton-Celles area by Horrocks' 30 Corps) would attack southeasterly toward Houffalize; Ridgway's XVIII Airborne Corps, pivoting on Malmédy, would attack east toward Vielsalm, recapturing the terrain it had only just relinquished; Huebner's V Corps would more or less remain in place on the Bütgenbach-Elsenborn front, serving as the hub around which Collins and Ridgway would wheel.

At about the same time the Allies were finalizing this plan, the Germans, also realizing the Ardennes offensive had failed, were debating what to do next. Model, who correctly foresaw Bradley's counterattack, urged a withdrawal to the Siegfried Line. But Hitler rejected that sensible plan as defeatist. He decreed that the German forces inside the Bulge would be regrouped to fight a war of attrition, delaying for as long as possible the Allied drive into Germany. As part of this plan, both the Fifth and the Sixth panzer armies would give up any further attempts to crack the north front, about-face and concentrate against Patton's more immediately threatening forces in the southern sector of the Bulge. The Germans would seize and hold Bastogne, attacking the city in utmost force from three sides. Accordingly, Model assigned the equivalent of eight (greatly depleted) German divisions to this task and, one by one, the divisions of the Fifth and Sixth panzer armies withdrew from the north shoulder and turned toward Bastogne to open a new and bloody chapter in the history of the city.[2]

The most daunting task in Patton's part of Bradley's plan proved to be that assigned to Middleton's VIII Corps: the drive northeast from Bastogne to Houffalize, where Middleton was to link with Collins' VII Corps. Patton thought it would be a cakewalk, that the area was practically devoid of Germans.

Troy Middleton's VIII Corps had been hastily reconstituted. In addition to Taylor's 101st Airborne (plus the attached armor and artillery in Bastogne), it consisted of three divisions from SHAEF reserve which had been posted behind the Meuse during the Bulge crisis and had not been in the battle. These were the 11th Armored, commanded by Ridgway's classmate Charles S. Kilburn; the 87th Infantry, commanded by Frank L. Culin; and Bud Miley's 17th Airborne. Kilburn's 11th Armored and most of Miley's 17th Airborne were green to combat; Culin's 87th, which had arrived on the Continent in December, had seen brief action in Patton's Saar campaign, but it had yet to be put to a real test.[3]

The VIII Corps, which gathered on the west side of Bastogne near Morhet, jumped off on December 30. The 11th Armored Division (reinforced by CCA,

9th Armored Division) and the 87th Division spearheaded the attack. Miley's 17th Airborne Division, hastily moving up from the Meuse, was held in reserve. Taylor's 101st supported the offensive with heavy artillery fire and by a limited attack of Chappuis' 502nd Regiment northeast toward Noville.

The weather was more bitterly cold than ever. Heavy snow had fallen; the temperature plunged to zero Fahrenheit. Some fields and woods were nearly waist deep in drifted snow; the roads were glazed with ice. For many men it was a struggle to merely stay alive, let alone fight. One officer recalled: "I wore woolen underwear, a woolen uniform, armored force combat overalls, a sweater, an armored force field jacket with elastic cuffs, a muffler, a heavy lined trenchcoat, two pairs of heavy woolen socks, and combat boots with galoshes over them—and I cannot ever remember being warm . . . The troops built little fires of anything that would burn, even within sight of the enemy, to try to warm themselves."[4]

The 87th and 11th armored divisions received a rude shock. They unwittingly attacked straight into the flanks of the several German divisions turning away from the north front to move on Bastogne. In this first taste of combat, Kilburn's 11th Armored was badly mauled and thoroughly disorganized, losing about one third of its tanks. In fact, it was in such bad shape that Middleton had to rush Miley's 17th Airborne Division from corps reserve in order to give the 11th time to reorganize and recompose itself. Patton was so angry at the division's performance that he considered relieving Kilburn of command on the spot.[5]*

Miley, too, was in for a surprise. His 17th Airborne Division was composed of four infantry regiments, two parachute (507, 513) and two glider (193, 194), plus three artillery battalions (466th Parachute; 680th and 681st glider), equipped only with 75 mm pack howitzers. In keeping with earlier airborne doctrine, the 193rd and 194th glider regiments had but two battalions each. However, the 550 Glider Battalion, from DRAGOON, was hurriedly attached to the 194, giving it three battalions. Of these units, only Edson Raff's 507 and Edward Sachs's 550 had seen combat.[6]

Rushing forward pell-mell and piecemeal to Morhet, occupying the 11th Armored Division positions, Miley elected to launch operations with two regiments: James R. Pierce's reinforced 194 gliderists on the left and James W. Coutts's green but well-trained 513 paratroopers on the right. The other two regiments, Raff's 507 and Maurice G. Stubbs's 193 gliderists, were held in reserve. Miley later wrote Ridgway that "General Patton was insistent that there was nothing in front of us and stated that we had to attack immediately." There was no time to get out reconnaissance patrols to check on Patton's intelligence reports. It was bitterly cold. A heavy fog drastically limited visibility. Miley could not use artillery effectively: "There was no observed fire," he

---

* Two months later, Patton did relieve Kilburn of command, telling him, as Patton noted in his diary, that he was "not suitable" to command an armored division, "due to lack of offensive spirit." Patton appended: "I should have relieved him in January."

explained. "We couldn't get stuff up close enough to our troops." Culin's 87th Division, positioned somewhere on Miley's left flank, was not in touch.[7]

Miley's two assault regiments jumped off from Houmont at 0815 on January 4. On the left, Pierce's three battalions advanced smartly through the fog, at first meeting little resistance. They captured Hubremont—then ran headlong into the German units attacking toward Bastogne. All hell broke loose. German artillery and tanks pounced on Pierce, inflicting heavy casualties. There was still no sign of Culin's 87th Division on the left. "Our left flank," as Miley put it, "was left dangling in the breeze." In the face of murderous fire, Pierce was forced back to the jump-off line. Pierce remarked: "God, how green we are —but we are learning fast and the next time we will beat them."[8]

On the right, Coutts's 513, advancing on the left flank of Taylor's 101, met resistance almost at once. The paratroopers entered a woods, fixed bayonets, and charged, doing, Miley said, "one hell of a fine job." Alton R. Taylor's 1st Battalion, on the left, reached Cochleval. On the right, Allen C. (Ace) Miller's 2nd Battalion hit the enemy hard in the woods beyond Mande, killing at least two hundred Germans, a fine action for which Miller was later cited. But the 513, too, was soon overwhelmed by a strong German counterattack. Both the 1st and the 2nd battalions suffered "heavily," Miley recalled, and were forced to withdraw, as Miley said, "almost back to where they started."

Patton had been wrong. The Germans were gathering in force. Miley, entering combat for the first time, had been forced by higher authority to attack blindly in foul weather and too hastily and had gotten a very bloody nose. In his diary, Patton later transformed this blunder into a triumph, writing: "They . . . ran right into the flank of a German attack. Had this not happened things [at Bastogne] could have been critical. As it was, we stopped the attack in its tracks. Historians will claim that such perfect timing was a stroke of genius . . . [but] I had no idea the Germans were attacking."[9]

Troy Middleton sent word for Miley to regroup, lick his wounds and prepare for another try. His second attack jumped off on January 7. This time he launched it with three regiments, line abreast. Stubbs's 193rd Glider on the right (abutting the 101); Coutts's 513 paratroopers in the center; Pierce's 194th Glider on the left. The key objective was the high ground at the town of Flammierge. Miley recalled: "The situation had not changed. The enemy was still out there—in the positions we had failed to take from him. The weather was as forbidding as ever. There was almost no visibility and no chance of air support. You still could not observe artillery fire. Third Army still insisted there was nothing in front of us."

The two flanking glider regiments encountered heavy resistance and were stopped in their tracks and hit hard. The 194, Miley said, suffered "terrific" casualties. But Coutts's 513, in the center, was not to be denied. The 513 paratroopers drove ahead hell-for-leather toward Flammierge. In a fine piece of work, Coutts's 3rd Battalion, commanded by Edward F. Kent, took the town, and Coutts hurriedly brought up his other two battalions, Taylor's 1st and Miller's 2nd. As they were digging in, Miley decided to reinforce Coutts with the 3rd Battalion of Raff's 507 (still in reserve), commanded by John T. Davis.

The next morning, the Germans counterattacked with, Miley recalled, "everything they had," including tanks and flamethrowers. The weather was still "terrible." The reinforced 513 took "terrible" losses. Taylor's 1st and Miller's 2nd battalions, Miley recalled, were "almost annihilated." They held until their ammo was spent; then the few survivors began withdrawing. Later, Miley ordered all units to fall back. In this bloody action, appropriately called "Dead Man's Ridge," the 507's 3rd Battalion commander, John Davis, was killed, temporarily replaced by Allen Taylor and permanently by Roy Creek. The 513's 3rd Battalion commander, Edward Kent, was severely wounded and replaced by Morris S. Anderson. The 513's 2nd Battalion commander, Allen Miller, was also wounded, but retained command. The 513's 1st Battalion commander, Alton Taylor, Coutts said later, "failed to meet my standards as a commander in combat" and was relieved, replaced by Harry S. Kies.[10]

Thus Miley's paratroopers, brought up to replace Kilburn's badly shattered tankers, were themselves badly shattered and forced to go over to the defensive. Patton was likewise angry with Bud Miley and for a time also considered relieving him. He wrote in his diary: "The 17th Airborne . . . got a very bloody nose and reported the loss of 40% in some of its battalions. This is, of course, hysterical. A loss for any one day of over 8 to 10% can be put down to a damn lie, unless the people run or surrender. General Miley did not impress me when I met him at Bastogne . . . He told me he did not know where his right regiment [193] was, yet he was not out looking for it . . . I can never get over the stupidity of our green troops."[11]†

In a letter to Ridgway, Max Taylor wrote: "Bud's division was committed to action alongside the 101st on January 3. Since that time it has been a source of deep concern to me. It was thrown into a very difficult tactical situation and in the course of a couple of days took very heavy losses and accomplished almost nothing. The morale of the entire organization has undoubtedly suffered heavily. I hope that the division can be withdrawn soon and allowed to settle down and reorganize. Meanwhile I do know that Bud is on the spot with General Patton and that personnel changes may well be forthcoming. General Patton has already spoken to me about the possibility of taking [101 ADC Gerry] Higgins for that division. I am sorry that you are far away and unable to give the 17th the benefit of your steadying hand."[12]

Taylor gave Ridgway the impression that Patton wanted to relieve Miley and put Gerry Higgins in his place. In a reply to Taylor's letter, Ridgway, believing Higgins far too junior for the job (he was West Point 1934), wrote that if a change of command in the 17th were to be made, he, Ridgway, would recommend that Tony McAuliffe get the job. However, there was never any intent to make Higgins commander of the 17th. As Patton's chief of staff, Hobart Gay, explained later, Patton had in mind that whether Miley was

---

† In fact, 17th Division casualties were appalling. One historian estimates they totaled about "one thousand a day."

relieved or not, Gerry Higgins should trade places with Miley's ADC, John L. Whitelaw, so that the 17th could benefit from Higgins' combat experience.

Upon reconsideration, Patton decided not to relieve Miley and also left Whitelaw (and Higgins) in place. ("One should not act too fast," Patton wrote in his diary.) Furthermore, without consulting Ridgway, Eisenhower plucked McAuliffe from the 101st and named him commanding general of Third Army's 103rd Infantry Division with a promotion to two stars.

Ridgway was miffed that Eisenhower had sent McAuliffe to command a regular infantry division without clearing with him. "While he is undoubtedly well qualified to command an infantry division," Ridgway wrote Taylor, "the government has too much of an investment in him as an airborne commander to justify his assignment to an infantry division in preference to an airborne division." At first Taylor wanted to give McAuliffe's job to Higgins and promote the deserving and able Bob Sink to ADC, but eventually Taylor drew William N. Gillmore, a nonparatrooper who had been artillery commander of the 1st Armored Division.[13]

The 101st Airborne Division, still anchored in Bastogne on Miley's right, remained in active defensive positions until January 9, skillfully repulsing several strong German attacks. Max Taylor was now back in full command; Mike Michaelis, partly recovered from the severe battle wounds he'd suffered in Holland, was named chief of staff. On January 10, in support of Middleton's VIII Corps drive on Houffalize, the 101st went over to full offensive operations, with the objective of capturing Noville and the surrounding high ground and woods. It turned out to be a very bloody fight, taking a far heavier toll of Taylor's senior commanders than the December Bulge action.‡

While the 101 attacked northeast toward Noville, Middleton ordered Bud Miley's 17th (to the left of the 101) to attack northeast toward Houffalize with a stop line at the Ourthe River. The reconstituted 11th Armored Division was positioned on Miley's right, between the 17th and the 101st, which was soon to be relieved from combat. Miley jumped off on January 13 with two regiments line abreast: Edson Raff's battle-hardened 507 and Bob Pierce's 194th Glider

---

‡ In the 501, the able commander, Julian Ewell, was severely wounded in the foot and replaced by his exec, Robert Ballard, who was replaced by Richard J. Allen. In Chappuis' 502, John P. Stopka, commanding the 3rd Battalion, was killed by an errant American bomber and replaced by Cecil L. Simmons. Thomas F. Sutliffe, commanding the 2nd Battalion, incurred a back wound or injury and later died in the hospital. He was replaced by James J. Hatch. In Sink's 506, the 1st Battalion commander, Robert Harwick, was severely wounded, as was his successor, Charles G. Shettle, who was replaced by Clarence Hester. In Harper's 327, Hartford Salee was wounded and temporarily replaced by George Nichols. Counting earlier Bulge action, the final toll in 101 senior commanders was as follows: two killed (LaPrade, Stopka); six injured (Inman, Ewell, Sutliffe, Harwick, Shettle, Salee), one fatally (Sutliffe). The division as a whole suffered about eighteen hundred casualties in the January fighting, bringing the total for the Bulge to about thirty-four hundred—about five hundred killed, twenty-five hundred wounded and four hundred missing or captured.[14]

Regiment. Coutts's badly mauled 513 was held in reserve. On January 15, Stubbs's 193rd Glider Regiment was attached to the infantry-short 11th Armored Division. Directly supporting the 17th was an unusual and highly regarded outfit: the 761st Tank Battalion, composed entirely of black tankers who had first been committed to action in November with Patton's Third Army.[15]

Miley's assault regiments vied to outdo one another. Up to this time, only the 3rd Battalion of Raff's 507 had been committed to combat in the Bulge. Now fully deployed, Raff was determined to show his stuff. Led by battalion commanders Pearson (1st), Timmes (2nd) and Creek (3rd), the regiment put on a dazzling performance. Against greatly diminishing German resistance, it blazed through Givry to Gives and reached the Ourthe River on January 15. No less impressive was Pierce's 194, determined to make up for the bloody nose it had gotten in its initial combat effort. Led by battalion commanders William S. Stewart (1st), Frank L. Barnett (2nd) and Edward Sachs (attached 550), it likewise blazed northeastward and reached the Ourthe on the same day. Fortunately there were no casualties among the senior commanders in either of the regiments and very few in the ranks.

Taylor, whose 101 was relieved of offensive responsibilities on January 16, wrote Ridgway: "Bud's outfit is definitely on the up-turn now and I hope my previous views were unduly pessimistic." Taylor was right. After a very shaky baptism of fire, the 17th Airborne Division had matured in a hurry.[16]

<h1 style="text-align:center">☆45☆</h1>

IN BRADLEY'S PLAN to trap the Germans in the salient, Montgomery was to coordinate Hodges' First Army counterattacks with Patton's attacks out of Bastogne. But Montgomery, misreading German intentions, feared the panzers might again attack Hodges' north front, and for that reason he insisted on a delay to absorb the possible blow. After it came, he would attack the Germans on "the rebound." While he procrastinated, the Germans pulled away from the north front and regrouped for the attack in the opposite direction, toward Bastogne.[1]

Eisenhower, Bradley and the American corps commanders—Ridgway, Collins and Middleton—were furious at Montgomery's delays and indecisions. Middleton later summed up the collective American opinion: "The leadership up there was poor. Montgomery should have moved in and launched a counterattack long before he turned his troops loose."[2]

Ridgway and Collins, who would bear the responsibility for carrying out the northern counterattack, were especially perturbed. They seriously doubted the Germans were capable of another counterattack. They wanted to get rolling as soon as possible with all the power and speed the Allies could mount. Otherwise, they feared, the Germans might slip away to fight again.[3]

Nor did they approve of the battle plan Montgomery was formulating. The plan was for Collins to attack east with four divisions from Marche toward Houffalize, while Ridgway, on Collins' left, pivoted the 82nd Division to the Salm River line. From the beginning, Ridgway and Collins had argued that Collins had been put in the wrong place—too far west—and that he should have been put north of the Malmédy area so he could attack due south to St. Vith. They still believed that. Collins now complained that an attack east out of Marche would be like "emptying the sack by pushing from the bottom" and would probably result in "another Falaise"—that is, most of the Germans would escape. Realizing there was no hope of relocating Collins at this late date, Ridgway proposed that his XVIII Airborne Corps be permitted not only to advance beyond the Salm River but also to attack St. Vith directly from the northeast and north with all available forces, including Hobbs's 30th and Hasbrouck's 7th Armored divisions.[4]

Ridgway pressed these views on Montgomery and/or Hodges during a series of meetings December 28 to December 31. On the twenty-eighth, he told Hodges that "the time has arrived or its arrival is imminent for offensive action on the most powerful scale we can mount" and his corps could be ready to jump off at daylight, December 31. The next day, Ridgway and Collins met with Hodges to insist that "the decisive direction" of the counterattack should be "as near as possible north-south" and that the "decisive objective was St.

Vith." Hodges, Ridgway wrote, "seemed inwardly to favor" their St. Vith plan (and directed them to prepare a formal one), but he reminded them that Montgomery was in charge and cautiously recalled that, near the end of World War I, the Germans had mounted unexpectedly strong offensives. In a meeting with Montgomery on December 30, Ridgway and Collins repeated the arguments for an attack on St. Vith. Montgomery, Ridgway wrote, "indicated his full agreement with the concept but was insistent that the time had not arrived for its execution"—"doubtless" it would come later. He was still fearful of a powerful German panzer attack on the north front.[5]

In the meantime, Eisenhower, reacting to the American impatience, was trying to build a fire under Montgomery. On December 29 and 31, he wrote Montgomery tactful but prodding letters, reminding him, among other things, that Horrocks' 30 Corps, "not yet employed, gives you great flexibility." Eisenhower insisted on "immediate attacks" from the north. "The one thing that must now be prevented," he wrote, "is the stabilization of the enemy salient with infantry, permitting him opportunity to use his Panzers at will on any part of the front. We must regain the initiative, and speed and energy are essential." In other words, Get going![6]

Montgomery, reacting to pressures from above and below, assured Eisenhower that if the expected German counterattack did not materialize, he would launch Collins and Ridgway on January 1. But still he procrastinated, delaying the jump-off to January 3. The final scheme for the attack was cautious in the extreme: As previously planned, Collins would attack east out of Marche with four divisions; on his left flank, Ridgway would pivot Gavin's 82nd Division eastward to the Salm River line. Horrocks' 30 Corps, committed at last (and which now included Bols's 6th Airborne Division which had not seen any Bulge combat), would cross the Meuse River and attack on Collins' right flank. The advance would be meticulously controlled by First Army, which would establish "phase lines." A last-minute plea from Ridgway to launch Hobbs's 30th Division southward toward St. Vith was rejected.[7]

In preparation for the offensive, Ridgway made two high-level changes in his corps headquarters. First he sacked his uncooperative corps-artillery commander, Theodore Buechler, replacing him with an old and close friend, Lemuel (Matty) Mathewson, who had been serving as Joe Collins' corps-artillery deputy commander. Mathewson was a brilliant, well-rounded officer who had begun his career as an infantryman and later converted to artilleryman. In the 1930s, he had become a Spanish language specialist and had worked with Ridgway in the Latin American section of War Plans and, upon Ridgway's departure, in early 1942, replaced him as chief. Ridgway had earlier tried to pry Mathewson out of War Plans and bring him to the 82nd Division at Camp Claiborne, but Thomas T. Handy, who replaced Eisenhower as chief of War Plans, had refused to release him. Later, Marshall had appointed Mathewson a military aide to President Roosevelt. Ridgway was nearly ecstatic at getting Mathewson; he considered him one of the ablest men in the Army. "The change in that XVIII Corps artillery was almost incredible," he wrote.

"Within twenty-four hours after Mathewson took over, the smooth efficiency, the alert response of that fire control center were perfectly manifest. Its whole character of operations changed, and from then on was conspicuously superior."[8]

Next, perhaps in response to criticism of his frequent absence from corps headquarters, Ridgway became determined to recruit an official deputy. He had earlier asked for the FAAA chief of staff, Floyd Parks, but Brereton had vetoed that; Parks was deemed indispensable to FAAA. Several other generals he proposed to Hodges had likewise been vetoed. The upshot was that Ridgway "just took Bill Hoge," the CCB, 9th Armored Division, commander, and put him in the job. Hoge moved into Ridgway's CP and laid out his sleeping bag "in the same room" with Ridgway.[9]

The corps G-3, Day Surles, recalled:

Ridgway was a great believer that even at corps level he should get down to battalions. That was his method of operation: personal visits to battalion commanders all day long. He couldn't get to all the battalions, so he had General Hoge take half one day and he'd go one way and Ridgway would go the other, and the staff would stay there and try to make plans and get ready for the next operation. Then Hoge would come back and report to him what he had found in various units—which were weak and not doing well and they'd switch and Ridgway would go visit those units the next day.[10]

Ridgway was more than pleased with Hoge. The unflappable Hoge, he said later, was "more likely to understate things than ever to exaggerate." Thus he did not waste Ridgway's time on nonessentials. Ridgway recalled, "I knew that if he came back and told me a situation was bad . . . I had better start doing something about it."[11]

The forces allotted to XVIII Airborne Corps for the counteroffensive were sharply limited, in keeping with its limited mission. Ridgway would command only two divisions: Hobbs's 30th and Gavin's 82nd. The other forces formerly assigned to the corps, Hasbrouck's 7th Armored Division, CCB of 9th Armored Division, the remnants of the "106th Division" (424th Regiment plus) now commanded by the former ADC of the 106, Herbert Perrin, the 112th Regiment of the 28th Division, and Tomasik's mauled 509th Parachute Battalion, were placed in corps or army reserve.[12]

Gavin's 82nd, which would carry the main weight of the offensive, had not yet received any replacements and was therefore considerably understrength. In order to beef it up, the disparate parachute elements on the north front were attached. These included the whole of Rupert Graves's 517 (plus its 460 Parachute Field Artillery Battalion) and Wood Joerg's independent 551st Parachute Battalion, which had been fighting with the 30th Infantry Division and was now attached to the 517. These additions gave Gavin a total of five infantry regiments, comprising sixteen battalions. Had all battalions been at full strength, the 82nd would have been one of the most formidable infantry outfits in the ETO. But owing to the manpower shortages, the division barely mustered its authorized strength.[11]*

As finally scheduled, Collins jumped off on January 3. His VII Corps had four fine, experienced divisions: two armored (Harmon's 2nd and Rose's 3rd) and two infantry (Bolling's 84th and the 83rd, commanded by a tough, able veteran, Robert C. Macon, who had fought the division all the way from Normandy). The weather was ghastly: bitterly cold and foggy. All aircraft were grounded, depriving VII Corps of close air support. The roads were glazed with ice. The tanks and other vehicles of the 2nd and 3rd armored divisions skidded and slipped and piled up, causing traffic jams. The withdrawing Germans blocked roads by felling trees and sowing mines and leaving behind enclaves of 88s at key road junctions. Progress was so slow that Collins had to bring up infantry regiments from the 83rd and 84th divisions to clear the way.[15]

Ridgway's XVIII Airborne Corps jumped off on the same day. Hobbs's 30th Division (with the 112th Regiment attached) made a feint, as planned, then dug in. Gavin, holding Tucker's 504 and Lindquist's 508 in reserve, attacked with three regiments: Ekman's 505, Billingslea's 325 and Graves's 517. The newly integrated 517 was positioned on the left flank, or the "inside" or hub of the wheel, near Trois-Ponts, which it soon captured. The other three regiments, having displaced toward the west, attacked in a southeasterly direction toward Vielsalm. It turned into a very tough fight. The weather was freezing cold, the snow very deep in places where it had drifted.[16]

In Gavin's opinion, the newly attached 517 "had difficulty getting off its line of departure," and he was forced to spend a good deal of his time in its sector, goading the men forward. One of the company commanders in Boyle's 1st Battalion was astonished by all this close attention. He recalled that during the first five days the 517 was attached to the 82nd, Gavin visited his company headquarters twice. "I suppose he was worried about us," the officer recalled, "as a unit new to him. But how he found the time and energy to be constantly with his front line troops and still direct the overall activities of the division was a mystery. He did it with outstanding success." Boyle, who won a DSC, was severely wounded on January 5, replaced by his exec, Donald W. Fraser.[17]

Gavin was not at all happy with the tactical plan for his division. In fact, he later bluntly described it as "infuriating." He had to adhere strictly to the First Army "phase lines" so that no division in either corps got too far ahead of another. Since the 82nd was accustomed to moving rapidly—and did so in spite of the snow and ice—it meant Gavin repeatedly had to rein in his advance units, losing many opportunities to inflict punishing attacks on the withdrawing Germans and, on several occasions, giving them time to dig in on favorable terrain. This occurred when the division approached the key high ground,

---

* Typical of the understrength: Boyle's 1st Battalion, 517, had suffered over 25 percent casualties (157 of 609 men) while fighting with the 3rd Armored Division, December 22 to December 26.[14]

Thier-du-Mont, near Vielsalm. Had he not been constrained by "phase lines," Gavin could have quickly seized it. But instead he had to hold up and watch helplessly while the Germans dug in.

Gavin's impatience with the "phase lines" was echoed by the 505 historian Allen Langdon, who wrote: "This was the worst battle I saw in the entire war. The resistance was tough—very tough. Even so, the 505 had the best advance of the day for any unit in First Army. There is no doubt in my mind that if it hadn't been adhering to the phase lines the 505 could easily have reached the Salm River on January 4. Each time we stopped at a phase line, it gave the Germans time to build up another defense, and most days we had to break through this thin defense each time we jumped off."[18]

The job of retaking Thier-du-Mont fell to Roy Lindquist's 508, which had first seized it on December 19 and knew the terrain well. The January 7 attack proved to be a tough job. The regimental historian wrote: "The worst part of the attack . . . was not that so many men were killed in the assault . . . but rather that many men who were wounded . . . died that night from exposure. The thermometer hovered around zero all day and then dropped much lower at night. The entire ridge was buried in two feet of snow, and the few paths that ran up the side of the hill were snowbound. Not even a jeep could get near the wounded. Search parties combed the thick woods all night in hope of finding some of the wounded, but many were not found until too late." One company lost sixty-seven out of one hundred men.[19]

As he closed on his objective—the Salm River—Gavin's losses were everywhere heavy. In the 325th, Billingslea's 2nd Battalion commander, Richard Gibson, was wounded and evacuated and would not return to the division. He was replaced by a Gavin favorite, West Pointer Edwin Ostberg, a former 507 battalion commander who had been wounded in Normandy at Chef-du-Pont (and who had won a DSC). With his appointment, three out of the four principal 325 commanders were now West Pointers, and two of them were paratroopers. (Billingslea and Ostberg and Oz Leahy were West Pointers; Billingslea and Ostberg were paratroopers.)

Nowhere were casualties heavier than in Wood Joerg's 551st Battalion, attached first to the 517, then to the 504. Fighting in deep snow and heavy woods near the Petit-Halleux area, Joerg's men met very heavy resistance every foot of the way. They fell by the score—dead, wounded or frostbitten. As in the 508, many wounded froze to death. Early on the morning of January 7, Joerg himself was killed by an artillery tree burst and replaced by his exec, William N. Holm. But Holm found he had few men left to command. A muster two days later showed that of 839 officers and men who entered battle on January 3, there were only 110 left. Appalled, Gavin withdrew the unit and sent it to the rear. Three weeks later, January 27, the outfit was deactivated, its few survivors reassigned to other units in the 82nd.[20]

On the day that Joerg was killed, the 505's 2nd Battalion commander, Ben Vandervoort, was severely wounded. It was Vandervoort's second wound in the Bulge. Earlier, on December 21, he had taken a Schmeisser slug in his right shoulder. This time, the wound was much more serious. A shell fragment from an 80 mm mortar penetrated his left frontal sinus and orbital ridge, destroying the eye. He was evacuated, never to return to the division. It was a loss that was shattering, both to Ridgway and to Gavin—and to every soldier who had known him. William R. Carpenter replaced Vandervoort in command of the battalion.[21]†

As the VII and XVIII Airborne Corps counteroffensive began to pick up speed, Hitler authorized a general withdrawal of all German forces in its path. This information soon reached the Allies (from sketchy code breaking and battlefield interrogations of POWs), and it persuaded Montgomery and Hodges to approve Ridgway's repeated requests to increase the power and scope of his XVIII Airborne Corps attack. It was finally agreed that on January 13, the 30th Infantry Division, operating in conjunction with the 7th Armored Division, would attack due south from the Malmédy area with the aim of recapturing St. Vith.[23]

In preparation for this far more muscular drive on St. Vith, there was a major realignment of XVIII Airborne Corps forces. Gavin's tired and battered 82nd Division (less the 517) was withdrawn from its positions along the Salm River and put in corps reserve, replaced by Fay Prickett's 75th Infantry Division. The three battalions of the 517 were scattered about, the 1st (Fraser) and 3rd (Paxton) to Hobbs's 30th Division, the 2nd (Seitz) to Hasbrouck's 7th Armored Division. Hoge's CCB (with Hoge) returned to its "home," the 9th Armored Division, as did the 112th Regiment of the 28th Division, which was later also awarded a Presidential Unit Citation. John B. Anderson, scheduled to command the new XVI Corps, temporarily replaced Hoge as Ridgway's deputy. Herbert Perrin's "106th Division", soon to be commanded by a veteran, Donald A. Stroh, remained in the corps.‡

Ridgway's renewed attack jumped off, as scheduled, at 0800 hours, January 13, by which time Collins and Middleton were closing on Houffalize from the southwest. Elements of the 30th and "106th" divisions—the 119th, 120th, 424th regiments—spearheaded the attack while Ridgway observed at the front. The vaunted 30th Division advanced about three thousand yards, then bogged down, infuriating Ridgway. Hodges' aide, William Sylvan, noted in his diary: "According to General Ridgway [German] resistance is nowhere near as stiff

---

† In a letter to Ridgway about this time, Taylor wrote that he was becoming desperately short of qualified battalion commanders and was "combing the files for possible candidates and directing every effort to intensify their training for a battalion command." Ridgway, also feeling the pinch, replied that he had asked Omar Bradley for permission to "canvass" regular infantry divisions for possible candidates (not to exceed two men from any one division) but that Bradley had denied the request. "At present," Ridgway wrote, "the only thing I know is to continue intensified effort to develop battalion commander material within the division."[22]

‡ These realignments and shifts gave XVIII Airborne Corps a total strength of about four and a half divisions: one armored (7th), three infantry (30th, 75th, 82nd), plus the two regiments, the 106's 424th, which would soon get a new commander, John R. Jeter, and Graves's 517th.[24]

as the soldiers would have people believe." Hodges, too, was scornful. Sylvan wrote: "General Hodges is not pleased with results since the 30th Division has [previously] pushed patrols out this distance in the past week and General Hodges said it could be considered they reached the patrol line and no farther."[25]

That evening, a smoldering Ridgway summoned Hobbs, his ADC, William K. Harrison, and his chief of staff, Richard W. Stephens, to the XVIII Airborne Corps CP. According to minutes of this meeting, Ridgway laid into Omar Bradley's good friend Leland Hobbs without restraint. Ridgway stated that he was "entirely dissatisfied with the 30th Division." He singled out in particular the "poor showing" of the 119th Regiment, stating he had "little confidence" in the regimental commander and that the 119th's failure "was due in large measure to the failure of all commanders, from the division commander on down, to influence the action by applying strong and positive leadership." Hobbs agreed that the 119 "had fallen down badly," particularly its 3rd Battalion, and that its commander, Roy G. Fitzgerald, "had been relieved on the spot." Ridgway concluded the meeting by stating that the 30th's initial objectives must be taken by noon the next day. No obstacles would be tolerated. "With proper leadership," he said, there was "no reason" why the job couldn't be done.[26]

There was trouble also in Fay Prickett's 75th Division, which had relieved the 82nd. Its initial mission was to hold behind the Salm River. However, on January 15, Ridgway ordered it to cross the Salm, attacking east and southeast in support of the 30th Division. The next day, Ridgway visited Prickett at one of his regimental CPs. After a good look around, Ridgway judged that the division was performing in "a satisfactory, though not highly creditable manner." When Ridgway asked Prickett (within the hearing of the regimental staff) what corps headquarters could do to help him, Prickett replied, "Nothing but pray for me."

Ridgway was shocked. Prickett's pusillanimous statement convinced him that the men of the 75th did not have "that forceful, aggressive, positive leadership to which they are rightfully entitled." Furthermore, he was equally dissatisfied with the division artillery commander, Albert C. Stanford, another of Ridgway's West Point classmates. In a letter to Hodges, Ridgway recommended that both men be relieved of command. Hodges, who had already expressed misgivings about Prickett, accepted the recommendation at once. Prickett was replaced by Ray E. Porter, Ridgway's classmate at the Command and General Staff School and an able non-West Pointer who had served under Eisenhower in North Africa but had been manning a Pentagon swivel chair (in G-3) for many months.[27]*

---

* Prickett, who retained his rank, was detailed to conduct an investigation into the careless loss of cryptographic gear in Dutch Cota's 28th Division. He recommended that Cota, his chief of staff and his G-2 be relieved of command. Higher authority reduced the punishment to a reprimand, thus sparing Omaha Beach hero Dutch Cota disgrace and professional ruin. Prickett wound up the war in command of the 4th

Meanwhile, Collins' VII Corps was slugging southeast through deep snow toward Houffalize. On January 15, elements of his leading division, Harmon's 2nd Armored, reached the high ground overlooking the town. That same day, leading elements of Middleton's VIII Corps, a unit of Kilburn's 11th Armored Division (with Stubbs's 193rd Glider Regiment attached) arrived from the southwest in company with Miley's 17th Airborne Division. The two corps formally linked at Houffalize on January 16, thereby reestablishing the continuous (but still bowed and jagged) Allied front which the Germans had bashed in exactly one month earlier. On the following day, January 17, Eisenhower returned Hodges' First Army (and its corps) to Bradley's control, but not Simpson's Ninth. The latter would remain under Montgomery for his long-delayed conquest of the Ruhr.[29]

The linkup of the First and Third armies at Houffalize hardly fazed Ridgway. His full attention was still fixed on the recapture of St. Vith. To him, and to the men of the 7th Armored Division, having lost St. Vith, it was now almost a matter of honor to regain it. But apparently it was also a matter of honor for the Germans to hold what they had captured. The fight for that battered road junction continued to be a hard struggle.

When Hobbs and Prickett had bogged down, Ridgway had urged Hodges to commit the 1st Division on Hobbs's left (or east) to help. But Hodges and the new V Corps commander, Ralph Huebner, were reluctant to do so because it would significantly weaken V Corps, which was still holding the north shoulder. However, after the junction of First and Third armies at Houffalize (and after the code breakers reported the withdrawal of Sixth Panzer Army behind the Siegfried Line), Hodges committed both Huebner's 1st and 2nd divisions to a southerly attack. This added power drove the Germans back on St. Vith and at last opened a path for Hasbrouck's 7th Armored Division.[30]

All this time, the 7th Armored Division had been resting, reequipping and remanning. Although he was suffering so badly from gallstones that he had to take pain killers, Bruce Clarke insisted on remaining in command of CCB for the triumphant reentry into St. Vith. William Triplet had replaced Dwight Rosebaum as commander of CCA, and while no personal honor was at stake in St. Vith, he was itching for a fight and his men were anxious to avenge the bloody nose they had gotten at Manhay. The pitiful but proud remnants of Tomasik's 509th Parachute Battalion (Tomasik and ninety-six others) were attached to Clarke's CCB to give Clarke more infantry. Richard Seitz's 2nd Parachute Battalion (of the 517) was attached to Triplet's CCA.[31]

This was an unforgettable moment in the history of the 7th Armored Division. It moved into attack position on January 19/20 and jumped off the following day. The weather was hideous. The snow, one tanker recalled, was "deep and cold as sin" and there was a "howling blizzard." When the snow cover reached thirty inches, Hasbrouck had to employ bulldozers to "plow"

Armored Division and later became deputy inspector general of the Army. Stanford, reduced to colonel, retired from the Army the following year.[28]

the roads. The men huddled in igloos and melted snow on tank exhaust pipes for drinking water. The tanks were camouflaged with white paint; the men wore white Belgian bedsheets over their uniforms.

In such weather, the division moved slowly—too slowly, in Ridgway's view. When Bruce Clarke's CCB bogged down in front of Born, Ridgway threatened to send Triplet's CCA to its assistance. Hearing this, Clarke got moving and took Born the next day. Nonetheless, Ridgway remained dissatisfied and complained to Hodges that the division was "sluggish." At one point, Ridgway told Hasbrouck that if he couldn't get the job done, he would order Hobbs's infantry to push straight through the 7th and take St. Vith.[32]

On the morning of January 23, the 7th Armored reached the high ground overlooking St. Vith. The honor of taking the city was given Clarke's CCB. CCA commander Triplet, learning that Ridgway was coming forward to observe the entry with his outfit, located an observation post (OP) in some German trenches on the forward slope of a hill, where the view was good. He sent his driver, O'Hare, to lead Ridgway to the OP on foot, so Ridgway's jeep caravan would not make a conspicuous target on the crest of the hill above the OP:

About 1330 hours, to my surprise, disgust and horror, here came O'Hare skidding along the road on the skyline with two other loaded jeeps skidding behind him. Ridgway and five of his staff dismounted and posed. I galloped up, reported and said, "General, I recommend we move down into those trenches. We're right on the skyline here." Ridgway looked over the lines of soldiers, tanks and destroyers huddled behind the houses or concealed behind the ridge and said, "I don't think that will be necessary." I told O'Hare to get the jeeps out of sight and he took off with enthusiasm. I'd have liked to have gone with him.

Just as I prophesied, the Jerries began slamming shells at us and whipped a few into our near vicinity . . . I was getting a stiff neck, starting to duck as usual for everything coming, passing, or going—but having to check the impulse rigidly on account of the general posing with the idea of "influencing the troops by his example." Finally an assault gun bracketed us with three very close rounds. "General," I said, "I've found a good trench down there." He said, "All right. I think we can move down there now." And we STROLLED LEISURELY to my selected OP. I had to stay with him. It wouldn't have been polite for me to make the 100 yards in seven seconds as I yearned to do.

At 1430, CCB started into town. It was like a good movie, in Technicolor, with sound effects. There wasn't much resistance—not more than 200 prisoners were taken, but it was a good show. Ridgway thanked me for the entertainment and left, whereupon I relaxed and resumed my cowardly practice of ducking for everything that I heard coming my way.[33]

Paratroopers were in on the final kill at St. Vith: 70 survivors of Tomasik's mauled and tattered 509 attached to Clarke's CCB. After the action, there were but 54 men, including Tomasik, left of the 745 who had departed France. Like the 551, the unit was deactivated. Tomasik went to the 13th Airborne Division, the 53 others to the 82nd.† Dick Seitz's 2nd Battalion (517), attached to Triplet's CCA, had helped pave the way to St. Vith—at terrible cost in killed and wounded. Triplet was forever grateful: "I was, and still am impressed by the quiet courage and capable, uncomplaining performance of Seitz and his crew." From the time he arrived to fight in the Bulge, Seitz had suffered about 400 casualties out of his force of 600—329 killed or wounded so badly they were evacuated.[35]

For Ridgway's XVIII Corps, Gavin's 82nd Division and the DRAGOON paratroopers, the Bulge ended with the recapture of St. Vith. For Max Taylor and the 101, the end came at about the same time, when the 101 was hurriedly withdrawn from Bastogne and shifted to Sandy Patch's Seventh Army in Alsace to help blunt a supposed German threat to Strasbourg. For Eric Bols's 6th Airborne, which had been used sparingly in Horrocks' 30 Corps, it ended on the Ourthe River.[36]

The Bulge lasted two weeks longer for Bud Miley's 17th Airborne Division. Hastily transferred south to John Millikin's III Corps, the 17th joined Millikin's 6th Armored and 90th Infantry divisions in a drive from Luxembourg northeastward to the German border at the Our River near Roderhause. The purpose was to clear all Germans out of the area. Raff's 507 led this drive and it cost him two fine battalion commanders: Roy Creek (3rd Battalion), severely wounded on January 21, and Ben Pearson (1st Battalion), seriously wounded a week later when his jeep hit a mine. During its Bulge action, the 507 suffered a total of seven hundred casualties—one hundred killed, three hundred severely wounded, three hundred seriously injured.[37]

When the Bulge ended, FAAA's four airborne divisions were literally scattered to the four winds, each serving with a different army. The 17th was with Patton's Third Army, the 82nd was with Hodges' First Army, the 101st was with Patch's Seventh Army and the 6th was with Dempsey's British Second Army. The three American divisions had incurred grievous casualties. No exact accounting was ever made, but one reliable estimate put the total at about ten thousand killed, wounded and missing plus another five thousand felled by trench foot, frostbite and other illness.[38]

† Back in the States, when Bill Yarborough learned the 509—"the finest parachute unit in the U.S. Army"—had been deactivated, he thought it was "tragic" and he was "heartbroken." He received "a number of anguished letters from 509ers whose world, they thought, had so unjustly come to an end." Many 509 survivors, including its "founder," Edson Raff, and its most recent historian, Charles H. Doyle, were extremely bitter at Ridgway, who approved the deactivation of the 509th. After the recapture of St. Vith, the 7th Armored Division was placed in reserve and Bruce Clarke left for England to have his gallstones removed. He was replaced by Joseph W. Haskell and did not return to the division until after V-E Day. In the postwar Army Clarke rose to four-star general.[34]

☆46☆

IN EARLY JANUARY, while the Allied counteroffensive was getting underway, the Combined Chiefs had agreed that when future large-scale ground operations against Germany were possible, the main effort would be made in the far northern sector by Montgomery. His 21st Army Group, consisting of Dempsey's Second Army and Crerar's First Canadian Army and reinforced by Bill Simpson's Ninth Army, would cross the Rhine near Wesel, encircle Germany's Ruhr industrial area and destroy the German Army, which it was believed would deploy to defend the vital Ruhr area to the last man. Bradley's 12th Army Group, consisting of Hodges' First and Patton's Third armies, would support Montgomery by conducting important but lower-priority attacks along the upper Rhine from Cologne to Mainz.

Bradley was not pleased with this strategy for a number of reasons. Not only did it give the most important role in the defeat of Germany to the British, whose contribution to the ground forces was about one third that of the Americans, but Bradley did not think Montgomery was sufficiently aggressive to pull it off. Moreover, the plan compelled Bradley to give control of his Ninth Army to Montgomery more or less permanently. He still firmly believed that a strong First- and Third-army thrust into the Cologne-Mainz area was necessary to prevent the German Army from concentrating decisively against Montgomery in the Ruhr and that all the Allied armies should draw up to the west bank of the Rhine River on a "broad front" before Montgomery was turned loose.

Bradley's broad-front strategy was supported by Eisenhower, and although Eisenhower assured the Combined Chiefs that Montgomery would receive the highest priorities in resources for crossing the Rhine, over the next several weeks he encouraged Bradley to utilize whatever resources he had available to advance the First and Third armies ever closer to the river.[1]

Eisenhower's first step in this unheralded process was to authorize a combined First- and Third-army offensive soon after the consolidation of the Allied front in the St. Vith area, on January 23. Bradley's plan, to be launched on January 28, was as follows. Hodges and Patton would attack, more or less line abreast, along a narrow, twenty-five-mile front (Monschau–Luetzkampen) into the Schnee Eifel, Losheim Gap and Monschau Forest, break through to the Siegfried Line and push east as far as possible—to the Rhine, it was hoped. Three corps would be employed north to south: Huebner's V and Ridgway's XVIII Airborne of First Army and Middleton's VIII of Third Army. Collins' powerful VII Corps with its two armored divisions would be held in First Army reserve to exploit a decisive breakthrough on either Huebner's or Ridgway's front.[2]

Ridgway's XVIII Airborne Corps was to make the "main effort"—lead the offensive. Ridgway would attack northeast out of the St. Vith area toward Schleiden and thence to Euskirchen, a city forty miles northeast of St. Vith and a mere fifteen miles west of the Rhine River at Bonn. Huebner's V Corps (on Ridgway's north flank) would attack eastward through the Monschau Forest toward Schleiden, where it would link with XVIII Airborne Corps for the attack toward Euskirchen. Middleton's VIII Corps (on Ridgway's south flank) would attack northeasterly through Prüm—and beyond.[3]

Although the offensive was hastily organized and the weather was still unfavorable for vehicular traffic, it was believed the Germans were fleeing east willy-nilly, and Bradley had good reason to expect a break-in. A quick, decisive American success in this area of Germany's border would achieve Bradley's goal of drawing the First and Third armies to the west bank of the Rhine before Montgomery launched his offensive. It also would go a long way toward restoring the prestige the American GIs had lost in the Bulge. Moreover, it also might persuade the Combined Chiefs to more evenly distribute resources for the invasion of Germany, giving Bradley's armies a more prominent role in the final victory. Conceivably, a Bradley success on German soil might cause the complete collapse of the Third Reich.[4]

When Ridgway received this new and important assignment, he was elated. Owing to the coldly hostile weather—it was developing into the worst European winter in forty years—airborne operations were out of the question for an indefinite time and XVIII Airborne Corps had nothing else to do. Moreover, Ridgway in his debut as a ground corps commander had been engaged largely in defensive operations. Too many of these had been frustrating, patchwork jobs with ragtag troops, and some had resulted in controversy and hard feelings. He welcomed this opportunity to lead his corps in a conventional, wide-open offensive drive with well-organized, well-manned divisions.

He was not unaware of the high military (and political) stakes involved and was thus determined to make the offensive successful. In planning his attack, he came up with an unorthodox scheme of maneuver. Owing to the heavy ice and snow, he would not employ armored divisions, only infantry divisions, which, if necessary, could advance through the deep, drifted snow on foot, supplied by small tracked cargo vehicles called weasels. His plan was to assign two infantry divisions to lead the attack, with two others immediately behind. When or if the two leading divisions ran out of steam, the two trailing divisions would leapfrog the leading divisions and carry the attack while the other two rested. Then the two rested divisions would leapfrog the leading divisions—and so on. In sum, infantry supported by jeeps, weasels and whatever armor and artillery (organic to infantry divisions) that could advance in the snow-covered terrain would carry the corps deep into Germany, perhaps to the Rhine.[5]

This unusual scheme required outstanding infantry divisions. Fortunately, First Army had two of the best at hand: the 1st Division, commanded by Clift Andrus, and Gavin's 82nd Airborne. These two would lead the assault, the 1st Division on the left (or north), the 82nd on the right. Leland Hobbs's 30th and Alex Bolling's 84th would come behind, ready to leapfrog into the van on a moment's notice.[6]

Gavin's 82nd Division had not yet received many replacements and it was still seriously understrength. For that reason, Graves's scattered 517 (and the attached 460 Parachute Artillery Battalion) was regathered and assigned to the 82nd, although the 517 itself had suffered severe casualties. Even though the addition of the 517 again gave Gavin five regiments (fifteen battalions), the 82nd remained far below its normal strength.[7]

Ridgway's two lead divisions jumped off as scheduled, before dawn on January 28. In order to achieve surprise, Ridgway withheld the usual artillery bombardment. It worked. The 1st found the Germans still sleeping in their bedrolls. The 82nd, Gavin reported, "caught the enemy at breakfast." Ridgway was ecstatic: "I don't think any commander ever had such a magnificent experience as to see those two splendid divisions, both veteran outfits, at their highest state of combat effectiveness, attacking side by side. It was a joy to see . . . like watching two great racehorses, drawing head and head to the finish line. All I had to do was give them their head, and then help them with all the means at the Corps's disposal, and with everything I could get from Army."[8]

However, Ridgway's elation was short-lived. Despite the surprise achieved, the divisions advanced only two miles the first day. The official Army historian, Charles MacDonald, wrote: "The story of these first attacks could be told almost in a word: weather. By the end of January the month's unusually heavy snowfall and low temperatures had left a snow cover one to two feet deep everywhere and in some places drifts up to a man's waist. Snow glazed the hills, choked the valleys and the roads, and hid the enemy's mines. On the first day it snowed again and into the night." There was only sporadic and light resistance, "yet men marching all day through the snow even without sight or sound of the enemy were exhausted when night came from sheer physical exertion."[9]

In the 82nd, Roy Lindquist's 508 was in reserve behind the attacking regiments. The extremely difficult conditions were vividly described by the regimental historian: "It was snowing hard and a high wind was blowing. Straining bodies leaned into the storm as the swirling snow worked itself under scarves and into boot tops, chilling the men to the bone. All day long the troopers moved forward, first warmed up by the rapid movement through deep snow under a heavy load, and then nearly freezing whenever the column made one of its frequent halts . . . Heavy snow made walking almost impossible with a heavy load. The trail breakers had to be changed frequently in order to keep them from dropping with fatigue. For the men in the middle of the column it was an old story. Run fifty steps, walk fifty then stop. Unshoulder a load, shoulder it again and move on. Up the steep mountainsides the men labored. Down icy trails they slithered. Through half-frozen streams they sloshed. Bodies became tired, minds became dulled from being constantly on the alert. When the forest began to shade the meager sun, a halt meant near freezing . . ."[10]

On the second day, January 29, progress was not much better. German resistance increased. Ridgway reported: "The enemy who now had recovered from the previous day's surprise . . . defended from infantry strong points to good advantage." The 1st Division captured Büllingen; the 82nd, angling northeasterly toward the Losheim Gap, captured Herresbach, Holzheim and Emmerscheid. At Herresbach, Tucker's 2nd Battalion, commanded by Edward Wellems, surprised and captured an entire German battalion, then occupied the town. These little Belgian villages were now highly prized for shelter from the cold, and as a result they were not pulverized with artillery. The men, Gavin recalled, "would encircle them, dig out the occupants with rifles and do everything they could to rout out the enemy so as to have the houses for their own use . . ."[11]

By the end of the fourth day of the offensive, January 31, Ridgway's elite troops had managed to advance only about ten miles. This had brought the XVIII Airborne Corps to the "west branch" of the Siegfried Line in the area between Udenbreth and Losheim. North of Ridgway, Huebner's V Corps, led by the veteran 2nd and 9th infantry divisions, had found German resistance lighter but had done only slightly better. South of Ridgway, Middleton's VIII Corps, delayed by a complex crossing of the Our River, had made even slower progress.[12]

Considering the weather and the state of the terrain, these advances were near-heroic achievements, but in Eisenhower's eyes not nearly enough for a decisive break-in. Ridgway was still thirty miles short of his main objective, Euskirchen. At his average rate of advance it would take another two weeks to go the thirty miles, if it could be done at all in the face of the snow and the sporadic but unexpectedly tough German resistance. Meanwhile, Montgomery was heatedly denouncing the offensive: not only was it militarily futile, it was delaying the buildup of his 21st Army Group for the "main effort."[13]

On February 1, when Eisenhower abruptly canceled the offensive, Ridgway was crushed. The next day, he wrote Hodges: "I feel the First Army attack has met with high success, has delivered a powerful, disrupting blow at the enemy's physical means and his will to fight; that his command and organization have suffered severe loss of control; that if continued for a few days longer, the First Army attack will reap its full fruits, will smash through all organized defenses in its zone, and be prepared for exploitation with its power substantially undiminished . . . I have complete confidence, which is shared by my division commanders, that with the forces now available to this Corps, and the continued assistance provided by the corps on my flanks, the Siegfried defenses can be captured and a complete break-through effected."[14]

But there was no appeal; Eisenhower's orders stood. Many American generals, including Hodges and Patton, were incensed. Patton wrote in his diary: "Damn this political war . . . I feel, and I believe Hodges also agrees, that our present attack, which is moving, has a better chance of getting to the Rhine first than has a new attack which will not start until February 10, if then . . . Neither of us has a very high opinion of the offensive value of British troops . . . Personally I think that this is a foolish and ignoble way for the Americans to end the war."[15]

The momentum of the attack carried Ridgway's XVIII Airborne Corps eastward for several more days. This enabled Ridgway's troops to enjoy the satisfaction—and publicity—of penetrating the outer edge of the famous Siegfried Line with its formidable-looking concrete "dragon teeth" tank barriers, barbed wire and interlocking concrete pillboxes. Both the 1st and the 82nd divisions made limited penetrations February 1 to 5. The Germans reacted with surprising fury, launching strong artillery and tank-supported infantry attacks, during which Edwin Ostberg, commanding Billingslea's 2nd Battalion, was killed. (He was replaced by the battalion's former commander, Tad Major, who had recovered from his battle wounds.) That action terminated the offensive. Owing to its abrupt termination, Ridgway never had an opportunity to leapfrog Hobbs's 30th and Bolling's 84th divisions into action.[16]

All attention now focused on Montgomery's "main effort" in the north. It grew into an enormous and complex operation which would be carried out in three steps. The first two steps were designed to position 21st Army Group on the west bank of the Rhine River in the Wesel-Düsseldorf area. In step one, Crerar's First Canadian Army, reinforced and spearheaded by Horrocks' 30 Corps, would attack southeast from the Nijmegen area toward Düsseldorf. In step two, to be launched almost simultaneously, Simpson's Ninth Army would attack northeast from the Aachen area toward Düsseldorf. When all the Germans had been cleared out west of the Rhine in the Wesel-Düsseldorf area, Montgomery would proceed to step three: a massive crossing of the Rhine near Wesel, followed by encirclement of the Ruhr and destruction of the German armies.[17]

Hodges' First Army, now positioned in the "center" of the Allied front, would support Montgomery's operations in a substantial way. First, Hodges would transfer sufficient divisions from his First Army to Simpson's Ninth to ensure that Simpson could field three corps, comprising a total of not less than ten divisions. Second, Huebner's V Corps would launch yet another attack into the Hürtgen Forest to seize the Roer River dams so that the Germans could not flood the lower Roer and impede Simpson's attack. Third, Ridgway's XVIII Airborne Corps and Collins' VII Corps would attack, line abreast, on the right flank of Simpson's Ninth Army, going through the Roer dams and the Hürtgen Forest area to Düren, then on to Cologne and Bonn.[18]

These First Army operations in support of Montgomery required considerable reshuffling and redistribution of forces and corps headquarters.* While the operations were being planned and carried out, Huebner proceeded with the urgent First Army task of trying (once again) to seize the Roer dams. For this

---

* Collins' VII Corps headquarters moved north to the Aachen area and linked with Simpson's right (or south) flank. Ridgway's XVIII Airborne Corps headquarters moved to the town of Zweifall (six miles southeast of Aachen), at the edge of Hürtgen Forest, and linked with Collins' right flank on the north and Huebner's V Corps left flank to the south. Ridgway's forces would consist of the 1st, 82nd and 78th Infantry divisions. Huebner stretched his right flank southward to Losheim, linking with Middleton's VIII Corps and filling the gap caused by the withdrawal of Ridgway's XVIII Airborne Corps.[19]

tough and dreaded job, he chose his northernmost division, the 78th, commanded by Edwin P. Parker, Jr. The outfit (inherited from Ninth Army) was relatively new to combat and would soon be assigned to the right flank of Ridgway's XVIII Airborne Corps. Parker jumped off on February 5, assisted by CCR of Hasbrouck's 7th Armored Division. The attack was launched south of Schmidt, where Craig's 9th Division and Cota's 28th Division had been mauled the previous October and November.[20]

The plan had been hurriedly and poorly conceived, and the initial results were disappointing. Both Hodges and Huebner rushed to the Hürtgen area to personally supervise Parker's maneuvers. But the presence of all this second-guessing brass rattled Parker and only made things worse. Huebner, fearing Parker might fail, ordered elements of his adjacent division, Edward Craig's 9th Infantry, to join in the battle, while Hodges ordered up a vast array of big artillery. As it turned out, Parker surmounted both the enemy at his front and the high-level quarterbacks at his rear, and the 78th, with Craig's timely assist, captured the dams. To add additional punch to the division, Hodges temporarily attached Graves's peripatetic 517th Parachute Regiment, which was assigned the tough task of capturing the big dam at Schmidt. However, the Germans outwitted the Allies. They cleverly demolished the floodgates of the dams so that the lower Roer was inundated by a slow, long-lasting flood which the Allies were powerless to stop. This would force a postponement of Ninth Army's jump-off, and that of VII and XVIII Airborne Corps.[21]

Ridgway activated his XVIII Airborne Corps headquarters on February 8, just as the dams were being seized. Gavin's 82nd Division, then in process of redeploying north, was temporarily assigned to V Corps to assist in securing the dams and to cut off German forces fleeing the area. Three of Gavin's regiments (Ekman's 505, Lindquist's 508, the reattached 517) were committed into the tail end of the battle north of the 78th's sector. They were to attack through Vossenach and Bergstein toward Schmidt. Typically, Gavin made a firsthand survey of the terrain before committing his troops in accordance with the V Corps plan. The shock of what he found stayed with him the rest of his life:

I proceeded down the trail on foot. It was obviously impassable for a jeep; it was a shambles of wrecked vehicles and abandoned tanks. The first tanks that attempted to go down the trail had evidently slid off and thrown their tracks. In some cases the tanks had been pushed off the trail and toppled down the gorge among the trees. Between where the trail begins outside of Vossenach and the bottom of the canyon, there were four abandoned tank destroyers and five disabled and abandoned tanks. In addition, all along the sides of the trail there were many, many dead bodies, cadavers that had just emerged from the winter snow. Their gangrenous, broken and torn bodies were rigid and grotesque, some of them with arms skyward, seemingly in supplication . . . Nearby were dozens of litter cases, the bodies long dead

. . . As darkness descended over the canyon, it was an eerie scene, like something from the lower levels of Dante's *Inferno.*[22]

Although Ridgway had no command responsibility at this time, he, too, toured this area:

I made a personal reconnaissance into these deep, wooded valleys where the 28th had been attacked and overwhelmed. It was a graveyard of war, a no man's land populated by ghosts . . . Tanks and trucks had been abandoned in country so precipitous and rugged they should never have been employed there in the first place. The winter snows were melting in the first warm days of spring, and from beneath the snow the bodies of the 28th Division dead were beginning to appear. They littered the ground in various stages of decomposition, lying singly and in little groups and clusters, just as they had fallen [three] months before . . . One of my most seasoned commanders suggested to me that during our attack we should make certain that the new units assigned to the corps should not be required to attack across this sector . . . A green unit, he felt, might be strongly affected by the sight of so many American dead, in such a condition, and should not have to undergo such an experience the first time they were committed to battle. It was a thoughtful suggestion.[23]

Gavin returned to V Corps headquarters boiling mad. He was convinced that inept and unrealistic headquarters planning by staff officers who had never seen the terrain had been responsible for the tragic losses of the thousands of men in the 9th and 28th divisions the previous fall. The V Corps plan for the 82nd Division was no less inept. The V Corps staff, Gavin wrote, was "remote . . . from the realities." He insisted on formulating his own scheme of maneuver, based on the realities of the terrain he had seen with his own eyes and which included some theretofore undiscovered good roads on high ground. As a result, the 505 and 517 (which had to negotiate a massive minefield) quickly seized Schmidt and other objectives with minimum casualties and then proceeded to the west bank of the Roer River. After that, the 82nd Division reverted to XVIII Airborne Corps control. Gavin laid plans to cross the Roer in concert with Ridgway's other divisions, and the 517 (and Ray Cato's attached 460th Parachute Artillery) was transferred permanently to the American 13th Airborne Division, newly arriving in France.[24]

Montgomery launched the first step of his offensive on February 8, the day Ridgway activated XVIII Airborne Corps at Zweifall. This was the attack of the Canadian First Army—spearheaded by Horrocks' 30 Corps—southeast from Nijmegen toward Düsseldorf. Step two, the attack of Simpson's Ninth Army northeast from Aachen toward Düsseldorf, had been scheduled to jump off two days later, on February 10, but owing to the flooding of the Roer River, had had to be postponed until February 23, a delay that Bradley described as "two long, utterly maddening weeks."[25]

If the Roer dams had been seized, destroyed or opened earlier, there would have been no flooding to contend with and Simpson could have attacked on schedule, with Collins' VII Corps and Ridgway's XVIII Airborne Corps jumping off on Simpson's right flank on February 10, heading for Cologne and Bonn. But the enforced delay that temporarily idled Ridgway's XVIII Airborne Corps led, in part, to a drastic change in the fortunes of Ridgway and the 82nd Division.

Except for the emergency air resupply missions to the 101st at Bastogne, Lewis Brereton's big and expensive FAAA had achieved nothing of consequence since MARKET-GARDEN, in September. There had been no paratroop operations; in the Bulge and thereafter, the four parachute divisions had been committed to ground action. The opening of Antwerp as a supply port in November had eliminated the need for using FAAA's fourteen-hundred-odd air transports for carting gasoline and ammo to the continent. The FAAA staff and its vast aerial resources were going to waste.

FAAA, however, continued to generate plans. Most of these were designed to support Montgomery, Bradley or Patch in crossing the Rhine River into Germany, but one—ECLIPSE (formerly TALISMAN)—was an American drop on Berlin, should the Third Reich suddenly collapse. Just prior to the Bulge, the airborne plans for crossing the Rhine had been reduced to three, in this order of priority: VARSITY (in support of Montgomery's crossing at Wesel); CHOKER II (in support of Patch's Seventh Army crossing at Worms); NAPLES II (in support of Bradley's crossing at Cologne).[26]

By February 1, circumstances and resources had focused FAAA planning on VARSITY. Montgomery had personally insisted on airborne support for his massive Rhine crossing at Wesel, and Eisenhower had approved. Brereton had assigned VARSITY planning to his new British deputy, Richard Gale (who also commanded British 1 Airborne Corps) and had appointed Gale provisional commander of the operation. Montgomery and the British Second Army commander, Miles Dempsey, who would spearhead the Rhine crossing, had drawn a plan utilizing three airborne divisions, which were chosen by Brereton and Gale: Eric Bols's 6th, which after the Bulge had been moved to a rear area in Holland; Bud Miley's 17th, still in the line at the Our River; and the newly arrived American 13th Airborne Division, commanded by Elbridge G. (Gerry) Chapman.[27]

Within a matter of a few days, however, these plans were altered significantly. After being briefed, Montgomery (or Dempsey, or both) vetoed Gale as the airborne commander, insisting that Ridgway instead command VARSITY. There were probably several reasons for this decision. Ridgway and his corps headquarters were far more experienced; British 1 Airborne Corps had been utterly useless or worse in MARKET-GARDEN; and there would be two American divisions and only one British division. Montgomery had worked closely with Ridgway during the Bulge and had utmost confidence in his ability. Montgomery's chief planners told FAAA that "21st Army Group would be delighted to have Ridgway and will make sure he is relieved within a week after commitment."[28]

On February 5 and 6, Eisenhower toured the front with Omar Bradley. On the 6th, Eisenhower, Bradley and Ridgway conferred at Huebner's V Corps CP, then drove in Eisenhower's staff car to the 78th Division CP. Along the way, Eisenhower dropped a bombshell: plans were "under consideration," he said, for two airborne operations, VARSITY and CHOKER II. VARSITY would employ the British 6th and the American 13th and 17th divisions; CHOKER II would employ the 82nd and 101st. It was Eisenhower's "intention" that Ridgway should command both operations, first VARSITY, then CHOKER II.[29]

By the next day, February 7, as Ridgway was establishing XVIII Airborne Corps headquarters at Zweifall, word of his impending departure—and that of the 82nd Division—from First Army was leaking through First Army headquarters. William Sylvan noted in his diary that day: "Gen. Ridgway was with the CG [Hodges] most of the day at this headquarters. It now appears that Gen. Brereton is trying to get Gen. Ridgway and his corps back in order that some airborne operations may be planned. Gen. Hodges and Gen. Kean, of course, are protesting against this suggestion, especially as it comes at a date when XVIII Corps is completely ready to assume its important place in our coming action, and when relief of it would be practically impossible. Gen. Ridgway concurred wholeheartedly in a letter which was signed by Gen. Hodges, asking that such a move be postponed indefinitely."[30]†

Why was Ridgway, the exemplar of airborne warfare, so stoutly resisting his assignment to VARSITY, the first Allied airborne operation since MARKET-GARDEN? There were probably several reasons: By then he had had a good taste of "conventional" warfare, had done very well at it and wanted to stay with it longer—at least until First Army reached the Rhine. He had also formed a close and highly satisfactory working relationship with Hodges, and Hodges had come to depend on Ridgway as much as he depended on Joe Collins. No doubt Ridgway knew by this time that Eisenhower had recommended him, after Collins, for the next available army command and may have believed his opportunity for such a promotion would be enhanced by remaining with "conventional," rather than "specialized," forces. Last, notwithstanding his public declarations to the contrary, Ridgway had little faith in the ability of most British generals and may have feared that Montgomery's Rhine crossing, like MARKET-GARDEN, would turn into a fiasco, or at least an inconclusive operation. For one thing, there was clearly a time squeeze: it seemed doubtful that even the highly flexible and capable XVIII Airborne Corps could properly plan and execute both VARSITY and CHOKER II, the latter immediately on the heels of the former.

As Ridgway saw it, it would be much more logical to assign Gale and his 1 British Airborne Corps to plan and execute VARSITY, allow XVIII Airborne

† The concluding paragraph of the letter—Hodges to Bradley—stated: "It is recommended that the XVIII Airborne Corps and the 82nd Airborne Division not be relieved from the First Army until the present operation to the Rhine is completed."[31]

Corps to remain with First Army until it reached the Rhine River, and finally transfer XVIII Airborne Corps to command and execute CHOKER II.

On the same morning, February 8, that Ridgway hand-carried the Hodges letter to Bradley at his new headquarters in Namur, Brereton and his chief of staff, Floyd Parks, had conferred with Eisenhower in Versailles to confirm—and solidify—Ridgway's appointment to command VARSITY. Eisenhower had told Brereton that Montgomery's offensive now constituted "the big push" behind which the bulk of Allied resources was to be placed and that he desired "the command set-up to conform to the wishes of Montgomery." In other words, if Montgomery wanted Ridgway for VARSITY, Montgomery would get Ridgway.[32]

By the time Ridgway conferred with Bradley, SHAEF had already told Bradley of Eisenhower's decisions, and Bradley knew it would be futile to try to overturn them. He made it clear to Ridgway that there was no appeal—but at the same time tried to reassure him. According to Ridgway's notes of this meeting, Bradley said Eisenhower had promised him that XVIII Airborne Corps would be withdrawn from VARSITY "almost immediately" so that Ridgway and the corps headquarters could take charge of the planning for CHOKER II. Moreover, Bradley said, after CHOKER II was concluded, he, Bradley, intended to assign an armored division to XVIII Airborne Corps and carry the corps "straight through with him" into the heart of Germany as a reserve force. In other words, Ridgway was not to worry, XVIII Airborne Corps would be in on the final kill.[33]

Eisenhower's—and Bradley's—final decision on this matter was another blow to Hodges. He had envisioned his two most aggressive corps commanders, Collins and Ridgway, who worked so well together, dashing side by side to the Rhine. He had made "every effort" to keep Ridgway and was "extremely sorry" to lose him. William Sylvan logged: "It now seems almost certain that we shall lose the XVIII Airborne Corps, much to our disappointment . . . It is not known when this change will take place but it is thought to be imminent." Informal word soon leaked down from Bradley's 12th Army Group that John Millikin's III Corps of Patton's Third Army would probably be transferred north to replace XVIII Airborne Corps.[34]

The next day, February 9, one day before Simpson's originally scheduled jump-off, Montgomery's planners called a meeting at 21st Army Group headquarters in Eindhoven to discuss VARSITY. Brereton had insisted that Ridgway attend and Ridgway did so, very reluctantly. He groused to Floyd Parks, who was representing FAAA, that he was "engaged in combat" and "involved in planning an operation for crossing the Roer River and could ill afford to be absent and would have much preferred to have sent a representative." He made it clear that, under the circumstances, VARSITY "should have been given to 1 British Airborne Corps."[35]

Ridgway continued to do his utmost to get out of the VARSITY assignment, to no avail. He turned over all VARSITY planning to Gale and requested a meeting with Montgomery to make his case. But Montgomery was at the front observing Crerar's attack toward Düsseldorf. In any case, Montgomery's chief planner told Ridgway, it would be futile; Montgomery had made up his mind he wanted Ridgway. Worse, owing to the flooding of the Roer dams, that day Simpson's jump-off was indefinitely postponed, fatally undermining Ridgway's case that he was "in combat." His appeals were shut off once and for all the next day, February 10, by a call from SHAEF to Floyd Parks at FAAA. SHAEF told Parks that Montgomery "definitely wants Ridgway to command VARSITY" and furthermore, neither Montgomery nor SHAEF desired that the planning be left to Richard Gale. Ridgway was to take over all aspects of VARSITY without further ado or delay.[36]

Events moved swiftly thereafter. On February 13, John Millikin's III Corps relieved XVIII Airborne Corps. Ridgway and the corps staff prepared to return to the former corps headquarters at Épernay, France, to commence VARSITY and CHOKER II planning. The three American airborne divisions (17th, 82nd, 101st) were withdrawn from combat and returned to their old bases near Rheims. Bud Miley's 17th and Gerry Chapman's 13th were formally designated for VARSITY. Gavin's 82nd and Taylor's 101st, both sorely in need of refitting and rest, were provisionally designated for CHOKER II or, if necessary, ECLIPSE, the airborne occupation of Berlin.[37]

Before leaving, Ridgway had a private "farewell" meeting with Courtney Hodges. The First Army commander was more morose than usual. The Roer was flooded; the First Army drive to the Rhine in support of Simpson's Ninth Army was indefinitely delayed. Looking back with some bitterness, Hodges faulted Allied strategy. If only Eisenhower had not mounted MARKET-GARDEN, and had kept the British "close" with First Army in the run through France and Belgium, the Allies could have crossed the Rhine in October. The further implication was that had the Allies crossed the Rhine, there could have been no German counterattack in the Bulge. Moreover, if Eisenhower had allowed Hodges to continue the most recent (February) offensive going above (south of) the Roer dams, First Army would be on the west bank of the Rhine by now. Hodges agreed with Bradley and Patton that Eisenhower's decisions to favor Montgomery in September 1944 and again in February 1945 were terribly costly errors in judgment.[38]

PART IX

Germany:

Destruction of the Third Reich

☆ 47 ☆

Ridgway and the XVIII Airborne Corps staff had been out of close contact with FAAA and airborne operations for nearly two full months. Now they had to simultaneously plan and prepare to command two major airborne operations, one for the British (VARSITY, with a D day of April 1) and one for the Americans (CHOKER II, with a D day of April 10). All plans had to be coordinated with widely dispersed British and American ground and air commands and with SHAEF, a tedious responsibility that compelled Ridgway and his key staffers to rush from one meeting to the next over the next five weeks.[1]

All those involved in this planning were determined to prevent a repetition of the Arnhem disaster. Several new airborne tactical policies had been adopted. First, all the airborne forces required to perform the assigned task would be delivered in one, single, massive lift. FAAA would not again rely on continuing good weather to bring in vital reinforcements on D+1 or D+2. Second, the forces required would be dropped as closely as possible to the key objectives. There would be no more "long marches" like those at Arnhem and Nijmegen. Third, all airborne operations would be conducted in daylight, escorted and protected by masses of Allied fighters and fighter-bombers. Fourth, no airborne operations would be conducted without absolute assurance of a firm linkup with advancing ground forces within twenty-four hours and preferably less, or beyond the range of medium Allied artillery.

Airborne planning was further complicated when, as a result of Ridgway's continued pressure from the field, AGF and George Marshall finally approved his ideas for reorganizing the American airborne division, to become effective March 1, 1945. The new airborne division was to consist of three regiments: two parachute regiments and one glider regiment (of three battalions each). Each of the three regiments would have one battalion of artillery permanently attached and would be redesignated a "combat team." In addition, there would be one or two battalions of "divisional" artillery to be brought in by glider and controlled directly by the division commander.[2]*

---

* The reorganization led to painful partings in Gavin's 82nd and Taylor's 101st. Roy Lindquist's 508th Parachute Regiment, "temporarily attached" to the 82nd (with the 507th) for Normandy, was released and sent back to France. Similarly, in the 101st, the "temporarily attached" 501st Parachute Regiment, now commanded by Robert Ballard, was detached and sent back to France. In Bud Miley's 17th Division, Maurice Stubbs's 193rd Glider Regiment and Sachs's 550th Glider Battalion were deactivated and the personnel utilized to fill out the three battalions of Bob Pierce's 194th Glider Regiment. Chapman's 13th Division, which had arrived in France with one parachute regiment, the 515th, commanded by Harvey J. Jablonsky, was assigned Graves's 517th Parachute Regiment. For the time being, the 13th retained its two

One factor complicating the planning was the new D-day "single lift" policy. In fact, it imposed a severe reduction on the size and scope of VARSITY and CHOKER II. FAAA still had only about fourteen hundred transports under its control. About seventy-five of these were new, larger-capacity American Curtiss C-46s, which could carry twice as many paratroopers as a C-47 (thirty-six, compared to eighteen). FAAA had also decided that American C-47s of IX Troop Carrier Command now moving to new bases near Paris would be close enough to the target to safely permit double towing of gliders, and some three hundred C-47s would do so in VARSITY. However, even with these innovations FAAA could provide sufficient lift for simultaneous delivery of only about six combat teams plus divisional artillery, medics, engineers and staffs—no more than a total of about seventeen thousand men.[4]

FAAA had originally earmarked three divisions for VARSITY: Miley's 17th, Chapman's 13th and Bols's 6th British. Owing to the airlift shortage, early in the more detailed—and realistic—planning it became clear that one full division had to be eliminated. Inasmuch as VARSITY was to be in support of Montgomery, the British 6th Airborne Division (then in process of transferring from Holland to England in order to utilize British aircraft) had to be retained in the lineup, and one American division had to be scrubbed. Because it was combat-hardened and most of it had not yet made a combat jump (the 507 had) Ridgway chose to keep Miley's 17th Airborne Division. The British 6th would consist of about seventy-five hundred men, the 17th of about ninety-eight hundred men—a total of about seventeen thousand.

From its inception, XVIII Airborne Corps headquarters had been designed to go into battle by glider, like the British 1 Airborne Corps in MARKET-GARDEN. Early in the planning for VARSITY, Ridgway changed his mind about that. As on Sicily, he (and the corps headquarters) would enter battle on the ground—after crossing the Rhine in landing craft. This decision evoked a sneer from Edson Raff, who said it proved Ridgway was not "a real paratrooper who would jump with his men." In fact, Ridgway's decision made good sense. As on Sicily, it was more important for him to maintain clear and close lines of communication with the British and American army commanders (Dempsey, Simpson) than to fling himself and the corps headquarters onto a confused battlefield where communications were likely to be poor or worse. Moreover, looming up immediately after VARSITY was CHOKER II. If Ridgway lost key corps staffers in VARSITY glider crashes (as seemed inevitable), he would be hard-pressed to recruit new men who could play a meaningful role in CHOKER II.[5]

Ridgway first met with Miles Dempsey to discuss VARSITY on February 14, the day after he departed First Army. It was not an auspicious beginning. Rather than asking for Ridgway's expert advice, Dempsey made the mistake of presenting Ridgway with a preconceived airborne plan. Ridgway, who believed

---

original two-battalion glider regiments, the 88th, commanded by Samuel Roth, and the 326th, commanded by William O. Poindexter.[3]

Dempsey's lack of aggressiveness on the ground was one main cause for the Arnhem disaster, and who had his own preconceived ideas about VARSITY, was not in the mood to be lectured or told precisely how to run an airborne operation, least of all by the man he believed had so badly failed in Holland.[6]

Dempsey began by giving Ridgway a broad outline of the plan for Montgomery's massive Rhine crossing. It was, in terms of ground forces, more massive than NEPTUNE. Montgomery would command three armies, comprising ten corps, totaling over one and a quarter million men. Dempsey's 12 and 30 corps and Simpson's XVI Corps would spearhead the crossing; the British in the north, Simpson in the south. Ridgway's XVIII Airborne Corps would be assigned objectives in the British 12 Corps sector, which would cross the Rhine between Rees and Wesel.

Ridgway had assumed that his airborne mission would be similar to that of the 101st at Utah Beach: a preinvasion jump at dawn on the east side of the Rhine to seize key objectives that would facilitate Dempsey's amphibious landings. But that was not what Dempsey wanted. He told Ridgway that his forces, which had had plenty of amphibious assault experience in Sicily, Italy and Normandy, did not need airborne help in getting across the river. He had such a preponderance of artillery, landing craft and air support, he had "written off" the idea of using the airborne to secure a bridgehead. Dempsey's idea was to drop the three airborne divisions farther inland and considerably later (ten hours after his amphibious landings).

These forces were to: seize a hill mass and the Diersfordter Wald, a dense forest five miles northwest of Wesel where the Germans had concealed artillery which overlooked—and commanded—the Rhine where Dempsey would cross; seize bridges across the Issel River and the town of Hamminkeln, just east of the Diersfordter Wald; seal off and seize Wesel by dropping one division considerably east of Wesel to cut the highway and railroad and the Lippe River, all of which ran east–west toward the town; and block all German counterattacks aimed at repulsing the 12 Corps invasion. All this would be done with a big bang—a single lift which would drop all three divisions nearly on top of their objectives simultaneously.

Ridgway was completely flabbergasted. Theretofore, Allied parachute drops had been structured to take advantage of the element of surprise by landing *before* the ground forces hit a beach (Sicily, Normandy) or jumped off (Holland). Dempsey's plan would reverse that procedure: a daylight parachute operation in an enemy sector already fully alerted to invasion. The Luftwaffe and the notoriously heavy flak installations in the area might well blast an airborne force out of the sky. Dempsey's rejoinder was that the massive artillery fire he could pour into the enemy (including the proposed airborne landing sector) by jumping off first far outweighed the advantage of momentary airborne surprise. Moreover, massive Allied bomber strikes had been programmed for several days prior to D day to destroy the fifteen Luftwaffe bases in the area (some of which had jet fighters), and on D day itself the airborne forces would be protected by some three thousand Allied fighters and fighter-bombers.

Ridgway, perhaps recalling the lack of all-out British drive in the invasions of Sicily, Salerno and Normandy, and in other tactical situations he had witnessed in Tunisia, Sicily, Italy (notably the Volturno River crossing), Normandy and Holland, bluntly asked Dempsey if his airborne forces could confidently count on a speedy linkup of the ground forces. For example, what if Dempsey's massive artillery bombardment, which would surely alert the Germans to an oncoming crossing, drew unexpectedly strong German reserves to the east bank of the river? What if the Germans had a secret plan for flooding the river as they had flooded the Roer? Dempsey, exuding confidence, assured Ridgway that, no matter what the Germans threw at him, he absolutely would have not less than two British infantry divisions in the airborne zone within forty-eight hours.

Ridgway raised two other major objections to the airborne plan. The first concerned operations north of Wesel between the Diersfordter Wald and the Issel River. Earlier FAAA VARSITY studies had concluded that DZs and LZs which could be utilized there were barely sufficient to accommodate one division. Dempsey's plan called for *two* divisions to jump and land in that area. The second objection concerned the operations to the east of Wesel, designed to seal off the city and cut the highway, the railroad and the Lippe River. Ridgway derided this idea as purely "a map problem," which some staff officer had cooked up without any consideration of the strength of enemy defenses or of the availability of suitable DZs and LZs, or the fact that the airborne lacked artillery heavy enough to attack Wesel from the east.[7]

Beyond that, Dempsey appeared to have only a slight grasp of aerial logistics. His plan called for the delivery of three airborne divisions simultaneously, and yet the maximum Allied airlift capability could deliver no more than one and a half divisions. He seemed not to understand that if his plans were accepted as drawn, it would automatically require multiple lifts, stretching over several days. If Dempsey's forces advanced east as promised, by the time all the airborne forces could be delivered, Dempsey's 12 Corps would have long since moved east of the airborne area, and the follow-up airborne drops would be useless.

Dempsey concluded the meeting with another utterly astonishing pronouncement. He frankly thought, he said, that Ridgway's XVIII Airborne Corps would remain with British Second Army "for sustained ground operations of an indefinite duration" and that the two American airborne divisions in VARSITY (by Dempsey's plan, Miley's 17th and Chapman's 13th) "would be retained" by Montgomery's 21st Army Group "for the duration of the war."

Ridgway must have been shocked by the ineptitude of Dempsey's airborne plan for VARSITY and even more so by the revelation that XVIII Airborne Corps (and the 17th and 13th divisions) would remain with the British until the end of the war. Both Eisenhower and Bradley had assured Ridgway that XVIII Airborne Corps would be withdrawn immediately after VARSITY. If Dempsey was correct, and there seemed little doubt in his mind, it meant that the American high command had seriously misled Ridgway.

On the very next day, February 15, Ridgway met with Brereton, Parks and other FAAA planners at FAAA's new headquarters in Maisons-Laffitte, outside Paris. He was highly disapproving of British tactical planning for VARSITY and incensed by Dempsey's suggestion that XVIII Airborne Corps might remain indefinitely under British control. Brereton, who shared Ridgway's concerns and who was apt to act impetuously, declared he would leave at once for Versailles to present Ridgway's objections to Eisenhower, but Ridgway and Parks wisely talked him out of it. They suggested that they should first study Dempsey's plan in more detail.[8]

Over the next several days, FAAA and XVIII Airborne Corps pored over Dempsey's VARSITY plan with hypercritical eyes. The Americans continued to find many features of it unacceptable, and on February 19, Brereton went to SHAEF to present a more well-reasoned case to Eisenhower. In a preliminary meeting with Bedell Smith and Montgomery's chief of staff, Francis de Guingand, and others, Smith prudently proposed that before Brereton barged in on Eisenhower, it might be better to fully discuss Ridgway's objections with Dempsey. Parks's diary recorded that Smith said, "Ridgway is 'not a British man' and usually was unable to come to an agreement with the British in initial conferences but that later, however, they usually found a common ground on which to meet." Furthermore, Smith said, "there is no intention of permitting 21 Army Group to retain the XVIII Corps or the [American] divisions indefinitely." Smith further declared that Eisenhower positively wanted Ridgway's corps "withdrawn promptly" in order to plan and execute CHOKER II.[9]

During the next two weeks, Ridgway and Dempsey and their planners met often, and as Smith had predicted, the two generals found a common meeting ground. After give and take on both sides, they agreed to the following revised plan. First, the operation would go on March 24, weather permitting. If necessary, Montgomery would wait "up to five days" for good weather. Second, the ground forces, in an all-out power drive, would precede the airborne forces by six hours (0400 hours to 1000 hours), and during the period 0930 hours to 1330 hours Dempsey would withhold all artillery and antiaircraft fire to avoid hitting friendly forces. Third, the proposed drop east of Wesel to "seal off" and/or attack the city would be eliminated (along with the 13th Airborne Division). Fourth, airborne operations in the crowded sector between the Diersfordter Wald and the Issel River would be carried out by airborne forces comprising six combat teams from the 6th British and 17th American divisions, delivered simultaneously by parachute and glider. These forces would seize the Diersfordter Wald, the town of Hamminkeln and several bridges over the Issel, and provide a forward "link" between Dempsey's Second British and Simpson's Ninth armies. Fifth, the 6th Airborne Division would remain with Dempsey, the 17th with Simpson, for the continuing drive east, but XVIII Airborne Corps would be relieved by another corps no more than six days following D day.[10]

While the VARSITY plan was being hammered out, the war with Germany was racing toward a dramatic climax. On January 12, the Russians, who had advanced to the Vistula River near Warsaw, had launched a massive offensive (ten armies, comprising seventy divisions). By February 24, these Russian armies had thrown the Germans back three hundred miles to the Oder and Neisse rivers. There, however, they had been stopped by an unseasonal thaw, which melted the ice on the rivers, making it easier for the Germans to defend them. But by March 1, the Russians were a mere forty miles from Berlin and Hitler was desperately stripping his western front of ground forces to defend the eastern front, which, to Hitler, seemed the greater threat.[11]

On the western front, Crerar's First Canadian Army attack toward Düsseldorf—spearheaded by Horrocks' 30 Corps—had also bogged down in the unseasonable thaw. After two weeks of tough, miserable fighting in quagmires of mud, Horrocks had advanced only seventeen miles, barely a third of the way to his initial objective. However, Crerar and Horrocks were helped immeasurably in this drive when, on February 23, Simson's Ninth Army was finally able to jump off, cross the receding Roer River, and race northeast toward Düsseldorf and beyond in what Bradley described as "one of the most perfectly executed" attacks of the war. Simpson's belated offensive unhinged the German defenses in front of Crerar and Horrocks, and the two armies linked on the west bank of the Rhine near Duisburg during the first week of March. They then concentrated their combined forces against a pocket of Germans that had formed on the west bank of the Rhine in front of Wesel, where Montgomery intended to cross.[12]

Simpson's drive had been so successful that he and his staff became convinced that Ninth Army could cross the Rhine on the fly and keep going through the Ruhr. On March 1, when Eisenhower and Bradley visited Ninth Army's CP, Simpson had outlined a plan for an impromptu Rhine crossing. Eisenhower had evinced "intense interest" in the plan, but it had been flatly turned down by Montgomery. The Ninth Army historian would later write: "So the course of history as it might have developed had Ninth Army leaped the Rhine early in March will never be known. Of one point Ninth Army men are certain—it could have been done, and done successfully."[13]

Closely coordinating with Simpson's offensive, Collins' VII Corps and Millikin's III Corps (substituting for XVIII Airborne Corps) jumped off on Simpson's right flank, as planned. In an equally remarkable performance, Collins crossed the Roer and Erft rivers and thundered east to Cologne. By March 3 he had encircled the city and was preparing to seize it. Millikin, advancing less spectacularly on Collins' right, drove toward Bonn and Remagen, with John Leonard's 9th Armored Division in the van. On March 7, advance elements of Leonard's CCB, still commanded by Bill Hoge, stunned themselves and the Allied high command with an impromptu seizure of the big Ludendorff railway bridge across the Rhine at Remagen.[14]

This wholly unanticipated Allied coup would profoundly change the course of the war on the western front. With Eisenhower's enthusiastic approval, Bradley immediately commenced exploiting the Remagen bridgehead. "This was one of the most rewarding moments of my life," Bradley wrote. "I was engulfed in euphoria. Monty had been preparing his massive . . . [Rhine crossing] for weeks. It was not to jump off for another two weeks. Our American troops had completely upstaged him, grabbing a bridge on the fly. Beyond that purely human reaction, and far more important, the opportunities that now lay before us were immense. If the crossing could be properly exploited, I could realize my long-sought strategic goal of a strong right hook into Germany—the old 'two thrust' concept."[15]

The Remagen bridgehead was not easily exploited. Hitler, who was furious at this Allied coup, ordered every available German division to repulse the Allies. Eventually Model threw twelve (understrength) German divisions (four of them panzer) against the Remagen bridgehead, and these forces did their utmost to push the Allies back across the Rhine. In this fierce battle, Hodges lost confidence in Millikin and, with Bradley's concurrence, relieved him of command of III Corps. He was replaced by Jim Van Fleet, who since Normandy had risen to command the 90th Infantry Division and had proved himself to be one of the ablest and most aggressive Allied battlefield generals. Subsequently Hodges added Collins' VII Corps to the battle to assist Van Fleet's III Corps in holding—and widening—the bridgehead.[16]

On the evening of March 7, when Bradley telephoned Eisenhower to first report the capture of the Remagen bridge, Eisenhower was at dinner at his new headquarters in Rheims. His guests for the evening were most of the principal airborne commanders: Ridgway, Doc Eaton, Gavin, Taylor and Gerry Chapman, commander of the newly arrived 13th Airborne Division. Eisenhower had summoned them to discuss future proposed airborne operations: CHOKER II, ECLIPSE, and a brand-new, huge and spectacular operation called ARENA.[17]

In their war memoirs, Gavin and Taylor both vividly recalled Bradley's mid-dinner phone call announcing the capture of the Remagen bridge, and the excitement it created. Ridgway, however, did not mention the incident in his memoir. Perhaps it was a moment he did not care to remember. If XVIII Airborne Corps had not been pulled out for VARSITY, against his wishes, it would have been his forces—not Millikin's—which captured the Remagen bridge, and Ridgway and XVIII Airborne Corps would have had the great privilege of exploiting the bridgehead with Joe Collins and VII Corps. Moreover, having been present when Eisenhower authorized Bradley to exploit the bridgehead, Ridgway knew that the whole course of the war was going to change, that the real push would now come in the center and that Montgomery's Rhine crossing—and VARSITY—would become an overstaged sideshow.[18]

When the excitement had died down, the talk at Eisenhower's dinner returned to a discussion of future airborne operations, with the focus on ARENA. Conceived by FAAA's fecund planning staff, it fulfilled George Marshall and Hap Arnold's long-standing desire for a big and decisive strategic airborne operation deep in enemy territory. During Max Taylor's visit to Washington in December, Marshall had once again urged such an operation. According to Taylor, Marshall had "damned without stint" Montgomery's

MARKET-GARDEN and had been "emphatic in speaking about the 'timidity' of our [airborne] planning." Marshall's idea of "proper airborne operations," Taylor reported, was still "to seize an air head and then pour in large quantities of troops." Now that the Allied armies were drawing up to the Rhine and Germany appeared to be tottering toward collapse, FAAA believed that the opportunity (and good flying weather) had finally arrived when a strategic airborne operation could be mounted.[19]

Breathtaking in size and scope, the plan for ARENA abandoned the conservative, newly adopted "one-lift" doctrine. Initially a force of four to six Allied airborne divisions, brought in by multiple lifts, would seize an airhead about a hundred miles east of the Rhine in an area of high ground lying between Paderborn and Kassel. In that area there were three well-organized and comparatively undamaged German airfields and numerous outlying landing strips. These would be utilized to fly in four or five more regular infantry divisions, making a total FAAA force of about ten divisions.

The airborne army thus assembled deep inside Germany might be given several principal missions depending on the battlefront situation. It could attack westward toward the Ruhr, helping Montgomery and Bradley trap the German armies. Or it could more or less stand pat, denying the German armies retreating from the Ruhr a place to make a last-ditch stand, while providing the armies of Patton and Patch a friendly enclave toward which to advance. Conceivably, so vast an Allied army landing so deep inside Germany could of itself cause the complete collapse of the Third Reich.

Ridgway had first learned about ARENA three days before, on March 3, in a meeting with Floyd Parks and Eisenhower's G-3, Harold R. (Pink) Bull. At that time, Parks had sketched a rough outline of the plan and had told Ridgway and Bull that Brereton intended to lay the whole thing out for Eisenhower within a few days. Ridgway had been astounded—and not a little put out. Brereton had promised to keep him abreast of FAAA planning; he had told Parks that he, Ridgway, should have been thoroughly briefed on ARENA before Brereton took such a plan to Eisenhower.[20]

Digging further into the plan over the next few days, Ridgway learned more details. FAAA intended, if possible, to utilize all six Allied airborne divisions (the American 13th, 17th, 82nd and 101st, and the British 1st and 6th) in the assault phase. These would be followed into the airhead by four regular divisions: Walter Robertson's 2nd, Alex Bolling's 84th, Tony McAuliffe's 103rd and one other (as yet undesignated). There would be three corps: XVIII Airborne, 1 British Airborne and one other for the regular infantry divisions. Maximum FAAA airlift would be utilized with all aircraft making two round trips a day from bases in France and Belgium. In addition, masses of Eighth Air Force heavy bombers would help fly in supplies at the rate of three hundred tons per division per day—that is, building to a total of three thousand tons per day.[21]

Despite his initial pique, Ridgway, like all airborne officers who were briefed on ARENA, was electrified by its scope and daring and fully endorsed it. However, he had several major reservations. Chief among these was the use of

British airborne forces. By then he knew that Dempsey intended to hang on to Bols's 6th Airborne Division for the encirclement of the Ruhr, and he was certain that Montgomery (hard-pressed for troops) would not willingly release it. The British had not pushed hard for the restaffing of the 1st Airborne Division after Arnhem. Ridgway doubted it could be fleshed out and trained in time by May 1, the date originally proposed for ARENA. In view of these factors, he suggested that ARENA be carried out strictly with American troops—with the airborne assault composed of the four American divisions organized into a single corps—his XVIII Airborne. However, Brereton vetoed this proposal, intending to do his utmost to bring the British 1st and 6th divisions (as well as Gale's 1 British Airborne Corps) into the operations.[22]

When Eisenhower was first apprised of ARENA, he, too, was enthusiastic. Perhaps recalling his long-standing promises to Marshall and Arnold, he commented that he "would dearly love to have one big airborne operation before the war ended" and thought ARENA "would really be fun to do." But he insisted that it be international in makeup—that the British airborne forces be used. He cabled the British high command in London requesting transfer of the British 6th Airborne Division to ARENA and a crash program to get the British 1st Airborne Division ready in time. He cabled Marshall in Washington to ask if it was possible to pry a regular infantry division from Mark Clark in Italy to serve as the fourth regular airlanded infantry division.[23]†

Thus it transpired that while Ridgway and XVIII Airborne Corps were fine-tuning the VARSITY plan, they were simultaneously working up detailed plans not only for CHOKER II but for ARENA as well. None of these plans was ever "final," but for several weeks the best solution seemed to be to scale CHOKER II down and assign it to Gerry Chapman's 13th Division and carry out ARENA with the 17th, 82nd and 101st divisions plus whatever British airborne troops London could—or would—make available. In any event, in the face of the challenge and promise of ARENA, VARSITY became increasingly insignificant, and Ridgway, more than ever, must have been disappointed at being saddled with it.

With the capture of the Remagen bridge, Bradley now had the psychological and political edge, and he determined to make the most of it. He would expand the Remagen bridgehead as rapidly as possible until it contained the whole of Hodges' First Army. At the same time, Patton's Third Army, farther south, would advance with all power toward Mainz, on the Rhine, cleaning the west bank of the river of Germans below Coblenz. When that was done, First and Third armies would launch a massive joint offensive into Germany, linking up near Marburg and thereafter swinging north to the Paderborn-Kassel area, encircling the Ruhr from the south, meeting with Montgomery's forces.[24]

† London replied that the British 1st Airborne Division could not be gotten ready until mid-May, and SHAEF delayed ARENA D day accordingly. Marshall refused to strip Clark of yet another division and mildly rebuked Eisenhower for even making the request.

The first steps of this plan were carried out with theretofore unheard-of American Army efficiency. By March 22, Hodges had crammed most of First Army inside the Remagen bridgehead with three corps poised to strike into the heart of Germany. In a classic campaign, Patton's Third Army, coordinating its attacks with Patch's Seventh Army on his right flank, swept through the Saar-Palatinate. On the evening of March 22, Patton's 5th Infantry Division, commanded by S. LeRoy (Red) Irwin, "sneaked" across the Rhine at Oppenheim (near Mainz). Patton's impromptu crossing would open the way for Patch's Seventh Army to cross near Mannheim within a few days.

Bradley's spectacular 12th Army Group maneuvers killed both CHOKER II and ARENA. Owing to Patton's brilliant campaign in the Saar-Palatinate, Patch's Seventh Army was able to leap the Rhine without assistance from the 13th Airborne Division. Bradley personally persuaded Eisenhower to cancel ARENA. He was now certain that once he launched Hodges and Patton toward Paderborn-Kassel, both armies would get there long before ARENA could be mounted. Since he intended to run wide open, he preferred to use FAAA's fourteen hundred-odd transports to bring in gasoline and ammo and evacuate wounded, as he had done in France. He could no longer spare the three or four regular infantry divisions ARENA would require. Since all of First Army would be committed in the drive, he needed the 82nd and 101st divisions to form a strategic reserve behind the Rhine, from Düsseldorf to Cologne, in the event the Germans trapped in the Ruhr attempted to break out (a la Bulge) to the west, and to serve as policemen in these newly occupied, devastated and possibly hostile Rhine cities.[25]

☆48☆

TEN MONTHS of unrelieved physical and mental strain had begun to sap Ridgway's vitality. In early January, during the Bulge, he had been briefly felled by another attack of malaria. On the eve of VARSITY, he had a "real bad back attack" that left him "just about immobile." The XVIII Airborne Corps surgeon, Wolcott Etienne, for the first time, gave Ridgway a shot of Novocain directly into his back muscles. This treatment afforded Ridgway "temporary relief," but he still had "some trepidation" that he might be immobilized for VARSITY.[1]

No one outside Ridgway's close battlefield "family" was aware of these setbacks; outwardly, he showed no change. He threw himself into preparations for VARSITY with his customary intensity and relentlessly aggressive outlook. He and Paul Williams were determined to make VARSITY the first letter-perfect airborne operation of the war, to forge a spearhead that would open a wide avenue on which the British could dash straight into the heart of the Ruhr.

So far in the war, no Allied airborne operation had been preceded by what Ridgway believed to be sufficient training of airborne and Air Force personnel. Now, owing to the delay imposed by relocating the 50th, 53rd and half of the 52nd troop-carrier wings to bases in France and a continuing requirement to hold two or three groups in reserve for possible emergency supply runs, the proposed, very stringent VARSITY training program, like all others before it, was not realized. A plan to practice-jump all six regiments had to be canceled. Of the American units, only Edson Raff's 507th made a full-scale mass jump. Nonetheless, Paul Williams' IX Troop Carrier pilots logged an impressive fifty thousand training hours in the air and every glider pilot made five practice landings per month. In all, the troop-carrier historian reported, the American paratroopers logged 20,000 practice jumps, and some 26,666 gliderists went aloft on training missions. The British 6th Airborne Division logged 4,128 practice parachute jumps and countless practice glider missions.[2]

Of particular interest to Ridgway and all other paratroopers was the new C-46 "Commando" troop-carrier aircraft. In addition to its ability to carry twice as many paratroopers as the C-47, its more powerful engines gave it a higher cruising speed, and it was thought to be more rugged than the C-47. It had exit doors on both sides of the rear fuselage (as opposed to one door on the C-47), which, in theory, enabled the enlarged stick to get out as fast as a stick could exit from a C-47. Thus the C-46 gave the airborne forces the capability of delivering a full platoon of men in one swoop, a feat that was considered to be a significant advance in airborne technology.

The question of which parachute outfit would be assigned to these flashy

Operation VARSITY

new planes caused no little discussion. Both Raff's 507 and Coutts's 513 were eager to be first to utilize them. It was finally decided that Coutts's 513, which had not yet jumped in combat, and which was "senior" in terms of service in the division, would go in them. However, inasmuch as there were only seventy-five-odd C-46s, there was not room enough for Coutts's artillery, the 466th Battalion, commanded by Kenneth L. Booth. The artillery was thus relegated to forty-five older C-47s, which would drop the artillerymen on the same DZ, in a second serial.

The C-46s were assigned to the 313th Group of Hal Clark's 52nd Wing, commanded by William L. Filer. Ridgway had hoped that Coutts's 513th could make a mass practice jump from Filer's new planes, but owing to the relocation of part of the 52nd Wing to France and other factors, this proved to be impossible. However, during a five-day period in mid-March, every paratrooper in the 513 made one or more jumps from C-46s, a total of 3,246 jumps. These "platoon jumps" were considered highly satisfactory. As a by-product, a warm camaraderie developed between Coutts's 513th and Filer's 313th Group. Even among the airborne elite, they were regarded as something special: innovators bringing the first new airborne "weapons system" to the battlefield.[3]*

As the time for Montgomery's pachydermal Rhine crossing drew ever closer, his four assault corps, comprising the equivalent of twenty divisions, with fifteen hundred tanks, backed by fifty-five hundred artillery pieces, made final and appropriately elephantine preparations. Horrocks' 30 Corps (six-plus divisions) would cross at Rees; the British 12 Corps (four divisions, six brigades), commanded by Neil M. Ritchie, would cross immediately south of Horrocks at Xanten and Wesel, opposite the Diersfordter Wald. Ridgway's XVIII Airborne Corps would jump and land east of the Diersfordter Wald, in front of Ritchie's 12 Corps sector. The American XVI Corps (five divisions) of Simpson's Ninth Army, commanded by John Anderson, would cross immediately south of Ritchie and Ridgway at Rheinberg.[5]

A host of Allied VIPs flocked to the front to watch this astounding spectacle. Churchill, Montgomery and their retinues converged on Montgomery's 21st Army Group and Dempsey's Second Army headquarters. Eisenhower and his retinue encamped at Rheinberg, where John Anderson had located his XVI Corps CP. Of the senior Allied commanders, only Omar Bradley was absent. He remained at his headquarters in Namur, making final preparations to launch Hodges and Patton—already well across the Rhine—on an all-out drive toward Paderborn on the next day, March 25.[6]

---

* The 513 (and other units) were also equipped with two brand-new field weapons: the forty-five-pound, shoulder-held 57 mm "recoilless rifle" and a larger, heavier version, the 114-pound tripod-mounted 75 mm "recoilless rifle." These weapons, available in limited quantity, were introduced late in the war to replace the puny and ineffective bazooka antitank weapon. Since Normandy, paratroopers and others had been using the superior (and larger) German bazooka, called a *Panzerfaust,* which they found or captured on the battlefield.[4]

For several days, Allied air power, almost unopposed in the skies, had been pounding Germany in mind-boggling numbers. On March 21 and March 22, 1,744 Eighth Air Force heavy bombers, escorted by 752 fighters, had dumped five thousand tons of bombs on the fifteen airfields in the sector immediately opposite Montgomery. Some 1,500 of these same bombers prepared to strike the same airfields with four thousand tons of bombs on D day. Another 1,500 heavy bombers (some based in Italy) would attack targets all over Germany. More than 2,000 fighters and fighter-bombers would strike bridges, railroads, troop formations and bases opposite Montgomery. Another 1,000 fighters would escort and cover the airborne forces.[7]

Ridgway, his battlefield "family" (Don Faith, Frank Farmer, Jim Casey) and advance elements of XVIII Airborne Corps camped at Xanten, adjacent to Ritchie's 12 Corps headquarters. Ridgway's party had three jeeps, one with a powerful radio. His D-day plan was to cross the Rhine in an amphibious craft with the leading elements of Ritchie's 15th (Scottish) Infantry Division, then drive on several miles through "no man's land" to Bud Miley's CP, at Flüren, where Ridgway intended to establish the XVIII Airborne Corps advanced CP.[8]

In the early afternoon of D−1, March 23, Montgomery's meteorologists reported that the weather would be nearly perfect for airborne operations on the following day. After hearing this good news, at 3:30 P.M. Montgomery gave the coded message to launch the attack as planned. The message was perhaps intended to be humorous or ironical: "TWO IF BY SEA." This was part of a famous American Revolution code alert to indicate the British were advancing on Boston by ship.[9]

Soon thereafter, the massive artillery barrage commenced. It was the greatest artillery show by the Allies in World War II. The American Army historian reported that the two thousand big guns supporting Anderson's XVI Corps fired 65,261 rounds in a period of merely one hour. The barrage went on in all assault sectors hour after hour. As if this were not enough, British Bomber Command, in a nice display of precision bombing, dumped eleven hundred tons of bombs on Wesel, reducing this small, lightly defended city of twenty-five thousand to a pile of rubble.[10]

The Rhine crossings commenced during the night of March 23/24. First to go was the 51st (Highland) Division of Horrocks' 30 Corps, which crossed and struck at Rees and Speldrop at 9 P.M. The troops achieved a good, firm landing, but, by dawn, the German 8th Parachute Division had struck back, fighting hard and isolating some British units at Speldrop. Next to go was the 1st British Commando Brigade, of Ritchie's 12 Corps, which at 10 P.M. crossed two miles downstream of Wesel. It fared better. By dawn the entire brigade was inside the rubble heap; the German commander had been killed and most of his headquarters staff captured. Last to jump off was Ritchie's 15th (Scottish) Division and two American assault divisions of Anderson's XVI Corps: Leland Hobbs's 30th and Ira Wyche's 79th. These three heavily reinforced divisions commenced crossing at 2 A.M. On the far shore, the Scots collided with the German 7th Paratroop Division and soon reported they were in a stiff fight between the Rhine and the Diersfordter Wald. Hobbs and Wyche, landing against slight or no opposition, suffered a mere forty-one casualties in the two divisions combined and began driving fast to the northeast (toward the south bank of the Lippe River), spreading out with immense power and speed.[11]

In Britain and France, the paratroopers and gliderists of VARSITY, who had been cloistered for several days at airfields, emplaned and departed on a meticulously drawn schedule. First into the air, at 0600 hours, was the slowest and most distant element of the air armada: the 440 aircraft of the British 38th and 46th groups, towing an equal number of Horsa and Hamilcar gliders from English bases. Aboard these gliders were Eric Bols and his division staff, the 6th Airlanding Brigade, commanded by R. Hugh Bellamy, and the British airborne artillery units. In all, 3,383 British troops plus 66 artillery pieces, 285 trucks and jeeps, 553 other vehicles and 3 Locust T-9 light tanks. En route to a rendezvous with other airborne units of VARSITY, some 35 of these heavily laden gliders aborted or broke loose from their tows, but the remaining 405 continued on in fine, clear weather over the English Channel.[12]

Next to take off were the two British parachute brigades (regiments) of the 6th Division, likewise based in Britain. These were the 3rd, commanded by S. James L. Hill, and the 5th, commanded by J. H. Nigel Poett. The 3rd comprised 1,920 paratroopers, the 5th 1,917, a total of 3,837 parachutists. They were lifted by three groups (61, 315, 316) of Hal Clark's 52nd Wing, comprising a total of 242 C-47s. There were no aborts.†

In sum, the British airborne armada for VARSITY comprised about 7,220 men (3,837 paratroopers and 3,383 gliderists) lifted in about 645 aircraft, 405 of the aircraft towing gliders. Of the total 645 aircraft, about 265 were American C-47s, the rest British, mostly Stirlings and Halifaxes. This contingent, which soon formed into a vast continuous aerial stream, was escorted by 213 RAF fighters. No enemy fighters attempted to attack the formation.

The lead American contingent in VARSITY was Edson Raff's 507th Combat Team, which included the 464th Parachute Field Artillery Battalion, commanded by Edward S. Branigan.

Branigan's 464 was new to the ETO. Until February 1945, it had been stationed in the States, giving tough readiness tests to the parachute and glider artillery battalions going overseas. Branigan, who had an engineering background (Brooklyn Tech), had helped devise a system of linking the air-dropped 75 mm pack-howitzer bundles with strong tape, making it easier to find the nine separate pieces on the ground. The recent "mating" of Branigan's 464 with the 17th Division had not gone smoothly. "Bud Miley and I did not have a good relationship," Branigan remembered. "Our outfit felt like bastard sons at a family reunion."[14]

In all, the 507 Combat Team comprised 2,479 men (about 2,100 infantry and 379 artillerymen). It was lifted by two groups (434 and 438) of 53rd Wing,

† The 3rd Parachute Brigade was composed of the 1st Canadian and the British 8th and 9th battalions. The 5th Parachute Brigade was composed of the British 7th, 12th and 13th battalions.[13]

using a total of 181 C-47s. The expert Air Force pathfinder pilot Joel Crouch flew in the lead plane, which also carried the combat-team commander, Edson Raff, and some of his staff. Bud Miley, who was also in this formation, would jump with the artillerymen in the rear serials. His ADC, John Whitelaw, was in charge of the large divisional land "tail" and would cross the Rhine like Ridgway, by landing craft.

By about 0730, Crouch's lead serial, of forty-six aircraft, was airborne. It carried the 507's 1st Battalion, now commanded by Paul F. Smith. Behind it came two other serials, carrying Charles Timmes's 2nd Battalion and Allen W. Taylor's 3rd Battalion, then a fourth serial with Branigan's artillery. The destination of this parachute armada was DZ "W," on the south edge of the Diersfordter Wald, adjacent to the town of Flüren, which was about three miles northwest of Wesel.

Next into the air was James Coutts's 513 Combat Team, which included Ken Booth's 466 Parachute Field Artillery Battalion. Coutts's combat team was almost exactly the same size as Raff's: 2,447 men (about 2,071 infantry and 376 artillerymen). However, owing to the larger capacity of the C-46s, only 117 planes were required to carry Coutts's team, seventy-two C-46s (of 313 Group) and forty-five C-47s (of 434 Group). Coutts and his infantrymen flew in the C-46s; the artillerymen flew in the trailing, slower C-47s. The destination of this parachute armada was DZ "X," on the east side of Diersfordter Wald, between the forest and the Issel River.

The last American contingents to get airborne were the massive glider formations. In all, 906 Wacos were assigned to the mission, two thirds of them (about 600) to be double-towed, a mix that required a total of about 606 C-47s.‡ To minimize the chances of the gliders colliding, one tow rope was about fifty feet shorter than the other. This new technique presented an added hazard in flight: the possibility of the short-rope glider yawing into the longer tow rope of the trailing glider. However, the risk was deemed to be within acceptable limits for an airborne combat operation.

The six hundred double-towed gliders were assigned to four groups (435, 436, 437, 439) of the 53rd Wing, utilizing a total of about three hundred C-47s. Despite all precautions—and extension of most runways to nearly six thousand feet—the takeoffs were, in Air Force jargon, "hairy." The troop-carrier historian wrote that observers on the ground held their collective breaths until the formations were airborne.

Circling nearby were the serials with Raff's 507 Combat Team. As one of the last of this group to get airborne, Ed Branigan's plane was still near the field. Branigan would never forget what he saw from his window: "One of the glid-

---

‡ Because CHOKER II had not yet been officially canceled, some 926 more Wacos were being held on alert to lift the glider combat team of the 13th Airborne Division to Worms. This requirement greatly intensified the already acute glider-pilot shortage. To temporarily solve the problem, Brereton had drafted about three hundred regular pilots from various outfits to serve as glider copilots in VARSITY. Ironically, CHOKER II was officially canceled that same morning.[15]

ers, loaded with an artillery piece and some men, had reached about three hundred feet. Suddenly its wings broke off. The fuselage plunged straight down into the ground. It was a horrible sight!"[16]

En route to the rendezvous, the tows and gliders encountered "extreme turbulence." Adriel N. Williams, commander of 436 Group, wrote that it was "the worst he had ever experienced." The gliders bounced crazily and were so hard to hold in proper position that the pilots and copilots had to rotate every fifteen minutes. The troops aboard were fearful—and airsick. Three short-rope gliders tangled with the long tow ropes. In these mishaps, two gliders crashed, killing all aboard; three cut loose and survived to land; one (long-rope) continued on minus its mate. Sixteen other gliders aborted en route for various reasons (loose or imbalanced loads, etc.), for a total loss of twenty-one gliders.

The remaining 578 double-towed gliders carried a massive load: Bob Pierce's 194th Glider Infantry Regiment, its attached 681st Glider Artillery Battalion, commanded by Joseph W. Keating; the 680th Glider Artillery Battalion (recently equipped with 105 snub-nose howitzers), commanded by Paul F. Oswald; the 155th Antiaircraft Battalion, commanded by John W. Paddock; miscellaneous engineers, medics, ammo and vehicles. In total, 3,492 men and 637 tons of cargo, which included 202 jeeps, 94 trailers and 78 mortars and artillery pieces. The glider armada was bound for LZ "S," situated on the southeast side of the Diersfordter Wald, at a point where the Issel River and the Issel Canal intersect, a mere two miles north of Wesel.[17]

Last came the conventional, single-tow glider formations: about three hundred Wacos, requiring an equal number of C-47 tows. These gliders were lifted by three groups (440, 441, 442) of the 50th Wing and one (314) of Hal Clark's 52nd Wing. They carried a total of 1,321 troops (the 139th Engineer Battalion, medics, signal men and most of the division staff) and 382 tons of cargo, including 143 jeeps, 97 trailers or ammo carts and 20 guns and mortars. These gliders also encountered extreme turbulence, making the troops airsick, but only one glider had to be cut loose. The destination of this formation was LZ "N," just north of the 513th's DZ "X"—and closest to the four British LZs around Hamminkeln.

In sum, the American airborne armada for VARSITY comprised about 9,777 men, of whom 4,964 were parachutists, 4,613 were gliderists. In total, about 900 airplanes and 900 gliders were required to lift the men and gear, which included thirty-six 75 mm pack howitzers and twelve 105 mm snub-nose howitzers. These American formations were escorted by about 330 fighters. But no enemy fighters attempted to attack the formation.

Over Wavre, Belgium (near Brussels), the British and American aerial armadas, operating on a precise timetable, more or less converged in beautiful weather to form a single massive stream of about 1,545 planes and 1,305 gliders flying on parallel tracks. In the lead were the two British and two American parachute regiments, comprising in total 8,801 paratroopers, who would jump first and help secure the LZs for the 8,196 gliderists, who were about fifteen minutes behind. The vast aerial convergence was marred by only one important mishap: the faster C-46s of 313 Group, carrying Coutts's 513th Regiment, had to perform a tricky maneuver to get into proper position in the stream, and during the maneuver the lead serial became temporarily disoriented. It was Coutts's belief that the Air Force 313 Group commander, William Filer, who flew the lead plane, never did regain an accurate orientation and thus the entire formation of seventy-two C-46s headed for DZ "X" was slightly off course. If so, it would help explain why the 513's drop would be the worst in VARSITY.[18]

On the west bank of the Rhine River, Eisenhower, Simpson, Brereton, Anderson, Ridgway, Richard Gale and more than one million other soldiers began scanning the western skies at 0930 hours. It was now an eerily quiet battlefield. On Montgomery's orders, all Allied artillery, mortar and antiaircraft fire (every weapon with a range of five hundred yards or more) had been shut down to avoid hitting the paratroopers. Perhaps in puzzled response, the German counterfire had tapered off.[19]

Jim Gavin, on hand as a sightseer, was first to spot the massive armada. He later wrote, "Never having viewed an airborne operation, I flew up from Sissonne in a . . . Troop Carrier transport." His plane was flying between two thousand and three thousand feet, slightly above the oncoming armada. "It was," he wrote, an "awesome spectacle."[20]

Another sightseer aloft was Omar Bradley. He later wrote, "I had flown up to Hodges' CP that morning and we loitered in the air as the long trains of C-47s and a few fat-bellied C-46s swarmed by." Bradley was by no means awestruck. He was quietly contemptuous of Montgomery's massive Rhine crossing and still angry that Montgomery had not earlier allowed Simpson to cross the Rhine on the run, as Hodges and Patton had done. He knew from code breaking and other intelligence sources that Hitler had greatly stripped the sector opposite Montgomery and sent the forces to attack Bradley's Remagen bridgehead. "Enemy resistance on the east bank of . . . [the Rhine, in Montgomery's sector] was disorganized and uninspired," Bradley wrote in his war memoir *A Soldier's Story*. Therefore, Bradley did not think VARSITY was necessary, that it was typical Montgomery overkill.[21]

As the lead serials approached the Rhine from the southwest, guided by electronics, the landmarks were clear and the course true, or almost true. But at the Rhine River, an unforeseen problem arose: the battlefield and many of the DZs and LZs were shrouded in a thick haze. The haze had been caused by the massive Allied artillery barrages and by smoke generators employed to conceal the Allied troops crossing the Rhine. The smoke makers had been shut down, but not soon enough. The haze disoriented or blinded a very large number of aircraft and glider pilots, with the result that once again Joel Crouch and other lead pilots had a tough time precisely locating the DZs and LZs, and not a few planes had to make two or more passes over the area.

Nor was that the only problem. Despite the thousands of Allied fighters up that day on flak-suppression and other missions, apparently only a few German antiaircraft emplacements had been put out of action. Perhaps many Germans had been deliberately withholding fire, expecting an airborne assault. Whatever the case, as the lead planes crossed the Rhine, at fifteen hundred feet, German flak suddenly erupted from scores of well-concealed guns in the Diersfordter Wald and in the towns of Hamminkeln and Brünen, Dingden and others east of the DZs and LZs. It would prove to be one of the heaviest flak barrages the airborne forces had ever encountered.

The four paratroop regiments jumped nearly simultaneously, between 0950 and 1000 hours. The troop-carrier historian wrote that the British 3rd and 5th brigades, aiming for DZ "A" and DZ "B," on the northeast and northwest corners of the Diersfordter Wald, respectively, received "an accurate and generally excellent" drop. But the German flak took a heavy toll. Of the 121 British troop-carrier planes, ten were shot down (after the paratroopers jumped) and seven others forced to crash-land, most damaged beyond repair. About seventy others were severely damaged, rendering them temporarily non-operational. There were no losses to friendly fire.[22]

The American parachute drops were far less successful. For once, Joel Crouch, leading the first serial, failed and failed badly. He dropped the 507 commander, Edson Raff, and about 493 other men, most of them from Paul Smith's 1st Battalion, more than two miles northwest of DZ "W," near Diersfordter Castle. The serial following Crouch dropped Smith and his remaining 200 men about a mile northwest of the DZ, southeast of the castle. The serial bringing Branigan's 464th Artillery Battalion and General Miley also erred, dropping some of its load about three fourths of a mile northwest of the DZ, not far from Paul Smith and his band of 200 men. But Miley and the majority of the 464 landed on DZ "W" as planned. The other two serials did far better. They dropped Charles Timmes's 2nd Battalion and Allen Taylor's 3rd Battalion squarely on DZ "W." The drop of Raff's 507 Combat Team was thus only 67 percent successful.

The 181 C-47s which dropped Raff and his men were lucky—perhaps because they were among the earliest arrivals. Only one aircraft was lost to flak—after it had dropped its men. Another thirty-five planes were hit but none seriously and no air crewmen were wounded. Another reason for the modest loss rate may have been that these C-47s (and most others in IX Troop Carrier Command) had (at long last) been fitted with plasticized "self-sealing" fuel tanks, which, when hit, did not leak gushers of highly inflammable aircraft gasoline.

Next in the American stream came the vaunted new weapons system: the seventy-two C-46 Commandos, carrying Coutts's 513th Regiment. By the time this formation arrived, perhaps slightly off course, the German flak was intense. The C-46s did not yet have self-sealing fuel tanks. Moreover, it was later discovered that when a wing fuel tank was hit, the leaking gasoline tended to trickle inside the wing toward the fuselage. As a result, a disaster ensued.[23]

As Gavin looked on from the sky and Miley from the ground, C-46s were seemingly exploding in flames all across the sky. In fact, nineteen of the seventy-two were lost and another (lucky) thirty-eight limped home severely damaged. Of the nineteen, fourteen had gone down in flames, some with paratroopers on board. When it slowed to drop, one C-46 stalled out and crashed nose first with its full load of paratroopers. One gave up and dropped its load near Ridgway on the west bank of the Rhine. A bundle stuck in a door prevented twelve paratroopers from jumping; eight others were brought home, most of them wounded. Some troopers who were already wounded jumped, rather than risk their lives another minute in a C-46.

One of the planes that caught fire was Group Commander Filer's, the lead plane in which Coutts and some of his staffers were riding. Coutts later wrote, "I suddenly realized we were catching a sizable share of German flak. The port engine broke out in flames. I glanced at my watch, wondering if the ship would get us there. It did. Our pilot kept us steadily in formation in spite of flak and flames for a little more than three minutes . . . We had flown in at about five hundred feet." Coutts and his men jumped before the plane exploded.[24]

Coutts's 2nd Battalion commander, Allen (Ace) Miller, who had been cited in the Bulge action for outstanding leadership, was one of the smallest men in the airborne: five feet, four inches. One observer wrote that "his helmet came down over his eyebrows and his jump boots almost reached to his knees." But he was also one of the coolest. After his C-46 crossed the Rhine, it ran into intense flak. The pilot was hit and badly wounded; the plane dropped to 350 feet. Miller yelled, "Jump!" and out went his stick. After his chute opened, Miller looked back and saw the left wing of his C-46 burst into flame. He did not have time to see it crash.

Miller landed on soft ground inside the fenced pigpen of a farm. There was German small-arms fire coming from everywhere, so much that it reminded him of a rifle range. He shed his parachute, drew his pistol and approached a shed. Peering around a corner, he saw a German machine-gun emplacement, manned by four Germans, not two feet away. Miller shot all four Germans, then ran into the main farmhouse. There he found Germans manning several machine guns at the sandbagged windows facing the field into which the 513 paratroopers were dropping. Miller bowled a thermite grenade down the hall toward the kitchen and a fragmentation grenade into the dining room. Before they exploded, he ran out of the house into the field, where he found many dead and wounded 513 paratroopers.[25]

The drop of the 513 was a shambles. Coutts, Miller and hundreds of others had been scattered two to three miles northeast of their DZ in the British zone, just south of Hamminkeln. Despite other courageous actions like Miller's, the Germans continued to rake the open fields with heavy fire, forcing Coutts and his men to lie flat or race for the woods. Scores were killed or wounded. For a long time, they had no clear idea where they were. It would take several hours to assemble the survivors and achieve a semblance of military organization.[26]

The rest of Coutts's combat team, Ken Booth's 466th Artillery Battalion, coming behind in forty-five "old-fashioned" C-47s, got a very good drop. Most of the men and weapons landed squarely on DZ "X" as planned, but here, too, the German fire was intense. Among these men were two VIPs from the States: Brigadier Generals Ridgeley M. Gaither (head of the Fort Benning Parachute School) and Josiah T. Dalbey (head of the Airborne Training Center). The generals and Booth's artillerymen felt decidedly naked without Coutts's infantry. While half the men set up the guns, the other half became instant infantrymen, returning the German fire. General Dalbey rounded up a group of strays in the field and personally led an attack on a German 20 mm gun battery. His small impromptu task force overran and silenced the battery, giving Booth a little more breathing room. But where was Coutts?[27]

Ten or fifteen minutes after the paratroopers were down, the awesome fleet of 1,305 American and British gliders appeared over the Rhine. First came the 405 British Horsas and Hamilcars, which were to land on four British LZs and on both British DZs. Since the British released their gliders from high altitude (twenty-five hundred to thirty-five hundred feet) and the Germans were concentrating fire on the lower, more vulnerable gliders, only 7 British towing planes were shot down; 32 were damaged. As the gliders descended, the Germans shot down 10 and riddled 284, killing and wounding many pilots and troops. However, 90 percent of the British gliders touched down on or very near the designated LZs and DZs, about half in terrifying crash landings. Almost all came under heavy German fire. Only 80 (20 percent) came through completely untouched.

The glider-pilot casualty rate was heavy: thirty-eight killed and thirty-eight wounded. A British gliderist in a Horsa carrying a platoon of engineers and a jeep with a trailer full of explosives recalled his descent:

While we were still quite high, about one thousand, a shell splinter penetrated the petrol tank in the jeep and set the whole center section of the Horsa ablaze. We did not have parachutes, of course, so there was nothing for it but to hope we might land before the machine broke up or went out of control. Seconds seemed like minutes, and minutes, hours . . . The pilot made his final turn . . . and approached to land. That is the last thing I remember . . . I regained consciousness to find myself lying on a haystack . . . All around where I lay . . . were the fragments of my Horsa, the wreckage of the jeep and the bodies of the passengers and crew. Of the trailer there was no trace. The fire must have reached it and at the crucial moment it had exploded.[28]

Next came the 578 American Wacos in double tow, bound for LZ "S." The 295 C-47 tows were hard hit: 12 were shot down and 14 so badly damaged they were forced to make emergency landings. Another, returning home, was lost in an accident; some 126 more were damaged by flak. Most cut loose their gliders at very low altitude: four hundred to eight hundred feet. Over half the gliders were savagely hit by flak and small-arms fire, but fortunately only about 6 were actually shot down. Owing to a poor release by 439 Group, about 83 gliders found themselves far north of LZ "S," in the British zone. But the other five hundred were released close to the proper LZ. The majority of the American gliders made the usual harrowing crash landings and immediately came under heavy German fire. Eighteen glider pilots were killed; eighty were injured or wounded.

Last came the three hundred American Wacos in single tow, bound for LZ "N," just north of the 513th's intended DZ "X." These serials arrived at noon, about two hours after the first parachute drops. Since the Germans were now grappling with the nearly sixteen thousand paratroopers and gliderists already on the ground, the flak and ground fire had subsided considerably. Only three tows were lost (forty-four were damaged) and the releases were fair to good. During the descent, one glider was shot down and about seventy-five were hit by small-arms fire, wounding a few troopers but killing none. Astonishingly, two thirds of the gliders landed in wildly scattered patterns on the LZ; another third scattered to the south of it, some as far away as LZ "S." About half were destroyed in crash landings, but the men and cargos survived. Many were immobilized by heavy German fire until Coutts's southbound 513 came through the LZ on the way to DZ "X." Fourteen glider pilots were killed, twenty-six wounded.

Hard on the heels of the airborne forces came the Eighth Air Force heavy-bomber resupply missions: 240 England-based B-24s, each with two and a half tons of bundles in their bomb bays. The lead planes arrived over the sector at 12:57 P.M., flying fast and very low—many at a hundred to three hundred feet. The drops to the Americans were poor: the 17th Division recovered only 50 percent of the bundles immediately. The drops to the British were considerably better: the 6th Division immediately recovered about 85 percent. (All bundles fell into friendly territory, so it is probable that Allied troops ultimately recovered 100 percent of the bundles in both sectors.) During these drops the B-24s, despite their speed and armor plating, suffered the astonishing—and shocking—loss of 15 planes shot down and 104 severely damaged. Since this was an unacceptable loss rate, all further air-resupply missions by heavy bombers were canceled.[29]

Brereton would later describe VARSITY as a "tremendous success" and rate it the most effective Allied airborne operation ever executed. In a broad sense this was true. FAAA's 1,545 airplanes and 1,305 gliders had delivered 17,000 paratroopers and gliderists and all their artillery and gear into a four-by-six-mile sector in daylight in a mere two hours of operations beyond the Rhine. The British airborne forces achieved remarkably good drops and glider landings, the Americans considerably less so. But the American errors, while serious, did not prove to be disastrous, as they had in Sicily and Normandy. Within two hours, both the 513 and 507 had formed themselves into fully organized regiments and were en route to their proper destinations or objectives with full command and communications.[30]

However, the cost of the delivery had been high. In all, about 77 Allied aircraft (including the 15 heavy bombers) directly involved in VARSITY had been lost to German flak and small-arms fire; 475 were damaged, many severely. Most of the 1,305 gliders were so badly shot up or otherwise damaged that they were left where they crashed for salvagers. (Only 148 Wacos and 24 British gliders were recovered for future use.) Brereton deemed these losses to be well within acceptable statistical limits for combat operations, and Eisenhower wrote that the loss of planes "was far lighter than we had calculated."

But others, including Ridgway, were deeply concerned, especially by the C-46 failure and the glider carnage. VARSITY had been conducted a mere three miles ahead of Allied lines manned by over a million men against what Bradley has described as slight, disorganized and dispirited German forces that had been pummeled for days by Allied air and for hours by the greatest artillery barrage in the war. By all odds, VARSITY should have been a cakewalk, but it was far from that. Ridgway summed up the more realistic airborne reaction: "We learned a lot from it, but it cost us dearly."[31]

☆49☆

IN A BROAD SENSE, Omar Bradley was right: the German forces defending the Rees-Wesel area were neither numerous nor aggressive. The German line was a thin crust of about eighty-five thousand hastily trained, ill-equipped, dispirited and exhausted German soldiers organized into about five divisions. It was, the German generals later conceded, a mere "shadow of an army" that "could only pretend to resist."[1]

The Germans had been told that an Allied parachute operation was probable, but it was expected at Emmerich, twenty miles to the northwest. Confronted with the sudden shock of the massive VARSITY vertical envelopment and aware that masses of Allied ground forces were already across the Rhine on their flanks, the Germans in the VARSITY sector gave up (or retreated eastward) within about five hours. Nor did they ever recover from the overwhelming shock of the envelopment in sufficient time to mount a meaningful counterattack.[2]

Such was the overview. However, for the paratroopers and gliderists who jumped or landed in VARSITY and survived to carry the fight on the ground, those five hours (or at least the first three) were another hellish nightmare. Although stunned and beset, the Germans initially had sufficient presence of mind to turn their small arms, machine guns, mortars, artillery and 88 mm flak guns directly against the aerial invaders on the open DZs and LZs and against the many British paratroopers who had the misfortune to land in trees in the northwestern edge of the Diersfordter Wald. The airborne forces sustained very heavy casualties in those first three hours.

In the British sector, James Hill's 3rd Brigade had jumped first into the DZ abutting the northwestern edge of the forest. Despite a "most accurate" drop, perhaps as many as a hundred of the two thousand men fell into the trees near the edge of the DZ. Many of these were shot dead where they hung. From well-concealed positions inside the woods, the Germans raked the British DZ with artillery, killing the commander of the 1st Canadian Battalion, Jeoffrey S. Nicklin. An incoming Horsa glider hit and killed three officers in the 8th Battalion and concussed its commander, G. Hewetson. However, by 1100 hours, the DZ was secured and all opposition near it silenced. While the 8th held the DZ, the Canadian 1st and 9th battalions invaded the forest and captured or killed the Germans. The action cost Hill's brigade 270 casualties.[3]

Nigel Poett's 5th Brigade dropped second, onto a DZ on the northeastern side of the woods, two miles west of the town of Ringenberg. Here the German counterfire was even more deadly. The paratroopers jumped high (one thousand to eight hundred feet), suffered casualties in the air, and came down on a DZ raked by the murderous fire of 88 mm flak guns. Even so, the men of the

13th Battalion romantically doffed their steel helmets, pulled on their maroon berets and assembled to cries of "Tallyho" and the blast of fox-hunting horns. Getting down to business, Poett's men (the 7th, 12th and 13th battalions) fanned out with "speed and dash" to silence the 88s and secure the DZ and the four British LZs surrounding Hamminkeln. By about noon the situation, although still hot, was well in hand. Poett, too, had suffered heavy casualties: about three hundred.

Hugh Bellamy's 6th Airlanding Brigade came in next in burning and crashing Horsas. The enemy fire on all four LZs was still vicious, and many men fell dead or wounded even before they got out of the gliders. But the survivors rushed the objectives: the town of Hamminkeln and a half-dozen bridges over the Issel River from Ringenberg southward. By midafternoon the gliderists had accomplished all their missions and more, but the 6th Brigade also suffered about three hundred casualties.

In the American sector, farther south, Edson Raff and the five hundred men of his 507 (mostly from Paul Smith's 1st Battalion), who had been badly misdropped to the northwest of the DZ, assembled quickly and immediately attacked east into the Diersfordter Wald, more or less without a plan other than to root out Germans and silence the concealed artillery. They killed fifty-five Germans and captured three hundred (including a full colonel) and a battery of big (155 mm) howitzers.

A little farther to the south, Smith and the rest of his 1st Battalion (about two hundred men), also misdropped northwest of the DZ, found themselves in good position to attack a fortress or castle (the Schloss Diersfordt), which was the assigned objective of Allen Taylor's 3rd Battalion. Smith, like Raff, chose to attack without a plan and launched his men at the fortress. About one hour later he was joined by Raff, leading his large force southward, and by Allen's 3rd Battalion, marching quickly and smartly northward from the DZ. Raff turned the mission over to the preassigned force—Allen and his 3rd Battalion—and led Smith and his 1st Battalion (and a swelling group of POWs) to the DZ. There, Charles Timmes's 2nd Battalion was clearing out Germans, and Ed Branigan's 464th Parachute Field Artillery Battalion had set up its 75 mm pack howitzers.[4]

These actions on the southwest and south sides of the Diersfordter Wald by Raff's 507 Combat Team were largely improvised and a touch ragged, but nonetheless highly effective. The sector was soon reduced and cleared of Germans. In all, the 507 took one thousand prisoners, destroyed five tanks and destroyed or captured several batteries of artillery. Raff established his regimental CP on the DZ. Shortly thereafter, Bud Miley established his CP in the nearby village of Flüren, to await the outcome of the battles of his scattered forces and to prepare for the imminent arrival of Ridgway. Raff's casualties that day totaled about a hundred fifty men.

In the meantime, the British 1st Commando Brigade had cleaned the rubble of Wesel of Germans without much difficulty. Shortly after noon, according to plan, the brigade commander sent patrols northwest out of Wesel toward Raff's

DZ "W." At 2:58 P.M., these patrols linked up with Raff's forces near DZ "W." This was the first juncture of the British 12 and American XVIII Airborne Corps and the fastest "linkup" of ground and airborne forces in the war: about five hours. The British commandos thenceforth came under Miley's command.

In the eastern sector of the American zone—the five-mile-long north-south corridor between Hamminkeln and Wesel—the situation was far more hectic and deadly. One reason was the disastrously poor drop of Coutts's 513, which had left Ken Booth's well-dropped 466th Field Artillery Battalion on DZ "X" under heavy fire with no infantry to protect it. As quickly as he was able, Coutts rounded up most of the survivors of his misdropped three battalions and maneuvered south toward DZ "X" more or less in proper military field formation and established radio contact with the besieged Booth. But along the way Coutts ran into "heavy resistance" and on several occasions the resistance "required considerable maneuvering to overcome it." Artilleryman Booth hastened Coutts's progress south with an unorthodox improvisation: he aimed his 75 mm howitzers to fire directly toward (but in front of) Coutts's advancing columns. This procedure, Coutts reported later, "worked very well and must have seemed very confusing to the Krauts." By about three-thirty, Coutts reached DZ "X," joined Booth's 466th, and shortly thereafter accomplished all his objectives. The combat team also suffered very heavy casualties but captured about fifteen hundred Germans and numerous artillery pieces (including two 88 mm batteries).[5]

To the south of DZ "X," Bob Pierce's 194th Combat Team, which included Keating's 681st Glider Artillery, had landed by glider on LZ "S" in fair shape. His operation represented another tactical innovation: no parachute troopers had landed before him to clear and protect the LZ. For the first time in the ETO, an American glider regiment (or combat team) entered battle entirely on its own. The German fire on the LZ was very, very heavy, but Pierce's men, dodging bullets, assembled amid the graveyard of smashed and burned gliders in timely fashion. By noon, Pierce reported that 75 percent of the combat team was under regimental control—notwithstanding a scattering of Robert Ashworth's 3rd Battalion and the loss of some artillery and ammo.

The "divisional" artillery, Paul Oswald's 680th Field Artillery Battalion, equipped with 105 mm snub-nose howitzers, had also landed on DZ "S." Three of its twelve guns went astray in the flight or landing, but Oswald's men wrestled the others, the jeeps and nine hundred rounds of 105 ammo from the unit's ninety-seven crumpled gliders in the face of a "withering cross-fire." In order to set up shop, Oswald's officers and men had to clear Germans from the area, temporarily assuming the role of infantrymen. In the process, they captured one hundred fifty Germans and two batteries of German artillery (105s and 155s). In this fine action, which earned the 680th a Presidential Unit Citation, Oswald's losses were heavy: nineteen killed and fifty-six wounded.

Knowing full well they were on trial, Bob Pierce's 194th Combat Team was determined to make a good mark and prove that gliderists could function in combat on a par with, or perhaps even better than, the vaunted paratroopers.

The team also did well. By 2 P.M., it had accomplished all its assigned missions except the capture of several bridges over the Issel River (to the east) and the Issel Canal (to the south) and the clearing of Germans from the Diersfordter Wald in the area between DZs "X" and "W." Although Pierce also suffered heavy casualties, his men captured 1,150 Germans and captured or destroyed about fifty artillery pieces and ten tanks. In the late afternoon, Pierce made contact with the 513th Combat Team, on his left flank, and the British commandos on his right, dug in on the east bank of the Issel River to repulse expected German counterattacks, and laid plans to take the bridges.[6]

There was yet another innovation in the 194th Combat Team operation. Theretofore the hundreds of American glider pilots and copilots assigned to airborne operations had not been given meaningful battlefield tasks after crash-landing their aircraft. In NEPTUNE and MARKET-GARDEN, some had been detailed to guard POWs and CPs and a few had been hastily drawn into combat in emergency situations, but most had wandered around, "getting in the way." However, the 875 American pilots and copilots in VARSITY had been pretrained in rudimentary battlefield tactics and weapons and were organized into a "provisional" battalion of four companies and given specific "infantry" missions. The outcome exceeded all expectations. On D-day night, one company effectively repulsed a German counterattack. "The performance of the pilots in their ground operations was superior," 194's new exec, David P. Schorr, wrote in an official analysis. "They were most enthusiastic about their mission, assembled promptly and executed the plan exactly as prescribed."[7]

In airborne operations, bizarre battlefield scenes were commonplace; VARSITY produced one of the oddest. A group of glider pilots who were assaulting a farmhouse full of Germans were flabbergasted when four or more paratroopers (two of them wearing black silk top hats) mounted on farm horses thundered out of the woods and began circling the house, firing through the windows and emitting Indian war cries. Perhaps no less flabbergasted, the Germans inside quickly surrendered. A glider pilot historian wrote that the mounted paratroopers turned the Germans over to the pilots "and trotted off in search of more palefaces to scalp."[8]

Bud Miley was understandably proud of the 17th's first airborne mission. Despite the two poor parachute drops, he reported, "the division mission was accomplished in every particular within a few hours after landing," with "very few casualties considering the nature of the mission and the opposition." In fact, Miley's total casualties that day were almost exactly the same as Bols's: about 1,000, of whom fortunately only 159 were killed.

Military historians would long argue the merits of VARSITY. For the limited gains it achieved, had the loss of aircraft and gliders (and aircrews and glider pilots) and some 2,000 men (506 dead) on the ground been worth it? The official Army historian, Charles B. MacDonald, and one troop-carrier historian, James A. Huston, did not think so, especially when VARSITY was compared to the easy Rhine crossing by the American 30th and 79th divisions, in which only a total of forty-one men were killed.

MacDonald wrote: "In view of the weak condition of German units east of the Rhine and the particular vulnerability of airborne troops in and immediately following the descent, some overbearing need for the special capability of airborne divisions would be required to justify their use. Although the objectives assigned the divisions were legitimate, they were objectives that ground troops alone under existing circumstances should have been able to take without undue difficulty and probably with considerably fewer casualties. Participation by paratroopers and glidermen gave appreciably no more depth to the bridgehead at Wesel than that achieved by the infantrymen of the 30th Division."[9]

In Huston's assessment, it did not "appear that the airborne phase was essential to the success of the river crossing operation. Indeed, had the same resources been employed on the ground, it is conceivable that the advance to the east might have been more rapid than it was."[10]

Ridgway had a very different view of VARSITY. In his official postbattle critique, he wrote that the "concept and planning were sound and thorough," the "execution flawless." He went on: "The impact of the airborne divisions, at one blow, completely shattered the hostile defense, permitting prompt linkup with the assaulting 12 Corps, the 1st Commando Brigade, and the Ninth Army on the south."

For Ridgway, VARSITY was merely the first important step in a larger plan that would make XVIII Airborne Corps's contribution to Montgomery's Rhine crossing decisive. As he envisioned it, the two airborne divisions, plus attached British armor, would be used for "maximum exploitation to the east." In fact, Montgomery's entire 21st Army Group assault into the heart of Germany would be spearheaded by the XVIII Airborne Corps, setting such a swift pace that the trailing British divisions would not dare poke along in their usual slow and often indecisive fashion.[11]

In this regard, the commander of the British 12 Corps, Neil Ritchie, with whom XVIII Airborne Corps would work most closely, was the subject of considerable talk and speculation. Neil Ritchie was, in the words of one military historian, "an excellent staff officer," but he had previously suffered a major career setback that certainly would have disqualified him for corps command in the American Army. In early 1942, at the age of forty-four, he had been appointed commander of the British Eighth Army, then in Egypt fighting Rommel. Ritchie, the historian wrote, proved to be "quite unable to command the Eighth Army effectively against the wiley Rommel" and had been sacked by the theater commander, Claude Auchinleck, who himself took command of Eighth Army in late June 1942, after the disastrous loss of Tobruk. (Auchinleck was later replaced by Montgomery.) Ritchie had been demoted to major general and sent to Scotland to command a division in training, his career apparently at an end. But the Chief of the Imperial General Staff, Alan Brooke, had a "soft spot" for Ritchie, who had earlier served him loyally at Dunkirk, and by the time of the Normandy invasion Ritchie was on the rise again, commanding 12 Corps.[12]

Ridgway's mind was fixed on his grand scheme when he and his "family" set off for the airborne battlefield, a mere two hours after the last glider drop. The execution of his grand scheme, of course, depended on how well the airborne drops had been carried out. If they had been poor—as in Normandy—there could be no immediate XVIII Airborne Corps breakout. If they had been good —as in Holland—XVIII Airborne Corps could jump off in a matter of a day or so, as soon as the British 6th Guards Armoured Brigade, which had been assigned to his corps, got across the river. Meanwhile, however, the battlefield haze had obscured his view and the outcome of the drop was not known.

Ridgway crossed the Rhine in a British amphibious tracked vehicle. As the craft approached the east side of the river, its .50 caliber machine gun raked the bank, but there was no answering fire of any kind. Once the jeeps were ashore, the small group of Americans moved inland. Ridgway went on foot, carrying his Springfield rifle. Coming around a bend, he froze. Fifty feet ahead he saw a German soldier in a foxhole, staring right at him. "He had me cold," Ridgway wrote, "and I stopped stock-still, just staring at him, and he stared back." Luckily, the German was dead.[13]

"Breathing a little heavily after that encounter," Ridgway moved more care-fully through the woods. Moments later, hearing a noise, he gave a signal for his men to take cover. Then, as he wrote, "I saw one of the strangest sights I have ever observed in war." One of the horse-mounted paratroopers was com-ing down the trail wearing his black silk top hat, rifle casually slung on his back. Bursting into laughter, Ridgway stepped out on the trail. He later wrote that the paratrooper "damn near fell off the horse. He didn't know whether to salute from the horse's back, wearing the hat, or dismount and present arms, or what the hell to do." Seeing Ridgway laughing, the paratrooper simply sat on the horse and grinned. "A typical paratrooper," Ridgway wrote proudly, "tough and brave with a certain what-the-hell dash about him."[14]

By then, as this comical encounter demonstrated, the west sector of the VARSITY operational area was largely secure and Ridgway made his way to Miley's CP without further incident, arriving at 3:26 P.M. Generally, the news seemed good. By then, Miley was in radio contact with all the combat teams. He found they were in full assembly and fighting as cohesive units and had achieved most of their objectives (except the bridges). It was deduced from this that the drops had been mostly good and the division was prepared for a drive to the east.[15]

At about 4 P.M., Ridgway radioed this good news to XVIII Airborne Corps headquarters in Xanten, with instructions to inform Dempsey and Brereton, adding tersely: "Miley okay . . . Resistance now light . . . No shelling, no mortar fire in the vicinity of the temporary division CP . . . casualties light . . . cancel resupply missions [for] tomorrow . . . will remain with Miley . . . send me a cub . . ." He intended to personally scout the enemy territory to the east in a small, Piper Cub observation aircraft. He did not include the further good news that his back pain was diminishing; the Novocain treatment had worked.[16]

Miley was not in radio contact with Bols and the British, so the outcome of the British airborne operation was still unknown at 17th Division. At twilight, Ridgway, with Miley in tow, set off in a three-jeep convoy to find Bols and get a report. "There was a lot of sporadic firing going on all about," he wrote, "and a confused tactical situation, which is normal in an airborne drop. We didn't know where our own people were, much less the enemy, so we had to move with a moderate degree of caution."[17]

Ridgway's route took him east of the Diersfordter Wald, through the sector held by Pierce's 194th Combat Team, and by Coutts's 513th Combat Team farther north. He stopped first in Pierce's area, in the graveyard of gliders, to talk with the commander and his men. Carl A. Peterson, who would later replace Schorr as the 194 exec, recalled: "Ridgway could indicate his desires in such clear terms that there was no room for misunderstanding and he would do it without any trace of bombast. He could also convey a sense of urgency without raising his voice. By that night the 194 had not captured [three of nine] bridges over the Issel River and Issel Canal. 'We *need* those bridges,' Ridgway said quietly, and that was all that was needed to get across the importance of the mission." The 194 seized its assigned bridges promptly.[18]

Proceeding north to DZ "X," Ridgway found Coutts at his CP. Despite the foul-up in the drop, he had seized his bridges and other objectives. They began with some good-natured battlefield banter. Coutts proudly told Ridgway he had taken two thousand prisoners—but had been forced to turn over half of them to the British because he could not feed them. "I hope you got a receipt," Ridgway joked. Then the talk turned more serious. Coutts described the poor drop he had received and the horror of the fire-prone, exploding C-46s, which the men had already dubbed "Flaming Coffins." Later Ridgway wrote: "After that tragedy, I gave orders that under no circumstances would we ever use C-46s as paradrop planes again. The ship was a fire trap."[19]

Ridgway found the British situation highly satisfactory. The British had linked up with advance elements of Ritchie's 15th (Scottish) Division, which was ponderously moving inland from the Rhine. FAAA's deputy commander, Richard Gale, who had also crossed the Rhine in an amphibious craft, was on hand and had relayed an upbeat report to Dempsey and Brereton. The British 6th Airborne Division was ready in all respects to join the 17th in a drive to the east.[20]

There was, however, one disquieting note. Horrocks' 30 Corps, crossing at Rees, was in trouble. It was not moving, and this was indeed worrisome. With the 21st Army Group's left (or north) flank uncovered, Montgomery might stall Ridgway's XVIII Airborne Corps and Ritchie's 12 Corps until Horrocks could get moving. Nonetheless, Ridgway continued with his plan to drive east. His route would be the Wesel–Münster highway, which ran parallel to the Lippe River and its adjacent canal. The offensive, which had to await the arrival of the 6th Guards Armoured Brigade and the two airborne division "tails," would go off at 0900 on D+2—March 26.[21]

Ridgway and Miley left Bols's CP at about midnight to return to Miley's CP. In the meantime, a heavy firefight had erupted on the battlefield, now bathed in the light of a half moon. Ridgway, riding in the lead jeep, ran head

During the Battle of the Bulge, Ridgway's XVIII Airborne Corps, together with Leonard T. Gerow's V Corps and J. Lawton Collins' VII Corps, held the "north front" of the German breakthrough. In the midst of the crisis, Ridgway and Collins (left) took a moment to pose with British General Bernard Montgomery, who temporarily commanded all Allied ground forces on the north front.

Gavin (lower left) and his 82nd Airborne Division played a pivotal role in holding the north front.
Anthony C. (Tony) McAuliffe (lower right), who temporarily commanded the 101st Airborne Division in a tough flight at Bastogne, joins Third Army commander George S. Patton to present Steve A. Chappuis, new CO of the 502nd Regiment, a Distinguished Service Cross for heroism at Bastogne.

Ridgway (wearing a grenade and first-aid kit on a parachute harness) and Gavin discuss plans for an Allied counterattack after the Bulge, which took Gavin's 82nd Airborne Division to the Siegfried Line.

Belgium: troops of the 504th Regiment, 82nd Airborne Division, go by way of firebreak in the woods as they lead the First Army attack toward the Siegfried Line.

(Top) after the Bulge, Eisenhower, Bradley (extreme left) and American First Army commander Courtney H. Hodges (rear) assigned Ridgway (extreme right) several new airborne missions designed to assist Allied armies in crossing the Rhine River and destroying the German Army.

(Below) only one of these missions was carried out: VARSITY, a jump across the Rhine at Wesel ahead of Montgomery's 21st Army Group. The mission was assigned to the American 17th Airborne Division, commanded by William (Bud) Miley, shown here conferring with First Allied Airborne Army chief of staff Floyd L. Parks just before takeoff.

(Top) VARSITY saw the first combat use of the new Curtiss C-46 troop transport, shown here during a rehearsal jump. The plane proved to be a "flying coffin."

(Below) in addition to Edson Raff, CO of the 507th, Miley's regimental commanders for VARSITY were James W. Coutts (left), CO 513th, and James R. (Bob) Pierce, CO 194th.

Portrait of Major General Matthew B. Ridgway.

(Top) in VARSITY, American Waco gliders were "double-towed" with good results, but many glider landings were, as usual, hair-raising (bottom).

(Top) after crossing the Elbe River, Ridgway (extreme right) and Gavin (center) linked up with Russian generals (at left) near the Baltic Sea.

(Bottom) after the victory over Germany, Gavin led the 82nd Airborne Division in a triumphant New York City parade.

on into a twenty-man German patrol. He leaped from the jeep, hip-firing his Springfield. Bedlam ensued with Germans and Americans and generals and sergeants firing and cursing, "so mixed up there on the ground that they couldn't tell friend from foe." Even so, Ridgway hit a German, heard him "squeal" and "saw him fall."

Ridgway emptied his Springfield, then hit the ground to reload. When he rolled to the side to get a clip out of his belt, his head came to rest on the outside rim of the front wheel of his jeep. At that instant a German grenade exploded under the engine of the jeep. Ridgway "felt the heat and sting of a fragment" in his shoulder. The jeep was completely wrecked, but, Ridgway wrote, "by the grace of God, the wheel was between me and the blast and all I got was one small chunk that hit me in the shoulder." After he had shoved in the new clip, he kept right on firing.[22]

The generals, their aides and sergeants soon routed the German patrol and then continued on their way to Miley's CP, this time a bit more cautiously. For this battle wound, Ridgway was later awarded a Purple Heart, but he refused a doctor's advice to have the fragment removed and never did. An X ray revealed it was crescent-shaped. Eisenhower wrote Ridgway: "Someone told me you were slightly wounded. Thank the Lord it wasn't serious."[23]

Despite all the tedious and meticulous planning, the massive backup and the weakness of the German defenses, Montgomery's Rhine crossing did not proceed with the promised dash and élan. Horrocks' 30 Corps remained bogged down at Rees for three long days, blocked by a single battalion of the German 7th Parachute Division. This setback in part delayed construction of military bridges at Rees. Despite the airborne help, Ritchie's 12 Corps was also moving sluggishly and was seriously delayed in getting a military bridge across the Rhine at Wesel. The Germans were floating mines downstream, timed to explode at the bridge site, and Ritchie was slow to recognize the gravity of this nuisance.

The military bridge at Wesel was vital to Ridgway's planned dash to the east. Since it was to be utilized to bring across the 6th Guards Armoured Brigade (and the "tails" for the two airborne divisions), until it was completed, XVIII Airborne Corps could not jump off. Later, Ridgway would claim in his official critique that XVIII Airborne Corps operations had "materially increased the rapidity of bridging operations," but the official Army historian found this hard to credit. At 1000 hours, on D+1 (March 25), Ritchie telephoned Ridgway to explain the reasons and apologize for the bridge delay, but assured Ridgway the bridge was now being built as rapidly as possible.[24]

During that day—March 25—Ridgway directed a limited expansion and consolidation of the airhead. Facing east along the Issel River bridgehead, he deployed Coutts's 513th Combat Team on the left, Pierce's 194th Combat Team in the center and Raff's 507th Combat Team on the right, with its right flank anchored on the Issel Canal. The attached British Commandos served as the division reserve. Paul Oswald's 680th Glider Artillery, with its nine snub-nose 105 mms, continued to serve as division artillery. During that day, Brereton radioed news that he was "sure" ARENA had been canceled, leaving XVIII Airborne Corps with no further missions beyond VARSITY. Probably because of that news, Ridgway felt a renewed sense of urgency about carrying out his grand scheme to spearhead 21st Army Group deep into Germany.[25]

Of the senior American generals assigned to Montgomery's Rhine crossing, none was more frustrated and exasperated by the British delays and setbacks— and especially the delay on the Wesel bridge—than the American Ninth Army commander, Bill Simpson. He was a tall, earthy and utterly bald Texan who was ordinarily gregarious and easygoing. But now Simpson was boiling mad— in an absolute fury—at everything British, and he had good reason to be.[26]

Simpson's Ninth Army had come late to the ETO. It saw its first real action during the Bulge, when Eisenhower assigned it to Montgomery. Simpson was a superb and aggressive battlefield leader, but he was not noted for intellectual achievement. He had a difficult time academically at West Point and nearly washed out, finally graduating third from the bottom of his class (1909, with Patton, who had been set back a year). However, what Simpson lacked in brains was more than made up for by his chief of staff, James E. Moore, whom Bradley characterized as "one of the least known yet ablest officers in the ETO." Both Bradley and Eisenhower were "immensely impressed" with Ninth Army and its staff. In his memoirs, Eisenhower wrote: "If Simpson ever made a mistake as Army Commander, it never came to my attention."[27]

For weeks, Simpson had been frustrated and denied. First his army's initial major offensive—from Aachen to Düsseldorf—had been delayed two weeks by the flooding of the Roer River. Second, when the opportunity came at the end of that offensive to cross the Rhine on the fly, Montgomery had refused to allow it. Third, in the early planning for Montgomery's Rhine crossing, Simpson's army had been relegated to a back seat. Only two of his eleven divisions were to be included in the assault.[28]

In Simpson's eyes, there could be only one reason for this waste of his powerful army in the crossing: Montgomery wished to create the illusion that his crossing was an "all-British" operation and claim all the glory for England. Subsequently, Simpson, bringing strong pressure on Montgomery to increase the American participation, had succeeded in enlarging it to include John Anderson's full (five divisions) XVI Corps. However, Montgomery had partially negated that Simpson victory by severely limiting Ninth Army's use of the Wesel military bridge: nineteen hours per day to Dempsey, a mere five hours to Simpson. In the assault, this restriction would make it very difficult for Simpson to get Anderson's 8th Armored Division across the Rhine to help Hobbs's 30th and Wyche's 79th infantry divisions. In the follow-up, or exploitation, phase, it would make it very difficult for Simpson to get his other two corps (XIII and XIX) across the Rhine.

When Simpson first received word that construction of the Wesel bridge had fallen behind schedule, he quite understandably flew into a towering rage. He foresaw an immense traffic jam on the west bank that would encroach on his five-hour daily use of the bridge, further delaying the crossing of his 8th Armored Division. He was right. The delay in building the bridge, together with the necessity of bulldozing a path through the Wesel rubble heap, threw everything seriously behind schedule.

As a result, Hobbs and Wyche were stranded without armor and heavy artillery in their ever-widening bridgehead. Nonetheless, Simpson, who was even now scheming a way to bypass Wesel, ordered both Hobbs and Wyche to continue advancing and expanding the Ninth Army bridgehead. As they did so, Simpson sent elements of his 35th Infantry Division, commanded by Paul W. Baade, across the Rhine on landing craft and treadway bridges. Hobbs struck east toward Dorsten, keeping to the south of the Lippe River and Canal (immediately south of Ridgway's XVIII Airborne Corps sector); Wyche angled southeast toward Essen. Near Dorsten, Hobbs was checked by the 116th Panzer Division. This notorious German division was a mere shadow of its former self, but it still had grit and a will to fight to save the Fatherland.[29]

The Wesel bridge finally opened for business on D+2, March 26. Among the first units to cross was part of the 6th Guards Armoured Brigade, for which Ridgway was waiting, followed by the "tails" of the two airborne divisions. These vast motorized formations moved at a snail-like pace through the rubble of Wesel. When they reached the eastern limit of the airhead, they ground to a halt in immense traffic jams, which, in turn, altogether stopped traffic on the Wesel bridge.[30]

Simpson was like an angry caged tiger. His headquarters diary for March 26 and 27 bristled with sarcastic and derogatory entries about the "slow, plodding" British Army: "The CG [Simpson] is very confident seeing the light and spotty resistance that an early break-out can be made—if we successfully fight our way through the Second British Army. Hard feelings growing here . . ." "The British, stopping at night to sleep, for tea, and moving slowly at best, are just wasting time with their ten-year war . . ." "There is just no comparison in the way in which the two armies operate, and for the Americans, the British pace and methods are simply archaic and nerve-wracking in their [slow] speed."[31]

By the morning of March 27, Ridgway's corps was ready to charge east. The 6th Guards Armoured Brigade, composed of three tank battalions, plus supporting forces, was divided between Bols's 6th Division and Miley's 17th. Bols drew one battalion, the Grenadier Guards; Miley drew the Scots Guards and the Coldstream Guards. Bols and the Grenadiers would advance on the left (or north), Miley on the right, along the Wesel–Münster highway. James Coutts's 513 paratroopers would ride the British Churchill tanks; Ace Miller's 2nd Battalion with the Scots Guards, Ed Kent's 3rd Battalion with the Coldstream Guards.[32]

The Scots Guards jumped off first, at 3 P.M. on the afternoon of March 27. Ace Miller rode on a tank commanded by Robert Runcie, who would one day in the distant future be the Archbishop of Canterbury. It was a wild ride through Germany in darkness. Soon the column reached the town of Dorsten —seventeen miles east of the Rhine. The Coldstream Guards, with Kent's 3rd

Battalion riding its Churchills, came behind, on the left flank of the Scots Guards.[13]

Ridgway was out in his jeep that night, trailing behind the Scots Guards. He had a very close call. While driving through one of the little German villages, he rounded a blind corner and found himself face to face with a "massive" German roadblock. Four years later he wrote a friend: "I still recall the feeling of nakedness at the moment, followed by a renewed appreciation of my own stupidity. Fortunately—or I wouldn't be writing this—the roadblock was not garrisoned."[14]

At Dorsten, Miller ran into heavy German fire from an 88 mm gun—or guns. He recalled:

Since it was after midnight and quite dark, I dismounted my paratroopers and attacked on foot. However, heavy machine-gun fire soon forced us into the buildings on both sides of the streets. We then proceeded to "mouse-trap" forward in order to get close to the 88s. Mouse-trapping consists of breaking a hole through the wall of the next building (if there was no entrance), then, if possible, heaving in a grenade, and blowing a hole through the next wall, etc.

Towards morning, as it was just beginning to get light, I was in a room with two troopers. We three were breaking out a hole when Ridgway crawled into the room from our previous hole. After standing and observing us for a moment, he asked where the Germans were. I pointed to the next room. He said, "Good. Keep after them," turned and crawled back through the hole through which we had entered.[35]

Dorsten fell to Miller and the Scots Guards at about 0700, March 28. The Scots Guards historian wrote that Ridgway sat on the tank of the Guards' commander, C. I. H. Dunbar, and wrote out a short dispatch announcing that "the Scots Guards of the 6th Guards Armoured Brigade . . . had captured the town of Dorsten." The message, duly encoded, was passed back to Dempsey's headquarters and "to the Battalion's surprise and delight, it was broadcast by B.B.C.'s one o'clock news from London only a few hours later."[36]

This bravado could not have pleased Simpson. He may even have felt humiliated that a lightly armed parachute regiment, riding Churchill tanks, had forged ahead of Hobbs's 30th and by doing so had actually rendered it assistance. In any case, Ridgway's dashing advance was not going to win the war against Germany. Sooner or later so puny a force would be blocked. Simpson had two more-powerful war-winning corps waiting at the Rhine and he was impatient to get them across that Wesel bridge.

Simpson met with Montgomery and Dempsey to demand a larger role for his forces. He was still furious, but he managed to keep his temper under control while he frankly criticized British operations. By then, Horrocks' 30 Corps had taken Rees, but only just barely, and Horrocks was days behind schedule. Most of Ritchie's swollen 12 Corps was jammed up at the Wesel bridge: Those 12 Corps divisions already across the Rhine were plodding slowly along, far behind schedule, and seemed incapable of capitalizing on Ridgway's XVIII Airborne Corps advance to Dorsten. Meanwhile, Simpson's two powerful mechanized corps sat idle behind the Rhine.

Simpson came away from this meeting a big winner. His headquarters diary noted that Montgomery "sided with Ninth Army on every count and ordered Dempsey to get moving." More important, Montgomery, dismissing vigorous protests from Dempsey, decreed that on March 31, Ninth Army was to have overriding priority on the Wesel bridge. The old priorities would be exactly reversed: Simpson could use the bridge nineteen hours a day, Dempsey five.[37]

That same afternoon, Simpson met with his corps commanders to lay out his plan for the Ninth Army breakout. He also invited Ridgway. After Ridgway had heard the plan, he demurred. He could understand Simpson's impatience, but he felt that Simpson was attempting to move too quickly. The roads leading west from Wesel which Simpson intended to utilize were already jammed solid with slow-moving British traffic; an alternate Simpson idea to bridge the Lippe, thereby bypassing Wesel, would only create further, perhaps insoluble, traffic jams.[38]

Ridgway proposed what he thought was a better idea. If his XVIII Airborne Corps, then halted at Dorsten on Dempsey's orders, was attached to Simpson's Ninth Army, and if Simpson permitted Ridgway to drive east another twenty miles or so to Haltern and Dülmen, this would open the American bridgehead wide, clear out traffic between Wesel and Dorsten and give Simpson room to bring in his XIII and XIX corps. The key to Ridgway's plan was the shift of the XVIII Airborne Corps to the control of Ninth Army. That would move the "boundary" between the British Second Army and the American Ninth Army to Ridgway's north flank, bringing the Wesel–Münster highway under exclusive Ninth Army control.[39]

Ridgway's plan was approved first by Simpson, then by Dempsey and Montgomery. On March 29, XVIII Airborne Corps, now operating under Ninth Army control, shot eastward again. In the northern sector, Bols took Lembeck and angled more northeasterly toward Billerbeck. Coutts's 513, still riding with the 6th Guards Armoured Brigade tanks, drove hard and fast to Haltern, then continued on down the highway another eight miles to Dülmen. Edson Raff brought up his 507 by truck and on foot to occupy and defend Haltern; Pierce trucked his 194 to Dülmen to occupy that place.[40]

The 194 exec, David Schorr, recalled:

Ridgway came up to the 194 CP. He asked Colonel Pierce whether the 507 had come up on the 194's right. (Or maybe it was left.) Pierce replied, "No." Ridgway then asked me to get General Miley on the phone, which I did. The "conversation" went like this: "Bud, this is Matt. I'm up at Pierce's place. He tells me that Raff is not as yet up on his right. Would you get him up there? Good." End of "conversation."

Never before or since have I heard an order given in such soft-spoken, matter-of-fact, conversational tone and yet be so unequivocally and insistently compelling—compliance being a foregone conclusion. It was then that I saw in Ridgway the attributes of a combat commander who wins.[41]

The 17th Division kept barreling up the road to Münster, the paratrooper spearhead still riding on the tanks of the Scots Guards and Coldstream Guards. On April 1, Easter Sunday, it reached its destination. When the German commander in Münster refused a surrender offer, Miley commenced maneuvers to take the city, which was fifty miles east of the Rhine. It fell, officially, on April 2. During this action, James Coutts was severely wounded and was replaced by his exec, Ward Ryan. Fortunately, there were no casualties among the other senior commanders.[42]

This spectacular eastward dash of XVIII Airborne Corps completely opened up the Ninth Army Rhine bridgehead and provided Simpson ideal positions from which to launch his rightward encirclement of the Ruhr. Even so, he had a tough time cranking up. Dempsey was still "blocking" his path and Simpson was "burning mad." A Ninth Army headquarters diary entry angrily stated: "The British are deliberately taking advantage of Ninth Army, blocking its passage so that they can be first—in their own good time at that—to get away and grab off the glory of a breakthrough . . ." Simpson telephoned Montgomery and "in no uncertain terms told him just what he thought, and felt, and wanted." Montgomery, the diary states, "agreed, again, in detail." When Simpson finally gained overriding priority on the Wesel bridge and control of the Wesel–Münster highway, he gave "direct orders" to his division commanders to "physically throw every British vehicle seen on the road into the nearest field and order it to stay there . . ." Simpson was "in deadly earnest about the boundary-careless, road-hogging British."[43]

During this same week, March 25 to March 31, Omar Bradley's 12th Army Group forces (Hodges' First Army and Patton's Third) broke out of their Rhine bridgeheads at Remagen and Oppenheim and commenced a spectacular deep-wheeling armored drive northeast and north toward Kassel and Paderborn. Collins' VII and Van Fleet's III corps spearheaded the First Army drive; Manton Eddy's XII and Walton Walker's XX Corps, the Third Army's. These vast, swift-moving forces linked line abreast at Giessen on March 28 and continued almost without pause. Collins' VII Corps, led by Maurice Rose's 3rd Armored Division, which advanced an electrifying ninety miles in a single day, reached Paderborn on March 31. On the following day (Easter Sunday) at Lippstadt, elements of Rose's 3rd Armored met Simpson's oncoming 2nd Armored Division, now commanded by Isaac D. White, which had jumped off from Ridgway's positions in Dülmen.[44]*

This dazzling maneuver by Bradley's 12th Army Group was one of the great achievements of the war. After all the tedious and heated debates on strategy for encircling the Ruhr, which ended with the "main effort" being placed

---

* At this moment of great triumph, Maurice Rose, leading his armor, was shot and killed near Paderborn by a German tanker.[45]

behind Montgomery, it was Bradley who actually encircled most of the area. By impromptu but forceful and rapid exploitation of the Remagen and Oppenheim bridgeheads, Bradley was able to speed around three quarters of the "circle," while Montgomery barely traversed one quarter. Had it not been for Ridgway's aggressive eastward drive to Haltern and Dülmen, which set the stage for springing White's 2nd Armored Division, Bradley's armor might well have come most of the way around the circle to Dorsten.

On March 30, the XVIII Airborne Corps was relieved of its duties and responsibilities by the British 8 Corps, commanded by Evelyn H. (Bubbles) Barker. Eric Bols's 6th Airborne Division remained with 8 Corps to fight as regular infantry. Bud Miley's 17th Airborne Division was transferred to similar duties in Alvan Gillem's XIII Corps and, later, Anderson's XVI Corps.[46]

By then, Nazi Germany was shattered and reeling. A mere two hundred miles separated the American and British armies from the Russian Army, which was closing on Berlin. Since Eisenhower had foresworn an American or British attack on Berlin (leaving that job to the Russians), the American Berlin airborne operation ECLIPSE, as well as ARENA, had been canceled. Although FAAA resolutely continued to grind out grandiose airborne plans (jumps into Bavaria and Denmark), only one seemed to have real merit: platoon-size jumps into camps inside Germany to safeguard Allied POWs.

Apart from the last-mentioned task, which was also "iffy," Ridgway and the XVIII Airborne Corps were now stranded high and dry with no combat role and no troops. But not for long. There were now an estimated 125,000 German soldiers and airmen encircled and trapped in the Ruhr. Bradley, who was soon to regain control of Simpson's Ninth Army, wanted to keep rolling east with the bulk of all three American armies (First, Third, Ninth), but he was concerned about leaving the massive "Ruhr pocket" in his rear. Accordingly, in reorganizing his armies, Bradley assigned three corps to reduce the Ruhr: Anderson's new XVI, Van Fleet's III and Ridgway's XVIII Airborne.[47]

The administrative responsibility for the Ruhr reduction fell to Courtney Hodges' First Army. On the evening of March 31, Ridgway reported to Hodges' CP. The headquarters diarist, William Sylvan, logged that Hodges "is as delighted to see General Ridgway again as the latter is delighted to serve under him."[48]

☆50☆

ON APRIL 2, the day the XVIII Airborne Corps headquarters became operational for the Ruhr campaign, Ridgway found himself something of a celebrity. *Time* magazine, in its issue dated that day, featured him on the cover, highlighting his role as "the world's No. 1 active airborne commander" in general, and VARSITY in particular. Tens of thousands of copies of a "pony" size edition of *Time* (devoid of advertising) were circulated to men serving in the ETO.

Time wrote that Ridgway "looks like a Roman senator and lives like a Spartan hoplite."* It described him as "ruggedly built" (5' 10½" tall, 175 lbs.) and "husky, aggressive, driving," with straight, dark brown hair sprinkled with gray, dark brown eyes and "expressive eyebrows." His deeply tanned face, *Time* wrote, had been variously described as "distinguished," "handsome" or "austere" and was "crinkled with the lines natural to an outdoorsman." The story stressed Ridgway's love of sports and the out-of-doors (tennis, riding, hunting) and said his chief off-duty recreation was reading (Kipling) and playing cribbage. He was "no hater of change or challenge" and had welcomed the assignment to airborne duty and command.[1]

Ridgway was of course flattered and grateful for *Time*'s unusual professional and personal tribute. He wrote *Time* war correspondent Will Lang, who had interviewed him for background: "As for the personal touch, I find my feelings hard to explain. Boyish pleasure, gratitude and the sober determination 'to meet with triumph and disaster, and to treat those two imposters just the same' are mingled. My deepest pleasure will come from that which my wife will feel."[2]

Apart from that considerable but ephemeral uplift, Ridgway may not have been in the most buoyant mood. Earlier in the year, Omar Bradley had given Ridgway the impression that after VARSITY and the now canceled CHOKER II, XVIII Airborne Corps would be given an armored division. Attached to 12th Army Group as a reserve corps, it would go "straight through" with Bradley into the heart of Germany. Things had turned out very differently. Bradley's three armies were now racing toward the Elbe for the final kill. Ridgway, with fellow corps commanders Anderson and Van Fleet, had been left behind to carry out a tough but far less glamorous task which would almost invariably be demeaned or trivialized in the histories of the war as the "Ruhr mop-up."[3]

The final Ruhr reduction plan was as follows. Simpson's Ninth Army (ele-

* A heavily armed foot soldier in ancient Greece.

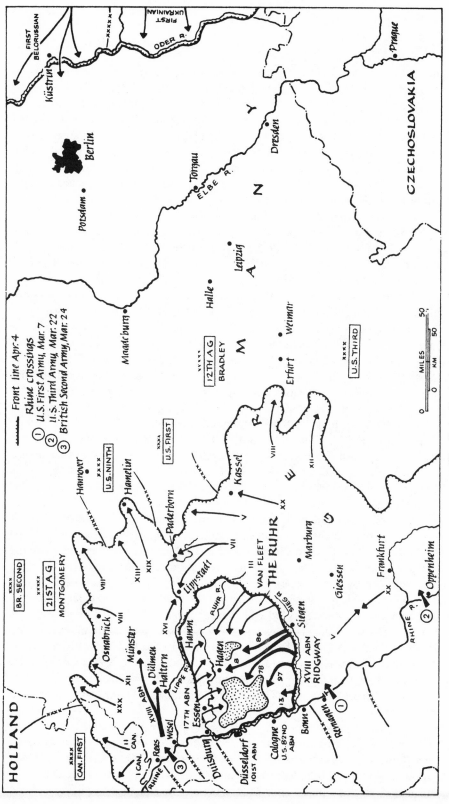

The Ruhr Encirclement

ments of XVI and XIX corps) would drive south to the east–west-flowing Ruhr River; Hodges' First Army (XVIII Airborne Corps and III Corps) would drive north. The idea was that these American forces would squeeze the Germans into a "pocket" on the east side of the Rhine River near Düsseldorf. Under the plan, Ridgway and Van Fleet had almost three times as far to travel as the Ninth Army forces, but the terrain in First Army's sector was less urbanized than that in the Ninth's, and it was believed that First Army could move faster than the Ninth, which would face heavy and perilous street fighting in the Ruhr industrial district.[4]

The XVIII Airborne Corps, Ridgway learned, was to be assigned four infantry divisions for its Ruhr campaign. Ridgway (and Hodges) naturally wanted —and asked for—the 82nd and the 101st, but Eisenhower and Bradley turned them down. The 82nd and the 101st had been positioned on the west bank of the Rhine in the Düsseldorf-Cologne area as strategic reserve, less Taylor's 501 and Gavin's 508, which had been detached and put on standby for possible platoon-size jumps into POW camps (Operation JUBILANT). Nor were the 17th and the 13th available. Simpson, hanging onto the 17th, intended to use it in his sector of the Ruhr campaign; the 13th was still on standby for a possible jump into the alleged Nazi redoubt in Bavaria (Operation EFFECTIVE).[5]

What Ridgway finally drew, initially, were four regular infantry divisions. Two were brand-new divisions that had never fired a shot in battle, both led by West Point classmates of Ridgway's: the 86th, commanded by Harris M. (Count) Melasky, and the 97th, commanded by Milton B. Halsey, a distant relative of Admiral William F. (Bull) Halsey. The other two (already in the line) were the 8th, commanded by Bryant E. Moore (who graduated in the second section of Ridgway's 1917 class), and the 78th, commanded by Edwin Parker, which had earlier fought adjacent to the 82nd Airborne Division in the Roer-dam area.[6]

The 8th Division had had, as Ridgway put it, many "ups and downs." In its baptism in the Cotentin, under command of Ridgway's classmate William McMahon, it had fallen on its face and in so doing had momentarily endangered Ridgway's 82nd Division. After McMahon, Don Stroh had led the division with conspicuous success from Normandy to the Hürtgen Forest. In late November, Stroh had been succeeded by the ADC of the 90th Division, the able and much-decorated Wild Bill Weaver, who had helped McLain salvage the 90th Division. Under Weaver, the 8th had been very badly mauled in the Hürtgen Forest. Owing to the bad experience the 82nd had had with the 8th in Normandy, Ridgway had asked Hodges not to assign it to XVIII Corps in the February Roer-dam fighting. On February 22, 1945, Weaver, one of the oldest division commanders in the ETO (class of 1912), had relinquished command to Bryant Moore.[7]

Thus, when Moore reported to Ridgway for the Ruhr campaign, he had commanded the 8th only six weeks. He had had considerable combat experience, however, first in the South Pacific, later in the ETO as ADC of the 104th Division, which had been loaned to Montgomery to help clear the Scheldt. The 8th was in an "up" phase after Moore took over, and Moore quickly became one of Ridgway's most trusted lieutenants. Ridgway called him "a superior combat commander in every way. He was quiet, dignified, a taciturn New Englander. Not a great talker but a solid thinker and an indefatigable and imperturbable worker and a great leader."[8]

Ridgway's XVIII Airborne Corps sector was a sixty-seven-mile stretch of terrain just south of the east–west-flowing Sieg River. It was anchored on the left (or west) near Bonn, on the Rhine, and on the right (or east) at Siegen, where it adjoined Van Fleet's III Corps. Facing north, Parker's 78th Division was deployed on the left, Moore's 8th on the right. For the offensive, Ridgway sideslipped Moore and Parker to the right (east) and inserted Milton Halsey's green 97th Division on the corps's left flank, along the east bank of the Rhine, with the "primary mission" of preventing a sudden German attack out of the Ruhr against the American Army Rhine bridges at Remagen. He deployed the other green division, Count Melasky's 86th, behind Moore's 8th, intending to leapfrog the 86th over the 8th when the right moment came. The 78th, 8th and 86th divisions would constitute the main corps attack.[9]

At that time, the 82nd and the 101st airborne divisions were a mere stone's throw from Ridgway's CP. Taylor's 101 was deployed on the west bank of the Rhine facing Düsseldorf and the area south to Worringen. Gavin's 82nd was deployed from Worringen, facing Cologne, and south almost to Bonn. In effect, these divisions were sealing the west side of the Ruhr "pocket" on a south–north line along the Rhine extending north from the XVIII Airborne Corps boundary.[10]†

Both Taylor and Gavin were eager to assist in the Ruhr campaign by attacking east across the Rhine at Düsseldorf and Cologne, more or less in front of Ridgway's northbound corps. Such an attack would no doubt have materially assisted Ridgway, unhinging the German defenses he faced, but Eisenhower and Bradley remained adamant: the 82nd and the 101st were to be held on a tight rein as "occupation troops." Unknown to Ridgway, Taylor or Gavin, SHAEF had tentatively earmarked the two divisions for transfer to the Pacific for the invasion of Japan, and Eisenhower did not want them to incur any further casualties.

Still, it was difficult to keep these two fine fighting units sitting idle. To assist Ridgway's attack, both Taylor and Gavin set up their artillery to fire across the Rhine into the west flank of the Germans facing Ridgway. This, in turn, unfortunately evoked counterbattery fire from the Germans. One German shell fell near Bud Harper's 3rd Battalion CP, severely wounding the battalion com-

† The 101 senior staff had suffered several recent misfortunes. The chief of staff, Mike Michaelis, still suffering from wounds incurred in Holland, had a relapse and was evacuated to the States, replaced by the G-1, Ned D. Moore, who had been acting chief of staff in the early stages at Bastogne. During a demonstration of a new (but defective) "baseball grenade," the G-3, Harry Kinnard, was "seriously wounded" in the stomach when a grenade exploded prematurely and he had to be hospitalized. He was temporarily replaced by Charles H. Chase. The same grenade (which killed one man) slightly wounded the ADC, Gerry Higgins, and fourteen other 101 staffers.[11]

mander, Ray Allen, who had led the battalion since before Normandy. Allen, who lost a leg, was the only casualty the battalion suffered in the Rhine duty and the last of the war. He was succeeded by his S-3, Robert J. McDonald.[12]

Both airborne division commanders had permission from their boss, newly appointed XXII Corps commander Ernest Harmon, to send night patrols across the Rhine to "probe" enemy defenses. These patrols grew ever larger and more aggressive; first platoons, then companies. In the 82nd, Tucker sent two of his 504 companies across simultaneously and captured the town of Hittdorf. The Germans reacted with furious counterattacks that inflicted heavy losses and drove Tucker's men back to the river. Harmon gave Gavin a royal chewing-out for exceeding his orders; thereafter, Gavin was more restrained. During one of these patrol operations, William R. Carpenter, who had replaced Vandervoort as commander of the 2nd Battalion of Ekman's 505, drowned in the Rhine, along with one of his company commanders, while going across to retrieve the body of one of his men who had been killed on a patrol. Carpenter was replaced by William R. Dudley, onetime exec of the independent 509th Battalion who had returned from duty in the States.[13]

The Allied squeeze on the Ruhr pocket commenced in earnest on April 4—first from the north. Four of Simpson's Ninth Army divisions (Wyche's 79th, Baade's 35th, Ray Porter's 75th, Bud Miley's 17th Airborne) attacked south from the Lippe River toward Duisburg and Essen, while the 95th and 8th Armored drove south from Münster toward Hamm. The Germans momentarily checked the drive at the Rhine-Herne Canal, then broke and fell back, defending some towns, but, bafflingly, not others. The truth was that the Germans in the Ruhr were in utter disarray and Model had but one, desperate idea: to break out directly to the east, toward Berlin. But that route was solidly blocked by other elements of First and Ninth armies.[14]

Bud Miley's 17th Airborne Division was in the thick of the fighting in the north. After the division had taken Münster, Bob Pierce's 194 was temporarily attached to the 95th Division, commanded by Harry L. Twaddle, which was attacking in the Hamm area in conjunction with John Devine's 8th Armored Division. During these operations, Pierce's glidermen captured a famous German statesman living in seclusion at his estate near Hirschberg: Franz von Papen, who had been chancellor of Germany before Hitler's rise. Farther west, the paratroopers of Edson Raff's 507 and Ward Ryan's 513 combat teams crossed the Rhine-Herne Canal on April 6. They marched into Duisburg and Essen (site of the vast Krupp steelworks), where they found few German soldiers and white flags of surrender strung up by the surviving civilians.[15]

In the south, Ridgway's XVIII Airborne Corps jumped off on April 6, one day behind Van Fleet's III. Ridgway was in a hurry. If the Ruhr campaign could be completed quickly, his corps might yet join Bradley's vast easterly push to the Elbe. In a meeting with his division commanders, he put it this way: "The sooner we get this job done, the sooner we will get into the real final kill of striking into the very heart of Germany and getting into Berlin."[16]

Ridgway's instructions to his division commanders were typical of him: "drive, drive, drive." In another staff meeting, he elaborated:

The minute a regiment is stopped for fatigue or battle losses or for any other reason the next one is to go through and keep it going day and night. Each commander must watch . . . [the young battalion commanders] and must try to anticipate where the crisis is going to be in his command and be there on the spot. Before then, he's done everything he can to anticipate the difficulties, to bolster up these youngsters, whose judgment needs it, and then when the time comes for action, he's present on the spot, ready to intervene, if he thinks it's necessary. I just can't emphasize this too much. These things are simplicity themselves. There's no tactical genius required. It's driving, constant, unrelenting pressure from the division commander down that produces results.[17]

The two veteran infantry divisions, Moore's 8th and Parker's 78th, led Ridgway's corps attack, driving north from the Siegen area toward Hagen, with the aim of cutting the pocket in half. However, the rural terrain in the southern sector favored the defense. It was hilly and densely wooded and cut by numerous deeply ravined streams. The official Army historian wrote: "The Germans defended in some degree almost every town and village and most ridge and stream lines."[18]

Owing to an acute shortage of riflemen in the 12th Army Group, Bradley had recently authorized the use of black soldiers in regular infantry divisions. The blacks would remain segregated by platoons, which were to be commanded by a white lieutenant and a white platoon sergeant. The platoons would be assigned to veteran infantry divisions. Hundreds of blacks, theretofore relegated to "service units" (on housekeeping duties or driving trucks, etc.) volunteered for these platoons, often taking a reduction in rank to qualify. In total, SHAEF fielded fifty-three black platoons.[19]

Both Moore's and Parker's divisions had been assigned hastily organized (and understaffed) black platoons: four in the 8th, three in the 78th. Six of the seven platoons fought in this early phase of the Ruhr offensive. After one week of combat, Ridgway's Corps G-1, Fred Schellhammer, conducted an analysis of this radical (and not widely popular) experiment. His conclusions helped shatter the age-old myth that "negroes can't or won't fight." Schellhammer found that the "morale and manner of performance of all platoons is excellent." Of a total strength of 253 blacks, 5 had been killed, 33 had been wounded and 5 were missing. The blacks had captured 82 Germans, and "several members" of the platoon assigned to G Company, 28th Infantry Regiment, 8th Division, were being "put in for awards."[20]

On April 8, Ridgway committed his reserve division, Count Melasky's 86th. Part of it leapfrogged a portion of Moore's 8th, the rest moved up on the 8th's right flank. When Ridgway visited Melasky's CP that day to see how things were going, he was not pleased. About two days later, he called Melasky to his own CP to tell him that the progress of the 86th Division was "thoroughly unsatisfactory" and that the power available to Melasky "was apparently not being used," or, at any rate, "the results were not being obtained." Melasky pointed out that his division was new to combat and was meeting "strong resistance." Ridgway scoffingly produced Melasky's own casualty figures. These he described as "negligible" and said the conclusion from them was inescapable: "enemy resistance was not the cause of unsatisfactory progress." Later, Ridgway would write that Melasky had "failed" in his duties and responsibilities as a division commander.

Melasky later sought to shift much of the blame for the failure of the division to his ADC, George van Wyck Pope, and requested authority to relieve Pope of command. Although Ridgway probably did not approve of Melasky's shifting the blame in this fashion, he did not have a high opinion of Pope himself and both he and Hodges concurred with Pope's proposed relief. When he checked with Omar Bradley, however, Bradley came to bat for Pope. Pope was an old friend and had been Bradley's chief of staff at Camp Claiborne in 1942. Bradley expressed the opinion that "while the recommendations might be well founded," Pope had "not been sufficiently tested in so brief a period of combat." He may also have questioned the judgment of Pope's accuser, Melasky. In any event, upon hearing Bradley's verdict, Ridgway "at once dropped the matter."[21]

Ridgway had another personnel problem on his hands at that time that was far more pressing. In early April, he had been assigned yet another division, the brand-new 13th Armored, commanded by Bradley's West Point classmate John B. Wogan. Early in its training, perhaps rashly, the division had thumbed its nose at the "bad luck" superstitions of the number thirteen by adopting a colorful shoulder patch which depicted spilled salt, an open umbrella, a broken mirror and a black cat. Colloquially, it was called the Black Cat Division.[22]

The official Army historian wrote that the 13th Armored Division had been rushed willy-nilly to the Ruhr front in two long road marches totalling 260 miles, with no time between them for rest or servicing equipment. By jump-off time on April 10, only two of the division's combat commands were in place (with little or no backup) and one of the commands had only half its tanks. Nonetheless, Ridgway needed armor to overrun the Germans who were blocking the advance of his infantry. He ordered Wogan to attack without delay with whatever he had and to "destroy" all German forces he encountered.[23]

Wogan, a field artilleryman, could not have been pleased by this sudden and rude introduction to combat. He may also have been a little baffled. Ridgway's order to "destroy" enemy forces ran counter to armored doctrine. Armor was used principally for speedy and surprise dashes behind the enemy to unhinge his defenses. Ordinarily the infantry following was utilized to "destroy" the enemy forces the tankers had unhinged—and unnerved. However, Wogan took his orders literally—perhaps too literally—and attacked at once, in beautiful weather, through Halsey's 97th Division, taking the *Autobahn* north toward Cologne.[24]

Total chaos ensued. Communication broke down; some tankers got lost and strayed. One combat team stopped at a stream to literally "destroy" an enemy enclave. (Ridgway rescinded the "destroy" order on April 12.) Dumfounded, Ridgway later reflected: "Wogan was gallant and probably as highly-trained as any officer [we had] . . . I always thought of him as a real fighting soldier—aggressive, powerful physique, bright . . . [but the men of the 13th] just weren't moving . . . The Germans were at a low ebb. The opposition wasn't heavy at all. In other words the progress of the division was thoroughly unsatisfactory." Up to then, Ridgway's XVIII Airborne Corps had commanded eighteen different divisions of all types. None, he thought, was "as generally inefficient in combat as the 13th." Its leadership, he stated, was "lamentable"; there was "a complete lack of aggressiveness."[25]

Doubtful that Wogan could exercise control of his division, Ridgway sent his corps artillery commander, Lemuel Mathewson, to help straighten out the mess. Mathewson was appalled. He officially reported to Ridgway: "As it stands today, I would say the division is thoroughly ineffectual as a fighting machine and drastically in need of a major overhaul." The division, he said, had been "totally unprepared to meet and accept the conditions and consequences of combat." He thought the division headquarters was "poorly staffed" and "with few exceptions" the subordinate commanders "were apparently incapable of providing forceful, aggressive leadership which the ordinary circumstances of combat require."[26]

Vigorous steps were taken to provide the unlucky 13th new leadership. Wogan requested the immediate relief of his CCA commander, a non-West Pointer, Brigadier General Wayland B. Augur, owing to his "lack of aggressiveness in combat." Augur was temporarily replaced by the division artillery commander, Alfred E. Kastner, then permanently by an experienced and decorated tanker who was yanked from the First Army staff, West Pointer Peter C. Hains III. At about the same time, 8th Division commander Bryant Moore recommended the relief of Wogan's CCR commander, non-West Pointer Frank R. Williams, because of his "ineffectiveness as a leader and conspicuous failure to achieve results." Moore also believed Williams' reports to him were "false and misleading." Williams was immediately replaced by another experienced and decorated tanker, West Pointer Charles G. Rau. Ridgway also had qualms about CCB commander Harold G. Holt, a non-West Pointer, but he kept him in command.[27]

The command chaos in the division was intensified on April 13 when Wogan was hit in the neck by rifle fire. The wound was so serious that he had to be evacuated and did not again return to battle. Ridgway named Lemuel Mathewson temporary commander of the division until Hodges could find a replacement. The replacement turned out to be John Millikin, whom Hodges had recently relieved of command of III Corps for failing to aggressively exploit the Remagen bridgehead. Later, when Wogan was recommended for a DSC for the action that led to his battle wound, Ridgway disapproved the medal. And still later, in the postwar years, Ridgway wrote that Wogan had "failed" as a commander in World War II.[28]

The new CCA commander, Peter Hains, recalled:

The division chief of staff [Herbert H. Frost] had also gone to the hospital and did not return to the division. When Millikin took over, he named me [to three jobs]: assistant division commander and chief of staff as well as commander of CCA, until we could get things organized. I went down to Holt's [CCB] CP. I found him and a number of his officers lounging around in chairs and chatting. I introduced myself and asked what was going on. He said they'd had a big battle and were reorganizing. I asked how many men had he lost. None. How many tanks knocked out. None. I commented, sarcastically, "It must have been some battle . . ."

Remembering what Doc Eaton, Ridgway's chief of staff, told me the night before, I told Holt to get the lead out, to start for Dusseldorf at once, to keep going till he got there without another stop. I said, "If you don't have Dusseldorf by dark, your throat will be cut from ear to ear, as will every man's in the command, including me." They moved out with alacrity and they did get to Dusseldorf.

Since Hains could not reasonably handle all three of his important jobs, he combed the division for a prospective chief of staff. He found a famous West Point football player and cavalryman, William H. Wood, commanding the division trains (or tail), and proposed him for the job. Wood said, "No way" would he take that job in that "disorganized" outfit. But, under heavy pressure from Hains, Wood agreed to be chief of staff. In time, under the direction of Millikin, Hains, Wood and Rau, the division got itself straightened out. Holt, who retained command of CCB, went on to win a Silver Star and Bronze Star for heroism.[29]

In the meantime, Moore's 8th Division had gotten up a full head of steam and was driving north, overrunning everything in its path. This was the kind of power drive Ridgway had been seeking, and he immediately drafted an official letter of commendation for Moore on the "smartness" of his outfit. That day— April 14—at Hattingen, a battalion of Moore's 13th Infantry Regiment reached the XVIII Airborne Corps objective: the Ruhr River. Moore's men jubilantly shouted GI obscenities across the river at the men of Wyche's 313th Infantry Regiment who were digging in on the opposite bank. The Ruhr "pocket" was now split in twain, leaving the bulk of the Germans completely cut off and stranded in the western half around Düsseldorf and Wuppertal.

Realizing all hope was lost, Karl Wagener, Model's chief of staff, urged Model to request permission from Hitler to surrender his forces. Although Model knew his situation was now hopeless, he could not bring himself to take that drastic and humiliating step. However, after a "struggle with his con-science," he decided, in the interest of saving the lives of his soldiers, to simply "dissolve" his command. As the official American Army historian explained: "There could be no formal surrender of a command that had ceased to exist." Before dissolving the command, Model issued orders officially discharging "all youths and older men" in his armies and put out the word that all others were free to try either to fight their way out of the pocket in organized groups or to slip out unarmed. It was every man for himself.[30]

Early on the morning of April 15, Ridgway decided the time was ripe to present Model with a "surrender demand." He drafted such a demand and a covering letter and sent them to Hodges for approval. At two o'clock that afternoon, Hodges replied favorably but with several provisos: that the demand was to be "peremptory in character," made in English, and that the surrender would be (in keeping with Roosevelt and Churchill's proclamation at Casablanca in 1943) "unconditional." In sum, Ridgway was to be iron-fisted with Model and not enter into any "deals" of any kind.[31]

In the meantime, Ridgway had dispatched his G-2, Whitfield Jack, and aide-interpreter, Frank M. Brandstetter, who spoke fluent German, to Model's headquarters. Going in under a flag of truce, Jack and Brandstetter conveyed to Model a "simple" message from Ridgway: Model was in a "hopeless situation" and "further resistance could only cause needless bloodshed." But the informal mission failed. Model would not consider any surrender proposal. He was, he said, "bound by a personal oath to Hitler to fight to the end," and (as Ridgway remembered it) "it would do violence to his sense of honor even to consider my message."

Nonetheless, Ridgway wrote later, he decided to "make one more try." He drafted a formal letter in which he recalled Robert E. Lee's "honorable capitulation" in the American Civil War, and went on to say:

This same choice is now yours. In the light of a soldier's honor, for the reputation of the German Officer Corps, for the sake of your nation's future, lay down your arms at once. The German lives you save are sorely needed to restore your people to their proper place in society. The German cities you will preserve are irreplaceable necessities for your people's welfare . . .[32]

Jack and Brandstetter returned to Model's CP with Ridgway's letter that same day, April 15. According to FAAA's chief of staff, Floyd Parks, who visited Ridgway's CP the following day, Ridgway told Jack to tell Model that if he agreed to the surrender terms, Ridgway "would put on a show of strength to give him an excuse for surrendering." If he would not surrender, Jack was to tell Model, then Ridgway "would attack vigorously and capture him dead or alive."[33]

It was all futile. Brandstetter and Jack returned with Model's chief of staff, Karl Wagener, in tow and said "it was no use." Ridgway recalled: "That was that. I could do no more. From now on the blood was upon Model's head. His chief of staff was a wiser man. I told him he could go back under a flag of truce and take his chances in the disaster that was sure to come. Or he could remain in our custody as a prisoner of war. He did not debate this option long. He chose to stay."[34]

Model, who had long been critical of Friedrich Paulus for surrendering at Stalingrad, faced the end stoically and resolutely. "A field marshal does not become a prisoner," he told his cohorts. "Such a thing is just not possible." After ordering his staff to disperse, he went with his aide and two other officers to a forest north of Düsseldorf. There, in the presence of his aide, he shot and killed himself. The aide buried him and marked the grave. After the war, Model's son disinterred the body and reburied it in a German soldiers' cemetery in the Hürtgen Forest.[35]

On April 16 and 17, the German soldiers in the Ruhr gave up and surrendered by the tens of thousands. The Niagara of prisoners nearly overwhelmed the Americans. They were, the official Army historian wrote, "young men, old men, arrogant SS troops, dejected infantrymen, paunchy reservists, female nurses and technicians, teen-age members of the Hitler Youth, stiffly correct, monocled Prussians, enough to gladden the heart of a Hollywood casting director." They arrived "in every conceivable manner," he wrote, "plodding wearily on foot; some in civilian automobiles; assorted military vehicles or on horseback; some pushing perambulators; one group riding bicycles in precise military formation; a horsedrawn artillery unit under faultless control; some carrying black bread and wine; others with musical instruments—accordions, guitars; a few bringing along wives or girl friends in a mistaken hope they might share captivity . . . Many a German soldier walked mile after mile before finding an American not too occupied with other duties to bother to accept his surrender." A GI from Parker's 78th Division started out for a compound in Wuppertal escorting sixty-eight POWs. By the time he arrived, the sixty-eight had grown to twelve hundred. The civilians, the historian wrote, "sought to ingratiate themselves with the conquerors by insisting that they had never been Nazis, that they were happy the Americans had come. There were no Nazis, no ex-Nazis, not even any Nazi sympathizers any more."[36]

Ridgway, Van Fleet and other American generals were stunned by the ever-mounting numbers. They had been told there were about 125,000 German troops in the Ruhr. In fact, there were two and a half times that many: 317,000, remnants of two German armies, three corps, and fourteen divisions. This was more men than the Russians had taken at Stalingrad or the Americans, British and French in Tunisia. Ridgway's XVIII Airborne Corps accepted the surrender of about half the total bag: 160,092, including 25 generals. In addition, the corps liberated some 200,000 slave laborers and 5,639 Allied prisoners of war. Among the many captured German Army vehicles was Model's posh Mercedes-Benz staff car, which Ridgway gave to Omar Bradley.[37]

On April 18, at 6:30 A.M., Ridgway reported to Hodges that the last organized resistance within the Ruhr pocket had been eliminated. When Brereton got this word, he noted proudly in his diary that the Ruhr operation had been "the largest double envelopment in military history." Omar Bradley sent Ridgway "congratulations" for the Ruhr operation and, a month later, recommended to Eisenhower that Ridgway be promoted to lieutenant general. It was at this time (April 15) that Eisenhower, in a cable to Marshall, described Ridgway as "one of the finest soldiers this war has produced." When Bradley's recommendation for Ridgway's promotion arrived at SHAEF, Eisenhower hastily endorsed it: "He has never undertaken a job that he has not performed in a soldierly and even brilliant way. He has commanded airborne operations and a corps in a normal battle line. Everyone with whom he has served speaks of him in the highest terms. Definitely a fighting leader." Ridgway's promotion to three stars would become effective on June 4.[38]

☆51☆

ALL THIS TIME, Bradley had been driving east and southeast into the heart of Germany with three American armies. Each army had advanced with phenomenal speed, meeting only occasional pockets of resistance. Simpson's Ninth, spearheaded by Ray McLain's XIX Corps, had reached the "stop line" at the Elbe River first, at 8 P.M. on April 11, near Magdeburg. Hodges' First, delayed by a fanatical pocket of Germans in the Harz Mountains, had arrived at the Elbe on April 20. Patton's Third, advancing in the extreme southern sector in concert with Hodges, had reached the stop line (the Mulde River) on the same day.[1]

On Bradley's left (north) flank, Montgomery's 21st Army Group had angled northeasterly from Münster toward the lower Elbe near Hamburg. Montgomery's mission was to protect Bradley's left flank, then cross the Elbe below Hamburg and advance to Lübeck-Wismar on the Baltic Sea, thereby "sealing off" Denmark, both from retreating Germans who might create a "redoubt" in Scandinavia and from the advancing Russians. Montgomery was displeased with this assignment. Reflecting the British view, he thought Marshall and Eisenhower had made a terrible (political) mistake in leaving Berlin for the Russians. Like Simpson, Hodges and Patton, Montgomery wanted to go to Berlin, not to the Baltic.[2]

Day by day, Montgomery fell farther and farther behind. Moreover, it was soon apparent that his planned Elbe crossing would not be an opportunistic jump but, rather, another Rhine-like extravaganza. Eisenhower, growing increasingly concerned, tactfully prodded Montgomery in letters and volunteered to give him American troops. Accepting only a northward extension of Simpson's boundary line, Montgomery declined all other offers of American assistance. Finally losing all patience, Eisenhower flew to Montgomery's CP on April 20 and insisted that Montgomery—then refining his elaborate, set-piece Elbe crossing—speed up his offensive by accepting his offer of American troops. By then the Russian armies were encircling Berlin. There was a good possibility that the Russian armies would beat Montgomery to Lübeck-Wismar and keep going right into Denmark.[3]

Bowing to this heavy face-to-face pressure from Eisenhower, Montgomery, in Bradley's words, "finally and reluctantly agreed" to accept help from the Americans. That help, Eisenhower told Montgomery, would be Ridgway's XVIII Airborne Corps, which had completed its Ruhr operations and as yet had no other assigned tasks. As Bradley later put it, Eisenhower had all but forced Ridgway's corps on Montgomery.[4]

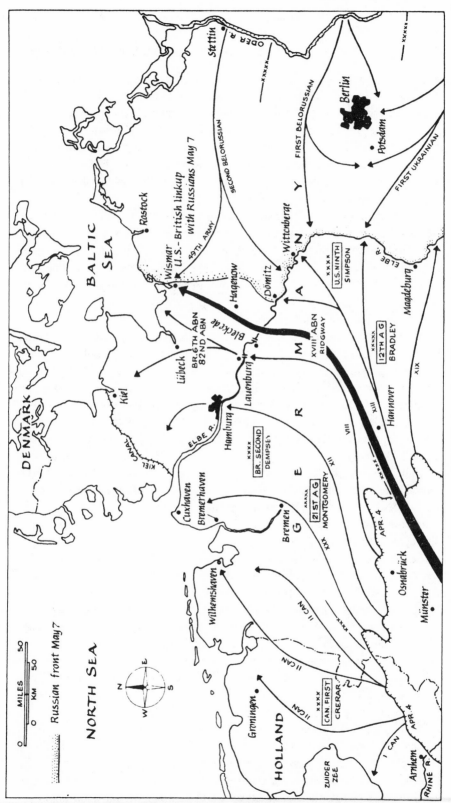

Allied Dash to the Baltic

On the day that Eisenhower was committing his corps to further action with 21st Army Group, Ridgway was taking a rare breather. His aide, Don Faith, had commandeered a "handsome, relatively modern" and "elegantly furnished" house in the "beautiful Westphalian countryside" south of the Ruhr River. Faith had moved its owner and his wife into a garage apartment and turned the house over to Ridgway. It was a welcome change from the "filthy, dirty places" where Ridgway had flopped down (usually in his sleeping bag) during the eighteen-day Ruhr campaign.[5]

Forty-eight hours after Ridgway had moved into the house, orders for the new assignment arrived from SHAEF headquarters. Ridgway wrote that he "hated to leave my comfortable little eyrie," but he welcomed another opportunity to have a crack at the Germans. Moreover, his corps objective was deep in the heartland of Germany, not too far from Berlin, where Ridgway, like every other American general, hoped to wind up even though the city was now exclusively a Russian military objective.

Ridgway left the eyrie at once by jeep, to find Montgomery and get his directive. It turned out that Montgomery's CP was twenty-five miles southeast of Hamburg. For Ridgway it was a brutal trip: 250 miles, the last few hours in sleet. Upon his arrival, at 6 P.M., Montgomery received Ridgway warmly—"he had great confidence in me, apparently," Ridgway wrote—and although himself a teetotaler, offered Ridgway wine with his dinner. Montgomery's directive to Ridgway was very broad and general: XVIII Airborne Corps, to be inserted between Dempsey's Second Army and Simpson's Ninth Army, would protect the right (east) flank of Dempsey's army in its advance across the Elbe to the Baltic. Later that same night, Dempsey outlined the plans in greater detail. After a few hours sleep, Ridgway returned 250 miles by jeep to his eyrie, completing in twenty-six hours what he would later describe as "as wearying a journey as I ever made."[6]

The next day, April 23, Ridgway visited Bradley at his advance CP. Bradley's staff drafted orders which formally attached XVIII Airborne Corps to Ninth Army for administrative purposes, but placed it "under control" of Dempsey's Second Army. In a private chat, Bradley outlined the reasons for this unusual mission—Eisenhower's dismay at Montgomery's turtle-like progress and his plans for an elaborate Elbe crossing—and made it clear that Ridgway's main task was to put some ginger in Montgomery's advance to the Baltic. As Bradley later wrote: "No one could build a fire under Monty better than Ridgway." The overriding consideration for the mission was thus speed—the more dazzling the better.[7]

Ridgway's first task was to select the divisions he would need and get them moving. All were to be drawn from the forces in the Ruhr, and here Ridgway had highest priority. His first choice was almost a foregone conclusion: the 82nd Airborne. It was no longer required for strategic reserve or occupation; it could move faster; it was still Ridgway's first love and he wanted it under his command in what would certainly be the last operation of the war.* His next pick was Bryant Moore's 8th Infantry Division, which had performed so well for him in the Ruhr campaign. The third was Bob Hasbrouck's 7th Armored Division, which had fought closely with the 82nd in the Bulge under XVIII Airborne Corps command and which had done an outstanding job for Van Fleet's III Corps in the Ruhr. In addition, Ridgway would be assigned Eric Bols's 6th British Airborne Division, which was already in the assembly area near Lauenburg.[9]

After issuing the necessary orders to get the American divisions cracking, Ridgway took a closer look at Dempsey's plan for the Elbe crossing. Briefly, it was as follows: Evelyn Barker's 8 Corps, which had relieved XVIII Airborne Corps after VARSITY, would lead the assault, on May 1, at Lauenburg. Barker would then build a bridge, as Ritchie had done at Wesel. The British would cross first, as they had at Wesel. After the British had crossed, XVIII Airborne Corps would be permitted to use the bridge, probably gaining access no earlier than D+5 (May 6) but more probably on D+6 (May 7). The first American division across the Elbe would then join the 6th Airborne Division, turn east to Bleckede and Darchau and build bridges in those two places to get the remainder of XVIII Airborne Corps across the Elbe. The plan was almost an exact duplicate of the Rhine crossing at Wesel, which had put the Americans firmly in the back seat.[10]

If the plan was allowed to stand as drawn, there was no way Ridgway could carry out his primary mission of building a fire under Montgomery. He would be stuck behind the Elbe (as Simpson was stuck behind the Rhine), crawling the walls while Barker's 8 Corps slowly inched ahead or stopped for tea, and the Russians would certainly beat Montgomery to Lübeck-Wismar and occupy Denmark.

The solution was to find a means to artfully "by-pass" the British at Lauenburg. With this in mind, Ridgway flew up to the Elbe to survey the situation at Bleckede, where he was to build a bridge in due course. He walked along the west bank of the Elbe, which was at this point about a thousand feet wide. There were plenty of Germans on the other side and they were "still full of fight," Ridgway wrote, but they had not yet organized at Bleckede to resist a river crossing. "I exposed myself as much as I thought necessary, but drew no fire," Ridgway went on. "Across the wide river, all was silent."[11]

During this reconnaissance, Ridgway conceived the solution to the problem: throw bridges across the Elbe at Bleckede immediately—before the Germans organized a defense. With its own bridges, XVIII Airborne Corps would not have to wait five or six days to cross the Elbe behind Barker's 8 Corps. It could

---

* He was also determined to have the 82nd selected as a part of the American occupation force in Berlin. Moving the division close to Berlin enhanced its chances of selection. George Marshall queried Eisenhower to ask why the 82nd, which had suffered so many casualties, was going back into combat, whereas the 13th Airborne Division had yet to be committed. Eisenhower replied that "all assignments to that corps were made in the interests of speed and economy in fuel and transportation."[8]

cross simultaneously with the British and then set a fast pace for Lübeck, hurrying the British onward by example.

Ridgway's solution, in turn, generated a considerable number of new problems for him. First, he had to further speed up the assembly of his corps forces, not at Lauenburg, as planned, but at Bleckede. This required a new blizzard of high-priority orders and much telephonic cajoling. Second, his corps engineer, Benjamin S. Shute, had to bring forward (at an unprecedented pace) bridging equipment and engineers to build the bridges. All this was further complicated when Montgomery—perhaps in part spurred by Ridgway's frenetic activity—advanced the British D day at Lauenburg from May 1 to April 29.[12]

Ridgway chose Gavin's 82nd Airborne Division to make the assault crossing at Bleckede. On the afternoon of April 29 (the British D day), the division, Gavin wrote, "was strung out, moving by truck and rail, more than 200 miles from Cologne." Leading the division was Ekman's 505, due to arrive by nightfall. Ridgway and Dempsey came to Gavin's CP, and Ridgway proposed the assault crossing immediately—that night, soon after the 505 arrived. Gavin wrote later that "it appeared to be a feasible undertaking, although a bit marginal and plans were made accordingly."

Ekman's 505 would go first during the night and secure the bridgehead. Work on the bridges would commence immediately thereafter. When Tucker's 504 arrived later in the day, it would come across. In the meantime, Ridgway would order Moore's 8th Division to send four infantry battalions to reinforce Gavin.[13]

Gavin designated two battalions of the 505 to lead the assault. These were Walter DeLong's 1st and the 2nd, newly commanded by William Dudley. They would cross in flimsy collapsible wood-and-canvas British assault boats like those Julian Aaron Cook had used to cross the Waal to capture the Nijmegen bridge. No lifebelts could be found. If a boat capsized, the swimmers would attempt to rescue the nonswimmers.[14]

The assault force, led by Bill Ekman, commenced crossing the Elbe at 1 A.M., April 30, in four waves aiming for four separate "beachheads." A 505 veteran recalled that the crossing was not carried out with wild enthusiasm. The 505, now beefed up with hundreds of green replacements, no longer had the old "cohesion or leadership" in the ranks. It was more like a group of strangers on a bizarre journey in the night. For the old hands, caution was the watchword. They knew the war would be over in a matter of days; nobody wanted to take risks now, or be the last man killed.

Apart from a few navigational errors, the crossing was made with ease. Ekman led his men ashore and routed the sleepy Germans out of their foxholes with rifles, using flashlights to find them. The only "surprise" encountered was a new German weapon: a magnetic mine which was preset to explode after so many vehicles had passed. One went off, throwing a jeep "high into the air, turning it over several times." Gavin recalled they had "never seen anything like it and it took us some time to figure out what kind of explosion it had been."[15]

By dawn, the 505 had cleared and "secured" the bridgehead. At 0530 hours,

XVIII Airborne Corps engineer Shute moved a small army of engineers forward to commence construction of the first bridge: a heavy pontoon structure 1,184 feet long. Two engineer combat groups (each consisting of four or more engineer combat battalions plus bridge-building specialists) were employed: the combat-experienced 1143rd, commanded by West Pointer Donald A. Phelan, and the green 1130th, commanded by Shute's West Point classmate James L. Green.

The Germans soon became aware of what was going on and attacked the bridge builders with heavy artillery. Ridgway, learning of this, hurried down to the bridge site. Later, in a letter to Bradley and Simpson, he described this rain of artillery fire (especially during one forty-minute period) as the heaviest and best directed he had experienced since Normandy.[16]

In his war memoir *Soldier,* Ridgway wrote that in the face of this intense fire, the engineers were less than heroic. They were "rather inexperienced engineer units," he said, "who had never been under fire" and didn't like it. "They left the river and took shelter" behind trees and in ditches "and all work came to a halt." Furious, Ridgway walked out on the finished portion of the bridge amid the rain of shells to prove (as he had on the Douve bridge in Normandy) that artillery shells exploding in water were relatively harmless—"a lot of noise, but not too much danger." He then, in no uncertain terms, ordered the engineer battalion commander to get his men back to work: "I don't see any reason why an engineer shouldn't get killed the same as a doughboy," Ridgway said, "and a lot of doughboys are going to be killed unless you get those bridges built."[17]

Later, the engineers would sharply dispute Ridgway's recollection of that incident. They pointed out to him that Phelan's 1143rd, which was assigned responsibility for the pontoon bridge, was not "rather inexperienced," but "combat-hardened." Its men had not bugged out but had continued the work right through the artillery barrage. Had they bugged out, as Ridgway claimed, there would have been no finished portion of the bridge for Ridgway to walk on. Furthermore, they argued, Ridgway may have misinterpreted what he saw. Men who appeared to be ducking for cover under the bridge decking were men who were required to be there, fitting the bridge pieces together. Men who appeared to be running off the bridge in fear were actually engaged in bringing forward preassembled bridge sections. There were no men seeking shelter behind trees or in ditches.[18]

Confronted with this explanation, Ridgway conceded he might have been in error in minor details, such as saying the engineers were "inexperienced," but he was "positive" of his major point: "at the time I appeared at the bridge site, work had been suspended and the men had taken cover."[19]

Regardless of who was right, Ridgway's stroll on the bridge in the face of that vicious rain of German artillery shells (which earned him a second Silver Star) caused considerable concern among his staff. Occurring this late in the war, it seemed a pointless risk, almost suicidal. When he heard about it, Doc Eaton gave Ridgway "a growl" (chewing out), but Ridgway "growled" back that it was his "duty." The aide, Don Faith, who had dutifully accompanied

Ridgway through countless such risks, was also on the bridge with Ridgway. Faith, Eaton recalled, had been "scared pink." The next day, Eaton said, Faith asked to be relieved of his job. Eaton recalled: "I told him, 'Your trouble is you're a little shell-shocked. I'll ask the Old Man to relieve you for one day. You stay here and sleep.' He got over it." Perhaps not quite: Faith ended the war with ulcers.[20]

Few in XVIII Airborne Corps fully understood how much that particular bridge meant to Ridgway. It was, of course, the key element in his alternate plan. The plan itself, as Gavin said, was "a bit marginal." If the engineers failed to quickly span the Elbe, Gavin and his slim force would be imperiled on the opposite bank and the principal mission of Ridgway's corps—to goad the British to Lübeck-Wismar—might fail.

Ridgway remained at the bridge site to whip the engineers along. He telephoned 82nd Airborne headquarters and in no uncertain terms ordered the division staff to get the artillery fire off the bridge site by counterbattery fire and aggressive attacks on the opposite shore. After five hours the German artillery petered out, then totally stopped, for reasons unknown—perhaps the artillerymen ran out of ammo. In any case, Shute and his army of engineers, in a remarkable feat, completed the big pontoon bridge in a record thirteen hours and, in addition, built a treadway bridge in a record six hours and fifteen minutes (suffering thirty-two casualties in the process).[21]

The bridges ensured the success of Ridgway's "marginal" alternate plan, and consequently he was very proud of the outcome. In letters to Bradley, Simpson and Dempsey, he praised his corps staff and Shute and his engineers to the high heavens for their "unique" and "remarkable" accomplishments. To Omar Bradley he boasted: "The corps is doing all but the impossible and will probably accomplish that too, as it has done in those previous missions you have been good enough to assign it."[22]

To the north, Barker's 8 Corps was crossing at Lauenburg. The British 6th Airborne Division, which was to cross there and join Ridgway's XVIII Airborne Corps for the all-out drive to Lübeck-Wismar, was assigned a low priority—after the British armor—but Eric Bols resorted to a clever ruse to get his men across first. The tankers wore black berets; the paratroopers, maroon berets—with black inner linings. The paratroopers turned their berets inside out—so they were black, not maroon—and on April 30, went across disguised as tankers. By means of this "damned smart stunt" (as Ridgway called it), the 6th got across the Elbe long before their assigned time and quickly joined XVIII Airborne Corps.[23]

On the day Ridgway was bridging the Elbe, April 30, Adolf Hitler, cowering in a beseiged Berlin bunker, committed suicide, and the doomed Third Reich "government" devolved to Grand Admiral Karl Dönitz. On the evening of May 1—as Gavin was rapidly expanding the bridgehead—Radio Berlin announced Hitler's death and Dönitz's appointment. After hearing this news, the German Army began surrendering, wherever possible to Americans and British, rather than to Russians.[24]

Gavin recalled that by late morning of the next day, May 2, "large groups of Germans began to appear . . . milling about indecisively" and "not particularly desirous to fight." After all these years of grim combat, Gavin found this to be an "eerie sight." Approaching cautiously—"taking our lives into our hands"—Gavin drove up to the groups in his jeep. "They wanted to surrender," he wrote. And they did, then and there, by the tens of thousands. Later that day, in a "cold and very proper" ceremony in Gavin's CP—the palace at Ludwigslust—Gavin had the astounding personal experience of accepting the surrender of the entire German 21st Army Group, commanded by Kurt von Tippelskirch. This force consisted of 150,000 German soldiers with all their impedimenta.[25]

In the meanwhile, the race to beat the Russians to Lübeck-Wismar proceeded. Under Dempsey's direction, Barker's 8 Corps angled the British 5th and 11th armoured divisions directly north to Lübeck; and they got there with astonishing speed. Ridgway's objective was Wismar, slightly to the east of Lübeck and, of course, closest to the oncoming Russians—the Forty-Ninth Army. Dempsey requested that for prestige purposes, Ridgway send Eric Bols's 6th Parachute Division to Wismar, thereby giving the British the glory of being first to link up with the Russians. At first Ridgway refused, but after reflecting on all the hardships the British had endured in the war, he changed his mind. Bols just barely beat the Russians to Wismar, but, as it turned out, in what was later described as an unplanned maneuver (but which was no doubt intentional) Jim Gavin's advance patrols had gotten there ahead of him by about one hour. However, Ridgway down-played the Gavin linkup, giving the long-suffering British nation an overdue ration of cheer.[26]

The XVIII Airborne Corps achieved its principal mission of spurring the British forward to "seal off" the Jutland Peninsula from the Russians. In the rush of end-of-the-war news, this operation received scant notice, but among the professionals, it was well remarked. In truth, it had been an astonishing achievement, surely breaking all records for speed and efficiency. In a mere seven days, Ridgway had organized a corps and moved it cross-country 250 miles to the Elbe. Within two more days he had forced a major river crossing under intense enemy artillery fire. In the next two days he had advanced sixty miles to the Baltic Sea. In the last phase, east of the Elbe, his corps had accepted the surrender of 359,796 German soldiers, including fifty generals. Bradley would later describe the operation as "remarkable"; George Marshall, not given to superlatives, as "sensational."[27]

The linkup between the Americans and the Russians was everywhere a momentous, and often riotous, occasion. In Ridgway's sector, the XVIII Airborne Corps confronted three Russian corps, each numbering about the size of one American division. A "neutral zone" about one kilometer wide was established, then Ridgway, Gavin and the other American generals exchanged visits with the Russian generals. The Americans found the Russians at first to have, as Ridgway put it, "a suspicious, stubborn, ill-mannered nature." But as the contacts increased, with lavish dinners and much liquor, the Russians became more amiable, and "a wary but fairly pleasant official and social relationship" ensued.[28]

One unforgettable meeting with the Russians was that of Charles Billingslea, commanding Gavin's 325th Glider Regiment. In a party with some Russian officers of his rank, as the vodka flowed freely, the Russians became more and more boisterous and eager to show how tough they were. One Russian officer ran up to the second floor of the house and jumped out the window. He landed without injury, slapped Billingslea on the back and pointed to the window. This was a challenge the tall and tough paratrooper Billingslea could not refuse, so he strode up the stairs and jumped. He landed upright on one foot—and broke his leg.[29]

As it developed, Taylor's 101st Airborne Division also got in on the "final kill." The foray proved to be no less interesting than Gavin's, but it took place in a far different setting.[30]

Eisenhower and Bradley remained convinced almost to the end that Hitler and his cronies would withdraw from Berlin to a "redoubt" in the mountains of southern Bavaria and wage a tough, bitter fight to the death. Chapman's green 13th Airborne Division had been put on standby for a possible jump into the "redoubt" area (Operation EFFECTIVE). But when Bradley commandeered IX Troop Carrier aircraft to support his April drive to the Elbe with ammo and gasoline, the jump had to be canceled, in part for want of airlift. Another reason for the cancellation was that Eisenhower and Bradley wanted a more powerful and experienced force to cut off or invade the redoubt. Accordingly, Patton's Third and Sandy Patch's Seventh armies were ordered to converge in southern Bavaria, near Munich.[31]

After the collapse of the Ruhr "pocket," when the 101st was no longer required as a strategic reserve, SHAEF assigned it to Patch's Seventh Army for the redoubt campaign, more or less in place of the 13th Airborne Division. Lead elements of the 101st (Bob Sink's 506) entrained on April 20 and traveled 145 miles to Merchingen. The rest of the division (Chappuis' 502, Harper's 327 and artillery) arrived by April 25. But the 101, which was sorely lacking in transport, was not really needed: the Germans were collapsing and frantically retreating, and the area was swarming with Patton's and Patch's tanks and motorized troops, which (as the 101 historian wrote) "advanced like lava, flowing down the roads, into valleys . . ."[32]

For the next week, the 101 was assigned limited "occupational" tasks. On April 28, Bob Sink's 506 moved into captured Landsberg (outside Munich), where Hitler had been imprisoned in 1923 after his unsuccessful *Putsch,* and where he wrote *Mein Kampf.* In this general area there were six Nazi concentration camps, including the infamous Dachau. Taylor's men were among the first to enter these wretched and ghastly places. Taylor wrote that the men "smelled the stench of the prisoner dead, many burned by the guards only a few hours before the arrival of American troops." The men who saw those camps, the 101 historian wrote, "would never forget them," and many tough paratroopers, looking on this horror, became physically ill.[33]

On May 4, Taylor at last received a combat mission, the final one of the war for the division: a 101 combat team would move forward and capture Berchtesgaden. Taylor gave this glamorous assignment to Bob Sink's 506. The men hoped to entrap many Nazi bigwigs there (and collect souvenirs), especially at Hitler's chalet, Ober Salzburg, and his famous mountain aerie, Eagle's Nest. The problem was, every unit of Third, Seventh and French First armies also wanted the honor of capturing Berchtesgaden, and a mad scramble ensued. Sink pushed his men hard through the mountains, but a motorized unit of the American 3rd Infantry Division got there first.[34]

In the days following, Taylor and his men "occupied" the Berchtesgaden area. They accepted the surrender of many German Army and Nazi notables, the prize being Field Marshal Albert Kesselring, who, after the loss of the Remagen bridge, had replaced Von Rundstedt as commander in chief of the western front. Taylor's men also found and impounded Hermann Göring's entire, priceless art collection, much of which had been taken from the museums of German-occupied countries. In addition, Taylor himself found the fabulous Salzburg musical-instrument museum, which had been moved to a private castle near Berchtesgaden to keep it safe from Allied bombers. The Eagle's Nest, however, proved to be "something of a disappointment"—unused by Hitler for the previous six months and "nothing really there" except a magnificent living-room rug.[35]

It was done now—the war with Germany was over. At 2:41 A.M., May 7, representatives appointed by Karl Dönitz signed a surrender instrument in Eisenhower's headquarters in Rheims. According to its terms, the surrender would take legal effect at 0001 hours, May 9. But at 0500, May 7, Bradley telephoned his army commanders and told them to "hold firmly in place and risk no more casualties."[36]

At that hour, the approximately sixty thousand American paratroopers in the ETO were deployed as follows:

● Ridgway's XVIII Airborne Corps at Hagenow, Germany, near the Baltic Sea. Gavin's 82nd Division (504, 505, 325 regiments) nearby at Ludwigslust.
● Taylor's 101st Airborne Division (502, 506, 327 regiments) at Berchtesgaden.
● Miley's 17th Airborne Division (507, 513, 194 regiments) in SHAEF reserve, performing occupation duty in the Ruhr near Essen.
● Chapman's 13th Airborne Division (515, 517, 88, 326 regiments) still on standby in Auxerre, France (near Troyes) for possible airborne operations.
● Ballard's 501 and Lindquist's 508 independent regiments on standby at French bases for possible POW-camp jumps.[37]

Two of the three Axis partners, Italy and Germany, had been crushed, but the third, Japan, hung on fanatically. As a final step in the Pacific war, the Combined Chiefs had approved a two-step amphibious invasion of the Japanese homeland: Kyushu on November 1, 1945, and Honshu on March 1, 1946. The invasion would be commanded by Douglas MacArthur. At Yalta, Stalin had agreed to enter the war against Japan within "several months" of Germany's collapse, and would begin with an attack on Japanese forces in Manchuria.[38]

MacArthur required vast reinforcements from the ETO for his invasion of Japan. Even before the Third Reich collapsed, SHAEF had been drawing "redeployment" plans. In choosing these reinforcements, the general policy guideline was that units (or GIs) that had fought in both North Africa and the ETO would be exempt from Pacific duty. As a result, the 82nd Airborne Division was not to go, but the 101st, 17th and 13th were possible candidates.[39]

MacArthur soon notified the War Department that he planned to utilize only two airborne divisions in the invasion of the Japanese home islands. He had one on hand, Joe Swing's 11th; he would need one other from the ETO. SHAEF chose Taylor's 101. At the same time, SHAEF decided that Gavin's 82nd would be deployed to Berlin (and Frankfurt) on occupation duty; Chapman's 13th would go to the Pacific as a regular (nonairborne) infantry division; and Miley's 17th would be utilized as a collection organization for "high point" paratroopers and gliderists eligible for discharge, shipped to the States and deactivated.[40]†

At first MacArthur expressed no desire for FAAA or XVIII Airborne Corps. SHAEF thus decided that the "American elements" of FAAA would be sent to the U.S. occupation zone in Berlin. They would be commanded by Ridgway. It was a job (he wrote later) that he "didn't look forward to with any great eagerness." He was tired—very tired—and what he wanted most at that time was furlough in the States with his wife.[41]

He made a personal request to Eisenhower for a week's furlough and it was "very graciously" granted. By that time, Ridgway had his own C-47, marked "Peggy R" on the nose and "The Barque Good Fortune" on the fuselage. His personal pilot, William M. Williams, and the crew chief, Harold T. Krick, rigged it with extra fuel tanks inside the cabin holding twelve hundred gallons. On May 26, Ridgway left for the States, taking his battlefield family: Don Faith, Jim Casey, Frank Farmer and several others. They flew by way of Scotland, Iceland and Greenland, arriving in Washington, D.C., on May 28.[42]

In Washington, one of Marshall's chief planners, John E. (Ed) Hull, had startling news for Ridgway: MacArthur had decided, after all, to employ Ridgway's XVIII Airborne Corps in the invasion of Japan. Ridgway was delighted by this "far happier" and "more challenging" assignment. The corps was ordered to return to the States by ship, reporting to Camp Campbell, Kentucky. FAAA's Chief of Staff, Floyd Parks, was designated commanding general of American forces in Berlin, replacing Ridgway.[43]

This new and wholly unexpected development had the effect of extending Ridgway's one-week furlough to about two months—until August 4. As was customary for returning high-ranking generals, he drew a two-week "assignment" to the fabulous Greenbrier resort (which the Army had taken over and temporarily named Ashford General Hospital) in White Sulphur Springs, West

---

† The point system was based on length of service, time in combat, awards for valor, dependents, etc.

Virginia. He and Peggy had a "delightful" time there, he wrote his driver, Frank Farmer, who, like Faith and Casey, was at home on extended furlough. "The bass season was closed," Ridgway wrote, "but tennis and hiking were at their best . . ." The Ridgways then spent the month of July "deep in the Maine woods," he wrote a friend.[44]

All during this time, Ridgway, who was in and out of Peggy's apartment at the Wardman Park Hotel in Washington, kept in touch with Doc Eaton and others at XVIII Airborne Corps by mail and cable. Doc Eaton's letters were lugubrious. He was ill and depressed—the injuries from the Normandy glider crash still plagued him—and he thought he would probably be placed on (limited) special duty. The corps artillery commander, Matty Mathewson, was also in a "bad way" (arthritis, bad back) and would probably "go out of the Army." Eaton was trying to get Charles L. Dasher, from the 75th Division, to replace Mathewson. The corps G-2, Whitfield Jack, was going home to his law practice in Shreveport; he would be replaced by a Ridgway favorite, Gavin's G-2, Walter Winton.[45]

In early August the XVIII Airborne Corps began arriving at Fort Campbell. By that time, Ridgway had decided to organize a small "advanced planning" party and fly ahead to MacArthur's headquarters in Manila. They would depart Campbell by commercial air on August 13 and San Francisco by military aircraft on August 14. The party would total twelve men: Ridgway; the new corps artillery commander, Charles Dasher; the new G-2, Walter Winton; the G-3, Day Surles; and his assistant, Hank Adams, recovered from his severe bout of malaria; the G-4, Bill Moorman; the signal officer, Lee R. Williams; the engineer, Benjamin Shute; plus Don Faith, Casey and Farmer, and an enlisted stenographer. Five of the eight officers in the party—Adams, Faith, Moorman, Surles, Winton—were the core of Ridgway's "inner circle."[46]

Doc Eaton would not go with them to Manila; he would remain at Campbell until the corps had departed, then go to other, less arduous duties. Ridgway would have to pick another chief of staff. Eaton felt "terrible" about letting Ridgway down: "I was crippled from Normandy. Because I wasn't getting enough exercise, what little brains I had were not working. I felt that I was falling down on him. I wasn't smart enough; I was a detriment. He was getting too big for me." But Ridgway had only respect for him: "Doc was a very, very modest man, one of the most modest I have ever seen. And completely honest. After the war he did not want to be a general officer."[47]

By the time Ridgway's party departed Campbell, Russia had attacked Manchuria, atomic bombs had been dropped on Hiroshima and Nagasaki and the Japanese Government was desperately attempting to arrange a surrender. The military transport took off from San Francisco on August 14, the same day Japan surrendered. Ridgway heard the news over the radio: "I sent a message to the pilot, suggesting he turn around and take me home. Quite properly, he refused. I didn't greatly care. The fighting was over. The world was at last at peace. I leaned back in my seat and went to sleep."[48]

Sources and Acknowledgments

The information presented in this book is derived from several principal sources: official government archives, interviews with and/or letters from participants, and published histories and memoirs.

Of the archival papers, the most valuable were those of General Matthew B. Ridgway, which are on deposit at the United States Army Military History Institute, at Carlisle, Pennsylvania (USAMHI). These extensive and well-organized papers, contained in sixty-plus boxes, include virtually all of Ridgway's official and personal correspondence, 82nd Airborne Division and XVIII Airborne Corps diaries, after-action reports, maps and histories, substantial biographical material, plus speeches, newspaper and magazine clippings, etc. In addition, there are half a dozen transcripts of taped interviews with Ridgway, most notably a long and thorough oral history conducted by John M. Blair (no kin to the author) in 1971 and 1972.

I and my wife, Joan, who worked side by side with me on this book as she had on many previous books, spent about two months at the USAMHI, immersed in the Ridgway Papers and others on deposit there and also in the stacks of the USAMHI Library. In every phase of this research we were ably and hospitably assisted by the USAMHI staff, headed by Colonel Donald P. Shaw. We wish to thank especially Archivist-Historian Dr. Richard J. Sommers, custodian of the Ridgway Papers and other papers, and his two assistants, Valerie Metzler and David Keogh.

Here, too, we wish to thank the Ridgways. Twice during the work with the Ridgway Papers, General and Mrs. Ridgway received us in their home. While these visits were not formal interviews, they proved to be invaluable in many ways. We found General Ridgway (nearing ninety years of age) to be in good health, vigorous, mentally keen and still history-minded. He suggested several research areas to explore which proved useful, provided us with research materials and later responded to a great many written queries from us which helped clarify certain murky or controversial points, not least the command muddle at St. Vith.

Other papers or oral histories at USAMHI which proved particularly useful were those of: Omar N. Bradley and his wartime aide, Chester B. Hansen; Floyd L. Parks (First Allied Airborne Army Headquarters Diary); Ralph P. (Doc) Eaton (a report on 82nd Airborne operations in the Mediterranean); Maxwell D. Taylor (oral history); Mark W. Clark (oral history); Hobart R. Gay (oral history); Charles LaChaussee (unpublished chronicle of the 1st Battalion, 517th Parachute Infantry Regiment); John P. Lucas (diary); William P. Yarborough (oral history); William C. Sylvan (First Army Headquarters Diary).

We also profited from visits to the George C. Marshall Research Library, in Lexington, Virginia, and the magnificent library at the United States Military Academy, West Point, New York. We especially wish to extend our thanks to the West Point Librarian, Egon A. Weiss, and to the Chief, Special Collections,

Robert E. Schnare, who valuably assisted us with guidance, cheer and research materials.

Following this archival research, with the help of World War II airborne alumni associations and the West Point *Register,* we were able to locate and interview and/or correspond with about one hundred fifty veterans of airborne operations in World War II. Particularly helpful to us in this search were airborne alumni activists Don Lassen, Dan Campbell, Joe Quade, Edward Siergiej, Jerry J. Hladik, George M. Rosie, George E. Koskimaki, Harry Phariss, Paul Brown and Richard L. Hoyt. The material developed by these interviews and letters proved to be invaluable in countless ways, not least in establishing the senior command sequences in the text (presented in chart form in the Appendix). Space limitations do not permit a list of all interviewees and correspondents; each, where quoted, is cited in the chapter notes. However, we extend special thanks to the following interviewees: James M. Gavin, Maxwell D. Taylor, Ralph P. (Doc) Eaton, Frank W. (Bill) Moorman, Walter F. Winton, Jr., A. Day Surles, Jr., Arthur G. Kroos, Emory S. (Hank) Adams, John H. (Mike) Michaelis, Ned D. Moore, and for assistance on Pacific airborne operations (see brief synopsis in Appendix), George M. Jones, Edward H. Lahti and George O. Pearson.

During the course of this phase of the research, we discovered that numerous historians, both amateur and professional, were at work on various aspects of World War II airborne operations. These men not only freely shared the fruits of their work with us but also responded to queries. We thank them all, and especially Allen L. Langdon, who is writing a long-overdue history of the 505th Parachute Infantry Regiment; Louis Hauptfleisch, who is amassing data on the 504th Parachute Infantry Regiment; Wayne Pierce, ditto the 325th Glider Regiment; Charles H. Doyle, who is writing a history of the independent 509th Parachute Battalion, and Dan Morgan, ditto the 551st Parachute Battalion. Additionally, we gratefully received from John W. Marr a hard-to-find history of the 507th Parachute Infantry Regiment, from Clark Archer his excellent monograph on the 517th Parachute Infantry Regiment, from X. B. Cox, Jr., a history of the 81st Antiaircraft Battalion, from Paul F. Oswald, portions of a history of the 680th Glider Field Artillery Battalion and from George M. Jones, a history of the 503rd Regimental Combat Team. Edson D. Raff, who is writing an autobiography, let us see those pages relevant to Ridgway and the 82nd Airborne Division. Philip Gowdy, who is writing a biography of Reuben Tucker, gave us background on his subject. William S. Triplet, veteran of the 7th Armored Division, kindly let us see portions of his autobiographical manuscript relating to St. Vith. We also profited by talks with John Duvall and Stuart Vogt, curators at the 82nd Airborne Museum, at Fort Bragg, North Carolina, and the Don F. Pratt Museum, at Fort Campbell, Kentucky, respectively.

We would like to extend our utmost gratitude to 505 historian Allen Langdon. He not only helped us in our initial research in countless ways, but also closely read the entire manuscript with an ex-paratrooper's critical eye. He flagged many technical and tactical errors, which we subsequently corrected.

Finally, published sources: We have freely used official and unofficial histories, biographies and memoirs. Space limitations prohibit the inclusion of a formal bibliography. Where such material is utilized, it is cited in the chapter notes.

On grand strategy, military politics and disputations, we drew heavily on our own *A General's Life*, which we recently researched and wrote in collaboration with Omar N. Bradley. In addition, we again mined the nine volumes constituting *The Papers of Dwight D. Eisenhower*, edited by Alfred D. Chandler and Louis Galambos, and Martin Blumenson's *The Patton Papers*, Volume II, as well as the official British and American army, navy and air-force histories of the campaigns in the Mediterranean and Europe. Additionally, we drew upon the recently published works focused on OVERLORD by John Keegan *(Six Armies in Normandy)*, Carlo D'Este *(Decision in Normandy)* and Max Hastings *(OVERLORD)*, as well as the two volumes of Nigel Hamilton's biography of Montgomery which have thus far appeared *(Monty* and *Master of the Battlefield)*.

Published memoirs by senior Allied paratrooper generals are plentiful. Towering over the lot is Gavin's memoir *On to Berlin*, which incorporates most of his previously published accounts of airborne combat operations *(Airborne Warfare* and *War and Peace in the Space Age)*. Ridgway and Maxwell D. Taylor provided further insights and personal experiences in their autobiographies *(Soldier* and *Swords and Plowshares*, respectively), but in each instance, regrettably, World War II was badly slighted. From the British, we have Richard N. Gale's *With the Sixth Airborne in Normandy* and Robert E. Urquhart's *Arnhem*, but, alas, nothing from Boy Browning. With permission of the publishers, herewith gratefully acknowledged, we have freely quoted from Gavin's *On to Berlin* (Viking) and Ridgway's *Soldier* (Harper & Row).

Two other American officers, both commanders of the independent 509th Parachute Battalion, have produced books, both on the same subject: the 509th's November 1942 jump into North Africa during Operation TORCH. These are Edson D. Raff's wartime quickie *We Jumped to Fight* and William P. Yarborough's later and more technical *Bail Out over North Africa*. Only those desiring close detail on this abortive operation will fully appreciate the literary labors of Raff and Yarborough.

From the American enlisted men, three noteworthy books emerged: *Those Devils in Baggy Pants*, by Ross S. Carter; *Currahee: A Paratrooper's Account of the Normandy Invasion*, by Donald Burgett; and *D-day with the Screaming Eagles*, by George E. Koskimaki. Taken together, these books provide a squad- or platoon-level view of airborne training and operations (and off-duty antics), but they are nonetheless quite fascinating to the student of airborne warfare and often deeply moving.

Each of the airborne divisions and some of the airborne regiments have published official histories. Most of these are disappointing—mere picture books and lists of names. Since they were not professionally written, all are error-prone and must be used with utmost care. The best by far is the 810-page 101 history, *Rendezvous with Destiny*, compiled by Leonard Rapport and Arthur Northwood, Jr., the most recent edition of which incorporates, in its entirety, S. L. A. Marshall's book *Bastogne*. Very disappointing is the 82nd Airborne Division history, a picture book entitled *Saga of the All American*, edited by Forrest W. Dawson. Also disappointing are Donald R. Pay's *Thunder from Heaven: The Story of the 17th Airborne Division, 1943–45;* William J. Blyth's *13th Airborne Division;* and (in the Southwest Pacific Theater) Edward M. Flanagan's *The Angels: A History of the 11th Airborne Division*. By and large, the published regimental histories are superior to the division histories:

The Devils in Baggy Pants (504th PIR); William G. Lord's *History of the 508th Parachute Infantry; Sky Riders, History of the 327/401 Glider Infantry,* by James L. McDonough and Richard S. Gardner, and Laurence Critchell's *Four Stars of Hell* (501st PIR). For more on Army airborne operations in the Pacific, see Harold Templeman's *The Return to Corregidor,* a history of the independent 503rd Parachute Regimental Combat Team.

Many American and British professional writers and/or historians have produced books about airborne operations in World War II. Among the Americans, the noteworthy volumes are *Night Drop* and *Bastogne,* by S. L. A. Marshall; *Paratrooper!* by Gerard M. Devlin; *Air Assault,* by John R. Galvin; *A Bridge Too Far,* by Cornelius Ryan (who, notwithstanding the film *The Longest Day,* slighted airborne operations in the book of the same title); *Glider Gang,* by Milton Dank; *Out of the Sky,* by Michael Hickey; *The Men of Bastogne,* by Fred MacKenzie; *Fighting Gliders* and *The Glider War,* both by James E. Mrazak. From the British, to name some, there are *Airborne at War,* by Napier Crookenden; *The Red Devils,* by G. G. Norton; *The Red Beret,* by Hilary St.G. Saunders; *Airborne to Battle,* by Maurice Tugwell.

From the Air Force or airmen, there are several noteworthy works, one of them outstanding. This is an official two-volume monograph by the Air Force troop-carrier historian, John C. Warren: *Airborne Missions in the Mediterranean 1942–1945* (Air University, 1955, 137 pages) and *Airborne Operations in World War II, European Theater* (Air University, 1956, 239 pages). These invaluable monographs have been republished by MA/AH Publishing, Eisenhower Hall, Manhattan, Kansas. In addition, there is *Out of the Blue: U.S. Airborne Operations in World War II,* by James A. Huston, which appears to have originated as an official Air Force troop-carrier history, but which was published in 1972 by Purdue University Press. Less valuable, and fatally canted where airborne operations are concerned, is the official *Army Air Forces in World War II,* by Wesley F. Craven and James L. Cate. Two memoirs were useful: Lewis H. Brereton's *Diaries,* and *With Prejudice,* by British Air Chief Marshal Arthur W. Tedder.

The photographs in this book, and on the jacket, were obtained from five sources, all governmental archives: the U.S. Army (USA), the U.S. Air Force (USAF), the USAMHI, the United States Military Academy (USMA), and the National Archives (NA). Most of the photographs are USA, obtained from the Department of Defense Audiovisual Agency (DAVA). Eleven USAF photographs were obtained from DAVA. Photographs from USAF, USAMHI, USMA and NA are credited in the layout; all others are USA.

Airborne Commanders

XVIII AIRBORNE CORPS HQ
Activated: 8/28/44

Commanding General
Matthew B. Ridgway

Corps Artillery
Theodore E. Buechler/Mathewson

Buechler relieved 12/19/44 by Lemuel Mathewson.

Chief of Staff
Ralph P. Eaton

Deputy Chief of Staff
James B. Quill

G-1 (Personnel)
Frederick M. Schellhammer

G-2 (Intelligence)
Whitfield Jack

G-3 (Plans)
A. Day Surles

G-4 (Logistics)
Frank W. Moorman

G-5 (Civil Affairs Officer)
Harry P. Cain

Air Officer
Jay G. Brown

Engineer
Benjamin S. Shute

82ND AIRBORNE DIVISION HQ
Activated: 8/15/42

Commanding General
Matthew B. Ridgway/Gavin

Ridgway promoted (8/28/44) to CG, XVIII Airborne Corps. Replaced by James M. Gavin.

Ass't Division Commander
William M. Miley/Keerans/Taylor/Gavin/Swift

Miley promoted (1/15/43) to CG, 17th Abn Div, replaced by Charles L. Keerans, KIA Sicily 7/11/43, replaced temporarily by Maxwell D. Taylor, replaced by Gavin 10/4/43, replaced by Ira P. Swift 12/10/44.

Division Artillery Commander
Joseph M. Swing/Taylor/March

Swing promoted (12/10/42) to CG, 11th Abn Div, replaced by Taylor, replaced by Francis A. March 2/22/44.

Chief of Staff
Maxwell D. Taylor/Eaton/Raff (acting)/Wienecke

Taylor to artillery commander, replaced 12/11/42 by Ralph P. Eaton. Eaton injured 6/6/44, temporarily replaced by Edson D. Raff, replaced 8/15/44 by Robert H. Wienecke.

G-1 (Personnel)
Ralph P. Eaton/Schellhammer/Ireland

Eaton to C/S 12/10/42, replaced by Frederick M. Schellhammer, replaced 8/15/44 by Alfred W. Ireland.

G-2 (Intelligence)
George E. Lynch/Jack/Winton/Berkut

Lynch to CO 142nd Inf 9/26/43, replaced by Whitfield Jack, replaced 8/15/44 by Walter F. Winton, replaced by Michael K. Berkut, 6/20/45.

G-3 (Plans)
R. Klemm Boyd/Jack/Turner/Wienecke/Norton

Boyd replaced 8/20/43 by Whitfield Jack, replaced 10/1/43 by Paul L. Turner, Jr., replaced 2/16/44 by Wienecke, replaced 8/28/44 by John Norton.

G-4 (Logistics)
Robert H. Wienecke/Zinn/Moorman/Marin

Wienecke replaced 2/16/44 by Bennie A. Zinn, WIA, replaced 6/7/44 by Frank W. Moorman, replaced 8/28/44 by Albert G. Marin.

325th Glider Infantry Regiment

States
CO: *Harry Leigh Lewis*
XO: *Jean D. Scott/Sitler*

1st Bn: *Herbert G. Sitler/Sanford*
2nd Bn: *Paul L. Turner/Swenson*

Scott relieved by Sitler, who was relieved by Teddy H. Sanford. Turner felled by severe ulcers, replaced by his XO, John H. Swenson.

North Africa-Sicily
CO: *Lewis*
XO: *Sitler*

1st Bn: *Sanford*
2nd Bn: *Swenson*

Salerno-Naples
CO: *Lewis*
XO: *Sitler*

1st Bn: *Sanford/Boyd*
2nd Bn: *Swenson*

Sanford replaced by R. Klemm Boyd (ex-82nd Div G-3) in October; Sanford reverted to Bn XO.

England
CO: *Lewis*
XO: *Sitler*

1st Bn: *Boyd*
2nd Bn: *Swenson*
3rd Bn: *Charles A. Carrell*

3rd Bn added, was ex-2nd Bn, 401 PIR.

Normandy
CO: *Lewis/Billingslea*
XO: *Sitler*

1st Bn: Boyd/Sanford
2nd Bn: Swenson/Leahy/Roy/Major
3rd Bn: Carrell/Gardner/Leahy

Lewis relieved of command, combat fatigue and ill; died the following year of cancer. Replaced by Charles Billingslea, former XO, 504, 8/21/44. Boyd injured in glider crash D+1, evacuated immediately, did not command in combat or return to 325. Replaced by his XO, Sanford. Swenson severely WIA and evacuated, temporarily replaced by Osmund A. Leahy. Leahy replaced by Roscoe Roy, former regimental S-3. Roy briefly in command, KIA, replaced by Charles (Tad) Major, former regimental S-4. Carrell relieved, replaced by Arthur W. Gardner. Gardner KIA and replaced by Leahy.

Medal of Honor: PFC Charles N. DeGlopper.

Holland
CO: Billingslea
XO: Sitler/Sanford

1st Bn: Sanford/Gerard
2nd Bn: Major/Ogden/Gibson
3rd Bn: Leahy

Sitler rotated to States; replaced by Sanford, who was replaced by Richard E. Gerard. Major WIA, as was his XO, Dave R. Stokely, and the next-senior officer, H. C. Tom Slaughter. All evacuated. Samuel Ogden temporarily commanded bn. Richard M. Gibson replaced Ogden.

Bulge
CO: Billingslea
XO: Sanford

1st Bn: Gerard
2nd Bn: Gibson/Ostberg/Major
3rd Bn: Leahy

Gibson WIA about 1/3/45, replaced by Edwin J. Ostberg, ex-507 PIR. Ostberg KIA 2/2/45, replaced by Tad Major returning from hospital.

Spring 1945 to V-E Day
CO: Billingslea
XO: Sanford

1st Bn: Gerard
2nd Bn: Major
3rd Bn: Leahy

504th Parachute Infantry Regiment

States
CO: Theodore L. Dunn/Tucker
XO: Reuben H. Tucker/Freeman

Dunn relieved by Ridgway 12/6/42. Tucker promoted to CO. Leslie G. Freeman promoted to XO.

1st Bn: Warren R. Williams
2nd Bn: William P. Yarborough
3rd Bn: Charles W. Kouns

North Africa-Sicily
CO: Tucker
XO: Freeman

1st Bn: Williams
2nd Bn: Yarborough/Danielson
3rd Bn: Kouns/Adams/Beall

Yarborough relieved 8/2/43, replaced by his XO, Daniel W. Danielson. Kouns captured while his bn attached to 505; replaced by the S-3, Emory S. Adams, Jr. Stricken with malaria, Adams was temporarily replaced by his XO, William R. Beall.

Salerno-Naples
CO: Tucker
XO: Freeman/Billingslea

1st Bn: Williams
2nd Bn: Danielson
3rd Bn: Beall/Adams/Freeman

Freeman, WIA, replaced by Charles Billingslea from Fifth Army staff. Adams, returning from hospital, resumed command from Beall, who was KIA about 10/1/43. Freeman, returning from hospital, appointed CO 3rd Bn. Adams reverted to S-3.

Volturno River to Venafro
Reinforced by 376th and 456th Para FA bns, redesignated 504th Regimental Combat Team (RCT)

CO: Tucker
XO: Billingslea

1st Bn: Williams
2nd Bn: Danielson/Blitch
3rd Bn: Freeman

Danielson injured 12/6/43; replaced by Melvin S. Blitch, Jr.

Anzio-England
CO: Tucker
XO: Billingslea/Williams

1st Bn: Williams/Harrison
2nd Bn: Blitch/Adams/Wellems
3rd Bn: Freeman/Cook

Blitch hospitalized and evacuated at Anzio, replaced by the S-3, Adams, who, in England, went to HQ, 82nd Abn Div, replaced by his XO, Edward N. Wellems. After Anzio, Freeman rotated to States, replaced by Julian Aaron Cook. On about 8/1/44, Billingslea assigned to command 325 GIR, replaced as XO by Williams, who was replaced by Willard E. Harrison.

Holland
CO: Tucker
XO: Williams

1st Bn: Harrison
2nd Bn: Wellems
3rd Bn: Cook

Bulge
CO: Tucker
XO: Williams

1st Bn: Harrison/Berry
2nd Bn: Wellems
3rd Bn: Cook

In January 1945, Harrison rotated to States, replaced by John T. Berry from XVIII Abn Corps.

Medal of Honor: Pvt. John R. Towle.

Spring 1945 to V-E Day
CO: Tucker
XO: Williams

1st Bn: Berry
2nd Bn: Wellems
3rd Bn: Cook

505th Parachute Infantry Regiment

States
CO: James M. Gavin
XO: Orin D. Haugen/Batcheller

1st Bn: Arthur F. Gorham
2nd Bn: James A. Gray
3rd Bn: Edward C. Krause

Haugen to CO, 511 PIR, 11th Abn Div, replaced by Herbert F. Batcheller.

North Africa-Sicily
CO: Gavin
XO: Batcheller

1st Bn: Gorham/Winton
2nd Bn: Mark J. Alexander
3rd Bn: Krause

Before Sicily, Gray relieved, and replaced by his XO, Alexander. Gorham KIA, replaced by his XO, Walter F. Winton.

Salerno-Naples-Volturno River
CO: Gavin/Batcheller
XO: Batcheller/Alexander

1st Bn: Winton
2nd Bn: Alexander/Vandervoort
3rd Bn: Krause

Gavin promoted to 82nd Div ADC, 10/4/43, replaced as CO by Batcheller. Alexander promoted to XO, replaced by Benjamin H. Vandervoort.

England
CO: Batcheller/Ekman
XO: Alexander

1st Bn: Winton/Kellam
2nd Bn: Vandervoort
3rd Bn: Krause

Batcheller relieved 3/21/44, sent to 1st Bn, 508 PIR; replaced by William E. Ekman, XO of 508. Winton injured knee, replaced by Frederick C. A. Kellam.

Normandy
CO: Ekman
XO: Alexander/Winton/Krause

1st Bn: Kellam/Alexander/Hagan
2nd Bn: Vandervoort
3rd Bn: Krause/Hagan/Krause/Kaiser

Krause WIA on D day, temporarily replaced by his XO, William J. Hagan III. Kellam KIA on D day, replaced by Alexander to 6/16/44, when Alexander became XO, 508 PIR. Hagan then replaced Alexander in command 1st Bn; Winton promoted to replace Alexander as XO, 505. Upon return to U.K., Krause replaced Winton as XO. James L. Kaiser replaced Krause in command of 3rd Bn.

Holland
CO: Ekman
XO: Krause

1st Bn: *Talton W. Long*
2nd Bn: *Vandervoort*
3rd Bn: *Kaiser*

Before MARKET-GARDEN, Hagan broke a foot and was relieved by his XO, Long.

Bulge
CO: *Ekman*
XO: *Krause/Long*

1st Bn: *Long/DeLong*
2nd Bn: *Vandervoort/Carpenter*
3rd Bn: *Kaiser*

Vandervoort severely WIA and evacuated 1/7/45, replaced by William R. Carpenter. Krause rotated to States; replaced as XO by Long, 3/6/45. Long replaced by Walter C. DeLong.

Spring 1945 to V-E Day
CO: *Ekman*
XO: *Long*

1st Bn: *DeLong*
2nd Bn: *Carpenter/Dudley*
3rd Bn: *Kaiser*

Carpenter drowned in Rhine River night of April 7/8, replaced by William R. Dudley, former XO, 509th Bn.

507th Parachute Infantry Regiment

Normandy
CO: *George V. Millett/Maloney/Raff*
XO: *Arthur A. Maloney*

1st Bn: *Edwin J. Ostberg/Pearson*
2nd Bn: *Charles J. Timmes*
3rd Bn: *William H. Kuhn/Davis/Maloney/Davis*

Millett captured, temporarily replaced by the XO, Maloney. On 6/15/44, Edson D. Raff to CO, 507, from Acting C/S, 82nd Abn Div. Maloney to CO, 3rd Bn. Ostberg severely WIA on D day, replaced by Ben F. Pearson. Ostberg later transferred to 325 GIR. Kuhn injured in jump, temporarily replaced by his XO, John T. Davis. Maloney, commanding 3rd Bn, severely WIA on 7/6/44. Permanently replaced by Davis.

After Normandy, regiment detached and transferred to 17th Abn Div.

508th Parachute Infantry Regiment

England
CO: *Roy E. Lindquist*
XO: *William E. Ekman/Harrison*

1st Bn: *Harry J. Harrison/Batcheller*
2nd Bn: *Thomas J. B. Shanley*
3rd Bn: *Louis G. Mendez*

Ekman transferred to CO, 505 PIR, replaced by Harrison. Herbert Batcheller, CO, 505, replaced Harrison.

Normandy
CO: *Lindquist*
XO: *Harrison/Alexander/Shanley*

1st Bn: *Batcheller/Warren*
2nd Bn: *Shanley/Alexander/Holmes*
3rd Bn: *Mendez*

Batcheller KIA 6/6/44, replaced by his XO, Shields Warren, Jr. Harrison relieved as XO and sent to 28th Div, replaced temporarily by Mark Alexander, XO of 505. Shanley WIA 7/3/44, replaced temporarily by Alexander. Alexander WIA 7/4/44, replaced by his bn XO, Otho E. Holmes. On about 7/13/44, Shanley returned from the hospital and became regimental XO.

Holland to V-E Day
CO: Lindquist
XO: Shanley

1st Bn: Warren
2nd Bn: Holmes
3rd Bn: Mendez

Medal of Honor: 1st Sgt. Leonard A. Funk, Jr.

Regiment detached from 82nd Abn Div on 3/1/45, transferred to France for special assignments.

101st AIRBORNE DIVISION HQ
Activated: 8/15/42

Commanding General
William C. Lee/Maxwell D. Taylor

Lee, felled by a heart attack, replaced by Taylor before the Normandy invasion, 3/10/44. Taylor retained command until after the war, 8/22/45, when he was appointed Superintendent of West Point. He was succeeded by the Division Artillery Commander, William N. Gillmore, who was succeeded on 9/25/45 by Gerald St. Clair Mickle (ex-CG 75th Inf Div), who commanded about two weeks, until relieved on 10/9/45 by Stuart Cutler, who remained in command until the division was deactivated.

Ass't Division Commander
Don F. Pratt/Gerald J. Higgins

Pratt KIA Normandy, 6/6/44, replaced by the C/S, Higgins, who was replaced after cessation of hostilities on 8/11/45 by Robert F. Sink.

Division Artillery Commander
Anthony C. McAuliffe/Thomas L. Sherburne/William N. Gillmore

McAuliffe, temporarily commanding the 101 Div in Bulge, was temporarily replaced by Sherburne. When McAuliffe was promoted to CG, 103rd Inf Div, he was permanently replaced, 1/10/45, by Gillmore, who came from the 1st Armored Division.

Chief of Staff
Charles L. Keerans/Higgins/Millener/Moore/Michaelis/Moore

Keerans to ADC, 82nd Abn Div, replaced by Higgins on 3/1/43. Higgins promoted to ADC 6/6/44, replaced by Raymond D. Millener, who committed suicide 12/7/44, temporarily replaced by G-1, Ned D. Moore, permanently replaced by John H. Michaelis (ex-502 PIR) on 12/28/44. On 2/10/45, when Michaelis was hospitalized with a relapse of battle wounds incurred in Holland and evacuated to States, Moore became C/S until division deactivation.

G-1 (Personnel)
Ned D. Moore/Brower

When Moore was named acting C/S in Bulge, he was replaced by Frank R. Brower, Jr., who reassumed the job in March 1945, when Moore was made permanent C/S.

G-2 (Intelligence)
Ralph N. Neal/Sommerfield/Danahay/Schweiter

Before Normandy, Neal transferred, replaced by his assistant, Arthur M. Sommerfield, replaced during Normandy by Paul A. Danahay, who though WIA in Holland, remained in the job until hostilities ceased, then replaced by Leo H. Schweiter.

G-3 (Plans)
Higgins/Millener/Hannah/Kinnard/Chase/Kinnard

When Higgins promoted to C/S, 3/1/44, Millener replaced him. When Millener promoted to C/S, 6/6/44, he was replaced by Harold W. Hannah, who was severely WIA in Holland and replaced by Harry W. O. Kinnard (ex-501). When Kinnard seriously wounded in grenade demo, 3/7/45, he was temporarily replaced by Charles H. Chase (XO, 506 PIR).

G-4 (Logistics)
William F. Kernan/Kohls

William F. Kernan replaced before Normandy by Carl W. Kohls, who remained until deactivation.

501st Parachute Infantry Regiment

Normandy
CO: Howard R. (Skeets) Johnson
XO: Harry W. O. Kinnard/Griswold

1st Bn: Robert C. Carroll/Kinnard
2nd Bn: Robert A. Ballard
3rd Bn: Julian J. Ewell

Carroll KIA 6/6/44, replaced by XO, Kinnard. George N. Griswold to XO.

Holland
CO: Johnson/Ewell
XO: Griswold/Ballard

1st Bn: Kinnard/Raymond V. Bottomly
2nd Bn: Ballard/Sammie N. Homan
3rd Bn: Ewell/Griswold

Johnson KIA 10/6/44, replaced by Ewell. Griswold to 3rd Bn. Ballard to XO, replaced by Homan. Kinnard to Division G-3, replaced by Bottomly.

Bulge to V-E Day
CO: Ewell/Ballard
XO: Ballard/Richard J. Allen

1st Bn: Bottomly
2nd Bn: Homan
3rd Bn: Griswold

Ewell WIA 1/9/45, replaced by Ballard. Ballard replaced as XO by Allen.

Regiment detached from 101st Abn Div on 3/1/45, transferred to France for special assignments.

502nd Parachute Infantry Regiment

Normandy
CO: George Van Horn Moseley, Jr./Michaelis
XO: John H. (Mike) Michaelis/Ginder

1st Bn: Patrick F. Cassidy
2nd Bn: Steve A. Chappuis
3rd Bn: Robert G. Cole

Moseley relieved 6/7/44; replaced by XO, Michaelis. Allen W. Ginder, S-3, to XO.

Medal of Honor: Lt. Col. Robert G. Cole.

Holland
CO: Michaelis/Chappuis
XO: Ginder/Cassidy

1st Bn: Cassidy/Hanlon
2nd Bn: Chappuis/Sutliffe
3rd Bn: Cole/Stopka

Michaelis WIA 9/22/44, replaced by Chappuis. Chappuis replaced by Thomas F. Sutliffe. Cole KIA 9/18/44, replaced by John P. Stopka. Ginder WIA 10/25/44, replaced by Cassidy. Cassidy replaced by John D. Hanlon.

Medal of Honor: PFC Joe E. Mann.

Bulge to V-E Day
CO: Chappuis
XO: Cassidy

1st Bn: Hanlon
2nd Bn: Sutliffe/Hatch
3rd Bn: Stopka/Simmons

Sutliffe WIA 1/1/45, replaced by James J. Hatch; Sutliffe died of wounds. Stopka KIA 1/4/45 (by American aircraft), replaced by Cecil L. Simmons.

506th Parachute Infantry Regiment

Normandy
CO: Robert F. Sink
XO: Charles H. Chase

1st Bn: William L. Turner/Foster/Patch
2nd Bn: Robert L. Strayer
3rd Bn: Robert L. Wolverton/Shettle/Harwick

Turner KIA 6/7/44, replaced by Franklin E. Foster. Foster WIA 6/7/44, replaced by Lloyd E. Patch. Wolverton and his XO, George S. Grant, KIA 6/6/44, temporarily replaced by Charles G. Shettle. Robert F. Harwick, a POW to D+5, escaped, returned, and took command. He was replaced in England by Oliver M. Horton. Patch was replaced in England by James L. LaPrade.

Holland
CO: Sink
XO: Chase

1st Bn: LaPrade
2nd Bn: Strayer
3rd Bn: Horton/Harwick/Patch

Horton KIA 10/5/44, temporarily replaced by Harwick, replaced by Patch.

Bulge to V-E Day
CO: Sink
XO: Chase/Strayer/Chase

1st Bn: LaPrade/Harwick/Shettle/Hester
2nd Bn: Strayer/Winters/Strayer
3rd Bn: Patch

LaPrade KIA 12/19/44, replaced by Harwick. Harwick WIA 1/9/45, replaced by Charles G. Shettle. Shettle WIA 1/10/45, replaced by Clarence Hester. Strayer temporarily replaced Chase, who temporarily replaced injured division G-3, Kinnard, 3/7/45. Strayer temporarily replaced by Richard D. Winters and reassumed command after return of Chase as XO.

401st and 327th Glider Infantry Regiments

England

401	**327**
CO: Joseph H. Harper	CO: George S. Wear
XO: Henry H. Leveck	XO: Curtis D. Renfro
1st Bn: Ray C. Allen	1st Bn: Hartford F. Salee
2nd Bn: Charles A. Carrell	2nd Bn: Thomas J. Rouzie

Before Normandy, the 401 PIR was split to provide temporary third battalions to the 325th and 327th GIRs. Harper was named beachmaster at Utah Beach for the 101's seagoing tail; Leveck, to Division HQ. Ray Allen's 1st Bn assigned to Wear's 327, Carrell's 2nd Bn to Lewis' 325. The merged 327 and 401 eventually became the 327th GIR.

Normandy
CO: Wear/Harper
XO: Renfro/Rouzie

1st Bn: Salee/Nichols
2nd Bn: Rouzie/Inman
1st Bn (401):   Allen

Wear relieved, replaced by Harper. Renfro, replaced by Rouzie, went to G-3, Section 101, and later, CO, 346th Inf, 87th Div. Rouzie replaced Renfro as XO; Rouzie replaced by Roy L. Inman. Salee, WIA 6/10/44, temporarily replaced by George P. Nichols.

Holland
CO: Harper
XO: Rouzie

1st Bn: Salee
2nd Bn: Inman
1st Bn (401):   Allen

Bulge to V-E Day
CO: Harper
XO: Rouzie

1st Bn: Salee/Nichols
2nd Bn: Inman/Galbraith/Inman
3rd Bn: Allen/McDonald

Inman WIA 12/20/44, temporarily replaced by Robert B. Galbraith. Salee, WIA 1/4/45, temporarily replaced by Nichols. Allen WIA (lost a leg) 4/5/45 in Rhine, replaced by Robert J. McDonald.

17th AIRBORNE DIVISION HQ
Activated: 4/15/43

Commanding General
William M. Miley

Ass't Division Commander
John L. Whitelaw

Division Artillery Commander
Joseph V. Phelps

Chief of Staff
Willard K. Liebell

G-1 (Personnel)
Lewis R. Good

G-2 (Intelligence)
Lyle N. McAllister

G-3 (Plans)
Edwin J. Messinger

G-4 (Logistics)
Charles W. Koester

193rd Glider Infantry Regiment

Bulge
CO: Maurice G. Stubbs
XO: David P. Schorr, Jr.

1st Bn: Robert L. Ashworth
2nd Bn: Harry Balish

On 3/1/45, 193 GIR abolished to conform to new T/O reducing airborne divisions to one GIR. Stubbs to G-1 Section, HQ FAAA. Schorr to XO, 194 GIR. Ashworth to newly created 3rd Bn, 194 GIR. Balish to HQ 17th Abn Div. Other personnel of 193 utilized as replacements in 194 GIR.

194th Glider Infantry Regiment

Bulge
CO: James R. (Bob) Pierce
XO: Clark N. Bailey

1st Bn: Frank L. Barnett
2nd Bn: William S. Stewart
550 Bn: Edward I. Sachs (temporarily attached)

On 3/1/45, 194 GIR reorganized to conform to new T/O reducing airborne divisions to one GIR. The independent 550 Bn was abolished and provided personnel for 3rd Bn, 194. Sachs to G-3 Section, 17th Abn Div HQ. Bailey sent to command 17th Abn Div Special Troops, replaced by David P. Schorr, ex-XO, 193 GIR. Ashworth, from 193 GIR, named to command new 3rd Bn, 194.

Rhine Crossing to V-E Day
CO: Pierce
XO: Schorr

1st Bn: Barnett
2nd Bn: Stewart/Balish
3rd Bn: Ashworth

Stewart, WIA, replaced by Balish, ex-193 GIR.

Medal of Honor: T/Sgt. Clinton M. Hedrick.

507th Parachute Infantry Regiment

After Normandy, Regiment attached to 17th Abn Div.

Bulge
CO: Raff
XO: Kuhn

1st Bn: Pearson/Smith
2nd Bn: Timmes
3rd Bn: Davis/Taylor/Creek/Taylor

Pearson WIA about 1/27/45, replaced by Paul F. Smith. Davis KIA 1/8/45, temporarily replaced by Allen W. Taylor; Taylor replaced by Roy E. Creek, who was wounded 1/21/45, whereupon Taylor assumed permanent command.

Rhine Crossing to V-E Day
CO: Raff
XO: Kuhn

1st Bn: Smith
2nd Bn: Timmes
3rd Bn: Taylor

Medal of Honor: Pvt. George J. Peters.

513th Parachute Infantry Regiment

States
CO: Albert H. Dickerson/Coutts
XO: Allen C. Miller/Ryan

1st Bn: John R. Weikel/Taylor
2nd Bn: Nicholas W. Willis/Miller
3rd Bn: Edward F. Kent

513 assigned first to 13th Abn Div, then to 17th Abn Div. Dickerson transferred to 13th Div HQ, replaced by James W. Coutts. Miller replaced as XO by Ward S. Ryan; Miller to CO, 2nd Bn, replacing Willis, who went to Div HQ. Weikel to 11th Abn Div, replaced by Alton R. Taylor.

Bulge
CO: Coutts
XO: Ryan

1st Bn: Taylor/Kies
2nd Bn: Miller
3rd Bn: Kent/Anderson

During Bulge, Taylor relieved, sent to HQ 17th Div, replaced by Harry S. Kies. Miller, WIA but not evacuated, retained command 2nd Bn. Kent, WIA 1/7/45, temporarily replaced by Morris S. Anderson.

Medal of Honor: Sgt. Isadore S. Jachman.

Rhine Crossing to V-E Day
CO: Coutts/Ryan
XO: Ryan

1st Bn: Kies
2nd Bn: Miller
3rd Bn: Anderson/Kent

Coutts, WIA 4/4/45, replaced by Ryan. Anderson jumped with bn, but replaced by Kent, returning from hospital.

Medal of Honor: PFC Stuart S. Stryker.

13th AIRBORNE DIVISION HQ
Activated: 8/13/43

Commanding General
George W. Griner/Chapman

Griner replaced by Elbridge G. (Gerry) Chapman November 1943.

Ass't Division Commander
Stuart Cutler/Monroe

On 5/25/44, Cutler assigned to 1st Army Group, ETO, later to FAAA; replaced by Hammond McDougal Monroe.

Division Artillery Commander
Eric S. Molitor

Chief of Staff
Richard P. Ovenshine/Harris

Ovenshine replaced by Hugh P. Harris.

Initial Units, States
513 PIR. *CO: Albert H. Dickerson. Transferred to 17th Abn Div.*

515 PIR. *CO: Julian B. (Jupe) Lindsey. Lindsey relieved before shipment overseas, sent to 101st Inf Rgt, 26th Div, replaced temporarily by XO, Harley N. Trice, on 2/12/45, permanently by Harvey J. Jablonsky.*

189 GIR. *CO: Walter S. Winn*

190 GIR. *CO: Rowland R. Street*

Note: On 3/1/45, the 326 GIR, commanded by Stuart Cutler, was detached from the 82nd Abn Div and sent to Alliance, Nebraska, where it was mated with the independent 88th GIR to form the 1st Independent Glider Brigade, commanded by Cutler, who was replaced as CO, 326, by William O. Poindexter. Robert C. Aloe originally commanded the 88 GIR, replaced by Joseph A. Hinton, replaced by Samuel Roth. In December 1943, Cutler's 1st Independent Glider Brigade was assigned to the 13th Abn Div, absorbing the embryonic 189 and 190 GIRs; Cutler became ADC, 13th Abn Div.

Combat Units, France (3/1/45)
515 PIR. *CO: Jablonsky*

517 PIR. *CO: Rupert D. Graves*

88 GIR. *CO: Roth*

326 GIR. *CO: Poindexter*

Note: The 13th Abn Div, assigned to XVIII Airborne Corps, was alerted for Operations VARSITY, CHOKER II and EFFECTIVE, but was not committed to combat and was frequently drawn on for replacements for the 17th, 82nd and 101st divisions. The 517 PIR was attached on 3/1/45. Selected for the invasion of Japan, the 13th sailed from France on 8/15/45, returned to Fort Bragg and, in October 1945, was deactivated.

Independent Airborne Infantry

NORTH AFRICA

509 Para Bn
CO: Edson D. Raff/Yardley
XO: Doyle R. Yardley/Dudley

Raff returned to States, replaced by Yardley, who was replaced by William R. Dudley.

AVELLINO (ITALY)

509 Para Bn
CO: Yardley/Yarborough
XO: Dudley

Yardley, WIA, captured. After Avellino, William P. Yarborough named CO; Dudley returned to States.

ANZIO

509 Para Bn
CO: Yarborough/Tomasik (acting)
XO: Edmund J. Tomasik (acting)

Bn attached to American Rangers, commanded by William O. Darby. Twice when Yarborough became ill with jaundice, acting XO, Tomasik, temporarily commanded.

Medal of Honor: Cpl. Paul B. Huff.

SOUTHERN FRANCE

517 PIR
CO: Rupert D. Graves
XO: George R. Walton/Zais

1st Bn: William J. Boyle
2nd Bn: Richard J. Seitz
3rd Bn: Melvin Zais/Forrest S. Paxton

Walton injured in D-day jump, replaced by Zais, who was replaced by Paxton.

509 Para Bn
CO: Yarborough/Tomasik
XO: John H. Apperson/Tomasik

Apperson KIA in postjump fighting, replaced by Tomasik. Yarborough returned to States, replaced by Tomasik.

551 Para Bn
CO: Wood G. Joerg
XO: Charles R. Hermann/Holm

Hermann temporarily replaced the XO, William N. Holm, who was ill on D day but later returned.

550 Gli Bn
CO: Edward I. Sachs
XO: James Wilson

All independent airborne units were attached to XVIII Airborne Corps in November–December 1944. The 550 Gli Bn to 194 GIR, 17th Abn Div, in England.

BULGE

517 PIR
CO: Graves
XO: Zais

1st Bn: Boyle/Fraser   (Presidential Unit Citation)
2nd Bn: Seitz
3rd Bn: Paxton

Boyle WIA 1/5/45, replaced by D. W. Fraser. Regiment attached to 82nd Abn Div for Siegfried Line and Roer River campaigns, afterward reassigned to 13th Abn Div.

Medal of Honor: PFC Melvin E. Biddle.

509 Para Bn   (Presidential Unit Citation)
CO: Tomasik
XO: Henry Howland

Howland KIA. Bn wiped out, deactivated. Tomasik to 13th Abn Div; other survivors to 82nd Abn Div.

551 Para Bn
CO: Joerg/Holm
XO: Holm

Joerg KIA 1/7/45, replaced by Holm. Bn wiped out, deactivated, survivors to 82nd Abn Div.

Airborne Artillery and Antiaircraft Units

Parachute artillery battalions with a total strength of about 550 men were composed of four batteries: HQ/Service and three firing batteries, A, B and C. They were equipped with 12 disassembled 75 mm pack howitzers, four weapons per firing battery.

Glider artillery battalions with a total strength of about 550 men were composed of four batteries: HQ/Service and three firing batteries, A, B and C. Most were equipped with 12 assembled 75 mm pack howitzers, four weapons per firing battery. Later, some battalions were equipped with 12 105 mm snub-nose howitzers. These units were composed of three batteries: HQ/Service, A and B, with 6 weapons per firing battery.

Antiaircraft battalions with a total strength of about 550 men consisted of a HQ/Service battery and 6 firing batteries: three batteries (A, B, C) were equipped with 24 antitank guns, eight per battery, and three (D, E, F) with 36 .50 caliber air-cooled machine guns, 12 per battery. Initially the antitank batteries were equipped with ineffective 37 mm weapons. Later they were equipped with the more powerful 57 mm gun, and still later (1944) with the British six-pounder gun, which fired the U.S. Army 57 mm projectile. These units actually saw very little A/A action. They were employed mainly in support of infantry.

SICILY (82nd Abn Div only)

376 Para FA Bn
CO: Wilbur M. Griffith

Jumped D+1 with 504 PIR. Aircraft riddled by friendly fire, many casualties. Thereafter supported 504 in Sicily campaign.

456 Para FA Bn
CO: Harrison B. Harden, Jr./Neal

Jumped on D day with 505 PIR. Badly scattered. Thereafter supported 505 in Sicily campaign. Harden relieved on Sicily. He was replaced by his XO, Hugh A. Neal.

319 Gli FA Bn
CO: William Harry Bertsch/Todd

Remained in North Africa during Sicily campaign. Owing to detachment of Bertsch to other assignments, the XO, J. Carter Todd, usually commanded the unit.

320 Gli FA Bn
CO: Paul E. Wright

Equipped with snub-nose 105 mm howitzers. Remained in North Africa during Sicily campaign.

80 A/A Bn
CO: Whitfield Jack/Singleton

Remained in North Africa during Sicily campaign. On 8/19/43, Jack promoted to G-3, 82nd Abn Div, replaced by his XO, Raymond E. Singleton.

SALERNO-NAPLES (82nd Abn Div only)

376 Para FA Bn
CO: Wilbur M. Griffith

Landed by ship at Salerno beachhead 9/23/44. Supported 504.

456 Para FA Bn
CO: Neal

Remained in Sicily/North Africa during Salerno-Naples campaign. Landed by ship in Naples about 11/1/43.

319 Gli FA Bn
CO: Bertsch/Todd

Landed by ship at Maiori in support of Darby's Rangers, 9/11/43, and fought through to Naples. On 10/6/43, when Bertsch named to XO, 82nd Abn DivArty, Todd promoted to CO.

320 Gli FA Bn *(snub-nose 105s)*
CO: Wright

Landed by ship at Salerno beachhead 9/23/43. Fought through to Naples.

80 A/A Bn
CO: Singleton

Batteries D, E, F (machine-gun) landed by ship at Maiori 9/11/43. Batteries A, B, C (57 mm antitank) landed by ship at Salerno beachhead 9/23/43. All fought through to Naples.

The 376 and 456 Para FA bns remained in combat in Italy in support of the temporarily detached 504 PIR through the Anzio invasion. During the early stages of Anzio, the 456 was ordered to send one firing battery (and the 456 unit designation) to England to rejoin the 82nd Abn Div. The remainder of the 456, left in Anzio, was redesignated the 463 Para FA Bn.

463 Para FA Bn
CO: Neal/Cooper

Fought at Anzio and in the liberation of Rome. Neal, WIA 5/13/44, replaced by John T. Cooper.

NORMANDY (82nd Abn Div)

456 Para FA Bn
CO: Wagner J. d'Allessio

Two pack howitzers jumped with airborne assault forces on D day. The rest landed by ship at Utah Beach on D+1 and D+2.

319 Gli FA Bn
CO: Todd

Landed by glider late on D day.

320 Gli FA Bn *(snub-nose 105s)*
CO: Wright/Lancey

Landed by glider late on D day. Owing to a mislanding of Wright, the XO, William S. Lancey, commanded temporarily.

80 A/A Bn
CO: Singleton

Part landed by glider with parachute assault forces on D day, the rest by glider late on D day.

NORMANDY (101st Abn Div)

377 Para FA Bn
CO: Benjamin Weisberg/Elkins

Jumped with airborne assault forces on D day, badly scattered. After Normandy, Weisberg relieved, replaced by his XO, Harry W. Elkins.

321 Gli FA Bn
CO: Edward L. Carmichael

Landed by ship at Utah Beach on D+1 and D+2.

907 Gli FA Bn
CO: Clarence F. Nelson

Landed by ship at Utah Beach on D+1 and D+2.

81 A/A Bn
CO: X. B. Cox

The three A/A batteries (D, E, F) and one antitank battery (C) landed by ship at Utah Beach on D day. Two antitank batteries (A, B) landed by glider on D day. (Cox was a Texan, named for a Confederate general of the same name. The "X. B." in his name does not stand for anything.)

SOUTHERN FRANCE

460 Para FA Bn
CO: Raymond L. Cato

Arrived in Italy with the 517 PIR several weeks prior to invasion.

463 Para FA Bn
CO: Cooper/Seaton/Cooper

After helping to liberate Rome, the unit was assigned to invasion. Cooper, who broke a leg in the jump, was replaced for about a month by his XO, Stuart M. Seaton.

HOLLAND (82nd Abn Div)

376 Para FA Bn
CO: Griffith/Neptune

Jumped on D day with assault paratroopers. On 9/25/44, when Griffith named XO, 82nd Abn DivArty, his XO, Robert H. Neptune, was promoted to commander.

456 Para FA Bn
CO: D'Allessio

Landed by glider on D+1.

319 Gli FA Bn
CO: Todd

Landed by glider on D+1.

320 Gli FA Bn *(snub-nose 105s)*
CO: Wright

Landed by glider on D+1.

80 A/A Bn
CO: Singleton

Part landed by glider on D day, part on D+1.

HOLLAND (101st Abn Div)

377 Para FA Bn
CO: Elkins

Three batteries (HQ, A, C) landed by glider on D day; one battery (B) by parachute on D+1.

321 Gli FA Bn
CO: Carmichael

Landed by glider on D+2.

907 Gli FA Bn *(snub-nose 105s)*
CO: Nelson

Landed by glider on D+2.

81 A/A Bn
CO: Cox

Landed by glider on D+2.

BULGE (82nd Abn Div)

376 Para FA Bn
CO: Neptune

460 Para FA Bn
CO: Cato

Arrived from southern France with the 517 PIR.

456 Para FA Bn
CO: D'Allessio

319 Gli FA Bn
CO: Todd

320 Gli FA Bn *(snub-nose 105s)*
CO: Wright

80 A/A Bn
CO: Singleton

BULGE (101st Abn Div)

377 Para FA Bn
CO: Elkins

463 Para FA Bn
CO: Cooper

Arrived from southern France independently, attached to 101st for Bastogne, remained with it for the rest of the war.

321 Gli FA Bn
CO: Carmichael

907 Gli FA Bn *(snub-nose 105s)*
CO: Nelson

81 A/A Bn
CO: Cox

BULGE (17th Abn Div) *(committed to combat 1/3/45)*

466 Para FA Bn
CO: Kenneth L. Booth

680 Gli FA Bn
CO: Paul F. Oswald

681 Gli FA Bn
CO: Joseph W. Keating

155 A/A Bn
CO: John W. Paddock

All FA and A/A bns fought through the Bulge and thereafter to February 1945. The 460 Para FA Bn was then reassigned to the 13th Abn Div, along with the 517 PIR. All other units remained attached to the airborne divisions shown.

RHINE CROSSING (17th Abn Div only)

464 Para FA Bn
CO: Edward S. Branigan, Jr.

Arrived in ETO from States in February 1945. Attached to 17th Abn Div for Rhine crossing and subsequent action. Jumped on D day with 507 PIR.

466 Para FA Bn
CO: Booth

Jumped on D day with 513 PIR.

680 Gli FA Bn *(snub-nose 105s)*
CO: Oswald

Landed b· glider on D day as "divisional artillery."

681 Gli FA Bn
CO: Keating

Landed by glider on D day with 194 GIR.

155 A/A Bn
CO: Paddock

Landed by glider on D day.

ARMY AIRBORNE OPERATIONS
IN THE SOUTHWEST PACIFIC

11th AIRBORNE DIVISION HQ
Activated: 2/25/43

Commanding General
Joseph M. Swing

Ass't Division Commander
Albert Pierson

Division Artillery
Francis W. Farrell/Dorn

Farrell, felled by illness 8/15/45, replaced by Frank Dorn.

Chief of Staff
Irvin R. Schimmelpfennig/Williams

Schimmelpfennig KIA 2/4/45 in Manila, replaced by Michael Williams.

511 PIR
CO: Orin D. Haugen/Lahti

Haugen died of wounds 2/22/45, replaced by the 511 XO, Edward H. Lahti.

187 GIR
CO: Harry B. Hildebrand/Pearson

Hildebrand, detached from division for special assignment, replaced by George O. Pearson.

188 GIR
CO: Robert H. Soule/Tipton

Soule promoted to brigadier general 3/1/45 and appointed ADC, 38th Div. Replaced by Norman E. Tipton.

OTHER UNITS:

457 Para FA Bn
CO: Douglass P. Quandt/Nicholas Stodherr

674 Gli FA Bn
CO: Lukas E. Hoska

675 Gli FA Bn
CO: Ernest L. Massad

152 A/A Bn
CO: John H. Farren

The 11th Airborne Division was deployed to the Southwest Pacific Theater in May 1944, but owing to a shortage of troop-carrier planes and gliders and other factors, it was never used in the airborne role for which it was conceived. It was first committed to combat in October 1944, by ship, as light infantry, on the island of Leyte. In northern Leyte, it engaged in bitter and bloody jungle fighting. On 12/4/44, it mounted its first primitive airborne combat operation: the jump of Battery A of the 457 FA Bn. (Two days later, 12/6/44, the division itself was attacked by a suicidal force of about three hundred Japanese paratroopers, the only instance in the war in which an American airborne division was directly attacked by enemy airborne forces.) In February 1945, the division was committed to the invasion of Luzon. The two glider regiments landed by ship, but the 511 PIR and 457 Para FA Bn jumped, staging from Mindoro, in a multiple-lift operation over two days. Thereafter the division, fighting as light infantry, attacked Manila from the south, incurring very heavy opposition, and casualties including the 511 CO, Orin Haugen, who was hit in the chest by a 20 mm dud and died of wounds. In a land-sea-airborne "raid," employing one air-dropped company of the 511 PIR, the division liberated 2,147 civilian internees (most of them clergy) from Camp Los Baños. Following the liberation of Manila, the division, still fighting as light infantry, was assigned the tough job of clearing southern Luzon of Japanese. On June 23, it staged its second (and last) large airborne operation: the parachute drop of a reinforced battalion of the 511 PIR, accompanied by Battery C of the 457 FA Bn at Aparri, in northern Luzon. In August 1945, the division was deployed, by air, first to Okinawa, then to Atsugi, Japan, thus becoming the first Allied occupation forces. The division remained in Japan until 1949, at which time its new commander, William M. (Bud) Miley, former CG of the 17th Airborne Division in the ETO, returned it to Fort Campbell, Kentucky.

Independent Airborne Forces

503 PIR
CO: Kenneth Kinsler/George M. Jones

The 503rd Parachute Infantry Regiment was deployed to the Southwest Pacific in the summer of 1943 as an independent unit. On 9/5/43, it jumped in daylight into Japanese-held Nadzab, New Guinea, as part of MacArthur's assault on Lae. Meeting only slight resistance, the regiment secured an airhead into which infantry of the Australian 7th Division was airlifted. Soon after this operation, Kinsler committed suicide, and his exec, George M. Jones, was named commander. When his 11th Airborne Division reached New Guinea, Joe Swing sought to incorporate the 503rd into the division, but MacArthur disapproved, preferring to maintain the 503rd in independent status for special tasks. In July 1944, the 503rd staged a two-battalion daylight jump into the Japanese-held island of Noemfoor, off the north coast of Dutch New Guinea, where it was reinforced (to become an RCT) by the 462nd Parachute Field Artillery Battalion. On December 15, 1944, the 503rd RCT, staging from Leyte, landed amphibiously on the lightly held island of Mindoro. Enplaning at Mindoro on 2/16/45, the 503rd RCT made a daring and dangerous daylight jump onto the fortress of Corregidor, in Manila Bay. Assisted by a battalion-size amphibious task force, the 503rd, commanded by Jones, reconquered Corregidor in a tough, bloody, ten-day fight. Subsequently, the 503rd RCT, temporarily commanded by Joe S. Lawrie and fighting as light infantry, participated in liberating the southern Philippine islands, landing by ship on Negros. Long after the war (in 1949), the regiment was finally incorporated into the 11th Airborne Division.

Notes

Foreword

1. General of the Army Omar N. Bradley and Clay Blair, *A General's Life* (New York: Simon & Schuster, 1983), p. 608.
2. Celebrityhood: See, for example, *Time* magazine (cover) profiles 3/5/51 and 7/16/51; *Newsweek* magazine (cover) profiles 1/8/51 and 4/30/51; Greg McGregor, "Front Line General," profile, New York *Times Sunday Magazine* 3/4/51; Gertrude Samuels, "Ridgway: Three Views of a Soldier," profile, New York *Times Sunday Magazine* 4/22/51; *Collier's* magazine 3/8/52, profile, "Ridgway: Will He Succeed Ike?" by John Denson, et al.; *Life* magazine (cover) profile 5/12/52, "A Tough Man for a Tough Job," by James Michener; *The Saturday Evening Post,* 10/25/52 profile, "Ridgway's Toughest Job," by Ernest O. Hauser.
3. James M. Gavin, *On to Berlin* (New York: The Viking Press, 1978; paperback ed. New York: Bantam Books, 1979), p. 245; Alfred D. Chandler and Louis Galambos, eds. *The Papers of Dwight D. Eisenhower,* 9 vols. (Baltimore, Md.: The Johns Hopkins Press, 1970). (Hereafter, Ike Papers.) Quotations cited here: Vol. IV, p. 2216, and Vol. VI, p. 79.

Chapter 1

1. The visit is described in *Soldier: The Memoirs of Matthew B. Ridgway,* by General Matthew B. Ridgway, as told to Harold H. Martin (New York: Harper & Brothers, 1956), pp. 48–49 (hereinafter, *Soldier).*
2. This period at Benning is described in *A General's Life,* pp. 85–103.
3. Ridgway (hereinafter MBR) was born March 3, 1895, at Fort Monroe, Va. He received his promotion to colonel on 12/11/41, per official biographical records, Ridgway Papers, United States Army Military History Institute, Carlisle Barracks, Penn. (hereinafter, RP-USAMHI).
4. Physical description: photographs, RP-USAMHI; author's observations during the early 1950s and interviews 4/25/80 and 5/29/84. Athletics: *Soldier,* pp. 24, 36; MBR oral history, Pt. 2, p. 31, RP-USAMHI; int. with MBR by John Child, 5/16/77, RP-USAMHI. At West Point, Ridgway sought a letter in athletics. He played on the (junior varsity) Collum Hall football team and tried out for shotput. But he did not get a letter. Never slouching or crossing legs: CB-Arthur G. Kross (aide) int. 2/6/83. "The force" from CB-Walter F. Winton int. 11/6/82.
5. CB-MBR ints. 4/25/80 and 5/29/84. West Point records of Thomas Ridgway and MBR; obit., Thomas Ridgway (by MBR) in 71st Annual Report, 6/10/40, Ass'n of Graduates, USMA, West Point. Thomas Ridgway, born in New York City 8/18/61, was the son of James and Esther Moliere Ridgway (of French descent, probably related to the author) of Brooklyn, N.Y. Thomas Ridgway graduated from USMA on June 13, 1883. He married Julia Starbuck Bunker on 2/12/90, in Garden City, Long Island. For details on MBR's upbringing, see *Soldier,* pp. 18–23 and MBR oral history Pts. 1 and 2, RP-USAMHI. MBR said that his mother was "practically a concert pianist" and "came from a lovely home with fine things."
6. MBR's military service: official biographical records, RP-USAMHI. He served as an instructor at West Point from 9/18 to 9/21. He was enrolled in the Company Commander Course at Fort Benning 9/24 to 6/25 and the Advanced Course 9/29 to 6/30. He attended the Command and General Staff School 8/33 to 6/35 and the Army War College 8/36 to 7/37. In *Soldier,* MBR described his 1918 orders to West Point as the "death knell of his military career" (pp. 32–33) and the failure to get to war "a blot on my record" (p. 49). In his oral history (RP-USAMHI), he says he got his "ears knocked back" for protesting his orders to West Point. His father, who had injured his eyes in a "laboratory experiment" which forced his retirement in 1919, did not get overseas in World War I either.
7. *Soldier,* pp. 33–34; MBR oral history, RP-USAMHI, Pts. 1A and 1B. MBR WP records. MBR described his reading in military history at WP as "prodigious," but owing to the diversions of athletics, he did not fully apply himself academically. Overall, he graduated 56th in his class of 139, but stood high in English, Spanish and law. On "half a dozen" Regular Army officers fluent in Spanish: CB-Maxwell D. Taylor int. 11/18/82.
8. Religious faith: ltr. George B. Wood (82nd Abn Div Chaplain) to author, 3/24/84: "Ridgway

was and is a deeply religious man." In 1946–47, while stationed in New York City, Ridgway was a vestryman at St. Bartholemew's Episcopal Church, in midtown Manhattan. Personal philosophy: various Ridgway speeches, letters and writings, RP-USAMHI. For example, remarks to the Company of Military Historians 9/20/80 and ltr. to Ambassador Charles W. Yost, 2/5/75, paraphrased here.

9. MBR oral history, RP-USAMHI; *Soldier.* Prior to 1942, MBR held the following troop commands: CO "F" Company 6/17 to 9/17 and CO HQ Co 5/18 to 9/18, both 3rd Inf Rgt; CO HQ Co, 15th Inf Rgt, 7/25 to 5/26; CO "E" Co, 9th Inf Rgt, 6/26 to 8/26; CO 1st Bn, 33rd Inf Rgt, 1/31 to 2/31; CO "G" Co, 33rd Inf Rgt, 2/31 to 5/31, per official biographical records, RP-USAMHI.

10. James Michener, "A Tough Man for a Tough Job," *Life* magazine, 5/12/52. A typescript draft of Michener's article, infinitely superior to the published version, is in Box 27, RP-USAMHI. It is the source for "right way . . . wrong way . . . Ridgway." The MBR working motto is from MBR oral history, RP-USAMHI.

11. CB-Russell P. Reeder, Jr. int. 7/30/84.

12. MBR memory for names: oral history, RP-USAMHI. See also James Michener typescript, p. 13.

13. "Black Knight": CB-John B. B. Trussell int. 12/8/82. First marriage: at USMA, West Point, 4/20/17, to Julia Caroline Blount, 21, daughter of A. C. and Clara Dorr Blount of Florida, New York. (Marriage license records, Orange County [N.Y.] Courthouse, Bk. 2, p. 682, entry 8404.) Children of this marriage: Constance, born 3/8/18 in San Antonio, Tex., and Shirley, born 7/10/20 at Highland Falls, N.Y. (ltr. MBR to author 8/3/84; Beverly L. Sullivan, Town Clerk, Highland Falls, N.Y.). The Ridgways were divorced 6/16/30 at Alameda County, Calif. (ltr. MBR to author 8/3/84). Second marriage: in New York City, 6/21/30, to Margaret (Peggy) Howard Wilson Dabney, widow of Henry H. Dabney (West Point, 1915) and daughter of New York City businessman Alexander Wilson. Peggy's daughter was named Virginia Ann. Ridgway legally adopted her in 1936. There were no Ridgway children from this marriage. (The Honorable David Dinkins, Clerk, City of New York. Ltr. MBR to National Cyclopedia of American Biography, 1946, RP-USAMHI; Who's Who in America, Vol. 24, 1946–47. Obit., Henry H. Dabney, 57th Annual Report, Ass'n of Graduates, USMA, 1926; ltrs. MBR to author 8/3/84 and 8/8/84.)

14. Various author interviews. MBR's comments on his sense of humor: oral history, Pt. 1, p. 41, RP-USAMHI.

15. CB-MBR int. 5/29/84.

16. *Soldier,* pp. 48–49.

Chapter 2

1. *Soldier,* p. 49.

2. Forrest C. Pogue, *George C. Marshall: Ordeal and Hope 1939–1942* (New York: Viking Press, 1966) (hereinafter *Pogue II),* pp. 39–40; MBR on Stimson: *Soldier,* p. 37.

3. Marshall bio: Forrest C. Pogue, *George C. Marshall: Education of a General 1880–1939* (New York: Viking Press, 1963) (hereinafter *Pogue I); "*austere . . .": *A General's Life,* p. 65; "occupy a place": *Soldier,* p. 42.

4. Marshall and the 15th Rgt: Leonard Mosley, *Marshall: Hero for our Times* (New York: Hearst Books, 1982), pp. 88–91 (hereafter *Marshall).* MBR assignment, condition of the regiment and trouble with the Chinese language: official biography and MBR oral history, Pt. 2, pp. 6–9, RP-USAMHI.

5. Marshall at Benning: *Pogue I,* pp. 247–69; "minor revolution": *A General's Life,* pp. 63–68; MBR's arrival and "top of the class": *Soldier,* p. 42.

6. 1936 maneuvers: *Pogue I,* pp. 290–92; MBR's role and illness: MBR oral history, Pt. 2, p. 26, RP-USAMHI; Marshall letter: Marshall Papers, Box 2, Folder 35, George Catlett Marshall Research Library, Lexington, Va. (Hereafter, Marshall Library.)

7. Brazil mission: *Pogue I,* pp. 338–44. MBR role: biographical records and oral history, p. 40, RP-USAMHI. Thomas Ridgway death: obit., 71st Annual Report. Ridgway's sister: WP records of Thomas Ridgway. Born 3/16/91, she was the only other sibling and lived in Pacific Beach, Calif. Her husband, Norton Meade Beardslee, born in New York 7/3/87, had retired from the Coast Artillery with a disability in 1920. Funeral arrangements, etc.: ltr. MBR to author, 6/3/83. Brazil mission secret aim: John Child-MBR int. 5/10/77, RP-USAMHI and MBR oral history, Pt. 2, p. 40, RP-USAMHI. Prior diplomatic missions on which MBR served were as follows: American Electoral Mission to Nicaragua, 12/27 to 12/28; Commission of Inquiry and Conciliation, Bolivia, Paraguay, 2/29 to 9/29; American Electoral Mission to Nicaragua, 6/30 to 12/30;

adviser to the Governor General of the Philippines, Theodore Roosevelt, Jr., 6/32 to 5/33, per biographical records and oral history. Follow-up on Brazil air routes: oral history, Pt. 4, pp. 36–37. Named to head Latin American section WPD: Child-MBR int.

8. CB-M. D. Taylor int.; Taylor oral history, USAMHI; Maxwell D. Taylor, *Swords and Plowshares* (New York: Norton, 1972); MBR oral history, Pt. 2, p. 40.

9. Memo 10/12/40 and letter GCM-MBR 10/14/40, Marshall Papers, Marshall Library.

Chapter 3

1. *Soldier,* p. 49.

2. Gerow: official bio. Bundy for Gerow and Bundy's death: *Pogue II,* pp. 235, 337. Ike's reluctance: Dwight D. Eisenhower, *At Ease—Stories I Tell My Friends* (Garden City, N.Y.: Doubleday, 1967), pp. 202–3. Ike relieved Gerow on 2/16/42: Dwight D. Eisenhower, *Crusade in Europe* (Garden City, N.Y.: Doubleday, 1948), p. 31.

3. Smith: *Current Biography,* 1953. Tannenberg drama: Transcript (and list of team), Box 2, RP-USAMHI. Taylor to Secretariat: CB-Taylor int. The Secretariat is described in *A General's Life,* pp. 83–92, and in J. Lawton Collins, *Lightning Joe—An Autobiography* (Baton Rouge, La.: Louisiana State University Press, 1979), pp. 95–99.

4. *Soldier,* pp. 49–50.

5. Ibid., p. 50.

6. Promotions: biographical records, RP-USAMHI; Ridgway views on Bradley: CB-MBR int.; MBR oral history, Pt. 2, p. 45, RP-USAMHI.

7. CB-Mark W. Clark int. 4/7/80. Tannenberg transcript, Box 2, RP-USAMHI.

8. Two hours: *Soldier,* p. 50. Burning papers: Box 45, RP-USAMHI. In a letter to a friend, MBR wrote, "I have many times since regretted this."

9. *A General's Life,* pp. 15–103; CB-ONB ints. 2/1/80.

10. *A General's Life;* biographical records, RP-USAMHI. Omicron Pi Phi: WP Archives. CB-MBR int. Ridgway recalled that while hunting at West Point, he and Bradley were nailed by a game warden for illegally shooting grouse.

11. Bradley views on MBR: *A General's Life,* p. 104; CB-ONB int.

12. CB-ONB ints.; CB-MBR int.

Chapter 4

1. *A General's Life,* pp. 105–6; *Soldier,* p. 51.

2. *A General's Life,* pp. 104–5; Peggy Ridgway illness: MBR ltr. to Walter Reed Hospital 4/24/42; Col. Arden Freer, at Walter Reed to MBR 4/28/42, both in Box 2A, RP-USAMHI. M. W. Clark to MBR 5/9/42, "Rosa has seen Peggy . . . glad she's improving."

3. *A General's Life,* p. 106; Omar N. Bradley, *A Soldier's Story* (New York: Henry Holt, 1951), pp. 14–15; T. B. Ketterson, "Official History of the 82nd Division," RP-USAMHI (hereafter Ketterson).

4. Ketterson; *A General's Life;* CB-M. Taylor int.; Swing official bio; *Howitzer,* 1915, WP Library.

5. CB-M. Taylor int.

6. CB-Frank W. Moorman int. 11/6/82; CB-Winton int.

7. *A General's Life,* p. 104. "One of the few . . .": CB-Taylor int.; CB-Ralph P. Eaton int. 1/9/83. Pope official bio.

8. *A General's Life,* pp. 104–5.

9. Here and below, CB-Eaton int.

10. Eaton's second wife was Eloise Lull, daughter of a career Army officer who was retired but recalled to active duty in World War II.

11. CB-Moorman int.

12. CB-Eaton int.; CB-Moorman int.

13. Box 2A, Box 9, MBR oral history, Pt. 2, p. 115, RP-USAMHI; ltr. MBR to author 8/3/84.

14. CB-ONB int. Easley and Cutler were soon promoted to brigadier general. Appraisal of George S. Wear: CB-M. D. Taylor int. and ltr., Curtis D. Renfro (West Point 1925) to author, 11/25/83. Renfro, who was executive officer—number two—of the 327th under Wear, wrote that Wear was "very ignorant and stupid, with little or no initiative . . . I soon learned that I would have to carry him on my back if we ever got any training done."

15. Ketterson; *A General's Life,* pp. 105–6.

16. *A General's Life,* p. 106; CB-Eaton int.

17. ROUNDUP: *A General's Life,* p. 119.

18. MBR oral history, Pt. 2, p. 45, RP-USAMHI.

19. *A General's Life,* pp. 106–7; *Soldier,* pp. 53–54.

20. Horses: ltr. MBR to author, 3/10/83. Long strides: ltrs. Stuart Cutler and Robert S. Palmer to author, 2/10/84 and 2/15/84. Stuart wrote that he had to "dog-trot" to keep up with MBR. Palmer wrote that MBR "spurned the regulation thirty-inch step and always took off with as long strides as he could." Wood chopping: ltr. MBR to author 2/21/84; ltrs. Edwin A. Bedell and Ralph M. Neal, 11/17/83 and 2/24/84. Bedell, a division engineer who supplied logs, recalled that MBR's log chopping "continued as long as he was with the division at practically every location where supply and circumstances permitted."

21. Ltr. Thomas J. Catanzaro to author 10/12/83.

22. Ltr. MWC to MBR 4/6/42, RP-USAMHI.

23. Sgt. York addressed Div on 5/7/42, per photo 82nd Abn Div Museum, Fort Bragg, N.C. For details: *A General's Life,* p. 107; *Soldier,* pp. 52–53. At MBR's urging, the hastily organized band was later formalized as the 501st Army Band and continued as such throughout the war (per ltr. to author from Cutler 2/20/84).

24. Ltr. MWC to MBR, 5/9/42, Box 9, RP-USAMHI.

25. *A General's Life,* pp. 107–8.

26. Personnel changes: *A General's Life,* p. 109. New personnel: Ketterson and CB-Eaton, Taylor, Gavin, Lynch, Matthews ints.; ltr. R. K. Boyd to CB, 3/23/83. Ridgway's promotion to major general was effective 8/6/42.

27. CB-Taylor int.

28. Change of command: Box 1, RP-USAMHI. MBR speech, 6/24/42, Box 4; ltr. ONB to MBR 7/28/42 and ltr. MBR to ONB 7/29/42, Box 2A, RP-USAMHI.

Chapter 5

1. CB-Taylor int.

2. Motorized: *Soldier,* p. 54; Ketterson.

3. Airborne: *Soldier,* p. 54; Ketterson. Parks: official bio.

4. Early parachute and airborne operations in the U.S.A. and abroad: James A. Huston, *Out of the Blue* (West Lafayette, Ind.: Purdue Univ. Studies, 1972); Gerard M. Devlin, *Paratrooper!* (New York: St. Martin's Press, 1979); James M. Gavin, *Airborne Warfare* (Washington, D.C.: Infantry Journal Press, 1947), reprinted 1980 by the Battery Press, Inc., Nashville, Tenn. (see especially introduction by William C. Lee); John T. Ellis, "The Airborne Command and Center, Study No. 25," Historical Section, Army Ground Forces, 1946, monograph on file at the Army War College Library, Carlisle, Penn.; "Air Infantry Training," *Infantry Journal,* July–Aug. 1940, pp. 324–31; "The Parachute Battalion," *Infantry Journal,* Nov.–Dec. 1940, pp. 554–59; William C. Lee, "Air Infantry," *Infantry Journal,* Jan. 1941, pp. 14–21.

5. The limitations and problems of airborne warfare are discussed in *Out of the Blue* and *Paratrooper!*

6. For a critique of the Crete operation (which also includes complicated naval actions), see *Paratrooper!* pp. 101–7; C. T. Schmidt, "The Airborne Conquest of Crete," *Military Review,* March 1949. On Hitler's shocked reaction, ibid. and *Out of the Blue,* p. 48. On breaking German military codes during Crete, see the official British history: Francis H. Hinsley, *British Intelligence in the Second World War* (New York: Cambridge University Press, 1979).

7. Lee: official bio. Gerard M. Devlin, op. cit., among others, describes Lee as "the father" of American airborne troops (p. 42). John T. Ellis, op. cit., agrees. William M. Miley concurs in CB-Miley ints. of 9/18/80 and 2/19/83, as did William P. Yarborough, an early paratrooper. Lee characterized in CB-Yarborough int. 2/19/83.

8. Devlin, op. cit., and Ellis, op. cit.

9. Miley bio: "Biographical Sketch" provided to the author; official Army biography; *Register;* "Parachute Infantry Fighting Men Are Proud of Their Commander," Charlotte *Observer,* Charlotte, N.C., 5/5/42. Contemporary quoted, CB-Yarborough int.

10. The new parachute battalions, their commanders and dates of activation were as follows: the 502nd, George P. Howell, Jr. (West Point 1923), 7/1/41; the 503rd, Robert F. Sink (West Point 1927), 7/15/41; the 504th, Richard Chase (Syracuse University 1927), 10/5/41. In addition, the Army activated two experimental "airlanding" battalions to work out the problems inherent in air-transporting regular (i.e., nonparachuting) infantry into combat. These were as follows: the 550th Infantry Airborne Battalion on 7/1/41, commanded by Harris M. Melaskey, and the 88th Infantry Airborne Battalion on 10/10/41, commanded by Elbridge G. Chapman. The first mass battalion jump is noted in James M. Gavin, *War and Peace in the Space Age* (New York: Harper, 1958), p. 46.

11. CB-Gavin int. 1/4/83.

12. "Broken back and cast": ltr., Gavin to 82nd Abn Museum, Fort Bragg, N.C. Ellis, op. cit., p. 10, states that Col. Lee was "hospitalized by an accident" ten days before Pearl Harbor. The change in Lee: CB-Gavin int. 9/28/82 and 1/5/83. Miley and Yarborough corroborated the seriousness of the accident.

13. Activation of PIRs and commanders: 502nd on 1/3/42, George P. Howell; 503rd on 3/24/42, William M. Miley; 504th on 3/24/42, Theodore L. Dunn; 505th on 6/25/42, James M. Gavin; 506th on 6/25/42, Robert F. Sink; 507th on 6/25/42, George V. Millett, Jr.

14. CB-Taylor int.; CB-Gavin int.

15. Choice of 82nd: CB-Gavin int.

16. Lee, Miley, Pratt, Swing, McAuliffe official bios, *Register.*

Chapter 6

1. Various interviews with 82nd Div staff.

2. *Soldier,* p. 54.

3. Ibid., p. 61. See also MBR oral history, Pt. 2, p. 48, RP-USAMHI; Ketterson.

4. Ketterson; various interviews. See also Devlin, Ellis.

5. *Soldier,* p. 55.

6. CB-Eaton int.; CB-Taylor int.; CB-Moorman int.

7. MBR back problem: CB-MBR int.; MBR oral history, Pt. 2, p. 18, Pt. 3, p. 10, RP-USAMHI; *Soldier,* pp. 24–25.

8. *Soldier,* p. 55; ltr. Williams to author, 4/5/83.

9. *Soldier,* p. 55.

10. Lt. Williams to author, 4/5/83.

11. *Soldier,* pp. 55–56.

12. Swing's reaction: CB-Moorman int.

13. Ltr. Ewell to author, 4/28/83.

14. CB-Moorman int.

15. "Bad knees," "not physically qualified": ltr. Williams to author. Gavin said in CB interview: "Ted Dunn was drunk most of the time, a big scandal. Everybody was talking about it. He had a habit of going off with a bottle to a hotel downtown and getting plastered for a whole weekend."

16. CB-Moorman int.; Taylor oral history, USAMHI.

17. Ltr. Charles W. Kouns to author, 4/9/83.

18. Tucker early bio. courtesy his ongoing biographer, Philip C. Gowdy, of Atlanta, Georgia, in ltrs. to author 11/12/84 and 11/30/84. Appraising quotes from CB-Moorman and CB-Winton interviews.

19. CB-Kroos int.; Kroos scrapbook contains photos of MBR wearing cap as described. "Golden eagle": CB-Chester B. McCoid int. 8/5/83; Ridgway salute: ltr. Wayne Pierce to author 8/24/83.

20. Review: Ketterson. MBR speech: Box 2A, RP-USAMHI.

21. Witness prefers anonymity.

Chapter 7

1. Charles W. Mason, "The 82nd Division Under Ridgway," unpublished article, Box 5, RP-USAMHI; MBR "early history": MBR oral history, Pt. 2, p. 47, RP-USAMHI; *Soldier,* p. 58.

2. Swing official bio.; Miley official bio.; CB-Miley int.; Ellis, "The Airborne Command and Center."

3. Keerans: *Register;* CB-Gavin int.

4. CB-Winton int.

5. CB-Eaton int.

6. CB-Taylor int.

7. CB-Eaton int.

8. Mason, "The 82nd Division"; CB-Lynch int.; CB-Boyd int.

9. Details here and below on 82nd and 101st and 17th airborne division artillery and "antiaircraft" battalions based on letters from and author interviews with: J. Carter Todd (CO, 319); William S. Lancey (XO, 320); Robert H. Neptune (CO, 376); Harrison B. Harden and Hugh A. Neal (COs, 456th); Arthur G. Kroos (battery CO, 80th); Clarence F. Nelson (CO, 907); John T. Cooper (CO, 463); Harry W. Elkins (CO, 377); X. B. Cox (CO, 81st); John W. Paddock (CO, 155th); Paul F. Oswald (CO, 680); Richard J. Long (XO, 681); Raymond L. Cato (CO, 460); Edward S. Branigan, Jr. (CO, 464); Kenneth L. Booth (CO, 466); Maxwell D. Taylor; James M. Gavin; Thomas L.

Sherburne; William N. Gillmore; T. E. Shockley; Harry Boyle; John G. Morgan; Thomas F. Magner.

10. Dunn's relief and Tucker's promotion: ltr. MBR–Bolling, 3/16/43, Box 2A, RP-USAMHI. Regimental approval of Tucker: Warren R. Williams ltr. to author 4/7/83, and others.

11. Easley promotion and departure: ltrs. R. Klemm Boyd to author 3/23/83, and Charles H. White, Jr., 5/10/83. Easley was subsequently killed in action on Okinawa. Re Scott: ltr. Gerald M. Cummings to author 10/20/83; CB-Eaton int.

12. Lewis' son, Robert L. Lewis, in 504: ltr. Louis Hauptfleisch (504 historian) to author. Lewis characterized: ltr. Wayne Pierce to author 10/4/83; CB interviews with Arthur G. Kroos 6/10/83, Paul L. Turner 8/7/83, John H. Swenson 8/7/83, Teddy H. Sanford 8/11/83 and Dave R. Stokely 9/11/83.

13. CB-Arthur G. Kroos int. 6/10/83. "Warm spot": CB-Sanford int. Cancer: CB-Swenson int.; ltr. Lewis to MBR 3/6/45, Box 3, RP-USAMHI. MBR ltr. to Robert L. Lewis 4/29/45 at his father's death. MBR wrote that Lewis was "a splendid officer" and "ever a faithful friend."

14. Huston, *Out of the Blue*, pp. 91–93.

15. Ibid., pp. 110–11. In MBR oral history, Pt. 2, p. 52, he commented that the division was "dreadfully short" of aircraft and gliders.

16. Dent: *Register*. MBR's glider ride, *Soldier*, pp. 56–57. MBR's second parachute jump occurred on October 22, 1942, at Fort Bragg. Taylor and the division Gs were in the stick. Ltr. Osmond A. Leahy to author 5/16/83.

17. *Soldier*, pp. 57–58. Murphy: Milton Dank, *The Glider Gang* (Philadelphia: Lippincott, 1977), p. 62.

18. Devlin, *Paratrooper!* pp. 119, 661.

Chapter 8

1. Here and below on grand strategy: *A General's Life*, pp. 117–26.

2. Huston, *Out of the Blue*, p. 97; MBR oral history, Pt. 2, p. 48, RP-USAMHI.

3. MBR oral history, Pt. 2, p. 48; Ridgway pressure on Marshall: CB-Gavin int.

4. Box 2A, RP-USAMHI; Ketterson; Mason, "82nd Division"; MBR "early history."

5. Official history, 13th Airborne Division, USAMHI Library. Cutler first took the 326th GIR to Alliance, Neb., where it was mated with the independent 88th GIR to form the 1st Independent Glider Brigade. This outfit became the nucleus of the 13th Airborne Division, to which was added the 515th PIR, then commanded by Julian B. Lindsey. (Per Cutler ltr. to author, 2/20/84.)

6. Ltr. Ridgway to Gavin, 2/9/43, Box 2A, RP-USAMHI.

7. Gavin here and below: CB-Gavin ints.; Gavin, *War and Peace in the Space Age*, pp. 21–46, has rather complete early bio. Additional Gavin bio.: Bradley Biggs, *Gavin* (Hamden, Conn.: Archon Books, 1980); Donald A. Davis (UPI), "Jim Gavin: Still Every Inch a Soldier," Los Angeles *Times*, 5/2/79. MBR quote: *Soldier*, p. 62.

8. CB-Winton int.

9. Various interviews; "jackals": CB-Eaton int.

10. *On to Berlin*.

11. CB-Gavin int.

12. CB-Moorman int.

13. Ibid.

14. Ibid.; CB interviews with Ridgway, Taylor, Gavin.

Chapter 9

1. Marshall summons and trip: *Soldier*, p. 58. Adams family and sons: CB ints. with Emory S. and James Y. Adams 9/25/84, 9/26/84 and 9/27/84.

2. Here and below, *A General's Life*, pp. 126–37.

3. *Soldier*, p. 59. *A General's Life*, p. 138. MBR arrival: Ike Papers II, p. 1017; "Eyes and ears" job: Ike Papers II, p. 951. Dinner, etc: Ike Papers V (Chronology), 3/10/43.

4. *Soldier*, pp. 66–67.

5. *A General's Life*, pp. 141–42.

6. *Soldier*, p. 58.

7. *A General's Life*, p. 98.

8. MBR oral history, Pt. 2, p. 105, RP-USAMHI.

9. *A General's Life*, p. 142.

10. Ward: *Register*.

11. *A General's Life*, p. 142; *Soldier*, p. 59

12. *A General's Life*, pp. 143ff.

13. MBR on Alexander: *Soldier*, p. 81.

14. *A General's Life*, p. 170. Dawley: ibid., p. 169; *Register*.

15. Sicily planning: *A General's Life*, pp. 160–68.

16. Sicily airborne planning: John C. Warren, *Airborne Missions in the Mediterranean 1942–1945* (hereafter Warren I), USAF Historical Division, Air University, 1955; Gavin, *Airborne Warfare;* Gavin, *On to Berlin*, pp. 15–18, 1–4; Huston, *Out of the Blue*, pp. 154–57; Devlin, *Paratrooper!* pp. 212–14. On "Boy" Browning see: *Soldier*, p. 66; CB-Gavin int.; Ike Papers II, p. 1100. Dank, *Glider Gang*, pp. 39–40; Michael Hickey, *Out of the Sky: A History of Airborne Warfare* (New York: Scribner's, 1979), pp. 82ff.

17. Gavin, *Airborne Warfare*, p. 4.

18. Warren I, p. 22; Box 5A, RP-USAMHI. The Taylor "advance party" is described in detail.

19. Clark and Gruenther: *Register;* Ike Papers II, pp. 824–25, 1181.

20. In *Soldier*, p. 65, MBR wrote: "I personally had selected the training sites on my . . . quick trip to Africa. . . ."; Ketterson; Mason, "82nd Division."

21. CB-Adams int.

22. Operations of Raff's 509 here and below: Warren I; Huston, *Out of the Blue;* Devlin, *Paratrooper!* pp. 138–90; Edson D. Raff, *We Jumped to Fight* (New York: Eagle Books, 1944); William P. Yarborough, *Bail Out over North Africa* (Williamstown, N.J.: Phillips Publication, 1979). Yarborough oral history, Yarborough Papers, USAMHI.

23. Eisenhower praise of Raff: Eisenhower, *Crusade in Europe*, p. 125. (Ike described Raff's operation as a "minor epic in itself.")

24. *Bail Out over North Africa*, p. 16; ltr. Charles R. Doyle (509 historian) to author 1/15/84. Ltrs. anonymous to author 1/14/84; Ben F. Pearson, Jr., to author 3/1/84.

25. Yarborough to 82nd Div: ltr. Lee to MBR 2/23/45, Box 2A, RP. Raff to States: Doyle ltr. to author. Yardley to CO 509: Devlin, *Paratrooper!* pp. 165, 215. William R. Dudley became the 509 XO: ltr. Dudley to author 10/28/83.

26. Yarborough oral history, USAMHI, p. 28; ltr. Yarborough to author, with enclosures, 6/15/83.

Chapter 10

1. *Soldier*, p. 59; Gavin, *On to Berlin*, pp. 7–8; ltr. MBR to Alexander Bolling, 3/26/43, Box 2A, RP-USAMHI.

2. *Soldier*, pp. 59–60; ltrs. MBR to Henry H. Arnold 4/12/43 and Arnold to MBR 5/5/43, Box 2A, RP-USAMHI.

3. MBR "early history"; CB-Winton int.; ltr. Harold L. Clark, CO, 52nd Troop Carrier Wing, to MBR 3/31/43, Box 2A, RP-USAMHI.

4. Ltr. Charles W. Kouns to author 4/9/83.

5. *Soldier*, p. 62; MBR oral history, Pt. 2, p. 47, RP-USAMHI.

6. Ltr. Robert L. Dickerson to author 9/20/83; Cummings to author 10/20/83; *Register*.

7. *Soldier*, pp. 61–62; MBR oral history, Pt. 2, p. 67; ltr. MBR to Maxwell D. Taylor 4/22/43, Box 2A, RP-USAMHI.

8. *Soldier*, pp. 62–63; MBR "early history"; Ketterson; Mason, "82nd Division." *The Devils in Baggy Pants; Combat Record of the 504th Parachute Infantry Regiment* (Nashville, Tenn.: Battery Book Shop, 1976). This official, oversized "picture book" should not be confused with *Those Devils in Baggy Pants*, by Ross S. Carter (New York: Appleton-Century-Crofts, 1951). Carter's book, republished in paperback by The Kingsport (Tennessee) Press, is a classic platoon-level "eyewitness" narrative of his three-year wartime service with the 504th.

9. CB-Eaton int.

10. Gavin, *On to Berlin*, p. 8; Mason; 82nd Division H.Q. Diary, 5/10/43, Box 5A, RP-USAMHI; *Soldier*, p. 65.

11. CB-Kroos int.

12. Devlin, *Paratrooper!* pp. 2, 5, 6; various interviews.

13. *A General's Life*, p. 686 (Notes).

14. Ibid., pp. 169–71; CB-MBR int.

15. *A General's Life*, pp. 164–65.

16. Warren I, p. 22; Martin Blumenson, *The Patton Papers* (2 vols.) (Boston: Houghton-Mifflin, 1972, hereafter *Patton Papers* I and II), p. 239. On May 3, 1943, Patton wrote: "I told them at once that I was going to land 4 divisions and 2 parachute regiments . . ."

17. Warren I, pp. 21–29.

18. Ibid.
19. Browning-Ridgway and tug-of-war: Taylor diary, North African trip 4/7/43, 4/8/43–4/10/43; Division HQ Diary 5/15/43, 5/18/43, 5/21/43, Box 5A, RP; "dilettante": CB-Alexander D. Surles int.
20. MBR oral history, Pt. 2, pp. 59–61, RP-USAMHI.
21. Ltr. MBR to Geoffrey Keyes, 4/25/43, Box 2A, RP-USAMHI.
22. *Soldier,* pp. 67–68; ltrs. Browning to Yardley 6/6/43, MBR to Browning 6/7/43 (not sent), Box 2A, RP-USAMHI.
23. *Soldier,* p. 68; MBR oral history, Pt. 2, p. 53, RP-USAMHI.
24. *Patton Papers II,* p. 254; *Soldier,* p. 68.

Chapter 11

1. Here and below: Warren I, pp. 22–28. Hopkinson plan: Hickey, *Out of the Sky,* pp. 98–101; Dank, *The Glider Gang,* pp. 63–67.
2. *Soldier,* p. 65. 82nd Div H.Q. Diary, 6/7/43, Box 5A, RP-USAMHI. Warren I, p. 28. The official 504 regimental historian wrote that these jump accidents "put nearly 30 percent of the regiment in the hospital with broken bones, sprains and bruises."
3. Warren I, p. 28; MBR "early history."
4. CB-Gavin int.; CB-Eaton int.
5. Ltrs. Gavin to author 7/25/84; Alexander to author 5/12/84; Gray to author 8/8/84.
6. Gavin, *Airborne Warfare,* p. 105.
7. Warren I, p. 28.
8. Gavin, *On to Berlin,* p. 8; Gavin, *Airborne Warfare,* p. 5.
9. "Ridgway—The Legend," brief article on MBR in *Static Line,* March 1983, by J. Aaron Cook.
10. Gavin, *On to Berlin,* p. 10.
11. Taylor, *Swords and Plowshares,* p. 49.
12. Ike Papers V, Chronology 6/16/43; Gavin, *On to Berlin,* p. 9.
13. Warren I, p. 24.
14. Ketterson; Mason; MBR "early history"; *Soldier,* pp. 65–66; Warren I, pp. 28–29.
15. *Soldier,* p. 66.
16. *The Devils in Baggy Pants* (unpaginated).
17. Ltr. Allen Langdon to author 11/12/84.
18. Ltr. Wayne Pierce to author, 10/4/83.
19. Warren I, p. 24; MBR memorandum, 8/2/43, "Reported loss of transport planes and personnel due to friendly fire," Box 2A, RP-USAMHI.
20. Route: Warren I, p. 24, and map opposite p. 39. MBR quoted in ltr. MBR-Chester B. Hansen 4/5/49—as background for Omar N. Bradley's war memoir *A Soldier's Story,* RP-USAMHI.
21. Warren I, pp. 37–39; MBR memorandum of 8/2/43.
22. MBR memorandum of 8/2/43.

Chapter 12

1. *Soldier,* p. 71; *Dictionary of American Naval Fighting Ships,* Vol. 1, p. 44; Vol. IV, pp. 419–20; Samuel Eliot Morison, *History of U.S. Naval Operations in World War II, Vol. IX, Sicily-Salerno-Anzio* (Boston: Little, Brown, 1959), pp. 61–62; CB-Adams int.
2. *A General's Life,* pp. 161, 175; Gavin, *On to Berlin,* p. 14.
3. Morison, Vol. IX, p. 67: "During the afternoon watch the wind increased from [Beaufort scale] force 3 to 6, some say 7; and a nasty, steep sea made up athwart the convoys' courses." At 2230 hours, Morison wrote, the "wind began to moderate." Force 6 on the Beaufort scale is 25–31 mph; force 7, 32–38 mph. Gavin, in *On to Berlin,* p. 22, puts the wind at "35 m.p.h." The official British historian, C. J. C. Molony, in *The Mediterranean and Middle East,* Vol. V (London: H.M.S.O., 1973), p. 54, puts the wind at force 6 (25–31 mph). Warren I, p. 33, puts the wind at 25–30 mph. MBR's estimate *(Soldier,* p. 69) of 35 knots (force 8) is far higher than most and was probably an unwitting exaggeration or misstatement.
4. Various 82nd Division histories, author interviews, and ltrs. Allen Langdon to author.
5. Devlin, *Paratrooper!* pp. 664–65.
6. Gavin, *On to Berlin,* p. 20 (complete text).
7. Warren I, pp. 29–37, has the most complete account of the Gavin mission. I have used it freely here and below, as well as Gavin's *On to Berlin,* pp. 19–47, which, in part, duplicates Gavin's *Airborne Warfare,* pp. 1–17, and Gavin's *War and Peace in the Space Age,* pp. 51–71. See also Devlin, pp. 108–48; Huston, *Out of the Blue,* pp. 154–67; Molony, pp. 83–84; Wesley Frank

Craven and James L. Cate, *The Army Air Forces in World War II* (Chicago: University of Chicago Press, 1948–58), pp. 446–49.

8. Ltr. Langdon to author 11/14/84.

9. The British glider operation at Ponte Grande is described in detail in Warren I, pp. 41–47. See also Molony, pp. 79–81.

Chapter 13

1. *A General's Life*, p. 180.

2. Gavin, *On to Berlin*, pp. 36–37.

3. Here and below: *Soldier*, pp. 71–72; MBR "early history."

4. Ltr. Willard R. Follmer to author 2/5/84.

5. Here and below: Warren I, pp. 34–37; Gavin, *Airborne Warfare*, pp. 1–17; Gavin, *On to Berlin*, pp. 24–47; Gavin, *War and Peace in the Space Age*, pp. 1–70. On Kouns's capture, ltr. Kouns to author 4/17/83.

6. Gavin quote: *On to Berlin*, p. 44.

7. Albert N. Garland and Howard McG. Smyth, assisted by Martin Blumenson, *Sicily and the Surrender of Italy* (Washington, D.C.: Office of Chief of Military History, 1965) (hereafter Garland and Smyth), p. 156.

8. Here and below: Gavin, *On to Berlin*, pp. 25–40; Gavin, *War and Peace in the Space Age*, pp. 55–67.

9. Warren I, pp. 42–47; Molony, *The Mediterranean and the Middle East*, pp. 79–81.

10. *A General's Life*, p. 187.

11. Gavin on Krause: *On to Berlin*, pp. 30–31; Gavin ltr. to author 4/5/83.

12. Ltr. Langdon to author 11/12/84.

13. Gavin ltr. to author 4/5/83.

14. Ltr. Langdon to author 11/12/84.

15. Ltr. anonymous to author 7/5/83.

16. On Conrath deciding to withdraw from Gela: Garland and Smyth, p. 173; *On to Berlin*, pp. 40–41.

Chapter 14

1. Here and below: Warren I, pp. 37–41; Garland and Smyth, pp. 175–84; various interviews; ltr. Williams to author 4/5/83; ltr. Yarborough to author.

2. Keerans in violation of orders: CB-Gavin int.; CB-Eaton int.

3. MBR at airfield: Ketterson. Warning antiaircraft gunners: MBR "Reported Loss of Transport planes and personnel due to Friendly Fire," Box 2A, RP-USAMHI.

4. Garland and Smyth, p. 179. Cook wounded: CB-Cook int. 6/19/83.

5. Garland and Smyth, p. 181.

6. Casualties: ibid. p. 182; 376th: CB-Neptune int. 8/4/84.

7. "Shaved heads": CB-Moorman int.

8. Ketterson.

9. *A General's Life*, pp. 184–86; Patton II, p. 283.

10. Huston, *Out of the Blue*, pp. 162–64; MBR "Reported Loss" memorandum.

11. Here and below: Warren I, pp. 47–54; Molony, *The Mediterranean and the Middle East*, pp. 95–97.

12. Nigel Hamilton, *Master of the Battlefield: Monty's War Years 1942–1944* (New York: McGraw-Hill, 1983), p. 311.

13. Warren I, p. 37; Bradley, *A Soldier's Story*, p. 127; Huston, *Out of the Blue*, p. 164.

14. Warren I, p. 37; Huston, *Out of the Blue*, p. 164; Gavin, *Airborne Warfare*, p. 16.

15. Huston, *Out of the Blue*, p. 164.

16. Memo. Taylor to MBR, 7/26/43; Memo. Gavin to MBR, 7/26/43; MBR memo. 7/31/43, Box 2A, RP-USAMHI. See also MBR memo. "Principles," Huston, p. 162.

17. MBR to Eisenhower 7/26/43, Box 2A, RP-USAMHI.

18. Lucas: Huston, p. 166; Eisenhower to Marshall, 7/20/43, Ike Papers III, p. 1440. McNair: Warren I, p. 54; Devlin, *Paratrooper!* p. 248.

Chapter 15

1. Here and below on Sicily strategy: *A General's Life*, pp. 186–90.

2. Patton's northwestward drive: *A General's Life*, pp. 191–92.

3. Staff lift: Ketterson; 9th Division artillery: Ernest B. Furgurson, *Westmoreland: The Inevitable General* (Boston: Little, Brown, 1968); *Soldier*, p. 73.

4. Taylor acting ADC: *Soldier*, p. 75. Beall: ltr. Kouns to author 4/17/83, and various interviews. Winton: CB-Winton int. and ltrs. Winton to author 4/5/83 and 4/21/83. Adams: CB-Adams int.; ltr. Adams to author 10/23/84.

5. Ltr. Ireland to author 2/20/84.

6. Garland and Smyth, p. 246; *A General's Life*, p. 192; Patton Papers II, pp. 419–21. Hobart R. Gay, oral history, pp. 28–29, Gay Papers, USAMHI.

7. *A General's Life*, pp. 192–93.

8. "Road March": Garland and Smyth, p. 250. "[M]ore like a maneuver": *Soldier*, p. 76. "Strange affair": Gavin, *On to Berlin*, pp. 48–49. Casualties and POWs: Ketterson. Speed of advance: *Soldier*, p. 76.

9. *Soldier*, pp. 73–74; MBR up front: Ketterson.

10. *Soldier*, p. 75.

11. MBR oral history, Pt. 2, pp. 105–6, RP, USAMHI.

12. CB-Gavin interviews.

13. Murray Schumach, "The Education of Matthew Ridgway," New York *Times Sunday Magazine*, 5/4/52.

14. Unpublished ms, William S. Triplet, kindly provided the author 1/13/84.

15. Ltr. Robert S. Palmer to author 1/15/84.

16. Yarborough oral history, pp. 30–39, Yarborough Papers, USAMHI; ltr. Yarborough to author 6/15/83. In the oral history, Yarborough stated that Ridgway said: "Your services are no longer required. You're a pain in the ass . . . You go back to Mark Clark and tell him that he should find another job for you." However, in ltr. to author, Yarborough stated that when he reported to Ridgway's CP, "Ridgway did not interview me nor did he see me on that occasion prior to my departure." Yarborough was given a sealed letter to Clark, recommending Yarborough's relief. In the oral history, Yarborough quotes Clark as saying: "Knowing your personality and that of General Ridgway, I should never have allowed you to be assigned to that outfit in the first place."

17. Ltr. Daniel W. Danielson to author 11/1/83.

18. Ltr. Williams to author 4/2/83.

19. Garland and Smyth, p. 255; Gavin, *On to Berlin*, p. 47.

20. Ltr. Boyd to author 3/14/83.

21. Ltr. Harrison B. Harden to author 3/12/84.

22. Ltr. Ireland to author.

23. Garland and Smyth, p. 255; *Soldier*, p. 76.

24. See especially Carter, *Those Devils in Baggy Pants*, pp. 32–34: "It was a very happy time . . ."

25. CB-Eaton int.

26. Ltr. Boyd to author 3/31/83.

27. *Register;* Jack profile, Shreveport *Times*, 8/21/83; CB-Kroos int. Jack attended Tulane and Yale law schools.

28. Here and below, *A General's Life*, pp. 194–95; proposed parachute operation on north coast: Gavin, *On to Berlin*, p. 58.

Chapter 16

1. Here and below: Italy invasion planning: Garland and Smyth, pp. 435–553; Martin Blumenson, *Salerno to Cassino* (Washington, D.C.: Office of the Chief of Military History, 1968), pages 3–58; Morrison IX, pp. 227–53; Sir Basil H. Liddell Hart, *History of the Second World War* (New York: Putnam's, 1971, hereafter Liddell Hart), pp. 447–75; Eisenhower, *Crusade in Europe*, pp. 183–91; Stephen Ambrose, *The Supreme Command: The War Years of General Dwight D. Eisenhower* (Garden City, N.Y.: Doubleday, 1970), pp. 237–63; Hugh Pond, *Salerno* (London: William Kimber, 1961), p. 38.

2. Limited aspect of Calabria: Field Marshal Viscount Montgomery of Alamein, K. G., *Memoirs* (Cleveland: World Publishing, 1958), pp. 171–73; Churchill "knee . . .": Chester Wilmot, *The Struggle for Europe* (New York: Harper & Brothers, 1952), p. 132.

3. Attack at Rome itself: Ike Papers III, p. 1453. DDE wrote Marshall: "We earnestly examined, during the month of August, the possibility of a landing at Rome instead of Salerno."

4. For a more detailed description of German troop deployments, see Blumenson, *Salerno to Cassino*, pp. 67–68.

5. Ronald Lewin, *Ultra Goes to War* (New York: McGraw-Hill, 1978), pp. 281–84; F. W. Winterbotham, *The Ultra Secret* (New York: Harper & Row, 1974), pp. 161–66.

6. Liddell Hart, pp. 473–75.
7. Blumenson, *Salerno to Cassino*, pp. 32–33, speculates on the reasons behind the choice of the 36th Division.
8. Pond, *Salerno*, p. 43. Montgomery on McCreery: Hamilton, *Master of the Battlefield*, p. 425.
9. 46th: George F. Howe, *Northwest Africa: Seizing the Initiative in the West* (Washington, D.C.: OCMH, 1957), pp. 350, 402. Freeman-Attwood: Pond, *Salerno*, p. 43. According to Pond, the security violation occurred in a personal letter in which Freeman-Attwood wrote to his wife: "I hope I shall be drinking a bottle of champagne somewhere in Italy on our wedding day." 56th: Hamilton, *Master of the Battlefield*, pp. 236–37. Montgomery cabled Alexander on April 29, 1943: "56 repeat 56 Division gave very bad showing today under heavy shell fire and I must accept the fact that the division has little fighting value."
10. Montgomery, *Memoirs*, pp. 171–73. Hamilton, *Master of the Battlefield*, pp. 385–432.

Chapter 17

1. Here and through the division landings at Salerno: "Contact Imminent, A Narrative of Pre-campaign Activities of the 82nd Airborne Division, July–September 1943," prepared by the 82nd Airborne Division General Staff, Fifth Draft, 12/26/43, Ralph P. Eaton Papers, USAMHI. (Duplicate in Box 2A, RP-USAMHI.) See also: MBR ltr. to Commander-in-Chief, "Lessons of Airborne Operations in Italy," with five enclosures, 10/25/43, Box 2A, RP-USAMHI. (See especially enclosure No. 2, "Description of Operation from Planning Phase to Execution"); "Report of Arrival of Units in Italy," by Paul L. Turner, AC of S, G-3, 82nd Abn Div, RP-USAMHI; MBR Memorandum "Development of Operation Giant," 9/9/43, Box 2A, RP-USAMHI. Also: Gavin, *Airborne Warfare*, pp. 18–28; Gavin, *On to Berlin*, pp. 59–71.
2. Ike Papers V, Chronology, 7/29/43. CB-Yarborough int. and ltr.
3. Maxwell D. Taylor, *Swords and Plowshares* (New York: Norton, 1972), p. 52.
4. "Contact Imminent," p. 3.
5. MBR ltr. to an acquaintance, 2/23/56, Box 41, RP-USAMHI, amplified in MBR ltr. to author 6/3/83.
6. More on Nocera-Sarno mission and cancellation in Warren I, pp. 56–57.
7. Pathfinders and gear described in Warren I, pp. 59–60.
8. Gavin designation: Gavin, *Airborne Warfare*, p. 21.
9. Additional data on Volturno River mission and cancellation: Warren I, p. 57; *Soldier*, p. 94; commanders' meeting: Ike Papers V, Chronology.
10. Eisenhower negotiations: Garland and Smyth, pp. 435–81.
11. Cunningham reaction: Morison IX, p. 239. High-level endorsements: Ike Papers II, pp. 1377, 1378–81. First choice British 1st Abn: ibid., p. 1378. Eisenhower wrote: "In view of fact 82nd Division has been integrated with AVALANCHE from beginning, believe it better to count on 82nd supporting X Corps while British division does Rome job but I am having the implications examined."
12. "Hare-brained scheme": *Soldier*, p. 83.
13. Garland and Smyth, pp. 485–89. See also Gavin analysis in *Airborne Warfare* and *On to Berlin*.
14. Mark W. Clark, *Calculated Risk* (New York: Harper & Brothers, 1950), p. 181. Hamilton, *Master of the Battlefield*, pp. 413–15.
15. *Calculated Risk;* "Contact Imminent," pp. 7–8.
16. Morison IX, pp. 234–35; Blumenson, *Salerno to Cassino*, pp. 52–53.

Chapter 18

1. Garland and Smyth, pp. 482–85.
2. "Contact Imminent," p. 7 (see note 1, Ch. 17).
3. MBR memo "Development of Operation Giant," 9/9/43; *Soldier*, pp. 80–82.
4. "Development . . ."
5. Ibid.
6. Ibid.
7. MBR memo 9/9/43.
8. *Soldier*, p. 81.
9. MBR memo 9/9/43. Gardiner: Warren I, p. 58; Taylor, *Swords and Plowshares*, pp. 54–55; Ike Papers II, p. 1387n.
10. Plan: Garland and Smyth, p. 500.
11. Gavin, *Airborne Warfare*, p. 25.
12. Bertsch: *Register*.

13. Warren I, p. 60, apparently in error, states that the 325th was not flown to Sicily.

14. Taylor-Gardiner mission: Garland and Smyth, pp. 500–5; Taylor, *Swords and Plowshares,* pp. 56–63.

15. Garland and Smyth, pp. 505–9.

16. "Contact Imminent," p. 9.

17. Garland and Smyth, p. 508.

18. Ibid., p. 509; MBR memo 9/9/43; CB-Eaton int.

19. Garland and Smyth, pp. 508–21. Regarding the German takeover of the Salerno beach defenses, Major General John P. Lucas wrote that the announcement of the Italian surrender was "a serious mistake because it meant that before H-hour the Italians defending the beaches had been replaced by Germans—a difference not to be taken lightly." John P. Lucas diary, Pt. 2, p. 19, USAMHI.

20. CB-Eaton int.

21. Morison IX, p. 241.

22. Kesselring and Westphal quoted in Liddell Hart, p. 455.

23. Disposition of German forces: Garland and Smyth.

24. Gavin, *On to Berlin,* pp. 67–68.

25. Taylor, *Swords and Plowshares,* pp. 63–64.

26. *Soldier,* p. 82.

27. CB-Eaton int. In *Crusade,* Eisenhower, other than praising Taylor for the great risks he ran in Rome, dismisses the entire Rome airborne mission as follows: "One of these plots involved the landing of a large airborne force in the vicinity of Rome. At the last minute either the fright of the Italian government or the movement of German reserves as alleged by the Italians—I have never known which—forced the cancellation of the project." Eisenhower views on airborne division iterated: Ike Papers III, p. 1481. After the war, Bedell Smith and Eisenhower's British G-2, Kenneth W. D. Strong, continued to believe that the cancellation of Allied airborne operations on Rome had been a mistake. (Their fantastical views may have influenced historian Morison.) In retrospect, Smith regretted the choice of "specialist" Max Taylor as emissary. What was needed, Smith said, was a more forceful generalist, someone who would have shocked Badoglio into action with a statement such as: "See here, you signed this agreement—and if you don't live up to it—you will all be lined up against the wall and shot." (Smith and Strong quoted in Hamilton, *Master of the Battlefield,* pp. 399–402.)

Chapter 19

1. Salerno invasion operations, here and below: Blumenson, *Salerno to Cassino,* pp. 73–153; Morison IX, pp. 252–301; Chester G. Starr, *From Salerno to the Alps; A History of the Fifth Army* (Washington, D.C.: Infantry Journal Press, 1948), pp. 16–33; Clark, *Calculated Risk,* pp. 182–209; Pond, *Salerno.*

2. Morison IX, p. 253.

3. Ibid., p. 249.

4. "Come on in . . ." Clark, p. 188. Largest German air attack: Morison IX, p. 261.

5. Hewitt quoted in Morison, p. 278. Lange, misnamed John W. and misidentified as division artillery commander, quoted in Morison, p. 270.

6. Clark-Dawley disputation and premature mislanding of 157th Rgt: Blumenson, pp. 100–1.

7. Morison IX, p. 294.

8. The Taranto landing described: ibid., pp. 235–36; Blumenson, p. 94.

9. The 1st Division action at Taranto et seq. is recorded in Hilary St. George Saunders, *The Red Beret* (London: Michael Joseph, 1950), pp. 143–48; and G. G. Norton, *The Red Devils: The Story of the British Airborne Forces* (Harrisburg, Penn.: Stackpole, 1971), pp. 29–30. Hopkinson was one of 101 casualties—killed, wounded, or missing—in the action. He was replaced by E. E. Downs.

10. Return of 82nd to Clark: Ike Papers III, p. 1405; see also Blumenson, pp. 122–23.

11. Blumenson, p. 122.

12. "Contact Imminent," p. 11. Blumenson (p. 122) apparently did not realize the 325th embarked at Licata at 2000 hours September 13 and sailed first to Palermo. Beall for Adams: CB-Adams int. and other interviews.

13. Blumenson, p. 123.

14. Ibid. MBR memo 9/25/43, "Lessons of Airborne Operations in Italy," and enclosures (2) "Descriptions of Operations from Planning phase to Execution," Box 5A, RP-USAMHI.

15. Dawley quoted in Clark, *Calculated Risk,* p. 200. Middleton quoted in Pond, *Salerno,* p. 173.

On the withdrawal plans—and the controversy—see Blumenson, p. 116, Morison IX, p. 290, and Hamilton, *Master of the Battlefield,* p. 413.

16. Morison IX, p. 266. Vietinghoff quoted in Morison, p. 292. Morison estimated that during the Salerno operation naval vessels delivered "more than 11,000 tons" of shells in direct gunfire support of ships ashore—the equivalent of 72,000 Army 105 mm high-explosive projectiles.

17. Eisenhower reaction: Ike Papers III, pp. 1405–40. Blumenson, pp. 118–20; Morison IX, pp. 293–94.

18. Clark, *Calculated Risk,* p. 199. Blumenson, pp. 123–24.

19. Ridgway to Termini and Salerno: "Contact Imminent," p. 11; *Soldier,* p. 84; Gavin, *On to Berlin,* p. 71; Warren I, p. 60.

20. "Can do": Clark, *Calculated Risk,* p. 203.

21. Here and below: Warren I, pp. 61–65; Gavin, *On to Berlin,* pp. 71–72; Clark, *Calculated Risk,* p. 203; "Contact Imminent," p. 11.

22. Warren I, p. 65 and n. 29 (p. 124), says Tucker had about 1,300 men, which seems right for 82 planes with 16 paratroopers each. Both Morison IX, p. 291, and Craven and Cate II, p. 531, greatly understate number of men ("over 600" and "more than 600").

23. Tucker quoted in "Contact Imminent," p. 11. Jump injuries: *The Devils in Baggy Pants.*

24. Clark on Tucker: Clark, *Calculated Risk,* p. 203; Pond, *Salerno,* p. 174; Gavin, *On to Berlin,* p. 70.

25. Warren I, pp. 65–66; Gavin, *On to Berlin,* p. 72. Ltr. Langdon to author 11/12/84.

26. Avellino: Warren I, pp. 66–69; Gavin, *On to Berlin,* pp. 74–75; Gavin, *Airborne Warfare,* pp. 31–32; Blumenson, pp. 131–32; Devlin, *Paratrooper!* pp. 306–26. The Devlin account has the most detailed description of the ground fighting.

27. Yardley: Devlin, pp. 311–15. Dudley: ltr. to author 10/28/83; Kellogg: ltr. Paul L. Turner to author 9/8/83. DSC: Blumenson, *Salerno to Cassino,* p. 132n.

28. No more parachute drops: Starr, *Salerno to the Alps,* p. 32. Evaluation of Avellino: Clark, *Calculated Risk,* p. 206; Gavin, *On to Berlin,* p. 75; *Soldier,* p. 86; Warren I, p. 69; Blumenson, p. 132. Ridgway, describing the drop as a "tragic miscarriage" declined an evaluation: "They caused the Germans vast annoyance, but whether they had any real effect on the Salerno operation is a matter for military historians to debate."

29. "Contact Imminent," pp. 12–13. Paul L. Turner, "Report of Arrival of Units in Italy," 10/22/43, Box 5A, RP-USAMHI. Richard Tregaskis, *Invasion Diary* (New York: Popular Library, 1962), pp. 100–2. Tregaskis, a war correspondent, sailed to Salerno with Lewis. MBR crossing to Salerno: ltr. to author 6/13/84. No records can be found. However, MBR was certain that he crossed on the "first LST departing after Tucker took off." Thus, he probably crossed during the day of September 14.

Chapter 20

1. Blumenson, pp. 134ff; Morison IX, pp. 295ff.

2. Blumenson, p. 149; Taylor, *Swords and Plowshares,* p. 65.

3. Lange's relief: Ike Papers III, p. 1436; Blumenson, p. 126n. Dawley: Blumenson, pp. 148–52; Pond, *Salerno* (quoting Walker Diary), pp. 215–16; Clark, *Calculated Risk,* p. 208; Ike Papers II, pp. 1136, 1154; Ike Papers III, pp. 1428, 1436, 1439, 1447–48.

4. Gavin on Dawley: *On to Berlin,* p. 76. Quoted here: ltr. Gavin to MBR 9/1/78, RP-USAMHI.

5. "So as . . .": Ike Papers III, p. 1428. "Should not . . .": Blumenson, p. 152.

6. CB-Mark W. Clark int. 4/7/80.

7. DDE visit: Ike Papers V, Chronology; DDE to Marshall, as quoted: Ike Papers III, p. 1436. Blumenson doubts: Blumenson, pp. 151–52; Martin Blumenson and James L. Stokesbury, *Masters of the Art of Command* (Boston: Houghton-Mifflin, 1975), p. 371.

8. CB-Clark int.

9. Lucas and II Corps: *A General's Life,* pp. 207–8. MBR release from VI Corps: Ltr. M. W. Clark to MBR 9/20/43, Box 1 RP-USAMHI. MBR views on Dawley and Lucas: ltr. MBR to Superintendent USMA 6/9/58 in response to a questionnaire, Box 31, RP-USAMHI.

10. Gavin on Tucker: Gavin, *On to Berlin,* p. 72, and CB-Gavin int.

11. Here and below: Blumenson, *Salerno to Cassino,* pp. 135–36; Pond, *Salerno,* pp. 211, 216; Gavin, *On to Berlin,* pp. 72–74.

12. Ltr. Louis A. Hauptfleisch to author 3/6/84.

13. *Those Devils in Baggy Pants,* pp. 54, 64; Tregaskis, *Invasion Diary,* pp. 104–18. Tregaskis, who joined Tucker in the thick of the fighting, has a vivid account of the action. *The Devils in Baggy Pants* quotes Tucker as saying, "Retreat Hell! Send me my other battalion."

14. "Eight times . . .": Carter, p. 64. Tucker DSC: Blumenson, *Salerno to Cassino*, p. 135n.
15. CB-Adams int. *Register*. Other author interviews.
16. "Contact Imminent," p. 12; Turner report 10/11/43.
17. CB-Neal int. 8/13/84.
18. German plans: Blumenson, pp. 154–56.
19. Mutiny: Pond, *Salerno*, pp. 208–10. Lucas use of artillery: Blumenson, p. 158. 36th Division: Lucas diary. Lucas wrote that 36th Division losses at Salerno had been so heavy that the division had to be withdrawn from combat "for necessary reorganization and was in Army reserve."
20. Beyond Salerno: Blumenson, pp. 154–71; Starr, *Salerno to the Alps*, pp. 33–47; Clark, *Calculated Risk*, pp. 209–28.
21. Ridgway force: Blumenson, p. 164.
22. Ltr. Robert D. Dickerson to author 9/20/83.
23. Gavin, *On to Berlin*, pp. 76–77.
24. Ltrs. Warren Williams to author 6/3/83; Charles W. Kouns to author 6/12/83; CB-Julian A. Cook int. 6/19/83. The quoted description was provided by Kouns, then a POW in Italy, who heard it from a newly arrived 504 POW who had witnessed Beall's death. Other details: CB-Adams int.
25. MBR quote from *Soldier*, p. 87.
26. Entry into Naples: Blumenson, p. 165; Gavin, *On to Berlin*, pp. 77–78; Clark and publicity: *A General's Life*, p. 204; Martin Blumenson, *Mark Clark* (New York: Congdon & Weed, 1984); John Ellis, *Cassino* (New York: McGraw-Hill, 1984).
27. Clark, *Calculated Risk*, p. 214; *Soldier*, p. 88; Gavin, *On to Berlin*, p. 78.
28. *Soldier*, p. 89; Gavin, *On to Berlin*, p. 79.
29. *Soldier*, p. 90.
30. CB-Eaton int.
31. *Soldier*, p. 91; whorehouse: CB-Eaton int.
32. Plan sketchily described in Starr, *Salerno to the Alps*, p. 40; more fully in Warren I, p. 70.
33. *Soldier*, p. 96. Truscott's 3rd "reinforced" for crossing: Starr, *Salerno to the Alps*, p. 40.
34. Ltr. Paul L. Turner to author 5/5/83; CB-Turner int.
35. Here and below: M. J. Alexander ltr. to Wm. E. Ekman 10/5/78, copy supplied by Alexander to author. Other details from Starr, *Salerno to the Alps*, p. 44.
36. MBR "frequent" visits to the front: Truscott, *Command Missions*, pp. 272, 278. Ridgway considered as temporary replacement for Middleton: Lucas diary, Pt. 2, p. 61, USAMHI.
37. Ltr. Turner to author 9/8/83.
38. The validity of the Italian campaign has been widely debated. See Blumenson, *Salerno to Cassino*, pp. 455–56; Starr, *Salerno to the Alps*, pp. 442–52; Morison IX, pp. 380–84; Samuel Eliot Morison, *Strategy and Compromise* (Boston: Little, Brown, 1958), pp. 41–47. For Eisenhower's views at the time, see Ike Papers III, pp. 1529–30.

Chapter 21

1. Clark comments on Ridgway: *Calculated Risk*, p. 236. Discussions re retaining 82nd Div: Ike Papers III, pp. 1481, 1513–14, 1517, 1523.
2. Ltr. MBR to M. W. Clark 11/10/43; ltr. Clark to MBR 11/12/43, Box 2A, RP-USAMHI. See also unused draft of a letter MBR composed for Clark to send Eisenhower.
3. Blumenson, p. 220. History 504 PIR, Box 5A, RP-USAMHI. *The Devils in Baggy Pants.* Freeman for Adams: CB-Adams int.
4. Gavin on Tucker: *On to Berlin*, p. 80. Carter. *Those Devils in Baggy Pants.* Lucas diary, Pt. 2, p. 81, USAMHI.
5. Danielson WIA, replaced by Blitch: ltr. Danielson to author 11/1/83.
6. Gavin to ADC: *On to Berlin*, p. 80.
7. Batcheller appraisal: CB-Gavin int.
8. Alexander to executive officer and Vandervoort to CO 2nd Bn.: ltr. Mark J. Alexander to author 5/12/83.
9. Cable Marshall to Eisenhower for MBR 10/25/43 and cable MBR to Marshall 11/1/43, Marshall Papers, Marshall Research Library.
10. Gavin, *On to Berlin*, pp. 85, 90.
11. Lynch replaced John Forsythe as CO, 142nd Rgt, 36th Div. Ltrs. Lynch to author 3/24/83 and 6/5/83, Klemm Boyd to author 4/13/83, Turner to author 5/5/83. Lynch wrote that the 82nd was "a splendid group, a great division" and that Ridgway was "the greatest soldier I have known, a great man and leader."

12. 505 History, Box 5A, RP-USAMHI.
13. CB-Eaton int.
14. MBR visit to 504: ltr. MBR to Tucker 11/5/43; ltr. MBR to L. B. Keiser, C/S VI Corps, 11/6/43, Box 2A, RP-USAMHI. MBR and Clark quotes: See note 2.
15. Ltr. MBR to M. D. Taylor 11/7/43; ltr. MBR to G-1, Eisenhower's HQ, 11/8/43, Box 2A, RP-USAMHI. Churchill's plea for using the 504: Winston S. Churchill, *The Second World War,* Vol. 5, *Closing the Ring,* pp. 443, 486, 493. On 1/3/44, Churchill cabled the senior British military liaison officer in Washington, Field Marshal Dill, to say that Eisenhower was "reluctant" to keep the 504 in Italy any longer, and asked Dill to intercede with Marshall and Eisenhower to let the 504 do Anzio ("This one fine and critical job") before moving to the British Isles for OVERLORD.
16. A more detailed account of Marshall's airborne ideas for OVERLORD will be found in the following chapters.
17. North Africa: The British airborne operation deep inside Tunisia was a drop of the 530-man 2nd Parachute Battalion of the 1st Parachute Brigade, commanded by John D. Frost, at Depienne, in late November 1942. Owing to the failure of Anderson's British First Army to break through to Tunis, the airborne outfit was cut off behind enemy lines. Frost and 180 of his men escaped to friendly lines, but the other 349 men were killed or captured. (Warren I, pp. 16–18.) Lae, New Guinea: Clay Blair, *MacArthur* (Garden City, N.Y.: Doubleday, 1977).
18. Swing Board: Devlin, *Paratrooper!* pp. 246–48; Huston, *Out of the Blue,* pp. 54–56, 99–100, 123–24.
19. MBR Memo: "Summary of Principles Covering Use of the Airborne Division," to Eisenhower on 11/27/43, copy to Ass't C/S, Operations and Plans Division, War Department, 12/2/43, Box 5A, RP-USAMHI.
20. MBR memo "Airborne Training" to Ass't C/S, Operations and Plans Division, War Department, 11/6/43, copy to Eisenhower 11/7/43, Box 5A, RP-USAMHI.
21. Ltr. MBR to author 6/3/83. He wrote that by then the strength of airborne divisions had been "arbitrarily" fixed at about 11,000 men, but that combat had demonstrated this was "too low."
22. Glider pay: MBR, Clark and Eisenhower ltrs. 5/19/43; 6/8/43; 12/2/43. Jump refusal: MBR ltrs. 8/21/43; 12/2/43, all in Box 2A, RP-USAMHI; MBR oral history, Pt. 2, p. 97, RP-USAMHI.
23. Knollwood described in Devlin, *Paratrooper!* pp. 247–48; McNair quoted in ibid., p. 248.

Chapter 22

1. Here and below for detailed accounts of OVERLORD planning, see the official American and British army histories: Gordon A. Harrison, *Cross-Channel Attack* (Washington, D.C.: OCMH, 1951), pp. 1–127 and 158–95; Lionel F. Ellis, *Victory in the West,* Vols. 1 and 2 (London: H.M.S.O., 1962, 1968), pp. 1–91; and the semiofficial American naval history: Samuel E. Morison, *History of U.S. Naval Operations in World War II,* Vol. XI (Boston: Little, Brown, 1959), pp. 3–74.
2. Here and below, Marshall-Arnold airborne plan: Pogue II, pp. 379–83; Huston, *Out of the Blue,* pp. 274–75; Ike Papers III, pp. 1736–40ff.
3. Warren II, p. 6.
4. For an insightful contemporary statement of the airmen's skeptical views on OVERLORD, see Max Hastings, *OVERLORD* (New York: Simon & Schuster, 1984), pp. 41–42, quoting Spaatz.
5. Warren II, p. 6. Leigh-Mallory's American deputy commander, Hoyt S. Vandenberg, likewise opposed this plan and other airborne plans for NEPTUNE, Hastings, *Overlord,* p. 42.
6. Huston, *Out of the Blue,* pp. 274–75.
7. Troop movements: Rapport, *Rendezvous with Destiny;* Devlin, *Paratrooper!* various interviews. Gliders: Warren II, p. 19; Dank, *The Glider Gang.*
8. *A General's Life,* pp. 213–14.
9. Ibid., pp. 216–17.
10. FORTITUDE: ibid., pp. 219–20.
11. Ike Papers III, pp. 1880–81.
12. Arthur William Tedder, *With Prejudice* (Boston: Little, Brown, 1966), pp. 564–65, 572. Hamilton, *Master of the Battlefield,* p. 551; Hastings, *OVERLORD.* p. 44, quoting American airman Elwood Quesada.
13. Brereton: official biography and *Register,* USNA; loss of Brereton's air forces in the Philippines and the ensuing disaster was not ever officially investigated, as was the disaster at Pearl Harbor. Brereton blamed the loss on the confusion and indecision in MacArthur's headquarters; MacArthur blamed Brereton. See Clay Blair, *MacArthur* (Garden City, N.Y.: Doubleday, 1977); Lewis H. Brereton, *The Brereton Diaries* (New York: Morrow, 1946).

14. Clare Boothe, Brereton profile, *Life* magazine 6/1/42. CB-Quesada int. 3/13/80. Brereton File, G. C. Marshall Papers, Marshall Library. Marshall's letter of rebuke was seen by author, but it was later restricted owing to the controversy caused when it was published in full in Mosley, *Marshall,* p. 241.

15. Omar Bradley oral history (conducted by Charles K. Hanson), Bradley Papers, USAMHI. Bradley, *A Soldier's Story,* pp. 248–49. CB-Eaton int.

Chapter 23

1. For early NEPTUNE airborne planning, see: Harrison, *Cross-Channel Attack,* pp. 73, 75; Warren II, pp. 2–9. Gavin's reaction: *Airborne Warfare,* pp. 37–41; *War and Peace in the Space Age,* pp. 71–73; *On to Berlin,* pp. 90–98.

2. Title: Gavin, *On to Berlin,* p. 91.

3. Ibid., pp. 90–91; CB-Gavin int. Browning's title: Maurice Tugwell, *Airborne to Battle: A History of Airborne Warfare: 1918–71* (London: Kimber, 1971), pp. 208–9.

4. "Unkind remark": Gavin, *On to Berlin,* p. 91.

5. Brereton, *Diaries,* entry for 12/9/43, published in Gavin, *On to Berlin,* p. 91.

6. Gavin, *Airborne Warfare,* p. 41.

7. CB-Taylor int. Similar views are expressed in Taylor oral history, USAMHI.

8. Bradley on Gavin: Bradley oral history, USAMHI. Gavin on Bradley: *On to Berlin,* pp. 92, 96.

9. Assault corps commanders and shifts: *A General's Life,* pp. 223–24.

10. For Clark's help to Eisenhower, see Martin Blumenson, "Ike and his Indispensible Lieutenants," *Army,* June 1980, and Blumenson's *Mark Clark;* CB-Collins int.; CB-Clark int.

11. CB-Eaton int.

12. Ibid. For the phase of NEPTUNE airborne planning here and below, see Warren II, pp. 6–9; Harrison, *Cross-Channel Attack,* pp. 183–85; Rapport, *Rendezvous with Destiny,* pp. 55–60; Roland G. Ruppenthal et al., *Utah Beach to Cherbourg.* Army Dept. Historical Division (Washington, D.C. 1947), pp. 1–13. CB-Eaton int.

13. Collins, *Lightning Joe,* pp. 202–3.

14. *Soldier,* p. 12; Warren II, pp. 7–9; Harry C. Butcher, *My Three Years with Eisenhower* (New York: Simon & Schuster, 1946), p. 475. Butcher wrote that at the first big NEPTUNE planning session, January 21, 1944, "Leigh-Mallory felt that it would be wrong to use the airborne on the Cotentin Peninsula and that losses will be seventy-five to eighty percent."

15. Warren II, pp. 9–10; Leigh-Mallory quoted in Ellis, *Victory in the West,* p. 138.

16. Warren II, p. 10.

17. Huston, *Out of the Blue,* pp. 274–75.

18. Ibid., pp. 275–77; Ike Papers III, pp. 1736–40.

19. Ike Papers III, pp. 1767–68. In a letter to author, 8/18/83, Gavin wrote: "Marshall and Arnold had an interesting idea . . . Marshall had good grounds for observing that we were beginning to use airborne troops in penny packets, as we used armor in World War I. Only when we made mass out of armor did it become truly effective, as we demonstrated in World War II . . . Unfortunately Marshall's idea was not valid with the state of the antitank art then in being. The problem was that we had no effective antitank weapons for the paratroopers. The small bazooka was ineffective against German armor. The 37 mm [antitank gun] was likewise not powerful enough. The British 57 mm [six-pounder antitank gun] was good and we got as many of those as we could borrow . . . [but] it took a glider to take one of them in. When we joined up with the main landings, of course, we could get tank and antitank weapons of much larger caliber but we had to depend on link-up in time to get them. So we could see the Orleans Gap [Évreux] chewed to pieces by German Panzers long before link-up could occur. [The plan] is an interesting example of how a concept can be postulated by those who look on combat as a theoretical exercise."

Chapter 24

1. Measures discussed in Harrison, *Cross-Channel Attack,* p. 184.

2. Box 5, RP-USAMHI; Rapport, *Rendezvous with Destiny,* pp. 32, 45.

3. Howell: *Register;* Harrison, *Cross-Channel Attack,* p. 402n.; Ruppenthal, *Utah Beach to Cherbourg,* pp. 53, 61. In a letter to author, 8/19/83, Gavin wrote of Howell: "Officers coming into the combat zone with high grade and no combat experience were facing a difficult situation in any event. Most experienced battle commanders would sooner pick a junior officer with combat experience rather than take a senior without the experience." Howell personality: CB-M. D. Taylor int. Taylor said: "I knew George well at West Point. He didn't get along with anybody."

4. Split-up of the 401: James Lee McDonough and Richard S. Gardner, *Sky Riders: History of the*

327/401 Glider Infantry (Nashville, Tenn.: Battery Press, 1980); ltrs. Harper to author 7/2/83, 9/25/83, 10/31/83.

5. Ltr. Carrell to author 8/31/83; ltr. Lee C. Travelstead to author 10/4/83. Travelstead, an officer in 2nd Bn (401), wrote of Lewis: "He seemed old to us. He reminded me of the even older officers around basic training units in the States . . . He was distant and the few times I even saw him he appeared excitable, bombastic—sort of the proverbial 'bantam rooster.' It was 'our' (those of us of the 2nd Bn., 401) perception that he [Lewis] regularly favored original 325 over us, resulting in us getting the tough and dirty jobs."

6. McDonough, *Sky Riders*, pp. 12ff.

7. CB ints. with John T. Cooper 8/9/84 and Hugh Neal 8/13/84.

8. Ltr. Alexander to author 6/9/83; CB-Gavin int.

9. Harrison: *Register;* CB-Thomas J. B. Shanley int. 6/14/83; ltr. Alexander to author. Gavin quote: CB-Gavin int.

10. CB-Gavin int.; ltr. Allen Langdon to author 10/17/83.

11. CB-Gavin int. Gavin elaborated on Lindquist's record-keeping: "He knew where everything was in his supply room to several decimal points and how much he had of everything."

12. Ltr. "Anonymous" to author 1/14/84.

13. Ltr. McCoid to author 1/19/84.

14. Ltr. Raff to author 7/17/84, enclosing part of a draft of a book ms (hereafter, Raff ms).

15. Raff ms, pp. 12–13.

16. Ibid., pp. 13–14.

17. Ltr. Turner to author; CB-Winton int. Kellam: *Register.*

18. CB-Casey int. 9/26/83; taped self-interview provided to author 11/1/83; ltr. 3/19/84. CB-Arthur G. Kroos int. 6/10/83.

19. Ike Papers III, pp. 1717–19; Taylor, *Swords and Plowshares,* p. 70; McDonough, *Sky Riders,* p. 24. Lee went before an Army medical board in early June 1944 and was permanently retired for physical disability: ltr. Lee to Miley 5/30/44, kindly furnished in 1983 by Miley to author. Lee died of the heart ailment in the postwar years.

20. Taylor, *Swords and Plowshares,* p. 70.

21. Ibid.

22. Various interviews and letters to author and, where available, regimental histories or records.

Chapter 25

1. William G. Lord, *History of the 508th Parachute Infantry* (Washington, D.C.: Infantry Journal Press, 1948), p. 13.

2. Gavin, *War and Peace in the Space Age,* pp. 74–75; ltr. Gavin to Louis A. Hauptfleisch (504 historian) 8/17/81.

3. Ninth Air Force and IX Troop Carrier Command buildup and personnel: Wesley Frank Craven and James L. Cate, *The Army Air Forces in World War II,* Vol. 2: *Europe: Torch to Pointblank* (Chicago: University of Chicago Press, 1949); Warren II.

4. Warren II, pp. 8, 18–19.

5. Ibid. For more detailed accounts of the glider buildup, see Dank, *The Glider Gang,* and James E. Mrazak, *The Glider War* (New York: St. Martin's Press, 1975). For technical data on military gliders in WWII, including specifications, cutaway drawings, photographs, etc., see Mrazak. The "acute shortage of glider pilots for the rest of the war" is from CB-Gavin int. Horsas equipped with saws: Raff ms.

6. For British troop-carrier buildup, see Norton, *The Red Devils,* p. 224. Warren II, p. 4, is source for 48 Group planes being "borrowed" from RAF Transport Command.

7. Division history, Box 5, RP-USAMHI; Rapport, *Rendezvous with Destiny,* p. 55; Lord, *History of the 508th,* pp. 13–14.

8. *Soldier,* pp. 99–100.

9. CB-Eaton int.

10. Warren II, p. 23.

11. "Time and time . . ." Warren II, p. 26; MBR visit to battalion: MBR oral history, Pt. 2, p. 68, USAMHI.

12. Gavin, *War and Peace in the Space Age,* p. 78; Lord, *History of the 508th,* p. 14.

13. Warren II, p. 26; Rapport, *Rendezvous with Destiny,* p. 67.

14. Warren II, p. 26.

15. "Direct appeal": ltr. MBR to Louis Hauptfleisch 8/31/81.

16. Anzio: Blumenson, *Salerno to Cassino;* Ike Papers III, pp. 1730–32.

17. Frontispiece, *The Devils in Baggy Pants.*
18. *Soldier,* p. 92.
19. Ltr. Gavin to Hauptfleisch 8/7/81.
20. Ltr. Allen Langdon to author.
21. *The Devils in Baggy Pants;* Carter, *Those Devils in Baggy Pants,* p. 133. Carter wrote that twenty-five "of our boys" (enlisted men) volunteered for "detached service" in Normandy and that seventeen of them were killed in action. Billingslea: CB-Adams int. Adams: MBR correspondence, RP-USAMHI; CB-Adams int. Harrison: Gavin, *On to Berlin,* p. 110. Neptune: CB-Robert H. Neptune int. 8/4/84.

Chapter 26

1. German forces: Harrison, *Cross-Channel Attack,* Ruppenthal, *Utah Beach to Cherbourg;* Gavin, *Airborne Warfare.*
2. For the intelligence "failure" on 352, see *A General's Life,* p. 244, and Ralph Bennett, *Ultra in the West* (New York: Scribner's, 1980), p. 45. Bennett wrote: "352 Division, a field division of good quality, which moved into the Cotentin in March and right up to Omaha Beach a few days before the landing, received only a single mention in Ultra [1/22/44] before the fighting began." This single mention did not locate the division, Bennett wrote. For the intelligence *coup* on the 91st Airlanding Division, see Bennett, pp. 45–46. The movement of the 91st to the Cotentin, Bennett wrote, was picked up "very promptly indeed."
3. Ellis, *Victory in the West I,* p. 138, is source for the date, May 25.
4. Here and below on the impact of the news and the debate that followed: Ellis, *Victory in the West I,* pp. 138–39; Warren II, pp. 10–11; Harrison, *Cross-Channel Attack,* p. 186; Ruppenthal, *Utah Beach to Cherbourg,* pp. 8–9; Tedder, *With Prejudice,* p. 543; Eisenhower, *Crusade in Europe,* pp. 246–77; Butcher, *My Three Years,* p. 551; *Soldier,* pp. 12, 100–1; Gavin, *On to Berlin,* pp. 106–7.
5. *On to Berlin,* p. 103.

Chapter 27

1. CB-Kroos int. Back: *Soldier,* p. 25.
2. Parachute jumps and glider flights: ltr. MBR to author 6/3/83. Snatch: MBR oral history, Pt. 2, pp. 15–16, and memo, Box 5, RP-USAMHI. Snatching described in James E. Mrazek, *Fighting Gliders* (New York: St. Martin's Press, 1977), pp. 155–58.
3. Malaria: Eaton memo 10/22/44; ltrs. Lewis Brereton to MBR and MBR to Brereton 10/22/44, Box 5 RP-USAMHI.
4. CB-Eaton int.
5. CB-Kroos int.
6. Ltrs. Alexander to author 5/12/83 and 10/5/83.
7. Ltrs. Talton W. Long to author 9/12/83 and 10/18/83.
8. Ike Papers V, Chronology, January 15 to June 6, 1944; Hamilton, *Master of the Battlefield,* p. 508.
9. Taylor, *Swords and Plowshares,* p. 75.
10. Ibid., pp. 75–76; Eisenhower, *Crusade in Europe,* pp. 251–52; Ike Papers V, Chronology, June 5, 1944.
11. On the American airborne flights into Normandy, here and below, Warren II (pp. 32–80 and his tables pp. 224–25) is the best possible authority.
12. The route is shown in Map 1, p. 13, Warren II.
13. MBR oral history, Pt. 2, pp. 92–93, USAMHI.
14. Marshall, *Night Drop,* pp. 5f.
15. Shock and sleepiness, etc.: John Keegan, *Six Armies in Normandy* (New York: Viking, 1982), pp. 91–92.
16. George E. Koskimaki, *D-day with the Screaming Eagles* (New York: Vantage Press, 1970), pp. 84–87; Lord, *History of the 508th,* p. 17; Donald Burgett, *Currahee! We Stand Alone; A Paratrooper's Account of the Normandy Invasion* (London: Hutchinson, 1967), p. 77.
17. Taylor, *Swords and Plowshares,* p. 77.
18. "Bill Lee!": ibid.
19. CB-Everett G. Andrews int. 8/4/84. Weisberg relief: CB-Edward S. Branigan int. 8/4/84 and Thomas L. Sherburne int. 8/5/84.
20. Koskimaki, *D-day with the Screaming Eagles,* p. 87.
21. Burgett, *Currahee!* p. 85.

22. Taylor, *Swords and Plowshares,* pp. 80, 83; CB-J. H. Michaelis int. 4/24/84. *Register.* Moseley's father (West Point, 1899) had been Deputy Chief of Staff of the Army under Chief of Staff Douglas MacArthur, 1930–33; he retired in 1938. The younger Moseley retired from the Army disabled in 1945, and in postwar years became a civilian aide in MacArthur's Tokyo headquarters.
23. Taylor, *Swords and Plowshares,* p. 79; CB-Taylor int.
24. Dank, *The Glider Gang,* pp. 119–20.
25. CB-Taylor int. Millener: *Register.*
26. British airborne operations: Ellis, *Victory in the West,* pp. 149–56. See also Tugwell, *Airborne to Battle;* Hickey, *Out of the Sky;* Warren II, pp. 78–80. John Howard "Dropping in on Pegasus," *The Illustrated London News,* June, 1984, pp. 69–71.

Chapter 28

1. *Soldier,* pp. 2–3. Clover, prayer book: RP-USAMHI.
2. Return to quarters: CB-Kroos int.; softball: *Soldier,* pp. 25–26.
3. Warren II, p. 48. Addition of nine aircraft for regimental HQ and three for engineers: ltr. Allen Langdon to author 9/22/83. Ridgway wrote in *Soldier* (p. 7) that he had jumped with Ben Vandervoort's 2nd Battalion in the first serial, but Alexander, Langdon, the jumpmaster (Dean L. Garber) and the troop-carrier historian (Warren) dispute this. An aircraft manifest, kindly provided by Garber (ltr. to author 10/31/83) confirms their memories. It shows that Ridgway's plane, "No. 49," in the third serial, departed from Spanhoe. The plane was one of those in 310th Squadron of 315 Group, which also lifted the 505 regimental HQ from Spanhoe.
4. Aircraft manifest provided by Garber. The aircraft tail number was 42-108912. Other aircrew: copilot Wilford F. Simmons, navigator James Boddia, Rebecca operator James T. McMurphy, radio operator George J. Cooke, Jr., and crew chief Emanuel J. Przybylinski. The four bodyguards were Sgt. Emit V. Conner, PFC James J. Ward, Pvt. Robert A. Brust and Pvt. Ryan R. Howard.
5. Devlin, *Paratrooper!* pp. 378–79. Ltr. Langdon to author 9/22/83: "This was a Gammon grenade that went off in Hdqs. Co., 1st Bn, and you could hear it all over the airfield. Everyone that was there remembers it." Delay: Warren II, p. 48. In ltr. to author 11/17/83, MBR wrote: "I heard it as I was standing outside the C-47 to which I was assigned. I did not learn until much later of the casualties." The fact that MBR heard this explosion is further proof that he flew from Spanhoe, with the 505's third serial, not with Vandervoort's 2nd Bn., which left from Cottesmore.
6. The drop of the 82nd into Normandy is described in detail in Warren II, pp. 48–58 and 64–65, plus tables pp. 224, 225. Additional, personal details are from notes of a "Debriefing Conference—Operation Neptune" (hereafter, Debriefing) on 8/13/44, from Roy E. Lindquist Papers, USAMHI. Participants: Vandervoort, Krause, Ekman, Mendez, Warren, Lindquist, Ostberg, Kuhn, Timmes, Shanley, Boyd, Sanford, March, Gavin, Singleton.
7. *Soldier,* p. 4. Vandervoort: Debriefing.
8. Vandervoort: Debriefing. Injury: ltr. Vandervoort to author 7/5/83.
9. Krause: Debriefing.
10. Ekman: Debriefing. Alexander: "Notes" on Normandy, a diary Alexander kindly provided the author.
11. *Soldier,* p. 8. "Hal Clark's boys had not failed us. They had put us down on the button."
12. Gavin, *Airborne Warfare,* p. 45: "Sicily and Italy had taught us that it was undesirable to blacken our faces or use crickets as signals. We decided to rely solely on oral challenge and responses, and a quick response it had better be." In a ltr. to author 7/19/83, Gavin wrote that crickets "were just a nuisance. They started teaching people to use one click for a challenge, expecting two clicks in response. That didn't work because once you made one click, if you thoughtlessly released it, it clicked itself again." He added that paratroopers lost their crickets in the jumps, or couldn't find them in their pockets when they were needed. "You couldn't walk around all night with a cricket in your hand, but you always had your voice. The 101 used crickets but to the veterans of the 82nd, they seemed pretty silly."
13. *Soldier,* p. 5. Some accounts say the password was "Lightning," the countersign "Thunder."
14. Casey, taped self-interview; CB-Kroos int.
15. Ltr. Follmer to author 2/5/84. *Soldier,* p. 6.
16. *Soldier,* pp. 6, 9–10. Ltrs. Vandervoort to author 9/5/83 and 9/25/83. On Vandervoort's injury: Ryan, *The Longest Day,* pp. 127–28; CB-Kroos and Casey interviews. The fact that the first men Ridgway encountered on the ground were Vandervoort and his men may have led to his mistaken recollection that he had jumped with Vandervoort's 2nd Bn.
17. CB-Moorman interview.

18. Warren II, p. 50. Soften policy: memos, Box 5, RP-USAMHI.
19. Gavin, *On to Berlin*, pp. 109, 113. Stick manifest at the 82nd Abn Div Museum, Fort Bragg, N.C.
20. Mission: Lord, *History of the 508th*, pp. 16–17. Falley: Warren II, p. 59; Gavin, *Airborne Warfare*, p. 65.
21. Here and below: Gavin, *On to Berlin*, pp. 113–15; Lindquist: Debriefing.
22. Ltr. Palmer to author 1/5/84.
23. Lord, *History of the 508th*, p. 21.
24. Mendez, Batcheller, Warren, Shanley: Debriefing; CB-Gavin int.
25. "Sorry state . . .": Warren II, p. 55.
26. Size of Millett force: "History of 507 PIR," provided by John Marr. Ltr. Paul F. Smith to author, with enclosures, 10/5/83. Apparently part of Millett force drifted away. Smith, who was part of the group, put it at "approximately 250" in an official after-action report. "Cut the guts . . .": CB-McCoid int.
27. Ostberg, Maloney, Kuhn, Timmes: Debriefing.
28. Gavin, *On to Berlin*, p. 117.
29. Ltr. Langdon to author 10/17/83.
30. Gavin, *On to Berlin*, pp. 115–17.
31. Walton quoted in a sidebar to Tim Clark's profile of Gavin in *Yankee Magazine*, June 1984.
32. Ireland mission: "History of 505" ms, by Allen Langdon.
33. CB-Eaton int.; ltr. Eaton to author 9/17/83; *Soldier*, pp. 9–10.
34. Ltr. Eaton to author 10/6/83.
35. Allen Langdon, "505" ms.
36. Eisenhower, *Crusade in Europe*, p. 247; Butcher, *My Three Years*, pp. 566–67. In Butcher's account (he took the phone call), Leigh-Mallory reported the loss of 29 planes (21 American, 8 British) of the 1,250 American and British planes employed. These figures closely match those in Warren and other official American histories.

Chapter 29

1. The D-day operations of the 101, here and below, are described in Rapport, *Rendezvous with Destiny*, pp. 89–137; Ruppenthal, *Utah Beach to Cherbourg*, pp. 14–30; Harrison, *Cross-Channel Attack*, pp. 278–89; S. L. A. Marshall, *Night Drop*, pp. 153–324. Note: Marshall, later Military Editor of the Detroit *News* and author of several books on Army combat, was in 1944 an official Army historian assigned to record the operations of both American airborne divisions. His reports, based on interviews with participants, supplied most of the background for the official Army accounts (Ruppenthal and Harrison). Many years later, in 1962, utilizing his interview notes, Marshall published *Night Drop*, a very close and detailed account of 82nd and 101st operations for the first three or four days in Normandy. Many veterans of the 82nd Division (among them regimental historians) have faulted *Night Drop* for inaccuracies, for his "101 bias" and for "considerable literary license."
2. Taylor, *Swords and Plowshares*, p. 80. Taylor's account of Normandy is sketchy, a mere four and a half pages.
3. CB-Taylor int.; USNA *Register*.
4. Landing of the 327 on D day: Rapport, *Rendezvous with Destiny*, p. 150. Hold-up of artillery; ibid., p. 151; McDonough, *Sky Riders*, pp. 35–36.
5. Ltr. Renfro to author 11/25/83.
6. *Rendezvous with Destiny*, pp. 135, 138, 150.
7. For a brief outline of Utah and Omaha beaches operations, see *A General's Life*, pp. 247–52. For more extensive accounts, see Harrison, *Cross-Channel Attack*, and Morison XI.
8. On British landings, see Ellis, *Victory in the West, I*. The quote is from pp. 212–13. Bradley wrote: "In sum, the British and Canadian assault forces sat down. They had Caen within their grasp and let it slip away."
9. Operations of 82nd Division in Normandy here and below are from: Ruppenthal, *Utah Beach to Cherbourg*, pp. 30–42ff; Harrison, *Cross-Channel Attack*, pp. 289–300ff; *Soldier*, pp. 6–16 (a disappointingly brief account); Gavin, *Airborne Warfare*, pp. 54–62; *War and Peace in the Space Age*, pp. 78–80; *On to Berlin*, pp. 115–22; Marshall, *Night Drop*, pp. 5–152ff; after-action reports, Box 5, RP-USAMHI, and numerous interviews with participants.
10. CB interviews with Eaton, Winton, Moorman, Finkel. Ltrs. Palmer and Bedell.
11. CB-Moorman int.
12. Gavin, *War and Peace in the Space Age*, p. 79. Gavin wrote that Ridgway told him D-day

night: "I have heard rumors that the amphibious landings did not come in on account of weather. We may have a hard time of it." Gavin continued: "We discussed this a bit further and decided, as far as possible, to keep it from the troops and to make the best of things."

13. Marshall, *Night Drop; Soldier,* p. 10.

14. Ryan, *The Longest Day,* p. 117. Sir Napier Crookden, *Airborne at War* (New York: Scribner's, 1978). The 505 historian, Allen Langdon, rejects many "facts" in both accounts. The account here is based on Langdon.

15. Vandervoort ltrs. to author 9/5/83 and 9/25/83. Vandervoort meeting with Ekman: ltr. Allen Langdon to author 8/16/83.

16. Marshall, *Night Drop,* pp. 78, 89. Various author interviews.

17. Anonymous 505 officer, ltr. to author 7/5/83. Gavin views: ltrs. to author 4/5/83 and 8/22/83.

18. Various letters, Langdon to author. Krause DSC: Harrison, *Cross-Channel Attack,* appendix.

19. According to Langdon, Turnbull held out for a shorter period than the official histories indicate. MBR on Vandervoort: *Soldier,* p. 7. *Nevada* Assistance: Langdon.

20. *Dictionary of American Naval Fighting Ships,* Vol. 5, p. 52.

21. Owing to the confusion, the shock of battle and the lack of record keeping, the paratrooper action at the Merderet on D-day morning presents the historian with special difficulties. Those who were present are highly condemnatory of the S. L. A. Marshall research on which the official Army accounts and most popular accounts are based. Allen Langdon, who was present—and wounded—during the action, has spared no effort to track down and interview as many survivors as he could find in order to establish a "true" account. He was kind enough to share the fruits of his research with me, as well as a meticulously detailed critical analysis of previously published accounts. Here and below, where accounts differ or are in conflict, I have followed Langdon's 505 ms. However, the judgments about the tactical command failures are strictly my own.

22. Langdon asserts that S. L. A. Marshall (and other writers) have made far too much of this brief action at Le Manoir.

23. Gavin, *On to Berlin,* pp. 118–19. Gavin's account of Merderet action that day is all too brief and contains errors, but there seems no doubt of his faith in the men at La Fière.

24. Gavin, *On to Berlin,* pp. 118–19. Gavin writes that he went on toward Chef-du-Pont to find an alternate crossing of the Merderet, but he does not explain why he did not first attempt to force a crossing of the La Fière causeway.

25. MBR confidence and calm: numerous author interviews with those present in the battle. These unanimous views contradict Ruppenthal (p. 56), who wrote (based on S. L. A. Marshall): "Among the commanders who were on the ground and whose units were in contact with the enemy there were uncertainty and anxiety on the night of D day."

Chapter 30

1. Plans: Harrison, *Cross-Channel Attack;* Collins, *Lightning Joe.*

2. Raff ms.

3. Accompanying Raff was New York newspaper publisher *(P.M.)* Ralph Ingersoll, one of Omar Bradley's staffers. His account is in Ralph Ingersoll, *Top Secret* (New York: Harcourt, Brace, 1946).

4. Warren II, pp. 65–69.

5. Ingersoll, *Top Secret,* pp. 131ff.

6. Warren II, p. 69.

7. Ibid., p. 79.

8. CB-Lancey int. 8/12/84.

9. Marshall, *Night Drop,* pp. 73–74.

10. Harrison, *Cross-Channel Attack,* p. 297.

11. CB-Winton int.; Collins, *Lightning Joe,* p. 203.

12. *Soldier,* p. 10.

13. Gavin, *On to Berlin,* p. 120.

14. Ibid., pp. 120–21; *Soldier,* p. 11.

15. MBR oral history, Pt. 2, pp. 120–21, RP-USAMHI.

16. Harrison, *Cross-Channel Attack,* p. 344; Collins, *Lightning Joe,* p. 203; Marshall, *Night Drop,* pp. 93ff.

17. Ingersoll, *Top Secret,* p. 133.

18. Ruppenthal, *Utah Beach to Cherbourg,* pp. 62–63; On Van Fleet's courage: *A General's Life,* p. 263.

19. Ltr. Gavin to author 4/15/83.
20. Roosevelt's combat background: *A General's Life*, p. 224.
21. Roosevelt's Normandy role: Harrison, *Cross-Channel Attack*, p. 304n.; Ryan, *The Longest Day*, pp. 178–79, 222, 225; *Soldier*, p. 11; CB-Kroos int.
22. *Soldier*, p. 11; MOH: Harrison, *Cross-Channel Attack*, p. 304n.; Roosevelt and McCoy assistance to MBR at C&GSS: MBR oral history, Pt. 2, p. 18, RP-USAMHI.
23. D+1 glider mission: Warren II, pp. 69–72.
24. Ltr. Boyd to author 3/23/83; ltr. Sanford to author 8/4/83: "No one commanded the 1st Bn in combat [in Normandy] but me."
25. Ltr. Vandervoort to author 11/11/83.
26. Hupfer: Harrison, *Cross-Channel Attack*, p. 344. Raff arrival: Marshall, *Night Drop*, pp. 93–94. Collins/Van Fleet arrival: Collins, *Lightning Joe*, p. 204. Marshall estimated that Raff arrived at about midday on D+1.
27. Marshall, *Night Drop*, pp. 94–100, has a good account of Hupfer's serendipitous linkup.
28. Vandervoort DSC: Harrison, *Cross-Channel Attack*, p. 475.
29. Harrison, *Cross-Channel Attack*, p. 345; Gavin, *On to Berlin*, p. 124; Marshall, *Night Drop*, pp. 66ff.
30. Quoted in Gavin, *On to Berlin*, pp. 124–26.
31. Marshall, *Night Drop*, p. 69; Langdon ms.
32. Harrison, *Cross-Channel Attack*, p. 386.
33. Raff ms, pp. 16–18. MBR on Raff: ltr. to Eaton 6/10/44, Box 5, RP-USAMHI.
34. Harrison, *Cross-Channel Attack*, p. 396; Ruppenthal, *Utah Beach to Cherbourg*, pp. 120–21.
35. Ingersoll, *Top Secret*, pp. 142–43. Ingersoll (p. 141) writes that Raff force had arrived only "an hour or so before me," but this is erroneous.

Chapter 31

1. Ruppenthal, *Utah Beach to Cherbourg*, pp. 95–104; Harrison, *Cross-Channel Attack*, pp. 386–96; Collins, *Lightning Joe*, pp. 205–7; Alexander, "Notes."
2. CB-Swenson int. 8/7/83; ltr. Leahy to author 8/16/83.
3. CB-H. C. Slaughter int. 8/10/83; corroborated in CB-Teddy H. Sanford int. 8/11/83.
4. Slaughter, Swenson, Sanford interviews.
5. *Soldier*, p. 14. Nearly thirty years later, on May 13, 1972, Ridgway stated in a letter to Mark Alexander: "That was the hottest single incident I experienced in my combat service, both in Europe and later in Korea." Copy courtesy Alexander.
6. Ruppenthal, *Utah Beach to Cherbourg*, pp. 119–21; Harrison, *Cross-Channel Attack*, pp. 396–401; Marshall, *Night Drop*, pp. 106–16; Lord, *History of the 508th*, p. 23.
7. *History of the 508th*, p. 23.
8. Ruppenthal, *Utah Beach to Cherbourg*, p. 121.
9. Ltr. anonymous to author 10/5/83.
10. Gavin, *On to Berlin*, p. 127.
11. Ltr. Leonard F. Fleck to Wayne Pierce, passed to author 11/1/83; ltr. Pierce to author 11/1/83.
12. *A General's Life*, p. 259; Collins, *Lightning Joe*, p. 206.
13. Gavin, *On to Berlin*, p. 127; CB-Gavin int.
14. Ruppenthal, *Utah Beach to Cherbourg*, pp. 121–25; Harrison, *Cross-Channel Attack*, pp. 398–400; Marshall, *Night Drop*, p. 117.
15. Devine: *Register*.
16. CB-Norris int. 3/7/84.
17. Ltr. McCoid to author 1/16/84.
18. CB-Norris int.
19. "At a loss": CB-Gavin int.
20. Gavin, *On to Berlin*, pp. 128, 130; CB-Gavin int.
21. Ltr. Wisner to author 1/20/84.
22. Gavin, *On to Berlin*, p. 128; CB-Gavin int.
23. Marshall, *Night Drop*, pp. 118–19.
24. CB-Gavin int.
25. Ltr. MBR to Eaton 6/23/44; ltr. Carrell to author 8/31/83.
26. Ltr. Lee C. Travelstead to author 10/4/83.
27. Marshall, *Night Drop*, pp. 117, 119.
28. Ibid., p. 122.

29. MBR oral history, Pt. 2, p. 18, RP-USAMHI.
30. CB-Norris int.
31. Marshall, *Night Drop*, p. 130.
32. Ibid., pp. 133–34; Gavin, *On to Berlin*, p. 128.
33. *On to Berlin*, p. 129.
34. Various ints. with 325 senior officers; CB-Gavin int.
35. MBR oral history, RP-USAMHI; on Lewis' death by cancer: CB-Sanford int. Lewis died on 4/16/45.
36. Lewis to MBR 8/22/44; MBR to Lewis 9/13/44, MBR Correspondence, Box 5, RP-USAMHI.
37. Marshall, *Night Drop*, pp. 139–40.
38. Gavin, *On to Berlin*, p. 130.
39. Ibid.; CB-Gavin int.
40. Lord, *History of the 508th*, p. 25.
41. Ibid., p. 26; *Soldier*, p. 8.
42. CB-Gavin int.
43. Ltr. Timmes to author 6/16/83.
44. Ruppenthal, *Utah Beach to Cherbourg*, pp. 79–85; Rapport, *Rendezvous with Destiny*, pp. 165ff; Taylor, *Swords and Plowshares*, p. 83.
45. Wear's relief: CB-Taylor int.; ltr. Harper to author 9/25/83; McDonough, *Sky Riders*, pp. 42–43.
46. Harrison, *Cross-Channel Attack*, pp. 351–65; Ruppenthal, *Utah Beach to Cherbourg*, p. 89; Collins, *Lightning Joe*, p. 205; *A General's Life*, p. 256.
47. Ruppenthal, *Utah Beach to Cherbourg*, pp. 88–90; McDonough, *Sky Riders*, pp. 42ff.
48. Ruppenthal, *Utah Beach to Cherbourg*, p. 92; *A General's Life*, pp. 259–60.

Chapter 32

1. Harrison, *Cross-Channel Attack*, pp. 388, 401.
2. Ibid., pp. 402–4; Collins, *Lightning Joe*, pp. 207–9; Gavin, *On to Berlin*, p. 131.
3. Nave: *Register;* Clarke: *Register*. The revolving-door senior leadership in the 90th Division was explained to the author, in letters 9/28/83 and 10/4/83, by a participant who requested anonymity.
4. CB-Gavin int. Nave KIA, DSC: *Register.*
5. Collins, *Lightning Joe*, p. 208. "Former commander" identified by anonymous source. Terrell's further duties described in Ike Papers I, pp. 406–7. Terrell was not promoted, nor did he serve overseas in World War II, source says.
6. *A General's Life*, p. 262; Collins, *Lightning Joe*, pp. 208–10; Ruppenthal, *Utah Beach to Cherbourg*, p. 129. The sequence of commanders in the 357th, 358th and 359th regiments provided by anonymous source. Bacon, Barth, McNary, Partridge: *Register*. Clarke's DSC: *Register*.
7. Harrison, *Cross-Channel Attack*, p. 403; Ruppenthal, *Utah Beach to Cherbourg*, pp. 132–33; Collins, *Lightning Joe*, pp. 210–11.
8. Harrison, *Cross-Channel Attack*, p. 402; Ruppenthal, *Utah Beach to Cherbourg*, p. 133.
9. Ltr. Shields Warren to author 10/24/83.
10. Ruppenthal, *Utah Beach to Cherbourg*, pp. 134–44.
11. "507 History in Normandy," courtesy 507 veteran John W. Marr.
12. CB-Kroos int.
13. Ltr. Alfred W. Ireland to author 3/31/84; ltrs. Henry H. Leveck to author 2/16/84, 2/18/84; ltr. J. H. Harper to author 10/24/83.
14. Ltr. Ireland to author 3/31/84. "Plot": CB-Gavin int.
15. Raff ms., pp. 18–20.
16. Ibid., pp. 20–21; ltr. Gordon K. Smith to author 9/26/83; CB-Eaton and CB-Moorman interviews.
17. Several strong disapproving ltrs. to author from senior 507 officers who preferred anonymity; CB-William D. Bowell int. 1/25/84. Bowell recited entries from his private diary, noting that at first he "hated" Raff.
18. Bowell int. In retrospect, Bowell thought the 507 was "lax" and Raff was the "tough, abrasive commander it needed," and that he was a "standout" in combat. Ltrs. Timmes to author 1/16/84, McCoid to author 1/19/84.
19. Alexander's "Notes"; Ruppenthal, *Utah Beach to Cherbourg*, p. 137.
20. Ibid. ". . . even before": 82nd Division history, Box 5, RP-USAMHI.

21. Diary, William C. Sylvan, 6/16/44, Sylvan Papers, USAMHI.

22. Ltr. Alexander to author 6/9/83; Alexander, "Notes"; "One of the finest . . .": ltr. MBR to G. H. Weems, Infantry School, 8/13/44, copy provided by Alexander.

23. Winton: CB-Winton int. Hagan: various interviews; *Register*.

24. Ltr. Alexander to author 6/9/83.

25. Ltr. Leahy to author 8/16/83; ltr. Ireland to author 3/31/84. Technically, no orders were ever cut naming Ireland to command of battalion.

26. Harrison, *Cross-Channel Attack*, pp. 408–16; Ruppenthal, *Utah Beach to Cherbourg*, pp. 145–49.

27. *A General's Life*, p. 262; Ruppenthal, *Utah Beach to Cherbourg*, pp. 150–51; Collins, *Lightning Joe*, p. 216.

28. *A General's Life*, p. 263.

29. Harrison, *Cross-Channel Attack*, p. 415; Ruppenthal, *Utah Beach to Cherbourg*, p. 149. Date of transfer to VIII Corps: Sylvan diary, 6/19/44.

30. Lord, *History of the 508th*, pp. 30–31.

31. CB-Kroos int.

32. Citation, Bronze Star Medal, Arthur G. Kroos: General Orders No. 35, HQ 82nd Abn Div, 15 July 1944.

33. CB-Slaughter int. 9/27/83.

34. CB-Kroos int.

35. Lord, *History of the 508th*, p. 31.

36. XIX Corps: *A General's Life*, p. 259.

37. Montgomery's opposition: ibid., p. 265.

38. Bradley's plan: ibid., p. 266.

39. Carlo D'Este, *Decision in Normandy*. (New York: Dutton, 1983), pp. 165–71. Hamilton, *Master of the Battlefield*, pp. 633–48.

40. Troop-carrier diversion to cargo: Warren II, pp. 84–85; *A General's Life*, p. 264.

41. Withdrawal of 101: Taylor, *Swords and Plowshares*, p. 83; Rapport, *Rendezvous with Destiny*, pp. 248–49. Other: *A General's Life*, pp. 269–70; Elbridge Colby, *The First Army in Europe* (Monograph, U.S. Senate, Doc. 91-25, 91st Cong., 1st Sess., U.S. Govt. Printing Office, 1969), pp. 41–47.

42. CB-Gavin int.; ltr. Gavin to author 8/6/84; Raff ms., p. 23.

43. *Soldier*, p. 15. Ltr. MBR to author 8/6/84: "The protest against attacking with the entire division toward La Haye-du-Puits was made to me personally by Gen. Gavin, the Ass't Div. Comdr. . . . neither of the two regimental commanders, Lindquist and Raff, made any protest personally to me . . . There was nothing wrong with Gavin's action in lodging that protest. Whether or not he endorsed it, or was merely presenting the views of the two regimental commanders, I do not know"; CB-Gavin int.; Raff ms, p. 23.

44. Gavin disapproval: CB-Gavin int.; ltr. Gavin to author 8/6/84. Raff disapproval: Raff ms, pp. 23, 36–37.

45. Colby, *First Army in Europe*, pp. 44–47.

46. Ibid., pp. 44–45; Gavin, *On to Berlin*, p. 131; Alexander, "Notes"; Sylvan diary 7/3/44 and 7/4/44. Sylvan wrote: "The 82nd A/B occupied all their objectives and withstood a counterattack on Hill 95."

47. CB-Shanley int.; Alexander, "Notes."

48. Alexander, "Notes"; ltr. Alexander to author 5/12/83. Holmes: Lord, *History of the 508th*, pp. 40ff.

49. Ltr. Gordon K. Smith to author 9/26/83; Maloney wounds: ltrs. Timmes 6/16/83, 8/16/83, and Paul F. Smith 10/5/83. Maloney retirement: *Register*. Kuhn as exec: Timmes, Gordon Smith and Paul Smith ltrs.

50. *A General's Life*, p. 271; Collins, *Lightning Joe*, pp. 227, 230.

51. *Lightning Joe*, p. 210; *A General's Life*, pp. 269–70. Changes in 90th: anonymous 90th Division senior officer. Weaver: *Register*. For more on Williams' relief, see Ernest N. Harmon, Milton MacKaye and William R. MacKaye, *Combat Commander* (Englewood Cliffs, N. J.: Prentice-Hall, 1970), p. 250. Williams served on the Nazi War Crimes Commission and was nicknamed "Hanging Sam"; still later, he was a lieutenant general in Vietnam.

52. Casualties: No figures ever exactly agree. Devlin (p. 416) is the source for 5,245; Gavin, *War and Peace in the Space Age*, reports that of 11,770 men landed in Normandy, 6,545 returned to England. Ridgway, in *Soldier* (p. 15), reports 1,282 KIA, 2,373 seriously wounded. Gavin, *On to Berlin*, reports an aggregate loss of 46 percent killed, missing and evacuated wounded.

53. Author's summary from interviews, letters from participants, official reports and published histories.

54. CB-Eaton int.; MBR oral history, Pt. 2, p. 100, RP-USAMHI.

55. The 101 losses are from Rapport, *Rendezvous with Destiny,* and various interviews and letters from 101 commanders.

56. Ltr. Omar Bradley to MBR 7/18/44, Box 5, RP-USAMHI; ltr. J. Lawton Collins to MBR 6/26/44; ltr. Troy Middleton to MBR 7/8/44, Correspondence, Box 3, RP-USAMHI.

57. Various interviews and letters; Gavin, *On to Berlin,* p. 158.

58. CB-Taylor int.

59. Ltr. H. R. Bull to MBR 7/18/44, Correspondence, Box 3, RP-USAMHI. The brief statement is reprinted in full in *On to Berlin,* p. 132.

60. Ike Papers III, pp. 2001, 2616.

Chapter 33

1. Ike Papers III, p. 1947 with n.1.

2. Ibid. Gavin said later in CB interview: "Ridgway had learned his lessons from George Marshall and John J. Pershing in World War I to watch out for the British taking over. Every time you turned around they'd take over command of your troops and that'd be the last you heard of them. We had four American airborne divisions in the U.K. or on the way there and if Boy Browning got his way he'd be the commander. So Ridgway, Bill Lee and I got together and decided we ought to organize an [American] airborne corps, for the simple reason of protecting our own interest. And we did. We organized an American corps [on paper]. Maybe it could be called a political move. But we were absolutely sincere that it was a sound *military* move, that we had to have an American command to take care of American airborne troops in combat."

Stuart Cutler, onetime commander of Ridgway's 326th Glider Infantry Battalion and founding ADC of the 13th Airborne Division, had come to England in late May 1944 to serve as an airborne adviser and planner on Bradley's 1st Army Group (later 12th Army Group) staff. He recalled in a letter to author 1/3/84: "Soon thereafter SHAEF sent me to [Montgomery's] 21 Army Group HQ, where I reported to Boy Browning for two weeks. I heard several remarks about combining all British-American airborne troops under Browning. Shortly thereafter SHAEF sent a letter to FUSAG [1st Army Group] stating the British had suggested forming a combined British-American Airborne Troop Headquarters and asking for remarks. Bradley was away . . . and his FUSAG [1st Army Group] Chief of Staff Levan Allen bucked the paper to me [to handle]. I told him that . . . the British were endeavoring to get control of our airborne divisions. I suggested an alternate plan: that SHAEF activate an American Airborne Corps with Ridgway in command and that British airborne troops be consolidated as a British Airborne Corps under Browning and that an American senior airborne general be named commander of the two airborne corps. Allen had me write that up as an endorsement for his signature and it went back to SHAEF that way."

3. Ike Papers III, p. 1988; Warren II, pp. 81–83. Cutler, named "Acting Chief of Staff" of FAAA, with orders to locate and staff the HQ, recalled in his letter to author: "On 10 August 1944, while riding in Eisenhower's train to review the 82nd Airborne Division, Brereton tricked Eisenhower into agreeing that the combined British-American airborne headquarters should be named First Allied Airborne Army."

4. "Felt strongly": Warren II, p. 81.

5. Ike Papers III, pp. 1947, 2001, 2002, 2008, 2013.

6. Bradley criticism of Normandy drops: Warren II, p. 58; "Thank goodness": ONB oral history, Pt. 5, USAMHI.

7. Brereton, *Diaries,* pp. 308–9.

8. Ranks of Brereton and Browning: Warren II, p. 81.

9. Ike Papers III, pp. 2013–14, 2022; Parks: official bio. Parks was a graduate of Clemson (1918).

10. Ridgway reaction: *Soldier,* p. 17; CB-Surles int. In response to the Ridgway-Brereton relationship, Surles said: "Let's put it this way. Ridgway and Brereton were never hot buddies."

11. *Soldier,* p. 18.

12. MBR to CG, ETOUSA, 7/19/44, and MBR to W. Bedell Smith 9/20/44, Box 5, RP-USAMHI.

13. CB-Gavin int. 9/28/82.

14. MBR to R. W. Barker, SHAEF, 7/23/44; Lynch to MBR 10/27/44, Box 5, RP-USAMHI; Lynch to author 3/24/83.

15. Ltr. Paul F. Smith to author 10/5/83.

16. CB-Gavin int.; various other interviews.

17. Krause: CB-Gavin int.; ltr. Alexander to author 6/9/83. Kaiser and Long: ltrs. Kaiser to author, Long to author; other interviews.
18. Ltr. Travelstead to author 10/12/83.
19. Gavin, *On to Berlin*, p. 158; interviews with Winton, Moorman, Casey, others.
20. CB-Surles int. 12/22/82. Morris: *Register*. Surles, Sr.: *Register*.
21. CB-Surles int.; Quill: *Register;* Buechler: *Register*. See also Brereton, *Diaries* and diary of Floyd L. Parks, Chief of Staff FAAA, Parks Papers-USAMHI. On Howell: Parks diary, various entries July–August 1944.
22. Robert H. Ferrell, *The Eisenhower Diaries* (New York: Norton, 1981), p. 140.
23. CB-Surles int.
24. Memo, MBR to Eaton 7/28/44, RP-USAMHI. On Marshall's recommendation, the Congress enacted a pay raise for glierists on 7/4/44.
25. Ike Papers V, Chronology; *Soldier*, pp. 16–17. Ridgway officially departed the 82nd Division and took command of the XVIII Airborne Corps on 8/27/44, Box 1 ("201 File"), RP-USAMHI.
26. CB-Taylor int.

Chapter 34

1. *A General's Life*, pp. 272–88.
2. McNair and other casualties: *A General's Life*, p. 280.
3. For Ike's defense of Leigh-Mallory: Ike Papers IV, pp. 2145–46, 2195. Brereton's demotion: Brereton *Diaries*, pp. 330–31.
4. Ike Papers IV, p. 2146.
5. On Mortain counterattack: *A General's Life*, pp. 291–304.
6. Ibid., pp. 307–18.
7. Ike Papers III, pp. 1975–76, 1983; Warren II, p. 83.
8. Here and below, DRAGOON operations: Craven and Cate, *Army Air Forces in World War II*, pp. 408–38; Warren I, pp. 77–110; Saunders, *The Red Beret*, pp. 285–87.
9. *A General's Life*, p. 334; Bennett, *Ultra in the West*, pp. 158–59. Bennett wrote that although Ultra was scanty on August 17 and 18, the code breakers picked up orders from Hitler for the immediate evacuation of southern France.
10. DRAGOON: Warren I, pp. 77–110. "Left behind": Saunders, *The Red Beret*, p. 279.
11. CB-Neal and Cooper interviews.
12. *Register*. Frederick was born 3/14/07, Gavin 3/22/07.
13. *Register*.
14. Graves: *Register*. See also Graves Papers, USAMHI. Prichard: Tugwell, *Airborne to Battle*, p. 222; Norton, *The Red Devils*. Artillery: Clark Archer, *Chronicle of the 517 PIR* (privately published, n.d.).
15. Joerg: *Register;* Sachs: *Register*.
16. Craven and Cate, *Army Air Forces in World War II*, pp. 428, 431.
17. "85 to 90 percent accurate": Warren I, p. 100.
18. CB-Cooper int. Apperson-Tomasik-Yarborough: ltrs. Tomasik, Doyle and Yarborough to author and Yarborough official bio.
19. *A General's Life*, p. 290.
20. Ibid.; Brereton, *Diaries*, p. 330; Warren II, p. 85; Parks diary, numerous entries in August.
21. Parks diary 8/7/44; Brereton, *Diaries*.
22. Warren II, p. 85.
23. Brereton, *Diaries*, pp. 332–33; various entries, Parks diary. For Bradley's supply problems, see *A General's Life*, p. 320.
24. *A General's Life*, pp. 318–19.
25. Warren II, p. 87; Parks diary 8/26/44, 8/30/44.
26. Robert E. Urquhart, *Arnhem* (London: Cassell, 1958), pp. 13–15.
27. MBR's reaction to Browning's appointment: *Soldier*, p. 108, describing his "bitter disappointment." In a letter to Cornelius Ryan 6/24/73 (in RP-USAMHI), who was researching his book *A Bridge Too Far*, Ridgway wrote: "I also, no doubt, still harbored a sense of deep disappointment, if not of resentment, that command of the operation of the Airborne Corps had been given to General Browning." While these comments referred to Browning's command of MARKET (see below), Browning's appointment to command LINNET evolved into his command of MARKET; they are thus appropriate.
28. Cornelius Ryan, *A Bridge Too Far* (New York: Simon & Schuster, 1974), pp. 126–27. MBR letter to Ryan 6/24/73. MBR wrote: "I had a topflight, well-organized corps staff in being.

Browning, I believe, did not, though of this I am not sure. I think he had only a pickup and makeshift staff at that time." In his oral history (Pt. 2, p. 80), MBR said: "As I remember it, Boy Browning really did not have a well-organized corps staff."

29. Bradley, *A Soldier's Story*, pp. 401–3; *A General's Life*, p. 320.
30. *A Soldier's Story*, p. 402; Hansen diary entry, 6/19/44, quoted in Russell F. Weigley, *Eisenhower's Lieutenants* (Bloomington, Ind.: Indiana University Press, 1981), p. 291.
31. LINNET II: Warren II, p. 87; Parks diary, August entries.
32. Ike Papers IV, pp. 2121–22, 2124–25.
33. Brereton, *Diaries*, p. 340.
34. *A General's Life*, pp. 323–24.
35. Warren II, p. 87; Brereton, *Diaries*, pp. 337–38.
36. Brereton, *Diaries*, pp. 337–38.
37. Time of LINNET cancellation: Warren II, p. 87. For Eisenhower's talk with Montgomery, see *A General's Life*, pp. 323, 328–30; Tedder, *With Prejudice*, pp. 587–91; Eisenhower, *Crusade in Europe*, pp. 305–7.
38. COMET: Warren II, p. 87; Urquhart, p. 17; Browning unresigning: Brereton, *Diaries*, p. 338.

Chapter 35

1. Optimism: *A General's Life*, p. 319. TALISMAN (ECLIPSE): Brereton, *Diaries*, p. 340; MBR as CG, Berlin: Parks diary, 11/14/44.
2. *A General's Life*, pp. 319–20.
3. Brereton, *Diaries*, pp. 340–41.
4. Ryan, *A Bridge Too Far*, pp. 30–59, 114–17; Urquhart, *Arnhem*, pp. 19–24.
5. Bennett, *Ultra in the West*, pp. 149–58.
6. *Patton Papers II*, p. 527.
7. Warren II, p. 88.
8. MARKET-GARDEN planning here and below: Warren II, pp. 88–100; Ellis II, pp. 29–32; Ryan, *A Bridge Too Far*; Urquhart, *Arnhem*; Gavin, *On to Berlin*, pp. 158–68. See also: Rapport, Huston, Hickey, Tugwell. Delayed by 8 Corps: *A General's Life*, pp. 330–31.
9. *A General's Life*, pp. 326–33.
10. Ibid., p. 326.
11. Ibid., p. 333.
12. Gavin quote: *On to Berlin*, p. 165.
13. Ltr. Cutler to author 2/20/84.
14. Ibid. See also Warren II, p. 89; *Swords and Plowshares*, pp. 86–87; *On to Berlin*, p. 165.
15. Split of the 377th: CB-Roger E. Kling int. 8/14/84; CB-Everett G. Andrews int. 8/5/84; CB-Thomas Sherburne int. 8/4/84; Warren (Vol. II) is in error when he writes (p. 106 and p. 119) that no 101 artillery came on D day or D+1.
16. CB-Robert Neptune int. 8/5/84; CB-J. Carter Todd int. 8/11/84. Todd said: "Bertsch had no stomach for airborne warfare. He was supposed to go in with my battalion [the 319th]. Ten minutes before takeoff, he found a surgeon who took him off—out of the operation."
17. The Browning-Ridgway divided-command setup, not theretofore discussed by any of the participants or historians, is mentioned briefly in Parks diary, 9/19/44. That day, according to his diary, Parks briefed Bedell Smith on how it was to be done. Parks wrote: "Told General Smith of our plans to make two corps of the force as soon as the 52nd Div. was committed—one British [corps] composed of British troops under General Browning and one American [corps] composed of 82nd and 101st under General Ridgway." Ridgway's reaction: note 27, Chap. 34.
18. *A General's Life*, pp. 330–31.
19. MARKET operations on D day: Ellis II, pp. 32–35; Gavin, *Airborne Warfare*, pp. 68–122; Warren II, pp. 101–17. For more colorful detail, see Ryan, *A Bridge Too Far*. MBR to 82nd: *Soldier*, p. 108.
20. MBR flight in B-17: *Soldier*, p. 109; Brereton, *Diaries*, 9/17/44.
21. British commanders: Urquhart, *Arnhem*, Appendix, pp. 223–26.
22. Gavin quote: *On to Berlin*, p. 172. A Dutch priest, Father Thuring of Groesbeek, who is a writer and historian, has spent years researching the exact times and order of jumps in the 82nd Division. He gave the results of his research to Allen Langdon, who shared them with the author in ltr. 12/10/84.
23. Gavin quote: *Airborne Warfare*, p. 39. Kroos: CB-Kroos int. Later, when Ridgway learned that Kroos was a POW, he was much stricken and sent a letter to Kroos's wife. "Your husband," Ridgway wrote, "is one of the finest characters I know, a man of sterling worth, high principles,

devotion to duty and family and a delightful companion. I released him from duty as aide with great regret in order that his demonstrated ability might be recognized with the promotion I knew he would win but which would have continued to have been denied him as an aide."

24. Rapport, *Rendezvous with Destiny.*

25. Cronkite: Ryan, *A Bridge Too Far,* p. 216n. Edward R. Murrow, CBS Radio, flew in a troop carrier for an on-the-spot broadcast.

26. Warren II, Appendix "Statistical Tables," pp. 226–27. No two official sources ever agree on exact figures. Numbers here reconcile (or average) conflicting figures.

27. Parks diary, 9/17/44; MBR quote: *Soldier,* p. 109. Brereton wanted to recommend Ridgway for an award of an Air Medal for the B-17 flight, but Ridgway refused to consider it.

Chapter 36

1. *Soldier,* p. 109; MBR oral history, Pt. 2, pp. 75–76, RP-USAMHI. Weather: Warren II, p. 117. CB-James Casey int. 11/1/83.

2. Hickey, *Out of the Sky,* p. 160.

3. For continuing MARKET-GARDEN operations and enemy reaction, see Warren II, Gavin, Ellis, Ryan, Urquhart, Rapport, et al.

4. Gavin, *On to Berlin,* pp. 178–83. In a letter to author 11/21/83, Gavin wrote: "The allocation of missions was very carefully considered by myself and members of the staff before leaving England. To us, before leaving UK, our first priority had to be to get the bridge at Grave. Otherwise we would be in very serious trouble in not being able to link up and get armor support. For that reason the mission was given to Tucker. He had far more combat experience than Lindquist and was a very tough fighter. His capture of the bridge at Grave was a masterpiece, and very few commanders could have done it as well . . . I directed the 505 to help him on the Canal bridges in addition to taking on the extensive front from Molenhoek through Groesbeek. The 508th attack on to Nijmegen was going to be a difficult one. For that reason I took Lindquist aside before we left UK and told him to avoid going through the city, but after landing, to move out on to the flatlands east and north of Nijmegen. A study of the maps and photos indicated that he could then move directly on the bridge under cover of darkness and capture the southern end of it. Apparently with the best of intentions he sent Major Warren and his 1st Battalion, to capture the bridge, and talked with a member of the Dutch Underground and got deeply bogged down in the streets of Nijmegen. I talked to Lindquist shortly after daylight, at which time he was uncertain as to where his 1st Battalion was, and my heart sank. If he thought he could go through the city to get the bridge, despite the warnings that I gave him, he was in very deep trouble; so was the division. I tried to use some of his regiment to get the southern end of the bridge anyway, as his record will show. At that very hour, we were very concerned about clearing the glider landing zones. So the final capture of the bridge had to await the linkup."

Shields Warren in ltr. to author 12/3/83 wrote: "I was called to the Regimental CP at about 1800 hours. [6 P.M., D day] An English-speaking native of Nijmegen was there. He stated that the highway bridge over the Waal was defended by [only] one N.C.O. [noncommissioned officer] and seventeen men. I was ordered by the Regimental CO [Lindquist] to take A and B Companies and half my heavy weapons, move into Nijmegen and secure the bridge, leaving my C Company and remaining heavy weapons in regimental reserve. By the time my units were assembled, it was night . . . I discussed the best route to the bridge with the Dutchman. I wanted to go directly to the bridge [via Galgeveld] but he stated that the headquarters of the Dutch Resistance was in the vicinity of the traffic circle in downtown Nijmegen east of the railroad station. He reasoned that information re current German strengths at the bridge would be available there and of value to my operation. Since the traffic circle was not that great a distance from the bridge, and he knew the city and its people better than I did, I agreed to this plan. The approach march to the traffic circle was made without incident, but as my lead scouts arrived at the circle, they became aware of men unloading from vehicles on the other side of the circle. A fire-fight quickly developed and in spite of pressing the attack in the face of what became very determined resistance, we were able to move only 200–300 yards toward the bridge during the night." Warren called for his reserve C Company and the rest of his heavy weapons, but Lindquist denied them. He "had not seen the Dutchman, who was with the lead scouts, since the initial fire-fight broke out and had word he had been hit in the initial exchange of fire." In the meantime, Lindquist had sent G Company of Mendez's 3rd Battalion to assist Warren by attacking along the riverbank. Gavin arrived at Warren's advance CP at about daylight on D+1 just as Warren was preparing an all-out attack on the bridge. By that time, a strong German attack was developing from the east (out of the Reichswald), threatening the LZs, and Gavin ordered Warren to delay his attack until that situation clarified. At 10:30 A.M.,

Warren said, "I received word that I was to disengage, march to the LZ and clear it," leaving a platoon-size unit, which had been cut off by Germans near the bridge. At the same time, G Company, 3rd Battalion, had to be withdrawn to meet another German threat in the Beek area. Warren thought that he had too many jobs to do, that "we were spread too thin," that "one [full] regiment should have been given the primary mission of securing the bridges of the Waal," one battalion dropped north of the river, the other two south of the river. "Simply put," he wrote, "the troops were dropped too far from the [Nijmegen] bridges, giving the Germans time to react."

5. D+1 MARKET operations: see Warren II, pp. 117–27.

6. Gavin quote: *On to Berlin*, p. 186.

7. CB-Lancey int.

8. Brereton, *Diaries*, 9/19/44; *Soldier*, p. 109.

9. Taylor observation: Rapport, *Rendezvous with Destiny*, p. 329. Cole KIA: *Register*.

10. Brereton, *Diaries*, 9/19/44.

11. D+2 MARKET operations: Warren II, pp. 127–33.

12. CB-Nelson int.

13. George V. McCormack, "History of the 81st Airborne Antiaircraft Battalion," n.d., kindly provided the author by X. B. Cox, Jr.

14. ". . . offer not . . .": John R. Galvin, *Air Assault* (New York: Hawthorne, 1969), p. 189; first news from Arnhem: Warren II, p. 112.

15. Brereton, *Diaries*, 9/19/44; *Soldier*, pp. 110–11. The "back attack" is also mentioned in MBR oral history, Pt. 2, p. 11, RP-USAMHI. It was "quite painful," MBR said, and "heat and rest" was the "only help."

16. *Soldier*, p. 111; MBR views on British overcaution: oral history, Pt. 2, pp. 75–79, RP-USAMHI. Taylor's CP: Rapport, *Rendezvous with Destiny*, p. 326.

17. Taylor's meeting with Brereton: *Rendezvous with Destiny*, p. 326.

18. MBR briefly—and inexplicably—wrote in *Soldier*, p. 111, that he found the 82nd Division that day in "fine shape."

19. Gavin, *On to Berlin*, pp. 188–89.

20. The day's action and the Ridgway-Gavin tiff are discussed in correspondence between Cornelius Ryan, Ridgway and Gavin, in 1973, as background for Ryan's *A Bridge Too Far*, but not included in the book itself. Ltrs. Ryan to MBR 6/19/73; Gavin to MBR 6/27/73; MBR to Gavin 7/3/73; MBR to Ryan 6/24/73, RP-USAMHI. On day's action, see also Gavin, *On to Berlin*, pp. 190–96.

21. Ryan, *A Bridge Too Far*, has a graphic account of the Waal crossing and Vandervoort's attack.

22. Gavin, *On to Berlin*, pp. 196–98.

23. On Tucker's anger, see Ryan, *A Bridge Too Far*, p. 478; the quote here is from Gavin, *On to Berlin*, p. 200.

24. Rapport, *Rendezvous with Destiny*, pp. 326ff.

Chapter 37

1. D+4 MARKET operations: Warren II, pp. 136–40.

2. Ibid., pp. 141–45.

3. Ridgway was later awarded a Silver Star Medal for his trip into Holland, Box 1, RP-USAMHI. Arrival at First Army HQ: Sylvan diary 9/21/44, USAMHI.

4. Sylvan diary 9/22/44.

5. *A General's Life*, pp. 335–37.

6. Gavin promotion: Parks diary 10/11/44; Brereton, *Diaries*, 10/21/44; Gavin concern: CB-Gavin int.

7. Ltr. Kaiser to author.

8. Ltrs. Brereton to MBR 10/22/44 and MBR to Brereton 10/22/44, Box 5, RP-USAMHI.

9. Dempsey quote: Brereton, *Diaries*, 10/21/44; Brereton quote and SHAEF pressure on Montgomery: Brereton, *Diaries*, 11/4/44. American withdrawal dates: Parks diary 11/14/44 and 11/24/44.

10. British losses: Ryan, *A Bridge Too Far*, p. 599, and other sources. The British figures also include hundreds of RAF glider pilots trapped in Arnhem. American losses: Charles B. MacDonald, *The Siegfried Line Campaign* (Washington, D.C.: OCMH, 1963), p. 206. On 10/10/44, Parks noted in his diary that the 101st had suffered a total of 3,275 casualties and was continuing to lose "100–200 men per day." The division remained in combat more than a month beyond that date, but the casualty rate in late October and November dropped off substantially.

11. Interviews with or letters from Leahy, Stokely, Slaughter, Sanford; CB-Gerard int. 8/14/84.

12. Taylor, *Swords and Plowshares*, pp. 94–95.

13. CB-Taylor int.; Rapport, *Rendezvous with Destiny*, pp. 260–422; author ints. with participants.

14. Browning departure: Parks diary 11/28/44; Gale appointment: Brereton, *Diaries*, 12/9/44. Assignment of 13th Airborne Division to FAAA: Parks diary 10/5/44.

Chapter 38

1. *A General's Life*, pp. 340–42.

2. MacDonald, *Siegfried Line Campaign*, pp. 328–74.

3. *A General's Life*, pp. 342–43.

4. Casualties: MacDonald, *Siegfried Line Campaign*, p. 356.

5. *A General's Life*, p. 343.

6. Ibid., pp. 343–48.

7. Here and below on the Battle of the Bulge, see *A General's Life*, pp. 349–78. Also: Blumenson, *The Patton Papers II;* Colby, *The First Army in Europe;* Hugh M. Cole, *The Ardennes: Battle of the Bulge* (Washington, D.C.: OCMH, 1965); Eisenhower, *Crusade in Europe;* John S. D. Eisenhower, *The Bitter Woods* (New York: Putnam, 1969); Ellis, *Victory in the West II;* William D. Ellis and Thomas J. Cunningham, Jr., *Clarke of St. Vith* (Cleveland: Dillon/Liederbach, 1974); Gavin, *On to Berlin;* Liddell Hart, *History of the Second World War;* Charles B. MacDonald, *The Mighty Endeavor* (New York: Oxford University Press, 1969); Charles B. MacDonald, *A Time for Trumpets* (New York: William Morrow, 1985); Samuel L. A. Marshall, *Bastogne: The Story of the First Eight Days* (Washington, D.C.: Infantry Journal Press, 1946); Robert E. Merriam, *Dark December* (New York: Ziff-Davis, 1947); Montgomery, *Memoirs;* Rapport, *Rendezvous with Destiny;* John Toland, *Battle* (New York: Random House, 1959); Weigley, *Eisenhower's Lieutenants;* Wilmot, *The Struggle for Europe.*

8. 106th Division: R. Ernest Dupuy, *St. Vith: Lion in the Way; The 106th Division in World War II* (Washington, D.C.: Infantry Journal Press, 1949). Jones: biography and other material, courtesy Alan W. Jones, Jr., ltr. to author 5/17/84.

9. *A General's Life*, pp. 352–53.

10. Ibid., pp. 349–50.

11. Model quoted in MacDonald, *The Mighty Endeavor*, pp. 359–60.

12. The complex plan may be found in detail in Cole, *The Ardennes*, pp. 1–74.

13. MacDonald, *A Time for Trumpets*, pp. 32, 86–87, 162.

14. *A General's Life*, pp. 353–54. Ralph Bennett, a wartime code breaker, has recently argued in his memoir *Ultra in the West* that the code breakers did in fact provide many messages in the fall of 1944 pointing to a German attack, but that these warnings were ignored or dismissed, as had been the warnings about panzer divisions at Arnhem. However, even in this hindsighted analysis, there is no evidence that the code breakers forcefully and unequivocally warned that a German attack was imminent.

15. MacDonald, *A Time for Trumpets*, pp. 162, 182, 189.

16. Ibid., pp. 191–92, 370–71.

17. Gerald K. Johnson, "The Black Soldiers in the Ardennes," *Soldiers* magazine, February 1981.

18. On the 7th and 10th armored divisions' contingency plan: *A General's Life*, p. 354.

19. Sylvan diary 12/17/44, USAMHI. Some would later assert that Bradley had recently soured on Ridgway, by pointing to a document prepared by Bradley on December 1, 1944. On October 25, 1944, Eisenhower had sent a memo to Bradley, Bedell Smith and Tooey Spaatz requesting they draw up a list of "25 to 35 lieutenant generals and major generals of the ground and air forces . . . that have, in your opinion, contributed most by their personal leadership and professional qualifications to the successful progress of the war . . ." Bradley's list (excluding army commanders, airmen and staff officers) "ranked" the ground field commanders as follows: Joe Collins, Gee Gerow, Troy Middleton, Manton Eddy, Wade Haislip, Pete Corlett, Walton Walker, Edward H. Brooks, Ray McLain, Ralph Huebner, Ernest N. Harmon, Ridgway (# 31 on Bradley's list of 32) and James Van Fleet. Most of the men on Bradley's list preceding Ridgway were senior corps commanders who had indeed made very substantial contributions to the successful progress of the war. Collins, Gerow, Middleton, Eddy, Haislip, Corlett and Walker had been corps commanders during OVERLORD and/or the dramatic race through France. Brooks had ably commanded the 2nd Armored Division in OVERLORD and beyond, and in mid-October had been appointed commander, VI Corps, in Patch's Seventh Army. McLain had "saved" the 90th Division, and replaced Corlett as XIX Corps commander in October. Huebner had commanded the 1st Infantry Division under Bradley in Sicily and at Omaha Beach and beyond and was at the top of Bradley's list for command of a corps and, in fact, had temporarily commanded V Corps during Gerow's

absence in the States. Harmon, who had commanded 2nd Armored Division in Patton's invasion of Casablanca in *TORCH*, and later the 1st Armored Division in Bradley's decisive drive on Bizerte, and still later in Italy (notably Anzio), had replaced Brooks as commander of the 2nd Armored Division and was also at the top of Bradley's list for command of a corps. On October 25, 1944, when Eisenhower requested the ranking, Ridgway had been commander of XVIII Airborne Corps for only two months and had not yet commanded it in combat. His principal combat service directly under Bradley had been in the Sicily landings and in the ETO as commander of the 82nd Airborne Division during the thirty-three-day conquest of the Cotentin Peninsula.

20. MBR, "Summary of Operations, XVIII Corps," 12/18/44 to 2/15/45, dated 3/1/45, Box 5, RP-USAMHI. (Hereafter "Summary.")

21. Swift: *Register;* official bio; CB-Gavin int.

22. Ltr. Tomasik to author 11/5/83; ltr. Richard J. Seitz (Bn CO, 517 PIR) to author 10/21/83; ltr. Graves to author 11/14/83.

23. CB-Cooper int.

24. Here and below: J. M. Gavin, "Division Commander's Report," Box 5, RP-USAMHI; *On to Berlin,* pp. 226–40.

25. CB-Thomas L. Sherburne int. 8/4/84.

Chapter 39

1. "Summary"; *Soldier,* pp. 112–13.

2. Parks diary 12/19/44; ltr. Miley to MBR 1/23/45, Box 5, RP-USAMHI.

3. "Summary"; *Soldier,* pp. 113–14.

4. *Soldier,* pp. 113–14. CB-Surles int. Surles said, "General Ridgway was disgusted, not with Middleton, who was a fine man, but with the obvious defeatism that was present in VIII Corps headquarters."

5. *Soldier,* p. 113.

6. Ibid., p. 114.

7. Ibid., p. 115. In his oral history, Ridgway put it a different way: "Someone said the Germans were already there," in Houffalize, so he took the road to Marche. The "someone" was probably Middleton. The various roads and German advances are shown in Cole, *The Ardennes,* Map IV, back matter.

8. Sylvan diary 12/19/44; *Soldier,* p. 115.

9. *A General's Life,* pp. 94–95. For a more detailed bio of Hodges, see G. Patrick Murray, "Courtney Hodges: Modest Star of WW II," *American History Illustrated,* Vol. VII, No. 9, January 1973.

10. *A General's Life,* p. 363.

11. Sylvan diary 12/18/44. He wrote: "Cheerful news, however, came this morning that we are to get Gen. Ridgway and two A/B Divs . . ."

12. On Bulge tactical operations here and below, see sources cited note 7, Chapter 38. Cole's *Ardennes* is indispensable, as is MacDonald's more recent *A Time for Trumpets,* which, as popular history, supersedes Eisenhower's *The Bitter Woods* and others.

13. XVIII composition: "Summary" and Cole, *The Ardennes.* Prickett: *Register;* Bolling: Cole, *The Ardennes.*

14. On the counterattack plans, see *A General's Life.* On Bradley's telephone contact with Hodges 12/18/44, see Cole, *The Ardennes,* p. 424.

15. *A General's Life,* p. 357.

16. Patton's counteroffensive plans: ibid., pp. 357–59.

17. Montgomery's political maneuvers: ibid., pp. 362–65.

18. Ibid.

19. Caulfield-MBR int., p. 25.

20. CB-Surles int.

21. Ltr. Seitz to author 10/21/83.

22. MBR oral history, Pt. 2, pp. 83–85, RP-USAMHI.

23. Ibid., pp. 81, 120–21.

24. Gavin, "Division Commander's Report."

25. Ibid.; Gavin, *On to Berlin,* pp. 246–49. "Senseless": MacDonald, *A Time for Trumpets,* pp. 448–49.

26. MacDonald, *A Time for Trumpets,* pp. 238–40.

27. Gavin, "Division Commander's Report"; MacDonald, *A Time for Trumpets,* pp. 454–55.

28. MacDonald, *A Time for Trumpets,* p. 90 and elsewhere.

29. Gavin, "Division Commander's Report"; CB-Todd int.; Lord, *History of the 508th.*

30. Ltr. Allen Langdon to author 12/26/84, with map outlining horseshoe.
31. Gavin, "Division Commander's Report"; Langdon map.
32. Hobbs: *Register;* official bio; *A General's Life,* p. 270; CB-Surles int.
33. Rose: official bio; Collins, *Lightning Joe,* p. 215; *Soldier,* p. 115.
34. No 3rd Armored Div CCR: MacDonald, *A Time for Trumpets,* p. 444. (Nor did the 2nd Armored Div. have a CCR. All other armored divisions did.) Disposition of the little task forces: ibid., p. 535 (map); Cole, *The Ardennes,* pp. 345ff; XVIII Abn Corps "Summary."
35. Ex-DRAGOON dispositions: ltrs. to author from Tomasik 11/5/83 and 1/17/84; Seitz 10/21/83; Dan Morgan (551st historian) 1/12/84. In addition: Clark Archer, "chronicle" of the 517 PIR; Charles LaChaussee (1st Bn, 517) ms, LaChaussee Papers, USAMHI.
36. *Soldier,* p. 116; CB-James B. Casey int. Omar Bradley, in his oral history, USAMHI, pp. 50–51, relates approximately the same story about Ridgway. "Lucky": Caulfield-MBR int., p. 25.

Chapter 40

1. CB-Gavin int.
2. Hoge: *Register;* oral history, USAMHI. Nelson: *Register;* John Eisenhower, *The Bitter Woods.* Devine: Cole, *The Ardennes;* John Eisenhower, *The Bitter Woods.*
3. 7th AD problems and command: MacDonald, *Siegfried Line Campaign,* pp. 237–47; Ellis, *Clarke of St. Vith.* Hasbrouck: official bio; *Register;* "ice water": ltr. William S. Triplet to author 1/13/84.
4. Dupuy, *St. Vith: Lion in the Way,* has detail on the 106th tactical movements, as has MacDonald's *A Time for Trumpets.* The Jones command "problem" is discussed extensively in *The Bitter Woods;* Toland, *Battle;* Cole, *The Ardennes;* and other sources. Alan Jones, Jr.: *Register;* "You two . . .": *The Bitter Woods,* p. 355.
5. *The Bitter Woods,* p. 357; Cole, *The Ardennes,* pp. 394–95.
6. Text of Hasbrouck letter: *The Ardennes,* pp. 393–95.
7. XVIII Abn Corps HQ Diary 12/20/44, Box 5, RP-USAMHI.
8. Cole, *The Ardennes,* p. 395.
9. XVIII Abn Corps HQ Diary 12/21/44 (complete text Hasbrouck letter).
10. Ibid.
11. *The Bitter Woods,* p. 367 (complete text Hasbrouck letter).
12. Ltr. Hasbrouck to author 2/5/84; *On to Berlin,* p. 254.
13. *A General's Life,* p. 365.
14. "[T]idy show": *The Bitter Woods,* p. 359.
15. MacDonald, *Mighty Endeavor,* p. 384.
16. Counteroffensive: Collins, *Lightning Joe,* pp. 282–85; Cole, *The Ardennes,* pp. 426–29.
17. *A General's Life,* p. 366.
18. *Lightning Joe,* p. 291.
19. Ibid., pp. 282–83; XVIII Abn Corps "Summary."
20. *Lightning Joe,* p. 284; CB-Collins int.
21. For Bastogne see: Cole, *The Ardennes;* Rapport, *Rendezvous with Destiny;* Marshall, *Bastogne;* Toland, *Battle;* McDonough and Gardner, *Sky Riders;* Fred MacKenzie, *The Men of Bastogne* (New York: Ace, 1968); MacDonald, *A Time for Trumpets.*
22. Cole, *The Ardennes,* pp. 294–98; 459–60.
23. Ibid.; Rapport, *Rendezvous with Destiny,* pp. 796–97; MacDonald, *A Time for Trumpets,* p. 502; Johnson, "The Black Soldier in the Ardennes"; ltr. Sherburne to author 1/5/84.
24. Rapport, *Rendezvous with Destiny,* describes difficulties of cohesion, p. 503.
25. Initial deployment of 101: ibid., maps pp. 506–7.
26. LaPrade: ibid., p. 469; *Register.* Author ints. with participants.
27. Rapport, *Rendezvous with Destiny,* pp. 509–13.

Chapter 41

1. Bulge tactical operations: see note 7, Chapter 38.
2. Cole, *The Ardennes,* pp. 405–6; Ellis, *Clarke of St. Vith,* p. 124. Cole wrote that four armored infantry companies were lost in the withdrawal: "The troops east of St. Vith simply had to be written off (at least 600 officers and men) although some later would be able to work their way back through German lines." In a ltr. to MBR, Hasbrouck wrote (XVIII Abn Corps HQ diary 12/22/44): "The withdrawal of CCB . . . was expensive. So far we are missing at least one half the infantry of Clarke's force." More recently, MacDonald, in his meticulously researched *A Time for*

Trumpets, arrived at the figure of nine hundred. XVIII Abn Corps HQ diary 12/21/44, entry at 2237 hours, gives Hoge "discretionary authority" to readjust his lines.

3. XVIII Abn Corps HQ diary 12/21/44, entry at 2345.
4. XVIII Abn Corps HQ diary 12/21/44, MBR-Kean telephone call at 2350.
5. Goose egg: Cole, *The Ardennes,* p. 407.
6. Ellis, *Clarke of St. Vith,* p. 129. Hasbrouck's objections are quoted in Cole, *The Ardennes,* p. 407.
7. CB-Surles int.
8. The message is published in full in John Eisenhower, *The Bitter Woods,* p. 374.
9. The first historian who wrongly interpreted the message was Chester Wilmot in *The Struggle for Europe,* p. 596. Citing the gist of the message, Wilmot wrote: "Ridgway relieved him [Hasbrouck] of command." Other historians followed his lead. These included Gavin, *On to Berlin,* p. 232. When Gavin's book was published, Ridgway wrote Gavin that he was wrong. Ridgway also wrote Hasbrouck for supporting evidence, which he obtained and sent to Gavin. (See ltrs. Gavin to MBR 9/1/78; MBR to Gavin 9/8/78; MBR to Gavin 10/6/78; Hasbrouck to MBR 10/18/78; Gavin to MBR 10/25/78; MBR to Gavin 10/30/78; and MBR to Director, USAMHI, 10/31/78.) In the last, MBR, referring to Gavin's *On to Berlin,* wrote: "I hereby state that this reported relief of command of General Hasbrouck is completely contrary to the fact" and requested that this statement be incorporated with the XVIII Abn Corps HQ diary, RP-USAMHI. In ltr. to author 1/11/84, MBR wrote: "Not once did I even entertain any thought of relieving General Hasbrouck of his command. Any statement or rumors to the contrary are false." Despite all, Gavin, in CB-Gavin interview, continued to insist that Ridgway relieved Hasbrouck. In CB-Surles int., Surles said, "Gavin in *On to Berlin* is completely wrong and misinformed about Hasbrouck."
10. Ltrs. MBR to Gavin 10/6/78; Hasbrouck to MBR 10/18/78; CB-Surles int.
11. XVIII Abn Corps HQ diary. Quill report 11:35 A.M.
12. Hasbrouck to MBR, XVIII Abn Corps HQ diary 12/22/44 at 11:50 A.M.
13. Ibid., MBR (radio) to CG 106th Division at 12:25 P.M. Telephone call from Kean at 1400 hours; CB-Surles int. Cole, *The Ardennes,* p. 413, implies that Ridgway did not approve Hasbrouck's request for withdrawal until 1500—after Kean's telephone call relaying Montgomery and Hodges orders, but this is in conflict with XVIII Abn Corps HQ diary.
14. *Soldier,* p. 120.
15. Ibid., pp. 119–20.
16. Ibid., p. 120; Cole, *The Ardennes,* p. 413; XVIII Abn Corps HQ diary 12/22/44.
17. *On to Berlin,* pp. 257–58; CB-Gavin int.
18. *Register.*
19. Jones heart attack: Toland, *Battle,* p. 196; ltr. Alan Jones, Jr., to author 5/7/84. Jones (Jr.) wrote: "My father suffered a major heart attack, diagnosed later as coronary occlusion and infarction of myocardin, 23 December 1944. Evacuated by ambulance to 365th Station Hospital, vicinity Liege. Wounded in V-1 attack on hospital 26 December. Mild recurrence [heart attack] 15 January 1945. Returned to U.S. . . . Walter Reed General Hospital, 20 March 1945 . . . Retired 31 October 1945, incapacitated for active service . . . He was generally immobile for several years. Partial recovery slow. Treatment continued throughout remainder of his life. Died 22 January 1969 of carcinoma and arteriosclerotic heart disease." "[F]ailed": ltr. MBR to WP Superintendent 6/8/58.
20. *The Ardennes; Battle,* pp. 200–1; Ellis, *Clarke of St. Vith,* p. 133.
21. *The Ardennes,* pp. 582–83; *Soldier,* p. 120; XVIII Airborne Corps "Summary"; MBR oral history, Pt. 2, p. 85, USAMHI.
22. Ltr. Hasbrouck to author 2/5/84.

Chapter 42

1. On tactical operations, see note 7, Chapter 38.
2. MacDonald, *A Time for Trumpets,* pp. 534ff.
3. XVIII Abn Corps "Summary." Paratroopers: "Summary"; Clark Archer, 517 "Chronicle"; ltrs. to author from Tomasik and Charles H. Doyle (509 historian).
4. Gavin, "Division Commander's Report," here and below; Gavin, *On to Berlin,* pp. 258–61; Allen Langdon 82nd Div deployment map; MacDonald, *A Time for Trumpets,* pp. 543–46 (and map, p. 535).
5. Transfer of 3rd AD to VII Corps: XVIII Abn Corps "Summary" and HQ diary 12/23/44, entry at 1520 hours. Collins, *Lightning Joe,* p. 286.
6. Gavin, *On to Berlin,* pp. 260–63; Eisenhower, *The Bitter Woods,* pp. 373–74.

7. CB-Eaton int.

8. 7th AD plus: XVIII Abn Corps HQ diary 12/23/44, entry at 1850 hours; Hoge: XVIII Abn Corps HQ diary 12/24/44, entry 0652; Gavin, *On to Berlin*, p. 263.

9. Clarke, here and below: Ellis, *Clarke of St. Vith*, pp. 136–37, 144.

10. *Soldier*, p. 118.

11. XVIII Abn Corps "Summary."

12. Gavin, *On to Berlin*, p. 261; Gavin, "Division Commander's Report"; Langdon map.

13. XVIII Abn Corps HQ diary 12/24/44, entry at 0615 and others.

14. XVIII Abn Corps "Summary."

15. Sylvan diary 12/23/44, USAMHI.

16. MBR oral history, Pt. 2, p. 102, USAMHI.

17. Ibid.; Gavin, *On to Berlin*, pp. 264–65; Gavin, "Division Commander's Report."

18. 82nd withdrawal: Gavin, *On to Berlin*, p. 265; Gavin, "Division Commander's Report"; Cole, *The Ardennes*, Map VIII, back matter; Lord, *History of the 508th*.

19. Gavin, "Division Commander's Report"; Gavin, *On to Berlin*, pp. 266–67; MacDonald, *A Time for Trumpets*, pp. 462–63.

20. Cole, *The Ardennes*, pp. 585–90.

21. Ltr. Hasbrouck to author 2/15/84.

22. Ibid.; ltrs. Triplet to author 1/13/84, 3/4/84.

23. CB-Surles int.

24. Caulfield-MBR int., p. 25.

25. XVIII Abn Corps HQ diary 12/25/44.

26. Cole, *The Ardennes*, p. 590.

27. 424 and 112: ltr. MBR to Kean 12/25/44, Box 5, RP-USAMHI.

28. Cole, *The Ardennes*, pp. 583, 587; Collins, *Lightning Joe*, p. 286.

29. Ltr. MBR to Hodges 1/18/45, Box 5, RP-USAMHI.

30. The legend was published by Julian Aaron Cook in the airborne newsletter *Static Line*, March 1983. The 3rd Bn exec, who requested his name be withheld, punctured the legend in a letter to author dated 8/24/83.

31. *Soldier*, p. 122.

32. Ibid., pp. 121–22.

33. Cole, *The Ardennes*, pp. 595–96; 597–98.

34. 517 "history" provided by Seitz; Paxton: ltrs. Seitz and Graves to author; Clark Archer, 517 "Chronicle."

Chapter 43

1. Bulge tactical operations: see note 7, Chapter 38.

2. Cole, *The Ardennes*, pp. 445–81; Rapport, *Rendezvous with Destiny;* Marshall, *Bastogne;* McAuliffe's account in Brereton, *Diaries*, pp. 378–86. Air-resupply figures vary widely—Cole, p. 468, used here.

3. Rapport, *Rendezvous with Destiny*, pp. 536–38.

4. Cole, *The Ardennes*, map, p. 473.

5. Rapport, *Rendezvous with Destiny*, pp. 548–60.

6. Battle: Cole, *The Ardennes*, pp. 570–81; 12/26/44 air drop: ibid., p. 468.

7. Operations of III and XII Corps: Cole, *The Ardennes*, pp. 509–55; MacDonald, *A Time for Trumpets*, pp. 514–33.

8. *Patton Papers II*, pp. 604–5.

9. Taylor: *Swords and Plowshares*, pp. 98–100.

10. Cole, *The Ardennes*, pp. 672–73.

11. Ltrs. and statements of Manteuffel kindly provided to author by Bruce Clarke 1/15/84.

12. Montgomery to Bradley, 1/12/45, quoted in *A General's Life*, p. 385; Hodges to MBR 2/23/45, Box 1, RP-USAMHI; *Soldier* (citation), p. 337; Bradley endorsement undated. A second endorsement by Brereton stated: "I wish to add my commendations to those of Lieutenant General Bradley. By your military excellence, while serving with the ground troops under his command, you have well upheld the high tradition of the Airborne Troops." Ridgway was awarded a Bronze Star Medal for heroism during the Bulge; a recommendation for a third DSC was not approved. Generally, the Army was very conservative in awarding decorations for this defensive phase of the Bulge. Eisenhower's "I think you would . . .": Ike Papers IV, p. 2427; he also praised Hasbrouck for "a brilliant job." Gavin appraisal of MBR: CB-Gavin int.; *On to Berlin*, p. 245. On February 1, 1945, Eisenhower forwarded to Marshall a list of senior officers, ranking them by "the value of

services each officer has rendered in this war." It was a list similar to the list Bradley had drawn the previous December 1 (before the Bulge). Ridgway had moved up the list dramatically. Excluding Bradley, army commanders (including newly appointed Gerow), staffers and airmen, Eisenhower's ranking was as follows: Collins, Ridgway, Brooks, Walker, Haislip, Eddy, McLain, Huebner, Harmon and Van Fleet. (Ike Papers IV, pp. 2466–69.)

13. Ike Papers IV, p. 2442. Marshall also recommended that Collins be promoted to three stars. Eisenhower did not think it was wise to promote Collins to three stars until 12th Army Group commander Omar Bradley, who still wore three stars, got a fourth star. After Bradley's promotion, Collins and other "outstanding" corps commanders would get three stars. Collins' promotion was thus delayed. Marshall and Eisenhower agreed that owing to Ridgway's relatively brief (four months) tenure as corps commander he should not be considered for promotion to three stars at this time.

14. Parks diary 3/3/45.

15. Ike Papers V, Chronology; Butcher, *My Three Years*, pp. 772–73.

16. Ike Papers VI, p. 508.

17. Ltrs. Tomasik to author 1/17/84; Clark Archer, 517 "Chronicle"; ltr. Bruce Clarke to author 1/15/84, enclosing CCB P.U.C. dated 7/12/48.

18. Ellis, *Clarke of St. Vith*, pp. 333–34.

19. 101 casualties: Cole, *The Ardennes*, p. 481; 82 casualties: author's estimate.

Chapter 44

1. *A General's Life*, pp. 369–78, wherein these extraordinary events are extensively discussed.

2. Charles B. MacDonald, *The Last Offensive* (Washington, D.C.: OCMH, 1973), p. 28.

3. Third Army's ongoing offensive, which also included Millikin's III and Eddy's XII corps, is described in Cole, *The Ardennes*, pp. 606–48.

4. Weather described in Cole, *The Ardennes*, Patton Papers II (p. 610) and elsewhere. Officer quoted: Ralph Ingersoll in *Top Secret*, p. 251, reprinted in Rapport, *Rendezvous with Destiny*, pp. 590–91.

5. The action of VIII Corps is described in *The Ardennes*, pp. 617–27, 643–47, and *The Last Offensive*, p. 35. See also Patton Papers II, pp. 627, 653. Kilburn was replaced by Holmes E. Dager on 3/8/45.

6. On 17th Abn Div composition and personnel: ltrs. to author from James W. Coutts (2/5/84, 2/8/84, 2/20/84); Allen C. Miller (2/7/84); David P. Schorr (2/8/84); Edward I. Sachs (2/29/84); Ward S. Ryan (2/27/84); Robert L. Ashworth (2/28/84); Joseph Quade (2/20/84).

7. 17th Abn Div action in Bulge, here and below: ltr. Miley to MBR 1/23/45, Box 5A, RP-USAMHI; Miley, after-action int. 1/19/45 and Stubbs after-action int. 1/20/45 kindly provided by Joseph Quade (17th Abn Assoc.). See also: Donald R. Pay, *Thunder from Heaven* (official division history).

8. Pierce quoted in MacDonald, *The Last Offensive*, p. 38.

9. *Patton Papers II*, pp. 615, 627.

10. Coutts on Taylor: ltr. Coutts to author 2/20/84.

11. *Patton Papers II*, p. 610.

12. Ltr. Taylor to MBR 1/11/45, Box 5A, RP-USAMHI.

13. Ltr. MBR to Taylor 1/13/45, Box 5A, RP-USAMHI; Hobart Gay oral history, p. 24, USAMHI; *Patton Papers II*, p. 627; McAuliffe assignment: Ike Papers IV, pp. 2427–28. Gillmore: ltr. Taylor to MBR 1/11/45; ltrs. Gillmore to author 1/5/84, 2/20/84; Parks diary 1/26/45.

14. 101 action, losses and replacements in *Rendezvous with Destiny*, pp. 586–665; ltrs. 101 personnel to author; Sherburne (2/24/84) ltr. to author. Sutliffe: ltrs. to author John Hanlon 2/27/84 and James J. Hatch 3/9/84. In a ltr. to MBR 1/11/45, Taylor reported his total losses in the Bulge to be "approximately 3,000." The division was in combat for another week after that (RP-USAMHI).

15. See notes 6 and 7. Attachment of the 761st Tank Bn: Johnson, "The Black Soldier in the Ardennes"; 761st Battalion history, *Come Out Fighting*, pp. 52–54, excerpts kindly provided by Joseph Quade; David Williams, *Hit Hard* (history of the 761) (New York: Bantam Books, 1983). The 761 was awarded a Presidential Unit Citation; see New York *Times* 9/5/83.

16. Ltr. Taylor to MBR 1/17/45.

Chapter 45

1. Ike Papers IV, pp. 2383–85.

2. Frank James Price, *Troy H. Middleton: A Biography* (Baton Rouge: Louisiana State Univ., 1974), p. 391.

3. The Ridgway-Collins arguments are set forth at length in XVIII Abn Corps HQ diary, December 28, 29, 30, 31, 1944.

4. "Another failure" and "emptying sack": ibid., December 29, 1944.

5. See note 3.

6. Ike Papers IV, pp. 2382–85; 2388–89.

7. Ellis, *Victory in the West II;* XVIII Abn Corps HQ diary 12/31/44.

8. Mathewson: *Register,* official bio.; *Soldier,* p. 118; ltr. MBR to Hodges 12/24/44, Box 5, RP-USAMHI; MBR oral history, Pt. 2, pp. 101–2, RP-USAMHI. Early attempts to get Mathewson into 82nd: ltrs. MBR to M. W. Clark and Mathewson, 5/18/42, Box 5, RP-USAMHI and MBR to Alexander R. Bolling (G-1, AGF) 3/26/43, Box 2A, RP-USAMHI.

9. Ltr. MBR to Brereton (re Parks) 12/21/44, Box 5, RP-USAMHI. Other requests: MBR oral history, Pt. 2, pp. 110–11; Pt. 3, pp. 54–60, USAMHI.

10. CB-Surles int.

11. MBR oral history, Pt. 2, pp. 110–11, USAMHI.

12. XVIII Abn Corps "Summary" and HQ diary.

13. Archer, 517 "Chronicle"; XVIII Abn HQ "Summary."

14. Archer, 517 "Chronicle."

15. MacDonald, *The Last Offensive,* pp. 26–33; Collins, *Lightning Joe,* pp. 293–94.

16. Gavin, *On to Berlin,* pp. 276–81.

17. LaChaussee ms, LaChaussee Papers, USAMHI. Charles LaChaussee was a company commander in William Boyle's 1st Bn, 517 PIR. His brief ms traces the 1st Bn (and 517) from birth to Italy to DRAGOON to Bulge. Boyle: Archer, 517 "Chronicle"; *Register.*

18. *On to Berlin,* p. 277; ltr. Langdon to author 12/26/84.

19. Lord, *History of the 508th,* pp. 69–71.

20. Joerg: *Register;* ltr. Holm to author 12/5/83. Losses: ltr. Dan Morgan (551 historian) to author 1/12/84.

21. Wounds: ltr. Vandervoort to author 7/5/83.

22. Ltrs. Taylor to MBR 1/11/45 and MBR to Taylor 1/13/45, Box 5A, RP-USAMHI.

23. Withdrawal: *The Last Offensive,* pp. 39–41; XVIII Abn Corps offensive, HQ Diary 1/5, 1/6, 1/7, 1/8, 1945.

24. XVIII Abn Corps HQ diary and "Summary." Anderson: MBR oral history, Pt. 2, pp. 59–60; Sylvan diary 12/27/44; Stroh, Jeter: Dupuy, *Lion in the Way,* pp. 213, 219.

25. XVIII Abn Corps HQ diary 1/13/45; Sylvan diary 1/13/45.

26. XVIII Abn Corps HQ diary 1/13/45. In an earlier HQ diary entry (12/22/44 at 2110) Ridgway was quoted as telling Bill Kean that Hobbs "has more stuff than any other division and yet he's always crying for more."

27. Relief of Prickett and Stanford: XVIII Abn Corps HQ diary 12/31/44 (Hodges wanted to relieve Prickett then, but Ridgway urged that he be given a full "test in battle"). Ltr. MBR to Hodges 1/18/45, Box 5A, RP-USAMHI; Sylvan diary 1/24/45. On Porter: Ike Papers II, p. 1134; IV, p. 2371.

28. *A General's Life,* pp. 389–90.

29. Linkup of VII and VIII corps: *The Last Offensive,* p. 42; *Lightning Joe,* p. 294. Stubbs: After-action int. 1/20/45. Control of First and Ninth armies: Bradley, *A Soldier's Story,* p. 492.

30. *The Last Offensive,* p. 46; *Lightning Joe,* p. 294. Collins wrote that V Corps entered the fight "belatedly, in my judgment."

31. Here and below: 7th AD attack on St. Vith based on material supplied by Triplet 1/13/84. Ltr., unpublished 48-page ms, poem "Saga of CCA," by Cpl. Ben Maugham. Also after-action report of 2nd Bn, 517, kindly supplied by Seitz. Richard Spencer (of 2nd Bn 517) ltr. to Seitz 1/24/84 is source for the 509 paratroopers in St. Vith. He was sent into the city to "see who the paratroopers were that were reported in that town in bitter fighting . . . When I got there I found it was the 509." Clarke's gallstones: *Clarke of St. Vith.*

32. "Sluggish": Sylvan diary 1/21/45.

33. Ltr. Triplet to author, 1/13/84.

34. Ltr. Yarborough to author 7/28/84; Doyle to author 3/18/84. Ellis, *Clarke of St. Vith;* ltr. Clarke to author 1/15/84.

35. 509: ltrs. Tomasik to author 1/17/84, 3/10/84; Charles Doyle to author 3/18/84.

36. 101: Rapport, *Rendezvous with Destiny,* pp. 666–95.

37. 507 history. Interviews with and ltrs. from participants.

38. Based in part on Parks diary 1/16/45: "Cumulative casualties for airborne troops during Bulge." However, the Parks figures appear to be understated. The 551st Battalion, for example, is shown as having an "effective strength" of 313, the 509th Battalion, 505; whereas both outfits had

already been virtually wiped out. Parks puts the killed, wounded and missing in the 101st at 3,067 as of 1/16/45, whereas Rapport, *Rendezvous with Destiny*, p. 801, has 3,458 as of 1/14/45, and the 101 fighting over the next week added several hundred more. Curiously, the casualties in all three divisions were very nearly the same.

Chapter 46

1. Bradley's views on the broad-front strategy: *A General's Life*, pp. 372–73; 379–80.
2. Ibid., pp. 386–87.
3. MacDonald, *The Last Offensive*, pp. 60–62; XVIII Airborne Corps "Summary."
4. *A General's Life*, pp. 372–73.
5. *Soldier*, pp. 127–28.
6. XVIII Airborne Corps "Summary."
7. Archer, 517 "Chronicle."
8. Ibid.; *Soldier*, pp. 127–28.
9. *The Last Offensive*, p. 63.
10. Lord, *History of the 508th*, p. 75.
11. XVIII Airborne Corps "Summary"; Gavin, *On to Berlin*, p. 283.
12. *The Last Offensive*, pp. 63–65; XVIII Airborne Corps "Summary."
13. Montgomery objections: *A General's Life*, p. 387.
14. Cancellation of offensive: ibid., p. 392; ltr. MBR to Hodges 2/2/45, Box 5, RP-USAMHI.
15. Patton's view: Blumenson, *Patton Papers II*, pp. 632–63; Hodges' view: an MBR entry in the XVIII Corps diary on 2/13/45 quoted Hodges as saying if the offensive had not been called off, First Army "would have been on the Rhine by this time."
16. XVIII Airborne Corps "Summary"; *Soldier*, p. 128. Ostberg: *Register;* various interviews 325 GIR personnel.
17. *A General's Life*, pp. 393–94.
18. *Soldier*, p. 131; *The Last Offensive*, p. 69. The mission of XVIII Airborne Corps in support of Simpson's offensive has usually been minimized in the official and unofficial histories and even in Ridgway's memoir *Soldier*. Ridgway erroneously limited it to: "We were to join VII Corps in an attack against the Roer dams." In fact, the mission of XVIII Airborne Corps was first to assist in the capture of the dams; second, cross the Roer River; third, drive to the Rhine toward Bonn on the right flank of Collins' VII Corps.
19. Colby, "The First Army in Europe," pp. 133–34; XVIII Airborne Corps "Summary."
20. *The Last Offensive*, p. 71; map, p. 76. For earlier 9th and 28th division attacks, see MacDonald, *The Siegfried Line Campaign*, pp. 323–24. 517: Archer "Chronicle."
21. *The Last Offensive*, pp. 71–83. 517: Archer "Chronicle."
22. *On to Berlin*, pp. 288–92.
23. *Soldier*, p. 132.
24. *On to Berlin*, pp. 294–95, 297–98; *History of the 508th*, pp. 81–82. 517: Archer "Chronicle."
25. *A General's Life*, pp. 395–96, 399.
26. Brereton, *Diaries*, pp. 340–41; Parks diary 12/1/44.
27. Brereton, *Diaries*, 2/1/45; Parks diary 2/1/45.
28. Parks diary, 2/5/45.
29. XVIII Airborne Corps HQ diary 2/6/45; Ike Papers V, Chronology.
30. Sylvan diary 2/7/45.
31. Ltr. Hodges to Bradley 2/7/45, Box 5A, RP-USAMHI. See note 18: This letter makes clear that the XVIII Airborne Corps mission was not merely to attack the Roer dams, but also to go all the way to the Rhine.
32. Ltr. Hodges to Bradley 2/7/45, Box 5A, RP-USAMHI. Doc Eaton wrote on the file copy of the letter: "Delivered in person to Gen. Bradley 1100, 8 February, by Gen. Ridgway." Brereton, *Diaries*, 2/8/45; Parks diary 2/8/45.
33. XVIII Airborne Corps HQ diary 2/8/45.
34. Sylvan diary 2/8/45. Hodges quoted: XVIII Airborne Corps HQ diary 2/14/45.
35. Parks diary 2/9/45.
36. XVIII Airborne Corps HQ diary 2/9/45; Parks diary 2/10/45.
37. Colby, "The First Army in Europe," p. 134; XVIII Airborne Corps "Summary"; *On to Berlin*, p. 296; Rapport, *Rendezvous with Destiny*, pp. 694–95. The 17th Airborne Division was withdrawn on February 10; the 82nd on February 17 and the 101st on February 23.
38. XVIII Airborne Corps diary 2/13/45.

Chapter 47

1. VARSITY and CHOKER II planning: Warren II, pp. 156–74; entries, Parks diary and Brereton, *Diaries,* 2/1/45 to 3/20/45; entries XVIII Abn Corps HQ diary 2/14/45 to 3/20/45; XVIII Abn Corps "Summary," dated 4/25/45. The original D-day dates for VARSITY and CHOKER II: ltr. MBR to O. N. Bradley 2/7/45, RP-USAMHI. This letter assigns 6th, 13th and 17th divisions to VARSITY; 82nd and 101st to CHOKER II.

2. Max Taylor's visit to Washington in December 1944 helped persuade AGF and others to adopt Ridgway's reorganizational scheme. On December 18, 1944, Marshall wrote Ridgway that as a result of Ridgway's repeated requests (the most recent being 12/4/44) and of requests by Eisenhower and Taylor during his visit, "A new organization has been adopted which I understand from Gereral Taylor is in all probability wholly acceptable to you and your associates . . ." On return from Washington, Taylor wrote Ridgway 1/7/45: "Insofar as organization and equipment are concerned, I felt that the War Department is willing to do anything for us that the Theater will support." Ltrs. MBR to Marshall 12/4/44; Marshall to MBR 12/18/44; Taylor to MBR 1/17/45, Box 5A, RP-USAMHI. Effective date: MacDonald, *The Last Offensive,* p. 229.

3. Interviews with and letters from participants. When the 17th Division's 193rd Glider Regiment was deactivated, the commander, Maurice Stubbs, was transferred to FAAA; the exec, David P. Schorr, Jr. (West Point, 1932) replaced Clark M. Bailey as exec of the 194. The 193rd's 1st Bn commander, Robert L. Ashworth, became CO of the new 194 3rd Bn. The 193 2nd Bn CO, Harry Balish, was transferred to 17th Div HQ (per ltr. Schorr to author 2/8/84). The deactivated 550th Glider Bn CO, Ed Sachs, who had been hospitalized with pleurisy, returned to 17th Div HQ for a time and was rotated to the States (per CB-Sachs int. 11/27/83 and ltr. Sachs to author 3/5/84).

4. Capacity of C-46: Warren II, p. 158. Double towing, ibid. In February/March, 50th Troop Carrier Wing moved to an area near Chartres; the 53rd to Voisenum, and part of the 52nd to fields near Amiens. Three groups of the 52nd remained in southern England to lift the 6th British Airborne Division.

5. Raff's view on Ridgway and Rhine crossing: ltr. Raff to author, 11/1/83.

6. The Dempsey-Ridgway dispute on VARSITY plans is most clearly set forth in Parks's diary and XVIII Abn Corps HQ diary. See especially Parks diary 2/9/45, 2/10/45, 2/15/45, 2/19/45; XVIII Abn Corps HQ diary 2/14/45, 2/19/45, 2/20/45, 2/23/45.

7. Parks diary 2/15/45: Parks wrote that under Dempsey's plan part of the airborne force would land east of Wesel, seize the "high ground" and take the town from the east. Ridgway, he recorded, objected that this was not a "suitable" airborne mission, that the ground east of Wesel was "not a feasible" place to land or operate and that there were not sufficient "heavy weapons" to attack Wesel.

8. Parks diary 2/16/45.

9. Ibid., 2/19/45.

10. See note 1.

11. *A General's Life,* p. 416.

12. Ibid., p. 399.

13. Ibid., pp. 399–400.

14. For a detailed account of the capture of the bridge: *The Last Offensive,* pp. 208–35.

15. *A General's Life,* p. 406.

16. Ibid., pp. 407–8.

17. Ibid., p. 407; Eisenhower, *Crusade in Europe,* p. 380; Ike Papers V, Chronology.

18. Gavin, *On to Berlin,* pp. 304–5; Taylor, *Swords and Plowshares,* pp. 105–6. Ridgway wrote John Leonard a letter of congratulations for seizing the Remagen bridge. In response, Leonard said that all credit should go to Bill Hoge, "as he was the driving force that pushed the task force across." Leonard concluded: "Courtney [Hodges] sings your praises. I know he hated to lose you." Ltr. Leonard to MBR 3/18/45, Box 3, RP-USAMHI.

19. ARENA plan: The most complete description may be found in the transcript of an Army War College critique on airborne warfare given in 1945 by Lewis Brereton with Ridgway participating. Copy of transcript in Box 9, RP-USAMHI. See also: Huston, *Out of the Blue,* pp. 216–18, who cites planning documents and Ridgway's comments thereon. See also Parks diary 3/3/45, 3/7/45, 3/8/45, 3/12/45, 3/17/45, 3/19/45, 3/23/45, 3/25/45, 3/26/45. Marshall's comments on MARKET-GARDEN and strategic airborne operations: ltr. Taylor to MBR 1/17/45, Box 5A, RP-USAMHI.

20. Parks diary 3/3/45.

21. *Out of the Blue,* p. 217.

22. Brereton veto: ltr. Brereton to MBR 3/15/45, Box 1, RP-USAMHI.

23. Eisenhower reaction: Parks diary 3/12/45. Follow-up action: Ike Papers IV, pp. 2524–26; 2529; 2547–48.

24. *A General's Life*, pp. 406–15.

25. Ibid., p. 409.

Chapter 48

1. Malaria: 201 File, Box 1, RP-USAMHI. A medical report dated 1/2/45 stated Ridgway had "malarial parasites." Back: MBR oral history, Pt. 3, p. 11, USAMHI.

2. VARSITY training: Warren II, pp. 168–70. Groups held in reserve: ibid., pp. 82–169. These two or three reserved groups were familiarly known as CATOR (Combined Air Transport Operations Room, which controlled and dispatched them).

3. Warren II, pp. 169-70.

4. Recoilless rifles: MacDonald, *The Last Offensive*, p. 299. *Panzerfaust:* Gavin, *On to Berlin*, pp. 145, 205.

5. Details here and below on Montgomery's Rhine crossing (Operation PLUNDER) from Ellis II, pp. 285–92; *The Last Offensive*, pp. 294–315.

6. Ike Papers, Vol. V, Chronology; Eisenhower, *Crusade in Europe*, pp. 387–90; *A General's Life*, pp. 412–14.

7. See note 5; Warren II, p. 171.

8. *Soldier*, pp. 133–34.

9. *The Last Offensive*, p. 303. The full American Revolution code signal was "one if by land, two if by sea." The alarm was to be conveyed by hanging either one or two lanterns in a Boston church tower.

10. *The Last Offensive*, p. 305.

11. Ibid., p. 307; Ellis II, pp. 288–89.

12. VARSITY operations: Warren II, pp. 174–95, and chart, pp. 228–29.

13. Saunders, *The Red Beret*, p. 301.

14. CB-Branigan int. 8/4/84.

15. Reserved gliders: Warren II, p. 158. Cancellation of CHOKER II: Parks diary entry at 1107 hours 3/24/45: "SHAEF called and said CHOKER II definitely off."

16. CB-Branigan int.

17. Ibid.; interviews and letters from Oswald and Paddock.

18. *The Last Offensive*, p. 309, erroneously states that 1,696 transport planes and 1,348 gliders lifted 21,680 paratroopers and gliderists into battle. These erroneous figures are repeated in Gavin, *On to Berlin*, p. 309. In a much earlier work, *Airborne Warfare* (p. 135), Gavin's figures almost exactly match those of Warren: 17,122 paratroopers and gliderists lifted into battle. MacDonald's figure of 21,680 may well have inadvertently included the "tails" of the 6th and 17th airborne divisions, which later crossed the Rhine by landing craft and joined the divisions on the battlefield.

19. Eisenhower watching: *Crusade in Europe*, p. 390. Ridgway watching: *Soldier*, p. 133. Brereton watching: Parks diary 3/24/45; Brereton later had lunch with Montgomery and Dempsey, during which Montgomery said he would release the 17th Division "in about ten days."

20. *On to Berlin*, p. 309.

21. Bradley, *A Soldier's Story*, p. 524.

22. Warren II, p. 176.

23. Weakness of C-46 fuel tanks: ibid., p. 180; *Soldier*, p. 133.

24. Coutts after-action report, reprinted in part in *Airborne Warfare*, p. 136.

25. John Toland, *The Last 100 Days* (New York: Bantam Books, 1967), pp. 301–5.

26. Coutts after-action report.

27. Galvin, *Air Assault*, p. 244.

28. Quoted in Tugwell, *Airborne to Battle*, p. 275.

29. Resupply: Warren II, pp. 188–90. The loss of so many B-24s was never satisfactorily explained.

30. "[T]remendous success": Warren II, p. 192. Eisenhower *(Crusade in Europe*, p. 390) wrote that VARSITY "was the most successful airborne operation we carried out during the war." Lost and damaged aircraft and gliders, in a list compiled from individual actions, described in Warren II. See also summation, p. 194. Warren concludes that the VARSITY aircraft losses were "moderate," not high.

31. Warren II; Eisenhower, *Crusade in Europe*, p. 390; Ridgway, *Soldier*, p. 134.

Chapter 49

1. MacDonald, *The Last Offensive*, p. 301.

2. Ibid., pp. 309–13.

3. British VARSITY operations, here and below: Saunders, *The Red Beret*, pp. 300–7.

4. American VARSITY operations, here and below: *The Last Offensive*, pp. 309–13; Warren II, pp. 177–88; Donald R. Pay, *Thunder from Heaven; The Story of the 17th Division 1943–45* (Nashville, Tenn.: Battery Press, 1980), pp. 31–43; David P. Schorr, "Airborne Assault Crossing of the Rhine," *Military Review*, June 1948, pp. 48–55; official after-action report of William M. Miley, RP-USAMHI; XVIII Abn HQ diary and "Summary of Operations," dated 4/25/45, Box 5A, RP-USAMHI. See also: Dank, *The Glider Gang;* Tugwell, *Airborne to Battle;* Galvin, *Air Assault.*

5. Coutts quoted in after-action report, excerpts in Gavin, *Airborne Warfare*, pp. 135–37.

6. Operations of 194 CT described best in Schorr. Operation of 680: ltr. Oswald to author 8/27/84, enclosing unit history and copy of citation.

7. Schorr, "Airborne Assault Crossing of the Rhine."

8. Dank, *The Glider Gang*, pp. 250–51.

9. *The Last Offensive*, pp. 313–14.

10. Huston, *Out of the Blue*, p. 215.

11. XVIII Abn Corps "Summary of Operations."

12. Carlo D'Este, *Decision in Normandy* (New York: Dutton, 1983), p. 61; Nigel Hamilton, *Monty: The Making of a General* (New York: McGraw-Hill, 1981), pp. 543, 597, 629–30.

13. *Soldier*, p. 134.

14. Ibid.

15. MBR arrival time at CP: Warren II, p. 190.

16. XVIII Abn Corps HQ diary 3/24/45.

17. *Soldier*, p. 135; XVIII Abn Corps HQ diary.

18. Ltr. Peterson to author 3/6/84.

19. Ltr. Coutts to author 2/8/84; *Soldier*, p. 133. In his oral history, Pt. 2, pp. 89–90, Ridgway called the C-46s "flaming coffins."

20. Gale: Saunders, *The Red Beret*, p. 307.

21. Offensive: XVIII Abn Corps HQ diary 3/15/45.

22. *Soldier*, pp. 135–36.

23. Purple Heart: *Register;* MBR biographical records and decorations, USAMHI. X ray: ltr. MBR to author 2/21/84. Ltr. DDE to MBR 4/4/45, Box 3, RP-USAMHI.

24. XVIII Abn Corps HQ diary, entry 1000 hours, 3/25/45: "General Ritchie called at 0930 and stated they were having considerable trouble on the left because 30 Corps was not advancing. The bridging is behind schedule for which he is very sorry. Last night 20 heavy mines came down the river which were exploded before they got to bridging site. He is sending a battalion up the river to clear out the enemy." Wesel bridging operations: XVIII Abn Corps "Summary of Operations"; refutation in *The Last Offensive*, p. 315.

25. 17th deployment: Pay, *Thunder from Heaven*, p. 46. Cancellation of ARENA: XVIII Abn Corps HQ diary 3/25/45.

26. Simpson: *A General's Life*, p. 395.

27. Ibid.; *Register.*

28. Only two divisions: *A General's Life*, p. 402.

29. Bridge priority: ibid., p. 422. See also Ninth Army HQ diary, 3/22/45, Simpson Papers, USAMHI: "The original agreement gave the bridge to the Ninth Army for the first 5 hours after completion to get food, ammunition and gas over to the 17th Abn Division, then to the British for 10 days."

30. *The Last Offensive*, p. 314, states that work on the Wesel bridge *started* at 0915 hours, March 25 (D+1).

31. Ninth Army HQ diary 3/26/45 and 3/27/45.

32. XVIII Abn Corps offensive: *The Red Beret*, pp. 307–9; *Thunder from Heaven*, pp. 45–46; XVIII Abn Corps HQ diary 3/21/45: "Will attack at 0900 tomorrow, the 27th of March." D. H. Erskine, *The Scots Guards* (London, 1956). Michael Howard and J. H. A. Sparrow, *The Cold-stream Guards, 1920–1946* (London: Oxford, 1951). Ltrs. Coutts, Miller and Schorr to author.

33. Ltr. Miller to author 2/7/84.

34. Ltr. MBR to Frank Brandstetter, 3/22/49, Box 11, RP-USAMHI.

35. Ltr. Miller to author 2/7/84.

36. *The Scots Guards*, p. 429.

37. *The Last Offensive*, p. 319; Ninth Army HQ diary 3/27/45.

38. XVIII Abn Corps HQ diary 3/27/45: "General Simpson informed me that he would like me at CP XVI Corps at 1600 today to hear his plans." *The Last Offensive,* p. 318: "General Ridgway promptly discouraged the plan."

39. Ltr. MBR to author 2/21/84.

40. *The Scots Guards; The Coldstream Guards; Thunder from Heaven;* XVIII Abn Corps diary 3/27/45: "Gen. Dempsey told me he was very sorry to report that he was turning me over tomorrow morning . . . to Ninth Army." The turnover of XVIII Abn Corps to Ninth Army occurred on the night of March 27/28, per orders, Box 3, RP-USAMHI.

41. Ltr. Schorr to author 2/8/84.

42. *The Scots Guards; The Coldstream Guards;* ltrs. Coutts, Peterson, to author.

43. Ninth Army HQ diary 3/29/45, 3/31/45.

44. *A General's Life,* pp. 414–15.

45. Collins, *Lightning Joe,* pp. 313–14.

46. XVIII Abn Corps HQ diary and "Summary of Operations"; *The Red Beret,* p. 310; *Thunder from Heaven,* pp. 46–47.

47. *A General's Life,* p. 423.

48. Sylvan diary 3/31/45.

Chapter 50

1. XVIII Airborne Corps: "Summary of Operations, 1 April to 18 April, 1945," dated 5/4/45, Box 5, RP-USAMHI; Sylvan diary 4/2/45. Corps HQ was established in Dillenburg, Germany, at 6 P.M., April 1, and became operational at noon, 4/2/45. *Time* magazine, issue of 4/2/45. The article, which had only slight biographical material, stated that MBR was "avid for mail from his blonde wife . . . and their daughter, wife of a lieutenant colonel now on duty in Europe." This was a reference to Peggy Ridgway's daughter, Virginia Dabney Ridgway, adopted by MBR, who was married to West Point (1936) infantryman Claude L. Crawford, who was first a battalion commander, then G-3, 102nd Infantry Division. The 102, assigned to Alvan C. Gillem's XIII Corps, was then part of Ninth Army's drive to the Elbe River. *(Register; Last Offensive,* pp. 387–400.) That same week, Ridgway was awarded two high decorations: the Army's Distinguished Service Medal and the British Order of the Bath. (Parks diary 4/2/45; ltr. MBR to Montgomery 4/3/45, Box 3, RP-USAMHI.)

2. Ltr. MBR to *Time* correspondent Will Lang, 4/9/45, Box 3, RP-USAMHI.

3. ONB's promise, see page 435.

4. XVIII Abn Corps "Summary"; *The Last Offensive,* pp. 344–72 (see battle map p. 363); Colby, *The First Army in Europe,* pp. 165–68; *Soldier,* pp. 139–40.

5. 82nd and 101st: Sylvan diary 3/31/45; ltr. MBR to Brereton (and reply) 4/10/45. 501, 508 and 13th Division in JUBILANT and EFFECTIVE: Parks diary 3/30, 4/2, 4/4/45.

6. 86th and 97th "never fired a shot": Sylvan diary 4/3/45. Melasky, Halsey, Moore: *Register;* official bios. Halsey kinship to Admiral Halsey: ltr. to author from General Halsey's son, Milton B. Halsey, Jr., 4/20/84.

7. 8th Division history, Stroh and Weaver: MacDonald, *The Siegfried Line Campaign,* pp. 448–63; *Register.* Moore: obit, *Assembly* (USMA alumni magazine), April 1951.

8. Moore, obit, *Assembly;* MBR on Moore: oral history, Pt. 3, p. 11, RP-USAMHI.

9. XVIII Abn Corps "Summary"; *The First Army in Europe;* orders, MBR to Halsey, 4/5/45, Box 5A, RP-USAMHI.

10. Rapport, *Rendezvous with Destiny,* p. 704; Gavin, *On to Berlin,* pp. 309–11.

11. Ltr. Michaelis to author 2/17/84. Grenade: Parks diary, 3/7/45; ltr. Higgins to author 2/16/84; ltr. Kinnard to author 2/26/84. The "baseball grenade," far more powerful than the British Gammon grenade, was designed as an antitank weapon. In a demonstration for Lindquist's 508 PIR at about the same time, another exploded prematurely killing one paratrooper and wounding several (Lord, *History of the 508th,* p. 84).

12. *Rendezvous with Destiny,* p. 708.

13. Ibid., pp. 708–13; *On to Berlin,* pp. 311–12; Harmon, *Combat Commander,* pp. 250–51; ltrs. Dudley to author 10/28/83, Langdon to author 12/26/84.

14. *The Last Offensive,* pp. 363–64.

15. Ibid., p. 370; Pay, *Thunder from Heaven,* pp. 47, 74. Ltr. Coutts to author 2/7/84.

16. *The Last Offensive,* p. 365; *The First Army in Europe,* p. 166; XVIII Abn Corps HQ diary 4/8/45.

17. XVIII Abn Corps HQ diary 4/8/45.

18. *The Last Offensive,* p. 365.

19. Ibid., pp. 334–35.

20. Report, Schellhammer to Eaton, "Negro Troops," 4/8/45, Box 3, RP-USAMHI. Based in part on this experience, Ridgway later (in the Korean War) became a leading advocate of desegregation in the Army.

21. The 86th Division and Pope problem: ltrs. Melasky to MBR 5/22/45, MBR to Melasky 5/24/45, and Melasky to MBR 5/31/45, Box 5, RP-USAMHI. By the end of May, Melasky's 86th Division, then in Third Army, had been reassigned to the Pacific, and Melasky again sought Ridgway's help in sacking Pope. Ridgway agreed Pope should be sacked but also took pains to say, in effect, that the division's failure was not all Pope's fault. Melasky "failed": ltr. MBR to Superintendent, USMA, 6/9/58, Box 31, RP-USAMHI.

22. 13th AD Records, National Archives, Record Group 94, Boxes 16256 to 16267. Wogan: *Register.*

23. *The Last Offensive,* p. 367.

24. Ibid.

25. 13th AD problems here and below: MBR oral history, Pt. 2, p. 100; Report, Mathewson to MBR 4/18/45; Report J. T. Mozley (Asst. G-3, XVIII Abn Corps) to MBR 4/18/45; Report, MBR to Hodges 4/20/45; memo, Wogan to MBR re relief of Augur 4/13/45; Box 3 and Box 5, RP-USAMHI. Ltr. Moore to MBR recommending relief of Williams 4/16/45, Box 5, RP-USAMHI.

26. Report, Mathewson to MBR 4/18/45, Box 3, RP-USAMHI.

27. Ibid., 13th AD Records, NA, RG 98, Boxes 16256 to 16267. (And see notes 25 and 29.)

28. Wogan wounds: *The Last Offensive,* p. 367; MBR oral history, Pt. 2, p. 100. MBR disapproval of Wogan's DSC: endorsement, 9/25/45, Box 8, RP-USAMHI. Wogan "failed": ltr. MBR to Superintendent USMA 6/9/58, Box 31, RP-USAMHI.

29. Ltrs. Hains to author 9/26/84; Rau to author 9/14/84.

30. *The Last Offensive,* pp. 368–70.

31. Surrender demands: ltr. MBR to Hodges 4/15/45, Box 5A, RP-USAMHI; *Soldier,* pp. 139–40.

32. Ltr. MBR to "The General Officer Commanding Army Group B," Box 5A, RP-USAMHI (excerpted in *Soldier,* p. 140).

33. Parks diary 4/17/45.

34. *Soldier,* p. 140.

35. *The Last Offensive,* p. 372.

36. Ibid., pp. 370–71.

37. 317,000: ibid., p. 372; XVIII Abn Corps achievements: Corps "Summary" 5/4/45. Model's car: *A General's Life,* p. 423.

38. Campaign conclusion: Corps "Summary." Brereton, *Diaries,* 4/18/45. Bradley to MBR: "Congratulations on the way you are helping clean up the Ruhr" (ONB to MBR 4/11/45, Box 3, RP-USAMHI). Recommended promotion: Hansen Papers (list of 5/17/45) USAMHI. Ike endorsement of promotion: Ike Papers VI, p. 79. Bradley had finally been promoted to four stars on March 12. This cleared the way to promote other generals in the ETO. Patton was promoted to four stars on April 14, Hodges to four stars on April 15. Other corps commanders promoted to three stars (lieutenant general) were as follows: Walton Walker (April 15), Wade Haislip (April 15), Joe Collins (April 16), Alvan Gillem (June 3), Troy Middleton (June 5). (Ike Papers IV, pp. 2600, 2617.)

Chapter 51

1. *A General's Life,* p. 424; Collins, *Lightning Joe,* pp. 310–26; Colby, *The First Army in Europe,* pp. 170–71.

2. *A General's Life,* p. 426.

3. Ibid., pp. 433–34; Ike Papers V, Chronology.

4. *A General's Life,* pp. 427, 434; for a more detailed account of Eisenhower's offer of help to Montgomery and his dissatisfaction with Montgomery's progress, see Ike Papers, Vol. IV, letters to Marshall, Montgomery, Alan Brooke et al., pp. 2593–94, 2615, 2617, 2640, 2649, 2650–52, 2655.

5. *Soldier,* pp. 141–42.

6. Ibid., XVIII Abn Corps "Summary of Operations 27 April to 3 May 1945," dated 5/20/45.

7. "Summary of Operations 27 April to 3 May 1945," dated 5/20/45; *A General's Life,* p. 427.

8. 82nd to Berlin: ltrs. MBR to Bradley 4/8/45, and Bradley to MBR 4/11/45. Box 3, RP-USAMHI. Marshall to Eisenhower re 82nd vs. 13th: Ike Papers IV, p. 2669.

9. "Summary"; MacDonald, *The Last Offensive*, p. 363.

10. "Summary."

11. *Soldier*, pp. 142–43.

12. "Summary." On new D day: *The Last Offensive*, p. 461; Ellis, *Victory in the West II*, p. 337.

13. Gavin, *On to Berlin*, pp. 316–17.

14. Ltr. and enclosures kindly provided by Allen Langdon (who made the assault crossing) to author 1/3/84. The enclosures included maps, official regimental reports, etc.

15. Gavin, *On to Berlin*, p. 317.

16. *Soldier*, pp. 143–44; "Summary"; ltrs. MBR to Bradley, Simpson, Dempsey 5/1/45 and 5/2/45, Box 3, RP-USAMHI.

17. *Soldier*, pp. 143–44.

18. Ltr. a senior engineer to MBR 3/2/56, Box 3, RP-USAMHI, following publication of excerpts of *Soldier* in *The Saturday Evening Post*, 2/18/56. Ltr. senior engineer, who requested anonymity, to author 3/6/84.

19. Ltr. MBR to senior engineer 3/15/56, Box 3, RP-USAMHI.

20. Ltr. Eaton to MBR 3/12/56 (responding to senior engineer's letter), Box 3, RP-USAMHI; CB-Eaton int. Silver Star: 201 File, Box 1, RP-USAMHI. Faith ulcers: ltr. Faith to MBR 1/9/46, Box 9, RP-USAMHI.

21. Ltr. senior engineer to MBR 3/2/56. Engineer casualties: ltr. MBR to Simpson 5/2/45.

22. See note 16. The boasting is in ltr. to Bradley 5/1/45.

23. *The Last Offensive*, p. 463; *Soldier*, p. 144; Saunders, *The Red Beret*, p. 314.

24. Radio Berlin on Hitler's death: Weigley, *Eisenhower's Lieutenants*, p. 723.

25. *On to Berlin*, p. 321.

26. *The Last Offensive*, p. 462; *Soldier*, pp. 145–46.

27. "Summary"; Bradley: *A General's Life*, p. 434; Marshall: Foreword to *Soldier*.

28. *Soldier*, pp. 149–50; *On to Berlin*, p. 324.

29. The Billingslea anecdote is condensed from Edith Steiger Phillips' memoir *My World War II Diary*, kindly provided (and confirmed) by Lee C. Travelstead of the 325th in his ltr. to author.

30. Rapport, *Rendezvous with Destiny*, pp. 719ff; Taylor, *Swords and Plowshares*, pp. 106–10.

31. Redoubt: *The Last Offensive*, pp. 407–42; *A General's Life*, pp. 418–19. Cancellation of EF-FECTIVE: Parks diary 4/19/45. Southern offensive: *A General's Life*, pp. 430–31.

32. *Rendezvous with Destiny*, pp. 723–24.

33. Ibid., p. 726; *Swords and Plowshares*, p. 106.

34. *Swords and Plowshares*, p. 109; *The Last Offensive*, p. 442.

35. Kesselring for Von Rundstedt: *The Last Offensive*, p. 222. His surrender: *Swords and Plowshares*, pp. 107–8. Göring art, Salzburg Museum, Eagle's Nest: ibid., pp. 109–10.

36. *A General's Life*, p. 436.

37. Rapport, Pay, Lord, Parks diary, and Brereton, *Diaries*, various entries 5/1/45 to 5/9/45.

38. *A General's Life*, p. 435.

39. Ibid., pp. 434–36.

40. Galvin, *Air Assault*, p. 249.

41. FAAA to Berlin: Ike Papers IV, p. 2678. Ridgway's opinion of job: *Soldier*, p. 150.

42. *Soldier*, p. 150; orders 5/26/45, 201 File, Box 1, RP-USAMHI; CB-Casey int.; ltr. Harold T. Krick to author 9/4/84; other aircrew: Edward Renner, copilot; Edward Lynn, navigator; Wayne D. Foster, radio operator.

43. Hull: official bio. News from Hull: memo 5/28/45, Box 5, RP-USAMHI. XVIII Corps orders 6/14/45: Box 1, RP-USAMHI. *Soldier*, pp. 150–51. Later, Parks wrote Ridgway in part: "You sure ducked a man-sized headache when you got out of this assignment . . ." Infuriated, Ridgway responded: "Let me put you right. I have never ducked any job in my life, headache or no headache, and I had nothing whatever to do with the change of assignments . . ." Parks hastened to write: "I apologize if you felt I insinuated you had requested the change. I meant to say that you were fortunate to escape it. I know that you are too good a soldier to ask for release from any assignment . . . [and that] you would enjoy a combat assignment in the Southwest Pacific much more than an occupational role here."

44. Ltrs. MBR to Frank Farmer 6/20/45; MBR to J. C. H. Lee 8/7/45; both in Box 8, RP-USAMHI.

45. Ltr. Eaton to MBR, Box 8, RP-USAMHI. Dasher: *Register;* CB-Winton int.

46. Makeup of party: ltr. MBR to W. D. Styer 9/20/45. Departure date: ltr. MBR to Lt. Gen. George (Air Transport Command) 8/7/45. Both in Box 8, RP-USAMHI. CB-Adams int.; CB-Surles int.; CB-Moorman int.; CB-Winton int. After the war, Bill Moorman married the sister of Day Surles's wife. The sisters were granddaughters of a West Point general, Thomas H. Barry

(class of 1877), who was superintendent of the USMA 1910–12, and daughters of another West Point (1904) general, William Bryden, who was George Marshall's deputy chief of staff for operations early in World War II. Adams, Moorman, Surles and Winton would continue to serve Ridgway off and on during the period 1945–55, and all but Adams, who said he was "not ambitious," became generals. In late 1950, during the Korean War, Don Faith, a lieutenant colonel and commander of a battalion of the 32nd Regiment, 7th Infantry Division, in the Chosin Reservoir area, was killed in heroic action for which he was awarded a Medal of Honor.

47. Eaton: ltr. Eaton to MBR 8/20/45, Box 8, RP-USAMHI. CB-Eaton int.; MBR oral history, Pt. 3, p. 36. Ridgway and Eaton would remain close. On 2/17/83, Ridgway wrote the author: "In many ways he [Eaton] exemplifies many of the finest character traits of Omar Bradley, whom he deeply admired. Doc was my ideal of what a chief of staff should be, and he was just that in the 82nd Airborne Division and the XVIII Airborne Corps."

48. *Soldier,* p. 151.

Index

Italicized page numbers refer to maps.

The Naval Institute Press is the book-publishing arm of the U.S. Naval Institute, a private, nonprofit, membership society for sea service professionals and others who share an interest in naval and maritime affairs. Established in 1873 at the U.S. Naval Academy in Annapolis, Maryland, where its offices remain today, the Naval Institute has members worldwide.

Members of the Naval Institute support the education programs of the society and receive the influential monthly magazine *Proceedings* and discounts on fine nautical prints and on ship and aircraft photos. They also have access to the transcripts of the Institute's Oral History Program and get discounted admission to any of the Institute-sponsored seminars offered around the country.

The Naval Institute also publishes *Naval History* magazine. This colorful bimonthly is filled with entertaining and thought-provoking articles, first-person reminiscences, and dramatic art and photography. Members receive a discount on *Naval History* subscriptions.

The Naval Institute's book-publishing program, begun in 1898 with basic guides to naval practices, has broadened its scope to include books of more general interest. Now the Naval Institute Press publishes about one hundred titles each year, ranging from how-to books on boating and navigation to battle histories, biographies, ship and aircraft guides, and novels. Institute members receive significant discounts on the Press's more than eight hundred books in print.

Full-time students are eligible for special half-price membership rates. Life memberships are also available.

For a free catalog describing Naval Institute Press books currently available, and for further information about subscribing to *Naval History* magazine or about joining the U.S. Naval Institute, please write to:

Membership Department
U.S. Naval Institute
291 Wood Road
Annapolis, MD 21402-5034
Telephone: (800) 233-8764
Fax: (410) 269-7940
Web address: www.navalinstitute.org